LIFE
OF THE
AMIR DOST MOHAMMED KHAN
OF KABUL

MOHAN LÀL, K.L.S.

LIFE

OF THE

AMIR DOST MOHAMMED KHAN OF KABUL

WITH HIS POLITICAL PROCEEDINGS TOWARDS THE ENGLISH, RUSSIAN, AND PERSIAN GOVERNMENTS

INCLUDING THE

VICTORY AND DISASTERS OF THE BRITISH ARMY

IN AFGHANISTAN

MOHAN LAL

IN TWO VOLUMES

VOL. I

WITH 11 ILLUSTRATIONS

Published by

Facsimile Publisher
12 Pragati Market
Ashok Vihar, Ph-2
Delhi-110052
facsimilepublisher.com

Distribution Network
gyanbooks.com
India, USA, Canada, UK, Australia, France

ISBN : 978-93-5324-437-8 (Set)
ISBN : 978-93-5324-438-5 Vol. 1 (HB)
First Published, London, 1846

2nd Impression 2020

Printed at: Gyan Press, Delhi.

LIfe of the Amir Dost Mohammed Khan of Kabul
Author: Mohan Lal

LIFE

OF THE

AMIR DOST MOHAMMED KHAN,

OF

KABUL:

WITH HIS POLITICAL PROCEEDINGS TOWARDS THE

ENGLISH, RUSSIAN, AND PERSIAN GOVERNMENTS,

INCLUDING THE

VICTORY AND DISASTERS OF THE BRITISH ARMY

IN

AFGHANISTAN.

BY MOHAN LAL, ESQ.,

KNIGHT OF THE PERSIAN ORDER OF THE LION AND SUN; LATELY ATTACHED TO THE MISSION IN KABUL.

IN TWO VOLUMES.

VOL. I.

LONDON:

LONGMAN, BROWN, GREEN, AND LONGMANS,

PATERNOSTER-ROW.

1846.

HER MOST GRACIOUS MAJESTY QUEEN VICTORIA.

DEDICATION

TO

HER MOST GRACIOUS MAJESTY QUEEN VICTORIA,

SOVEREIGN OF

GREAT BRITAIN AND OF THE INDIAN EMPIRE,

AND TO HER ROYAL CONSORT,

HIS ROYAL HIGHNESS THE PRINCE ALBERT.

SINCE the creation of the world it has been the custom and rule of the devoted loyal servants of every ancient and modern Government, that either on receiving marks of distinction, or the honour of being presented to their lawful Sovereign, they submit some present showing their homage and attachment to the Throne. This usage of submissive devotion has not been limited to human beings, but it has been adopted ever by other species of God's creatures, and has met with the approbation of the greatest in the world. If we trace back as far as three thousand years, we find, from tradition as well as from historical anecdotes, one of the most striking instances in an insignificant creature of God, namely, a small ant having secured a grain of rice in its forceps, crept some distance, and having gained an access into the presence of the wise and great Solomon, laid it under his feet, who accepted the said present!!

My fortunes have been bright, and I may say enviable, even in this land, by having the honour of being presented to your Majesty and to your Royal Highness, and also invited to your palace. The conversation which I had the good fortune to have with your Royal Highness, mingled with your detailed and minute knowledge of all the sad events of Afghanistan, did not only cause sensations of surprise in me, but was a source of proud gratification as showing that the conduct and zeal of public servants abroad, whether English or foreigner, are justly noticed and appreciated by so dignified a personage as your Royal Highness. Taking all the preceding points into consideration, I am utterly at a loss how to show my heartfelt gratitude, and in what manner to lay my unfeigned homage and devoted attachment at the feet of your gracious Majesty and your Royal Highness but by dedicating this work—the unworthy endeavours of my feeble pen in a foreign language.

If the honour so to dedicate this book is conferred upon me, it will at once show to the subjects of your Majesty's Indian Empire, that your Majesty knows how to appreciate their fidelity and devotion, and will lead them to the lofty consideration and appreciation of their present English Sovereign in a more dignified manner than they or their predecessors had ever enjoyed.

For my own humble part, I shall say no more; but conclude this dedication by adding that, while I live I shall consider myself the proudest and happiest servant by promoting the honour and interest of your mighty Government, and with heart shall ever pray, that as long as the oceans are filled with water, and the heavens decorated with sun and moon, the gracious shadow of your Majesty and his Royal Highness the Prince Albert may never be diminished from the heads of your British and Indian subjects, and both the kingdoms of England and India may never be deprived of the protection of your royal descendants.

MOHAN LAL, *Kashmirian.*

(*In the Service of the Honourable East India Company.*)

4, *George Street, Manchester Square,*
London, 20*th June,* 1846.

PREFACE.

The kind reception which my late publication, 'Travels in the Panjab and Afghanistan,' has met with from the public, deserves my hearty thanks. The greater part of my Travels having been published some years ago, had in some measure lost the interest of novelty; but the flattering mention made of them in the last edition of the valuable work of the Honourable Mountstuart Elphinstone,* a most

* "Mohan Lal, a (Kashmirian) gentleman of Delhi, accompanied Sir Alexander Burnes to Bokhara, and came back by Mashad and Hirat, has also published his travels. They appeared in English at Calcutta, and would have been invaluable if they had not been preceded by the works already mentioned. Even now they contain much new matter, and from the spirit of inquiry and observation as well as the command of a foreign language which they display, reflect high credit on the author and on the English Institution (now the College) at Delhi, where he received his education."—Elphinstone's *Kabul*, 1838.

talented and respected authority of this country, induced me to reprint them, with some additional information on the Commerce of the marts on the Indus.

Neither in the preceding publication nor in this, do I for a moment pretend to boast of the value of its information, eloquence, or style. On the contrary, I am fearfully conscious of abundant errors both in grammar, idiom, and, above all, of repetitions; but when I tell the public that I am a stranger to the customs, manners, and in great measure to the language of the English, and that I have written the MSS. and published these two volumes in a short space of time, without the assistance of a friend, as I had expected, I feel assured that I shall be excused on account of these great deficiencies. Whatever portion of the MSS. of these volumes (excepting about one hundred pages in the beginning) I was able to write every day, went to press immediately in the same way; and this will plainly account for errors and repetitions.

Besides the great expense incurred by the publishers in bringing out my late Travels, and these volumes, I beg to state, that about 300*l.* has been disbursed by me in employing a copyist, paper, and some of the portraits; a fact which will exonerate me from the imputation of having published them merely with the view of benefiting myself by their sale.

Whilst in Afghanistan I had prepared the 'Life of Dost Mohammed Khan,' both in English and Persian; and the information on which the MS. was prepared was supplied to me by his own courtiers and relations: but unfortunately all the MSS. were plundered during the insurrection of Kabul, and delivered to Mohammed Akbar Khan, who refused to give them back to me on any account. Afterwards it was out of my power to collect such satisfactory accounts as would place the circumstances of the Amir's life in a chronological series; and I therefore fear that these volumes will on many occasions be open to censure for misplacing the occurrences and the subjects contained in them.

The anecdotes inserted in the work, and especially in reference to the adventures and morals of the Amir Dost Mohammed Khan, &c., were generally communicated to me by the people with whom he associated. Not knowing what would be agreeable to the "English mind," and anxious as I was to avoid anything unpleasant of every kind, particularly when the Dedication was approved of by Her Majesty, and returned to me with only one correction, I wrote to the publishers and printers to erase such lines from the manuscripts as they might think not consistent with the rules of this country. To this, I am told, they kindly attended.

The Dedication to Her Majesty, and, I may say, the whole of the work, is written after the Persian style. Purity of idiom and eloquence in composition, which are at the command of the natives of this civilized land, are not to be expected from a foreigner of a limited education, like myself. The generosity of the impartial community at large will, on these considerations, forgive me for the blunders of every description which may disfigure the pages of these unworthy volumes.

The observations which I have made on our policy in Afghanistan, the reasons of sending an expedition, its means of success, and the cause of the disasters, are entirely the repetition of what I had despatched to the Government of India, in 1842, and which received the favourable notice of the Earl of

Ellenborough, then Governor-General of India. His Lordship writes to the Secret Committee at home in the following flattering manner.*

"In the letter from the intelligent Mohan Lal, which forms one of the enclosures of this letter, your Honourable Committee will be put in possession of the manner in which the King Shah Shuja-ul-Mulk was, on the 5th April, treacherously murdered by a son of Navab Mohammed Zaman Khan.

"Your Honourable Committee will peruse with deep interest the observations on the causes of the late insurrection at Kabul.

"Your Honourable Committee will find amongst the enclosures No. 24, an interesting paper by Mohan Lal, on the causes of the Afghan insurrection, and on the events which succeeded the outbreak at Kabul in November last.

(Signed) "ELLENBOROUGH."

The opinions so favourably expressed by this high

* 'Parliamentary Blue Book of Afghanistan,' pages 262, 264, 341.—I have left out many words, and omitted several other names, to make this extract as short as possible.

and talented personage then holding the reins of the empire of India, will, I am sure, be a sufficient ground for me to request the public to throw a glance on the contents of these volumes, and to grant forgiveness for the errors.

MOHAN LAL, *Kashmirian.*

30*th June*, 1846.

4, *George Street,*
Manchester Square, London.

CONTENTS OF VOL. I.

CHAPTER I.

CHAPTER II.

CHAPTER V.

CHAPTER VI.

CHAPTER VII.

CHAPTER VIII.

CHAPTER IX.

CHAPTER X.

PAGE

CHAPTER XI.

CHAPTER XII.

ILLUSTRATIONS OF VOL. I.

LIFE

OF THE

AMIR DOST MOHAMMED KHAN,

OF

KABUL.

CHAPTER I.

Sons of Abdal—Honourable Mountstuart Elphinstone, late Captain Arthur Conolly, and Sir Alexander Burnes—Predecessors of Dost Mohammed Khan—Origin of the Afghans—Sons of Rahimdad—Dost's Father becomes Chief—Promoted—Goes to punish the Momand Chief—Gets a title—Goes to fight the Osbeks—Places Zaman on the throne—Salary of Dost's father—Dost strikes coin so as to honour the name of his father—Envy of Vafadar Khan against Sarfraz Khan—Names of the Chiefs murdered with Sarfraz Khan—Folly of Vafadar Khan—Miracle of Dost's uncle.

ABDAL was the first and founder of the Abdali tribe. He left three sons, namely, Fofal, Barak, and Alako. If I were to mention the names and lineal descent of the offspring of Fofal and Alako, it would lengthen this book too much. The very valuable account of the kingdom of Kabul, by the Honourable Mountstuart Elphinstone, contains a correct and minute description of their descendants, as well as botanical, mineral, and animal information concerning that territory. In short, this interesting work has been a guide to many, and is as useful to travellers in Afghanistan as the mariner's compass is to voyagers on the seas. This honourable gentleman has made an everlasting impression on the minds of the people of Central Asia of his most amiable, kind, and noble disposition. It is a source of great pride to the travellers of Europe or British India to hear his name even into the remotest parts of Afghanistan with respect and tone of affection from the lips of those who are in general unaware of the names of the distinguished men of their own country. His generosity has gained for him the immortal name of "Hatim Tai,"* and his talents as a statesman the high appellation of "Socrates."† I can without any hesitation say that it was the name of "Ulfrishteen" (Elphinstone) which was the passport for the "army of the

* Famous for unlimited bounties in the old Persian histories.

† Celebrated minister and adviser of Alexander the Great.

Indus" to march through Afghanistan without any opposition. The valuable books of the late Captain Arthur Conolly and of Sir Alexander Burnes give us descriptions which also add to our knowledge of this celebrated and far-extended tribe. My object is to write about the early life, rise, and government of Dost Mohammed Khan, mentioning the names of his immediate predecessors, the sons of Barak, and not the sons of Fofal and of Alako.

Haji Jamal Khan, grandfather of Dost Mohammed Khan, was son of Usaf, son of Yaru, son of Mohammed, son of Omar Khan, son of Khizar Khan, son of Ismail, son of Nek, son of Daru, son of Saifal, son of Barak, the second son of Abdal. Tradition says that through successive generations Abdal descended from the Israelitish household; but to speak the truth, the origin of the Afghans is so obscure, that no one, even among the oldest and most clever of the tribe, can give satisfactory information on this point. Some of the Afghans, recognising their descent from the children of Israel, feel ashamed of their being related by blood to the Jews, upon whom they look as infidels. Concerning the obscurity of the true descent of the Afghans, if curiosity induces any one to desire to know more on that difficult subject, I can safely refer to and justly quote from the highly esteemed book by the Honourable Mountstuart Elphinstone. "After this cursory notice of the facts relating to the Afghans which are ascertained by authentic history, we may now examine what they say of themselves. The account they give of their own origin is worthy of attention, and has already attracted the notice of an eminent Orientalist. They maintain that they are descended from Afghan, the son of Irmia, or Berkia, son of Saul, king of Israel, and all their histories of their nation begin with relating the transactions of the Jews from Abraham down to the captivity. Their narrative of those transactions appears to agree with that of the other Mohammedans; and though interspersed with some wild fables, does not essentially differ from the Scripture. After the captivity (they allege that) part of the children of Afghan withdrew to the mountains of Ghore, and part to the neighbourhood of Mecca, in Arabia.

"So far this account is destitute of probability. It is known that ten of the twelve tribes remained in the East after the return of their brethren to

Judea, and the supposition that the Afghans are their descendants explains easily the disappearance of the one people and the appearance of the other. The rest of the story is confirmed by the fact that the Jews were very numerous in Arabia at the time of Mohammed, and the principal division of them bore the appellation of Khyber, which is still a district in Afghanistan, if not of an Afghan tribe. The theory is plausible, and may be true; but when closely examined, it will appear to rest on a vague tradition alone; and even that tradition is clouded with many inconsistencies and contradictions.

"The Afghan historians proceed to relate that the children of Israel, both in Ghore and in Arabia, preserved their knowledge of the unity of God and the purity of their religious belief, and that on the appearance of the last and greatest of the prophets (Mohammed) the Afghans of Ghore listened to the invitation of their Arabian brethren, the chief of whom was Khauled (or Caled), son of Waleed, so famous for his conquest of Syria, and marched to the aid of the true faith, under the command of Kyse, afterwards surnamed Abdoolresheed. The Arabian historians, on the contrary, bring the descent of Khauled from a well known tribe of their own nation, omit the name of Kyse on their list of the prophets, companions, or allies,* and are entirely silent on the subject of the Afghan succours. Even the Afghan historians, although they describe their countrymen as a numerous people during their Arabian campaign, and though it appears from a sarcasm attributed by those historians to the Prophet (who declared Pushtoo to be the language of hell), that they already spoke their national and peculiar tongue, yet do not scruple in another place to derive the whole nation from the loins of the very Kyse who commanded during the period of the above-mentioned transactions.

"If any other argument were required to disprove this part of the history, it is furnished by the Afghan historians themselves, who state that Saul was the forty-fifth in descent from Abraham, and Kyse the thirty-seventh from Saul. The first of these genealogies is utterly inconsistent with those of the Sacred Writings, and the second allows only thirty-seven generations for a period of sixteen hundred

* Ansaur, "Assisters."

years.* If to these facts we add that Saul had no son named either Irmia or Berkia, and that if the existence of his grandson Afghan be admitted, no trace of that patriarch's name remains among his descendants; and if we consider the easy faith with which all rude nations receive accounts favourable to their own antiquity, I fear we must class the descent of the Afghans from the Jews with that of the Romans and the British from the Trojans, and that of the Irish from the Milesians or Bramins."†

* This number is from the Taureekhee Sher Shaubee. The Taureekhee-Morussa give a much greater number, but then it introduces forty-five generations between Abraham and Jacob.

† This subject is briefly discussed by Sir William Jones, in a note on a translation by Mr. Vansittart (*Asiatic Researches*, vol. ii., Art. 4). That elegant scholar is inclined to believe this supposed descent, which he strengthens by four reasons. His first argument is drawn from the resemblance of the name of Hazaureh to Arsareth, the country whither the Jews are said by Esdras to have retired; but this reasoning, which was never very satisfactory, is destroyed by the fact that the Hazaurehs are a nation who have but recently occupied and given their name to a part of Afghanistan. The second argument is built on the traditions examined in the text, and on the assertion of the Persian historians, probably derived from those traditions, and at no time very deserving of faith. The third is founded on the Jewish names of the Afghans; but those they probably have derived from the Arabs, like all other Mohammedan nations. Their ancient names have no resemblance to those of the Jews.

It must be borne in mind that the Honourable Mountstuart Elphinstone's mission terminated at

The last argument is founded on a supposed resemblance between the Pushtoo and Chaldaic languages, of which the reader will hereafter be enabled to judge. Many points of resemblance between the manners of the Afghans and those of the Jews might be adduced, but such a similarity is usual between nations in the same stage of society; and if it were admitted as a proof of identity, the Tartars and the Arabs, the Germans and the Russians, might be proved the same.

It is also maintained by more than one European writer, that the Afghans are a Caucasian tribe, and particularly that they are descended from the Armenians. In the extent sometimes allowed to the name of Caucasus, the Afghans still inhabit that celebrated mountain; but if it be meant that they ever lived to the west of the Caspian Sea, the assertion appears to be unsupported by proof. Their Armenian descent is utterly unknown to themselves, though constantly in the mouths of the Armenians; and the story told by the latter people of the Afghans having become Mussulmans to avoid the long fasts prescribed by their own church, is too inconsistent with history to deserve a moment's consideration. I may add, that I have compared a short Armenian vocabulary with the Pushtoo, and could perceive no resemblance between the languages; and I once read a good deal of a Pushtoo vocabulary to a well-informed Armenian, who, though he strenuously asserted the descent of the Afghans from his countrymen, yet owned that he could not discover a word common to their language and his own. I have not had the same advantage with the language of other Caucasian tribes, but I compared about two hundred and fifty Georgian words with the corresponding ones in Pushtoo, and nothing could be more different; and I know no ground for connecting the Afghans with

Peshavar, and that he was never himself in Kabul. But the information given in his account of that

the Western Caucasus, except the assertion of a German traveller, whose name I forget, that he saw Afghans there during the last century, which proves too much.

Ferishta mentions that Kyse, the son of Haushem, and Huneef, the son of Kyse, were two of the earliest Arab commanders in Khorassaun (Briggs, Ferishta, vol. i., p. 3). He also states that Khauled, son of Abdoollah, being afraid to return to Arabia, settled in the hills of Solimaun, and gave his daughter to a converted Afghan chief (p. 5). It was probably from these facts that the names of Kyse and Khauled were suggested to the Afghan author, who first thought of ennobling his nation by connecting it with that of the Prophet.

I may here notice, that none of the ancient Afghan names bear the slightest resemblance to those of the Arabs or the Jews. The progenitors of four great divisions of the nation were Serrabun, Ghoorghoosht, Betnee, and Kurleh or Kuranee. The tribes immediately sprung from these are Abdal, Ghilzie, Khukhye, Cauker, &c. &c., and it is not till more recent subdivisions that we find Euzofzyes, Mahommedzyes, Solimaun Khail, and other Arabic and Hebrew derivatives. Professor Dorn, of Kharkov, who has translated a history of the Afghans, and has added many learned notes, discusses severally the theories that have been maintained of the descent of the Afghans: first, from the Copts; second, the Jews; third, the Georgians; fourth, the Toolks; fifth, the Moguls; sixth, the Armenians; and mentions more cursorily the opinions that they are descended from the Indo-Scythians, Medians, Sogdians, Persians, and Indians: on considering all which he comes to the rational conclusion that they cannot be traced to any tribe or country beyond their present seats and the adjoining mountains. 1838.

kingdom, as well as its immediate neighbourhood and more distant dominions, is so correct, and everything is described in such a manner, that all readers would at once think the honourable gentleman had himself been in the capital, had traversed the whole country, and examined all its wonders personally. Above all, his sojourn in Peshavar, while negotiating with the late Shah Shuja, his constant communication, directly and indirectly, with the people of all ranks, and his civil and liberal manners towards every one, created a most wonderful and noble reversion of respect for the generosity, truth, and justice of the British nation in the hearts of the inhabitants of that part of Asia, and on this account all European travellers have been well treated, and many of the Afghan chiefs offered their homage to Lord Keane when advancing upon Cabul. This high-minded gentleman describes the Barakzais, the tribe of Dost Mohammed Khan, as follows:—"The next clan to the Populzye, which it far exceeds in numbers, is the Baurekzyes. This great clan inhabits the country south of Candahar, the valley of Urghessaun, the banks of the Helmud, and the dry plains which that river divides. Those near Can-

HON MOUNT STUART·ELPHINSTONE.

dahar, and many of those in Urghessaun and on the Helmud, are led by the fertility of their soil to agriculture, and the industry of others has even produced caureezes and cultivation in the midst of the desert, but the greater part of the tribe is composed of shepherds. They are a spirited and warlike clan, and as Fatah Khan is now their chief, they make a much more conspicuous figure than any other tribe among the Afghans. At present the grand vizier and almost all the great officers of state are Baurekzyes, and they owe their elevation to the courage and attachment of their clan.

"Their numbers are not less than thirty thousand families."

Let us return to Haji Jamal Khan, son of Usaf. In the reign of Ahmad Shah Durrani, Haji Jamal Khan, the grandfather of Dost Mohammed, became a noble of great influence; and when Taimur Shah ascended the throne of Afghanistan, he died, and left four sons, namely: Rahimdad Khan, Payandah Khan, Harun Khan, and Bahadar Khan. His Majesty made the first of these chief of the Barakzai tribe, in the room of his father Haji Jamal. But he possessed a mean disposition, which induced all the tribe to stand against him; and they complained to the king that the chief, Rahimdad Khan, having a bad temper, does not invite his equals and followers to his table, and never dines in the company of the nobles, but alone in the house. Such conduct is disgraceful to the name of their chief, and therefore they are not willing to render him homage.

His Majesty accepted the appeal of the tribe, dismissed Rahimdad Khan from the chiefship, and appointed him keeper of the Government papers. He left eight sons, Abdul Khan, Abdulmajid, Abdul Kabir, Abdul Salem, Abdulhakim, Abdulhamid, Abdullah, and Abdul vahid Khan.

On the dismissal or death of Rahimdad Khan, Taimur Shah nominated Payandah Khan, the father of Dost Mohammed, as chief of the Barakzai tribe. His civil and liberal conduct towards the people made him popular. His fidelity and attachment to the state rendered him the favourite of the king.

Meanwhile Sardar Madad Khan set out to punish the obstinacy of Azad Khan, the governor of Kashmir; and Payandah Khan, the father of Dost Mohammed, embraced this favourable opportunity of distinguishing himself, and accompanied the Sardar on his expedition. He fought bravely with the governor, who was routed and subjugated. When the Sardar returned from Kashmir to Kabul, and waited upon the king, he mentioned the services of Payandah Khan with the highest praise. Having had previously a good opinion of this individual, and hearing now of his brilliant achievements at Kashmir, his Majesty ordered him to proceed to Shal and Quetta, and to collect the revenue of those districts. He performed this duty to the advantage of the state, and satisfaction of the populace. On this occasion every one spoke highly of the talents of Payandah Khan.

These successive and good services of Payandah Khan wrought upon the heart of the king, who not only rewarded him by adding the Ghilzai division to his flag, but also allowed him to stand near the throne, and thus his promotion was advancing continually.

In the meantime Prince Abbas, son of Taimur Shah, rebelled against his father, and Arsalan Khan Momand became his adherent. His Majesty ordered Payandah Khan to quell this disturbance. He marched at the head of an army, and on reaching Lalpurah he rode his horse through the river without fear of being drowned. His followers imitated the heroic conduct of their leader, and found themselves on the other side of the river without any loss. Arsalan Khan, having no power of opposing him, was obliged to fly. Payandah Khan, after gaining the victory, returned to the presence of the Shah.

The Shah, agreeably to the advice of Payandah Khan, went off for Peshavar; and he also accompanied the royal camp. On reaching the city, Arsalan Khan was summoned to appear, and was put to death in the court. The rebellious son, Prince Abbas, threw himself on the mercy of his father, the Shah, and after obtaining pardon for his misdemeanour, came back to Kabul with the king. His Majesty was so much pleased with the valuable services rendered by Payandah Khan that he honoured him with the title of Sarfraz (Lofty) Khan.

After some time the peace of the western frontier of Kabul was disturbed by the Ozbek tribe. This disturbance frightened the king to such a degree that he had determined to quit the capital and escape to Herat. On hearing of such a cowardly purpose in his Majesty, the father of Dost Mohammed Khan, who was entitled Sarfraz Khan, with his usual resolution and fidelity, persuaded the Shah to remain on the throne, and himself marched towards Balkh. In the exercise of his sagacity and sound wisdom, he made peace with the Ozbek chief, and returned to Kabul without having occasion to use his sword. The favour of the king increased daily towards him, but unfortunately his Majesty expired after a short interval.

On the death of Taimur Shah some of the Durranis were anxious to place Prince Abbas on the throne, and others wished that Mahmud should succeed him. In short, every chief was puzzled to determine on whose head the crown should be placed. Sarfraz Khan, however, gave the sceptre of the realm into the hands of Prince Zaman, afterwards called Shah Zaman. His Majesty therefore loved him as dearly as his own life, and daily bestowed upon him fresh marks of royal distinction.

The continued services of Sarfraz Khan made Shah Zaman so much attached to him that in addition to the command of the Barakzai tribe, and the division of the Ghilzais, his Majesty attached part of the Qizalbash force to his detachment, and appointed for him an annual salary of about eighty thousand rupees. How pleasing it would have been if Sarfraz Khan had lived to see the divine favour shown in behalf of his son Dost Mohammed Khan, who ascended the throne of the late Kabul kings, and employed many people equal in rank with his father! Nay, also his old uncles, the brothers of Sarfraz Khan, as Jabbar Khan, Mohammed Zaman Khan, and Usman Khan, acknowledged their young nephew as their superior, and received from him a higher salary than Sarfraz Khan got from the old king of Kabul.

As soon as Dost Mohammed Khan gained distinction, and became chief of Kabul, he stamped the following verse on the coin, and this honoured and gave permanence to the name of his affectionate father:—

> "Simo tila be shams o qamar medahad naved."
> "Vaq te ravaj Sikhai Payandah Khan rasid."

"Silver and gold give the happy tidings to sun and moon that the time has arrived for the currency of Payandah Khan's coin."

It would certainly be wonderful if Sarfraz Khan

could hear with his own ears that his enterprising son Dost Mohammed had become as celebrated as one of the kings, and that the ambassadors of the British, the Russian, the Persian, and the Turkistan governments waited in his court. It happens seldom in this sad and changing world that parents are alive to derive pleasure from the prosperity of their promising sons; and if they ever happen to be alive, still when the child has gained dignity, it is to be regretted that he seldom pleases them entirely by performing his filial duties according to their expectation.

When Vafadar Khan became the minister of Shah Zaman, he gained the highest favour of his Majesty by the use of his sweet words and intrigues in the court. Afterwards by his hypocrisy and false accusations he induced the king to treat all the nobles with contempt, and to look upon them with distrust; and prevailed on his Majesty to make him prime minister of the kingdom. When he was sure that Shah Zaman had become disgusted with his deceit with regard to the chiefs, he represented to the king that Sarfraz Khan was intriguing with Shah Shuja, with the view to dethrone his Majesty, and make Shah Shuja sovereign of Afghanistan. He added the names of some other chiefs as his adherents in this act of disloyalty. Shah Zaman, who was afterwards blind of both eyes, seemed blind of sense at this time, for as soon as he heard the false accusations of Vafadar Khan, he sent for Sarfraz Khan and put him to death without making any investigation into the facts or circumstances of the alleged treason. The envious conduct of Vafadar Khan did not cease upon accomplishing the murder of Dost Mohammed Khan's father, Sarfraz Khan. This was followed by that of other chiefs also, namely: of Mohammed Azim Khan Alakozai, of Qamruddin Khan, of Amin-ul-mulk babri, of Hazar Khan Ghilzai, of Amir Arsalan Khan, of Jafar Khan Javan Sher, of Zaman Khan Rekabashi, &c., who all fell victims to the envy of Vafadar Khan.

After the unjust massacre of the above named nobles, there remained not a talented and qualified man who could manage the affairs of the realm, and govern to the satisfaction of the people of all ranks. In short, the behaviour of the minister, Vafadar, was offensive to all. He oppressed the subjects, and he paid the forces in soap and red colours, instead of money; he made also many deductions in their pay, which at length caused every one to be thirsty for his blood, and at length this was shed most ignominiously.

When Sarfraz Khan was murdered, Harun Khan acted as governor of the district of Girashk for him. The latter died, and left two sons, namely, Shah Savar Khan and Amardin Khan. His brother, Bahadar Khan, was a man of much piety, and shunned all worldly affairs. He was day and night engaged in prayers. The ladies of the household of Sarfraz Khan mentioned that when he was in deep contemplation of the Almighty God, a heavy gold chain was generally coming out from his mouth and going into it again. He was said to be a stranger to the stratagems of the Afghans, and a lover of God. His son, Mohammed Rahim Khan, entitled Amin-ul-mulk, was also known to abhor the tyrannical habits of the Afghans, and by his amiable disposition had added honour to the good name of his father. He married a lady of Kashmir, whose virtues, love of her husband, and good conduct in the days of adversity, are worthy of my notice. I will mention them more fully in the proper place, and especially concerning her being forced to marry Dost Mohammed Khan when she was a widow.

CHAPTER II.

Brothers of Dost Mohammed Khan—Dost's early training—Shah Zaman—Dost becomes the confidential agent of Fatah Khan—Defeat of Shah Shuja—Youth of Dost Mohammed Khan—He returns to Kabul—His sister married to Shah Shuja—Fatah Khan's treaty with Mukhtar and with Qaisar—Intrepidity of Dost—He and Fatah leave Qandhar—They rebel from Shah Shuja—Are compelled to return to Qandhar—Fatah Khan is confined, and Dost escapes—Dost besieges Qandhar—Fatah is released—Dost and Fatah join Kam Ran—Dost gains a victory—Fights with Shuja—Makes peace, and allies himself with Shuja—Dost and his brother desert the camp—Shuja gains a victory—Measures of Dost—His bravery—He defeats his enemy—Shah Mahmud becomes king, Fatah Khan vizir, and Dost is dignified—Mirza Ali Khan—Mohammed Azim Khan—Dost is made Sardar—Expedition to Kashmir—Rebellion in Kabul—Suppressed—War with the Sikhs.

When the Sarfraz Khan was murdered he left twenty-one sons and several daughters. If I did not mention that they had different mothers, it might puzzle the reader to consider that so many children were born from one mother. The celebrated Vazir Fatah Khan, afterwards entitled Shah Dost by Mahmud Shah, was the eldest son of Sarfraz Khan. He, Taimur Quli Khan, and Mohammed Azim Khan were brothers from one mother, who belonged to the Nusrat Khail clan. Then Navabs Asad Khan, Samad Khan, and Turrahbaz Khan were born from the Barakzai mother. The seventh son of the Sarfraz Khan was Ata Mohammed Khan, who was the real brother of Yar Mohammed Khan, of Sultan Mohammed Khan, of Said Mohammed Khan, and of Pir Mohammed Khan. Their mother was from the Alakozai family. Purdil Khan, who was the twelfth son of the Sarfraz Khan, was brother to Sherdil, to Kohindil, and to Mehardil Khan. These descended from their mother of the Idu Khail clan of the Hutak Ghilzai. The well known Navab Jabbar Khan is said to be the seventeenth son of the Sarfraz, and is the only one from his mother, of whom mention is made in the book of Mr. Vigne.* The reputation

* "The Nawab Jubar Khan well deserves the name of the Feringis friend, was then about fifty-five years old, to judge from his appearance, standing about five feet nine, with a corpulent person, dark aquiline features, and somewhat of a Jewish look, having a very good tempered expression. His mother was a slave girl in the Zunana of Poyundu Khan; his father gave her in marriage to a water-carrier, but still continued his attentions to her. By the custom of these countries a servant marrying a slave becomes also a slave. When the Nawab was born the

of her character stands now high. Jumma Khan was born from an Afghan slave girl. Aslam Khan's mother was also a slave of the tribe of Kafar Siah-posh. The hero of my tale, Dost Mohammed Khan, was the twentieth, and his younger brother, Amir Mohammed Khan, was the twenty-first son of the Sarfraz Khan; their mother being from the Siah Mansur family, a branch of the Persian tribe, which was looked upon with disgrace and contempt, by the others, the Afghan wives of the Sarfraz Khan.

I must safely say that the mother of Dost Mohammed was the favourite wife of Sarfraz Khan. She accompanied him in the various campaigns, and would not allow him to rise early and march long after sunrise. For this she was blessed by the troops and camp followers, who did not like to start earlier in cold.

When the Sarfraz was no more, Fatah Khan, with the sons of his own uncles, namely, Abdul Sa-

waterman took the child to Poyundu Khan, and told him that he knew more about the child than he himself did. For many years the Nawab was running about the Bala Hissar of Kabul, and was called the waterman's son. Mohamed Azim Khan took notice of him, owned him as his brother, and procured him an appointment as governor of Dhera Ghaze Khan."

PEDIGREE OF DOST MOHAMMED.

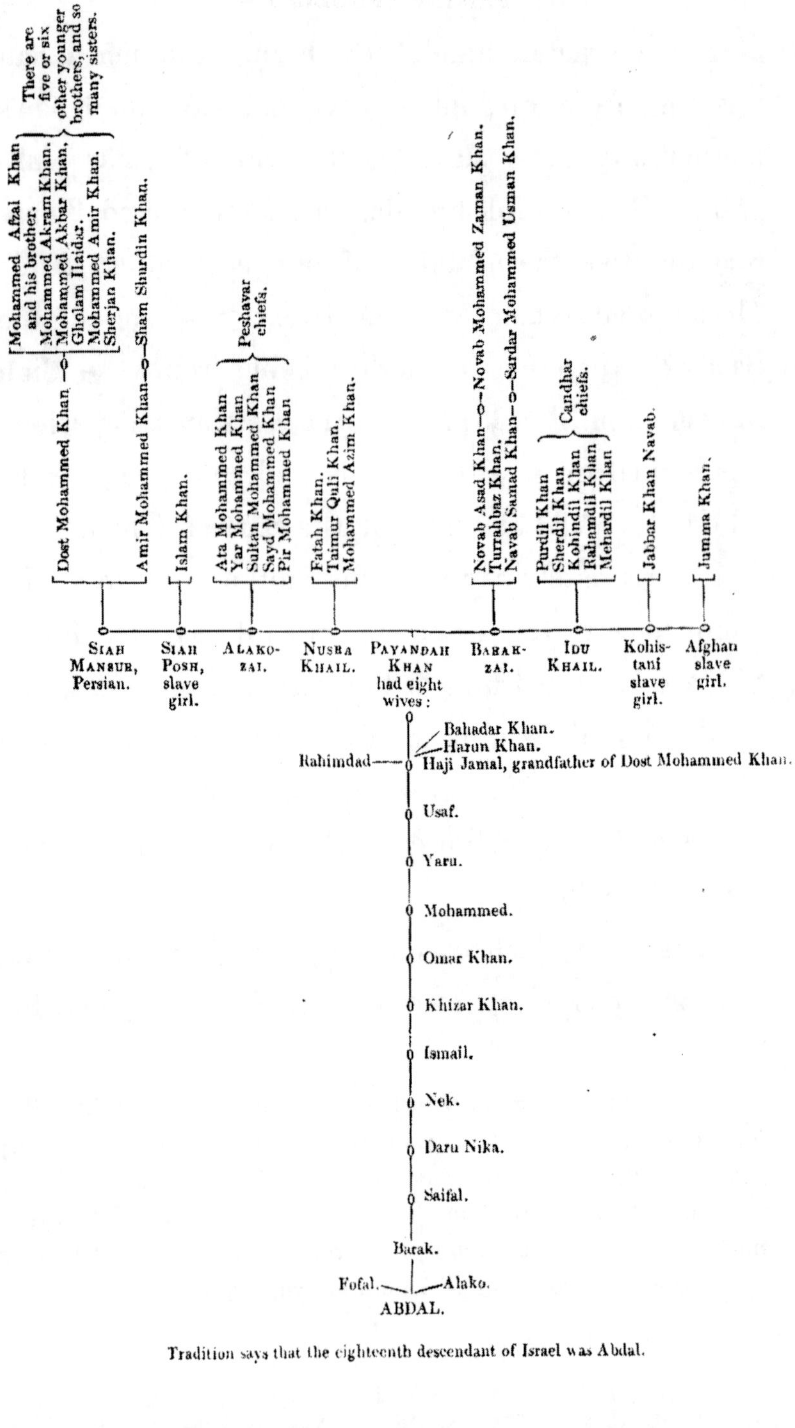

Tradition says that the eighteenth descendant of Israel was Abdal.

lam, Abdul Vahid, Mohammed Rahim Khan Amin-ul-mulk, and two other confidential men, made their escape through one of the bulwarks of the city of Qandhar to Girishk, and took up their abode in the fort named Sadat. After a short stay in that place, he went through Sistan to Persia, and joined Mahmud Shah in Kirman, whither he had fled through fear of Zaman Shah. These were the days in which the descendants and family of Payandah Khan suffered most miserably. They were begging from morning till night for pieces of bread. Many were prisoners, and others had taken shelter in the mausoleum of the late Ahmad Shah, with the view of gaining food which was daily distributed for charity's sake. No doubt my hero was included in the company and shared their miseries.

Abdul Majid Khan, son of the uncle of Dost Mohammed Khan, asserting his claim, after the Afghan custom, to inherit the widow of the nearest relation, forced the widowed mother of the latter to marry him. His brother Abdulamin Khan married the sister of Dost Mohammed Khan in the same forcible manner. While these unfortunate events were taking place in the family of the Sarfraz Khan,

Dost Mahommed Khan, with his younger brother Amir Mohammed Khan, lived four years in one of the forts of Maruf, which belonged to the new husband of his mother, called Abdulmajid Khan. At this time he was from seven to eight years of age.

Meanwhile Fatah Khan returned with Mahmud Shah from Persia, and encamped in the village of Amirbaldan, situated in the vicinity of Sistan. In this place he met with Mirakhor, who was one of the chiefs of Shah Zaman, and governor of Qandhar. The Mirakhor, without gaining any information of the strength of Fatah Khan's force, was overawed by the reputation of his rival's celebrated bravery, and was compelled to flee, leaving his tents and camp equipage in possession of Mahmud Shah. Now the stars of the descendants of the Sarfraz began to shine.

Fatah Khan, with Mahmud Shah, marched from Sistan and came to Girashk with pleasant spirits. Here he sent for his servant, named Mohammed, and gave his young brothers, Dost Mohammed and Amir Mohammed, into his charge, with injunctions to take very great care of them, and especially of the former. He also fixed a handsome income for the maintenance of his enterprising brother.

After doing good offices for the improvement of Dost Mohammed Khan, Fatah Khan, and Shah, Mahmud marched against Qandhar and laid siege to the city. While the siege and skirmishes were going on, Yayha Khan Barakzai fled from the town and joined Fatah Khan. The latter, after forty-two days' blockading, made numerous ladders and took Qandhar by escalade. Immediately after this he confined the Prince Haidar in the palace along with Yar Mohammed Khan, &c. &c., the chiefs of Shah Zaman's party. Fatah Khan asked Mahmud Shah to put Abdulrahim Khan Sadozai and his father to death, and to publish that the deed was done by the Durrani chiefs. By fabricating this story, Fatah Khan was anxious to excite the suspicion of Shah Zaman against the Durranis, and to form an attachment to himself and to Shah Mahmud. Any one who was reported to have a little wealth became a prey to Fatah Khan's extortion. He, as well as Mahmud Shah, hoarded up a great deal of money by oppressing the merchants and cultivators, who provided them with all supplies for the war. When fully prepared, they moved from Qandhar with arms towards Kabul to meet Shah Zaman.

At this time Dost Mohammed Khan had reached the twelfth year of his age. He obtained a situation under his brother Fatah, and attended upon him as "abdar," water-bearer, on every occasion. After some time he got an additional service, that of having the charge of preparing the smoking-pipe for Fatah Khan.

When Shah Zaman had intelligence of the movement of Mahmud Shah and Fatah Khan in the direction of Kabul, he left all the heavy and royal baggage in charge of Shah Shuja, and marched himself lightly equipped to oppose the enemy. On arriving at Mokar he inspected his army, and he found it consisted of nearly forty thousand foot and horsemen. Ahmad Khan Nurzai, who had one thousand horse under his command, was appointed to form the advance guard of the army. This commander made rapid intrigues with Fatah Khan, deserted Shah Zaman, and offered his services to Mahmud Shah. When this news reached Shah Zaman, he thought that all his chiefs and forces had become disgusted with him through the ill behaviour of his minister, Vafadar Khan,* and, instead of fighting for him, they would probably seize and deliver him up to the enemy. Already overcome by this fear, he was himself routed without a moment's opposition. On escaping from before Mahmud Shah's camp, his Majesty was informed that the inhabitants of Kabul had placed themselves on the road to this city, with the intention to plunder his Majesty. With this fearful view he took a different route to go down to Jalalabad, and thence to Peshavar. For the purpose of passing the night he stopped in the fort of Ashaq, who, having learned the deplorable flight and condition of the Shah, lost no time in receiving the person of his Majesty, and by express conveyed a report of the same to Mahmud Shah and Fatah Khan. They immediately dispatched Navab Asad Khan with directions to bring Shah Zaman

* Mohammed Osman Khan, the son of this unwise Vafadar Khan, was entitled Nazamuddaulah by the influence of the late Sir William Macnaghten and Sir Alexander Burnes, and was made minister of the late Shah Shuja in Kabul. This person imitated his father, and suggested such imprudent measures to the newly arrived functionary as caused disturbances, the loss of thousands of lives, honour, and also of Afghanistan. For particulars of the character of Vafadar Khan, see Major Hugh's 'Campaign in Afghanistan,' p. 378-9.

and his minister both as prisoners. He reached the fort of Ashaq, and brought the captives from thence to Jagdalak. Here he blinded Shah Zaman, and Vafadar Khan was put to death along with his brother in the Bala Hissar of Kabul.

Much has been said and known about the celebrated diamond of Kohi Nur (mountain of light), wherefore on this subject I add nothing more than that Shah Zaman, before he was taken captive, concealed it in the wall of the tower where he lived in the fort of Ashaq. He did not point out the place of its concealment to Shah Mahmud, but to his brother, Shah Shuja. When the latter ascended the throne he took out the precious diamond, and when his evil stars predominated he was deprived of it by force by Ranjit Singh.* This Lion of the Panjab, Naunelal Singh ("Hotspur"), and poor Sher Singh, tied that diamond on their arms on happy occasions. When the latter was murdered, and anarchy took deep root in Lahaur, Rajah Hira Singh, the late minister of Maharajah Dalip Singh, got possession of the diamond, and sent it to his father's stronghold in the Jammu Hills, where, no doubt, the

* Died in 1839.

present rajah, Golab Singh, has it in his possession. Rajah Hira Singh had also murdered Missar Beli Ram, the keeper of it, for fear of his saying that it has been received and sent by him to Golab Singh. Now if any inquiry be made with regard to this valuable gem, the Rajah will say he cannot find it, because it was in the charge of Beli Ram, who is now no more.

When the reign of Shah Zaman was at an end, Fatah Khan placed Mahmud Shah on the throne of Kabul, and admitted Dost Mohammed Khan into all the secrets of each party. This promising young man was in attendance upon him at all times, and never went to sleep till Fatah was gone to his bed. He stood before him all the day with his hands closed, a token of respect among the Afghans. It was not an unusual occurrence, that when Fatah Khan was in his sleeping-room, Dost Mohammed Khan stood watching his safety.

After some time had passed, Shah Shuja prepared an army to proceed against Mahmud Shah and Fatah Khan at Kabul, and to revenge the outrage done by them to his brother Shah Zaman. On hearing this, Fatah Khan and Prince Kam Ran, son of Mahmud Shah, quitted Kabul to check him. Near the village of Ishpan the armies fought with each other. In the beginning of the battle the warriors of Fatah Khan became dispirited, but at length Shah Shuja was routed and overcome. Whatever royal property and treasures were left to him by the late kings fell into the hands of the followers of Fatah Khan, and many of them were very much enriched. Shah Shuja fled, and the Vazir Fatah Khan, flushed with success, went down to Peshavar for the purpose of collecting the revenue of that place. At this time Mahmud Shah had very little force in Kabul, which induced Abdulrahim Khan Ghilzai to make the Logar people his partizans, and to rebel against his Majesty. He set out for Kabul, and the king, being alarmed, released Mukhtar-ud-daulah, Ahmad Khan Nurzai, and Akram Khan Ghilzai from custody, and sent them to oppose the refractory chief. These chiefs collected about three thousand men, while the enemy was at the head of twenty thousand horse and foot. A hard fight ensued between the Ghilzai rebels and the Durranis of the king, who lost Taj Mohammed Khan, Akram Khan Ghilzai, and Sher Mohammed Khan, who had much influence in the kingdom. Finally the Durranis were victorious: and the rebels, after losing numerous followers, retired to their native villages. The heads of the dead were cut off and brought by the Durranis into the presence of Mahmud Shah. He ordered them to be heaped up outside the palace, on the cliff known by the name of "Tapaïkhaki-balkh."

In the mean time Shahabuddin Tokhi, finding that the city of Qandhar was without troops, collected a large body of forces, and proceeded to take it. Abdul Majid Khan Barakzai, Saidal Khan Alakozai, and Salah Mohammed Khan Ghilzai, quitted the city to oppose the Tokhi chief on the road. The armies fought on "Puli Sangi," where two hundred Durranis and one thousand Ghilzais were killed. It was curious that the army of the king, fighting against rebels at two different places and far from each other, gained two victories in one day and at the same hour.

The Vazir Fatah Khan, in the beginning of spring, appointed Abdul Vahid Khan as governor of Peshavar, and Khojah Mohammed Khan Fofalzai was left with him. Prince Kam Ran and the Vazir Fatah

Khan returned to Kabul and dispatched Mukhtar-ud-daulah and Ahmad Khan Nurzai to strengthen the city of Qandhar. They were also directed by the above-mentioned chief to destroy all the Ghilzai forts which were situated on and in the vicinity of their march. They did the same, and after settling the disturbances of the southern kingdom, they came back to Kabul.

While peace was thus being established on the southern side, a fresh rebellion broke out in the East. "Fatah Khan Babakarzai" took up his residence in the house of the priests of "Ozbin," and besought them to take up his cause. They assembled a large body of plunderers, and with the aid of Jabbar Khail and Ahmadzai tribe, which in all amounted to about forty thousand men, they came with the above-mentioned rebel, and made breastworks near "Munar Chakri" to fight with the king's forces. The Vazir Fatah Khan moved with an army to punish this refractory multitude, which, after a little fighting, was defeated and dispersed. The Vazir cut off nearly one hundred heads of the rebels and brought them into the city. After this he went to collect the revenues of the country of Bannu, and on his way back was surprised by the arrival of the news that Prince Qaisar of Herat, being unable to wage war with the prince Haji Firoz, had fled, and had sought refuge and aid from the king of Persia; and that after passing some time in that country, he had marched to seize on the city of Qandhar. On this he immediately joined Prince Kam Ran at Qandhar, and marched to check the progress of Qaisar. They met and fought with each other at Kokran, in which place Akram Khan Ghilzai was killed on the part of Kam Ran, and Prince Qaisar was taken prisoner and carried to Kabul.

While Fatah Khan was engaged in suppressing the aforesaid disorders in the kingdom, the enterprising Dost Mohammed Khan was with him. His heroic conduct and persevering energy of mind were very pleasing in the eyes of the Vazir, and were the subject of jealousy of his older and younger brothers. His age at this time was fourteen years. As his intrepidity was the topic of the warrior's conversation, his beauty also rendered him a favourite with the people in those days.

After that time the Vazir Fatah Khan, along with Dost Mohammed Khan, directed his course back to

Kabul. This afforded a favourable opportunity for Shah Shuja at Peshavar, who, finding that the territory of Qandhar was left without forces, proceeded through the Vazir's country to take it if possible. Akram Khan Barakzai, Mohammed Ali Khan, and Mir Akbar were then with his Majesty. No sooner had Fatah Khan and Dost Mohammed Khan heard of the movement of Shah Shuja towards Qandhar, than they set out to assist Prince Kam Ran against his Majesty. When they reached that place they confined Ghafur Khan Barakzai, Saidel Khan Alakozai, and Khojah Mohammed Khan Badozai, believing that they were likely to go over to Shah Shuja. This intelligence alarmed Mukhtar-ud-daulah, who thought that the daily increasing power of Fatah Khan would some day ruin him; and to prevent this evil he excited the Mirvaiz, Khojah Khanji and Sayad Ashraf to take his part.

The seditious Mirvaiz assembled the inhabitants (Sunnis) of Kabul, and on religious pretence excited their animosity against the Kuzilbashes (Shias). He added that Mahmud Shah and Fatah Khan, contrary to their own religion, are protectors of the Shias, the annihilation of which tribe is incumbent on the Sunnis' faith. As the greater part of the Qizilbash force was advancing with Fatah Khan and Dost Mohammed Khan towards Qandhar, the Mirvaiz, finding their part of the town weakened in its defence, he ordered the Kabul, Kohistan, and Ghilzai people to make a sudden attack on it; and one of the divisions of the Qizilbash fort, occupied by the Khafis, was plundered, and Shah Mahmud besieged in Bala Hissar. At last his Majesty was taken prisoner, and Shah Shuja planted on the throne.

As soon as Fatah Khan was informed of his master's dethronement, he quitted Qandhar immediately with Dost Mohammed Khan, to fight with Shah Shuja in Kabul. About four miles from the city a battle took place between Shah Shuja and Fatah Khan, in which the latter was beaten, and compelled to join Prince Kam Ran at Qandhar. Shah Shuja being victorious returned to Kabul.

As Navab Asad Khan, uncle of Dost, was a prisoner in the Bala Hisar of Kabul, Mukhtar-ud-daulah supplicated his Majesty to release him, and allow him to be his guest. The Shah complied with his request, and Mukhtar-ud-daulah did every honour to Asad Khan. The Nawab being desirous to destroy all feelings of animosity between the Sadozai and Barakzai family, wished to make matrimonial connexions among them; consequently the sister of Dost Mohammed Khan was married to Shah Shuja. After this his Majesty requested Navab Asad Khan, Gul Mohammed Khan, the brother of Mukhtar-ud-daulah and Dost Mohammed Khan, to go to the Vazir Fatah Khan at Qandhar, and after assuring him of every attention and respect on the part of the king to induce him to relinquish all designs of supporting Mahmud Shah, and to attach himself to Shah Shuja. The latter also made an oath to restore him to the rank and privileges of his late father the Sarfraz Khan, and to treat him with all due consideration. The aforesaid chiefs went down to Qandhar, and delivered the messages of the king to Fatah Khan, who was pleased with this unexpected condescension in Shah Shuja, and immediately marched for Kabul. Prince Kam Ran was broken-hearted at this unhappy turn of affairs, and was obliged to take refuge in Hirat.

When the intelligence of Fatah Khan's departure from Qandhar reached Mukhtar-ud-daulah at Kabul, he went down to meet him at Ghazni, and conducted him to the presence of the king. Fatah Khan did not receive the favours of his Majesty as stipulated, nor was the Ghilzai division of the army placed under his charge. He was nearly two months in the house of Mukhtar-ud-daulah, who treated him with distinction and civility. In the meantime Akram Khan advised Shah Shuja to proceed to Peshavar, and there to put Fatah Khan and Mukhtar-ud-daulah into custody, and so to save himself from all fear of injury from them. One of the men who was aware of this secret went and said to Mukhtar-ud-daulah that Akram Khan and Shah Shuja had contrived to ruin them. Mukhtar-ud-daulah was lost in wonder at such ungrateful contrivances of Shuja, whom he had shortly before made king, after dethroning Mahmud Shah. He said to himself, that if he were to rebel openly just now, to prevent the ill designs of his antagonist, it would bring a load of disgrace to his own long-earned reputation. He therefore advanced seventy thousand rupees secretly to Fatah Khan, and told him to wait in Kabul on the excuse of procuring a marching equipage, while he himself would go with Shuja to Peshavar. He added also, that when Fatah Khan should receive the news of the Shah's arrival in Tezin, he should immediately commence proceedings as a foe to the king, and should cause the release of the chiefs, namely: Baqar Khan, Ibrahim Khan, Mirza Abul Qasim Khan, and Mardan Khan, and convey them to Shah Zadah Qaisar at Qandhar. These chiefs were the friends of Shah Mahmud, and therefore had been put into confinement by Shah Shuja. While Mukhtar and Fatah Khan were planning these proceedings against Shah Shuja, they entered into an agreement with each other, that the friends and enemies of the one should be friends and enemies of the other, and both should join when an antagonist appeared against either of them.

No sooner had Shah Shuja reached Tezin on his way to Jalalabad than he heard of the hostile views of Mukhtar and Fatah Khan. Immediately he issued orders that a strong cavalry force should return to Kabul, and bring the captive nobles of Shah Mahmud to his presence, along with the guard already with them. Before this cavalry had reached Kabul the brave Fatah Khan took all the chiefs out of custody, and conducted them to Qandhar, through

Lahogard.* Shah Zadah Qaisar was ruling in Qandhar at that time, and Ahmad Khan Nurzai was his minister. Fatah Khan, after long marches, reached the "Edgah" gate of Qandhar at midnight, and bribed the guard to report his arrival secretly to Agha Idrak, then confidential eunuch of the Shah Zadah. When he heard this he instantly waited upon Qaisar, and mentioned the arrival of Fatah Khan, with this message, "If the Shah Zadah had any intention of becoming a king, this seemed a good opportunity, and he (Fatah Khan) would place him on the throne; otherwise he should send him a quiet and plain answer."

As soon as Qaisar received the overtures of Fatah Khan he came at midnight to meet him at the gate, without being noticed by any one. Fatah Khan said to the prince, that if his royal highness would deliver to him Ahmad Khan Nurzai, and take an oath that he would be gratefully attached to him for ever, he would either shed all his own blood on his behalf, or would make him king of Afghanistan. Otherwise he would go to Hirat, and offer the same assistance to Prince Kam Ran.

* Commonly called Logar.

Shah Zahah Qaisar accepted the good advice of Fatah Khan, and both wrote an agreement on a leaf of the Qoran, under their respective seals, binding themselves to each other with perpetual attachment. When this was settled, Fatah Khan conducted the prince to his palace in the city, and ordered his two thousand horsemen to dismount and proceed under the command of Dost Mohammed Khan, to surround the house, and seize the person of Ahmad Khan Nurzai, by taking the "Char Suq" road. The hero Dost Mohammed Khan succeeded in opening the door of Ahmad Khan's house, and seized him while in bed. After this he tied his hands and feet, and imprisoned him in the house of Shah Zadah Qaisar.

In the morning the courtiers as well as the citizens did not see Ahmad Khan passing to "Darbar" as usual, and were astonished to perceive that in his place Fatah Khan and Dost Mohammed Khan had attended the court of Shah Zadah; and no one knew what had become of the unfortunate Ahmad Khan. This sudden change of the nobility created the utmost terror among the Afghan chiefs, and curiosity among the citizens. The latter proceeded to see the prisoner in the palace, to satisfy their curiosity; and the former persuaded Qaisar to put Fatah Khan in confinement. On this his royal highness, being forgetful of his solemn oath, made an artifice to seize Fatah Khan, and with this view asked him to give him a private entertainment in the garden, where he secretly made arrangements with the chiefs to shackle him immediately.

However, this fraud of the ungrateful Qaisar came to the knowledge of Fatah Khan, who begged Qaisar to allow him leisure of two days to prepare the articles of the entertainment, while he meant to manage his own defence. At this crisis he found no remedy but to appoint the brave Dost Mohammed Khan superintendent of the feast, and commandant of his personal guard. Consequently, he (Dost) decorated a most beautiful apartment to receive the prince, and being himself armed cap-a-pie, as well as at the head of five hundred good fighting soldiers, stood in the presence of his royal highness, and by his alert manners showed him that he was watching the safety of his brother the Vazir.

When the prince, as well as the Durrani nobility,

observed that their designs of catching Fatah Khan were frustrated by the vigilance of Dost Mohammed Khan, they pretended that the object of the meeting was to obtain the rescue of Ahmad Khan Nurzai. For this they also offered a present of one lakh of rupees to the prince and to the Vazir, on the part of the captive. They also married his daughter to the prince that day. This arrangement caused his release, and his reappointment to the situation of the lieutenant-governor of Qandhar.

Meanwhile Fatah Khan, with Dost Mohammed, Ata Mohammed, and Khowajah Mohammed Khan, proceeded to attack Kabul. When he reached Kaleti Ghilzai he was deserted by Ata Mohammed Khan, and other Nurzai chiefs, who went back and joined Ahmad Khan at Qandhar. Fatah Khan, relying on the intrepidity of Dost Mohammed Khan, cared very little for the faithless conduct of the deserters, and with his heroic brother continued his march towards Kabul. When he arrived at the village named Top, the news of the movement of Shah Shuja from Peshavar, as well as his arrival at Qilai Qazi to oppose him, spread in the camp of the Barakzai chiefs. On this, about midnight, Faizullah

Khan Fofalzai, along with five hundred horsemen, left Fatah and Dost, and joined Shah Shuja.

This desertion caused great consternation in the camp of Fatah Khan, whom Dost wisely advised to retrace his steps to Candhar. Before they reached Kalat they were informed that Prince Kam Ran was in possession of Qandhar, and that Ahmad Khan, the lieutenant-governor, without firing a shot, had stolen his way to his native fort in the adjacent country. As soon as Fatah and Dost heard this they sent Shah Zadah Qaisar in charge of Khowajah Mohammed to Dehlah, and themselves with the rest of their brothers waited upon Prince Kam Ran at Qandhar. They passed about two months in great distress with him, and at last begged him to advance them some money to distribute among their followers. The prince, notwithstanding that he had a great deal of wealth, swore that he had none to give them.

Fatah and Dost took immediate steps to intrigue with their former master, Prince Qaisar, against Prince Kam Ran, whom they, when every thing was in their own favour, turned out of the city; and they then invited the former to take his place. In these times of agitation Dost failed also in the respect which was due to the royal household, and omitted no opportunity to plunder and rob the royal ladies. After the Shah Zadah Qaisar, with the assistance of Fatah Khan and Dost Mohammed Khan, had seized the government of Qandhar, his royal highness dispatched Mohammed Ali Khan, and Mir Akbar, to Shah Shuja and Mukhtar-ud-daulah, and proposed that if he would allow him the possession of Qandhar, Shikarpur, and their dependencies, he would destroy Kam Ran, with Haji Firozuddin. He also suggested that if his Majesty suspected the attachment of his royal highness, and the fidelity of Fatah Khan and of Dost Mohammed Khan, he would immediately send their brother Mohammed Azim Khan as a hostage to the Shah.

Shah Shuja-ul-Mulk did not accept the offers of Shah Zadah, but continued his march to Qandhar. When the royal camp was near a village called "Chishmah Shadi," Dost Mohammed and Fatah Khan fled from the city to Frah, and the Shah Zadah, in company with Khowajah Mohammed Khan, proceeded to take shelter in "Dehlah." This intelligence disappointed his Majesty, who set out by express to get the Shah Zadah if possible. Mukhtar-ud-daulah secretly conveyed the news to the Shah Zadah, who quitted "Dehlah," to secure himself in some distant and out of the way place.

On this Shah Shuja entered the city of Qandhar, and offered the most kind and honourable treatment to Dost Mohammed and Fatah Khan, who immediately waited upon him. Four days afterwards Shah Zaman and Mukhtar-ud-daulah went and brought Shah Zadah Qaisar with Khowajah Mohammed Khan into the presence of his Majesty, who pardoned them for their past misdeeds and restored the government of Qandhar to them. Shah Shuja, in company with Dost Mohammed and Fatah Khan, proceeded to Sindh, where he received the usual tribute from the Meers, and bent his course by the Derajat and Peshavar to Kabul.

Meanwhile the Mir Alam Khan was deprived of the governorship of Derah Ghazi Khan, and Ata Mohammed Khan Nurzai was placed by Shah Shuja in that important situation. This alarmed Dost Mohammed and Fatah Khan to such an extent, that they found no safety for their persons but in flying towards Hirat. The Mir Alam also fled at the head of some good and brave cavalry, and gained employment under Shah Zadah Qaisar in Qandhar. In Hirat Dost Mohammed and Fatah Khan did all in their power to induce Shah Zadah Haji Firoz to attack Qandhar and Kabul, but he did not comply with their request. He said he had not ambition to rule the kingdom of Afghanistan, and was well satisfied with the present possession of Hirat.

The refusal of Shah Zadah Haji Firoz broke the hearts of Dost Mohammed and Fatah Khan, and even compelled them to return to Shah Zadah Qaisar at Qandhar. Here Khowajah Mohammed Khan Fofalzai, with the friendly assistance of the Mir Alam Khan Nurzai, began to insult Dost Mohammed and Fatah Khan with dispute about equality, and intrigued with Shah Zaman, who at this time was living with his son Shah Zadah Qaisar in Qandhar, to put them both in confinement.

With this view Shah Zaman begged the confidential servants of Shah Zadah Qaisar, who were the Mir Alam Khan Nurzai and Shah Navaz Khan Achakzai, to call upon Dost Mohammed and Fatah Khan, and state on the part of his Majesty that they should give him a grand entertainment. The quick-sighted Dost Mohammed Khan discovered the real object of the pretended familiarity and base affection of Shah Zaman, and both brothers apparently showed themselves highly honoured by such favour of Shah Zaman. They made preparations for three different entertainments; one on their own part, the second from Navab Asad Khan, and the third from Mohammed Azim Khan.

Upon the one hand Fatah Khan was preparing everything pompously to receive Shah Zaman in the beautiful garden of Maranjan, as if he were not aware of the conspiracy, and on the other, the active Dost Mohammed was secretly engaged in adding to the number of his body guard, and kept a piercing eye on all sides to secure the safety of his brother, Fatah Khan, and of himself, in case the conspirators should dare to injure them. His celerity and readiness to meet any blow showed Shah Zaman and Shah Zadah Qaisar the impossibility of making them the victims of the conspiracy, and therefore to remove every suspicion from the minds of Dost Mohammed and Fatah Khan, the Shah conferred the dress of honour on them. Thus the watchfulness of the hero of my tale frustrated the designs of the conspirators, who in great despair made all possible schemes to gain their mean object during the day, but availed nothing.

At last Shah Zaman and Shah Zadah Qaisar left the entertainment, and on returning to the palace gave orders that no chief should enter the court-yard accompanied by more than five attendants. During twenty days Fatah Khan managed to take about one hundred men with him, when he was waiting upon Shah Zadah, and thus secured his safety for such a period. At length, the Shah Zadah concealed some of his strong men in his garden, when he gave orders that his nobles should wait to pay their respects. This was done, and suddenly the Mir Alam Khan, the nephew of the Sardar Ahmad Khan, surnamed Saifuddaulah, lifted up Fatah Khan and threw him down on the ground, which broke two of his teeth, and immediately they made him a prisoner. After this the friends of Fatah Khan, namely, Navab Asad Khan, Mirza Mohammed Raza, and Agha Mehndi, were similarly treated; but the brave Dost Mohammed was fortunately aware of the impending danger, and lost no time, but called his followers, who amounted to about five hundred men.

It was not in the power of Shah Zadah to catch Dost Mohammed Khan, when thus protected.

It was impossible for a man like Dost Mohammed Khan to see his brother, Fatah Khan, suffering in custody without using his utmost energy to obtain the freedom of the dear captive. At the head of his followers he made a bold rush into the outer gate of the palace, but on reaching the door of the residence of the Shah Zadah, where Fatah Khan was confined, he was disappointed to observe that it was shut, and not only strongly defended, but all the walls and towers filled with matchlock men. They all at once fired at him, and he, having no means to ascend the walls, relinquished the attack. However, he besieged the palace; on which the Shah Zadah ordered Khowajah Mohammed Khan and the other chiefs to shut the gates of the city, and thus cut off the means of escape from Dost Mohammed Khan when thus reduced in the number of his adherents. One of the friends of Mohammed Azim Khan secretly sent this news to the Dost, and added also that the chiefs, with five hundred men each, had been ordered to take charge of the different gates and towers of the city against him.

On receiving this unpleasant intelligence, which might make to tremble almost the bravest leader, the hero Dost, with his usual perseverance and presence of mind, assembled his brothers and the heads of his small handful of men, with whom he held a council of war. He stated, "that the captivity of his elder brother, Fatah Khan, is of course painful to every one of the present party, and most heart-rending it is to leave him lingering in the hands of the enemy; but as the Shah Zadah has made every preparation either to destroy or to seize this small party, if his royal highness succeeds in either of his plans, we shall not only be sufferers, but shall also lose the hope of securing the liberty of Fatah Khan for ever. Consequently, we must draw our swords, and with energetic determination killing our opposers on the road, force our way through the gates, and go down to Girishk." The party accepted this advice as the best, and gladly followed him who gave it so wisely. On approaching the gate, Dost Mohammed killed some men of the guard stationed to impede his progress; and thus opening the gate made his escape to his stronghold in Girishk. On this, Shah Zaman advised his son, Shah Zadah Qaisar, to cut off the head of Fatah Khan in return for his being the instrument in blinding his Majesty and forcing him from the throne; but the Shah Zadah lent more attentive ears to the advice of Mukhtar-ud-daulah and Mohammed Khan, than to that of his father, and thus saved the life of his prisoner.

At this time a large caravan from Persia passed through Hirat for Qandhar, and had scarcely reached the vicinity of Girishk, when Dost Mohammed Khan with Mohammed Azim Khan placed himself in its way. When the store of booty was near and in his view, he galloped forward and deprived all the merchants of their goods and cash. He paid no attention to the heart-rending shrieks and complaints of the traders; and being in possession of about four lakhs of rupees, he raised troops, proceeded at the head of them, and laid siege to Qandhar. During nearly three months he surrounded the city so closely that all communication with the garrison was stopped, and the supplies of grain and ammunition were nearly consumed. While Dost Mohammed Khan was daily reducing the Shah Zadah to a dangerous perplexity by a regular and protracted siege, Mukhtar-ud-daulah was also not less active in favour of

Fatah Khan. Shah Zadah Qaisar had much regard for Mukhtar, who sent him a petition begging him to release Fatah Khan, "otherwise his brother, the brave Dost, will destroy the city of Qandhar, and I shall be able to secure no respect for the royal family when captured." He also asked Shah Shuja to write to Shah Zadah to the same effect. The Shah instructed the Shah Zadah that, on releasing Fatah Khan, he was to ask him to send Mohammed Azim Khan, with the Gholam Khanah (Persian troops), to remain as hostages with his Majesty, the Shah Zadah considering this a most lucky opportunity to please Shah Shuja by obeying his orders, and much more so to get rid of the Dost's siege, gave an immediate acquiescence to the request of his Majesty, and set Fatah Khan free, who also sent the demanded hostages to Shuja.

After some time Shah Shuja dispatched Mohammed Azim and Ata Mohammed Khan on special service to Multan, and on their return from that quarter they passed through Deratjat and Peshavar on their way to Qandhar. As soon as they arrived at that place, Dost Mohammed and Fatah Khan rebelled from Shah Shuja and Shah Zadah Qaisar, and declared themselves willing to support Shah Zadah Kam Ran against them. When his Majesty heard this sad news he immediately wrote to Shah Zadah Qaisar to proceed with four thousand horsemen and attack the rebels. Dost Mohammed and Fatah Khan, having been informed of the hostile steps of Qaisar, solicited Shah Zadah Haji Firoz of Hirat to lend them aid. To this his royal highness agreed, and dispatched Shah Zadah Milak Qaisar at the head of three thousand cavalry to their assistance. It was in the plain near the fort of Azim Khan where the allied forces under the Dost engaged with those of Shah Zadah Qaisar. After a fight, in which about two thousand men were killed and wounded on both sides, the hero of my tale, Dost Mohammed Khan, and his brother, Fatah Khan, were victorious, and the army of Shah Zadah routed.

When the intelligence of the defeat of Shah Zadah reached the Imperial court of Shah Shuja, he proceeded quickly in person to defend the city of Qandhar. On this, Fatah Khan and the Mir Alam Khan made preparations to oppose the progress of his Majesty. Since there was no other person so qualified as Dost Mohammed Khan, both in conducting political affairs and in the energetic duties of a field-marshal, the whole party unanimously elected the lion of my subject to undertake that important post.

The field-marshal, Dost Mohammed, with his accustomed alacrity and perseverance, led his troops to oppose Shah Shuja, whom he met near Qarahbagh, or rather in Obeh. A battle ensued, and both parties fought desperately, when the Sardar Ahmad Khan Nurzai became the medium of a negotiation between the Shah and Dost Mohammed Khan. War was changed into peace, on which Dost Mohammed returned to Girishk, and Shah Shuja, after replacing Shah Zadah Qaisar in the government of Qandhar, moved back to Kabul with Mukhtar-ud-daulah.

It was not long after the arrival of Shah Shuja in Kabul that his Majesty was surrounded with new difficulties, and thought to have recourse to the services of the brave Dost Mohammed and of Fatah Khan. The affairs of the capital took a most frightful aspect. The prime minister, Mukhtar-ud-daulah, in junction with the celebrated hypocrite, the Mir

Vaiz, the priest of Kabul, rebelled against his royal master, with the view to recognise Shah Zadah Qaisar, governor of Qandhar, as sovereign of Afghanistan. When this cheerless information reached the ears of his Majesty, he immediately sent a deputation consisting of the Durrani nobles of the realm, namely, the Sardar Madad Khan Is-haqzai, Ahmad Khan Nurzai, some members of the royal family, and holy descendant of the Prophet the Sadats, as well as other " Aq Saqal," silver-bearded people of respectability, to Dost Mohammed and Fatah Khan in Girishk.

The deputation of the Shah, after engaging and pledging themselves for the personal safety and good treatment of Dost Mohammed and of Fatah Khan, conducted them to Qandhar. As soon as this report spread in the country, Mukhtar-ud-daulah and the Mir Vaiz, as well as their followers, relinquished all their rebellious designs for the time. Shah Shuja felt very anxious to secure the closer alliance of Dost Mohammed and of Fatah Khan, and therefore he himself met them in Qandhar. His Majesty gave them every assurance of his favour and attachment, and delivered to them a sealed engagement written on the holy leaf of the "Qoran," and at the same time conferred the title of "Sardar i Sardaran" (chief of chiefs) upon Fatah Khan: he also gave a most valuable dress of honour, along with a superior horse with gold trappings, to Dost, and one lakh of rupees for their expenses.

After Shah Shuja had succeeded in obtaining the good will and services of Dost and Fatah Khan, he proceeded to raise tribute from the Meers of Sindh; but the Sindhians made preparations to fight with the Shah. On this the nobles of the court, namely, Akram Khan, &c. &c., petitioned the Shah to make peace on getting five lakhs of rupees from them; while the hero Dost Mohammed and Fatah Khan, relying on their intrepidity and sagacity, begged the Shah not to lend an ear to the proposals of Akram, but to leave the whole affair to their arrangement. They also added that, without using arms and sacrificing lives, they would get from the Meers and fill the royal coffers with thirty lakhs of rupees. However, Akram foolishly prevailed on his Majesty to follow his counsel; and going secretly to the Meers at night, brought only five lakhs of rupees, and made an arrangement with them.

This proceeding of Akram Khan, which was nothing but a tissue of folly and crooked understanding, not only showed the weakness of the Shah's powers to the Sindhians and caused a loss of twenty-five lakhs of rupees to the royal treasury, but it also excited the extreme displeasure of Dost Mohammed and Fatah Khan. They deeply lamented the damage sustained by the ill counsel of Akram Khan, and became exceedingly wrathful, that the Shah, instead of paying attention to their advantageous advice, followed that of their inferior and fool.

Dost Mohammed and Fatah Khan were so much disgusted with the above-mentioned proceedings, that they left Haidarabad and came up to Shikarpur. Hither the Shah followed them and apologized to them. He swore that nothing of the kind should happen in future, and that all the affairs of his government, whether internal or external, should be adjusted by their guidance. As nature had cultivated noble and independent notions in the head and heart of Dost, he therefore could not be estranged by ill usage of this kind, but was determined to oblige and serve the Shah evidently and openly, and agreed to fight with Shah Zadah Qaisar,

Mukhtar-ud-daulah, and Mir Vaiz, who had again assumed the character of enemies to the Shah.

In the mean time the news of the movements of Shah Zadah Qaisar and Mukhtar-ud-daulah towards Peshavar was brought to Shah Shuja, who proceeded with Dost and Fatah Khan to Derah Ghazai Khan, with the intention to strike a blow on the party of Shah Zadah Qaisar at Peshavar. Before the march commenced, the watchful Dost Mohammed directed his and Fatah Khan's family to steal their way to Qandhar, and the Navab Asad Khan was appointed to take charge of them; and he at the same time said that he would soon join them with Fatah Khan.

It should be recollected here that Mukhtar-ud-daulah was always on friendly terms with Fatah Khan and with Dost. He now, being the chief instrument of recognising Shah Zadah Qaisar, against whom Shah Shuja was proceeding, wrote secretly to Dost and to Fatah, that if they still adhere to the bonds of friendship and their oath with him, they are to desert Shah Shuja immediately, and kindle the flame of insurrection in the dominion of his Majesty in Qandhar, which no doubt would agitate and ruin the measures of the Shah beyond remedy. While

Shah Shuja was about six miles from Derah, Dost Mohammed and Fatah Khan deserted the royal camp and took their route towards Qandhar. The report of the desertion of Dost Mohammed and Fatah Khan thunderstruck Shuja, who, however, relying much more on the protection of God than on the assistance of the deserters, continued his march to Peshavar.

It was near the village of Tahkal, in the suburbs of Peshavar, where the force of Shah Shuja fought with that of Shah Zadan Qaisar. After a severe conflict Mukhtar-ud-daulah fell in the field, and his brother Haji Mir Ahmad and Khowajah Mohammed Khan also followed him. The victory was on the side of Shah Shuja, who at once set out for Kabul and put to death the fanatic ringleader the Mir Vaiz, priest of that city. As soon as his Majesty got rid of the said priest he started to punish Dost Mohammed and Fatah Khan at Qandhar, who had deserted him at Derah.

When Dost Mohammed and Fatah were informed of the hostile movements of Shah Shuja, they raised a large army, and under the royal shadow of Shah Mahmud and of Shah Zadah Kam Ran, set out to oppose Shah Shuja. Dost Mohammed volunteered to be the head of the advanced guard, and was accompanied by his step-brother Purdil Khan, and also by Nur Mohammed Khan, the brother of Khowajah Mohammed Khan, who was slain in the late battle of Tahkal, in Peshavar. The very moment he had reached Kalat i Ghilzai, Nur Mohammed Khan went over to Shah Shuja, and Ata Mohammed Khan Nurzai and Yahya Khan Bamzai, who were commanders of large bodies of troops, fled towards Dehlah and Murghab.

At the time these sad desertions took place, and the leader of the advanced guard remained alone, Shuja would not have hesitated a moment to seize and destroy him (Dost Mohammed) by surprise, but he knew his brave heart and wise head, and therefore avoided a skirmish with him. It is said by the people that at this crisis Dost Mohammed was afraid of Shah Shuja, because he was deserted and alone, and the Shah was afraid of the talents and heroism of Dost, lest he might cause dissension among his followers. These fears, entertained on both sides, prevented an immediate contest, and afforded a favourable opportunity to Dost Mohammed Khan to retrace his steps and join his brother Fatah Khan.

On the approach of Shuja's army, Mahmud Shah, being aided only by Fatah Khan and Dost Mohammed, found himself too weak to fight with Shah Shuja, and therefore in this low spirit he fled to Girishk.

After some time Dost Mohammed and Fatah Khan left Girishk and went to Sabzvar, where they remained for three months. During their sojourn in this place they were informed that Shah Shuja had left Qandhar for Kabul, and appointed Shah Zadah Yunas, with Azam Khan Nasakhchibashi and the Mir Alam Khan, governor of the former city.

Meanwhile Dost Mohammed and Fatah Khan heard that two large caravans were to pass near Khashrod, one from Qandhar to Persia, and the other from the latter country to the former. On this they placed themselves on the road of the caravans, and the very moment they encountered with them every article fell into the possession of these noble highwaymen. They gained plenty of money by this plunder from the merchants. Immediately after this they raised an army and prepared themselves to attack Qandhar.

Dost Mohammed and Fatah Khan met no opposition on the line of their march to Qandhar, which place they fortunately took with little trouble. The governor of this place fled, and joined his master Shah Shuja in Derajat; and Mir Alam Khan, the lieutenant-governor, being a relative of Pir Mohammed Khan Alakozai, threw himself on the protection of Shah Mahmud, who was again made nominal king by Dost and Fatah. After arranging the government affairs of Qandhar, Dost Mohammed and Fatah Khan proceeded to take Kabul, under favour of the name of Shah Mahmud. They succeeded in gaining possession of this capital, and sent Mohammed Azim Khan towards Peshavar to oppose Shah Shuja.

While Mohammed Azim Khan was encamped at Balabagh to intercept the progress of Shah Shuja, Dost Mohammed and Fatah Khan were strengthening themselves and weakening their adversaries in Kabul. Among them was the Mir Alam Khan, whom they confined and treated with barbarous cruelty. Shah Shuja, at the head of twenty-five thousand men, proceeded from Peshavar to Kabul. When the royal army reached Jalalabad, Mohammed Azim Khan, finding himself unable to oppose his Majesty, left the highway and took shelter in the different skirts of the Sufaid Koh.

No sooner had the above-mentioned intelligence reached Dost Mohammed and Fatah Khan than they marched down to Surkhab to bring Mahmud Shah with them. These three enterprising men had no more than three thousand soldiers, and knew the strength of the army they were going to fight with; but Dost Mohammed's bravery, mingled with policy, was always depended upon, and generally productive of the results of victory. On their arrival in the vicinity of the Lukhi of Surkhab, they thought that if the Durrani chiefs should cause the release of the Mir Alam Khan, he would probably succeed in joining Shah Shuja, and desertions might take place among the followers on both sides. To prevent this anticipated misfortune, Dost Mohammed and Fatah Khan murdered the poor prisoner.

Now Dost Mohammed and Fatah Khan held a council of war with their subordinate chiefs in the presence of Shah Mahmud, and stated that it was most contrary to the rules of policy and of war to appear in the open field with a small force of three thousand before a monarch or enemy of twenty-five thousand well mounted cavalry and well equipped infantry. The only thing they think now advisable to preserve warlike fame and gain honour is to avoid a general action, and then with determined spirit to attack the enemy by surprise. They also proposed that, until the enemy were perfectly routed, they should not divide themselves into small bodies, and commence to plunder their respective antagonists, as was usual with the Afghans, because this would cause great confusion among them, and probably the enemy would get the benefit of it. They also added that, though the enemy exceeded them in power and number of men, none of them ought to be disheartened and go over to him, believing that the victory would always attend his army, because such conduct would not only cause a disgraceful name for the man himself who should do so, but would also dishearten the rest of their followers.

These counsels of Dost Mohammed Khan were applauded by Mahmud Shah, Fatah Khan, and the chiefs, on which they left everything of peace and war to his sound and wise management. He remained all day concealed in the bushes or "lukhi," and about evening he marched with all his forces.

He made a long march under cover of the darkness of night, and about five in the morning he attacked the Sardar Madad Khan, Azam Khan, and Ghafur Khan, who commanded ten thousand foot and horse, and had been sent as an advanced brigade. Persons who were present in the field of battle told me that it was out of the power of any man's tongue to describe the matchless alacrity, prowess, and steadiness of Dost Mohammed Khan in this grand battle. In one moment he was seen making a havoc in the lines of the enemy, and then, forcing his way back, he was observed to encourage his followers to fight; and another time he was perceived to restore order among the undisciplined soldiers. Madad Khan and Azam Khan, commanding the opposite forces, now felt the narrowness of their situation, and at the same time were panic-struck to see that Dost Mohammed was causing great slaughter in their army, which was already much reduced in number and in power. At length Dost Mohammed Khan routed and dispersed the enemy, who suffered exceedingly both in men and in baggage.

When the report of the defeat of the strong royal force under Madad Khan, &c. &c., by a small body of troops under the personal command of Dost Mohammed Khan reached the camp of Shah Shuja, it not only incensed his Majesty, but alarmed him much, and made him proceed in person to check the progress of Dost Mohammed Khan. Shah Shuja had still fifteen thousand good soldiers under the command of the celebrated Akram Khan, who made the King believe that Shah Mahmud's forces were only three thousand men, and that they would not stand before him; and also that Dost Mohammed would soon lose the name of victorious, which he lately obtained in consequence of the ill management of Madad Khan. It appears that Akram Khan was either jealous, or had foolish brains to suppose that he could beat an army headed by Dost Mohammed Khan, who was never once known to leave a field of battle without gaining the victory, except some foresighted policy had induced him to do so. However, Shah Shuja made all necessary arrangements for waging war with Mahmud Shah and Fatah Khan, evidently proud of the superiority of his army, yet in heart extremely fearful of the energies of Dost Mohammed Khan. I heard from several credible people in Afghanistan that at this time of the war Shah Shuja said confidentially to his minister, that while Dost Mohammed is not captured, the victory is not to be expected; and while he is alive the crown will not be on his (Shuja's) head.* The forces on both sides were arrayed in the field, those of Shah Shuja commanded by the Sardar Akram Khan, and those of Shah Mahmud were guided by the personal and heroic directions of Dost Mohammed Khan. A battle ensued, and after a severe conflict the Sardar Akram Khan was killed, with many hundreds of Shuja's army. Some say that the deceased was cut down by Dost himself; and others add that he had received a ball from some of his own followers. The fall of such a high nobleman in the field, with so many hundred followers, produced an alarming feeling in the forces of Shuja. His Majesty was also himself frightened, and at last compelled to flee. All the rest of his followers also dispersed.

Shah Mahmud and Fatah Khan, happy in their success, and proud of the victory gained by their brave adherent Dost Mohammed Khan, returned to Kabul, and Mahmud was placed on the throne and acknowledged as King of Afghanistan. Fatah Khan,

* This appears to be a wonderful and true prophecy.

the elder brother of Dost Mohammed Khan, was appointed prime minister of the Shah, and he gave the charge of various important situations to his brothers. Since the qualifications for conducting war, unshaken courage and persevering generalship, as well as the talents for administering the affairs of the realm, prudent foresight and sound policy, were shining on the forehead of Dost Mohammed Khan, Mahmud Shah and the Vizir considered his presence with themselves of much value, and consequently he was selected as next person to the Vazir, but in reality he was first in everything.

The Vazir desired Mohammed Azim Khan to go with Shah Zadah Kam Ran, and take Peshavar, and he (Azim) therefore sent Jabbar Khan, with his secretary, Mirza Ali Khan, to collect the revenue of Derah Ghazi Khan. As the secretary possessed high talents for arranging the affairs of government, he was summoned by Mohammed Azim Khan, who desired him to take charge of every thing under him. Being a native of the civilized part of Persia, and a deep politician, his conduct and kind disposition obtained the praise of almost every man in the country. His credit and word were so much respected by the wealthy merchants that he was able to raise six lakhs of rupees in one day, which had never formerly been done by any one. He had full information of almost every thing in Afghanistan, and gained the highest favour of Mohammed Azim Khan, for whom he collected a great deal of wealth, and also caused every body to look upon him as the first noble in Afghanistan. This, however, excited great hatred against himself, especially that of Dost Mohammed and the rest of his brothers. They secretly said to the Vazir Fatah Khan that the intention of Mirza Ali Khan is to strengthen the power of his immediate master, Mohammed Azim Khan, to make you and every one of your brothers dependent upon him; and that the time is not distant when we may all be reduced to bondage under him. On this the Vazir Fatah Khan sent for Mirza Ali Khan, and requested him to get three lakhs of rupees for him from his master, as he intended to go to Kashmir. The Mirza delivered the message to Mohammed Azim, but got no satisfactory reply. He told him the same again, and even went so far in his conversation with Mohammed Azim Khan as to say that if he would not give the demanded sum quickly to the Vazir, he would bring himself into much difficulty. He then agreed to pay the sum next day.

Mirza Ali passed a very happy hour, thinking that his success in gaining the money from his master Mohammed Azim Khan would secure the good will of the Vazir Fatah Khan, and of Dost Mohammed Khan; but unluckily the Vizir had a wine party that night, and was a little intoxicated. Now the enemies of Mirza availed themselves of such a favourable opportunity of speaking against him to the Vazir; and added, that the Mirza would shortly induce Mahommed Azim Khan to stand up in opposition to the Vazir, because he had hoarded up an immense sum of money, and gained the attachment of every man for his master: adding, that if he were immediately put to death, then Mohammed Azim Khan, having no ill adviser like him, would never dare to offend the Vazir.

The Vazir was alarmed at this fabricated report of the enemies of Mirza Ali Khan, and as he was a little intoxicated he resolved at once to put an end to the life of the poor Mirza. Considering that no one could perpetrate the deed immediately but

Dost Mohammed Khan, he therefore sent for him, and said privately to him, that without fearing Mohammed Azim Khan, he was to go quickly and kill Mirza Ali Khan his secretary.

On receiving the orders of the Vazir, Dost Mohammed armed himself cap-a-pie, and taking six men with him went and remained waiting on the road between the house of Mohammed Azim Khan and the Mirza. It was about midnight when the Mirza passed by Dost Mohammed Khan, whom he saw, and said, "What has brought your highness here at this late hour? I hope all is good." He also added, that Dost Mohammed should freely command his services if he could be of any use to him. He replied to the Mirza, that he had got a secret communication for him, and would tell him if he moved aside from the servants. He stopped his horse, whereupon Dost Mohammed, holding the mane of his horse with his left hand, and taking his dagger in the right, asked the Mirza to bend his head to hear him. While Dost Mohammed pretended to tell him something of his own invention, and found that the Mirza was hearing him without any suspicion, he stabbed him between the shoulders, and throwing him off his horse cut him in many places. This was the commencement of the murders which Dost Mahommed Khan afterwards frequently committed.

When Mohammed Azim Khan was informed of the murder of his beloved and useful secretary, Mirza Ali Khan, by the hands of Dost Mohammed Khan, there were no bounds to his grief and anger against the perpetrator of this shocking deed. That very moment he ordered his followers to get ready for fight, and he came out of his house with them. Dost Mohammed immediately joined the Vazir, and told him that Mirza Ali was no more, and that his master was preparing to revenge himself upon him for the assassination. While he was speaking with the Vazir, information arrived that Mohammed Azim Khan was going to report to Mahmud Shah the unlawful conduct of the murderer, and beg him to co-operate in punishing the conspirators.

On this the Vazir Fatah Khan sent Mohammed Rahim, Ata-ullah Khan, and Shah Ghazi Dilavar, with the holy Qoran in their hands, begging Mohammed Azim Khan to pardon him and Dost for the past, and added to him, that if the Vazir was destroyed the result would be nothing short of the downfall of the whole family, as the good and ill fortune of Mohammed Azim Khan were closely connected with those of the Vazir, Dost Mohammed, and the rest of the brothers. He (Mohammed Azim), for the sake of the respect due to the Qoran, went back to his house, without going and reporting the case to Mahmud Shah, and remained quiet, though vexed.

After the lapse of three or four days the Vazir Fatah Khan, by the advice of the politic Dost Mohammed, went in person to apologise to Mohammed Azim Khan for the murder of his secretary Mirza Ali Khan; Dost Mohammed also accompanied him. They both pretended to express sorrow for the loss of his Mirza; they consoled him, and apologised to him exceedingly. Afterwards they all proceeded together to the palace, and stated before Mahmud Shah, that they were all one-hearted brethren, and that the past accident was all forgotten.

From time to time the Vazir Fatah Khan treated Dost Mohammed Khan with much consideration, and had a high opinion of his bravery, enterprising character, and experience, from which he had gained numerous advantages. He accordingly used his influence in the court, and at last succeeded in inducing Mahmud Shah to confer the title of Sardar, or chief, upon Dost Mohammed Khan, and to give him much more influence in the affairs of government. Now the Sardar of my tale became the object of more jealousy among his brothers. Every one of them feared and suspected him; and they, as well as the other chiefs, feeling alarmed, began to say among themselves, that it was not unlikely the Sardar Dost Mohammed Khan would soon send them also to join Mirza Ali Khan.

In short, the Sardar Dost Mohammed Khan established his plans so firmly, and grew so much in power, that he never acted on the advice of any individual, but managed affairs by his own mature deliberation. This established the affection and confidence of the Vazir in him much more than before, and his influence increased more and more daily. The Sardar was always present in the night parties of the Vazir, and bore a golden cup permanently in his hands. He filled it with water and sometimes with wine, as the Vazir requested, and gave it to him to drink.

It is said that when the Vazir was a little tipsy at these wine parties, he generally gave a hint to the Sardar Dost Mohammed Khan to enter his room (whence his beloved wife, named Bhagi, was witnessing the pleasures of the party) to prepare his bed. While the Sardar was engaged in performing this duty, his graceful, youthful, and comely person, had desperately won the love and heart of the above-mentioned lady. It was out of her power to keep her feelings secret any longer from the beloved object—the Sardar Dost Mohammed Khan, the pleasure of whose society she enjoyed till the Vazir, her noble husband, entered the apartment. It is not known whether the Vazir was aware of this fire of love between his wife and the Sardar, which was every day gaining strength. On many occasions the Vazir allowed him to remain in his private room to enjoy the advantages of his society and conversation. It must be remembered that neither Shah Mahmud nor his Vazir Fatah Khan could boast of their good morals. There was no limit to their most dissipated practices. Sardar Dost Mohammed Khan was undoubtedly a beautiful lad, and therefore a real favourite of the Vazir, who allowed generally his beautiful brother to remain in his palace, and thus gain the royal favours and power.

When the Vazir Fatah Khan received the required sum from Mohammed Azim Khan, he made the necessary arrangements for undertaking an expedition against the Governor of Kashmir, named Ata Mohammed Khan Bamzai, son of the late Mukhtar-ud-daulah. Before the army of the Vazir, under the immediate command of the sardar Dost Mohammed Khan, reached the suburbs of Kashmir, the said Governor sent overtures, and agreed to pay the tribute of three lakhs of rupees annually to the Kabul government; which promise was gladly accepted by the Vazir and the Sardar. Hence they sent their agents to receive the stipulated sum, and bent their course towards Multan.

Immediately after their departure the agents of the Vazir Fatah Khan, and of the Sardar Dost Mahommed Khan, were driven out of Kashmir by Ata Mohammed Khan, the governor of that place; and with all haste they joined their masters in the country of Multan. On their arrival they reported to the Vazir and to the Sardar that the said governor had treated them with disgrace, and refused to pay the tribute. On this the Vazir and the Sardar retraced their steps by the Esakhail route, and purposed to weaken the power of the refractory governor by besieging and reducing the fort of Atak.

In the mean time the unfortunate news came from Kabul that the Sayad Ashraf and Sayad Ata, the great fanatics, had placed Shah Zadah Abbas on the throne, and intended to excite their Sunni followers to attack the Persians. This not only frustrated all the plans of the Vazir Fatah Khan, and of the Sardar Dost Mohammed Khan, but created great confusion amid the Persian division of their army, —the foundation of their power. They came and stated to the Vazir and to the Sardar, that if they were not allowed immediately to return to Kabul for the purpose of protecting their fellow Persians against the intended attack of the Sunnis, their wives and children, now in Kabul, would be massacred, or made slaves by the bigoted enemies of their creed. The generals assured the Persians of their protection, and begged them to stay one month longer in their camp, to reduce the turbulent Governor of Kashmir; but they were so uneasy about their families, that against the wish of their masters they struck their tents and took the road to Kabul.

The departure of the Persian division of the army of the Vazir Fatah Khan and of the Sardar Dost Mohammed Khan weakened their power so much, that they had no remedy but to cross the Atak and follow them to Peshavar. Here a council of war was held between the wise Sardar and the Vazir; and it was resolved that the latter, with his nominal king Mahmud Shah, should remain in Peshavar, and that the former, along with Mohammed Azim Khan, and the head of the returning division of the Persians, should proceed to Kabul, whither the Vazir and Mahmud Shah should soon follow them. After speedy and double marches every day the Sardar Dost Mohammed Khan and his Persian party reached Kabul; and for ten days a hard fight continued between him and the rebels, headed by Shah Zadah, afterwards called Shah Abbas. In this battle the victory was won by the Sardar, and Shah Abbas was made prisoner. The principal factious chiefs, as Sayad Ashraf, with his tumultuous friends of Kohistan, were ordered by the Sardar to be executed. The other fanatic rebel Sayad Ata was laid down on his breast on the ground, and then an elephant was made to trample on him, which crushed him to death. Such was the end of Sayad Ata, a descendant of the Prophet!!

The Vazir Fatah Khan, and Mahmud Shah, on their return, found that every thing was quiet in Kabul, and that the wicked men had been annihilated by the Sardar Dost Mohammed and Mohammed Azim Khan. They all passed about one year in the arduous duty of restoring order, peace, and security, in the administration of the government. The reform and improvement in the revenue and mercantile matters introduced by the sagacious Sardar filled the empty chests of the government with money. The money coined in the temporary reign of the unfortunate Shah Abbas had much mixture of copper in it, and very little silver. To this the Sardar paid particular attention, and melting the whole of the bad coin, ordered that purer silver should be obtained and be struck into new coin of proper value.

No sooner had the affairs of the government improved, and the state treasury was a little filled, than the Vazir Fatah Khan and the Sardar Dost Mohammed Khan made preparations for an expedition against Kashmir, but it is said that the Vazir was not so quick as usual, and appeared very slow in his preparations for an immediate departure. This was at once observed by the sharp eyes of the Sardar, who addressed the following speech to the Vazir in open "darbar" or court. "It appears to me that the victory gained last year, the annihilation of the seditious chiefs, the confinement of Shah Zadah Abbas, the repossession of Kabul, and the elevation of our King Shah Mahmud to the throne of his forefathers, by the use of the sword, and by the wisdom of the members of our family, have been a sufficient source of gratification to those who are attached to our fortunes and to his Majesty Shah Mahmud. Not only this, but the citizens, fearless of the attacks of the lawless followers of the late rebel Sayad Ashraf of Kohistan, sleep comfortably: reform and improvement have been successfully introduced into the agitated affairs of government, may our King Shah Mahmud, and my noble brother the present Vazir, as well as the rest of chiefs, including myself, enjoy the fruit of our hard earned authority; but I regret to say that the luxurious habits of the king, and of my noble brother the Vazir, and the carelessness of the other chiefs, bid fair to cause that the present condition of the country be not a lasting one; and that the enjoyments of my superiors be not durable; and in this respect the most blind and foolish policy appears to prevail. One cause for every one of the above-mentioned individuals falling into luxurious indolence appears to be, that they forget the seditious conduct of Ata Mohammed Khan, governor of the rich valley of Kashmir, without the possession of which region no king of Afghanistan has been, or ever will be, able to maintain a large army and the royal dignity." The noble hearers, as well as the Vazir, made no opposition to the speech of the Sardar, but every one cried aloud the words "Bisyar Khub" (well done) with cheers. The Sardar added, "Notwithstanding the peace and pleasure which every one seems to enjoy, and that to imitate them there is an open field for me also, yet the rules of sound and foresighted diplomacy, which are always wandering in my heart and brain, have not allowed me to rest a moment, and I shall never be easy until some mature steps are taken to punish the hostile obstinacy of Ata Mohammed Khan, the governor of Kashmir, who turned the government agent, as well as that of my noble brother the Vazir, with disgrace out of the valley; and refused to pay the stipulated sum of tribute. It is not possible to defray the general expenses of the movements of an army under my noble brother the Vazir, to check the restless spirit of the discontented chiefs, unless the country of Kashmir be ceded to us." This speech of the Sardar Dost Mohammed Khan did not only cause the cheers of the assembly, but excited all the chiefs, and his noble brother the Vazir, to set out immediately for Kashmir.

On this a great number of horses were distributed among the chiefs, and the state treasury was opened to pay the troops, who went off with the Vazir Fatah Khan and the Sardar Dost Mohammed Khan for Kashmir. When they reached Atak, and were in the western part of the Panjab, they entered into an offensive and defensive alliance with the lion of this state, the late Maharajah Ranjit Singh. His Majesty the Maharajah assisted them with a large Sikh force to chastise the governor of Kashmir, named Ata

Mohammed Khan. The governor was busy making the necessary preparations to defend himself. When all negotiations failed, both armies were ordered to get ready for fighting the next morning. The Sardar Dost Mohammed Khan led the Kabul army with steadiness and order, and suddenly engaged with the enemy. A great action took place between the two Afghan chiefs, and after a great loss of men on both sides, the lion of Kabul was successful, and Ata Mohammed Khan, the governor, with his brother Gholam Mohammed, were totally routed and made prisoners.

After the rich and celebrated valley of Kashmir came thus into the possession of the Vazir Fatah Khan and of the Sardar Dost Mohammed Khan, they dismissed the Sikh general to return with his army to the Maharajah, and gave him some friendly presents for his Highness. As some intrigues were in existence between the prisoners and the Sikh general, he therefore begged the Vazir and the Sardar to have them released, and allow them to proceed with him to Lahore. The Sardar thoroughly disapproved, and gave his reasons for so doing. He also pointed out to the Vazir the harm which would undoubtedly follow if the prisoners were delivered over to the Sikh government; nevertheless the general succeeded in inducing the Vazir to allow Gholam Mohammed Khan to go with him, and to keep his brother, the late governor, still by him as a prisoner. This extremely annoyed the Sardar, who, in a tone of displeasure, said to his noble brother the Vazir, "Allow me to prophesy the calamity which the release of Gholam Mohammed Khan will bring upon our heads, and remorse to you for your unwise policy," &c. &c.

The day was not far distant when the symptoms of the misfortunes which the Sardar Dost Mohammed Khan had predicted, began to appear, on the very arrival of Gholam Mohammed Khan in the court of Ranjit Singh. He insisted upon his third brother Jahandad Khan, the commandar of Atak, selling that fort to the Sikh government; and his brother did so on receiving one lakh of rupees for it. The occupation of that important fort by the Sikh garrison provided the Maharajah with the key of the conquest not only of Kashmir after a short time, but of many other Afghan places on the western bank of the Indus. Now the Vazir repented of his folly in liberating Gholam Mohammed Khan, and giving him to the Sikh chief, which he had done utterly against the advice of Dost Mohammed Khan.

The Vazir Fatah Khan felt himself in a very complicated situation, and was lost in speculations how to repair his mistake, and put his affairs on a better footing. He appointed Mohammed Azim Khan governor of Kashmir, and himself, with the Sardar Dost Mohammed Khan, quitted that valley for Atak. Here they resolved to attack the Sikh garrison. On this the Lion of Panjab dispatched an army of thirty thousand men, under the command of Divan Mohkam Chand, Bhai Ram Singh, Dal Singh, and Ghaus Kham, with directions to destroy the Afghan force. This large army encamped on the bank Nilab branch of the Indus, and engaged in action with the Vazir and the Sardar. The latter was the hero of the field, and his exploits of that day were highly applauded by the Sikh generals. At last the Sikh army succeeded in depriving the Afghans of the place whence they were provided with water.

It was about midday that the sun grew hotter, and the weather exceedingly warm, whilst both armies were annihilating their respective antagonists. The thirst, in consequence of the scarcity of water, was sadly felt in the army of the Vazir and of the Sardar, on which the former begged the latter hero to take command of the Qizilbash or Persian cavalry, and at once rush into the main column of the Sikh army. On this occasion the Sardar and his Qizilbash fought so desperately that the Sikh heroes gave them the title of gallants of the first class, and the ornamental title of celebrated and matchless champions (Rustam and Afra si ab*) of the old days. The Sardar rushed into the main line of the enemy, captured some of their guns, and forced them to leave their ground and retreat; but unfortunately some of the Afghans, overpowered by thirst, made such a disorderly attack on the other division of the Sikh army, that they were repulsed with loss: and thus the Kabul army, under the Vazir and the Sardar, after gaining once victory and guns, was routed, and compelled to fall back upon Peshavar, and from thence they marched to Kabul. Here the news arrived that Shah Shuja, with the Shah Zadah Haidar, had collected a large force, and having fought with the Navab Jabbar Khan, the governor of Derah Ghazi Khan, were

* Fabulous warriors of Shah Namah.

defeated. Though this intelligence was acceptable to them, yet it excited the jealousy of the Navab's brothers, the Vazir and the Sardar, who proceeded to supplant him. On their arrival at Derah they said to the Navab that, with regard to the sum of three lakhs of rupees, the balance of the revenues of Derah, he was squandering all this to satisfy his vanity and idle pleasures; and that, therefore, they must dismiss the Navab, having done which they returned with Mahmud Shah to Kabul.

CHAPTER III.

Brothers envy Dost Mohammed Khan—He chastises the Kohistanis—Expedition against Hirat—Murder of the Vazir Fatah Khan—The Sardar takes up arms—Besieges the Bala Hisar—Takes Kabul, and makes Sultan Ali king, and himself minister—His intrigues—Murder of Shah Sultan Ali—Mohammed Azim Khan—The Sardar procures money from the Sindhians—He deserts—Takes Ghazni—Fights with Azim Khan—Corresponds with Ranjit Singh—Sikh force at Peshavar—Dost's treachery towards Azim Khan—Death of Azim Khan.

Although the Sardar Dost Mohammed Khan received kindness and honour from his principal brothers, as the Vazir Fatah Khan, &c., yet being born from a mother of a different creed, and not of a high Afghan family, he was looked upon with contempt by the other brothers, who boasted that they were descended from pure and noble parents. On several occasions the jealousy of the brothers threw him into all the distresses of poverty. His dependants and horses have often passed nights and days without a piece of bread for the human being or a blade of grass for the horses.

In spite of this cheerless state of life, Dost Mohammed Khan never departed from the perseverance of his mind, combined as it was with all the external appearances of sincerity, and real internal hypocrisy. He was trying to gain ascendancy by all means possible, and therefore in return for all the animosity of his jealous brothers his behaviour towards them was at all times civil and obliging. This sometimes made them exceedingly ashamed of their own conduct, and at the same time astonished at his superior wisdom and management. His sweet words were supported by flattery, and he showed himself regardless of that respect which his own age was entitled to receive from his younger brothers, who were prosperous while himself was poor; and by these means he had created and organised such sound schemes for his own success that none could dare to hope to annihilate him. I have heard with my own ears from the Sardar Dost Mohammed Khan, that he had gone without food for three or four days successively, and several nights, after taking only a morsel of dry bread or a handful of half-fried grain—that in the mean time he had often laid himself down on the bare ground, making the stone his pillow; and also, having no means to maintain servants, he had many times saddled his own horse. While his heart was wounded with these painful wants, his conversation was always refreshed by a lively wit and a smiling countenance, leaving behind an impression of admiration on the hearts of the chiefs under his brothers.

The Sardar Dost Mohammed Khan was excessively fond of drinking, and carried it to an extreme excess. It is said that he has emptied several dozens of bottles in one night, and did not cease from drinking until he was quite intoxicated, and could not drink a drop more. He has often become senseless with drinking, and has on that account kept himself confined in bed during many days. He has been often seen in a state of stupidity on horseback, and having no turban, but a skull-cap on his head.

It has been stated by the early companions of the Sardar Dost Mohammed Khan, and confirmed by his own mouth, that he had and still has an extraordinary taste for music. When pleased with drinking wine, he has often sung ballads, and played upon the "Rabab," a kind of fiddle. His intimate friend and supporter was Gholam Khan Populzai; and both these persons were considered in Afghanistan the first players on the "Rabab." The fort of Nanchi was the favourite seat where Dost Mohammed Khan formed his pleasure parties, and these were generally composed of Gholam Khan Populzai, Mirza Abdul Sami, and Agha Mohammed. The former, being richer than the Sardar, assisted him frequently in pecuniary matters, and clothed and fed him on many occasions. Gradually he gained rather more influence, yet was in the habit of drinking.

It was on the evening of a beautiful day in the spring, that the eldest son of the Sardar Dost Mohammed Khan, named Mohammed Afzal Khan, drank wine with his younger brother, Mohammed Akhbar Khan, and both of them met him drunk. He was incensed at their conduct, and determined to punish them. He seized and bruised them severely; and at last taking them up to the roof, threw them down on stony ground, by which he had nearly endangered their existence. On this his favourite wife, the mother of Mohammed Akhbar Khan, who is wiser than the other wives of the Sardar, was informed of the dangerous state of her son. She went to her husband and stated that he himself is desirous of drinking, while he punishes the sons, and persuades them to the contrary; and that this is not just, as the wise of former days have said that a son cannot well inherit the property unless he follows the example of his father, and that consequently they imitated him in drinking. Hearing these words from the lips of his favourite, the Sardar felt ashamed, and then swore not to drink wine any more.

At the time Mahmud Shah returned from Derahjat, the chiefs of Kohistan, especially the head men and priests of Istalif, made an open rebellion. The Vazir Fatah Khan formed an expedition against them, but was obliged to fall back unsuccessful, having spoiled their cultivation and gardens. This made the rebels suffer the risk of starvation, and they made a resolution and agreed with each other to revenge the loss by destroying the residence of the Vazir in Kabul, and ruining his garden by ploughing over the young plants with a plough drawn by asses, which they did immediately the Vazir quitted the capital to punish some other distant refractory chiefs.

The Shah Mahmud and the Vazir Fatah Khan did all in their power to induce the Kohistanis to come into allegiance by bribes, titles, and rewards; but all this was useless: and when any threatening preparations were made against them they ascended the mountains. This disorderly state of things continued for some time, when the Sardar Dost Mohammed Khan volunteered to undertake the government of Kohistan and to punish the ringleaders. The Shah and the Vazir gladly accepted the offer, and made him governor of that turbulent district. He left Kabul with his followers, and encamped at Nanchi the first day. Here he passed the night with his Qizilbash friends in drinking, singing, and dancing, and also committed some other idle acts unworthy of his dignity. Navab Asad Khan having heard of it, advised the Sardar not to do any base act of the kind hereafter, as it will fix an everlasting stigma on his character. To this he replied, that though he was guilty of folly, yet the charge is not so bad as the mean and covetous oppression of the Navab himself. The latter requested him to explain what he meant; on which the Sardar reminded him that on a certain time he saw at the court of the Navab that a woman complained against her husband. He was summoned, and proved clearly that he had been always partial to his wife, and had never given her any reason for dissatisfaction. After a long investigation, the Navab discovered that the old husband being careless of the rules of society, disgusted his wife. Here the Sardar stated that the Navab Asad Khan decided that both were guilty, and therefore commanded them to pay three hundred rupees as a fine to him, besides suffering a long imprisonment. When this was asserted by the Sardar as a sample of the justice distributed by the Navab with regard to the wife and her husband, he caused the whole assembly to laugh at the farce of his adviser, the Navab, who thenceforward ceased to interfere with the Sardar.

Next day, the Sardar Dost Mohammed Khan entered the valley of Kohistan, where he succeeded in seizing numerous robbers, whom he immediately executed. Also by his sweet and hypocritical words, as well as by all possible sacred oaths, he induced the various rebel chiefs to wait upon him, and then lost no time in murdering them. On his arrival at Charkar, the Sardar took up his quarters in the fort of Faiz Khan. He induced Aslam Khan and Saqi Khan by a solemn agreement to join him in Charkar with other chiefs; and they relied on his oaths and paid him their respects. In order to banish all suspicion of his evil intentions towards them, he married the daughter of Baqa Khan, one of the chiefs, and thus, after gaining their confidence, put the father of the new bride to death. This assumed garb of sincerity was, however, merely a mask; and while the chiefs were dining with him, the Sardar made a signal to cut off their heads. There was still one of his greatest foes alive, whom the Sardar wished to destroy, and while he was in existence the Sardar considered that the tranquillity would exist neither in Kohistan nor in Kabul, where the people of the Sunni sect always raise tumult by his aid. He sent deputation after deputation with solemn declarations written on the Qoran, and assured Khojah Khanji of his highest regard and respect towards him. He addressed him as a father, and stated that his intention was to give charge of the government of Kohistan to him, and himself go back to Kabul. All these flattering but false oaths produced no effect upon the cautious Khojah. Hereupon the Sardar Dost Mohammed Khan adopted a most novel measure to get hold of him at the sacrifice of another man. Khojah Khanji, like other chiefs of Kohistan, had many enemies, and one of the strongest was with Dost Mohammed Khan. He put him to the sword, and thus boasted the sincerity of his good wish towards the Khojah, as proved by destroying his enemy. This vile deed was perpetrated at Bayan, where he begged the Khojah to honour him with his company, to settle past differences at the place of the murder of his antagonist. Induced at length, and blinded by his destiny, he came with a large number of followers. No one of course was better able than the Sardar Dost Mohammed Khan to restore confidence by his sweet language, in the Khojah, whom he addressed on every occasion as his venerable father. In the evening the Sardar led his guest inside of the fort, on the pretence that he might survey the valuable property of his enemy, whom the Sardar just destroyed in order to ensnare the Khojah. As soon as he was within, the gates of the castle were shut in the face of his followers, and the Sardar praised the gun of the Khojah, and desired him to show it to him. . Immediately after this he ordered his Qizilbash companions to assassinate the Khojah, whom he at the same time called his father! and his head was thrown over the walls amid the large retinue of this unfortunate victim. At this sad occurrence his followers determined to attack the fort, and fired for a considerable part of the night; but in the morning they all dispersed, leaving the Sardar Dost Mohammed Khan to enjoy the triumph of his wilful murders. This was not the end of his dexterity in such deeds, for he massacred in one day eight of the chiefs at Charkar, and Sayad Ashrat of Opiyan, men of great influence and reverence, shared the same fate. When he had no more blood to shed, he engaged himself in arranging matters for collecting the revenues and distributing justice. In two months he completed these affairs and returned to Kabul.

While the Sardar Dost Mohammed Khan was employed in Kohistan, he was accompanied by Jai Singh, a Sikh chieftain, with whom he had become acquainted, when the latter was on a mission to Peshavar. Shah Mahmud and the Vazir Fatah Khan finding that the affairs in Kohistan were all satisfactorily settled by the Sardar Dost Mohammed Khan, they appointed a governor in Kabul, and themselves started for Peshavar. Hence they dispatched the Navab Asad Khan to Sardar Mohammed Azim Khan in Kashmir, demanding the sum of twenty lakhs of rupees, the arrears of the revenue of that valley. He delayed the payment of the sum, by which he hastened the departure of the army of the Shah to Kashmir. Mohammed Azim Khan, having heard of the hostile movements of his brothers under his Majesty, assembled all the chiefs with their forces, strengthened the fort of Muzaffarabad with a strong garrison, and afterwards encamped on the road between the two hills to check the progress of his enemy. The Sardar Dost Mohammed Khan was called upon to lead the attacking army. He found that the road was narrow, and closely occupied by Azim Khan, and that an attempt to force through would cause a great slaughter of his men. On mature deliberation he commands his followers to dismount from their horses and follow him to fight on foot in ascending the hills, and thus compel Azim Khan to fall back on Kashmir. The Sardar forced the garrison of Muzaffarabad to surrender, on which the enemy strongly occupied all the heights of the mountains which closely commanded the route of the Sardar's force. Here the Shah and the Vazir, as well as Dost Mohammed Khan, found themselves placed in a difficult position, and without any prospect of gaining a victory. Nevertheless the perfidy of the latter did more good to their cause than the swords of his party. He wrote letters to some of the chiefs in the camp of Azim Khan, stating that he had received all their letters, and laid them under the feet of Shah and of the Vazir. He added that these have appreciated their good will, and believe that they will fulfil their promised resolution by imprisoning and bringing the disloyal chief (Azim) into the presence of his Majesty early next day, while all in the camp are engaged in attending to their morning prayers. The cunning Sardar directed the bearer of the letters to pass by such a road and company on guard, so that he might be detected, and his letters and himself taken to Mohammed Khan. It was done accordingly, and caused in him the utmost alarm. He began to suspect that all his retinue were bribed, and that he would no doubt be delivered as a prisoner to the Sardar. In the mean time he continued his talk of fighting to the last, and yet on the other hand he secretly opened a negotiation with his foes. While this was going on, the winter and snow caused a great loss on both sides, and a treaty of peace was concluded on condition of receiving provisions for two weeks, and a sum of thirteen lakhs of rupees. Azim Khan came in person to the Sardar Dost Mohammed Khan, and there having tied a sword to his neck and the Holy Qoran on his head,* he accompanied the Sardar thence to the royal camp. The Vazir Fatah Khan, with the consent of his royal master, pardoned Azim Khan, embraced and kissed him as his brother. Such was the fruitful result of the Sardar's perfidious letters!

The army of Mahmud Shah returned to Kabul, and after passing the few months of the winter there, intended to go to Qandhar. The intelligence of the Sikhs having been attacked by Mohammed Azim Khan in Kashmir, and of their having been routed by him with great loss, inspired a joyful and fresh enthusiasm in the Vazir Fatah Khan and the Sardar Dost Mohammed Khan, and they prepared an expedition for defending Hirat against the Persians. On reaching Qandhar they received information that their nephew Abdul Vahid Khan, at the head of the Hirat army, had been defeated by the Persian prince Hasan Ali Mirza at Ghoryan, and probably taken prisoner.

* A sign of confessing to be guilty, and imploring pardon.

This news alarmed the Vazir Fatah Khan, who, leaving Mahmud Shah at Qandhar, set out with great haste to stop the Persians before they might come upon Hirat, and the Sardar Dost Mohammed Khan of course was with him. Mahmud Shah was not well disposed towards Haji Firozuddin, the prince and ruler of Hirat, in consequence of his not assisting him when routed by Shah Shuja, and thus gave secret encouragement to the Vazir for the purpose of punishing the Shah Zadah Firoz, who was his own brother. All the Afghans and other chiefs of Khorasan became attached to them by the liberality of the Vazir and the flattering tongue of the Sardar. A battle ensued; it was fought bravely, and the Vazir was slightly wounded by the Persian army or by his own adherents; but of this the certainty is not known. This wound, however, caused the Vazir to abandon the field of action, where Dost Mohammed Khan had distinguished himself to an amazing degree.

Shah Zadah Haji Firozuddin treated the Vazir Fatah Khan with marked distinction, and commanded all his chiefs to pay their respects every morning to the Vazir before they come to his Royal

Highness; but this generous feeling of the Shah Zadah made no favourable impression upon his guest. He directed the active Dost Mohammed Khan to enter the city of Hirat, under the pretence of being invited, and to place his Kohistan followers in small parties for the night, in the different houses of relations and friends. The Vazir added, that when the chiefs of the Haji should come to see him next day out of the city, he should make them prisoners, and Dost Mohammed Khan was to shut the gates of the city, and take possession of the palace "Arg" with the prince. He entered the city, as was arranged, with his retinue, and after the sun rose and the Shah Zadah's courtiers had gone out to Fatah Khan, as usual, the Sardar Dost Mohammed Khan massacred the palace-guard and seized the person of the Shah Zadah Firoz. Afterwards he commenced to plunder and to gain possession of all the jewels, gold, and treasure of the captive prince, and even went so far as to despoil the inmates of the household; and committed an unparalleled deed by taking off the jewelled band which fastened the trowsers of the wife of the Prince Malik Qasim, the son of the captive, and treated her rudely in other ways. The pillaged lady was the sister of Kam Ran, to whom she sent her profaned robe; and the Shah Zadah, or her brother, resolved and swore to revenge the injury. Fatah Khan was informed of the immense booty which the Sardar had taken, and also his improper conduct towards the royal lady; and the Vazir planned to take the plundered property from the Sardar Dost Mohammed Khan, and to chastise him for his deeds in the Palace. The Sardar having heard of this made his way through the mountains to join his brother Mohammed Azim Khan, the governor of Kashmir. He was there put under restraint by the direction of the Vazir, who was preparing again to wage war with the Persians.

The Shah Zadah Kam Ran reached Hirat, internally determined to have revenge, and yet externally he appeared very civil to the Vazir Fatah Khan. He advised him to procrastinate his second expedition against the Persians, and that it would be better to give rest to his army. In the mean time he laid a plot for the ruin of the Vazir; and many other Durrani chiefs, who had been reduced to subordination by the Vazir, and were jealous of his increasing power, joined him in planning the destruction of the Vazir. He was seized by Kam Ran at the consent of his father Mahmud Shah, and blinded by Ata Mohammed Khan Bamzai. His brothers contrived their escape from Hirat, excepting Purdil Khan, who was also released on the condition of his continuing loyal and obedient to the prince. No tragedy of modern days can be compared with that barbarous one that ended the life of the Vazir. He was conducted blind, and pinioned, into the presence of Mahmud Shah, whom he had elevated to the throne. The Shah asked him to write to his rebellious brothers to submit, to which he replied with fortitude, that he was a poor blind prisoner, and had no influence over his brothers. Mahmud Shah was incensed at his obstinacy, and ordered him to be put to the sword, and the Vazir was cruelly and deliberately butchered by the courtiers, cutting him limb from limb, and joint from joint, as was reported, after his nose, ears, fingers, and lips, had been chopped off. His fortitude was so extraordinary that he neither showed a sign of the pain he suffered, nor asked the perpetrators to diminish their cruelties, and his head was at last sliced from his lacerated body. Such was the shocking result of the misconduct of his brother the Sardar Dost Mohammed Khan towards the royal female in Hirat. However, the end of the Vazir Fatah Khan was the end of the Sadozai realm, and an omen for the accession of the new dynasty of the Barakzais, or his brothers in Afghanistan.

Mohammed Azim Khan wrote from Kashmir to Shah Shuja, and assured him of the united aid of his brothers, as well as of the Sardar Dost Mohammed Khan, against Shah Mahmud, who had ordered his brother the Vazir to be murdered. Shuja was joined by Nawab Mohammed Zaman Khan, and after defeating Samandar Khan, he took possession of Derah Ghazi Khan. The Sardar received the sum of three lakhs of rupees from his brother Azim Khan in Kashmir, and assembled a moderate force to join his brothers Yar, Sultan, and Pir Mohammed Khan in Peshavar, and these elevated and acknowledged the Prince Ayub, king of Afghanistan. The Sardar also made secret engagements with the Prince Sultan Ali, and secured his consent to make him sovereign if necessary. Mahmud Shah was frightened to death by the threatening news that the Barakzai had resolved to supplant him in the throne. In the mean time Ranjit Singh caused an alarm towards Atak, which forced the brothers of the Vazir to leave Peshavar and take shelter in Lalpurah. Hence the Sardar Dost Mohammed Khan sent a few beautiful horses, with some other presents, to the Lion of Panjab; and as soon as he returned towards his capital, the Sardar, with his brothers Yar Mohammed Khan, &c., came through the Khaibar upon Peshavar, and compelled Jahandad Khan, the Bamzai, to flee to the country of the Yusafzais.

On this Ata Mohammed Khan, the Bamzai, relation of Jahandad Khan, induced Mahmud Shah and Kam Ran to send Prince Jahangir, the son of the latter, with him, and to subdue all the Barakzai rebels, as he called Sardar Dost Mohammed Khan, the brother of the murdered Vazir. He succeeded in his proposals to the king, and came to Kabul with the prince. Immediately the Sardar wrote an offensive and defensive treaty on the margin of the Holy Qoran, and in an important article thereof he and his brothers bound themselves by a solemn oath to divide the kingdom for ever between themselves and Ata Mohammed Khan, if he agreed to lend no assistance whatever either to Shah Shuja, to Kam Ran, or to any other Sadozai. The Sardar dispatched this treaty in charge of a confidential adherent, and Ata Mohammed Khan, knowing that neither Shah Shuja nor Mahmud Shah, with Kam Ran, could shine in the presence of the brighter talents of the Sardar, he accepted the offers made in the treaty. He sent a secret letter to the Sardar Dost Mohammed Khan with a verbal token to make it more sincere, and which was in these words: "When the late Vazir Fatah Khan left you with Prince Kam Ran a long time ago in Qandhar, the friendship between us (Dost and Ata Mohammed) was strengthened by a solemn oath." If this was true, the Sardar Dost Mohammed Khan was to march for Kabul with easiness of mind, and at Khovajah Rivash he will meet and confer with the Sardar himself. At the arrival of such a flattering communication from Ata Mohammed Khan Bamzai, the Sardar made arrangements to leave Ayub Shah at Peshavar, and taking with him Shah Zadah Sultan Ali and Ismail, he set out for Kabul. The Sardar was well aware that the former Shah Zadah was the master of three or four lakhs of rupees, and he therefore renewed his promise and oaths of putting the crown of Kabul on his head, and gave hopes of the same nature secretly to the latter Shah Zadah.

After uninterrupted and rapid marches the Sardar Dost Mohammed Khan reached Butkhak with the Shah Zadahs,—and the Prince Jahangir ordered Ata Mohammed Khan, the Bamzai (who had already entered into intrigues with the Sardar), and Baqar Khan, to meet the Sardar with arms, and to shut themselves within the citadel of the Bala Hisar in Kabul, with a considerable store of provisions, with the view to be besieged by the enemy to resist till relieved by Mahmud Shah and Kam Ran his father. Ata Mohammed Khan pitched his tent near the village of Bibi Mahru,* and the Sardar Dost Mohammed Khan, with Navab Samad Yar and Pir Mohammed Khan, moved and encamped at Khovajah Rivash, as previously appointed, and about ten o'clock at night Hafizji, the son of Mir Vaiz, and Mulla Hidayat Ullah, effected a clandestine interview between the Sardar and Ata Mohammed, the head of the Jahangir's army. The treaty which had been formerly contracted through their respective

* Where the British troops under Brigadier Shelton were defeated at the outbreak in Kabul in 1841.

deputations, was now solemnly renewed personally. This treaty was resealed by the Sardar, Yar Mohammed, and by Navab Samad Khan, to Ata Mohammed Khan, who was to desert Jahangir, and allow the Sardar to attack the Bala Hisar. Ata Mohammed Khan desired that Pir Mohammed Khan should add his name and seal to this agreement, being one of the brothers of the same family as the Sardar Dost Mohammed Khan. As the object of the Sardar was to destroy Ata Mohammed Khan, after he had obtained his end, he therefore thought proper not to include Pir Mohammed Khan in the treaty, for the purpose of employing him against his meditated future enemy, with whom he was now contracting terms of friendship. With this view the Sardar stated repeatedly to Ata Mohammed Khan that Pir Mohammed Khan was young and not fit to be trusted with such important secrets, and that there was no need of his appearing to be a party in the treaty; but that he will, no doubt, follow the example of his brothers respecting the articles of the agreement. Ata Mohammed Khan outwardly harangued his followers, that if they relax in their exertions in promoting the cause of their royal masters, Shah Mahmud, Shah Zadah Kam Ran, or Shah Zadah Jahangir, and fail to punish the Barakzai rebels (Sardar Dost Mohammed Khan, &c.), the wrath of the Almighty God will fall upon them and curse them if they betray his cause. He continued his treacherous harangues for a few days, while secretly he exchanged a great many oaths of perpetual friendship with the Sardar Dost Mohammed Khan, and was thus betraying his own sovereign. It was agreed that they were to have a second interview with each other in the "Burj i Vazir," and ratify the agreements with much more satisfactory and solemn swearings and ceremonies. Ata Mohammed came accordingly, and as soon as he entered the door of the "Burj i Vazir" the Sardar Dost Mohammed Khan induced his brother Pir Mohammed (whom he had purposely kept out of the treaty), to throw down his newly and solemnly made friend, Ata Mohammed Khan, on the ground, and to pluck out his eyes; and he accordingly perpetrated this foul deed. The deprivation of sight drove away all ambitious thoughts from the head of the blind chief, who, while governor of Kashmir, had inflicted similar injuries on numerous persons, and had also taken a prominent part in blinding the late Fatah Khan.

The Sardar Dost Mohammed Khan, relieved from a powerful enemy, or an intriguing friend, resolved to besiege the Bala Hisar. Shah Zadah Jahangir was treacherously advised by some of his adherents (with whom Dost Mohammed Khan was intriguing) to evacuate the lower citadel, and to close himself, with his retinue, in the upper one; and the empty part of the Bala Hisar was instantly possessed by the enemy. A battle ensued, and Dost Mohammed Khan formed a mine and blew up part of the gate of the other citadel. Shah Zadah Jahangir then found himself in a dangerous situation, and being accompanied by his confidential friends, he stole his escape towards Ghazni.

Now, after such an extraordinary display of talent and perseverance of mind, after such intrigues and murders, and this surprising run of good luck, the Sardar Dost Mohammed Khan found himself master of Kabul;—but the peace of his mind was subverted by the arrival of the intelligence that Shah Mahmud and Shah Zadah Kam Ran were in progress from Qandhar to fight against him; and at the same time that Mohammed Azim Khan had left Kashmir with the view that he, being the eldest of the brothers, should not leave Dost Mohammed to become master of the capital of Afghanistan. He, nevertheless, being elated with his victory, and at the same time fearful of his enemies on the south, and of his jealous brothers on the east, he proclaimed Shah Zadah Sultan Ali as king of Kabul, and made himself his minister. This intelligence more stirred up the jealousy of Mohammed Azim Khan and of the other brothers. They invited Shah Shuja to join with them for their common advantage, but some difference occurred and caused a battle between the Shah and his inviters, in which the latter were victorious, and the former was put to flight. They dared not, however, to move upon Kabul without being under the nominal authority and shadow of the Sadozai Prince; and they therefore sought, found, and proclaimed Shah Zadah Ayub as king. The Sardar Dost Mohammed Khan, under his own appointed king, Shah Zadah Sultan Ali, now left Kabul to meet Shah Mahmud and Shah Zadah Kam Ran. He soon discovered that it was impossible to gain a victory against such a powerful army of the Shah, which was composed of all the principal Durrani chiefs; and he therefore thought it advisable to have recourse to his usual intrigues and stratagems. He accordingly forged seals and letters, as if they were from some of the high chiefs, which formed the army of the Shah Mahmud, and which stated their discontent in serving the Mahmud, and a desire to enter into the employment of the Shah Zadah Sultan Ali,—the king made by the Sardar. He also directed one of his confidential chiefs to enter into correspondence with the enemy, and to pretend to intrigue against him (the Sardar Dost Mohammed Khan), and, moreover, to enclose the forged letters for Mahmud Shah, in order to convince him of his own (the writer's) fidelity and attachment to the Shah, and of his hatred against his employer Dost Mohammed. This perfidy of the Sardar proved successful, so that Mahmud Shah and Kam Ran became suddenly alarmed, and showed the letters to the chiefs, whose seals and names had been forged, and which they now bore, and all of them solemnly denied being the writers of these letters. In the meantime Salu Khan, called Shah Pasand Khan, stated to Shah

Mahmud that all the Durrani chiefs intended to go over to the enemy; and it so happened about that time the Shah Ghasi Dilavar, with a few horsemen, deserted the Shah's camp and joined the Sardar Dost Mohammed Khan. This frightened Shah Zadah Kam Ran and his father to the utmost, and they fled through Hazarajat to Hirat, leaving all the artillery and camp-equipage to the Sardar. Purdil Khan, the other brother, got possession of Qandhar, which was under Gul Mohammed Khan, governor for Mahmud Shah. This was the commencement of Afghanistan into the hands of the Barakzais—Sardar Dost Mohammed Khan and his brothers; and he considered that his good fortune had thus gained for him the possession of Kabul a second time.

Mohammed Azim Khan marched from Kabul with his own assumed king, the Shah Ayub, and the Sardar Dost Mohammed Khan took possession of the stronghold of Ghazni, where he appointed his younger brother, Amir Mohammed Khan, as Governor, with the view that if overpowered by Mohammed Azim and Shah Ayub, he may easily defend himself in this impregnable fort. However the Sardar's position was far from securing to him the enjoyment of the possession of the capital, for he found himself at the same time threatened by his brothers at Qandhar, and by those with Mohammed Azim Khan. Numerous negotiations and altercations were exchanged: and at last it was arranged that Mohammed Azim, being the eldest of the brothers, should enjoy Kabul; that Yar Mohammed Khan should possess Peshavar, and Purdil Khan should receive Qandhar, and the Sardar Dost Mohammed Khan, Ghazni. Thus the country was divided between the brothers of this family, and the nominally proclaimed King of the Sardar was set aside. All appeared happy with this arrangement, and were occupied in planning to repel any external real or apprehended danger. But the Sardar Dost Mohammed Khan was discontented, and searching for an opportunity to secure his own particular advantage.

Mohammed Azim Khan, with Shah Ayub, left Kabul to proceed against Shah Shuja, who was organizing troops in Shikarpur. When the former passed Ghazni, the Sardar Dost Mohammed Khan returned to the capital, and reproclaimed Shah Sultan Ali as king; and this made Mohammed Azim Khan to retrace his steps. When he reached Kabul with his own appointed king, Shah Ayub, the monarch who had been set up by the Sardar abdicated and retired. It is a matter of great difficulty to determine here whether the Sardar did all in his power to subvert the designs of his rival brother, or joined him to dethrone Shah Sultan Ali, who undoubtedly was a prince of high talent and of some wealth. However, he waited upon Sultan Shah, and said to him, that if he was anxious to secure for himself the sovereignty, he must murder Shah Ayub. To this he replied with wrath, that he was not so inhuman as to steep his hands in innocent blood; and he even added, that he will try to destroy any man who shall ever perpetrate such a murder. The Sardar, after making him easy for a few days, persuaded him, for the safety of his person, to retire into the Bala Hisar, which he did. Mohammed Azim Khan explained to Shah Ayub the necessity which existed for putting an end to the life of Shah Sultan Ali,—on the promise that he (Mohammed Azim) will get rid of the Sardar Dost Mohammed Khan in the same manner, and with this view Ayub meanly agreed. Both of the Shahs were living together on friendly terms, till after an evening party the poor Shah Sultan Ali retired to repose, when Prince Asmail, son of Ayub Shah, strangled him to death; and now the cruel Shah requested his instigator, Mohammed Azim Khan, to fulfil his promise, of killing the Sardar Dost Mohammed Khan. To this request, however, he answered, "How can I murder my brother?" Such was the end of Shah Sultan Ali, by the intrigues of the Sardar who had once elevated him to the throne.

After some time the Sardar Dost Mohammed Khan commenced to contrive schemes for reducing the power of his elder brother, Mohammed Azim Khan, and for gaining possession of all his wealth, which he had hoarded up from extortions and all kinds of oppression when Governor of Kashmir. He pretended to appear as if he was really fond of his brother, and could not part with him even when he retired, adding, that he thinks proper to attend him always, and to guard him against his enemies, whereas, in secret, he intended to annihilate him at a favourable opportunity. He had nearly succeeded in his base design when, luckily, Navab Samad Khan became acquainted with the plot, and informed Mohammed Azim Khan immediately. He then increased the number of his personal guard; and to divert the attention of his brother the Sardar he marched with all his treasure and family towards Qandhar, with the intention to receive tribute from the Mirs of Sindh. The Sardar assembled his Qizalbash adherents, such as Mahmud Khan Bayat, &c., and stated that they had abandoned the legal cause of Mahmud Shah, and joined Mohammed Azim Khan in the hope that the wealth he had brought from Kashmir will be circulated amongst them in Kabul; and that now, on the contrary, he goes with it to Qandhar, and enriches its inhabitants. He would therefore advise them to use every energetic exertion and to follow him, and seize him with the Mammon he possesses. They all agreed to this, and started off. Meanwhile Mohammed Azim Khan precipitated his march, and took shelter in the fort of Ghazni; and as he had plenty of money he collected a large force to preserve himself. However, he induced Navab Samad Khan to dissuade the Sardar Dost Mohammed from such an act of hostility against his own brother. The Sardar accepted the terms of peace on condition that a sum of money should be advanced to him to distribute amongst his followers, which was gladly done.

Easiness of mind was restored to Mohammed Azim Khan by this peace, or rather truce, with the Sardar Dost Mohammed Khan, and he proceeded from Ghazni to Qandhar, where, leaving his cumbersome equipage, and being lightly equipped, he started to demand tribute from the Mirs of Sindh; and the Sardar, under the name of a coadjutor, followed him. When the army arrived at Shikarpur, negotiations began between the Mirs and the invader; and, when about to be satisfactorily concluded, here the arch-intriguer, the Sardar Dost Mohammed Khan, sprung his secret mine, and dispatched his uncle Alahdad Khan clandestinely to Mir Ismail Shah, the Minister of the Mirs of Sindh, with the proposal, that if he were to advance him only one lakh of rupees, in lieu of four lakhs which had been demanded by his brother Mohammed Azim Khan, that he, in conjunction with the other brothers, Sherdil and Pir Mohammed Khan, would march back to Qandhar; which deed, by diminishing the strength of the army, and depriving Azim of all brotherly support, would compel him to follow them with whatever the Mirs chose to give him, or even with nothing. The minister knew well that the stratagems of the Sardar Dost Mohammed have always been unquestionably successful; and that he was the first man who, for his own little personal advantage, would aptly sacrifice the material interests of his powerful brother. He therefore made the above-mentioned proposal known to the Mirs, and lost no time in sending the amount of money asked by the Sardar, who, being delighted with this success, which otherwise would never have attended him, deserted Mohammed Azim Khan; and Sherdil and Pir Mohammed Khan of course went with him. Now Azim Khan soon discovered that he was treacherously abandoned by his brothers, and by a larger number of forces than what he had with him: and he therefore considered it proper to fall back upon Qandhar, where Purdil Khan received the intelligence of his failure, by the conduct of the Sardar, before the latter reached the city. He received him coolly on account of this: and the Sardar thinking that Mohammed Azim and Purdil

Khan might join to destroy him, and consequently considered that it was the wisest plan for himself to go to the brothers at Peshavar.

On his route from Qandhar he plundered villages, caravans, &c., and extorted money from every one he met till he reached Kabul. Here he created a tumult, but Azim Khan followed to check his progress. The Sardar had already formed a party of his own in the city, and immediately went to Istaliff, for collecting the Kohistanis against Azim Khan. The Navab Samad Khan caused peace between them, on which the Sardar, plundering all he could on the road, came to Peshavar. Here the brothers of course were aware of the danger which would befal them if they were not liberal and polite to their embarrassing guest, and they instantly gave up the district of Kohat, with its revenues, for his support. Mohammed Azim Khan, with the king of his own creation, Shah Ayub, came to Peshavar, and demanded the revenue of that country for his Majesty from his brothers. When this was settled, he thought, imprudently, to leave the Sardar in the rear, in the possession of Kohat; and he promised he would give him a larger country, affording much more revenue, if he will come with him to Kabul. He then appointed Navabs Samad Khan in Kohat, and Mohammed Zaman Khan at Hashtnagar, he himself retiring to Kabul with the Sardar.

In Kabul the Sardar Dost Mohammed became again restless, and began to quarrel with his brother, Mohammed Azim Khan, and demanded larger sums of money than he could conveniently give. When he pressed hard, Mohammed Azim Khan unwisely said to the Sardar that he may go any where he likes, and that he does not want his services. This was the object of his desire, which proved highly beneficial to himself and injurious to Azim Khan. The Sardar hereupon quitted Kabul, and on the road contrived schemes how he might gain possession of the stronghold of Ghazni. He assembled all his brave followers, and desired them to enter the fort, four persons together; concealing their arms, and to continue so doing until he gives further orders. He added, that they are to avoid the suspicion of the commander at the gate, and if questioned, say they want to buy provisions. When the Sardar found that a sufficient number had gone into the fort for offensive operations, he himself, in disguise, with two servants, joined the party. The commandant of the guard at the gate was shot by him; and a skirmish took place, which, after some injury on both sides, gave the Sardar possession of the whole gate. He now easily hastened to increase the number of his retinue from his camp; and he soon proclaimed himself the master of Ghazni, and restored confidence and peace among the inhabitants. He engaged himself in repairing and strengthening the fortifications, and stored the place abundantly with ammunition and provisions. He then waited in confidence, ready for the assault of Mohammed Azim Khan.

The intelligence of the Sardar Dost Mohammed Khan's possessing Ghazni heightened the wrath of Mohammed Azim Khan; and at the head of a strong force, and with battering guns, he came and besieged that fort. For eight days a continued firing was kept up on both sides, and the guns from the citadel caused great slaughter in the camp of the enemy, who, at length, hopeless of subduing the garrison, thought best to negotiate with the Sardar. Navab Samad Khan was then deputed from the camp to confer with Dost for that purpose, but the

Sardar neither opened the gate nor asked him to come in; but hanging out a rope from the rampart he descended by it himself to meet the envoy outside of the fort. The ambassador used every sort of art to deprive the Sardar of the fort, but he swore that he will rather sacrifice his head than give up Ghazni to Mohammed Azim Khan. A second deputation was sent the following day, and another conference was held, in which it was agreed that the Sardar should continue to keep possession of the fort, but that he must come and wait upon Mohammed Azim Khan, as a token of his homage, and so prevent the appearance of disgrace and weakness to be attached to him (Azim). On this the Sardar appointed his younger brother, Amir Mohammed Khan, the governor; and manned every tower and bastion for defence. Having thus secured the place, the Sardar came out and had an interview with his besieger, and they both embraced, and yet accused each other for the breach of brotherly respect. A treaty of peace was thus concluded, and Mohammed Azim Khan again resolved to levy tribute on the Sindhians.

The Sardar Dost Mohammed Khan was now

strengthening himself much, and enjoying repose by the possession of Ghazni, the first stronghold of Afghanistan. Even now nothing could keep him in peace, nor induce him to secure the internal welfare of the country, and he planned to bring external embarrassment on his brother, and on the whole family. With this view he deputed a mission to the Maharajah Ranjit Singh, and kept an unceasing correspondence with the Lahaur court, and hoped by this alliance to elevate himself, and to subdue his brothers, and especially the powerful Mohammed Azim Khan. This excited the alarm of Mohammed Azim Khan, who lost no time to fall back upon Peshavar for the purpose of checking the progress of the Sikhs. The Afghan and the Sikh armies were now near enough to have occasional skirmishes; however, all the Barakzai brothers sent Yar Mohammed Khan as an envoy to the Maharajah Ranjit Singh. He betrayed the trust reposed in him; and with or without the advice of the Sikh invader, he wrote letters to Mohammed Azim Khan, that it was the intention of the Sikhs to take a different route, and to seize his family and treasure then left at Michni. The Sardar Dost Mohammed Khan was to be sure connected with the enemy for the destruction of Azim Khan; and these sad circumstances marred his intrepidity. Upon one hand he considered that he ought to prevent the seizure of the wives and treasure by the Sikhs at Michni, and on the other, that retiring from the face of the enemy without hazarding a battle, was a most cowardly deed. In the meantime his heart was bitterly wounded by finding that not only the Sardar Dost Mohammed Khan had attached himself to the Lahaur chiefs, but that nearly all the other brothers had followed his example. In this disturbed state of mind he sometimes resolved to fight and keep his ground; and at other times he thought best to break up the camp, for the purpose of preserving his wives and his money. Soon after this his followers became disheartened at the uncertainty of his determinations, and every one began to strike his own tent, and to leave the camp; while no one knew a sufficient cause for so doing. Mohammed Azim Khan, sadly vexed, plucked out his beard, and lamented for the treachery of the Sardar Dost Mohammed Khan, and of the other brothers; and for being thus compelled to retire with the outward show of weakness and disgrace. On his return to Kabul Azim Khan was attacked by dysentery, and soon after died broken-hearted.

CHAPTER IV.

Succession of Habib-ullah Khan—He is defeated by the Sardar—Peace is concluded between them—Habib-ullah's secret intentions—Flight of the Sardar—Sherdil Khan and the Sardar join against Habib-ullah—Policy of Dost—He takes the Bala Hisar—Intrigues and rupture between Sherdil and Dost—Siege of the Bala Hisar—Peace between the brothers—Death of Sherdil Khan—The Sardar sole master of Kabul—Sayad Ahmad's war with the Sikhs—Rebellion at Tagav, and defeat of the Sardar.

Sardar Mohammed Azim Khan, by the turn of fortune, was the first in wealth amid the sons of Sarfraz Khan, the brothers of the Sardar Dost Mohammed Khan. Knowing the incapacity of his son Habib-ullah Khan, he implored Navab Jabbar Khan, as he breathed his last, tó take care of his son, whom he requested and charged to wipe away the stigma he had sustained before the Sikhs. After his death Habib-ullah Khan succeeded him; and these two became his favourite and immediate advisers—Hafizji, son of the late

Mir Vaiz, and Aminullah Khan Laho-gardi.* He also wrote and invited Purdil Khan from Qandhar, and treated him with consideration and liberality.

It must not be forgotten that Shah Ayub, the sovereign created by the late Mohammed Azim Khan, was still in the Bala Hisar. He disbelieved his son Shah Zadah Ismail, and paid no attention to his prudent advice,—namely, to seize Habib-ullah Khan with the treasure of his father. Purdil Khan therefore entered the citadel by force, with a large retinue; seized the Shah, and killed the Shah Zadah. He set Ayub at liberty, however, after having caused him to pay the sum of one lakh of rupees; and he then made his way towards the Panjab.

Habib-ullah Khan, surrounded by the abandoned of all classes, immersed himself in base dissipation. The courtiers of his father's time became disgusted; some retired, and some were dismissed. Sardar Dost Mohammed Khan discovered that he had now an open field for his hypocrisy and ambition. Regardless of the difference of age, and of the dignity of an uncle towards a nephew, he pre-

* Who took a prominent part in the rebellion against the English in 1841.

tended to respect Habib-ullah Khan, as older and chief of the family, and therefore as superior to himself. He often ran, and even placed shoes under his nephew's feet, wiping them with his own handkerchief. While the Sardar was cunningly gaining ground and time for the display of his real object, Habib-ullah Khan was fool enough to pride himself by fancying that he already exceeded the power of his late father in reducing the Sardar to the condition of one of the vassals. There was no limit to the false and sweet words of his devotion and affection towards Habib-ullah Khan, and no bound to the pride and vanity of the latter on this occasion. However some old and experienced persons about him, as Aminoollah Khan, &c., always cautioned him against the mask of homage which the Sardar Dost Mohammed Khan had politically put on. At length he discovered that the Sardar was paying him a false homage, and was only watching for a favourable opportunity to upset his power. He thereupon disclosed his fears of the Sardar to his unwise companions; and with their consent resolved to seize the Sardar when he comes to his court, and to deprive him of his eyes. Dost Mohammed Khan proceeded to the Bala Hisar, as usual, in the morning, and it was fortunate for him that Haji Khan Kakar became acquainted with the plot, and on the Sardar's entering the room, where he sat with Habib-ullah, he caught the sight of the Sardar, and put his fingers on his own eyes; which sign the Sardar, of quick understanding, instantly knew meant that Habib-ullah had contrived and conspired to blind him, and consequently he lost not a moment to return and ride off on his horse.

The Sardar Dost Mohammed Khan induced Yar Mohammed Khan to take his part, and prepared to wage war with Habib-ullah Khan. The latter was supported by the son of Mir Vaiz and by many other influential citizens. The followers of both parties came out by the gate named Shah Shahid, and after a long fight the Sardar was victorious. The enemy was besieged, and would have been easily assailed had Dost Mohammed Khan not feared the plunder of his treasure and property, which the Sardar was desirous to procure for his own use. He therefore used his exertions in preventing his followers to enter the residence of Habib-ullah Khan, and stopped in the fort of Baqar Khan Moradkhani, hemming in the enemy all the night. Next day Amir Mohammed Khan came to aid his brother the Sardar, and Habib-ullah Khan also received reinforcements from Lahogard, when another battle ensued near the fort of Kashif. However, the nobilities interfered and put a stop to the bloodshed. It was agreed that the Sardar was to receive twenty thousand rupees and the revenue of Vardak in addition to that of Ghazni, and Habib-ullah Khan must remain the undisputed master of Kabul. On this the Sardar went to Ghazni and continued to improve the military strength of the place in every way for some time. But Habib-ullah, conscious of his sagacity, could not enjoy rest, for the constant fear of being destroyed by the Sardar was destructive of his happiness: consequently he dispatched agents with valuable presents to the Qandhar chiefs, and sought their alliance. Purdil Khan immediately came to relieve him from anxiety, and to lend him aid if necessary. After some days spent in festivals and parties of pleasure, the real Afghan character showed itself in a misunderstanding which took place between the host and the guest, and this presented an opportunity for the Sardar Dost Mohammed Khan to appear again as the enemy of Habib-ullah Khan. In the plain near the fort of Qazi both sides met for battle, but bloodshed was prevented by the interference of some silver-bearded chiefs. On this Habib-ullah placed the Sardar on the elephant with himself, and brought him into the city with every pomp and show of cordiality, as if he was reconciled heartily with him for ever, while yet he conspired for his murder. He presented him with a large sum of money to distribute among his forces, and thus pretended to show the sincerity of his disposition and attachment. The Sardar meanwhile became acquainted with the conspiracy, and while it snowed heavily he fled from the city, placing his family also on the elephant. The cold was so keen, and the rapidity of the flight was so necessary, that one of his little daughters fell down in that hurried march and expired immediately. Habib-ullah was informed of his escape, and immediately followed and overtook him. He had, however, secured a fort near Maidan for his head-quarters, and was able to sally out and thence to skirmish with his pursuers. Amir Mohammed Khan, the younger brother of the Sardar, started from Ghazni to relieve him; but Habib-ullah, having known of this, met and routed him on the road. The Sardar now thought proper to leave the fort in the dark of the night, and go to his brother at Ghazni unseen by the enemy.

Meanwhile Sherdil Khan was invited by Habib-ullah, and the quick-sighted Sardar Dost Mohammed Khan, found that their union with each other would be injurious to his own advancement. He therefore left Ghazni for Kohistan, where he remained for a few months, making the chiefs his partisans, and thus prepared to render himself strong enough to encounter his united foes. Sherdil Khan was not less active in the city. He was intriguing to proclaim himself the principal chief, and to destroy Habib-ullah Khan, for whose assistance he had originally come. The latter's influence was merely a shadow of the nominal chiefship, while Sherdil Khan managed the affairs of government. He allowed thirty thousand rupees per month for his private expenses, and appointed Khodai Nazar Khan, his own maternal uncle, deputy governor in Kabul. His habits were tyrannical, and he very soon made the whole population disgusted with the existing rule of Sherdil. Many people began to hold correspondence with the Sardar Dost Mohammed Khan, and assured him of their co-operation in his behalf. The Sardar came to Kabul, and adopted his usually successful policy of adjusting matters by stratagem rather than with the sword. He asked for an interview with Sherdil, and after a long-continued discussion on the propriety and importance of the past and present conduct of each other, a new agreement was made, in which it was arranged that Sherdil Khan was to remain the paramount Lord of Kabul; while the Sardar was to keep the government of Ghazni, Maidan, and Kohistan, marrying at the same time the widow lady of Mohammed Azim Khan, with all her property. She was the daughter of Sadiq Khan Javan Sher, and the step-mother of Habib-ullah Khan. Although Sherdil was considered a braver man, as well as a shrewd diplomatic character, yet after all he could never penetrate into the deep-bottomed hypocrisy of the Sardar. He was quite senseless, indeed, not to apprehend the great influence which Dost Mohammed gained by his connexion with the widow lady. He obtained through this marriage quarters and friends among the very warlike and heroic Qizalbashes, where he could raise brave and numerous cavalry, and where in adversity he could shelter himself against any of his powerful brothers.

After the conclusion of this agreement the Sardar Dost Mohammed Khan thought that nothing could advance his interest farther than to cause a struggle in the town. He therefore presented a series of fictitious alarms relating to perfidious dangers from Habib-ullah to his new ally Sherdil Khan, and induced him at last to make the other his prisoner. The Sardar, to show his sincerity in the cause, counselled Sherdil that he should confine him also (the Sardar) with Habib-ullah, which will show the other party that they are not united, and which will thus give him the opportunity of promoting his pretensions secretly! This was accordingly done, and the mother of Habib-ullah Khan was exasperated as well as distressed at the custody of her son; and closing the gates of the Bala Hisar, she declared war against Sherdil. Thus happened what the Sardar Dost Mohammed Khan wanted; and as Sherdil found himself in an awkward position, he asked counsel of the Sardar, then his prisoner, on mutual understanding. He was immediately released, made deputy governor under Sherdil, and commenced to negotiate with the warrior-lady. He sent to her deputations repeatedly, and after assuring her, with his usual solemn oath, of his fidelity towards her, and promising her safe escort with her treasure, as well as the wealth of her son Habib-ullah, he succeeded in having the gates of the citadel opened, and lost no time in placing his guards on the different towers. On this Sherdil Khan immediately repaired to the Bala Hisar, and placing the widow lady of Mohammed Azim, the step-mother of Habib-ullah, on an elephant, sent her to Sardar, who married her according to the concealed agreement. The Sardar resolved not to violate the oaths he had made with the lady when she caused to be opened the gates of the Bala Hisar for him, and not to satisfy his perfidious avarice by plundering her himself; but he induced and gave opportunity to Sherdil Khan to do this, on the condition of equal shares in the spoil. The pillage took place accordingly, and went so far, that every woman of the family was searched and deprived even of her dress, if it was not torn. Sherdil possessed himself of the whole remaining mammon of the late Mohammed Azim Khan, and drove every member of the household of Habib-ullah with infamy out of the citadel. Sherdil now became avaricious of this very considerable booty, and determined not to give even a little to the Sardar Dost Mohammed Khan, as had been originally stipulated. To effect this object of his imprudence, he sent off Habib-ullah Khan as prisoner into the distant fort of his Mama, and then contrived schemes to blind the Sardar Dost Mohammed Khan, if not to destroy him altogether. In the mean time the brothers, chiefs of Peshavar, also arrived in Kabul to take advantage of the disorder, and to share the riches if possible. Sherdil intended to seize the Sardar and perpetrate his deed of cruelty when he attends his court, but he was again informed of the plot, as before, by the motion of Haji Khan Kakar; and instantly leaving the presence of Sherdil, on the pretence of ablution, he rode off on his horse and came to his residence. This was the second time when the Sardar had a providential escape from his deadly enemies but pretended friends.

It was now evident that Sherdil Khan could not remain in the enjoyment of his ill-gotten power, as the Sardar Dost Mohammed Khan could not be entrapped. The latter lost no time in collecting a strong body of men at the expense of his new rich wife; and, exasperated at the faithless behaviour of Sherdil Khan, he insisted upon having his own will for the delivery of Habib-ullah Khan. He then laid siege to the Bala Hisar, and all the brother chiefs of Peshavar joined him with the view of enriching themselves from the plunder of the besieged. Sherdil Khan also sent an express to his brothers at Qandhar, intimating to them that he was possessed of considerable wealth, which, if he were not protected by those who were his real brothers, would fall into the hands of the Sardar Dost Mohammed Khan and the chiefs of Peshavar, and would make them extremely powerful in the family. This communication stirred up the chiefs, and they left Qandhar immediately for the purpose of defending their brother Sherdil Khan in Kabul. They arrived at length to aid the besieged, but the Sardar had surrounded the citadel so closely that provisions began to diminish; and in the mean time he sent a message to Sherdil Khan that the brave never shut themselves up in a house or fort, but come out and feel a proud desire either to fall or to gain in the open field. It is well known that Sherdil Khan was really a person of great intrepidity, and braver than all the sons of Sarfraz Khan. This message stirred him up and he sallied out. Many days at first passed in skirmishes, and at last a general action was intended. Sherdil arrayed the line of his forces towards the tomb of Shah Shahid; and the Sardar, with the flower of his Qizalbash adherents, appeared on the opposite hillock, called Tappah Maranjan. The Qandhar chiefs, after reconnoitring the position of the Sardar, discovered that there would be only useless bloodshed in fighting with him while supported with such well-equipped cavalry and in possession of such a commanding position. Sherdil Khan, just like an Afghan, came into the camp of the Sardar, and stopped at the tent of the Navab Mohammed Zaman Khan. Counsel after counsel continued for many days, and the leaders of both parties were cherishing themselves on fruits and rich dinners together, while their respective followers were fighting for their employers in the field.

It would be tiresome to the reader to detail here the numerous treaties which were concluded and then violated, the struggles which were renewed and which again ceased,—oath after oath being exchanged, till finally it was settled that the Navab Samad Khan should be empowered by both parties to adjust their differences. He proposed that neither Sherdil nor Dost Mohammed Khan should possess Kabul, which should be entirely left to be governed by the influential citizens, headed by the Sultan Mohammed Khan, one of the brother chiefs of Peshavar. It was further arranged that Sherdil Khan with his brothers must retire to Qandhar, and the Sardar to his government seat at Ghazni or Kohistan. This peace, however, was soon disturbed, for the followers of the Qandhar chiefs fell into a quarrel with those of the Sardar, and this ended not without much bloodshed. In the mean time, the widows of the late Mohammed Azim Khan deafened the ears of the hearers by shrieks, and begged the Sardar and the Navab to revenge on Sherdil Khan the insult and disgrace he had shown to the ladies of their deceased brother, demanded that he should be compelled to liberate their sons, Habib-ullah and Akram Khan. The Sardar again, exclusive of his other brothers, went and made a secret agreement with Sherdil Khan, that the Sardar will join him against any one who may attempt to impede his progress, or may wish to seize his property which had belonged to Habib-ullah Khan, on the condition that Sherdil Khan will bind himself to assist the Sardar against the Peshavar chiefs, if necessary, and will give up his prisoners into his hands. On this Sherdil Khan loaded on beasts of burden all the moveable wealth from the Bala Hisar, and after delivering Habib-ullah Khan to the Sardar, set out for Qandhar.

The Sardar Dost Mohammed Khan meanwhile knew that the brother chiefs of Qandhar and of Peshavar, in concurrence with each other, had established Sultan Mohammed Khan Governor of Kabul, with the view of having influence in the capital, and that he himself was set totally aside. Consequently he insisted upon leaving Habib-ullah Khan with Sultan Mohammed Khan on his part in the city; and he succeeded in doing so. Some time, however, passed before the Sardar could recruit his means and troops in Kohistan, and in the interval the death of Sherdil Khan happened. The talents and bravery of this chief of Qandhar were respected and dreaded by the Sardar, who now found that no one else remained in the family capable to frustrate his designs in any way. Sultan Mohammed Khan was exceedingly partial to the citizens of the "Sunni" sect; and to counterbalance this, the Sardar took the "Shias," or Qizalbashes, under his wings; and he employed clandestinely emissaries to kindle religious misunderstanding and offences between the two parties. In the meantime Habib-ullah Khan left Kabul, annoyed with the treatment of Sultan Mohammed Khan, and this created a fine excuse for the hostilities of the Sardar.

Finally, the Sardar Dost Mohammed Khan communicated to Sultan Mohammed the alternative to leave Kabul, or to be ready to fight with him. The latter, however, treated this message with ridicule, till the Sardar actually had opened a fire on the city. The citizens made a few skirmishes, and at length Sultan Mohammed Khan consented to evacuate Kabul; and so the Sardar entered the Bala Hisar by one gate, while the Sultan went out by another. The Sardar was now so fortunate as to be the sole sovereign of Kabul, where he ruled till the British Government dethroned him; and he is now again ruling where his English enemies could not govern. He was proud of having the chief seat and government of the capital of Afghanistan; but he was not happy in his new position. He was sure that as soon as the brother chiefs of Qandhar and of Peshavar had no fear of attacks from Kam Ran and the Maharajah Ranjit Singh, they will not allow him to remain in the undisputed possession of Kabul. He therefore entered into correspondence with the fanatic Sayad Ahmad, who had raised a religious war on the Sikhs, in the Yusaf Zai country; and who kept the chiefs of Peshavar also engaged so as to prevent their attempts to disturb the Sardar. By this diversion of the attention of the Peshavar chiefs he had nothing to fear from the East; but his brothers on the South marched from Qandhar to oppose him. He thereupon led forth a large force, and met his antagonists near Qarabagh. A few skirmishes took place between the Kabul and Qandhar armies, which were obliged to fall back on their respective capitals by the sudden appearance of the cholera.

The Sardar Dost Mohammed Khan made a discovery that Habib-ullah was intriguing with the ill disposed chiefs to supplant him from the throne of Kabul, and he thought the best and safest mode of putting off this impending danger, was to bribe and induce the followers of Habib-ullah to desert their master, and to join him. He succeeded in this, and afterwards confiscated all his estate. Annoyed at this, he went over to the chiefs of Peshavar, where he received a district yielding one hundred and twenty thousand rupees for his support, yet after a year he quarrelled with them and returned again to Kabul. The Sardar, however, paid him no attention, and this induced him to go to Qandhar with all his family. Distress from want, and the neglect of the ruling uncles, broke and deranged his spirits, and he became quite insane. Even then he did not stop much longer there, notwithstanding the chiefs offered him twenty-five thousand rupees a-year for his maintenance, but he crossed the Ghoeleri range of mountains with his families, and on reaching the Esa Khail district near Derah Ismail Khan, he massacred all his wives and children, and threw them into the Indus. Such was the dreadful deed and sad fall of one who was once respected, flattered, and dreaded by the Sardar Dost Mohammed Khan, and by the other uncles.

The Sardar Dost Mohammed Khan had not firmly established his authority in Kohistan, for robberies and murders were still in practice, and some persons in existence there, who threatened death to his collectors and magistrates. He therefore assembled a select force, but, avoiding every occasion for the use of arms, he, with his natural sweetness of tongue, ensnared the ringleaders, as Nurak Shakardarari, Sayad Baba Qushqari, Zaman Istalafi and Mazu Tagavi, &c., assassinated them all, and forced the petty ones into banishment.

The inhabitants of Tagav, in the meantime, rebelled against the Sardar Dost Mohammed Khan and subverted the tranquillity of the suburbs of Kabul. The Sardar collected a good force and placed over it the Navab Jabbar Khan to punish the rebels. The Navab remained for some time in Tagav negotiating with them, and thought that he will be able to settle the disturbance without having recourse to arms, but it proved to be quite contrary. The Tagavis made a night attack upon the Sardar's army, which, with its leader Navab Jabbar Khan, was defeated and dispersed. All the camp equipage fell into the hands of the rebels, and the remains of the forces returned successful to Kabul. This failure did not incense the Sardar Dost Mohammed Khan, but created in him an apprehension that rebellion would soon appear on every side, if the honour of his arms was not recovered, and if the Tagavis were not punished.

CHAPTER V.

Haji Khan joins the Sardar—The Sardar punishes the rebels—Takes Bala Bagh and Jalalabad—Jealousy of the brothers—His escape from assassination—Marches against Shah Shuja—His letter to the British political agent at Loodianah—Sir Claude Wade's answer—The Sardar writes to Shah Shuja—Reaches Qandhar, and defeats Shah Shuja-ul-mulk — Correspondence discovered among the spoils—Ingratitude of the Qandhar chiefs towards Dost Mohammed Khan—The Sardar's interview with his dying brother—Flight and evil designs of the Peshavar chiefs—Haji Khan Kakar.

WHILE the Sardar Dost Mohammed Khan was making preparations for marching an army in person against Tagav, his principal and secret object was to subdue Bala Bagh, Jalalabad, and the people of Zurmat and of Bangash. The Sardar had at this time with him Haji Khan Kakar, a man of great treachery and hypocrisy, similar to himself. This person was formerly in the service of Habib-ullah Khan, and then in that of Sherdil Khan the Qandhar chief. He knew well that among all the brothers Dost Mohammed Khan was the only man to prosper, and therefore, on two former occasions when he informed the Sardar of the plots which his (Haji) master had laid for blinding and killing him. Knowing also that at length the Sardar will gain the paramount power over the other brothers, he stole his escape from the camp of the Qandhar chief, his employer, and took shelter in the shrine of "Shah Ashqan Arefan," and pretended to be tired of this world, and to devote the remainder of this life for gaining the happiness of the next. The Qandhar chiefs did everything to induce him to follow them, but he seemed determined to retire from the world and live quiet in the mosque, yet this was merely a pretence. The Sardar went to him after the Qandhar chiefs went away, and persuaded him to quit the Mausoleum, and to co-operate with him for the aggrandisement of his power and of his country. Haji Khan accompanied the Sardar to his residence, and commenced a new career under a new master, as he had anticipated, and he will be found, on many occasions, to play a double part and to abound in treachery. Haji Khan advised the Sardar Dost Mohammed Khan first to proceed towards Zurmat and Bangash; and, though the Sardar at first thought it not good to undertake this expedition, yet at length it proved successful. He destroyed many rebellious forts, collected revenues, punished the refractory, and established peace and governors in that district. The cholera in the mean time spread and affected the Sardar; and fearful of the result, he returned to Kabul. Some time afterwards he declared war against Tagav, as he had originally intended. This declaration made Sultan Mohammed Khan and the other brothers alarmed on account of his increasing power, and they communicated to the Navab Mohammed Zaman Khan their earnest desire and urgent advice to make himself ready to oppose the Sardar, who after the conquest of Tagav would certainly subdue his country of Jalalabad. While the Navab was preparing for defence, repairing the fortress, and storing up provisions at Jalalabad for siege, the Sardar was engaged in razing the strongholds of the Tagav rebels. They fled to the mountains, and the Sardar possessed himself of their very considerable flocks, and of all their various quadrupeds. From that day no one from that country ever attempted to give him any offence, and the captured guns of the Navab Jabbar Khan were also restored to the Sardar.

SARDAR MAHOMED AKBER KHAN.

The Sardar Dost Mohammed Khan now turned his attention to the projected conquest of Bala Bagh and of Jalalabad. The former was ruled by Mohammed Osman Khan, and the latter by the Navab Mohammed Zaman Khan. After a siege of two days, the chiefs of Bala Bagh surrendered, and then the fort of Jalalabad was invested by the forces of Dost Mohammed Khan. Here the siege continued for a few days, and then the Sardar commanded his Kohistan force to mine the fort. It was accordingly mined and blown up, when his army made an assault and captured Jalalabad. The Navab Mohammed Zaman Khan entered the room of his wife, who was the daughter of the late Vazir Fatah Khan, and thought himself safe under her protection. On this the Sardar gave orders to his son, Mohammed Akhbar Khan, to go in, seize, and conduct the good Navab to his presence. Regardless of the respect due to him, he forced the Navab to leave his lady's protection; and with no turban on his head he was conducted by Akbar Khan into the presence of his father, who brought him away and gave him as his state-prisoner a sufficient allowance to live upon.

It must be borne in mind that the daily increase of power and influence, and the aggrandisement of territory by the Sardar Dost Mohammed Khan, was the source of the odious jealousy of his brothers, both old and young, the chiefs of Peshavar and of Qandhar. Knowing their own weakness they left and acknowledged him to be the master of Kabul, but yet they always murmured on account of the great expenses incurred by them on various occasions in proceeding to Kabul, and in restoring order there before the Sardar possessed it; and consequently they wrote to him to repay to them certain sums of money, and sometimes they asked for protection against Kam Ran and Ranjit. The Sardar always laughed at these reckless and murmuring demands for money and aid; but said, in reply, that he had nothing to give them, and that if it was convenient to him he will lend them military assistance against any real and general enemy. The Sardar Dost Mohammed found out that the Navab Jabbar Khan, instead of adjusting differences between him and the other chiefs, increased the difficulties for him by his unceasing intrigues with the malcontents. He thought best therefore to deprive him of the Ghilzai country, and to fix for him an adequate and respectable stipend in the city. He stated to the Navab he has received numerous complaints from his (Navab's) subjects, and that for the stability of his rapidly and progressively increasing government, he thinks to take up the administration of that district himself, and to provide for him in lieu of it by some other means. This made the Navab feel more hostility towards the Sardar, who had always been successful against the base conspiracies and intrigues of his brothers, of the Navab, &c. It has been said that while at Jalalabad the Sardar found a person armed and concealed at night in his private tent, who was bribed to murder him. The Sardar felt or rather heard the breathing of a man under his bed; and without making any noise, he got up in the manner as if he was to retire for a minute, and then to return to his bed immediately. He then very quietly took the arms from the guard at the door of his tent, and pointing the musket in the direction of his bed, he commanded the culprit to come out. He was seized, yet at the interference of the Navab, and of the Peshavar chiefs, he was pardoned, or else he would have been blown up by the firing of a gun.

It was immediately before or soon after the Sardar gained possession of Jalalabad, that the Shah Shuja, the ex-king of Kabul, appeared and raised an army at Sindh, with the intention to try to recover from his repeated failures of fortune in recovering his dominions and invading Qandhar; but the chiefs of this place wrote and applied for the assistance of the Sardar Dost Mohammed Khan. He knew that if he was not to proceed at their call, his brothers will not be able to oppose and to frustrate the designs of the Shah, who if once in the possession of that city, would place him in a most dangerous situation in Kabul; and he therefore prepared an army, to start forth with it towards Qandhar. The Navab Jabbar Khan, with the rest of the discontented chiefs, was in correspondence with Shah Shuja, who had agreed to restore the Ghilzai district to him, and in like manner to restore Jalalabad and Bala Bagh to their respective masters, the Navab Mohammed Záman and Usman Khan; and they had resolved to join the Shah, when the Sardar Dost Mohammed Khan arrives suddenly before the Shah's camp at Qandhar. The Navab was of opinion that Shah Shuja had resolved to recover his lost kingdom under the auspices of the English government, and he had inculcated a similar belief into others. To effect the purpose of his intrigues, or to secure his profit, he planned of course numerous schemes, and at last on arriving at Ghazni he supplicated the Sardar Dost Mohammed Khan to allow him to go on with his plans and to make some favourable terms with the Shah for him, as he was sure that he (the Shah) would at last be victorious. The Sardar, knowing that the Navab wished to go over to the Shah, and believing that then all the chiefs from his own camp and from the Qandhar camps would follow his example, leaving him alone in the field, replied thus: "Lala,* there will be plenty of time for your negotiations if I be defeated."

Dost Mohammed Khan thought it advisable to ascertain whether this expedition of Shah Shuja (as rumour described it) was framed by the desire of the British government; and he therefore addressed a letter to Sir Claude Wade, then political agent at Loodianah, and requested that functionary to inform him whether the Shah was supported by the English

* An affectionate term for addressing personally to a brother, and sometimes to a very intimate friend.

government to invade Afghanistan, or was marching thither on his own account only. He added, that if the former was the case, he would take all these matters into his own deliberate consideration; and if the latter, that he was on the way to meet the Shah with arms. Sir Claude Wade replied that the British government had no participation in this expedition of the king against the Barakzai chiefs, but that he wishes him well. Dost Mohammed Khan dispatched also a letter to Shah Shuja, saying that his brothers, the chiefs of Qandhar, are not capable to meet the wishes of his Majesty, and that he (the Sardar) is making rapid marches, and trusts to settle all differences satisfactorily. This mode of writing seemed to promise that he will fight with and defeat the Shah, which his brothers at Qandhar were unable to do. The Sardar had also written to Gulistan Khan, the Hazarah chief of Qara Bagh, to reinforce him against Shah Shuja; although he had one year before shown designs of revolt, but had not actually taken up the cause of the Shah. Whether he did not or could not spread dissensions in favour of the monarch, is a matter of investigation; yet it is evident that he made a very fair excuse for not accompanying the Sardar Dost Mohammed Khan to Qandhar. He stated that he was moving with followers for the assistance of the Sardar, and on the road met some Afghan maliks,* with their heads cut on their shoulders, who advised him not to proceed; but he paid no attention to them, thinking that probably they wished to mislead him by false advice. He continued marching on, he said, till he met Mir Yazdan-bakhsh,† with his head also in his hand, who cried out and said to me, "Oh unfortunate man! where are you going? Do you wish to fall into the mouth of a serpent? Is not this head disunited from my shoulders a warning to you?" The chief added, that when he heard the above words from the lips of a Hazarah, he could not hesitate a moment to disbelieve him; and that he therefore was obliged to go back to his home with his followers, and thought it safest not to accompany the Sardar. The most remarkable thing in the Hazarah's answer is, that he showed his Afghan ruler (by mentioning the Afghan and the Hazarah men with their heads cut in their hands) that the Sardar being an Afghan was not to

* Head men of the villages.

† Whose account will hereafter be found.

be believed, and that therefore he could not trust himself to him.

On arriving at Qandhar the Sardar thought it prudent to fight at once with Shah Shuja-ul-mulk, rather than allow his troops to recover from the fatigue of their rapid marches. He was wise enough to know the duplicity of certain chiefs and relations in his camp, and thought even the least delay might mature their intrigues and induce them to abandon him. Shah Shuja-ul-mulk had occupied a very strong post opposite to the city, but his vanity, and the idea of securing a safe route, excited him to quit his entrenched camp and to choose another place for battle in spite of his wiser counsellor, Samandar Khan. Dost Mohammed Khan on his side made the disposition of his army, and the plan for attacking the Shah; and he placed his son, Mohammed Akhbar Khan (renowned as the murderer of the late Sir William Macnaghten, the British Envoy), at the head of his well-mounted cavalry; and the infantry was commanded by Nayab Abdul Samad Khan,* as

* A Persian adventurer, who came into Bombay as a horse merchant, and thence went to Sultan Mohammed Khan at Peshavar. He entered his service, and raised a regiment of

well as by his other sons. Dost Mohammed Khan, being always the first for cunning in Afghanistan, now desired to know, and tried to find by some hypocritical manœuvre, whether the troops that were with him had any design to support him or to abandon him. He drew his sword consequently, and galloped forward as a general towards the enemy. He had not proceeded more than fifty yards when he stopped to find whether the troops followed him with or without hesitation. He then looked at his forces, and what he read from their countenances it is impossible to say; but he ordered Mohammed Akbar Khan to make an immediate attack with his cavalry. The battle was very hard fought, and the infantry of the Shah, under Mr. Campbell, though in a very weak state, made a brave resistance. It defeated at once the Barakzai force, and the chiefs entered the city of Qandhar. Sardar Dost Mohammed Khan was,

infantry. Afterwards he fled to Kabul, and received a similar command under Dost Mohammed Khan. He continued with him for some years, and then finding his position dangerous he stole his escape to Bokhara, and gained the favour of an infantry regiment from the half-mad monarch, the Amir of Bokhara, where his proceedings in regard to the British authorities shall be mentioned in their proper place.

however, still keeping his post, and Mohammed Akbar Khan causing great havoc by his cavalry and by his intrepidity amid the line of the Shah. The Sardar having discovered that the army of the Sadozais with the Shah was gaining, and his brothers the Qandhar chiefs had retreated into the fort; determined either to lose or to gain, he, with his son, Mohammed Akbar Khan, made a general attack upon his Majesty, and after a desperate resistance and loss they at last succeeded to defeat and disperse the army of the enemy. The weak but brave regiment under Mr. Campbell was still in the engagement, and at last surrendered when it was known that Shah Shuja with his Khavanins (nobles) had run away, and that their commander, Mr. Campbell, had fallen wounded on the field. He was taken prisoner by Dost Mohammed Khan, and was handsomely treated by him. All the tents, guns, and camp equipage of the ever fugitive Shah Shuja, fell into the hands of the Lion of Afghanistan, and a large bundle of the papers and correspondence of various chiefs in his country with the Shah. Among these he found many letters under the real or forged seal of Sir Claude Wade to the address of certain chiefs, stating that any assistance given to Shah Shuja shall be appreciated by the British government.

Nayab Abdul Samad Khan, the commander of the infantry of Dost Mohammed Khan, had sent a letter to the Shah by his own orderly; and when detected, he (the orderly) was blown up by a gun to prevent the disclosure of his master's intrigues with the Shah.

The chiefs of Qandhar prepared to pursue and seize the person of the fugitive king, and begged the Sardar Dost Mohammed Khan for leave to do the same. He replied that he would not take the trouble to pursue the Shah; but that he would be delighted to get possession of Shah Zadah Mohammed Akhbar, the son of the fugitive Shah by his own sister, whom in time of necessity he could make a useful instrument, and under his royal shadow advance his own interest. It was evident that the defeat of the Shah and the preservation of the Qandhar chiefship was owing to the active intrepidity and brisk assistance of the Sardar Dost Mohammed Khan; and yet the chiefs, forgetful of this cause for gratitude, began to treat the wishes of their champion with contemptible neglect and disinterestedness. They boasted of their superiority and bravery, after the battle had been fought and gained by him for them, and even did not trust him so far as to enter the city of Qandhar. Perhaps herein they were influenced by the remembrance of the mode and success of his stratagem in taking possession of the fort of Ghazni; and thus were mistrustful of his designs, and too fearful of the probable consequences to allow him to come into the citadel.

The prospect of appearing disorders in Kohistan, and the cold treatment he received from the chiefs of Qandhar, as also the arrival of the unwelcome intelligence of the serious illness of his brother, Amir Mohammed Khan, compelled the Sardar Dost Mohammed Khan to return to his capital, Kabul. On the road he thought it prudent and politic to connect himself with the Tukhi Ghilzai chief, and he proposed the connexion and instantly married his sister, in order to make an addition to the circle of his wives, and at the same time to establish confidence in the Ghilzai chief. When he reached Kabul he found his dear brother, Amir Mohammed Khan, just breathing his last. He was able only to say to his brother the Sardar what he had purposed to do, for the selling his old grain from Ghazni, and for storing up the new crop; and desired him to see that the money is received, and that all sorts of pecuniary matters are duly settled, for these he was ever most passionately fond of.

Before we make mention of the preparations made for his next expedition, it would be necessary to describe the circumstances which led to it. While the Sardar Dost Mohammed was engaged at Qandhar, his brothers the Peshavar chiefs, Sultan and Pir Mohammed Khan, were deprived of the government at Peshavar by the Sikh army; they were compelled to return and take refuge at Jalalabad. They were led to believe that the Sardar Dost Mohammed Khan would be routed by Shuja, which would give them an opportunity to gain possession of Kabul, and they had actually sent and placed their own governors in some of the districts; but the news came that the Shah was defeated, and that the Sardar was returning successful. This was, to be sure, sad tidings for them, which destroyed all their prospects and all the castles the deposed chiefs, the brothers of Peshavar, had built in the air. In the mean time, showing the usual fraudulent character of an Afghan, they fired a salute to celebrate the victory at Qandhar, and accused their own officers of taking the possession or the management of certain villages belonging to the Sardar, pretending that it was contrary to their wish and order. They proceeded towards Kabul, and went to meet the victorious Dost Mohammed Khan on his way back from Qandhar. The interview was nothing apparently but indicative of cordiality and brotherly unanimity. Here it is worthy of notice that the double-game player Haji Khan Kakar bowed lowly to him. This will show the feelings and disregard of honour characteristic to an Afghan, while having no shame or repentance for his past ill conduct, but repeatedly committing himself to similar disgraces and making excuses if necessary. This person had deserted Sherdil Khan to join the Sardar, and then deserted the latter to connect himself with the Peshavar chiefs, who were now deposed; yet his personal safety was secure as being under their protection. In the meeting, however, the Sardar said to this deserter that it was evident that his brothers of Peshavar could expect little good from him after his past conduct towards himself; to which Haji Khan replied, that if he had deserted him he had gone to his brother, and not to any Sikhs or other strangers.

CHAPTER VI.

Preparations for a new expedition against the Sikhs—Design of the Sardar to assume the Royal title—He is surnamed Amir-ul-momnin—His method of procuring money—Barbarity exercised towards a rich trader—New coinage—The Sikhs depute Dr. Harlan to Sultan Mohammed Khan—The Amir is incensed, and threatens Dr. Harlan—He encamps at Shekhan—Truce with the Sikhs—The Amir's treacherous designs—His violent altercation with Pir Mohammed Khan—His plans and counsellors—Ranjit Singh arrives, and sends an embassy to the Amir—Oath of friendship between the Amir and Sultan Mohammed Khan—The Amir seizes the Sikh envoys—Breaks up his camp—Sultan Mohammed takes the captive envoys with him—Rage of the Amir.

The Sardar Dost Mohammed Khan stated on his return from Qandhar, that he had got rid of one enemy in the person of Shah Shuja, now defeated, but another was powerfully wounding his heart and honour by the constant turn of affairs, and by the remembrance of the inroads made by an infidel into the Mahomedan land. In this he alluded to the conquest and possessions of the Sikh army at Peshavar; he planned to declare a religious war, in the view that having no money himself to levy troops, he

AMIR DOST MAHOMED KHAN.

could hardly persuade the people to take up his cause; whereas, under the name of a war for the sake of religion, he might be successful. The priests were accordingly consulted, and all the chiefs, as well as his counsellors, and Mirza Sami Khan, concurred in the opinion that the Sardar Dost Mohammed Khan should assume the royal title, and proclaim himself as king; because the religious wars, fought under the name and flag of any other than a king, cannot entitle the warriors to the rights and honours of martyrdom, when they fall in the field. The Sardar was not altogether disinclined to assume royalty; but the want of means to keep up that title, and the unanimous disapproval of his relations, prevented him from adopting the name of a king. The Sultan Mohammed Khan was so jealous of the Sardar's taking the royal title, that he left Kabul on the pretence of going to Bajaur. In the meantime the Sardar, without any preparation or feast, went out of the Bala Hisar with some of his courtiers; and in "Idgah" Mir Vaiz, the head priest of Kabul, put a few blades of grass on the head of the Sardar, and called him "Amir-ul-momnin," or, Commander of the faithful.

The change of title from Sardar to the higher grade of Amir-ul-momnin, made no change nor produced any effect upon the habits, conduct, and appearance of Dost Mohammed Khan, except that he became still plainer in attire, and in talk, and easier of access. The only difference we find now is that of addressing him from this time as Amir. Before the Amir came to the final determination of extortion, the head priest, Khan Mulla Khan, satisfied him by saying that it was not contrary to the Mahomedan law to snatch money from infidels, such as Hindu bankers, if it was disbursed amongst warriors of the true faith. As the Amir was really in pecuniary wants, and had the sanction of the priest, he therefore seized all the Shikarpuri merchants, and demanded three lakhs of rupees from them. The Amir sent openly, as well as clandestinely, his confidential men into all parts of the country, who spared no time in forcing the payment of the demands of their employer; and where he had given orders to raise a certain sum from certain bankers of a district, the persons employed on this occasion did not forget to fill their own pockets besides. Those who fell into the hands of these official banditti were tortured and deprived of their health before they would part with their wealth; and those who escaped suffered by the confiscation of their moveable property. Sham-shuddin Khan at Ghazni, Mohammed Usman Khan at Balabagh, and Mohammed Akbar in Jalalabad, as well as the other petty governors of the various small districts, received instructions from the Amir to follow his example in seizing and torturing, and thus depriving the wealthy of their money. This method of extortion did not remain limited in application for the infidels alone, but gradually it involved the Mahomedans. In the city many principal persons suffered, and among them a rich trader of the name of Sabz Ali, who was commanded to pay thirty thousand rupees, and having refused the payment of so large a sum, he was confined in prison, and torture of every horrid description was inflicted on him by the Amir. Some days he was branded on his thighs, and on other days, cotton, dipped in oil, was tied over his fingers, and burnt as a torch; and after many days of agony the poor man expired. On this occasion the Amir only uttered a word, that he wanted his money and not his death; which, however, could not make him a loser, for he forced the relatives of this victim to pay, and thus obtained this sum. The whole country at this time was an appalling picture of extortion and torture, and he continued to spread havoc all around till a sum of five lakhs of rupees was thus unjustly gathered up for the religious war of the faithful.

The title and the money were now provided for the Amir, but another conversation took rise amongst the learned Mirzas of the court before the "Commander of the faithful" could march; and it was discussed what words or verse should be struck with the name of the Amir on the coin. Numerous persons of skill in verse exhibited specimens of their own composition, and the one which Mirza Sami Khan, the prime minister, formed, at length succeeded in being struck on the coinage. The gold coin was scarce, but many pieces of silver and copper were circulated, bearing the stamp of Dost Mohammed Ghazi. The value of the silver was twelve sharis, each of which was formed of the value of five copper pence.

Intelligence of these preparations for a religious expedition by the Amir Dost Mohammed Khan against the Sikhs reached Peshavar; and the Maharajah Ranjit Singh deputed Dr. Harlan* to the Sultan Mohammed Khan, who was not on good terms with the Amir, hoping that by gaining him over to himself he would succeed in making a division in the Mahomedan camp. This did not escape the notice of the Amir Dost Mohammed Khan, who dispatched the Navab Jabbar Khan with the view to frustrate the designs of the Sikh mission, and to induce the Sultan Mohammed Khan to join his camp with the Bajaur militia. On the arrival of the Amir the Navab joined him with the Sultan Mohammed Khan, and with Dr. Harlan from Bajaur. It was now evident that the Sultan Mohammed was bought by Dr. Harlan for the Sikhs, and therefore the Amir accused him sharply for interfering and causing differences between his brother Sultan Mohammed and himself. Dr. Harlan found that he was not in a safe position after being suspected by the camp followers, and accused by the Amir, whom he could not induce to listen to him like the Sultan Mohammed Khan. He therefore went at night to

* An American gentleman.

the Amir with the "Qoran," as a token of supplication; and next day he considered himself fortunate to get permission to pass safely to the Sikh camp at Peshavar. The Amir quitted Dakka, and encamped at Shekhan, in the plain of Peshavar, opposite to the mouth of the Khaibar pass.

The Maharajah Ranjit Singh had not then arrived, and is said to have sent orders to his general to lull the designs of the Amir Dost Mohammed Khan by exchange of negotiations until he himself joins the camp; and these were accordingly commenced. The Navab Jabbar Khan and Agha Husain were the negotiators of the Amir, who had enjoined the latter to watch the former. The Agha was found to be bribed by the Sikhs to cause a truce; and at length the Sultan Mohammed Khan went to the Sikh camp, and became a medium for maintaining the truce until the arrival of the Maharajah. Meanwhile the Amir had refused to give the Government of Peshavar to Sultan Mohammed, whether it were taken by arms or obtained by negotiations; and he was likewise denied when he proposed to have Jalalabad. He therefore now thought that it was right, and that he was free to seek for his own interests while in the Sikh camp.

The Amir Dost Mohammed Khan was sensible of his own danger, from the presence of his discontented brother in the enemy's camp; and, contrary to the rules of the truce, he clandestinely stirred up some of the Ghazis to attack the Sikhs with the most foul and dishonest view, namely, to endanger his life. There were, in consequence of this, several desultory assaults made by the Afghans, who brought some heads from the enemy's side, along with some little plunder from their tents. The Sikh army only waited the attacks, and thus obeyed the commands of the Maharajah to stand on the defensive. Pir Mohammed Khan, brother of Sultan Mohammed Khan, who had remained in the camp of the Amir, pretending to be unwell, now waited on him, with a drawn dagger in his hand, and threatened to stab it into his own breast, adding his own opinion of the baseness of his act in causing this hostility in spite of the existing truce; alleging that it would excite the Sikh general to cut the head off his brother in retaliation. The Amir replied, and even swore falsely, as usual, that he had never given any such directions, and that he had no control over the Ghazis—the champions of the true faith. However, he affected to say that they should preserve the truce, while in the mean time he excited their avarice by pointing out to them the golden bangles which will fall into their hands by killing a Sikh soldier. The advanced guard was changed every day by the Amir; and when Pir Mohammed Khan's turn came, the Amir commenced negotiation with the Sikh of such a tenour that a severe conflict occurred;—but Pir Mohammed Khan being a good soldier, as well as commander, behaved bravely, and said that that atrocious scoundrel (the Amir) had brought a heavy calamity upon him, but that he had got well out of it.

It was not an easy task for the Amir to decide what course to pursue. His prime minister, Mirza Sami Khan, supported by Mohammed Afzal Khan and a few other chiefs, was advising the Amir to wage war; and Abdul Samad, the commander of his infantry, stated boastingly that he would defeat the whole Sikh army with his own regiments, and would bring Avitabile prisoner. On the other hand the Navab Jabbar Khan, considering the

MIRZA ABDUL SAMEI KHAN

superiority of the enemy, proposed to retire without the hazard of battle, and the Amir wisely agreed with him.

Meanwhile the Maharajah Ranjit Singh arrived in the camp from Lahaur, and his appearance gave fresh and bold spirits to the Sikhs. He lost no time in arranging the troops and the plan of attack, if necessary; but at the same time he sent his confidential physician or minister, Faqir Aziz-uddin, along with Dr. Harlan and the Sultan Mohammed Khan, to the Amir Dost Mohammed Khan, with the message either to retire or to fight. While the agents were conferring with the Amir, intelligence was brought that the Sikh army had already surrounded the Afghans with a heavy park of artillery, and that there was no chance of success by waging war, but of much good by retreat. However, the Amir was fearful that his followers might become disorderly at sounding the retreat, and then he might lose his guns and ammunition, which would reduce him to the level of his rival relations, as Mohammed Zaman Khan, &c. He consulted at this crisis with his minister Mirza Sami Khan, and during the conversation he fixed on a scheme for carrying

N

off the Faqir Aziz-uddin and Dr. Harlan, the Sikh agents, to Kabul. He thought that this arrangement would compel the Maharajah to give up Peshavar, or at any rate a very large sum, for the ransom of the Faqir, without whom the veteran ruler of the Panjab could not live. The Amir, however, thought at the same time that this act of seizing the envoys would bring an everlasting disgrace on him, and therefore he resolved to gain his object by casting the odium on the head of his brother the Sultan Mohammed Khan. He sent for him, therefore, and referring to all past misunderstandings and discord between them, he made a new engagement; and swearing on the Qoran, he solemnly bound himself to maintain a perpetual friendship and brotherhood. The Sultan Mohammed Khan learnt and knew immediately that the intention of the Amir was to gain the persons of the envoy at the expense of his disgrace, yet he feigned, and also swore, to adhere to the wishes and plans of the Amir. The latter gave up the charge of the Faqir and Dr. Harlan to him, stating his wish to keep them as hostages till the Maharajah restores half the territory of the Peshavar to him, and sends a sum of money besides for his own expense, proclaiming at the same time that he had not come to fight with the Maharajah, on whom he looks in the light of a father, but to establish peace with him for the future. The Sikh envoy begged in vain to permit him to return to the Maharajah in the first place for the purpose of informing his Highness of the agreement he had concluded with the Amir; but the latter replied that this can easily be done by means of a letter.

The camp of the Afghans was now broken up, and the Amir Dost Mohammed Khan used great caution and exertion to see that his guns and ammunition had passed safe to the mouth of the Khaibar, but he could not prevent the Ghazis from plundering the bazar and his own camp equipage. When he was quite safe and far within the valley he heard the firing of cannons from the Sikh camp, in their rejoicing at his flight. The Amir, believing that he had treacherously secured his game in the persons of Faqir Aziz-uddin and Dr. Harlan, the Sikh envoys, and that they were following him in the custody of the Sultan Mohammed Khan, turned his face towards the Sikh camp, ridiculed their firing, and expressed his own pride that he had carried off the soul (the Faqir) of Ranjit Singh. In this, however, he himself was the person deceived. In the mean time he continued his march; and the Sultan Mohammed Khan, conscious of the evil intentions of the Amir, and having a favourable opportunity to gain the kindness and attachment of the Maharajah Ranjit Singh, conducted the envoys, the prisoners of the Amir, to his own camp, instead of securing them in that of Dost Mohammed Khan. At night the Amir encamped at Jabar-ghi, and next morning made inquiries where his brother the Sultan Mohammed Khan had put up with the Sikh envoys. No one could find him or them in the camp, but still the Amir continued his search. Meanwhile the arrival of a messenger from the Sultan Mohammed Khan was announced, and a letter was delivered to him. The contents were a tissue of violent abuse; and after naming him the most faithless and the most treacherous, with everything which was bad, threatened to attack his country if he would not instantly send his guns and his brother Pir Mohammed Khan. This appalling news wounded the feelings of the Amir most bitterly. There were no bounds to the sweat of shame and folly which flowed over his face, and there was no limit to the laughter of the people at his being deceived and ridiculed. His minister Mirza Sami Khan was so much distressed by this sad exposure of his own trick, and still more by the failure of his plan in losing the Faqir, that he hung down his head with great remorse and shame, and then throwing away his state papers, he exclaimed that he would avoid all interference in the government affairs hereafter. In a tone of anger he stated to his master that his conduct was very unwise, and that he did not pay attention to his counsel when he advised him to fight with the Maharajah Ranjit Singh, adding, that his followers, the Ghazis, will never believe him that he had any intention of carrying on a religious war, and that none in future will come to support him. After a long-continued talk about right and wrong, and in referring to past intercourse with the Sikh camp, the Amir marched towards Kabul, and could neither keep his followers in order nor persuade them to allow him to review and thank them before they should depart for their respective districts. Such was the termination of the religious war of the commander of the faithful in Afghanistan. It commenced with extortion and oppression, and ended in an expensive rendezvous, gaining nothing but contempt and the ridiculous title of "Amir" to add to the name of Dost Mohammed Khan.

CHAPTER VII.

Difficult situation of the Amir—Duplicity of the Qandhar chiefs—The Amir designs to seize some nobles—His plan betrayed by Akhundzadah—He arrests Abdullah Khan Achakzai—Releases him—Sisters of the Amir—Saddu Khan murdered by a Kohistani bribed by his wife.

The Amir Dost Mohammed Khan, after returning to Kabul, was not easy in his mind, nor was his authority respected. Theft, plunder, slaughter, disobedience to him, were the predominant features of the time. He always indulged in the idea that he was betrayed by his own relations and brothers, in the late expedition against the Sikhs; and that in consequence of their increasing treachery he could not execute his wishes in the arrangement of the affairs of his own government. He was also surrounded by many chiefs and followers of the Sultan Mohammed Khan, who from the time that Peshavar fell into the hands of the Sikh rulers, had sought for maintenance from the Amir. He did not know how to restore confidence into his former adherents, and to provide for the newly arrived Khavanins.* He communicated all these difficulties to the brother chiefs of Qandhar, and they sent their confidential "Mashir," Counsellor Mulla Rashid Akhundzadah, apparently to promote the interests of the Amir, but secretly instructed and advised to counteract them. This Counsellor arrived at Kabul, and by his famous possession and practice of hypocrisy, gained the entire confidence of the Amir, for he gave ready approbation and compliance to all his measures. The first object of Dost Mohammed Khan was to reduce the number and allowances of his former dependants, so that he might be able to support the Peshavar arrivals; and every one groaned at the appearance and application of this project, and above all there were no bounds to the hard and ill language of Haji Khan Kakar. The Amir then planned to seize his relations, with a great many other men of rank, and, after getting rid of them, finally to establish his own authority. His minister, Mirza Sami Khan, prepared a list of the persons who were to be imprisoned, and whose property was to be confiscated. He went himself into the country

* Petty chiefs.

on the excuse to look after his estate, but in reality to keep himself free from the odium of taking an apparent share in the plot; if it proved successful he would appear to be perfectly unaware of its existence, and if it failed, he would become a mediator to restore peace and order. While the minister thus secured his own object, Mulla Rashid, who was daily becoming more and more a confidant of the Amir's plot, was not forgetful of his own peculiar benefit. He kept the opposite party alert, and acquainted with the proceedings of Dost Mohammed Khan, whose secrets and confidence he possessed. He filled his own coffers with the presents which he received from the Navab Jabbar Khan, and from the relations of the Amir and other chiefs about him, for betraying the secrets he knew, and making them watchful of impending dangers from his conspiracy. When the Amir thought that the plan was mature, and time had arrived to secure the fruits of his perfidy, he sat with a dismal and anxious countenance waiting for his confidential accomplice, Akhundzadah. Hereupon the latter appeared, and, throwing his turban before him on the ground, feigned to pluck at his own beard; and in a fearful and agitated tone of voice explained to the Amir that his relations, the Navab, &c. have in some way been informed of his plot laid against them, and have collected their respective followers to frustrate his designs. The penetrating Amir instantly knew that the Akhundzadah was the very first person who made the opposite party acquainted with his proceedings; and he wrathfully showered a heavy load of abuse on his head, calling him a traitor coming from Qandhar to destroy his measures instead of furthering them. The Akhundzadah, by remaining quiet, pacified the furious Dost Mohammed, and then gradually began to advise him by saying that his violence in such critical circumstances was perfectly childish, and would probably produce serious injury by making it manifest that he had really conspired for the ruin of his brothers and relations, who, being alarmed and losing confidence in him, will then join to upset him. Whether the counsel of the double-faced Akhundzadah, or the necessity of the time, moved the Amir to swallow his own repentance, we cannot say, but it is certain that he instantly waited upon his brothers, and pretended to be uneasy in his inquiries for the reason of assembling their retinue, and assuming a warlike aspect. He commenced his old and accustomed series of false excuses in a garb of solemnity, with an oath that he had never thought of any deliberate treachery against them. The plot which he had planned, he said, was to get hold of Abdullah Khan Achakzai, with his property, and not to injure them. He thus cleared himself of the suspicion of his relations, and then set about to make schemes to seize and gain possession of the person and wealth of the Achakzai chief. He instructed his wives to send an invitation to the whole number of the females of Abdullah Khan; who, of course, will come as usual adorned with jewels, of which he will deprive them without any difficulty. He also directed Mohammed Akbar Khan to send for the chief personally, on pretence of consulting him about some state affairs, and when in the room to seize him immediately, accusing him that he has been corresponding and intriguing with the Prince of Hirat, the enemy of the Barakzai family, whom he serves. This measure proved successful, the Achakzai chief was apprehended, and his horses and property confiscated. Now, however, the Amir discovered that his expectations are not realized, and that all he had gained by this act of treachery, the seizure of Abdullah Khan, was nothing but a few horses, old carpets, and worn-out furniture. He thereupon thought that the odium and disgrace was heavier on his head than these things are worth, and therefore he set the chief at liberty, restoring to him his plundered property.

It has been stated before that the Amir Dost Mohammed Khan had only one brother, named Amir Mohammed Khan; and here we speak of his four sisters, because their character and deportment is worthy of notice. The eldest one was married to Shah Shuja-ul-mulk when in possession of the kingdom. She had four royal children, three daughters and one son.* The second was forced to be wife of Abdul Amin Khan Tobschibashi, at the time when she, with her mother, brothers, and sisters, were in distress on the murder of their father Sarfraz Khan. The Tobschibashi had by her seven children, and one of them was Abdul Rashid Khan.† Abdul Rasul Khan married the

* He was named Shahzadah Akbar, and died when the Shah was placed by the British on the throne of Kabul.

† He was bought by me to desert Haidur Khan at Ghazni,

third sister, who has four sons. She is a widow, and known by the name of the mother of Madad Khan. This lady resembles very much her brother the Amir of Kabul, and bears an enterprising character. She used every exertion to induce our authorities to allow her, with her other sister, to remain in Kabul, after the whole family of the Amir were sent prisoners to India. She was aware that her brother, though an exile in Toorkistan, might return, and that then a general commotion would arise in the country. With this view she continued to pay her visit to all the principal chiefs in the country, and when the Amir appeared fighting with us in Bamian and Kohistan, she was day and night engaged in marching from one village to another, and in supplicating the head men of the place, with the holy "Qoran" in her hand, to rise against us, the infidels,—and to join her brother, the Commander of the Faithful. When the Amir surrendered, she made a wonderful escape to Jalalabad, and thence to

and came to the late Sir Alexander Burnes: his services were appreciated by Lord Keane and by Major Thomson, the engineer officer, in the capture of that fort, and rewarded by a pension of five hundred rupees.

Peshavar, in spite of our exertions to detect her while intriguing. Her conduct in other respects is not altogether without suspicion. The fourth sister of Dost Mohammed Khan was married to Saddu Khan, and had one daughter and one son, Mohammed Hasan Khan. Neither the behaviour of the husband nor wife was free from rebuke. His habits were very objectionable and mean. He was always stupified with opium and with all sorts of intoxicating things. His conduct towards his own daughter was unfather-like, brutal, and odiously abominable; and such, that at last it compelled him to take her far from the capital, and to put an end to her existence. He was passionate and dissipated, and his wife was equally regardless of the virtuous modesty of her own sex. She bribed a Kohistani to murder her own husband!! and while he was returning from a visit to the Amir at night he was shot in the Shor Bazar, and the culprit was seized. The Amir made the necessary investigations, and inquired after the reason which led him to assassinate a person of Saddu Khan's position, being a relative to himself. The guilty man replied that he had been desired to do this by his own wife, the sister of the Amir, who promised him a large reward, adding that he never dreamt that such a bold and desperate step of a female against her own comforter of life—her husband, would have originated in herself; but that, undoubtedly, there were some political circumstances which must have obliged the Amir to ask his sister to cause the annihilation of her own husband. The Amir made no further questions, and appeared sadly ashamed of his sister's conduct, while surrounded by the courtiers. However, he ordered the guilty one to be executed, and he was hanged near the gate of the Bala Hisar.

CHAPTER VIII.

The Amir fears the Hazarahs—History of Yazdan Bakhsh—Dost Mohammed's plan for seizing the Hazarah chief—Courage and devotion of his wife—Both are seized by the Amir—They negotiate for their release—The Mir escapes, and afterwards his wife—He consolidates his power—Haji Khan and Mir Yazdan Bakhsh—The Khan plans the ruin of the Hazarah Mir—His scheme to entrap him—Fails—He makes Haji Khan Governor of the Hazarahjat—Becomes suspicious of him—Haji Khan seizes Mir Yazdan Baksh—Plunder of the Hazarahs—The Mir is strangled—The Sardar's relations with Persia—His education—He humbles his rival relatives, and increases his own power—Disgrace of Haji Khan—The Amir's administration of justice.

It has been briefly described in the commencement of the elevation and fame of the Amir Dost Mohammed Khan that his career was marked with deeds of tragedy and perfidious bloodshed in Kohistan, and that he had no cause to be alarmed from that quarter, except that he was not free from the fear of a Hazarah chief of extraordinary character named Mir Yazdan Bakhsh. To shorten the history of his descent, and of the superiority and destruction of his elder brothers and rivals, it may be sufficient to say that he was the younger son of Mir Vali Beg of Karzar, who was slain by a petty chief. On the death of his father, the eldest son Mir Mohammed Shah became the master of Behsud; Mir Yazdan Bakhsh assembled a large force, and prepared to revenge the wrongs of his family on the assassin of his father,—and he apprehended him and slew him on the very spot where the blood of his own father had been shed. His attention was now turned to subvert his elder brother, whom he defeated, and he then made himself the principal chief or Mir of Behsud. The more he grew in power in his Hazarah tribe, and extended his territorial possessions, the more did apprehensions arise in the mind of the Amir Dost Mohammed Khan. He justly thought that the Golam Khanah, a powerful body in Kabul, are connected by the ties of their faith with the Shia sect and with the valiant Mir of the Hazarah; and that as they were principally the instruments of his prosperity, they might turn against him and join the Mir to seek his adversity and destruction, and he found no other way to entrap the object of his apprehension but to cultivate for himself a deeper confidence in the Shias of Kabul. He accordingly showed them all attention and civility, and at length persuaded them to establish a closer alliance between him and the Mir Yazdan Bakhsh by his visit to Kabul. He wrote all the sacred oath and solemn obligations of swearing on the Holy Qoran, and affixing his own seal to it, he assured the Mir of his personal safety and respectable treatment, and the Shias of Kabul became responsible for the veracity of the engagement. When the Besut Mir received that communication of the Amir, guaranteed by the people of his own creed, he prepared to set out for the city. One of his wives, however, the daughter of a Dehzangi chief, dissuaded him from such a hazardous visit. She was a woman of the most extraordinary qualifications and natural powers of mind. She used to put on a masculine robe, and ornamented herself with a sword and shield, a bow and arrows, a spear, a dagger, and a matchlock. She appeared in the field of battle with her husband, and shared the laurels by his side: thus, at home, she gave her lord comfort and counsel,—and in the field of battle she killed his enemies. Being wiser than himself in doubting the fidelity of the Afghans, she always advised him not to trust himself to them. On this occasion she found that she could not succeed in forbidding her husband to accept the invitation; and, therefore, with her usual attachment and boldness, she accompanied him to Kabul, attired as a brave soldier. The Amir Dost Mohammed Khan received them civilly, but soon seized the opportunity to make his guests his prisoners. The perfidious Dost Mohammed Khan would have killed the Mir without loss of time, but the more talented prisoner knew well that gold was the only thing which would melt the strong feelings of the Afghan, and especially of their treacherous host. He offered him, therefore, one lakh of rupees if immediately liberated, and permitted to go and collect from his own country, and in the meantime to make the Shias of Kabul security for the payment. The Amir, being always notoriously in exigence, contracted the orders for his execution, so that he might secure for himself possession of the money. While the arrangements were going on for obtaining the security of the Gholam Khanah, with regard to the payment of the offered sum, the captive Mir contrived his escape from the prison.

When this became known to the Amir Dost Mohammed Khan, there was no restraint to his wrath and disappointment. He had still, however, the brave wife of the fugitive in his custody, whom he summoned into his presence and rebuked very severely. The Hazarah fair, turning towards the Amir Dost Mohammed Khan, in the court, exclaimed in a heroic tone of voice—" Oh, son of Sarfraz Khan, dost thou not feel ashamed to match thyself against a female?" It is said, that on hearing this, the Amir and all his Afghan courtiers hung down their heads and were abashed. They applauded the spirit of the lady, and said to the Amir that they will not permit him to offer her any violence: and the Amir having recovered his senses, agreed to place her in the custody of the Shias, thinking that she will be treated by them better than by her former Afghan guard, and she was conducted to the Persian or Shia quarter—Chândaul. After some days she made her escape from the gaol, and dressing herself like a man, well armed and mounted, set off towards the high and bleak hills of the Hazarahs. The Amir was soon informed of her flight, and dispatched immediately a party of horsemen to seize her: she was overtaken, but succeeded in keeping off her pursuers by firing her gun and pistols towards them. The skirmish continued while she was sometimes halting, and at other times ascending the valley, till at last she reached the boundary of her own country, and the party sent by the Amir was now obliged to go back to Kabul, ashamed of not being able to secure a female; while the enterprising lady joined her husband with deep sensations of satisfaction. The Hazarah chief, however, never showed any ill will towards the Amir of Kabul, never interfered with his extortions, and the abuse which he made of his power in other districts of the Hazarahs. He was, moreover, very prudent in paying his tribute,—but at the same time engaged in erecting a very strong fort, and storing it with provisions and ammunition, with the view to have safe refuge in it when necessary.

Upon the other hand, the Amir Dost Mohammed Khan had not lost sight of the increasing power of his fugitive visitor, Mir Yazdan Bakhsh, the Hazarah chief. He was watching his progress with bitterness of mind, and searching for a favourable opportunity to check and destroy it. He now appointed Haji

Khan Kakar governor of Bamian. By this he convinced him of his lasting gratitude in bestowing a reward on him for the services he had rendered in informing him of the intention of Sherdil Khan to deprive him of sight; and at the same time he thus placed an Afghan, one of a different creed, to watch the conduct of his neighbour, the Mir Yazdan Bakhsh. This person, by his cunning manners, had cultivated a friendly sentiment and intimate connexion with the Shias of Kabul; and had secured their confidence by pledging himself to support their cause against the Amir if circumstances required it. In consequence of this they always wrote to Mir Yazdan Bakhsh, advising him to rely on the word and counsels of Haji Khan, who, on the other hand, gained the sincere friendship and intimacy of the Hazarah Mir, by binding himself to destroy all the ill intentions of the Amir towards him; and he even said that he would stand by his side if he was to rebel from necessity. After some time, the agent of Haji Khan, at Bamian, entered into some agreements with the Tartar chief of Saighan, the enemy of Mir Yazdan Bakhsh. This frightened the Mir, who thought that this proceeding was a league made for his destruction, and that not without advice from Kabul. He therefore turned out all the Afghan soldiers from all forts where he had himself formerly placed them. He subdued and took possession of all the castles of the petty Hazarah chiefs dependant on the Afghans, and he became the ruling master of the Bamian valley. This alarmed the Amir of Kabul; and Haji Khan, whose interests were connected with the Bamian territory, showed him the necessity of reducing the Mir Yazdan Bakhsh, and he also took upon himself to settle the matter. He showed himself liberal on every occasion to the Hazarahs, the tribe of the Mir; and through the Qizalbashes of Kabul he convinced the Hazarah Mir that his agent at Bamian had acted contrary to his orders; and in order to show the sincerity of his false friendship, he dismissed Rahimdad Khan, and appointed a new governor. He also sent the "Qoran" with oaths that the past is forgotten, and that the future will daily increase their mutual friendship and confidence. He proceeded with the Amir Mohammed Khan, the brother of the Amir of Kabul, towards Hazarahjat; but Mir Yazdan Bakhsh did not join their camp, but instead of that he went on a pilgrimage to Band Barbar.

After the Mir Yazdan Bakhsh had discharged his religious duties, he bent his attention to arrange his political affairs. He accordingly came with a large force to subdue Mohammed Ali Beg, the Tajak chief of Saighan, but the latter shut himself up in a fort, and showed no inclination to fight. Another year rolled on, but neither the Amir of Kabul nor Haji Khan were careless about the means of weakening the Hazarah Mir, whom they could not entrap during the last season. In 1832, Haji Khan again volunteered to collect the revenues of the Hazarahjat, and to establish the authority of the Amir in Bamian on a firmer footing. Dost Mohammed Khan allowed him two years to effect this purpose, reinforced him with two thousand troops, and gave him an elephant in present; and Haji Khan farmed the whole country of the Hazarahs for forty thousand rupees, from the Kabul government. He then proceeded thither, and through the medium of Khan Shirin Khan, the Hazarah Mir made known that he agreed to co-operate with the governor, whose aim was to ensnare the Mir by professions of cordiality, and of good understanding with him, and with the people of his creed. In the mean time, a religious conflict took place between the Shias and the Achakzai Afghans of Kabul, and Haji Khan cunningly took the side of the Shias. In so doing he had two objects in view; firstly, to convince the Shias of his attachment to them, and by this also to entrap the Mir Yazdan Bakhsh; and, secondly, if the Javan Shers or Shias should gain the ascendancy in this warfare, the subversion of the power of Dost Mohammed Khan will take place of course; and this was his principal desire. However, these affairs ended at last in a peaceable manner: but this duplicity of the Khan, as well as his correspondence with the Uzbeks, the Panjab, and the Biloch chiefs, did not escape the penetration of the able Amir, who naturally grew suspicious of the Khan. Sometimes, therefore, he thought to deprive him of the power he held, at other times he determined to put him to the sword; but while he continued in this state of irresolution, Haji Khan became acquainted with the alarming fact that he now held no safe position. The Mir Yazdan Bakhsh in the mean time paid him all the revenues, and waited upon him, and this meeting seemed likely to give perfect satisfaction on both sides; for it induced all the other chiefs in the Hazarahjat to send in their revenues that were due to the Khan, who thus collected sooner and more than his predecessor, the brother of the Amir.

Haji Khan now set out for an expedition towards Saighan; and, finding himself well supported and able to execute his long nourished desire, he summoned Mir Yazdan Bakhsh and his relations in the morning to come to his tent; and as soon as the brother of the Khan, with a strong body of armed men, came in, Haji Khan took an angry tone of voice and accused Mir Yazdan Bakhsh of intriguing against him: and forgetting all the often-repeated oaths of friendship, he seized the Mir with all his relatives. The merciless Afghans began to plunder the Hazarahs, who, notwithstanding the inclemency of the cold, were even deprived of their clothes. The faithless Haji Khan allowed only the Mir Yazdan to be left in his usual attire, and even his relations were obliged to give up their robes. It was a heart-rending sight to see the poor Hazarahs, barefooted and without clothes, pursued in all directions by the Afghans, who were now desirous to inflict on them wounds and every act of tyranny, because they were Shias. Mir Yazdan Bakhsh was pinioned with his adherents, and their feet bound with fetters; and the locks were fastened with melted lead, to prevent them from being opened by any one, and the chief of Saighan advised Haji Khan to execute his captive. The perfidious Khan accordingly ordered the "Pesh-khid-mat" to put an end to the life of the chief who only a few days before held sway over the whole country, and commanded a large force. The Qizalbashes of Kabul, now with Haji Khan, made a clamorous remonstrance against his dishonesty and treachery towards the Hazarah Mir; but this availed nothing, and the unfortunate Yazdan Bakhsh was strangled to death. It is said that he met his fate with extraordinary composure of mind, and that no sign of fear or sadness was found in his appearance. Haji Khan said to the Qizalbashes that he was obliged and compelled by Dost Mohammed Khan to put the Mir Yazdan Bakhsh to this end. Such, however, was the termination of the life of the Hazarah chief, and thus was the Amir of Kabul relieved from the fear of the only remaining antagonist left in his kingdom.

It must here be stated that the elevation of the Amir Dost Mohammed Khan to power was procured merely by the adherence and assistance of the Persians. The grand point of the policy of Nadir Shah was to colonize the distant regions he subdued from his own extensive country of Persia. On his death Ahmad Shah Durrani, who first held and strengthened the sceptre of the realm of Afghanistan, wisely took these foreigners under his protection, and trusted them with his personal safety and with the charge of the royal family; and they were surnamed Gholam Khanah, or the household slaves. He treated them with every consideration, and by a course of unceasing cordiality he attached them to himself, and thus showed his Afghans that he had the warrior Qizalbashes to put them down if they ever stirred against him. Dost Mohammed followed the same policy; and the Qizalbashes, strangers in land, in customs, in habits, and in faith, thought it prudent to attach themselves to him when he was nothing, and was looked on with jealousy by his most powerful and rival brothers. They supported his cause in every extremity, and he was at last so successful as to become the superior of all in Afghanistan. Through their arms he reduced all the old and influential men of his own tribe and blood, and then patronized young adventurers of obscure origin in order to diminish the strength of those to whom he owed gratitude at least for his prosperity. These Qizalbashes were twelve thousand families in number in former days, all men of arms, and not of trade; but now they are reduced to plough the land and to sell vegetables, and are craftily managed and placed by the Amir Dost Mohammed Khan against each other. Their clans are different, and they bear various names, as Javan Shers, Afshars,* Rikas, Kurds, Bakhtyaris; and, in fact, they thus show their origin and descent from every tribe of Persia.

The chiefs in Afghanistan do not value education as the first quality, for they must only know how to ride, fight, cheat, and lie; and whoever excels in these acquirements gains the renown of the time. Amongst the sons of Sarfraz Khan, the brothers of the Amir Dost Mohammed, few knew the letters of the alphabet. Their early life was spent in poverty, danger, treachery, and bloodshed; but when they came to power, the constant sight of the orders

* The tribe of the great Nadir Shah.

submitted by the Mirzas (Secretaries) for their signature at last enabled them to read plain writing. Mehardil Khan, one of the Qandhar chiefs, qualified himself more than the others. He composed poetry, and made himself distinguished by his literary taste in Persia; yet there are some of his brother chiefs who can neither write nor read. The Amir Dost Mohammed Khan learnt the "Qoran" only at the meridian of his glory, and Nayab Amir Mohammed Akhundzadah was his tutor. However, his local knowledge, and the information he possesses in ancient and modern history, in proverbs, and in adventures, as well as in the administration of various distant kingdoms, will not fail to show him as being well stored with extraordinary talents and science. He speaks Persian, Pashto, Turkish, Panjabi, and the Kashmir languages.

Haji Khan Kakar, the perfidious murderer of Mir Yazdan Bakhsh, came from Bamian on a visit to Kabul; and on his arrival in the city he went straight to pay his respects to the Amir Dost Mohammed Khan. He, with polite attention, took the Khan, his visitor, into the palace, and introduced him to his favourite wife, the mother of Mohammed

Akbar Khan, with a cheerful voice; and to show him a false respect, he said to her that her father had arrived, whom she was so long desirous to see. The crafty Haji Khan knew instantly that this flattering title from the Amir was not destitute of some treachery. He waited the result, therefore, with anxiety, and the next day he was informed by the Amir that his wife, who looks upon him (the Khan) as her father, has begged of him a favour; and that he will not disapprove of her appointing Haidar Khan to the Government of Bamian, and the Amir will equally provide the Khan with a larger yearly sum in cash. This awoke Haji Khan from mental slumber, and he thought that his fortune was now commencing to decline; wherefore, after some days, he waited upon the Amir Dost Mohammed Khan, and showed symptoms of being deeply offended and discontented with these measures. The Amir hereupon angrily accused him of the atrocious murder of the Mir Yazdan Bakhsh, on which the Khan inquired whether it was not perpetrated by his own orders:—" No," replied Dost Mohammed Khan; " it was never my wish that you should take a false oath, and kill the man afterwards. I repeatedly wrote to you to be kind to him, and induce him to come to Kabul, and to give him many dresses of honour. I would have been friendly to him, and permitted him to go back to his own country." Haji Khan then continued his remonstrance by saying, that it is most surprising that the Amir should accuse him of false swearing, and asked him how he had himself entrapped, and then had cut off the heads of the Kohistan chiefs. The Amir replied, by his own expertness, because he always sent a piece of wood wrapped up instead of the Holy Qoran. While this altercation was going on, the Amir did not tell him to disband his dependants, as he thought it would create an illiberal idea of his own feeling towards the soldiers; while Haji Khan, having no means to maintain them, would disband them himself. The Khan, however, retained them still, for he entertained for some time the hopes of having back Bamian; but he at length was compelled to discharge his followers.

There are no courts of justice in Kabul, and the matters of consequence are therefore all decided by the Amir Dost Mohammed Khan himself: hence a great criminal, or murderer, has a general hope of being released unpunished, if money, and sometimes influence, may interfere with his decision. The petty offences, and religious business, are entrusted to the care of the Mulla, or head of the Shara, or the Mahomedan law. He has appointed a kotval, or constable, who keeps watch at night, and has the privilege to seize the persons who may be found committing adultery, drinking wine, gambling or stealing. He puts such persons into prison, or "Bandikhanah," without limiting the time, and they can be released only through the medium of some man of rank, or by the discharge and payment of a certain sum. The criminal is neither fed nor clothed in the winter by the government, wherefore his subsistence depends upon begging alone. Even in these two departments of the "Mulla" and "kotval," if there is even the slightest chance of squeezing money from any sort of offender, he will not escape the tortures, long imprisonment, and even threats of the Amir personally. A most singular case happened a little before the arrival of the English mission in Kabul. The wife of Khairuddin, the son of Mulla Badruddin, the great merchant of Kabul, whom the Amir respected and called by the appellation of father, bore only a suspected character, and the Amir got information of her being out of doors at a late hour of the night. He was aware that her seizure would be productive of a very large sum, and he dispatched a person of trust to apprehend her when she returns from her visit, and to conduct her into his presence; and this was accordingly done. The Amir kept her very close and concealed, and the relations felt disgrace as well as anxiety from her prolonged absence; and knowing her habits, were still more vexed to think that she was in custody. However, the Amir, for his own sake, allowed her to communicate her apprehension to her husband, but said, as she was a lady of a rich family, she was to pay him ten thousand rupees before she would obtain her liberation. Mulla Badruddin, although he was every day in court with the Amir, yet feeling ashamed to speak on such a disgraceful subject as his daughter's imprisonment, never uttered a word to Dost Mohammed Khan. He, on the other hand, being aware that the delicacy of the case will seal the old rich merchant's mouth, persisted not to diminish ought of the demanded sum. The absence of the lady from home was now the talk of all the neighbours;

and to put an end to this, the relatives were compelled to send her the amount secretly into the prison. She gave it all to the Amir, who, after depriving her of the jewels and shawls with which she was covered, dismissed her from custody. A similar case in some respects followed this deed of extortion.

There was a young man of moderate income, related to Sufi Naqshbandi, who is the only person that repairs watches and other European articles of the kind in Kabul. He fell in love with a handsome girl of a rich Khatri, whose heart was also won. She left the house of her parents, who were grieved at her choice, and unwilling to see their child married to a person of a different religion, and of strange customs; while he, on the other hand, bribed the Amir, and requested his interference. The girl was accordingly caught, and ordered to be sent to the palace. She remained there for a considerable time in charge of Dost Mohammed Khan; and the parents, considering that she was not worthy to mingle with them any more after living in the "Haram serai" of the ruler, where she must have drunk and eaten with Musalmans, showed no anxiety to have her restored to them. On this the Amir communicated his will to her paramour, that if he will give him a certain sum of money, he may have the possession of the fair object of his desire. The money was accordingly paid; and the young damsel, after thus causing the coffers of the Amir to be filled by the plaintiff and by the defendant, was sent out of the palace. Such is a sample of the mode in which the Amir Dost Mohammed Khan sometimes distributes justice.

When Haji Khan Kakar was governor of Bamian, he had made a close alliance with the Tartar chiefs of Turkistan. He went among them and had conference with several of them, and in particular he paid a friendly visit to Mohammed Morad Beg, Mir of Qunduz, and on his coming to Kabul, the Uzbek envoys accompanied him. The Amir did not wish to recognise their mission to him, as he thought it was framed by the advice of Haji Khan, for his own purposes; yet at the same time he received them in his court, and was civil to them until he had secured to himself the presents brought for him. After they left his presence, he neither gave them a residence nor appointed any person to entertain them; and they thus were left to the feeding and maintenance of Mulla Badruddin, and of Haji Khan himself, whose repeated applications to show them civility made no effect on the Amir.

CHAPTER IX.

The Wives of the Amir—Their jealousies—Cruel treatment of one of them by the Amir—An anecdote—A Kashmirian wife—Her escape from the Amir—Bitter enmity entertained towards the Amir by Sultan Mohammed Khan—Wives, Sons, and Daughters of the Amir—His policy of depressing his brothers and raising his sons to power—Expedition against the Sikhs—Mirza Abdul Sami Khan arrives at the camp—Victory of the Afghans—Honours bestowed on Akbar Khan—How to estimate the sons of the Amir—State of the Amir's dominions—Revenues—Encouragement of Commerce—Character of the Amir—His military force.

It should not be omitted to mention that while the Amir Dost Mohammed Khan was occupied by day in endeavouring to increase his power and territory, he was not less active at night in planning the augmentation of the number of his wives, that he might complete the cabinet of his pleasures. In some instances, however, his matrimonial connexions were merely political expedients, and not for any domestic comforts. The number of his married wives is not under fourteen, besides the numerous retinue of slave girls. At present the mother of Mohammed Akbar is his favourite, and takes the freedom to give him her opinion on important occasions. She is descended from a high family, but is very jealous of the other wives of the Amir. Every one of them has a separate allowance, a slave girl, and a slave boy, and they occupy different rooms in the Palace or Haram Sarai, which is encircled by a high wall. Only one door is there for communication, where a few men, generally of old age, "Qabchis," are stationed. When the slave boy is absent, the slave girl brings orders from her mistress to the "Qabchi" for a purchase, or for any other purpose from the inside. If I remember the name well, one of the wives of the Amir who is named Bibi Gauhar, excited the great jealousy and animosity of the mother of Akbar Khan, who always sought for an excuse to create the suspicions and the wrath of the Amir against the rival lady. One evening there was a demand of firewood in the establishment of Bibi Gauhar, and her slave boy brought a quantity of it piled on the back of the seller. His eyes were, on entering the palace door, blindfolded, and his face wrapped in a cloth while he was conducted by the boy. After unloading the burthen from his back, he was in the same manner brought back and let out of the Haram Sarai. Hereupon the penetrating and jealous mother of Akbar Khan thought this the best opportunity to excite some abusive, but unjust suspicion of her character in the heart of the lord. The Amir was quietly asked in through Mohammed Akbar Khan, and the mother of the latter, taking him aside, stated that it was a disgraceful thing that her "Ambagh," rival wife of the Amir, was visited by her paramour, who came in under the disguise of a wood-seller; and she then fabricated sufficient stories to make the Amir prepared to meet her object, for he appeared incensed, and considered that it was not a fabrication; and the poor lady, who a little before was the charming idol of the Amir, was sent for and ordered to be punished for her misconduct. Her assertions of truth were not listened to, and he told Mohammed Akbar Khan to wrap her all in a blanket, and throwing her on the ground to strike her with sticks. The son was now perfectly aware of the jealousy of his own mother against her, and did not fail to inflict many most severe and cruel blows upon her. She was not released until she fainted, and appeared quite motionless in the bloody blanket. After some time when she recovered, the Amir found that he had been deceived by his wife, the mother of Akbar, and he apologized to the sufferer for his sad mistake, and punished the fair inventor of the story (Akbar's mother), only by not going to her apartments for a few days. Bibi Gauhar was the widow of Mahmud Shah, afterwards of Mohammed Azim Khan, and is now one of the Amir's wives.

At breakfast one day the Amir Dost Mohammed Khan asked one of his guests to eat an egg, to which he replied that he had already eaten a considerable number of slices of roast mutton, and feared an egg might cause an attack of indigestion. This made the Amir burst into laughter, and he said that the Amir Bangashi's wife bore a more masculine taste and appetite for eggs than his noble guest, who appears to yield in this affair to a female. In an amusing tone of voice Dost Mohammed Khan entertained the circle of his courtiers with the following anecdote:—When I went to the Bangash country to collect the revenues of that district, political circumstances induced me to marry the daughter of the chief, afterwards known as the mother of Mohammed Afzal Khan. According to the custom of the Afghans, the parents of the lady place several baskets of fruits and of sweetmeats, and one or two of boiled eggs, coloured variously, in the chambers of the newly-married pair. After the dinner was over the Amir with his bride retired, and while amusing themselves with conversation, he took a fancy for some grapes, and the bride handed him an egg, which he found in fact to have a better taste than any he had ever had before. He added that he saw his bride using her fingers with admirable alacrity in taking off the skin preparatory to swallowing an egg, and that this activity continued till she finished the whole basketful, to his astonishment, and he remarked that there were not less than fifty eggs in the basket!

Before we speak of the other ladies of the Amir Dost Mohammed Khan it would not perhaps be uninteresting to the readers to mention a singular instance of fidelity and perseverance in duty of a Kashmirian wife, named Bibi Karmi, in the face of danger and of every temptation. I have already mentioned her being formerly married to Mohammed Rahim Khan Amin-ul-mulk. When this chief was confined by Kam Ran at Qandhar, his son Prince Jahangir heard much said in commendation of the prisoner's wife, and he endeavoured to get possession of her. His threats and his offers of good fortune were equally received with contempt by the lady, who at length was informed that the prince had sent a party to seize and conduct her to the palace. Without saying a word to her dependants she left the house immediately, and threw herself into an adjacent well, in order to preserve her chastity and to avoid the dishonour of violation by her royal captor. Fortunately the well was dry, and was filled with rubbish, &c.; and although she suffered several bruises, yet she remained alive, and unseen by all, except by one merchant, who was standing at the time on the roof of his house. He had heard the report, and became convinced that the female who had thrown herself into the well must be Bibi Karmi, wife of the Amin-ul-mulk. He was also aware that there was in it no water, and therefore he secretly conveyed to her some meal and water at night. Jahangir could not find anywhere the object of his rash passion, and he plundered the houses of the neighbours when they failed to give him accurate information of her movements. The prisoner chief was forgetful of his own sufferings at the idea of the capture of his fair wife, which was bitterly marring the peace of his heart, for he did not know that she was safe, though suffering a strange kind of safety in the well. After some days the husband was liberated on paying two lakhs of rupees to Kam Ran, and permitted to proceed to Kabul. He was on his way overtaken and joined by his wife Bibi Karmi, after her wonderful escape. The merchant who had fed her in the well for his own good will, and expecting a high reward from Amin-ul-mulk, brought a horse, and mounting the Bibi Karmi on its back, started off from the city, and after a continued march of sixty hours, delivered the lady to the Khan, who felt no bounds to his unexpected joy, and rewarded the man liberally. On the death of Amin-ul-mulk the Amir Dost Mohammed Khan communicated the wish of his marriage to her, which was received with great hatred by the Kashmirian widow. The Amir, stimulated by the reputation of her beauty and wealth, determined to possess her, and ordered his counsellor, Agha Husain, to proceed to her residence, and placing her forcibly in the "jampan" (a kind of open litter), to escort her to his "haram sarai." The order was accordingly executed, and the qazi, or the priest, was desired to solemnize the ceremony of marriage, while the sad shrieks of the widow were rending to the ears of the hearers. When the party broke up and the Amir retired, he was overpowered by the charms of her beauty. Now as to Bibi Karmi, she was never at rest from the moment she was married without her own consent, and her tears flowed in torrents. All the endeavours of the Amir to make her his friend were fruitless, and she plainly told him that she would rather poison herself than allow him to approach. She stated that in her opinion it would be a most disgraceful and cold affectation to profess to enjoy his society, and to forget all the good and love of her deceased husband; adding, that it is an unbecoming and vain hope of the Amir to expect love from her; but that if he was desirous to possess the property she has, she would be glad to give him all. On this she placed all her jewels before the Amir with her slave girl, who was also admirably well favoured, and left the room. In short, when he had well considered that nothing could gain the favour and attachment of the lady towards him, he kept her jewels, and she was permitted to leave the palace after an unpleasant stay of a few months. She is now in Kabul, respected and liked by all, and her fidelity has become a proverbial saying among the Afghans.

In the number of his wives the Amir Dost Mohammed Khan has one from the royal family, which case is unprecedented in record or even in rumour, for no one ever was allowed to make a matrimonial connexion with the royal or Sadozai females. On the contrary, it was considered a great honour if any descendant of the Sadozai would marry a female from the Barakzai tribe, namely, that of the Amir, or indeed of any other tribe besides their own. When the decline of that dynasty commenced, she attracted the sight and attention of the Sultan Mohammed Khan, the brother chief of the Amir, at Peshavar, and a correspondence began between them. She prepared to leave Kabul to be married with her intended husband, under whose escort she was proceeding. The Amir had also lost his heart for her beauty, and got hold of her by force and married her immediately. This at once created, and has ever since maintained, a fatal animosity between the brothers; and the Sultan Mohammed Khan has often been heard to say that nothing would afford him greater pleasure, even at breathing his last, than to drink the blood of the Amir. Such is the nature of the brotherly feeling now existing between them; and the Amir has often and justly mentioned that these three words, commencing with the Persian letter "ze," and pronounced like *z* in English, are the principal and deadly causes of quarrel among men, namely, "zan" (female), "zar" (money), and "zamin" (land).

Descent or Relationship of the Wives of the Amir Dost Mohammed Khan.	Sons.	Names.	Daughters.
1. Sister of Mulla Rashid			
2. Daughter of Mulla Sadiq Ali, the Bangash Chief	2	Mohammed Afzal and Azam Khan	
3. Daughter of Baqa Khan, the Parvan Chief	1	Mohammed Akram Khan	
4. Daughter of Khojah Khanji, whom the Amir murdered in Kohistan, as is already mentioned	. .	. .	1
5. Widow of Shah Mahmud, and afterwards of Azim Khan . .	3	Mohammed Aslam, Hassan and Husain Khan.	
6. Granddaughter of Jahangir Khan, Tori Chief	1	Vali Mohammed Khan.	

Descent or Relationship of the Wives of the Amir Dost Mohammed Khan.	Sons.	Names.	Daughters.
7. Daughter of Prince Abbas, who caused enmity between the Amir and Sultan Mohammed Khan	3	. .	1
8. Daughter of a wealthy merchant, Nazir Khair-ullah.*	. .	. .	1
9. Sister of Mehtar Mosa, Chief of Zurmat			
10. Daughter of Sadiq Khan Javan Sher, widow of Azim Khan .	1	Sultan Jan, Step-son.	1
11. Sister of the Chief of Kalat and Ghilzai			
12. Bibi Karmi of the Amin-Ul-mulk, who acted as above related			
13. Daughter of Haji Raihmat-ullah-Khan, famous for being the mother of Akbar Khan, and favourite of the Amir . .	5	Mohammed Akbar† Ditto Haidar. Ditto Sherali. Ditto Amin. Ditto Sharif Khans.	1
14. Daughter of the Chief of Morad Khani, married on his restoration to Kabul or returning from India in 1843.			

The Amir Dost Mohammed Khan's best policy

* He left Kabul for fear of being seized and deprived by the Amir of his riches, and resided at Bokhara. Amir married his daughter to soothe his fear, and thus induce him to return to Kabul, and plunder him. He knows the Amir's craft, and will not come back.

† This son of the Amir is well known to the world for his treacheries, cruelties, and murders.

for the security of his authority is very judicious, though it has made him disliked by his rival relations. In the commencement of his power we find him occupied in bestowing the administration and charge of various districts upon his relations, or in some instances allowing them the enjoyment of their own possessions. Thus Navab Mohammed Zaman held Jalalabad; Mohammed Usam Khan, Bala Bagh; Jabbar Khan, Laghman and the Ghilzai; Shamshuddin Khan, Ghaznin; Haji Khan, Bamian; and so were also the other petty districts shared among them: but when he gained the stability of his position, he deprived every one of them of all authority, placing his own sons in their places. These feared him more than the others, and followed his example in the administration of their respective territories. Now at length the Amir was firmly established, and looked upon as the supreme Lord of Afghanistan. He was of course surrounded by his intriguing and dissatisfied brothers at home, but yet he entertained no fear of their upsetting him. The alarms, however, were daily increasing from the fear of an enemy abroad,—the powerful ruler of the Panjab.

The Sultan Mohammed Khan, brother of the Amir Dost Mohammed Khan, influenced by the Sikhs, commenced intrigues and designs for taking Kabul. The Amir ordered Mohammed Akbar Khan to proceed to Khaibar, and then he reinforced him by means of his eldest son, Mohammed Afzal Khan. He did not take this step merely as one frightened by rumours, but he had actually received repeated communications from the chiefs of the Khaibars, demanding the dispatch of some troops, and offering him their co-operation against the Sikhs, stating that otherwise they will be obliged to acknowledge the authority of Ranjit Singh. The army of the Amir encamped at the mouth of the Khaibar Pass, towards Peshavar, and every day skirmishes took place between the Afghans and the Sikh force garrisoned at Jam Road. The Amir considered it proper that his sons and the army should have some person of good judgment to regulate their conduct and the plan of the battle or of the negotiations. He was well aware that he had no more trusty servant nor any wiser man than his minister Mirza Abdul Sami Khan, and him he commanded to join his sons. The Mirza arrived in the camp, and observed that a large number of Mahomedan fanatics had assembled under the standards of Mohammed Akbar and of Afzal Khan, whether stimulated by religious feelings, or moved thereto by their avarice of plunder; but at the same time he was sure of sustaining one or two very strong battles with the Sikhs then present. He determined on attacking the enemy, and reported all the circumstances and prospects to the Amir at Kabul, and he sent fresh reinforcements under the Navabs Jabbar Khan, Usman Khan, and Shamshuddin Khan. The fort of Jam Road was besieged, and the garrison prevented from fetching any water or grass from outside the citadel. They wrote to Sardar Hari Singh at Peshavar, telling him of their distressed and fearful condition, and solicited his immediate succour. The Sikh chief, with an army of about ten thousand men, twenty pieces of artillery, and a great quantity of ammunition and provisions, came to the relief of the garrison at Jam Road. He attacked the Kabul forces, and compelled Mohammed Akbar Khan to quit his ground; while Mohammed Afzal Khan, his brother, with his conspicuous bravery and judgment, managed to penetrate into the left wing of the Sikh troops, on which

Hari Singh retraced his steps. He then, however, assailed the Navab, defeated him, and captured two of the guns. Many Afghans were fleeing back towards Kabul; but Shamshuddin Khan, noted for bravery, happened to reach the place at this crisis, and by a most daring assault regained the lost field. Hari Singh was mortally wounded, and soon after died; and this gave the Afghans the victory. The Sikhs, after losing their leader, entrenched their position round the fort of Jam Road, and the army of the Amir of Kabul was recalled.

It is a general topic of conversation that, had not Mohammed Afzal Khan shown his judicious valour, and Shamshuddin Khan his rash boldness, the victory would never have been gained by the Afghans. However, all the merits and praise due to them were attributed by the Amir Dost Mohammed Khan to Mohammed Akbar Khan, the son of his favourite wife. She gave feasts and illuminated the city in commemoration of the victory gained by her son, and prevailed upon her husband to think and say that every honour and all applause was due to him. Since that period the eldest son of the Amir, Mohammed Afzal Khan, with other heroes of the family, is very much disheartened. No feeling of pure regard has since existed between the father and these sons; and Akbar Khan continues gaining the favour and strength of the Amir.

It is a matter of unquestionable truth, that Mohammed Akbar Khan, by his most extraordinary and successful intrigues, cruelties, and murders has gained the highest pitch of influence in Afghanistan and renown in England, but Mohammed Afzal Khan is the first of all the sons of Dost Mohammed Khan who possesses a sound judgment and the laudable quality of heroism. On the death of the Amir there will be no doubt a general commotion in Kabul. If Sultan Mohammed Khan, the ex-chief of Peshavar, or any of the present chiefs of Qandhar, be in existence at that period, no doubt he will then exert himself to become the master of the capital, and many chiefs, and even the sons of the Amir, will co-operate with any of these against Mohammed Akbar Khan. On the other hand, none of the sons of the Amir stands so high in the estimation of the population and of the chiefs, and the Barakzai family, as Mohammed Afzal Khan, and all these will join him against Akbar Khan. Mohammed

Azam Khan, also the brother of the former, will not hesitate to intrigue for killing the latter, while Akram Khan, and the other sons of the Amir, will unite with him. Akbar Khan will have no supporters but his own younger brothers, as Haidar Khan, &c. The whole dominion of Kabul, now under the possession of the Amir, will be divided into small principalities, governed by his sons, and independent of each other; and continued warfare, intrigues, assassinations, and plundering of the merchants, will be the predominant features of the government.

It is well known that the Amir Dost Mohammed is not the master of the whole of Afghanistan. He has, of course, seated himself on the throne, or in broad words, in the capital of that dominion—Kabul. The city is divided by the river "Jue Shir," which springs from Sirchashmah, on the road to Bamian; has a population of about sixty-five thousand souls; lat. 34° 30′, long. 69° 6′. The whole province of Kabul, or the authority of the Amir Dost Mohammed Khan, extends from Hindu Kush-Parwan, lat. 35° 10′, long. 69° 12′ on the north, to Mukar, south of Ghuzni, lat. 32° 52′, long. 67° 41′, and little higher from Bamian in the west, lat. 34° 50′, long. 67° 48′, to the Khaibar pass in the east, lat. 33° 58′, long. 71′ 30′,* making a length of two hundred miles from east to west, and the breadth of about one hundred and seventy miles from north to south. All the distances above detailed are often traversed by the Amir's cavalry from three to five days. The principal towns and marts of the country are Jalalabad, Ghazni, and Charkar, with some other petty places of renown, as Istalif, Shakardrah, &c. &c.

On the revenues of the province of Kabul a great many assertions are in existence, varying from each other very considerably. My information on this point is derived from the records of the chief collectors of the Amir Dost Mohammed Khan, as Mirza Sayad Husain, Divan Mitha upon one side, and Divans Birbal and Daya Ram on the other. These parties, however, differ in the total sum, but the connexion of Sayad Husain with the minister of the Amir, is the manifest reason of his pocketing large sums undetected from the revenues, while the latter Divans proved the truth on their own side, by putting

* Thornton's 'Gazetteer of the Countries adjacent to India.'

down the additional sums only on the paper which were realized for the government, and paid in accordingly. By the Sayad's account, the annual sum of money derived from the land, custom-house, extortion, and other unjust sources (Bidat), amounts to 2,431,271 rupees, while Divan Birdal collected 2,509,238 lakhs. It would be better and perhaps the shortest way to put down here the list of the collections of the latter, and I shall mention the amount of the revenue under its proper heading or name by which it is raised, namely, "Asal," or just, and "Bidat," or unjust. The accounts of Divan Birbal make an additional sum of 77,967 rupees in favour of the government.

Names of the ——, or of the Places the Revenue is collected from.	"Asal," or just Amount of the Revenue.	"Bidat," or unjust Amount of the Revenue.	Total Sum in Kabul Rupees.
Duties from Custom House	207,580	92,340	299,920
Vajah Shahganj, Arghande, &c. &c. .	109,054 and 2 abbasi	11,920 and 1 sannar	120,975
Bilok-i-Kohdaman, Char Yakar, and Lahogard	389,914 and 3 shahis	23,635 and 1 shahis	413,549 and 1 abbasi
Istalif	24,834 and 1 abbasi	1,525 and 6 shahis	26,360
Khalsah, Government Land	159,179	..	159,179
Rezah Kohistan and Bulaghain . . .	18,831	2,805	21,636

Names of the ——, or of the Places the Revenue is collected from.	"Asal," or just Amount of the Revenue.	"Bidat," or unjust Amount of the Revenue.*	Total Sum in Kabul Rupees.
Ghorband	23,480	2,732	26,212
Tajakyah Maidan	21,825	921 and 5 shahis	22,746
Charkh	23,306	1,000	24,306
Ghilzai	222,595 and 1 senar	7,631 and 1 shahi	230,226 and 3 shahis
Behsud and Bamian	69,964	..	69,964
Ghaznin	397,971 and 7 shahis	37,451 and 3 shahis	435,423
Taefah Kharauti, Shinvari, &c.	18,321	740	19,061
Zurmat, Gardez, and Kharvar	64,240 and 2 abbasi	950	65,190 and 8 shahis
Hazarah Turkam, and Parsa	6,599	..	6,599
Khurm and Khost	95,000	..	95,000
Jalalabad and Lamghan-i-Tajakyah	435,588	29,940	465,528
"Darkat-i-Mut-faraqah Havai,"	5,870	3,850 and 6 shahis	9,720 and 6 shahis
Total	2,292,380	216,902	..
Grand Total	..	..	2,509,238

The Amir Dost Mohammed Khan has acquired great celebrity for the encouragement of commerce in comparison with the conduct of his brothers, the chiefs of Qandhar and Peshavar; and in this he has acted wisely, both for his own benefit and for that of the merchants. The roads under his government are safer than they were in former days; and there are no further demands on the merchandise made by the petty officers of the customs, as there were under the Sadozai dynasty. But I have heard from Mulla Rahim Shah, Gholam Qadir, and Gopaldas Shikarpuri, merchants of first rank, that the consumption of goods, and the circulation of money, was upon a much larger scale under the disturbed state of the late kings' governments only in Kabul than it is now under the Barakzai chiefs, including Qandhar and Peshavar, as well as Hirat.* The chief of Kabul has established some new duties on the exports, the imports, and the transit of goods in Kabul, under various names, commonly called "Bidat," which has already been stated under the head of revenues. The Amir has encouraged commerce indeed, but yet he has often forcibly extorted large sums of money from the merchants, wherewith to maintain his troops for sake of the extension and stability of his government. Whenever traders with shawls from Kashmir, or horses from Bokhara, pass on their way through Kabul, the Amir avails himself of the first descrip-

* Independent of the Barakzais.

tion of the articles, and of the animals, and giving no value to all the cries of the owner, he pays any sum he likes; which, of course, is much less than the original price. The merchants bring a great quantity of gold in Russian ducats, and the Bokhara tilas for Amrat Sar and India; but a good deal more from the former place. They bring these openly in the smallest quantity only, for fear of being seized by the Amir; and being thus forced they practise smuggling. At one time, while the British mission was in Kabul, a Lohani merchant was seized, if I remember well, with twenty thousand ducats; and on application made on his behalf several times by the late Sir Alexander Burnes, the Amir reluctantly restored some portion of it to the merchant.

Amount of duties levied at the different offices of customs in the province of Kabul, given to me by Mirza Sami, the minister of the Amir:—

Names of Places.	Amount in Kabul Rupees.
Kabul	212,000
Ghazni	80,000
Bamian	55,000
Kafshan	4,500
Charkar	10,000
Istalif	6,000
Sarae Khojah	4,000
Arghande	16,000

Names of Places.	Amount in Kabul Rupees.
Jalalabad	7,000
Basaval or Hazarah nau . .	2,500
Gandumak	2,500
Lahogard	6,000
Sardari	6,000
Goshi Qandhar	2,000
From the city gates called "Chiraghi" (lamp)	2,000
Total . .	415,500

It must be understood that the above mentioned sum is included in the revenue of the government, and the total amount of 2,509,238 rupees is nearly equal in Company's rupees to 2,262,943, or about 226,294*l.* sterling. All the government and mercantile accounts are received and paid in Kham rupees, equal to ten shahis each. This is not a current coin, but is used in the accounts.

In the person, in the manners, and in the public proceedings of the Amir Dost Mohammed Khan, there is manifest the existence of every thing imaginable most suitable to support his own view. He is calm, prudent, and wise in cabinet, and an able commander in the field. In treachery, cruelty, murder, and falsehood, he is equally notorious. He is not at all a popular ruler, but he is the first man in Afghanistan who knows how to keep his authority undisturbed, and to deal effectually with the vagabond Afghans. He is certainly very much liked in regard to one thing, namely this: any man seeking for justice may stop him on the road by holding his hand and garment, once his beard, may abuse him for not relieving his grievances; and the Amir will continue to listen to him without disturbance or anger. Upon several occasions people in companies come near to the palace, and by the shouts of "Dad," justice, deafen the ears of the hearers; but seldom do they receive what they want. On the whole, whatever odium may be attached to the Amir of Kabul, it is an unquestionable fact that he is the only person fit to rule Kabul. Dost Mohammed Khan is of the Sunni religion, being the son of an Afghan; but as his mother is a Shia, he is therefore suspected to be of her creed, though he does not confess it openly. He has indulged in all sorts of dissipation, and experienced all kinds of hardships. When he gained power, he prohibited the sale and the use of wine, and prevented dancing girls from remaining in his kingdom, while the dance performed by boys was considered lawful! One day he was informed that some women were drinking and dancing privately in the house of Husain, the servant of Nayab Abdul Samad, on which the Amir sent people to seize them. The punishment inflicted upon them for drinking wine against the Mohammedan law and his own notification was the infliction of deformity instead of their beauty, in order to prevent them from appearing again in drinking parties. Their heads were shaved, and the beard of the host was burnt by the flame of a candle! The Amir Dost Mohammed Khan always gets up before it is dawn, takes a bath, makes his prayers, and reads a portion of the "Qoran" every morning. After that Mahmud Akhund Zadah gives him some lessons in history as well as poetry. He receives afterwards the state people privately in the dressing-room of the bath, and then comes out to hold his court. He sits there generally till 1 P.M. Now he had his breakfast, or I may say his dinner, as it is just the same as he receives after sunset. When he has finished his breakfast or mid-day meal he sleeps till 4 P.M. He then discharges his prayers, and proceeds usually to ride, sees his stud, and returns to the palace, where he dines with his immediate courtiers and friends.

There is then some talk of his early proceedings and of his future plans; and the wonder, the jealousy, and the ascendancy of foreign powers are discussed. Sometimes chess, and at other times music, were the favourite amusements of the evening. He amused himself generally in this manner till one hour past midnight. All the chiefs are then dismissed, and on retiring the Amir resides in the apartments of his wives. They live in separate parts, and the Amir pays a visit to one lady one night, and to another wife the next night, and no one is visited two nights successively except the mother of Mohammed Akbar Khan.

The military strength of the Amir Dost Mohammed Khan does undoubtedly exceed and excel that of any other of the chiefs of Afghanistan; and if I am rightly informed, the Sadozai kings never had such a large park of well-mounted guns as the Amir has. Whatever his occupations were during the day or night, his sole aim was bent towards the improvement and increase of his military power. He had fifty pieces of cannon, some of them well cast, besides those which were captured from the Sikhs when Sardar Hari Singh fell in the battle of Jam Road;

he has also about two hundred of "Shahnaks," good ones of their kind; these being light and small are placed on the backs of camels, and used by the driver. His cavalry amounted to twelve thousand in number, and is composed of two different brigades, the one called "Khud Aspah," riders of their own horses, and the other, "Amlah Sarkari," mounting the government horses. These are placed under the petty "Khavanins," in various numbers, from two to two hundred horses, and then attached to, and commanded by, some one of his own sons. Mohammed Akbar Khan usually leads two thousand, Mohammed Afzal Khan six hundred, Gholam Haidar Khan one thousand, and so on, the other sons and the Navabs, and the rest of the relations of the Amir, have few followers. He has also more than two thousand of "Jazayarchis," or infantry, bearing a large musket, like a wall piece of ordnance, which they use with a rest. This arm has gained great improvement under Mohammed Akbar, and his best and most confidential Ghilzai are armed with them, and he superintends the manufacture of them in person. The infantry of the Amir, organized by Nayab Abdul Samad, Mr. Campbell, and Dr. Harlan, cannot be compared to the cavalry of that chief, but as they are generally the men of the mountains, they are by the position of their country and mutual warfare well adapted to fight under the shelter of bushes, walls, and hollow places, where the uniform movements of our foot regiments will not permit them to exercise their discipline as the Afghans can. Their muskets are also better for throwing balls to a long distance than those of England. This portion of the Amir's force is limited to about fifteen hundred men.

The pay of the troops is not properly distributed, for neither the cavalry soldiers nor commanders, "Khavanins," receive an equal sum; the increase of pay and rank both depend entirely upon the influence and patronage of their friends. They are paid yearly in cash, grain, grass, sheep, blankets, and butter, which, after obtaining an order from the paymaster, they get from the local collectors and the headmen of the villages in the country. The general pay of a horseman is 12 tomans, or 120 Kabul Kham rupees, that is about 10*l.* a-year, which feeds and clothes him with his family, as well as his charger—such is the wonderful cheapness of provisions in that country. The foot soldier has no more than 84 rupees, or 8*l.* a-year, in the same manner, but a greater number of them are engaged for only about 6*l.* per annum.

CHAPTER X.

Connection of the British with Afghanistan—Policy of Russia—Her alliance with Persia—The Afghans lean towards the British Government—Claims on Peshavar—Policy of Lord William Bentinck—Of Lord Auckland—Letter from the Amir to the Governor-General—Reply of the latter—Mission of Sir Alexander Burnes—The Amir demands the restoration of Peshavar—Sir Alexander's Reply—Dissatisfaction of Dost Mohammed Khan—His letter to the King of Persia—His plan of balancing Russia, Persia, and England against each other.

I HAVE now fully related the adventurous commencement of the career of the Amir Dost Mohammed Khan, and brought him gradually to the zenith of his glory. It is evident that the Afghans never put any circumstances on record, nor do they take the trouble to keep past events fresh in their memory. Whatever they do remember is preserved by the memory only, in the rudest manner. My informants always failed in giving the precise dates, or even the years of the Amir's progress, as noticed in the preceding pages, and therefore no blame can be justly attached to this narrative for misplacing the events of his career. I shall now begin to describe the circumstances which opened the way for making the British more familiar with Afghanistan, and which also made the Amir Dost Mohammed Khan desirous to correspond with the Indian authorities.

Upon the one hand the English Government always sought for information in an independent state, lying between the confines of the Indian Empire and the Caspian Sea, and its officer felt an anxiety to secure that object. That political foresight was even worked upon so far back as 1808, when the mission of the Honourable Mountstuart Elphinstone was directed and proceeded to that quarter. The valuable "Account of the Kingdom of Kabul," published by that functionary, opened the eyes of the British nation to explore its curiosities, and in a political view the attention of the Government was most earnestly directed to that part of the globe. Hence also some Englishmen of mature sense and much ambition were induced to penetrate into that despotic country, and thought that, by making important and improved additions to the already gained knowledge of that extensive tract, and close familiarity with its vast number of inhabitants, they might gain the patronage of their Government and high estimation in their own country. With these deliberate views of advantage, therefore, they set out to carry their objects into effect. First of all Mr. Moorcroft entered Afghanistan, but unfortunately he expired on the other side of the Hindu Kush. Mr. Sterling, Captain Arthur Conolly, and after all the late Sir Alexander Burnes,* walked in the same path as marked out by his predecessors. The more new knowledge we gained of that region the more interest we felt in relation to its importance, both in a political and commercial point of view. For this purpose the navigation of the river Indus was opened, and a favourable alliance made with the Sindhians, the Daud potrahs, and the Sikhs.

Upon the other hand, the Persians and the Afghans having much more inland communication with each other, and dwelling on the frontiers of Russia, nourished a magnified idea of her ambitious policy, of her great power, and of her jealous eyes towards British India, and thus they considered themselves

* When the author of these Memoirs accompanied him.

the fortunate favourites of both these rival nations. The Persians, being wiser and nearer than the Afghans, set the example of acting on this universal feeling, allied herself to Russia, while she continued to profess the holding of intimacy with England, and in this manner thought she obtained her wishes. The Afghans, though not so polished as their neighbours in Persia, were not altogether unaware of the interest which the English took in their extensive country, which commanded the passes or doors leading to India. With this thought the late King Shah Shuja sought asylum in British India, and hoped to be supported by us, and in this he was not disappointed. Also in the same opinion the late celebrated Vazir Fatah Khan sent communications to the Indian Government. The same impression was on the heart of the Amir Dost Mohammed Khan, but his crafty manœuvring brought all the secret designs of the parties concerned in them to light, and he thought that he possessed the key of Hindustan, which no doubt will be too dearly bought by the English if there should happen the slightest shadow of another bidder.

With these well matured sentiments he desired to

make himself known to the governments of India, Persia, and Russia; and while his brother, the Sultan Mohammed Khan of Peshavar, was alive, and held the Kohat and Hasht-nagar districts of that province under his acknowledged superior, Maharajah Ranjit Singh, the Amir Dost Mohammed Khan, whom both always despised and feared, made claims upon Peshavar. There were always warfare and negotiations between him and the Sikhs upon this subject, and the Amir despatched communications and agents to the governments of British India, Persia, and Russia, soliciting the interference of each of these powers to recover the Afghan territory from the ruler of the Panjab, and promised his alliance and services to them (of course against each other) if there should happen the necessity of employing such services in future.

The late Lord William Bentinck, however, did not take a prominent interest in the politics of Afghanistan. In fact there did not seem any necessity during his government to demand attention so seriously in that quarter as it unavoidably happened to require in the time of his successor. The regretted Governor-General nevertheless seemed inclined to share so far in the politics of that country that he appointed Sayad Karamat Ali,* Mr. Masson, and myself † in Afghanistan to convey to him information of the passing events in that state. This produced an easy way for the Amir to effect his long-nourished objects, and he therefore lost no time in corresponding with the British government. His communications to his Lordship and Sir Claude Wade, the political agent, implored the mediation of their authority to adjust differences between him and his powerful enemy the Maharajah Ranjit Singh. He had strong reasons for fearing that he might be subverted by his foe, who, through the influence of his brother Sultan Mohammed Khan, now with the Sikhs, could injure him (Dost Mohammed) even in Kabul.

In the mean time the Earl of Auckland arrived as the new Governor-General of India, and the Amir Dost Mohammed Khan addressed a congratulating epistle to his Lordship.

* Fellow traveller with the most deeply regretted and distinguished Captain Arthur Conolly.

† I never joined that situation at Qandhar, being appointed in the meantime to settle the disputes between the subjects of Lahore and Bahavalpur during the absence of Major Mackinon.

The Amir Dost Mohammed Khan of Kabul to the Governor-General of India.

(After compliments.)

"As I have been long attached to the British Government by the ties of friendship and affection, the late intelligence of your Lordship's arrival, enlightening with your presence the seat of government, and diffusing over Hindustan the brightness of your countenance, has afforded me extreme gratification; and the field of my hopes, which had before been chilled by the cold blast of wintry times, has, by the happy tidings of your Lordship's arrival, become the envy of the garden of Paradise.

"It may be known to your Lordship, that, relying on the principles of benevolence and philanthropy which distinguish the British Government, I look upon myself and country as bound to it by the strongest ties, and the letters I have received from that quarter have all been replete with friendly sentiments and attention,—and to the effect that, in the time of need, the obligations of friendship should be fulfilled. The late transactions in this quarter, the conduct of reckless and misguided Sikhs, and their breach of treaty, are well known to your Lordship. Communicate to me whatever may suggest itself to your wisdom for the settlement of the affairs of this country, that it may serve as a rule for my guidance.

"I hope your Lordship will consider me and my country as your own, and favour me often with the receipt of your friendly letters. Whatever directions your Lordship may be pleased to issue for the administration of this country, I will act accordingly."

This letter was followed by many others similarly expressive of his anxiety and fear of the Sikhs; and his alarms were truly increased when an army of fifty thousand from Lahaur arrived at Peshavar, intending to revenge the sudden attack of the Afghans upon Jam Road, and the fall of the Sardar Hari Singh in that battle. The Earl of Auckland sent to the Amir Dost Mohammed Khan a very kind answer, and at the same time resolved to relieve him from the continued fear of the Sikhs, under the name of holding a commercial alliance with him.

The Earl of Auckland to the Amir Dost Mohammed Khan.

22*nd August*, 1836.

(After compliments.)

"I HAVE had the pleasure to receive your friendly letter, which was transmitted to me through Sir Claude Wade, and I am gratified at the opportunity which it affords so shortly after my assumption of the Indian government, to convey to you the assurances of my unfeigned regard and esteem.

"It is my wish that the Afghans should be a flourishing and united nation; and that, being in peace with all their

EARL OF AUCKLAND G.C.B.

neighbours, they should enjoy, by means of a more extended commerce, all the benefits and comforts possessed by other nations, which through such means have attained a high and advanced state of prosperity and wealth.

"My predecessor, aware that nothing was so well calculated to promote this object as the opening of the navigation of the Indus, spared himself no pains in procuring this channel for the flow of industry and enterprise; and it shall be my study to second his philanthropic purpose, and to complete the scheme which he so successfully commenced. I feel assured that you cannot but take a lively interest in the success of this undertaking, so especially conducive as it must be to the prosperity of the people over whom you rule.

"It is probable that I may, ere long, depute some gentlemen to your Court, to discuss with you certain commercial topics, with a view to our mutual advantage.

"I have learned with deep regret that dissensions exist between yourself and the Maharajah Ranjit Singh. My friend, you are aware that it is not the practice of the British Government to interfere with the affairs of other independent states; and indeed it does not immediately occur to me how the interference of my Government could be exercised for your benefit. I shall be happy, however, to learn from you by what means you think that I can be of any assistance; and in the meantime, I have only to hope that you will be able to devise some mode of effecting a reconciliation with the Sikhs; it being not only for your own advantage but for the advantage of all the countries in the vicinity, that two nations so situated should ever preserve the unimpaired relations of amity and concord.

"Begging that you will accept my renewed assurance of friendship and regard,

"I am, &c. &c.

(Signed) "AUCKLAND."

The receipt of this letter excited a great sensation in Dost Mohammed Khan, and served as a new reason for him to employ his tact in order to second his own objects, by intriguing with Persia and Russia. On the other hand the Governor-General of India made preparations for sending a special mission to his court, and Sir Alexander Burnes was selected to conduct it. The equipage of the mission and the presents for the Amir were nothing in comparison to those of the Honourable Mountstuart Elphinstone when deputed to Shah Shuja-ul-mulk: however, Sir Alexander Burnes, in company with his assistants, Major Leech, Lieut. Wood, and Dr. Lord, of the Bombay Presidency, ascended the Indus, and I was ordered by the Supreme Government to join him on that river.

The mission was well received at Haidarabad,

Khairpur, and Bahavalpur, on its way up the river; and in the latter place Sir Alexander Burnes received a letter from Mr. Masson, the news-writer in Kabul, stating that the Amir has been delighted to hear that he was nominated to confer with him; and he added that whatever the objects of the mission might be, whether commercial or political, they will meet an unreserved welcome from the Amir Dost Mohammed Khan. The more near the British mission approached Afghanistan, the more frequently the Amir of Kabul despatched letters to Sir Alexander Burnes, conveying the expression of his delight at the prospect of the interview, and his readiness and desire to attach himself to the British government by any terms the Governor may think proper to propose. On entering the Khaibar Pass the mission was met by a deputation from the Amir, and a salute was fired; and it was honourably conducted and escorted by Shah Ghasi Gul, Mirza Aghajan, and Sadat Khan, the Momand chief, towards Kabul. Dost Mohammed Khan sent another deputation, headed by Nazir Ali Mohammed Khan, who had directions to provide the mission with all the Afghan cookery and the other luxuries of Kabul, and to wait upon us all the way to Kabul. After some marches it reached Butkhak, and next day Mohammed Akbar Khan, with a large retinue, came to receive and conduct the mission into the city. The procession in entering was very grand, and we were placed on elephants together with him, and thus proceeded onwards between lines made on both sides by the spectators and the respectable citizens, who were requested by the Amir to welcome us. The anxiety and pleasure of Dost Mohammed Khan at the arrival of the English envoy was so great, that he desired his son to conduct us at once to his own presence. He received us most cordially; and near his own palace a beautiful garden, surrounded with the most comfortable apartments, was allotted to us as our place of residence.

On the 21st of September the Amir Dost Mohammed Khan assembled his nobles and received the mission formally. Sir Alexander Burnes submitted his credentials from the Governor-General of India to the Amir, and they were opened by himself, and read aloud by his minister Mirza Abdul Sami Khan; and the Amir seemed really flattered by hearing the contents of them in the presence of those

THE LATE SIR ALEXANDER BURNES KT. C.B.

chiefs who, being older, and having seen the late kings of the Sadozai family, had never dreamt that Dost Mohammed Khan, one of the humblest of the sons of Payandah Khan, could become a person of such consequence as to be respected by the English power.

The credentials were these:—

The Earl of Auckland to the Amir Dost Mohammed Khan.

Fort William, 15*th May*, 1837.

(After compliments.)

"In my letter to your address, dated 2nd August, 1836, I intimated my intention of deputing an officer to confer with you as to the best means of promoting the interests of commerce, and facilitating the intercourse of traders between India and Afghanistan.

"To your enlightened mind it cannot fail to be obvious, that commerce is the basis of all national prosperity, and that it is commerce alone that enables people of one country to exchange its superfluous commodities for those of another; to accumulate wealth, and to enjoy all the comforts and blessings of civilized life.

"The general diffusion of these blessings and comforts among neighbouring nations is the general object of the British Government. It seeks for itself no exclusive benefits, but it ardently desires to secure the establishment of peace and prosperity in all the countries of Asia.

"With this view the British Government prevailed upon

the powers occupying the banks of the river, to open the navigation of the Indus; and to this object, indeed, have all its efforts been invariably directed.

"I now send Sir Alexander Burnes, who will deliver this letter, to confer with you as to the best means of facilitating commercial intercourse between Afghanistan and India. I have no doubt that he will meet with a friendly reception at your Court, and that his personal communication with you will be attended with all the advantages which I anticipate.

"In conclusion, &c.,

(Signed) "AUCKLAND."

For a few days the Amir Dost Mohammed Khan continued to show us every civility, and appearing to act with perfect sincerity and candour; and in his conversation with Sir Alexander Burnes he always showed a moderation in his demands. Sir Alexander Burnes wrote at that time as follows:—"Up to this time my communications with the Amir have been confined to matters of compliment and ceremony, but I shall take an early opportunity of reporting on what transpires at this court, merely observing at present, from what I have seen and heard, that I have good reason to believe Dost Mohammed Khan will set forth no extravagant pretensions, but will act in such a manner as to enable the British Government to show its interest in his behalf, and at the same time to preserve for us the valued friendship of the Sikh chief."

However, the moderation of the Amir Dost Mohammed Khan was of short duration. He forgot that the presence of the British mission in his capital had prevented the Sikh army from revenging the sudden attack of Akbar Khan upon Jam Road, and placed no value on the mediation of the English, which was intended to secure his interests. The tenor of his previous correspondence and conversation was anxiously expressive of his fears of an attack from the Sikhs; but now, changing his views and his mind, he longed for the possession of Peshavar, and he accordingly demanded of Sir Alexander Burnes to write to his government to cause the restoration of that province to him. Sir Alexander Burnes replied to the Amir that Peshavar was never under his authority; and that his brothers, Sultan Mohammed and Pir Mohammed Khan, were the rulers of that part of Afghanistan, and had still "jagirs" in that district, granted to them from the sovereign of the Panjab. He added, also, that the Maharajah Ranjit Singh was a faithful ally of the English,—was powerful both in arms and in money; and had lost his commander-in-chief, Sardar Hari Singh, in an unprovoked assault of the Afghans upon his handful of forces at Jam Road. The British Government, he said, being desirous to establish peace for the extension of commerce as far as to the markets of Central Asia, and finding by the Amir's letters and words that he was always involved with alarms, resolved to adjust differences between him and the Sikhs by amicable terms; that is to say, the Amir will have no further necessity by extortions to make himself unpopular, to raise troops and to shed blood in fighting with the forces of the Panjab. On the contrary, that he will enjoy the comforts of his authority without fear, and will reign in prosperity. Sir Alexander Burnes continued, that his Government will induce the Maharajah, by friendly advice, to give up Peshavar to its former master, the Sardar Sultan Mohammed Khan, the brother of the Amir; but that the alliance, which so faithfully is maintained by the Maharajah, cannot permit the British Government to use its authority directly on this subject.

In my own presence the Amir Dost Mohammed Khan replied, that this was not the good offices of the English which he had expected; that his hopes were quite different; that he had now a turban of muslin on his head, but that on entering into a friendly relation with the British he had sanguine hopes that he would have a shawl one in lieu of muslin. On the contrary, he finds that the English wish to keep the old material on his head, with the obliging promise that they will not allow any other power to deprive him of it. To this act of amity he attaches not much importance, as he was not afraid that any one will ever wrest it from him. The Amir continued, that the restoration of Peshavar to the Sultan Mohammed Khan will not be a token of the British entertaining good wishes towards himself,—nay, it will hasten the ruin of his government in Kabul. He added, that his brother, Sultan Mohammed, though one of the family, and of one blood with himself, was a more fatal enemy to him even with a small force than the Sikhs with their large army. The Sikhs will lend his brother money, and, under his Mahomedan name, will send forth their intrigues to the very heart of his capital.

Now, also, the Amir Dost Mohammed Khan was informed of the progress of the Persian mission towards Afghanistan, bearing presents and letters in answer to those which he and his brothers the Qandhar chiefs had despatched to the king, and which affair the Amir had kept till this time unspoken.

It must here be said with propriety that when he had communicated his grievances to the British Government, he conveyed the same to the other western powers of Russia and Persia, with the view of gaining his object by playing these three states against each other.

Letter from the Amir Dost Mohammed Khan to His Majesty Mohammed Shah, King of Persia.

(After Respects.)

"SINCE in former days the chiefs of my family were sincerely attached to the exalted and royal house of your Majesty, I, too, deem myself one of the devoted adherents of that royal race; and considering this country as belonging to the kingdom of Persia, I on a former occasion despatched Haji Ibrahim to your Majesty's presence with the object of explaining certain affairs connected with this nation. I crave permission to state, that the cause of my addressing in the present instance is the following:—Your Majesty is the king of 'Islam,' yet throughout these territories disturbances and misery are caused by that detestable tribe, the Sikhs.

"Although four hundred thousand families of the tribe of Afghans, and the neighbouring tribes, wear the collar of obedience in subjection to this sincere well-wisher, my inability for the employment and arrangement of this multitude limits my forces to twenty thousand excellent horse and ten thousand foot, and fifty guns, which are ready at my capital, Kabul.*

"I have been long engaged in war against one hundred thousand horse and foot of the wicked infidels, who have three hundred guns; but, by the grace and assistance of God, I have not yet been subdued by this faithless enemy, and have been able to preserve the true faith; but how long shall I be able to oppose this detestable tribe, and how long shall I be able to resist their aggressions?† Without doubt an account of the difficulties of my situation has reached your Majesty; and your Majesty must have heard that, notwithstanding the inferiority of my power, I am perpetually engaged in war with the wicked Sikhs, without a moment's cessation. As the noblest of cities, Qandhar and the capital Kabul, and the countries bordering on Khora-

* Exaggeration. For the proper number, see his military power in the preceding pages.

† This is sufficient to show that the Amir feared the aggression of the Sikhs, but never considered that he had a right to seize upon Peshavar, and that it should be given to him, and not to his brother, Sultan Mohammed Khan, is not also known of this.

san, as well as the province of Khorasan, and the country dependant on the above places, form part of the Persian territory, and are within the kingdom of the King of Kings, the misery and welfare of those dominions cannot be separated from the interests of the Persian government. Even if my affairs should fall into disorder, and even if your Majesty should not direct your attention to the condition of these countries, nevertheless I shall persist in contending with the Sikhs as long as I am able; but should it prove that I be unable to resist that diabolical tribe, then I have no choice, and must connect myself with the English, who will thus obtain a complete authority over the whole of Afghanistan; and it remains to be seen hereafter to what places, and what extent the flame of the violence of this nation may be carried.

"I considered it imperative on myself to represent these circumstances to the King of Islam. As for the rest, your Majesty will act as seems expedient to your royal understanding. All other affairs will be narrated by Mohammed Husain Khan, who is a trusty person attached to your well-wisher."

This letter will clearly show that the Amir, without having waited the answer of his former communication, sent through Haji Ibrahim, despatched Mohammed Husain Khan with another letter in the mean time into Persia; and from this proceeding the reader will perceive that the Amir Dost Mohammed

Khan was not desirous to form any connexion with the British government, unless the Shah of Persia should relinquish his cause. He had also sent a letter to the Emperor of Russia by Husain Ali, stating that since Mahomed Shah, the centre of the faith, had closely connected himself with his Imperial power, desiring the advantage of such alliance, that he also being a Mahomedan, was desirous to follow his example, and to attach himself to his Majesty. In that letter the Amir gave an exaggerated account of his own military power and of his successful opposition to the Sikh army, whom he described as commanded by English and French officers. He added that if he was not assisted by the Emperor, the Sikhs, who are in alliance with the English government, will at last overpower him, and that their influence in Afghanistan will be a foundation for that of the British, who, under a commercial name, will become the superiors of this country, and will annihilate the trade which is now so briskly conducted between Moscow, Bokhara, and Kabul.

He then added, "that Husain Ali will fully explain to your Imperial Majesty the feelings of my respect and attachment to your august government, and the advantages which are likely to result to us all, Russia, Persia, and Afghanistan, from being heartily united, and considered to be but one body." This letter was recently shown to me by the son-in-law of Mirza Sami Khan, with the one which is already published in the Afghanistan correspondence.

The chiefs of Qandhar, the brothers of the Amir of Kabul, had also deputed Taj Mohammed Khan to his Excellency Count Simonich, the Russian ambassador in Persia, and his credentials were expressive of similar sentiments of concord and attachment to the Russian government as the letter of Dost Mohammed Khan, alluded to and given above. It is plain enough to observe that the Amir was raised to the supremacy which he enjoyed, by his bloody and treacherous but successful intrigues, and by the adherence to him of the Persian sect in Kabul. He was now, therefore, persuaded by his confidential counsellors, Mirza Sami Khan, Agha Husain, Mahmud Khan Bayat, and Haji Mirza Khan of Nanchi, not to come to a definite alternative in his negotiations with Sir Alexander Burnes, but to wait the arrival of the answers from the Russian and Persian governments.

CHAPTER XI.

A Persian Envoy arrives at Qandhar—The Chiefs of that place make a treaty with him—Letter from the Shah of Persia to the Amir—Instructions of the Persian Envoy—Mr. Ellis's despatch to Lord Palmerston—Sir John Macneil at the Persian Court—The Shah marches against Hirat—Despatches of Sir John Macneil—Russian intrigues—Various letters to the Chiefs of Qandhar—Their treaty with the Shah, under the guarantee of Russia—Negotiations of Sir A. Burnes at Kabul—The Russian Envoy, Capt. Vikovich—Diplomatic etiquette in Asiatic courts—Letters relating to Capt. Vikovich—His proceedings at Kabul—Progress of Russian influence there—The English mission retires—Various documents.

THE information which the Amir Dost Mohammed Khan had previously received of the progress of the Persian ambassador was now confirmed by his arrival at Qandhar, which induced him to take open steps with regard to particulars which he had hitherto kept secret. He knew the weight and value of the influence of his old adherents, the Javanshers of Kabul, and was aware that the government of Persia, advised by Russia, was marching against Afghanistan, or at least Hirat, the gate of India. Qambar Ali

Khan, the ambassador of his Majesty Mohammed Shah of Persia, along with Mohammed Husain Khan, the agent of the Amir, had in the mean time arrived in Qandhar. The chiefs in this place detained the Persian envoy to enter into alliance with them; and being jealous of the Amir of Kabul, and desirous to gain the conspicuous favour of the Shah of Persia and of the government of Persia for themselves alone, they prevented him from prosecuting his journey to Kabul until they themselves had concluded a treaty of alliance with him.

"The Treaty which I, Qambar Ali Khan, here made with the respected Sardars, Kohandil, Rahamdil, and Mehardil Khan, on the part of His Majesty Mohammed Shah, is as follows:—

"In case the Sardars should send one of their sons to His Majesty, I promise to the Sardars the following in return:

"1. That the country of Hirat, whether it be taken by the power of the servants of the Persian Government, or by that of the Sardars, must be left to the latter; and that the Shah should not expect anything from them in return but service, and likewise should make no interference of any kind with their country or tribe in Afghanistan.

"2. His Majesty is not to form any connexion with the Afghans of any description, great or small, and also not to employ them in case of any business with the Afghans; but in such case His Majesty is to have recourse to the Sardars.

"3. His Majesty is never to make friendship with Shah Zadah Kam Ram and Yar Mohammed Khan.

"4. On the arrival of the son of Sardar Kohandil Khan, His Majesty is to order the army at Meshid to march towards Hirat; and if Kam Ram and Yar Mohammed Khan resolve to take Qandhar, the Shah should prevent them by coming to Qandhar; and if they do not agree to this, then the Shah should come to Hirat.

"5. The Shah is also to give the Sardars means to pay the expenses of twelve thousand cavalry and infantry, and twelve guns, and the extra expenditure of the troops in the capture of Hirat; and, if the war lasts long, the Shah must furnish the expenses of the army.

"6. In case any harm befal the country of the Sardars, the Shah is to give them, in his own country, land equal to the value of their loss.

"7. The Treaty which I have now made with the Sardars, is to be approved of by His Majesty, and to bear the signature of Haji Mirza Aghasi, Mirza Masud (the Minister for Foreign Affairs), and also of the Ambassadors of Russia and of England, to secure confidence to the Sardars.

"QAMBAR ALI."

When Mohammed Husain Khan, the envoy of

the Amir of Kabul, who had returned from Persia with Qambar Ali Khan, discovered that the Sardars would not permit his companion to go to Dost Mohammed Khan, and had made an engagement with him, taking all the credit to themselves, and casting altogether the interests of his employer, the Amir, aside, he quitted Qandhar, and returned to Kabul. Dost Mohammed Khan, when informed of what had been done, secretly told him that he (Mohammed Husain) was not to pay any attention to what he (the Amir) might speak slightingly of the result of his mission, of his own letter, and of the power of Mohammed Shah; for such things would be said by him in order to make the British envoy believe that he did not care for the alliance of Persia, but was desirous to connect himself with the English, and this deceit was to be continued until he received the reply to his letter from "Petarpur" (St. Petersburgh). In secret he wrote, at the desire of Mohammed Husain Khan, to the chiefs of Qandhar, desiring them to send Qambar Ali Khan to him in Kabul, and upbraiding them that they had made a treaty with him for their own advantage, without consulting him at all, or making him a partisan in it. Now the cunning Amir, according to his arrangement with his envoy, made as if he looked upon the result of his mission as a matter of trifling importance, and did not show him much respect. He deceitfully pretended, in the presence of the British envoy, and of Mr. Masson the newswriter, to be dissatisfied with the terms of the letter (farman) which the King of Persia had sent him in answer to his letter (arizah), while privately he felt proud of the arrival of such an honourable token of His Majesty's favour on his behalf, and sent a copy of it to the King of Bokhara, with whom he was in correspondence on terms of equality.

Letter from His Majesty Mohammed Shah, King of Persia, to the Amir Dost Mohammed Khan of Kabul.

"His Excellency, the repository of honour and glory, the most Noble of Nobles, the opponent of infidels, the Amir Dost Mohammed Khan, Lord of Kabul, is honoured with our auspicious royal correspondence, and informed that the two letters addressed by His Excellency have been conveyed to our Royal presence by the hands of Haji Ibraham and Mohammed Husain Khan. The contents of each, displaying the rectitude of the intentions of that receptacle of dignity, have been perused by us from the beginning to the end, and the objects and wishes of his Excellency have also been explained to us by the above messengers. All these circumstances being proofs of sincerity and purity of intention, they gave entire satisfaction to our Royal mind, and disposed us to feel confidence in his devotion.

"With regard to your representation of your connexion with this never-ending government, and with regard to your observations that Kabul is to be considered as one of the countries dependant on the kingdom of Persia, and that you are incessantly engaged in war with the infidels, notwithstanding whose superior strength you had hitherto been able to oppose them, and to preserve those dominions from subjection, but that if you did not receive assistance from us, you will be obliged to seek aid elsewhere, in order that an end might be put to these disorders; in truth these observations are written with sincerity, and it is apparent to our kingly mind that your Excellency is a distinguished warrior of Islam, who fights with valour for the faith, most surely expecting to prosper, both on account of his dependence on this never-ending government, and for the protection of Islam, and for the defence of our kingdom and religion; and from kingly generosity we deem it imperative on us to hold that refuge of dignity under the standard of our protection, and not to grudge or withhold from him assistance of any kind. Thus, before the arrival of the messengers of your Excellency, we had firmly resolved to march to Hirat, and to convey every description of aid to your Excellency. We commenced our march from our capital, Tehran, with this intention. After our arrival at Bootan, it was represented to the ministers of this haughty state, that the cholera was raging with violence throughout the cities of Khorasan. We, therefore, for the sake of change of air, and in expectation of the cessation of this malady, moved to a healthy situation, and halted some days in the plains of Kalpoosh. In the meantime, it was represented to us, that Makhdum Quli, the Yamut (Turkman), having formed an alliance with Ala Quli Khan (chief of Khiva), had arrived at Karakala, which is situated near the Desert, with twenty thousand horse, the flower of the Usbeg and Turkman cavalry; and having fortified himself in that position, was waiting for the opportunity of the absence of our conquering army to produce disorder and tumult on the confines of our dominions. When this intelligence reached us we despatched our beloved brother, Feridun Mirza, with eight thousand regular infantry and four thousand cavalry, and twelve guns, to chastise these marauders. As soon as they became acquainted with the arrival of our troops, their courage failed them; and, not daring to oppose our forces, they abandoned their provisions and stores, and fled into the deserts. Our brother followed in pursuit of this wicked tribe; and near Qirchul, the cavalry, and some of the infantry, overtook and attacked them. From morning until night the fire of war was in a blaze, but the affair terminated in the defeat of the Turkmans. The greater part were killed, some were captured, and the remainder fled into the barren deserts, and escaped from our warriors. After chastising this tribe we halted some time at the river Gurgam to arrange the affairs of that frontier; and then winter, and the season of snow and rain having arrived, it was impossible to continue the campaign. We despatched twenty thousand horse and foot, and forty guns, with ordnance and stores, to Khorasan, to be in readiness to march in the beginning of spring to Hirat; and we have resolved to march, with the assistance of God, with the remainder of the army, towards Khorasan, after the festival Nauroz. As there has been some delay in the advance of the victorious army, we have despatched Qambar Ali Khan to your Excellency; and have sent a diamond-hilted dagger to your Excellency, which is to be worn as the ornament of your faithful waist. We have commanded Qambar Ali Khan to detail the full extent of our royal favour towards your Excellency, and your Excellency will explain to Qambar Ali Khan your wishes and intentions, in order that they may be represented to us on his return."

Written in the month of Shaval, 1252.

Qambar Ali Khan, while detained and negotiating at Qandhar, was very brisk in his intrigues and correspondence with Mahmud Khan Bayat, and other Persians of influence, and in the confidence of the Amir. He had also employed secret emissaries to collect information of the resources of the country, and particularly about the provisions. He had also requested the rich merchants of the Persian tribe to secure supplies for the army of Mohammed Shah, who, by his statement, was to penetrate Afghanistan in company with the Russian ambassador, as soon as Hirat had tendered submission. He possessed the following instructions, bearing the seal and signature of Mohammed Shah, and of his prime minister Haji Mirza Aghasi, the copy of which he gave, with his own agreement, as a security to the various merchants. Among them was Mulla Nasu, a wealthy trader, in the confidence of the chief Kohandil Khan, who secretly gave the copy of it to my newswriter, Mohammed Tahar.

Translation of a Copy of Instructions from the Persian Government to Qambar Ali Khan, envoy to Kabul.

"When you pass beyond the boundary of Qayan, at each stage that you reach you will detail the following particulars in a book which you will present to His Majesty on your return, namely, the state of the towns and villages, and population, with an account of all circumstances that happen during your journey, an estimate of the population and the strength of the tribes at each place, as of the Sistanis, Biloches, Afghans, and Qazalbashes, and an account of the revenue and expenditure of those countries,—their produce, their principal articles of cultivation, and from what course of cultivation the most profit is made, and an account of the taxes levied from the people, and the imports or commerce: finally, whether there is water on the road, and whether the latter is level or mountainous. In passing through Bilochistan you must raise great expectations of the munificence and benevolence of His Majesty in the minds of the Khans of Belochistan and of Sistan. If these persons are favourably disposed towards Kam Ran, you should endeavour to persuade them to attach themselves to the service of this government, and try to inspire them with perfect confidence. You should, in particular, éxtol the generosity of His Majesty to Ali Khan, and declare to him that tidings of his services had reached His Majesty. All these Khans should assemble and prepare their troops, &c., at the time of the arrival of the fortunate camp, for they are to join the Royal Stirrup. At Qandhar he will deliver the firman and robes of honour to Kohandil Khan, and to his brothers, and excite his hopes of the generosity of His Majesty. He will attach himself strongly to Kohandil Khan, and he will inquire from him why, after the arrival of that letter (some former one), he did not send his brother and his son. Kohandil Khan must endeavour to send one of his brothers in advance to this court, while he himself will remain in his present situation, and await the arrival of the Royal army. He will get his troops in readiness, and prepare as much cavalry as is practicable, for, please God, the campaign of Hirat will be entrusted to him. Qambar Ali Khan will declare to Kohandil Khan that if he has incurred any losses in the service of this government, reparation shall be made for them, and he shall experience His Majesty's generosity. Qambar Ali Khan will form an acquaintance with all the persons in authority, and with the Afghan and Qazalbash Khans, as well as with the Qazalbashes in general; and his object will be to excite their hopes of His Majesty's generosity. If they feel apprehensions, on account of the religious differences of Shias and Sunnis, he will endeavour to dispel their apprehensions, and will give them assurances that the justice and benevolence of His Majesty will not permit any distinction whatever to be made between them, and thus he will endeavour to render all persons desirous of serving this government. When he has finished his affairs in Qandhar he will proceed to Kabul, and deliver a dagger as a mark of His Majesty's favour to Dost Mohammed Khan, and he will convey the auspicious robes of honour to Navab Jabbar Khan. He will use the utmost endeavours to inspire them with earnest confidence in the sincerity of His Majesty's favour for them; and he will give them the strongest assurances that, after the arrival of the Royal army in those countries, favours of every description shall be unsparingly lavished upon them. Publicly he will declare that the object of his mission is to convey an answer to the petition

T 2

of Dost Mohammed Khan, and to deliver the auspicious robes of honour, but in private he will expatiate on the connexion of Dost Mohammed Khan with this country, and he will declare that, please God, Dost Mohammed Khan shall enjoy the royal favour to such an extent that those countries shall be placed completely in his possession, and he shall have entire control over them. Qambar Ali Khan will declare to Dost Mohammed Khan, that if he will avow his intimacy with this government, and will send one of his brothers or his sons to this court, it will prove of the highest advantage to him. In fine, his hopes of assistance from this country are to be excited, and he is to be persuaded that his only hope of safety is from this government. He is to be urged to prepare his troops, and he is to expect the arrival of His Majesty in spring. If the Amir is desirous of obtaining from Qambar Ali Khan a document declaring his connexion with this country, and prohibiting the Sikhs from molesting him, he is permitted to grant it."

While the Persian and the Afghan envoys were entering into alliance, and exchanging treaties for their respective governments, the Shah and his minister were not indifferent about other affairs, but busied themselves also in giving proof to the British ambassador that the court of Tehran was not only resolved to subdue Hirat, but that the reduction of the whole kingdom of Afghanistan into subjection was talked of and intended. The Right Honourable Mr. Ellis, who was sent from England to congratulate the Shah on his ascending the throne of Persia, writes to Lord Palmerston in the following manner:—

"I thought it desirable to bring again formally before Haji Mirza Aghasi, and the Minister for Foreign Affairs, the views of His Majesty's Government in respect of the foreign policy best suited to the actual condition of Persia; but they both protested against considering the Afghans as a government or consolidated state, with whom relations of peace or of equality were to be maintained. They declared that a large portion of Afghanistan belonged to the Shah of Persia, and that he was at liberty to decide for himself how he would deal with the Afghans, as being his subjects.

"I inquired how far they considered the dominion of Persia to extend, and their reply was, to Ghazni.

"I feel quite assured that the British Government cannot permit the extension of the Persian monarchy in the direction of Afghanistan, with a due regard to the internal tranquillity of India, for that extension will at once bring Russian influence to the very threshold of our empire.

"The success of the Shah in this undertaking is anxiously wished for by Russia, and her Minister here does not fail to press it on to early execution. The motive cannot be mistaken. Hirat, once annexed to Persia, may become, according to the commercial treaty, the residence of a Russian consular agent, who would from thence push its researches and communications, avowed and secret, throughout Afghanistan. Indeed, in the present state of the relations between Persia and Russia, it cannot be denied that the progress of the former in Afghanistan is tantamount to the advance of the latter, and ought to receive every opposition from the British Government that the obligations of public faith will permit.

"Aziz Khan (the Qandhar Envoy) held the same language to me as he had undoubtedly done to the Shah and his Ministers, namely, that the whole of Afghanistan was, with the exception of Hirat and its dependencies, ready to come under feudal submission to the State, who, in a fortnight, with the aid of the Afghans, like Nadir Shah, could push his conquests to Delhi.

"That the Russian Minister had had a long audience with the Shah on the preceding day, when the subject of discussion was the expedition against Hirat, in which the Russian Minister had recommended perseverance this year, on the ground that what now could be effected with ten thousand men, might not next year be practicable with a much larger force.

"It appears from the correspondence that Dost Mohammed Khan, on the 17th of September, despatched an agent, Haji Ibrahim, with letters to the Shah of Persia, placing himself, his country and its resources, at the disposal of the Shah, offering to co-operate in an attack upon Hirat, and seeking generally the protection of the Shah against the Sikhs."

SIR JOHN Mc NEIL. BART. G.C.B.

On the departure of the Right Honourable H. Ellis, Sir John Macneil was appointed by the Government of England the envoy extraordinary and minister plenipotentiary at the court of Persia. His long residence in that country and acquaintance with the feelings and politics of its people, promised fair that the intrigues of Persia, guided as they were by the Russian ambassador, will not be permitted to pass without detection; for as the latter continued still unchanged in his designs towards Afghanistan, Sir John Macneil, in his various despatches to Lord Palmerston, gives a full detail of the united policy of the Persian and Russian states. The British minister did all he could to dissuade the Shah from undertaking the hazardous expedition against Hirat, and reminded his Majesty that such proceedings will be contrary to the expectation of her Majesty's Government, and will, in fact, be injurious to the interests of British India. Nevertheless the campaign was formed, and the Shah marched against Hirat. The messenger of her Majesty's embassy in Persia, bearing letters from Major Pottinger, was seized, maltreated, and deprived of his letters and property. The Russian minister was in the meantime urging the Shah to prosecute his journey towards Hirat, and promised, on the part of his government, that if Persia takes possession of Hirat, she shall be released from the balance of the debt due to the cabinet of St. Petersburgh. Colonel Stoddart, accompanying the camp of the Shah, took always an opportunity to beg his Majesty to come to amicable terms with Hirat; but such remonstrances were of no avail. Ghuryan was taken, and Hirat besieged. Such disregard to the advice of the British representative was productive of serious injuries and insults to the agents of that government in all parts of Persia; and the inhabitants of the Residency at Bushir were threatened to be massacred by the populace. At length Sir John Macneil determined to proceed to the camp, and try to persuade Mohammed Shah fervently to accept the terms of the defenders of Hirat, and induce him to withdraw his army from the siege of that place. His Excellency Count Simonich, the Russian ambassador, wrote to the foreign minister of his Majesty to prevent Sir John Macneil from joining the camp; and Mirza Masud really directed a communication to him on the subject, and desired him at least to postpone his departure till the instructions of the Shah were received; nevertheless he sent no answer, but set out to his quarters. On arriving at Ghuryan he received an official letter from the deputy foreign minister, conveying the orders of the Shah not to proceed beyond that place. Yet he joined the camp, and induced the Shah to allow him to mediate, and to adjust the differences. Then treaties were framed; at one time agreed to, and at another time refused through the advice of Count Simonich. In the meantime the British ambassador was not respected nor treated with the usual cordiality, and was thus compelled to leave the court and camp of the King of Persia.

Extracts from the Despatches of Sir John Macneil, Envoy Extraordinary and Minister Plenipotentiary at the Court of Persia.

"YET in this state of things, the Russian minister, as late as the 23rd ult., still continued to urge the Shah to undertake a winter campaign against Hirat, an enterprise which, even were the army in the best condition as to feeling and preparation, would be extremely hazardous.

"Agreeably to intelligence communicated to me by Colonel Stoddart, it appears, that when one of my couriers was returning from Hirat to the capital, some horsemen were despatched from the royal camp in pursuit of him, who prevented him from continuing his journey, and brought him to the camp, where he was treated with great violence and indignity. Subsequently, when Colonel Stoddart had waited on His Excellency the Hajee, and explained to him that the above person was in my service, and when the Persian government was apprised that he was attached to my establishment, even then an order was issued for placing him in guard, and he received extreme ill-treatment from Hajee Khan Karabreghee, who used every description of threat towards him.

"It is reported and believed at Tehran, that the Russian minister has announced the intention of his government, if the Shah should succeed in taking Hirat, to release Persia from the engagement to pay the balance of the debt due by her to Russia; and the reason assigned for this act of grace is, that the Emperor desires to contribute that amount towards defraying the expenses of the campaign.

"I have the honour to enclose a copy of a communication I received a few days ago from the officiating resident at Bushire, by which your Lordship will perceive that a threat of exciting the populace to commit violence, with an allusion to the massacre of the Russian mission, has been held out by the government of Bushire.

"The most obvious impediment to the interference of Great Britain in the quarrel between Persia and Hirat is the stipulation contained in the ninth article of the treaty of Tehran; but it can hardly be argued that this article binds us to permit the unjust and wanton destruction by Persia of the most valuable defences of India, while the Shah appears to be acting in concert with, and promoting the influence in those countries of, that very power whose exclusion from them has become the chief object of the alliance with His Persian Majesty.

"And as I find that the government of India entertains the opinion that the preservation of the integrity of Hirat is of vital importance, I have determined to proceed to the Shah's camp, and to endeavour, by every means in my power, to induce His Majesty to conclude a treaty with Shah Kam Ran, and to raise the siege of Hirat.

"Count Simonich has contented himself with despatching a messenger, and with inducing Mirza Masud to address me a letter, remonstrating against my going to the camp, on the pretext that, from the opinion entertained by people generally of the views on which I act, my presence in the camp will tend to strengthen the Afghans, which will be injurious to the Persian government.

"'According to what you yesterday mentioned verbally in

the apartment of His Excellency the Beglarbegi, it would appear that you intend speedily to proceed to the camp of His Majesty, &c., &c., the Shah; and as, in consequence of certain circumstances which have occurred, and of certain others which friends and enemies have conjecturêd and imagined to be connected with these, your Excellency's presence during the siege of Hirat will certainly and undoubtedly produce greater confidence and resistance on the part of the besieged, and this is obviously injurious to the interests of this proud and ever-enduring empire, and the British government certainly cannot desire to cause an injury to this state; therefore I request your Excellency, if possible, to abandon this journey, or to postpone it for a time, till instructions on this subject can be received from His Majesty the Shah.'

"At Ghuryan I received a letter from the Deputy Minister of Foreign Affairs, conveying to me the Shah's desire that I would not advance beyond that place, as my presence could not fail to encourage the Hiratis in their resistance. I replied, that my duty to my own government, and even to the Shah, precluded the possibility of my complying with His Majesty's requests, which I greatly regretted, as it was at all times my anxious desire to comply with the wishes of the Shah. Next day I came in one march to the camp. All the attentions usually paid on such an occasion were omitted; and I have reason to believe that all my acquaintances in camp were either directly forbidden to visit me, or received hints to the same effect which could not be misunderstood; yet I took no notice of these slights.

"On the morning of the 20th, before I had yet left the town, I heard of the arrival of Count Simonich in the camp, and I ceased to hope that the adjustment of the differences between Persia and Hirat was on the point of being effected. On my return to the camp, I found the Shah's views had undergone an important change: his manner was more abrupt and peremptory; and he at once rejected the proposed agreement.

"In about an hour the firing recommenced; and from that time the siege was prosecuted with renewed activity; for Count Simonich gave his advice as to the best manner of conducting it, and employed an officer of the Etat-Major, belonging to his suite, to construct batteries, and to carry on other offensive operations against the town. The Shah became elated with success. The Russian minister furnished a sum of money to be given to the Persian soldiers; and his countenance, support, and advice confirmed the Shah in his resolution to grant no conditions to the Afghans of Hirat.

"I have had the honour to report to your Lordship that more than one attempt at negotiation had failed.

"I need not repeat to your Lordship my opinion as to the effect which such a state of things would necessarily have on the internal tranquillity and security of British India; and I cannot conceive that any treaty can bind us to permit the prosecution of schemes which threaten the stability of the British empire in the East. The evidence of concert between Persia and Russia, for purposes injurious to British interests, is unequivocal, and the magnitude of the evil with which we are threatened is, in my estimation, immense, and such as no power in alliance with Great Britain can have a right to aid in producing."

Now I must come back to the proceedings of Qambar Ali Khan, the Persian envoy, in connexion with the chiefs at Qandhar. A treaty of an offensive and defensive nature was formed between them, and the chiefs despatched their agent with him to wait upon his Majesty the King of Persia in his camp at Hirat. The credentials were submitted to the Shah with the treaty, and the letters of the chiefs delivered to M. Goutte, the Russian assistant ambassador, and General Bronski, with the camp of Mohammed Shah. The latter officer, although Polish, and in the service of Persia, was intimately connected with the Russian embassy in this country, and was intriguing with the Afghans, in order to promote the interests of the cabinet of St. Petersburgh. M. Goutte promised the approbation and protection of Count

Simonich, and which was finally despatched to the chiefs. After perusing such documents, which contain the avowal of the Russian agent, and seeing that the Russian ambassador becomes a guarantee in arrangements concluded between Persia and Qandhar, there remains no place for any doubt concerning the aim and the intentions of the Russian Government. The treaty to which he becomes a party or guarantee must of course be thought to be good for himself. On consulting these matters deliberately, the Shah and the Russian functionaries addressed letters to the chiefs, approving of the treaty they had sent by their agents with Qambar Ali Khan.

Mohammed Shah to Sardar Kohandil Khan, Chief of Qandhar.

(After compliments.)

"ALAHDAD KHAN has arrived in my camp, and made known your requests, and the favour of the king towards you has increased. Whoever shall in confidence come to me shall meet with nothing but kindness, and shall gain his ends, and if you are still firm and true to your word, you may consider the favour of the king firm to you too. Always write the state of your wishes and hopes to me, and consider that you will gain all your ends."

M. Goutte, the Russian Agent with the Shah, to Kohandil Khan.

(After compliments.)

"ALAHDAD KHAN and Mir Mohammed Khan have delivered your letter to me, and I was much delighted at its contents. You wrote to tell me you had determined on becoming subservient to Mohammed Shah, and had sought his protection. You may depend upon my fulfilling the engagements I have entered into with you, and consider it to be advantageous to yourself to perform any service to the government. I cannot express, in writing, my friendship for you, and care for your welfare. Regarding your making Russia the guarantee in this connexion, your wishes will meet the Russian ambassador, to whom I have forwarded your letter, and with it I have written my own opinions on the subject. I have cultivated your friendship at the suggestion of Haji Aghasi. It is better to despatch Omar Khan without apprehension, and I will write to the Persian government, to remove all apprehensions at your sending your son. He will be treated with great distinction by the Shah and his nobles. When you have despatched your son, the treaty, drawn up by Qambar Ali, will be entered into by the means of Hajee

Aghasi, and I, as your friend, tell you to be under no apprehension at sending your son. After he arrives, everything you wish will be done through Haji Aghasi; send your son quickly, and trust him to God. When I receive an answer from the Russian minister (Simonich), I will forward it."

Major-General Bronski to Kohandil Khan.

(After compliments.)

"ABDUL WAHAD BEG and Alahdad Khan have arrived with Qambar Ali Khan, and have extolled to me your acts and nature. Consider the subjects on which Captain Vikovich conversed with you, connected with your welfare; besides these, I have other subjects to speak on. You have done well in seeking the protection of Persia; this Alahdad informed me you had done, and I am much pleased with your messages. Alahdad Khan has requested me to write to you; he has himself witnessed my influence here, and has been himself favourably received by the Shah, and asked to know in what favour the Sardars of Qandhar were with him (the Shah). Nothing but good will result from this your connexion with the Shah; so much good, indeed, that I cannot put it to paper. Be convinced that your serving the Shah will turn out every way to your advantage. The Shah treats every one according to his deserts, and your deserts are above all others. By all means send Mohammed Omar Khan speedily; he will be treated with nothing but kindness, and on this subject the assistant to the Russian minister, M. Goutte, has written, as also Haji Aghasi, who has written to confirm what Qambar Ali had done (at Qandhar). By the fortune of the Shah, Maimana, the Hazarahs, and Char Adinak (Annak) have been subdued as completely as could have been wished; and as the Asif of Mashed had written, no doubt the son of Mizrab Khan Wali, and the brother of Sher Mohammed Khan, and Gurdzanum Khan and others will come over to the Shah (as hostages). Persia is not what it was; I wish your connexion with Persia were speedily accomplished. Mohammed Shah has hitherto avoided taking Hirat out of kindness to its Mahomedans: but, by the blessing of God and the fortune of the king, Hirat will be taken; everything will be for the best. It will be all the better the speedier you despatch Mohammed Osmar Khan."

Copy of the Draft of a Treaty sealed by Kohandil Khan, or the proposed Terms of a Treaty between His Majesty Mohammed Shah and Kohandil Khan, the Sardar of Qandhar, under the sealed guarantee of His Excellency Count Simonich, the Russian Ambassador.

"I, as Minister Plenipotentiary of the Russian government at the Court of Persia, guarantee the fulfilment of the following conditions of treaty between His Majesty Mohammed Shah, and the Sardar of Qandhar.

"I. The principality of Hirat to be bestowed by the Shah

on the rulers of Qandhar, as a reward for their faithful services performed to him since his accession to the throne of Persia.

"II. The territories and tribes at present subject to the Sardars of Qandhar to be preserved to them free of violence, injury, or confiscation.

"III. The Persian government in no way to amalgamate with their own subjects any of the Afghan tribes, great or small, nor to employ them upon service unconnected with their own affairs, and all business relative to the Afghan states to be submitted by the Persian government to the rulers of Qandhar.

"IV. The Prince Kam Ran and his minister Yar Mohammed Khan to be excluded from all participation in the councils of Persia.

"V. Should any hostile movement be made against Qandhar by Shah Shuja-ul-Mulk, the English, or the Amir of Kabul, aid to be afforded by the Shah to the Sardars.

"VI. In the event of the sons or brothers of Kohandil Khan coming with an auxiliary force to the royal camp, no violence or injury to be in any way offered to the persons or property of them or their followers, and none of them to be detained as hostages, with the exception of a single son of Kohandil Khan, who will always remain in the service of the Shah.

"VII. A contingent of twelve thousand horse and twelve guns to be supplied by the Qandharis to garrison Hirat, receiving pay and rations from them, and to assist the Shah on occasion of service.

"VIII. On the arrival of the treaty duly ratified at Qandhar, Mohammed Omar Khan to be immediately despatched to the royal presence.

"IX. After the presentation of this prince, the necessary money for the outfit of the horse and artillery to be made over by the Persian government to the Sardars of Qandhar; Sardar Mehardil Khan to be then sent with a thousand horse to the royal camp. This prince being presented, and mutual confidence being established between the Shah and the Sardars, no other demand to be made upon the Qandharis by the Persian government than that of military service.

"Should Mohammed Shah fail to fulfil any of these several conditions, or depart in any way from the stipulations, I, as Minister Plenipotentiary of the Russian government, becoming myself responsible, will oblige him, in whatever way may be necessary, to act fully up to the terms and conditions of the treaty."

I have brought the lengthened arrangements of the Qandhar chiefs with the Persian and the Russian governments to a plain conclusion; and it would be desirable now to turn our attention to the affairs of Kabul, and the negotiations of Sir Alexander Burnes with the Amir Dost Mohammed Khan. Agreeably to mutual understanding, as has already been stated, he pretended to be angry with the style of the letter of the Shah, and did not come to a final settlement with the English envoy, waiting the arrival of the Persian army in Hirat, and an answer from the Emperor of Russia to his letter. He was always in possession of the daily progress of the Russian minister; and through the Hazarah country received secret communications concerning the movements of the Russian agent towards his capital. He kept this under very strict secrecy; and if any talk was made of the power of Persia, and the influence of Russia, by any one in his court, while he knew that there was a person to inform us of it, he simply treated such ideas with contempt and laughter, calling the Russians and Persians "Lotis," or buffoons. In short, he always tried to keep off despair from Sir Alexander Burnes by his pleasing manners and eloquence, and thought that his craft was not known to him. This was, however, not the case, for the British envoy knew his meaning, and told and wrote to him several times to come to an immediate understanding; but he put off from day to day, writing letters to the chiefs of Qandhar and Qunduz, making mention of his feigned intention to establish friendship with the British.

At length the expected news came of the arrival of Captain Vikovich, the Russian agent, in Ghazni, on his way to the court of the Amir Dost Mohammed Khan. Hereupon the Amir, and his minister Mirza Sami Khan, planned privately, and it was soon conveyed by his "peshkhidmat" to Sir Alexander Burnes secretly, that Dost Mohammed Khan was to call upon the British envoy, and reporting the progress of the Russian agent towards Kabul, offer to act as guided by him (Burnes). If the latter did not approve of his coming to the city, then the Amir was to secure for himself a document from Sir Alexander Burnes, binding his government to pay him money, and aid him with forces on the plea of giving an insult to the cabinet of St. Petersburgh; and after having that paper he was at liberty to receive Captain Vikovich, and attach himself to Russia or to the English, whichever offered him the highest proposals. However, the Amir called upon Sir Alexander Burnes, who, hearing his sayings, and knowing previously the meaning of his conversation and of his visit, said that the Amir would commit no wrong in receiving Captain Vikovich, and, on the contrary, will make known his own hospitality and good sense in distant regions. Here the Amir was disappointed at the failure of his scheme; yet still persevering in his design, he tried to induce Sir Alexander Burnes to commit himself in some other way. In our presence he spoke to his minister in a manner that showed as if he felt no interest in the mission of St. Petersburgh, and that he therefore thought it was better to place him in the house where the other Persian lier (Mohammed Husain) was living, and again feigned to ask the opinion of Sir Alexander Burnes on the subject. He still adhered to his former sentiments, and replied that the Amir was ruler of Kabul, and knew best to treat and receive agents and guests in his own house. Finding that Sir Alexander Burnes was not a man to become the subject of his fraudulent proposals, he adopted at last what he had always meant. He was aware that his brother Navab Jabbar Khan, and also other relations, and certain chiefs, were in favour of the English mission, and might make intrigues with Captain Vikovich also. He therefore found no better place and charge for the Russian agent than that of his confidential minister Mirza Sami Khan. He knew that the people whom he suspects will be known there, and will thus fear to visit him in his house; and that this will keep his communication with the Russian envoy entirely secret. He was accordingly treated with great respect and civility, and was allowed to go and meet the Amir clandestinely in the private apartments of the minister. As he had not his own equipage, the son of the Mirza always accompanied him to sights and to the places of chief note, which attention was similarly shown to Sir Alexander Burnes for three days after his arrival in the Bala Hisar. This was the kind of honour paid to the envoy of the Emperor, which the British news-writer, Mr. Masson, mentions in his book, saying that he was under surveillance.

Captain Vikovich delivered his credentials, which consisted of a letter from the Emperor of Russia, and another from His Excellency Count Simonich, the Russian ambassador. These were written in the Persian and in the Russian languages. The Amir had no bounds to his joy and pride inwardly, but outwardly he feigned to show the English envoy and news-writer that he never knew till that very moment that he had even written a letter to St.

Petersburgh. He denied the transmission and the proceedings of Husain Ali, and of Mirza Sami Khan; and the latter took the credit upon himself (as Mr. Masson says) of gaining another ally for the Amir. All this ignorance of the Amir Dost Mohammed Khan, and the writing of the letter by the Mirza without his knowledge, was nothing but a fabricated invention of them both to mislead the English functionaries. By adopting this cunning line of policy he created a difference of opinion among a number of the persons who formed the mission of Sir Alexander Burnes, and at the same time he resolved to show them that he is an object so valuable and dearly sought by the united great powers of Russia and Persia, that the Emperor and his ambassador had addressed to him such flattering epistles while he never thought of seeking their friendship.

The Russian part of the Emperor's letter was copied by Major Leech, and the Persian was translated by me, which translation was unfortunately plundered from me at the time of the insurrection of Kabul, and could not be recovered afterwards, although I procured and purchased some of the papers in Kabul. Mr. Masson says it bore no sig nature, and was written directly by the Emperor himself; which affirmation, according to him, raises some doubts of its authenticity. On the contrary, according to Asiatic usage, these are the very reasons for confiding in the veracity of the letter. In all countries of despotic government, as Afghanistan, Turkistan, and Persia, and their neighbour the Russians, letters are forwarded under the seal and not under the signature. There were several letters of the Emperor of Russia shown to us by the late minister, Qoshbegi, to the address of the King of Bokhara, written direct from his Majesty, never from his secretary. The letters addressed by the minister do not stand so high in the estimation of the Asiatic monarchs as those written from the sovereign himself. It is considered a most strong feeling of regard and friendship, and confidence on the part of the writer. The cabinet of St. Petersburgh being aware of such a prevailing custom, and desire of its neighbours the Ozbegs and Persians, generally writes to them under the seal and name of the Emperor: and so in the same way was the letter written to the Amir of Kabul.

It is worthy of making such a remark in this place, and further to prove this, to the end that it may be clearly known how much the Asiatic monarchs are offended in being addressed by the minister or secretary, and not from the Sovereign himself. On the restoration of Shah Shuja to the throne of his predecessors, and the detention of Colonel Stoddart, the British Government was, on several occasions, obliged to begin communication with the King of Bokhara. More than fifty letters from Sir William Macnaughten, the British representative, and several others from the Earls of Auckland and of Ellenborough, were sent by special and highly paid messengers to the Amir of Bokhara; but he was always displeased at their arrival, and never returned an answer to any of them, and dismissed the bearers without any reply. He always told them, and also Colonel Stoddart, that he was an independent king, and should like to correspond with the British Sovereign directly, and not with the British representatives at Kabul, and the Governors-General of India,—(farman farma), whom he called the servants of the state. In the same manner it was felt by the Amir Dost Mohammed Khan. He considered the letter of the Emperor of so much more value and importance than that of Count Simonich, that the letter of the ambassador did not even stand in the first rank.

The contents of the letter from the Emperor of Russia to the Amir of Kabul, as far as I remember, from the translation I made of it at the time, to be sent to the government of India, were not of any political nature. It plainly acknowledged the receipt of the Amir's letter, and assured him that all the Afghan merchants shall be well received in the empire of Russia, justice and protection shall be extended towards them, and their intercourse will cause to flourish the respective states.

I have heard many people in their talking, say, that if the letter of the Emperor touched upon no other points but those of trade, there was no necessity for taking such alarm at its appearance in Kabul, and that it was exaggerated in importance,. as it appeared to be felt by the Indian government. Though I do not boast of being well versed in the histories of India written by talented English authors, but from what I have learned from them I come to the conclusion that the disguised word or appellation for politics is commerce, and that commerce is the only thing which expands the views and policy of territorial aggrandisement. To my great surprise I read from the book of Mr. Masson the doubts he entertained of the true character of the mission of Captain Vikovich. These doubts must have arisen from some extraordinary sources of information, or else from the ambitious motive of making himself conspicuous in differing from the opinions of those who had more apparent, wise, and just means to consider that agent a true representative of the court of St. Petersburgh. Count Nesselrode is the best authority on such a subject, and he has plainly acknowledged this mission to Kabul, and the following letters will further show that he was not an adventurer, but an accredited envoy from Russia.

Mohammed Shah of Persia to the Amir Dost Mohammed Khan of Kabul.

(After compliments.)

"AGREEABLY to my affection and kindly feelings towards you, I wish to bestow great favours on you, and anxiously wait to hear from you.

"In these days the respectable Captain Vikovich, having been appointed by my esteemed brother the Emperor of

Russia, to attend your Court, paid his respects on his way, stating that he had been honoured by his Imperial Majesty to deliver some messages to you: on this I felt it incumbent on me to remember you by the despatch of this Raqam, to convince you that your best interests are deeply engraven in my mind.

"Concerning the favours of my brother Majesty attached to you, let me hear occasionally from you; and by rendering good services to him you will obtain the protection of this Royal house."

His Excellency Count Simonich, the Russian Ambassador at Tehran, to Amir Dost Mohammed Khan of Kabul.

"THE respectable P. Vikovich will wait upon you with this letter.

"Your agent Haji Husain Ali has been attacked by a severe illness, and therefore he stopped at Moscow: when the intelligence of his bad health was conveyed to the Emperor, a good physician was ordered to attend, and endeavour to cure him as soon as possible. On his recovering I will not fail to facilitate him in his long journey back to Kabul.

"Knowing your anxiety to hear from this quarter I have hastened to despatch the bearer to you. He was ordered to accompany your agent to Kabul, and I hope on his arrival at your court that you will treat him with consideration, and trust him your secrets. I beg you will look upon him like myself, and take his words as if they were from me. In case of his detention at Kabul you will allow him often to be in your presence, and let my master know, through me, about your wishes, that anxiety may be removed.

"Though the great distance has often prevented the regularity of my correspondence with you, I am always very happy to respect and serve your friends, in order to show my friendly opinions towards yourself.

"The cause of our often hearing from each other merely depends upon friendship and acquaintance.

"I have some Russian rarities to forward to you: as the bearer (P. Vikovich) is lightly equipped, it was beyond his power to take them along with him; but I will take the first opportunity to convey them safely to you, and now have the pleasure to send you the under-mentioned list of them.

First Kind of Samur.

	Piece.
Gilt and silvered cloth	1
Cloth with do. flowered	1
Ditto with gilt do.	1
Ditto with green gilt flowers	1
Zari Abi, with gilt do.	1
Ditto qirmiz of gold	1
Ditto do. of silver	1
Parcha hazir, red and white	1
Ditto painted	1

		Piece.
Parcha hazir, white with gold flower	. . .	1
Alachah with do.	. . .	1
Ditto yellow with silver do.	. . .	1
Ditto red and green	. . . .	1
Ditto light blue	. . . .	1
Ditto with red flower	. . . .	1
Ditto green	. . . .	1
Ditto banassh	. . . .	1
Ditto red and light blue	. . . .	1

Before we proceed to notice the negotiations of Captain Vikovich in Kabul, it will be desirable to describe here briefly his conference with the chiefs of Qandhar. He told them that the King of Persia does not pay any attention to the advice of the British ambassador, but has attached himself to the Russians, who avowedly and secretly will lend him every aid to promote his object. Major Leech also reports thus:—

"Regarding the Russian officer, now in Kabul, with a letter from the Emperor, Mehardil Khan informed me that the following were his messages to them from the Emperor: that if they would make friends with the Amir Dost Mohammed Khan, the Russians would assist them with money to make war upon the Sikhs, and to regain Multan and Derajat; and that they would also aid them in regaining Scinde; that Mohammed Shah owed them one and a half crores of rupees, and they would give an order on him for that sum, the money to be divided between the Amir and them equally, as also the countries thus gained; that the Russians could not furnish men, but would furnish arms; that they in turn expected the Sardars to become subservient (farman bardar), and to receive a Russian resident; that they were to make war when desired, and make peace equally at the Emperor's will. This officer told them that the English had preceded the Russians in civilization for some generations; but that now the latter had arisen from their sleep, and were seeking for foreign possessions and alliances; and that the English were not a military nation, but merely the merchants of Europe. Sardar Mehardil Khan also informed me that several merchants had seen that officer in Bokhara, but were ignorant of the object of his visiting that city."

"With regard to the active part that Russia is taking in the movements of Persia, the Sardar assured me he had good authority to state that Russia had taken measures to keep the kingdom of Mohammed Shah tranquil in his absence, by means of letters where they were feared, and of troops where they were not feared."

The residence of Captain Vikovich in the house of the minister was very favourable to his general deportment and secret negotiations or intrigues.

His intercourse and negotiations with the Amir, conducted only through his confidential Vazir, were not made public, as were those of the British envoy. With him the communication was held sometimes through the Navab Jabbar Khan, or the Mirza Imam Vardi, and sometimes the Nayab Amir. If anything was ever known to us of the proceedings of the Russian envoy, it was only through the secret information of the Peshkhidmat of the Amir, and of the minister. In some circumstances the intelligence gained by Mr. Masson, the news-writer, was satisfactory, and without the slightest doubt. The Russian envoy told the Amir Dost Mohammed Khan that he has been instructed by his government to assure him of using its influence to adjust matters with the Sikhs, and to request the Court of Lahaur to restore all the Afghan territories to the ruler of Kabul. On the day of the festival of Nauroz (equinox) the minister Mirza Sami Khan had a party of some selected persons of state, to which Captain Vikovich was also invited. In the middle of their enjoyments, it was considered by him that his not asking the English envoy, while the Russian agent was present, will openly reflect a suspicious and uncivil light on his conduct, and on this consideration he sent his son to ask Sir Alexander Burnes to favour him with his company. He justly refused to accept the invitation, saying that if the Mirza did not think proper, for his own convenience, to invite him previously, like his other guests, he need not take the trouble to join his assembly. After a long and frequent intercourse Sir Alexander Burnes asked me to go to the minister. Here all the Persian and the Ghilzai chiefs were present. The minister and Captain Vikovich sat a little higher than the others, on the "Nihali;" and the former, to show his civility, removed from his seat, where he placed me by the side of the Russian envoy. While the music was going on, the minister was conversing on politics, sometimes with M. Vikovich and sometimes with me, inquiring the number of the English troops stationed at Lodiana; the distance between the divisions of Karnal, Merat, and Kanpur; and whether the Mahomedans were the major part of the army, or the Rajputs; and what were the feelings of the natives of India towards the decayed household of the great Taimur. Understanding the manner in which the inquiries were made, I came to the conclusion that every question was put to me according to arrangements made previously to my joining the party; and therefore, confining myself only to the answer of his questions, without commenting on politics, I pretended to show my astonishment at the great demand for Kashmir shawls in the Russian dominions. This afforded an opportunity to Captain Vikovich, who said, although the valley of Kashmir was nearer to the boundary of British India, yet the good treatment which the merchants receive from his government, along with the high price for their commodity in Moscow and at St. Petersburgh, had gained good will for the inhabitants of this valley. He then said to the minister it is wonderful that the Amir of Kabul lays his claims upon Peshavar, while he keeps the name of Kashmir exclusively to himself, though it is a principal source of the wealth of the Durrani empire. The minister replied that the policy of the Afghans is different from that of the other nations. They first catch hand, and then the arm, meaning, let us first gain Peshavar, and the claims on Kashmir will soon follow. Captain Vikovich said that, if it pleases God, his presence in Lahaur with the letters of the Emperor and of the Shah of Persia, of which he was the bearer, will induce the ruler of the Panjab to accede to the terms of the Amir in giving Multan, Derehjat, Kashmir, and Peshavar to their original masters, the Afghans. He added that he was authorized to say to the Maharajah Ranjit Singh, that if that chieftain does not act in a friendly manner towards the Afghans, Russia will send money easily to Bokhara, whence the Amir can make arrangements to bring it down to Kabul to raise troops, and to fight with the Sikhs for the recovery of his country. The Russian agent also issued a report that fifty thousand men of Russian regiments were in readiness to land in Astrabad, in order to keep peace in the rear of Mohammed Shah, who would then march towards the Panjab; that such movements would rouse all the discontented chiefs of India to rebel; and that the English, who are not soldiers, but merely mercantile adventurers of Europe, would not dare to assist Ranjit Singh, knowing that the Afghans are succoured by the warlike nation of Russia.

The presence and the promises of the Russian envoy changed now even the outward deportment of the Amir towards the British mission. He demanded a written bond for the restoration of Peshavar, besides a large sum of money to enable him to make himself the Supreme Lord of Afghanistan. In the mean time Captain Vikovich stated that the law of England does not permit the Governor-General of India to act without consulting the Council and the three authorities; whereas he and Count Simonich, or any other Russian agent, had the same power as the Emperor himself, and need not seek nor wait for the advice of the others. All these proceedings were communicated to the Governor-General of India, who judiciously placed not much credence at first in the professions of the mission; but when the state of things took an unfavourable attitude for the preservation of the tranquillity of India, he was then obliged to treat the whole subject not slightingly, but as an important affair. Some people, who do not know the real character of the Afghans, and especially that of the Amir Dost Mohammed Khan, say, "Why did not the Earl of Auckland give the small sum of money demanded by the chiefs of Qandhar or the Amir?" but there are hundreds of old nobles living in Kabul who will agree with me, that the refusal of the money from the Governor-General was judicious and wise. It would not have served to bind the Amir to co-operate with the British, nor to promote their interests; but it would have afforded him ample means for using his arms against the Sikhs and against our interests.

The Sardar Mehardil Khan, one of the brother chiefs of Qandhar, advised by the Shah of Persia and by Count Simonich, arrived at Kabul with the avowed purpose of frustrating the designs of the British envoy, and inducing the Amir to give him his dismissal and to settle his affairs with the Russian agents. He and the Amir now began to talk thus, that they really want a written engagement from the British government, not only to protect them against Mohammed Shah, but also pledging its influence, money, and arms to force Ranjit Singh, a faithful ally of the English, to give up all the Afghan territory, which, on the other hand, the Russians and Persians have offered to recover for them.

The winter was now past, and still the Amir did not dismiss the Russian agent from his court, as he had promised in his intercourse with Sir Alexander, and had written in his letter to Count Simonich. On the contrary, he entered more and more into close intimacy and conversation in public with him, and invited him openly to pass evenings and have dinners in the palace with him. Now it became evident that the Amir of Kabul was unfeignedly attaching himself to the Russian government, and that the further stay of Sir Alexander Burnes was not honourable to the name and credit of his government. He made his last report, therefore, of the steps which the Russian agent had taken, and of the throwing off of the mask which the Amir had hitherto assumed and worn to deceive us, stating circumstantially the proofs that he and his minister had become colder in their manners towards us, and warmer in their intercourse with Captain Vikovich. At last the letter of the Governor-General arrived for the Amir, stating that if he was inclined to attach himself to the other powers, he had better give leave for departure to Sir Alexander Burnes, which alternative was readily accepted. Our failure in the negotiations soon became public, and the people, especially the traders, feared to deal with the mission. The bankers would not lend the money necessary for our journey, and the muleteers refused to supply conveyances unless permitted by the Amir. Two or three days passed without any progress in the preparations for the return of the mission to Peshavar, and at length I waited upon the Amir with a note from Sir Alexander Burnes. After I had dined with him I delivered it into his hands, and Sardar Mehardil Khan read it before him. The tone and the words of the letter were written strong, but just, and worthy of the British envoy. This naturally roused the mind of the Amir and of his party, and after assuring me of orders to supply us with everything the mission wanted, the only word I heard him saying to his adherents and to the Qandhar chief was that he had not anticipated that matters would go so far, nor that the Russian government would come so openly forward to further his ends in spite of the English. He continued, smilingly, that as the British envoy was offended, he should not lose time to stir up Vikovich to inform his government of the state of affairs at Kabul.

Moreover I am astonished to read in Mr. Masson's work that the Amir Dost Mohammed was exalted at the submissive humility of Sir Alexander Burnes, who always addressed and answered him with his hands closed and the word of "Gharibnavaz," and that he (Masson) had never given information of Vikovich having letters for the Lahaur chief. I had more opportunities than Mr. Masson to be present when Sir Alexander Burnes had interviews with the Amir and with many other independent rulers of Asia, but I never heard him accosting any of them in the humble manner described by this worthy gentleman. His tone of voice with the Amir of Kabul and with the chiefs of other places was conspicuous, and bore the accents of dignity worthy of his government and rank; and I have heard the chiefs myself saying that his "Guftar va Kirdar" (meaning his sayings and doings) bespeak of his talent and his high notions. With regard to his misrepresenting the information which Mr. Masson gave him, I can only say that no British officer charged with such high functions of his government, and entrusted with the welfare of his country, as Sir Alexander Burnes was, would commit such a gross act as to misrepresent the information in order to support his own views. Every line of the four volumes of the valuable work of Mr. Masson speaks of the author's sound judgment and independent character, it cannot be denied; but not one human being on the face of the earth will impartially admit that his opinions did always stand firmer and wiser than those of the other men who at that time conducted their arduous duties honourably, and who are now no more to defend themselves. I rejoice to see the independence of Mr. Masson duly estimated; but if that independence were accompanied by the least shadow of that gratitude which he owed for the patronage he received from Sir John Macneil, Sir Alexander Burnes, Sir Claude Wade, Sir William Macnaghten, and other functionaries, it would have reflected a laudable credit upon him. But alas, they are now of no use to him, and the work is published. In broad words, if an obliged Englishman were to make such return to his obliging and national friends as Mr. Masson has made, what then can be expected from an Asiatic like myself? I have great regard for the person, talent, and character of Mr. Masson, but I beg to say that I do not like his principles as displayed in throwing loads of disparagement on the memory of those who lost their lives in the service of their country, and are not now able to answer the remarks of Mr. Masson or of any one besides. He quotes some lines of the various notes from Sir Alexander Burnes, Sir William Macnaghten, and the then chairman of the India House, &c., to prove the authenticity of his opinions; but unfortunately they are not alive to give publicity to the notes which Mr. Masson wrote to them at that time. They are dead, and the valuable work comes out. May success attend the sale, and the second edition appear with alterations!

Captain Vikovich made a very long and interesting report of his negotiations with the chiefs of Qandhar and the Amir of Kabul, and despatched it for his Excellency Count Simonich, the Russian ambassador with the Shah of Persia. Our agent, however, found means to obtain a copy of that interesting document before it reached its destination.

The Russian Ambassador at Tehran, to Amir Dost Mohammed Khan, of Kabul.

(After compliments.)

"In these happy days the respectable Haji Ibrahim Khan, one of your people, arrived at the door of His Majesty the Shah. He has now got leave to return to you, and I embrace the opportunity to write to you, being induced to do so by the praises which I am always hearing concerning you, and the friendly conversation which has passed between your man and myself. Through him, therefore, I send this friendly letter, and hope that you in future will keep up a correspondence with me.

"Considering me your friend, I trust that you will strengthen the bonds of friendship by writing to me, and freely commanding my services, as I shall be happy to do anything for you.

"Look upon me as your servant, and let me hear from you.

(Sealed) "GRAF. IWAN SIMONICH,
Minister Plenipotentiary of the Russian government."

Letter to the Amir of Kabul, forwarding the preceding from Haji Ibrahim, his Agent at Tehran.

(After compliments.)

"I REACHED the camp of the Shah in the month of Jamadi-ul-aval. When His Majesty learned the contents of your letter he was happy and kind to me; at that time the Shah was at Chashma Ali, seven marches from Tehran, near Dam Ghan; he stated that on arriving at Khalpush he would discharge me with some messages for you. On his reaching Khalpush he went to punish the Turkmans, and I accompanied His Majesty as desired. When we returned to Sharood the winter set in, and the Shah, by the advice of his counsellors, left his artillery there, abandoned the intentions of going to Hirat this year, and returned to Tehran. He ordered his nobles to get ready by Nauroz, for an expedition to Hirat.

"The Shah directed me to inform you that he will shortly send an Elchi, who, after meeting you, will proceed to Ranjit Singh to explain to him, on the part of the Shah, that if he (Ranjit Singh) will not restore all the Afghan countries to you, the Amir, he must be prepared to receive the Persian army. When the Shah takes Hirat he has promised to send you money and any troops you may want.

"The Russian ambassador, who is always with the Shah, has sent you a letter, which I enclose. The substance of his verbal messages to you is, that if the Shah does everything you want, so much the better; and if not, the Russian government will furnish you (the Amir) with every thing wanting.

"The object of the Russian Elchi, by this message, is to have a road to the English in India; and for this they are very anxious. He is waiting for your answer, and I am sure he will serve you. The letter you sent by Agha Mohammed Kashi pleased the Shah very much, and he (Mohammed Husain) will soon return to you.

"The Asef-ul-Daulah, the ruler of Khorasan, has written to the Shah that he saw Yar Mohammed Khan on this side of Farah; he says he has not power to oppose the

Shah, but he will not serve him until the Shah gives him money to take Qandhar and Kabul.

"I send you the letter (Firman) of the Shah, which will, I trust, meet your approbation."

Major Mackeson, British Agent, Camp Shekwan, to Sir Claude Wade, political Agent, Lodiana.

"The Russian envoy at Kabul gave out that he intended to visit Lahaur, in order to have some friendly conversation with Maharajah Ranjit Singh, and to send an account of his Highness's military power and resources to the Emperor."

Major Mackeson to Sir Claude Wade.

Camp Khanpur, 12*th Feb.*, 1838.

"His Highness next adverted to a letter he had received from Peshavar, mentioning that the Russian envoy intended to come on to Lahaur."

Sir Alexander Burnes to Sir William Macnaghten.

Kabul, 4*th March*, 1838.

"I have the honour to report, for the information of the Right Honourable the Governor-General of India, that I have more grounds for believing that Captain Vikovich, the Russian agent at Kabul, is charged with letters from his government to the Maharajah Ranjit Singh. I observe that

Colonel Stoddart mentions this as a surmise to Sir John Macneil; and a few days ago Mr. A. Ward wrote to me from Peshavar, to know if the 'on dit' of M. Vikovich's going to the Panjab were true.

"I have made every inquiry on this subject, and in the course of yesterday Mr. Masson was informed that the Russian agent had letters for the Maharajah, and that the purport of them was to the effect, that if his Highness did not withdraw from Peshavar, the Russian government would compel him."

Sir Claude Wade to Sir W. H. Macnaghten.

21st March, 1838.

"I HAVE the honour to transmit an open letter to your address from Sir A. Burnes, dated the 4th instant, repeating, from Kabul, the report which had formerly reached Peshavar, that the mission of Captain Vikovich would extend to Lahaur."

Sir Alexander Burnes to the Earl of Auckland.

Kabul, 3rd Dec., 1837.

"IN the despatches, which I forward by this opportunity to Sir W. Macnaghten, your Lordship will find a report of the extraordinary circumstance of an agent having arrived at this capital direct from St. Petersburgh, with a letter from the Shah of Persia and from the Count Simonich, the Russian ambassador at Tehran.

"Before I enter upon the messages delivered by the

agent to the Ameer, it is proper to state the information which has reached me regarding what has passed at Qandhar. In my official communication of the 9th September last, your Lordship will remember that I reported the departure of one Haji Mobin on a mission to Persia; and, as it was believed, in pursuance of the advice of the Russian ambassador. That individual accompanied Mohammed Shah to Khorasan, and was requested by His Majesty to await the arrival of Captain Vikovich, and to proceed with him to Qandhar. The connexion between Russia and Persia in this part of the transaction leaves little doubt of the whole being a concerted plan between these powers. The statement made by the emissary to the Sardars of Qandhar was to the effect that Russia had full influence in Persia: and that they should assist the Shah, and draw on him for money, and if their drafts were not paid, that the Russian government would be responsible for their discharge; but that they should follow the wishes of Mohammed Shah, if they sought the Emperor's good offices, and on no account ally themselves with the English nation. This declaration, if true, is certainly most explicit; but though it has been communicated to me by a man whose other reports entirely tally with all that is passing in Qandhar, and who is the individual that made known to me five months ago the then inexplicable nature of Haji Mobin's mission, I should not wish your Lordship to give to it that confidence which I seek to place on the report of events that have transpired at Kabul.

"On the evening of the 20th inst. the Amir received the Russian messenger. On the agent's producing Mohammed Shah's raqam, the Amir felt a degree of irritation which he could hardly control, and said, in Afghani, that it was an insult to him, and a proof of Mohammed Shah's being guided by advisers; for his master, the Emperor, wrote him a letter, and the subservient Shah of Persia arrogated to himself the right of sending him a raqam, or order, with his seal in the face of the document. The agent was then dismissed, and invited to the Bala Hisar on the following day.

"The communications which passed on this second occasion have also been made known to me, and are of a startling nature. M. Vikovich informed Dost Mohammed Khan that the Russian government had desired him to state its sincere sympathy with the difficulties under which he laboured; and that it would afford it great pleasure to assist him in repelling the attacks of Ranjit on his dominions; that it was ready to furnish him with a sum of money for the purpose, and to continue the supply annually, expecting, in return, the Amir's good offices. That it was in its power to forward the pecuniary assistance as far as Bokhara, with which state it had friendly and commercial relations; but that the Amir must arrange for its being forwarded on to Kabul. The agent stated that this was the principal object of his mission; but that there were other matters which he would state by-and-by; that he hoped the Amir would give him a speedy answer to despatch to St. Petersburgh, and that with reference to himself, he would go, if dismissed, along with it, though he gave the Amir to understand (and under which impression he still continues) that it was his wish to remain, at least for a time, in Kabul. The report of this interview has been communicated to me from two sources, and they both agree in the substance of what passed.

"Having thus laid before your lordship these strong demonstrations on the part of Russia to interest herself in the affairs of this country, it will not, I feel satisfied, be presumptuous to state my most deliberate conviction that more vigorous proceedings than the government might wish or contemplate than have been hitherto exhibited are necessary to counteract Russian or Persian intrigue in this quarter.

"By one class of politicians everything regarding the designs of Russia in this quarter has been disbelieved. By another, the little which has transpired has excited immediate, and, in consequence, what may be termed groundless alarm. For the last six or seven years I have had my attention directed to these countries, and I profess myself to be one of those who do believe that Russia entertains the design of extending her influence to the eastward, between her dominions and India. With her commercial operations, she has invariably spread the report that her designs were ulterior; and the language of her agents has lately been, that as the affairs of Turkey and Persia are adjusted, she sought an extension of her influence in Turkistan and Kabul.

Such reports would deserve little credence if unsupported by facts; but assisted by them, they gather higher importance, and exhibit views which, but for the greatest vigilance, might have eluded notice for years to come.

"There being, therefore, facts before us in the transactions passing at Kabul, it seems impossible, with any regard to our safety, to look on any longer in silence. If Russia does not entertain inimical feelings directly to the British in India, she avows that she wishes for the friendly offices of the chiefs on our frontier, and promises them her own in return; so that it is useless to conceal from ourselves that evil must flow from such connexions, for this is, indeed, casting before us a challenge. It is a true maxim that prevention is better than cure, and now we have both in our hands. We might certainly wish to delay a while longer before acting; but it is now in our power, by the extended and immediate exercise of our already established influence, to counteract every design injurious to us.

"I trust that the free expression of my sentiments will not prove displeasing to your Lordship: I am emboldened by the confidence which has placed me here to speak according to my conviction."

Sir W. H. Macnaghten to Sir Alexander Burnes.

20th January, 1838.

"His Lordship attaches little immediate importance to this mission of the Russian agent, although he will bring all the circumstances connected with it to the notice of the home authorities, as it undoubtedly marks a desire, which has long been known to exist on the part of the Russian government, to push at least the influence of their name to our Indian frontier; and the proceedings, especially of the Russian envoy at Tehran, in regard to it, are open to much observation.

"His Lordship is much gratified at the deference to our views shown by Dost Mohammed Khan, in requesting your advice as to the reception of this agent; and he entirely approves your having sanctioned his being admitted to the presence of the Amir, and treated with becoming civility. If he be not already gone from Kabul, you will suggest to the Amir that he be dismissed with courtesy, with a letter of compliments and thanks to the Emperor of Russia for his proffered kindness to the Kabul traders. His mission should be assumed to have been, as represented, entirely for commercial objects, and no notice need be taken of the messages with which he may profess to have been charged.

"This of course will be recommended by you, in the event of the Amir being firmly disposed to abide by our good offices. If he should, on the other hand, seek to retain the agent, and to enter into any description of political intercourse with him, you will give him distinctly to understand that your mission will retire; that our good offices with the Sikhs on his behalf will wholly cease; and that, indeed, the act will be considered a direct breach of friendship with the British government. It has been before at different times stated to you, that the continuance of our good offices must be entirely dependant on the relinquishment by the Amir of alliances with any power to the westward."

From the Amir Dost Mohammed Khan of Kabul to His Excellency Count Simonich.

"YOUR friendly letter was delivered to me by the respectable Captain Vikovich, and I was delighted to read this your second epistle.

"If I were to offer full thanks for such kindness, it would be as impossible as to confine the river in a small vessel, or to weigh its water with stones.

"I fully understand the messages which you had sent to me through Captain Vikovich, and confidently expect that your imperial government will support and defend my honour, and by doing so, it will be easy to win the hearts of friends.

"I thank you for the offer you made to arrange my affairs, and further for your informing me that you do not merely tell me so; but that you will fulfil your promise. I expect much more from your friendly government, and my hopes have been increased. Though the distance between us is great, it does not prevent our approach in heart. My mind is put in peace by your friendly messages, and I hope it will continue so.

"Before the arrival of the agent of your government

(Captain Vikovich), the English government had deputed Sir Alexander Burnes, who is now with me in Kabul. That officer is sowing the seeds of friendship between Ranjit Singh and myself; nothing is yet settled, however, but let us wait the result.

"On the winter ceasing, and the roads opening, I will despatch Captain Vikovich by any road he prefers. At present, on account of the snow, I have postponed his departure.

"I hope you may continue to enjoy happy days."

From Captain Vikovich to Count Simonich.

"HAVING departed from Qandhar 2nd (or may be the 27th) November, of the past year, 1837, I arrived at Kabul on the 8th of December. The reception of Dost Mohammed Khan, and his condescension towards me, were sufficiently marked—polite as kind.

"I was lodged in the house of the first minister, Mirza Abdulemi (probably Abdul or Abdallah) Khan, and after three days' (waiting), I demanded an audience, when I delivered the imperial credentials [literally the most high letter] and the letter of your Lordship; and to that I added verbally, that the object of my coming was to evince to him, and to the rulers of Qandhar, the very gracious wishes (or inclinations) of the Emperor; and to declare that His Majesty the Emperor was pleased to return a gracious reply to the letter of Dost Mohammed Khan, and vouchsafed to him protection and friendly alliance; that the rulers of Afghanistan having made up or reconciled their differences among themselves [this passage is rather guessed at, being unintelligible] should acknowledge or place themselves under the dominion of Persia, with whom Russia is connected by truly friendly relations.

"The Amir (Prince), in showing his satisfaction at the imperial letters (credentials), gave me to understand that a friendly treaty (on the part) of the Afghans with the Persians could not be (subsist), because an English envoy, Sir A. Burnes, now here, has concluded (or was concluding) a mutual treaty. That Dost Mohammed Khan having collected as large an Afghan army as possible (should go, or was to go) to the assistance of Kam Ran against the Persians besieging Hirat; and by that treaty the English bound themselves to give (supply) to the Afghans twenty thousand muskets [I cannot exactly make out the word thousand; but suppose it. Some words here about the Russian alliance not legible]; and to make over to the possession of the Afghans, Peshavar, and the other conquests of Ranjit, on the right bank of the Indus; and that the treaty was despatched to Calcutta, for the information of the Governor-General of India, Lord Auckland. Thus terminated my first interview with the Amir Dost Mohammed Khan, but his vizier Mirza Abdool (Husain) Khan almost daily comes to me, and makes various inquiries regarding the power of Russia and of the other European governments. In the meantime Sir A. Burnes departed (went) for Qandhar, accompanied by the lieutenant of artillery, Leech, in order to (induce) the Qandhar rulers (to enter into) a treaty, and (to withdraw themselves) from friendly relations with the Shah. The English have established between Kabul and Qandhar a kind of (letter-post); and they have written (or it has been written) that the Persians are defeated, have retreated to Meshid, and have suffered extremely from hunger (want of provisions). All this has occasioned Dost Mohammed Khan to conduct himself very coldly towards me; and then, as he daily (converses) with Burnes, from my arrival here to the 20th February, I have hardly (or two or) three times been in his presence. Having discovered (or learnt) from Mirza Abdul Khan that he [I do not make out whether Abdul Khan is here meant, or Dost Mohammed] had a secret distrust of (or dislike to) English influence (or connexion), I endeavoured, as much as possible, to strengthen it, and succeeded in shaking his previous (or at a former time) confidence in and friendship towards them.

"In the meantime, on the 21st February was received from Lord Auckland a reply distinctly (decidedly) to cancel (refuse) all that Burnes had negotiated (or agreed upon); but in his letter (not clearly made out) he does not advise (dissuades) the rulers of Afghanistan to enter upon any alliance with Persia or with other powers; that the Afghans were in a great measure indebted for their independence to the support of the English, who restrained Ranjit Singh from conquest.

"The true cause (reason) for such proceeding of Lord

Auckland, as Burnes declares, is the following:—Ranjit having received from the Company a proposal to give the Afghans Peshavar, and other conquests, that he would willingly comply with the wishes of the Company upon receiving intimation to that effect [some reference here to the territories between the Indus and Kashmir, and securing the succession to his heirs, but I cannot make connected sense of it]. On receiving such proposition from Ranjit, Lord Auckland replied, that in consequence of (or on the occasion) the approach of the Persian Shah to Hirat, he decidedly (objects) and advises Ranjit to retain Peshavar, and to oppose himself to the movements of the Shah, who, as reported, is resolved to extend his march (or conquest) on the borders of India. Dost Mohammed Khan abandoning his hopes of assistance (not clearly made out) on the part of the English, has sent to Qandhar (the purport) of the letter received from Lord Auckland, and requested for consultation and co-operation one of the Sardars of that place; Sir A. Burnes, on his part, has written to Lieut. Leech (being) at Qandhar, that he should by all means endeavour to dissuade the Sardars from going to Kabul, and with Dost Mohammed Khan. But the ill-conducted intrigues of Leech have been disclosed, and roused the Sardar Kohen Khan, and led the Afghans to adopt the contrary course—to join Dost Mohammed Khan, and break off all connexion with them (the English), and place themselves under the sway of Persia, with the guarantee of Russia; that the Shah should supply (one hundred thousand) muskets for the equipment of Kabul and Qandhar army, and that after taking Hirat, the Shah himself with his troops should advance into Afghanistan, for the recovery of the provinces conquered by Ranjit. In demonstration of the sincerity of this proposal, the Amir Dost Mohammed Khan, and the Sardar Kohen Khan,—as one of their proceedings. Mirza Abdul Khan, who not only possesses the entire confidence of Dost Mohammed Khan, but influences all affairs in Afghanistan particularly,—and the Sardar Mehir Khan. They request me to set out (in the course of a month) to forward (or obtain from your Lordship) the guarantee—that the Persians shall fulfil the conditions upon which the Afghans agree to submit themselves to the sway of Persia; and for that purpose I intend leaving Kabul on the 26th or 27th April. Sir Alexander Burnes has frequently demanded of Dost Mohammed Khan, that I should be immediately dismissed, and that the rulers of Afghanistan should engage not to enter into any negotiations (or relations) with Persia and Russia; but seeing that now affairs have taken entirely another turn, he does not wait for the arrival of his companions, who, last autumn, went into Turkistan, and having instructed Lieutenant Leech to proceed from Qandhar to Shikarpoor and Hydrabad, (where he probably) suspects that the ruler of Sindh may enter into the confederation forming between Persia and Afghanistan, he left Kabul on the 19th (or may be 17th) instant (April); and went through Peshavar to Lahaur. I have the honour to present for the favourable consideration of your Lordship, a brief description of Afghanistan. I venture to infer (conclude) that with some pains and discretion the Russian government (administration) — here — as well as in commercial, as political relations. The geographical position of Afghanistan makes it the only — through which a conqueror can — from Qandhar to the very shores of the ocean; — barren desert, which can never be passable by any kind of military force (or detachments); on the north and north-west the road (way) from Turkistan is bounded (closed) by the strong pass of Hindu Kush, which has only two roads hardly passable for the space of four (I cannot make out whether the next word is months, or some term implying distance, I think the former), (several words here not legible)—for military stores, or supplies of an army. The people of Afghanistan are warlike, and if the mutual animosities existing between the several authorities (ruling powers) were reconciled, they could oppose the united forces of all India. Being a place where it is difficult (as it is in all such places) to display (or enforce) the maritime power of Russia; it nevertheless participates (lends its aid) in the reliance and influence which your Lordship has ably succeeded in diffusing throughout Persia. In these countries your ———, which extends as far as the exploits of the Persian armies, accompanies the name of your Lordship, and no one of the inhabitants of Kabul, nor of Qandhar, doubts that the Shah, when leaving Tehran, gave over to your Lordship the reins of government—for my part, I do not doubt, that, by the aid of this, something permanent may be done (established here); the

English have appreciated the full importance of this country in a political point of view (bearing), and they have spared neither trouble nor expense to gain a footing (or to instal themselves) in Afghanistan, as, without doubt, is known to your Lordship. Their successes, in respect to the defence of Hirat, and this mission of Sir Alexander Burnes, as it appears (to have been), cost him (or them), as far as I can ascertain, three hundred rupees, he (or they), during eight years residence here, (or possibly it may be 'when here eight years ago'), made purchases to the extent of one hundred and fifty rupees. From the year 1832 there has been here an established English agent, receiving a salary of one thousand rupees. He left Kabul, together with Sir Alexander Burnes. On my arrival at Tehran, I shall have the honour more particularly to lay before your Lordship the affairs of Afghanistan. At present I venture to beg most humbly that the desired guarantee (by the Afghans) should be acknowledged by your verbal condescension in the camp of the Shah.

(Signed) "VIKOVICH, Lieutenant."

CHAPTER XII.

The British Mission leaves Kabul—Iniquitous counsels given to the Amir respecting it—He rejects them—The Amir attaches himself wholly to Russia—Departure of Captain Vikovich—Honours paid him—Affairs of Sindh—Opinions current in Hindustan relative to Russia—The Asiatics anticipate reverses for the British power in the East—Correspondence, and other Documents—Reasons for the advance of the Army of the Indus—Negotiations set on foot by the British Government.

HAVING delivered the last letter of the Governor General to the Amir Dost Mohammed Khan, and had an audience of leave with him, the British Mission quitted Kabul on the 26th of April, 1838, and his son Gholam Haidar Khan escorted us to a distance of four miles from the city. The minister Mirza Sami Khan came to Butkhak, and presented Sir Alexander Burnes and myself with three horses in a most miserable condition. He remained and dined with me, and during the night we had a long conversation with that officer. He stated that Captain Vikovich has promised positively the pecuniary aid of Russia and the military assistance of Persia for furthering the objects of the Amir; and the minister then trying to make us believe his regret at our departure, and his neutrality of feeling in regard to the success of the Russians at the court of Kabul, said to Sir Alexander Burnes that all this was brought about by the Sardar Mehardil Khan of Qandhar. When it was pointed out to him that wisdom cannot permit one to place much credence in the extravagant proposals made by distant powers to the Amir, the minister replied that it is not Persia that we rely upon, but Captain Vikovich in Kabul, and Count Simonich in the Persian camp, who is a legally authorised representative of the Emperor of Russia. These he said have become guarantees, and have made agreement to support the Amir in recovering the Afghan territory from the Sikhs. Since Russia is one of the greatest powers of Europe, and her representative with the Shah of Persia is reckoned to be an Emperor, and that this race of men is celebrated for adhering to their word, as is well known in Khorasan, all this leaves little room to doubt that the Russian ambassador could have proposed and agreed to anything which was not authorised by his government, and that the cabinet of St. Petersburgh will not act accordingly. He says that the letter of the Amir to the address of the Governor-General will follow us, and shortly afterwards we bade adieu to the minister and came to Tezin. The Mission was escorted to Jelalabad safely by Nazir Ali Mohammed, and yet various reports were privately received from Kabul that some of the chiefs, as Mohamud Khan Bayat and Agha Husain, were advising the Amir to massacre the Mission, or at least to detain it till a large sum of money is paid by the English government for its ransom, which will furnish him with the means of defence against his impending danger. The Amir wisely paid no attention to such rash counsels of his friends; and Dr. Lord and Mr. Wood, who were invited by Mir Mohammed Morad Beg of Qunduz, returned to Kabul after the Mission had departed from that city. They suffered no molestation, but being received coldly by the Amir Dost Mohammed Khan, they were sent away safely to Jelalabad, and thence followed us by the Kabul river to Peshavar. Lieut. Wood had also heard from authentic sources, and observed on his way through Kabul, that the Amir and Captain Vikovich had grown very familiar with each other, and that the former had attached himself without reserve to Russia.

There is no doubt that although the Mission of Sir Alexander Burnes proved to be unsuccessful in its chief purpose, yet it afforded ample information at the time of the proceedings and the steps which the Russian government had openly taken into the politics of Afghanistan. The Sardar Mehardil Khan and the Amir addressed letters respectively to Mohammed Shah, King of Persia, stating all the circumstances of the negotiations, and of the failure and departure of the British envoy. Captain Vikovich told the Amir that he will transmit a sum of fourteen lakhs of rupees to him; and the Russian ambassador in Persia requested the Shah to accede to all the terms of the chiefs of Qandhar and of the Amir of Kabul, since they had entered into alliance and friendship with Russia.

The Amir at length dismissed Captain Vikovich with all honour; and appointing Habbu Khan an agent on his part to go with him, he desired Mehardil Khan to take them safe to Qandhar. Here, on this occasion, the Russian agent was treated with much more distinction than he was on his way to

Kabul. The chiefs, at his request, unanimously wrote letters and treaties for the satisfaction of the Russian ambassador at the Persian court, who had made himself guarantee on the part of his government that he will not only make these chiefs masters of Hirat, but will cause Mohammed Shah to give Ghuryan also to them; and they on their part sent Mohammed Omar Khan with about two hundred and fifty horse to wait upon the Shah and Count Simonich. The Amir also, though becoming much more unpopular by his alliance with Persia and with Russia, was engaged in repairing the Bala Hisar of Kabul and the fort of Ghazni, and in urging the Shah and Count Simonich to subdue Hirat and to push on to Kabul. The arrival of Mohammed Omar Khan, the son of Kohandil Khan, the principal chief of Qandhar, in the Persian camp, and the seizure of Frah by Mohammed Saddiq, another son of the chief, gave no proof of want of vigour nor any encouragement to the Afghans in their hopes of now defending Hirat; and many were desirous to desert, and even to surrender it to the Qandhar party in the Persian camp, if any one would venture to make such a communication to them. Captain Vikovich returned again from Hirat to Qandhar, and supplied the chiefs with ten thousand Russian ducats, which Kohandil Khan distributed amongst his troops. He also informed him that Mohammed Shah had given permission to Count Simonich to bring Russian forces to reduce Hirat and to send money to the chiefs in Afghanistan; and that, according to the European law, his presence in Qandhar will prevent the Governor-General of India and its allies from taking any hostile attitude towards that city. That officer wrote also to the Amirs of Sindh to keep themselves easy, and promised that he, with the Sardars, will in three months hence be on the banks of the Indus with them. Such communications undoubtedly would not be favourable to the cause of the British in Sindh; and moreover the chiefs of Qandhar publicly declared that they are paid and requested by the Shah and by Russia to proceed against the territory of Hirat, and that if Qandhar during their absence was attacked by any inimical power, the Russian government, acting on its agreement and guarantee, will supply them with money to recover it from the enemy. When the chief started on his march towards Hirat, Captain Vikovich supplied him with grain brought from the villages under the authority of Persia; and he had cunningly spread a report that he was acting under the authority of Count Simonich and of the Shah of Persia, who is the ally of his master the Emperor. He accordingly accompanied the camp of the Sardar, and the Shah of Persia promised to send Agha Sayad Mohammed with money to the Amir of Kabul, and the Russian ambassador sent at this time some presents to the Amir (perhaps those left behind by Captain Vikovich). The intelligence of this despatching of the letter of the Russian agent to the Sindhians was found by Sir Henry Pottinger to be true, and there was no doubt that the Russian name and influence was materially injurious to British interests even as far as to the eastern side of the Indus. The rumours of the power and bravery of the Russians, exaggerated by distance and talked of in Oriental style as it passed from one person to another, had given ample reasons for restlessness in the minds of the discontented chiefs of India. This was indeed not limited to Mahomedans only, but extended to the Rajput chiefs also of that country; and every one of them was looking forward with anxiety for the expected reverses of the English. Tired of tranquillity, and aspiring and longing for that pomp which all Asiatics enjoy during public confusion, they were whispering their wishes and preparing themselves to be ready at a moment's call, and to throw off the mask of quiet discontent against the rule of the British government.

Lord Auckland to Amir Dost Mohammed Khan.

Simla, 27th April 1838.

(After compliments.)

"I HAVE received your letter, and fully comprehend its contents.

"It has been a source of much regret to find that your views of what is most for your advantage have led you to decline the good offices which I have tendered, for the purpose of effecting a reconciliation between you and Maharajah Ranjit Singh, on the only terms on which I could, consistently with what has appeared to me just, engage to exercise my mediation for the settlement of the unhappy differences existing between you.

"With the explanation, however, of your sentiments which you have now afforded to me, my further interposition in this affair could not lead to beneficial results; and as, in so unsettled a condition of things, the continuance of Sir A. Burnes, and of the officers under his orders in Afghanistan, would not be conducive to the good ends which I had hoped to accomplish by their deputation, I have now issued orders to them to return to India; and they will accordingly set out, on receiving from you their dismissal, for which their immediate application will be made to you.

"I have to express to you my acknowledgments for your attention and kindness to these officers while residing in your dominions.

"(Signed) AUCKLAND."

Sir Alexander Burnes.

"On the night of the 25th April, I had the honour to report for the information of the Right Hon. the Governor General, that I had had my audience of leave with the Amir of Kabul; and I quitted the city on the following day (the 26th), being escorted about two miles from its gates by three of the Amir's sons; and also accompanied to the first halting-place, Butkhak, by Mirza Sami Khan. It is now my purpose to lay before his Lordship such additional particulars as illustrate the opinions of Dost Mohammed Khan, and the views which it seems he has in contemplation, and which, since we can no longer act with him, will, as it appears to me, require counteraction. I inquired into the truth of these reports in circulation regarding the Amir having actually gone over to Persia, and sought the security of Russia. The reply was, that they were too true. I asked what had really occurred, and learned that some of the Amir's family, or that of his brothers at Qandhar, were to be sent with letters to the Shah; that Captain Vikovich had promised to get the guarantee of Russia to all their arrangements; and that when Hirat fell, either to send part of the Persian force through the Hazarahjat to Kabul, or furnish the Amir with money to expel the Sikhs from Peshavar, which, he had said, was the more easily to be exacted from the Shah, who was a large debtor to Russia.

"It will be remembered that the Amir, in my last interview with him, offered no palliation of the intercourse which he had had within the last few days with Captain Vikovich.

"I have had intelligence of it that leaves little or no doubt on the subject.

"Captain Vikovich has already asked leave to set out forthwith to Hirat.

"Whatever are the plans of Persia and Russia, it will now be no fault of the chief of Kabul if they come not to maturity. He still gives out that he would not trust Persia alone, but seconded M. Goutte and Captain Vikovich, he considers the Russian guarantee will gain for him all his ends, and, besides being able successfully to contend with the Sikhs, as certain of ministering to his ambition, and fixing his supremacy."

Amir Dost Mohammed Khan to Lord Auckland.

(After compliments.)

"ALL the conversation which has passed between Sir A. Burnes and myself from the day of his arrival is well known to your Lordship, and consequently it is needless to repeat it.

"I also wrote a second time respecting the determination of the King of Persia, and the expectations of this friendly nation (Afghans) for the protection and enlargement of their possessions, which it had hoped from the British Government for a long time.

"It is well known to your Lordship that the Afghans expected very much from the English, from the day the Honourable Mountstuart Elphinstone came to Afghanistan, for that gentleman made a treaty with the Afghans of an offensive and defensive nature:

"Since Sir A. Burnes discovered that the Afghans were quite disappointed, and he has no powers from your Lordship to satisfy this nation, he is now returning to India with my permission.

"When Sir A. Burnes reaches India he will minutely speak to your Lordship on all the circumstances of this place. There are many individuals who have enjoyed the favour of the British; but our disappointment is to be attributed to our misfortune, and not to the want of the British Government."

From Lieutenant Wood.

"The non-arrival of our baggage detained us a few days in Kabul, during which we had an ample opportunity of observing how far recent events had influenced the public mind. The Qizalbash or Persian parties, numbering many of the most respectable citizens of Kabul, rejoiced at what had occurred; but the mass of people, Afghan and Tajik, were at no pains to conceal their discontent.

"Dost Mohammed Khan was engaged at chess when we entered the apartment; and while the interview lasted, he affected to be more intent on his chess-board than on the political game which we well knew was the uppermost in his mind. His manner was at first cold."

Sir Alexander Burnes.

"With reference to Russia, her proceedings are open to so much remark, after Count Nesselrode's disavowals, that, I presume she must either disavow Captain Vikovich and M. Goutte as her emissaries, or be made responsible for their proceedings. I have only again to repeat my most deliberate conviction, founded on much reflection regarding the passing events in Central Asia, that consequences of a most serious nature must, in the end, flow from them, unless the British Government applies a prompt, active, and decided counteraction. I do not offer these as my opinions, founded on the periodical publications of all Europe (though the coincidence of sentiment in all parties does not want in weight), but as formed on the scene of their intrigues; and it is my duty, as a public servant, earnestly to state them to my superiors.

"As I am despatching this commission from Jelalabad, half way to Peshavar, I have received good information that the Amir has been constantly with Captain Vikovich since I left, and that officer has earnestly solicited permission to proceed to Hirat by the direct road of Hazarajat, and offered the solemn pledges to do all which the Amir wishes, under a month. He has also bound himself to address Maharajah Ranjit Singh, after retiring from Peshavar; and when Dost Mohammed Khan asked if he had authority to do so, he replied that he had a letter to that potentate which would soon set matters right.

"Explaining further the plans of the chiefs of Kabul and Qandhar, consequent on their new alliance with Persia and Russia.

"The day after you left Kabul the Amir had a private meeting with the Sardar Mehardil Khan, Reshid Akhundzadah, and Mirza Sami Khan. They have settled that Mohammed Azim Khan (the Amir's son), and Mirza Sami Khan, should leave Kabul, and having joined Mohammed Omar Khan and Mulla Reshid, at Qandhar, proceed to Hirat, and wait upon Mohammed Shah on the part of the Kabul and Qandhar chiefs.

"Sardar Mahardil Khan has addressed a letter to Mohammed Shah, which, after being sealed by his brothers at

Qandhar, will be sent by express. The contents of the letter are as follows:—

" 'On the arrival of Qambar Ali Khan, your Majesty's agent, at Qandhar, it was resolved that Mohammed Omar Khan should wait upon the Shah on the part of the Qandhar chiefs. Meanwhile, Sir Alexander Burnes reached Kabul, as an agent of the British Government, on which our elder brother Dost Mohammed Khan sent a letter, preventing us sending Mohammed Omar Khan to his Majesty on the following grounds: the British Government and Ranjit Singh are very near the Afghans, and Mohammed Shah is a distance of three months' journey; and that Amir feared these two powers may be offended, and endeavour to ruin him, which his Majesty could not prevent. Regarding the superiority of our brother (the Amir), and seeing the good of the governments, we recalled Mohammed Omar Khan from Giriskh, on account of the confusion; when we received authentic information of his Majesty's arrival at Hirat, I left Qandhar, and came to Kabul, and brought about the dismissal of Sir A. Burnes, and induced the Amir to send his minister Mirza Sami Khan to his Majesty, and from Qandhar Mohammed Omar Khan, and Mulla Reshid, to wait upon his Majesty.'

" The contents of the Amir's letter to Mohammed Shah are as follows:—

" 'When Qambar Ali Khan reached Qandhar, Sir A. Burnes also came to Kabul, on the part of the English Government. He prevented my entering into an alliance with your Majesty. As the Shah was at a distance I kept Sir A. Burnes in evasive discourse, and having the sure information of your Majesty's arrival at Hirat, I dismissed him instantly. I have now appointed my son Mohammed Azam Khan to wait upon your Majesty. I will obey the orders (amar) of his Majesty in future.'

"The chappar has been despatched with the above letter to Hirat.

"This proposal of the Mirza to the Amir originates in his sagacity, for he has settled every thing with Captain Vikovich, who has promised that on reaching the camp of Mohammed Shah he will send the Amir the sum of forty lakhs of rupees. The above officer is boasting very much what he will do to protect and exalt the Amir, but it is needless to mention those affairs minutely.

"After your departure from this place, the Amir sends for Captain Vikovich daily to his court, and makes arrangements with him which are as yet not written.

"On Tuesday evening a man by the name of Bahar, in the service of Kohandil Khan, came to Kabul with letters from the Russian agent with Mohammed Shah to Captain Vikovich. Alladad, who had accompanied Qambar Ali Khan, has also returned to Qandhar, with other letters from Mohammed Shah and the Russian agent, to the address of the Qandhar chiefs.

"His Excellency has instructed the Shah to satisfy the chiefs of Qandhar, and the Amir of Kabul, at any rate, and give whatever they want, since they have written to him (the ambassador) through Captain Vikovich, and accepted the friendship of Russia.

"The Amir has dismissed Captain Vikovich with all honour and respect; and that officer has proceeded to Qandhar, along with Sardar Mehardil Khan, accompanied on the part of Dost Mohammed Khan by Hubu Khan Barakzai, enjoying the Amir's confidence.

"The Qandhar family will wait on the Shah without delay, and be introduced through Captain Vikovich; and it is understood at Kabul, that the Amir will send his own subsequent messengers direct to Hirat by the Hazarah road.

"(Signed) A. BURNES."

"After perusing the treaty the Russian envoy took it to Mohammed Shah, who agreed to every article of it. The envoy made himself guarantee for the fulfilment of its articles, and sent it back to the Sardars, along with his own letter, the contents of which are as follows:—

"'Mohammed Shah has promised to give you the possession of Hirat, and I sincerely tell you that you will also get Ghoryan, on my account, from the Shah. It is, therefore, advisable that you send your son Mohammed Omar Khan to Hirat, where you must also afterwards come.

"'When Mohammed Omar Khan arrives here I will ask the Shah to quit Hirat, and send your son along with his Majesty to Tehran; I (the Russian envoy) will remain here with twelve thousand troops; and when you join, we will take Hirat, which will be afterwards delivered to you!'

"On the arrival of this letter the Sardar had no bounds to his joy, and sent it to Kabul. The report was, that it did not please the Amir at all.

"Sardar Mehardil Khan has returned to Qandhar. The Russian Agent (Vikovich), who accompanied him from Kabul to this place, was received here with honour, since the Russian Envoy at Hirat had written strongly to the Sardars, that they must treat Vikovich with all sorts of consideration; and believe his tongue, oath, and words, as if they were from him (Russian Envoy).

* * * * * *

"The Sardars have sent Mohammed Omar with two hundred and fifty horsemen to Hirat, to wait upon Mohammed Shah, and have sent an elephant for His Majesty, and some shawls for the Russian Envoy.

"The Sardars have sent one hundred and fourteen letters, &c., ordering the heads of Sistan, Farah, Sabzvar, and other Afghans, to join their son Mohammed Saddiq Khan at Farah. They have also informed them that the Russian Envoy has made them the 'Mir Afghan,' and has promised to give them possession of Hirat, when, if any of them will not obey our (Sardars') orders, he will be banished from the country for ever.

"You must also know that the days in which you saw

Dost Mohammed Khan are departed. He is no longer popular. His joining the Russians has utterly ruined him in the eyes of all Mahomedans.

"This has quickened Dost Mohammed Khan's plans; he has set out about repairing the Bala Hisar of Kabul, and the fort of Ghazni; he has also increased his taxes in the Kohistan; and, as you know, this only increases his difficulties. He now sends messenger after messenger to the Russian Ambassador and the Shah, urging them to settle affairs at Hirat, and come on to Kabul, when the country will be theirs.

"You take no notice of the fire which has been kindled in Khorasan and Afghanistan. You will see how far it extends in the course of six months.

"Mohammed Shah has written a letter to the Sardars of Qandhar. The contents of the letter were much; but tell you the result of it.

"Since the arrival of Mohammed Omar Khan, His Majesty has become sure of the attachment of the Sardars at Qandhar, to Persia, and that they should be at ease on account of their son, Mohammed Omar Khan; after taking Hirat, His Majesty will send Vikovich to them, and the Amir Dost Mohammed Khan, with the amount of nine lakhs of rupees, and then they must hold themselves ready to receive the orders of the Shah.

"This letter was sealed by the Shah, his Minister Mirza Haji Aghasi, and the Russian Ambassador.

"Mohammed Omar Khan was received by ten thousand

Persian cavalry, and presented with four guns and five pairs of dresses of honour. The Shah has given him a place near his own tent, and his Agent, Alladad Khan, lives with the Russian Ambassador. Mohammed Omar Khan gets two hundred ducats every day for his expenses; and the Shah has told him that he will do much more for the Sardars than he told them in his letters.

"This intelligence was sent by Mohammed Omar Khan to his father Kohandil Khan, through Khodadad Khan, chappar (courier), who arrived here in eleven days from Hirat.

"Two days after the arrival of Mohammed Omar Khan, the Persians made an assault on Hirat, and lost four hundred people, besides two hundred or three hundred wounded. Borowski and Samsan have been dreadfully wounded, and the former nearly killed. The head of one of the Russian officers was cut off and taken into the city by the Afghans. After this engagement both parties returned to their own quarters.

"The arrival of Mohammed Omar Khan at the Persian camp has deeply disheartened the Afghans at Hirat. Many of them have turned against each other, and if the Sardars at Qandhar write to Mohammed Omar Khan, he would easily take Hirat, for the Afghans would likely surrender it to him.

"Mohammed Sadiq Khan, the eldest son of Kohandil Khan, has possessed Farah, and is repairing it.

"On the 18th October, I wrote to Captain Leech about

Captain Vikovich, the agent of the Russian Ambassador, on which you are also informed.

"On the 26th of the above month, Captain Vikovich reached Qandhar, having left Mohammed Shah at Kosan, on the other side of Ghoryan. Sirdar Kohandil Khan wanted to send his son Mohammed Omar Khan, and three hundred horsemen for his reception, but Captain Vikovich prevented the Sardar doing so. He entered the city alone, and put up in the house of Mirza Yaha.

"Captain Vikovich told the Sardars that he was the bearer of sixty thousand ducats. Out of the above sum he has a bill for forty thousand ducats on the treasury of Kirman, and that money will be paid in three months hence to Dost Mohammed Khan; ten thousand ducats he has in cash for the Sardars, who will get ten thousand more from Qayn, when they go with their army of Hirat.

"After a long discussion on both sides, the Sardars took the ten thousand ducats from Captain Vikovich, and divided them. Kohandil Khan has pitched one coss from the city on his way to Hirat, and troops are daily assembling to join him.

"The Russian Ambassador then asked the Shah his opinion of taking measures about Hirat: he told him to send money to the Afghan chiefs. The Shah said, 'When the Afghans come against Hirat, I will also order my forces in Khorasan to join them in attacking that city.' On this the Ambassador told the Shah if the city of Hirat was not even taken by the combined arms of the Afghans and Khorasan, what then was the mode to reduce it; the Shah pointed out to the Ambassador that it was not according to Treaty, that Russian forces should pass through Persia, but now His Majesty would make no objection if that Government should send their army through it to reduce any country they liked. This permission from the Shah was received by the Ambassador with great thanks and pleasure. The Ambassador has gone with the Shah.

"The Sardars told Captain Vikovich that they were now quite satisfied about Hirat, but they feared for Qandhar, which may be taken by the English. He answered then, that it was not the law among Europeans that one nation should dare to conquer a foreign land in the presence of an officer from another, and therefore his (Vikovich's) presence will prevent the English coming. These words have made the Sardars totally fearless of any ill luck.

"On this the Sardars and also Captain Vikovich wrote separate letters to the Mirs of Sindh, saying that they should remain quiet for three months, and the Mirs will soon see them on the Indus with their army.

"The proceedings of Captain Vikovich at Qandhar are matters of notoriety here, and may have a prejudicial effect at Hyderabad. I also find that the Russians have sent presents to Ali Khan, the Bilochi chief of Sistan. I keep Colonel Pottinger informed on these matters, and indeed on all that is going on."

To Major R. Leech.

"I YESTERDAY asked Kohandil Khan what he meant by proceeding towards Hirat in the present crisis of affairs, and what was to be done with the English? He said that if the English were encamped on the plains of Qandhar, he could not help going as far as Farah. He said his only plan was to remain at Farah, as the Persians and Russians had told him; and if Qandhar in the interim should be taken or besieged, the Russians would have the blame; that the Russians would give money and troops to them, that they might come back and fight at Qandhar; and that if they did not find the English there, they might employ the resources put at their disposal to subdue Hirat.

"Sardar Kohandil Khan has left Qandhar, having distributed ducats to his army; he expected to arrive at Farah on the 9th of November.

"Captain Vikovich has brought one thousand kharvars of grain for the Sardar, that was in the fort of Shamshuddin Khan.

"Aladad Khan and Captain Vikovich arrived at Qandhar on the 17th October, bringing with them ten thousand ducats, which Kohandil Khan immediately applied for. The Russians answered, that it rested with Aladad Khan, to give the money as soon as the Sardars should start.

"On the 21st October, the Sardars pitched their pesh khanah (advanced tents), and received the ten thousand ducats. Sardar Kohandil Khan took for his share two thousand seven hundred ducats; Sardar Rahamdil and Mehardil Khans took the same; Mir Afzal Khan received nine hundred and fifty ducats; and Mohammed Sadiq Khan the same sum.

"On the 22nd October, four messengers arrived from Amir Dost Mohammed Khan, saying that Sir A. Burnes and Lieutenant Wood had arrived at Peshavar with thirty regiments; that the Sikhs had retired from Peshavar, and urging the Sardars not to quit Qandhar.

"Sardar Kohandil Khan showed the letter to Captain Vikovich, who said that they were at liberty to act as they pleased. The Sardars said they would start in four days."

Sir Alexander Burnes.

"This agent does not wish to figure as a Russian, but as a Persian; he gives out that his proceedings are guided by Mohammed Shah's orders, whose ally and friend is his master the Emperor.

"Sardar Mehardil Khan has pitched at Vashien, Sardar Kohandil Khan (in company with Captain Vikovich) at Kishknakhued; and Sardar Rahamdil Khan, near the Hauz Madad, twelve coss from the city. All the troops are preparing to follow and join them.

"Abdul Saheb Khan, the servant of the Russian ambassador, passed through Qandhar on his way to Kabul, in charge of the dress of honour for Dost Mohammed Khan.

"Our intelligence from Qandhar has been all along accurate, and you will see that the letters sent from Qandhar to Hyderabad, under Captain Vikovich's instigation (if not by himself), have at last come to light, as stated in the sixth paragraph of Colonel Pottinger's letter of the 23rd instant (November, 1838), now forwarded. It now turns out that the chiefs of Qandhar have offered a portion of their Russian bribe to the chief of Kelat, and such is the unhappy fatality hanging over these disunited chiefs; which throws considerable light on the intrigues of Russia in that quarter, and in which Captain Vikovich is represented to have taken a prominent part.

"Captain Vikovich has given ten thousand ducats to the Sardars of Qandhar, and promised them ten thousand more when they arrive at Farah, and the same number again on reaching one march on this side of Hirat, and twenty thousand ducats on besieging that city. The Sardars have consequently left Qandhar, and arrived at Farah. Mehardil Khan has been sent back to Qandhar; for he was afraid of the Ghilzais making an insurrection, because the heads of that tribe, Abdulrahman Khan, and Sultan Mohammed Khan, the sons of Shahabuddin Khan, and Gul Mohammed Khan, the son of Khan, had received letters from Shah Shuja; and because in the city there were Haji Khan, Sohbat Khan, and Mama, in whom the Sardars had but little confidence.

"The Russian agent, who lately came to Dost Mohammed Khan, presented six hundred yards of long cloth and a few pieces of broad cloth. He has put up at Mirza Sami Khan's.

"On the 11th December Sardar Mehardil Khan invited Captain Vikovich to a party at his house, where there were present Mulla Nasu, Nazar Mohammed Khan, and Haji Husain Alli Khan, the Persian ambassador. The Sardar told Captain Vikovich that he (the Captain) had told them (the Sardars) that on that side of the Indus was the British government, and on this side that of Mohammed Shah, who owes allegiance to Russia; that since they had also submitted themselves to Russian allegiance, it behoved him to assist them against the English, who are now going to invade Afghanistan. Captain Vikovich answered that they were not in allegiance of Russia, because though he had given them ten thousand ducats to set out for Hirat, they had not yet travelled twenty-five cosses during fifty days, and that when they arrived at Hirat he could assist them against any enemy. He also added that he was deputed to Amir Dost Mohammed Khan, and that the Amir had sent his letter to Russia by his man Habbu Khan, declaring himself a servant of the Russian government, and given an unsealed copy of it to himself; that the man had come as far as Qandhar, and then disappeared; that he sent the copy of the letter to his government, and received a letter for the Amir to the effect that he (the Amir) was not a servant but a friend; that if he wanted the Russian friendship he should write so, and it would send to him four lakhs of ducats and four officers skilled in artillery and infantry exercise; and that he was waiting for an answer to that letter from the Amir, after the receipt of which he would return to Russia.

"He also stated that the Russian government had more reliance on Dost Mohammed Khan's intellect and power than on the chiefs of Qandhar, because he, notwithstanding his poverty, and being without means, is fighting against the Sikhs who are provided with everything."

CHAPTER XIII.

Reluctance of the Indian Government to interfere with Captain Vikovich—Proceedings of Count Simonich—Sir A. Burnes and Sir J. Macneil urge the necessity of vigorous measures—The north-western Frontier—Lord Wellesley's opinion—Policy of the British government—Shah Shuja—Correspondence, and extracts from various sources illustrative of British policy in Afghanistan—The British government resolve to restore Shah Shuja—Mission to Ranjit Singh—Tripartite Treaty—Preparations—Declaration of the Governor-General—Letter to the Shah of Persia.

It has been well known to all, and published in various papers, and in the government despatches, that the Earl of Auckland, then the Governor-General of India, did not attach much importance to the mission of Captain Vikovich and the Russian intrigues in Afghanistan; and judiciously considered that the whole matter should be decided by the authorities of England in Europe. But yet the circumstances, which were daily assuming more and more and now wearing constantly an unfavourable aspect, would neither dictate nor approve the policy of his Lordship to treat always a subject of such magnitude thus slightingly. His Excellency Count Simonich, the Russian ambassador, with his other colleagues, was not only superintending and planning the assault upon Hirat, against the advice of the British minister, but was actually deputing agent after agent, and sending money and grain to the Amir of Kabul and the chiefs of Qandhar. Sir John Macneil was in the meantime dismissed by the King of Persia, and Sir Alexander Burnes by the Amir of Kabul. Both of these functionaries, well versed and experienced in the politics of the East, and noted for their knowledge of the feelings of that country, well proved also in their anxiety for the welfare of British India, and in their zeal to preserve the national honour, urged upon the Governor-General the consideration of the necessity so apparent for taking immediate steps to counteract the openly united intrigues and encroachments of the Russian ambassador and of the Shah of Persia, which had most effectually made their way into Sindh and the interior of India. It is unnecessary for me to beg the readers to trace their way back in the histories of former times, and in the records and publications which are so numerous, and which all bear a prompt witness that whenever any rumours of invasion from the west of the Indus have been afloat they have always excited very much the people of India. Even Zaman Shah contemplated at one time the plan of an expedition to proceed towards Lahaur, with the view to cross the Sutlej, and his correspondence with the Tipu Sultan were topics of great deliberation and interest to the British authorities of that day. Notwithstanding that barrier of British India was admitted by Lord Wellesley to be the territory of Ranjit Singh, yet his Lordship, in consideration for the safety of the English possessions, made a capital remark, regardless of all ties of friendship which might be in existence with the rulers of that country: "I consider that we have nothing more between us and the most desirable frontier everywhere but the territory of Ranjit. If we were threatened on the north-west, for example, by an invasion of the Russians, we should, in self-defence, be obliged to take possession of the country to the foot of the hills, as we could not leave an intermediate space in which the enemy might establish themselves." The Earl of Auckland was also informed that the letters of Sir John Macneil, despatched to Sir A. Burnes through the Bombay government, "proved all previous conjectures to be well founded, and that M. Vikovich was what he had given himself out, an agent from the Emperor of Russia." Meanwhile the reports of the unpopularity and the internal dissensions of the government of the Amir Dost Mohammed Khan had frequently reached the ears of our government. Taking all these points into one deliberate view, it became necessary that a friendly government should be established in Afghanistan, and the Barakzai chiefs, who are inimically disposed towards the British, must be removed from the usurped authority of Afghanistan.

It is well known that the British government in India, alarmed at the startling advance of Napoleon, had deputed the Honourable Mountstuart Elphinstone for this purpose, and had entered into alliance with Shah Shuja-ul-mulk, who, by adverse circumstances, was since obliged to leave his dominions, and to take refuge in Lodianah. He had tried several times to accomplish the recovery of his throne, but through want of resolution had repeatedly failed in his attempt. All the princes of India, and particularly those of Central Asia, nay, even some of the Barakzai, I have heard saying that Shah Shuja was driven away by his own servants, and sought refuge among, and the protection of, the English. They added, that these, by the rules of honour and as a powerful nation, were bound to replace him on the throne; that they would have done in this no more than was done by a former king of Persia, in the case of Dara Shikoh, when he fled through the fear of Aurangzeb. Though Shah Shuja, by his long inactive life and private residence at Lodianah, had lost the abilities of a sovereign, yet his name and person, and the hereditary right, were not only considered by the Governor-General to constitute him the best instrument for gaining the end in view, but were also recommended as such by the best authorities and of the largest experience. Sir Alexander Burnes, after his departure from Kabul, writes to the Earl of Auckland in these terms:—*

June 3, 1838.

"It is clear that the British government cannot, with any credit or justice to itself, permit the present state of

* Sir John Hobhouse's Speech, page 33.

affairs at Kabul to continue. If this be left undone, they will succumb to Persia and Russia, and become the instruments for whatever those powers desire. I therefore distinctly state that the evil lies beyond Afghanistan itself, and must be dealt with accordingly.

"If it is the object of government to destroy the power of the present chief of Kabul, that may be effected by the agency of his brother, Sultan Mohammed Khan, or of Shah Shuja-ul-mulk; but to ensure complete success in the plan, the British government must appear directly in it, that is, it must not be left to the Sikhs themselves.

"Of Sultan Mohammed Khan, the first instrument at command, you will remember that his brother, Dost Mohammed, plainly confessed his dread of him if aided by Sikh gold, and with such aid the ruler of Kabul may be readily destroyed; but Sultan Mohammed has not the ability to rule Kabul: he is a very good man, but incapable of acting for himself; and, though fit as an instrument for getting rid of a present evil, he would still leave affairs as unsettled as ever when fixed in Kabul; and he is consequently a very questionable agent to be used at all.

"As for Shuja-ul-mulk personally, the British government have only to send him to Peshavar with an agent, and one or two of its own regiments as an honorary escort, and an avowal to the Afghans that we have taken up his cause, to ensure his being fixed for ever on his throne."

The opinions of Sir John Macneil with regard to

the right of the Sadozai family, or of Shah Shuja, are expressed in this manner:*—

"Though the sovereignty of the Afghans has passed out of the hands of Ahmed Shah's descendants, the Durrani tribe, it appears, maintain an undoubted ascendancy in the nation. The Barakzais have usurped the greater portion of the power of the Sadozais; but the latter family still maintains itself in Hirat, and has a strong hold on the prejudices, if not on the affections, of a large portion of the Durranis.

"That the Barakzais, holding Kabul and Qandhar in independence, would not appear to have conciliated the attachment of the Durranis, who depend in a great measure for their power on influences foreign to their tribe. To force their rule therefore on the people would not only be a difficult operation in itself, but, if sought to be effected through the mediation of the British government, would require a degree of support from us which we cannot, in my opinion, afford to give to the present possessors of power in Afghanistan, or rather to the ruler of Kabul, without bringing new elements of discord into action, productive of more evil to the peace of Afghanistan, and of the whole country, than the preservation of the sovereignty of the Afghans in the Sadozai family would be worth."

Sir Claude Wade, the political agent at Lodianah, having continued a rapid communication and inter-

* Correspondence relating to Afghanistan, No. 5, page 20.

course with all the chiefs of Afghanistan, and by this means possessing a full knowledge of the feelings of the inhabitants, who frequently visited Shah Shuja,* preferred that His Majesty should be placed on the throne in the room of the Amir Dost Mohammed Khan.

"In this letter Sir Claude Wade endeavoured to impress upon Lord Auckland the opinion that Shah Shuja-ul-Mulk ought to be preferred to Dost Mohammed,—and stated why he differed from Sir Alexander Burnes on that point. Gentlemen would do well to peruse that important document, the facts stated in which, and the inferences drawn from them, are directly at variance with what was said by that Honourable Gentleman on the opposite side. In one place Sir Claude Wade says, 'My own sources of information, which have been repeatedly authenticated both by natives and Europeans, who have visited Kabul, lead me to believe that the authority of the Amir (Dost Mohammed) is by no means popular with his subjects, and many instances in confirmation of the fact might be adduced from the reports of Mr. Masson, even when that individual has been willing to render every justice to Dost Mohammed Khan's abilities."

As quoted by Sir Claude Wade,† who sums up his advice by these words:—

"I submit my opinions with every deference to the

---

* Sir John Hobhouse's Speech, p. 37. † Ibid., p. 39.

wisdom of his Lordship's decision; but it occurs to me that less violence would be done to the prejudices of the people, and to the safety and well-being of our relations with other powers, by facilitating the restoration of Shah Shuja, rather than by forcing the Afghans to submit to the sovereignty of the Amir."

Above all the authority of Mr. Masson, from his long intercourse with the Afghans, and from being the news-writer of the Indian government, will undoubtedly appear a predominant feature in the evidences already quoted.*

"The British government," said one of those on whose information that government acted (Mr. Masson), "could employ interference without offending half-a-dozen individuals. Shah Shuja, under their auspices, would not even encounter opposition; and the Amir (Dost Mohammed Khan) and his friends, if he has any, must yield to his troops or become fugitives. Another presumed recommendation of Shah Shuja was this—pointed out by the same authority. No slight advantage, were Shah Shuja at the head of government (in Afghanistan), would be that, from his residence among Europeans, he would view their intercourse in these countries without jealousy, which cannot be expected from the present rulers, but after a long period, and until better acquaintance may remove their distrust."†

* Thornton's History of British India, vol. vi. p. 150.

† Correspondence relating to Afghanistan, No. 5, p. 20.

"The failure of Shah Shuja is now most sincerely lamented by all reflecting minds: I myself, however, rejoiced at it at the time, but the course of events seems to prove that his success would have been felicitous to the country, and the wishes of all classes even now turn to his restoration.

"I must confess," writes Mr. Masson to Sir Claude Wade,* "I am not very sanguine as to any very favourable result from negotiations with the Barakzais (that is Dost Mohammed and his brothers). They are chiefly indeed their own enemies; but their eternal and unholy dissensions and enmities have brought them to be considered as pests to the country, and the likelihood is that affairs will become worse rather than better while they remain."

Mr. Lord and Lieutenant Wood, on their return from Qandarz, secured the unanimous voice of the population in Kabul against the Amir, and in favour of the Shah; the latter of whom thus expresses his own opinion:—

"Annoyed at Dost Mohammed's reception of Vikovich, the Russian emissary, and disquieted by the departure of the British agent, they looked to the Amir as the sole cause of their troubles, and thought of Shah Shuja and redress."

On these various and unquestionable evidences, given by the authorities well versed in the politics

* Sir John Hobhouse's Speech, p. 38.

of that quarter, where the danger was impending, the Earl of Auckland resolved to establish Shah Shuja on the throne, and thus to extinguish the flame of the united intrigues of Russia and of Persia on the west side of the Indus, before it extended to the eastern bank of that river. It was considered desirable, previous to forming an expedition for that purpose, to make the Maharajah Ranjit Singh, the ruler of the Panjab, a party in this important undertaking. Shah Shuja, who was watching with extreme anxiety the proceedings of Sir Alexander Burnes's late mission in Kabul, and, as he said himself, praying for its failure, was now informed that the British government were to restore him to his dominions, using both their money and their arms in his favour.

The Governor-General of India deputed Sir William Macnaghten, Bart., on a mission to the Court of Lahaur; and Sir Claude Wade and Sir Alexander Burnes were also directed to co-operate with him. The mission was favourably received by the Maharajah,* and the negotiations commenced with good designs, and ended successfully. The

* See 'Ranjit's Court,' by the Hon. Captain Osborn.

THE LATE MAHARAJAH RUNJEET SINGH

form of the agreement was in great portion the copy of that into which the ruler of the Panjab and the Shah had entered in 1833-4, with the exception of the third party—the British—which had now become an accomplice in the affair, and which agreed that while the Sikh and English troops engaged and encamped together to promote the cause of the Shah, the slaughter of the kine should not be permitted, as being against the religion of the Sikhs. The following is the copy of this tri-partite treaty, which must be borne in mind, and referred to on the release and departure of the Amir Dost Mohammed Khan from the British territory, through the Panjab, escorted by Captain Nicolson.

Treaty between the British Government, Ranjit Singh, and Shah Shuja-ul-Mulk, concluded at Lahore on the 26th June, 1838.

"WHEREAS a treaty was formerly concluded between the Maharajah Ranjit Singh and Shah Shuja-ul-Mulk, consisting of fourteen articles, exclusive of the preamble and conclusion: and whereas the execution of the provisions of the said treaty was suspended for certain reasons: and whereas at this time Sir William H. Macnaghten having been deputed by the Right Honourable George Lord Auckland, G.C.B., Governor-General of India, to the presence of the Maharajah Ranjit Singh, and vested with full powers to form a treaty in a manner consistent with the friendly engagements subsisting between the two states, the treaty aforesaid is revived and concluded, with certain modifications; and four new articles have been added thereto, with the approbation and in concert with the British government, the provisions whereof, as contained in the following eighteen articles, will be duly and faithfully observed.

"1. Shah Shuja-ul-Mulk disclaims all title on the part of himself, his heirs and successors, to all the territories lying on either bank of the river Indus that may be possessed by the Maharajah, viz., Kashmir, including its limits E. W. N. S., together with the fort of Attak, Chach, Hazara, Khebel, Aub, and its dependencies, on the left bank of the aforesaid river, and on the right bank Peshavar, with the Usafzai territory, Khataks, Hasht Nagar, Michni, Kohat, Hangu, and all the places dependant of Peshavar, as far as the Khaibar Pass; Bannu, the Vazivi territory, Daur, Tank Gorak Kalabagh, and Khushalgar, with their dependant districts, Dera Ismail Khan and its dependencies, together with Dera Ghazi Khan, Kot Mittan, Omar Kot, and their dependant territory, Sanghur, Harand, Dajal, Hajipur Rajanpur, and the three Kachis, as well as Munkera, with its district, and the province of Multan, situated on the left bank. These countries and places are considered to be the property, and to form the estate of the Maharajah; and the Shah neither has, nor will have, any concern with them; they belong to the Maharajah and his posterity, from generation to generation.

"2. The people of the country on the other side of Khaibar will not be suffered to commit robberies and aggressions, or any disturbances, on this side. If any defaulter on either state, who has embezzled the revenue, take refuge in the territory of the other, each party engages to surrender him; and no person shall obstruct the passage of the stream which issues out of the Khaibar defile, and supplies the fort of Fatahghar with water, according to ancient usage.

"3. As, agreeably to the Treaty established between the British Government and the Maharajah, no one can cross from the left to the right bank of the Satlej without a passport from the Maharajah, the same rule shall be observed regarding the passage of the Indus, whose waters join the Satlej, and no one shall be allowed to cross the Indus without the Maharajah's permission.

"4. Regarding Shikarpur and the territory of Sindh, lying on the right bank of the Indus, the Shah will agree to abide by whatever may be settled as right and proper, in conformity with the happy relations of friendship subsisting with the Maharajah through Sir C. Wade.

"5. When the Shah shall have established his authority in Kabul and Qandhar, he will annually send the Maharajah the following articles, viz. fifty-five high-bred horses, of approved colour and pleasant paces, eleven Persian scymitars, seven Persian poniards, twenty-five good mules, fruits of various kinds, both dry and fresh, and Sirdas or musk melons, of a sweet and delicate flavour (to be sent throughout the year), by way of Kabul river and Peshavar; grapes, pomegranates, apples, almonds, raisins, pistahs or chesnuts, an abundant supply of each; as well as a piece of satin of every colour; choghas of fir, kim khabs wrought with gold and silver, and Persian carpet, altogether to the number of one hundred and one pieces; all these articles the Shah will continue to send to the Maharajah every year.

"6. Each party shall address the other on terms of equality.

"7. Merchants of Afghanistan who may be desirous of trading to Lahaur, Amratsar, or any other parts of the Maharajah's possessions, shall not be stopped or molested on their way; on the contrary, strict orders shall be issued to facilitate their intercourse, and the Maharajah engages to observe the same line of conduct on his part with respect to Afghanistan.

"8. The Maharajah will yearly send to the Shah the following articles, in the way of friendship—fifty-five pieces of shawls, twenty-five pieces of muslin, eleven dupatahs, five pieces of kim khab, five scarfs, five turbans, fifty-five loads of barah rice (peculiar to Peshavar).

"9. Any of the Maharajah's officers who may be deputed to Afghanistan to purchase horses, or on any other business, as well as those who may be sent by the Shah into the Panjab for the purpose of purchasing piece goods or shawls, &c. to the amount of eleven thousand rupees, will be treated by both sides with due attention, and every facility will be afforded to them in the execution of their commissions.

"10. Whenever the armies of the two states may happen to be assembled at the same place, on no account shall the slaughter of kine be permitted to take place.

"11. In the event of the Shah receiving an auxiliary force from the Maharajah, whatever booty may be acquired from the Barakzais in jewels, horses, arms great and small, shall be equally divided between the two contracting parties. If the Shah should succeed in obtaining possession of such property without the assistance of the Maharajah's troops, the Shah agrees to send a portion of it to the Maharajah by way of friendship.

"12. An exchange of missions charged with letters and presents shall constantly take place between the two parties.

"13. Should the Maharajah require the aid of any of the Shah's troops, in furtherance of the objects contemplated by this Treaty, the Shah engages to send a force, commanded by one of his principal officers. In like manner the Maharajah will furnish the Shah, when required, with an auxiliary force, composed of Mahomedans, and commanded by one of his principal officers, as far as Kabul, in furtherance of the objects contemplated by this Treaty. When the Maharajah may go to Peshavar the Shah will depute a Shahzada to visit him, on which occasion the Maharajah will receive and dismiss him with the honour and consideration due to his rank and dignity.

"14. The friends and enemies of each of the three high powers, that is to say, the British and Sikh Governments and that of Shuja-ul-Mulk, shall be the friends and enemies to all and to each of them.

"15. Shah Shuja-ul-Mulk engages, after the attainment of his object, to pay without fail to the Maharajah the sum of two lakhs of rupees, of the Nanak, Shahv, or Kaldar currency, calculating from the date on which the Sikh troops may be despatched for the purpose of reinstating His Majesty in Kabul, in consideration of the Maharajah stationing a force of not less than five thousand men, cavalry and infantry, of the Mahomedan persuasion, within the limits of the Peshavar territory, for the support of the Shah, and to be sent to the aid of His Majesty whenever the British Government, in concert and counsel with the Maharajah, shall deem their aid necessary; and when any matter of great importance may arise in the westward, such measures will be adopted with regard to it as may seem expedient and proper at the time to the British and Sikh Governments. In the event of the Maharajah requiring the aid of any of the Shah's troops, a deduction will be made in the subsidy, proportioned to the period for which such aid may be afforded; and the British Government holds itself responsible for the punctual payment of the above sum annually to the Maharajah so long as the provisions of this Treaty are duly observed.

"16. Shah Shuja-ul-Mulk agrees to relinquish, for himself, his heirs, and successors, all claims of supremacy and arrears of tribute over the territories now held by the Mirs of Sindh (which will continue to belong to the Mirs and their successors in perpetuity), on condition of the payment to him by the Mirs of such a sum as may be determined, under the mediation of the British Government, one million five hundred thousand of rupees, and of such payment being made over by him to the Maharajah Ranjit Singh on these payments being completed. Article 4, of 12th March, 1833, will be considered cancelled, and the customary interchange of letters and suitable presents between the Maharajah and the Mirs of Sindh shall be maintained as heretofore.

"17. When Shah Shuja-ul-Mulk shall have succeeded in establishing his authority in Afghanistan, he shall not attack nor molest his nephew the ruler of Hirat, in the possession of the territories subject to his government.

"18. Shah Shuja-ul-Mulk binds himself, his heirs, and successors, to refrain from entering into negotiations with any foreign state without the knowledge and consent of the British and Sikh Governments, and to oppose any power having the desire to invade the Sikh or British territories by force of arms, to the utmost of his ability.

"The three powers, parties in this Treaty, viz. the British Government, the Maharajah Ranjit Singh, and Shah Shuja-ul-Mulk, cordially agree to the foregoing articles. There shall be no deviation from them in any way whatever, and in that case the present Treaty shall be considered binding for ever, and this Treaty shall come into operation from and after the date on which the seals and signatures of the three contracting parties shall have been affixed.

"Done at Lahaur, this 26th day of June, in the year of our Lord 1838, corresponding with the 15th of the mouth of Asarh, 1895, æra Bikarmajit.

(Signed) "AUCKLAND,
"RANJIT SINGH,
"SHAH SHUJAH-UL-MULK."

While the Governor-General was ratifying the above-mentioned treaty with the Maharajah, and with Qazi Mohammed Husain, on the part of Shah Shuja-ul-Mulk, and was framing the plan of the projected expedition, the arrival of advices from England, "characterized doubtless by Lord Palmerston's usual vigour,* led to the renewed considera-

* I forgot to mention in the preceding and proper place, when I was invited by the minister of the Amir of Kabul, in the presence of M. Vikovich, the conversation turned on the composition, taste, and love of poetry. The Russian agent said to the minister that Europeans consider the taste for poetry a sign of lazy habits, but the scientific inventions productive of wealth; and the tact of the principal leaders of the politics of the states are the national amusement and talk of the day. The Mirza replied that if that was the case, no nation in Europe can boast of excelling in science more than the English; and their successful career in India, China, and Barmis says much for the excellence of their politics. Here M. Vikovich hesitatingly replied that Russia has now roused from slumber, and her mi-

QUAZI MAHOMED HUSSAN KHAN

tion of the plan for establishing a British influence at Kabul, by the restoration of Shah Shuja," strengthened and confirmed the determination of the Earl of Auckland, and thus the expedition of Afghanistan was resolved on.

On the return of Sir William Macnaghten from the Court of Lahaur, preparations were made to put the contemplated schemes of policy into immediate execution, and the declaration of war was proclaimed and circulated in all parts of India and Afghanistan.

Declaration on the part of the Right Honourable the Governor-General of India.

Simla, 1*st October*, 1838.

"The Right Honourable the Governor-General of India having, with the concurrence of the Supreme Council, directed the assemblage of a British force for service across the Indus, his Lordship deems it proper to publish the

---

nister Count Nesselrode is considered at the present age to be matchless in politics, and would shake the whole of Europe if there was not one rival for him, "Vazir i daval i Kharajah Inglisyah (the English minister for the foreign affairs), Lord Palmerston." He also added that Louis Philippe, King of the French, is the wisest sovereign, but fears Count Nesselrode, who has not yet acknowledged him as King of that nation.

following exposition of the reasons which have led to this important measure.

"It is a matter of notoriety that the treaties entered into by the British government in the year 1832 with the Mirs of Sindh, the Navab of Bahavalpur, and the Maharajah Ranjit Singh, had for their object, by opening the navigation of the Indus, to facilitate the extension of commerce, and to gain for the British nation in Central Asia that legitimate influence which an interchange of benefits would naturally produce.

"With a view to invite the aid of the *de facto* rulers of Afghanistan in the measures necessary for giving full effect to those treaties, Sir Alexander Burnes was deputed, towards the close of the year 1836, on a mission to Dost Mohammed Khan, the chief of Kabul. The original subjects of that officer's mission were purely of a commercial nature. Whilst Sir Alexander Burnes, however, was on his journey to Kabul, information was received by the Governor-General that the troops of Dost Mohammed Khan had made a sudden and unprovoked attack on those of our ancient ally the Maharajah Ranjit Singh. It was naturally to be apprehended that His Highness the Maharajah would not be slow to avenge the aggression; and it was to be feared that the flames of war being once kindled in the very regions into which we were endeavouring to extend our commerce, the peaceful and beneficial purposes of the British government would be altogether frustrated. In order to avert a result so calamitous, the Governor

General resolved on authorising Sir Alexander Burnes to intimate to Dost Mohammed Khan that if he should evince a disposition to come to just and reasonable terms with the Maharajah, his Lordship would exert his good offices with his Highness for the restoration of an amicable understanding between the two powers. The Maharajah, with the characteristic confidence which he had uniformly placed in the faith and friendship of the British, at once assented to the proposition of the Governor-General, to the effect that, in the meantime, hostilities on his part should be suspended.

"It subsequently came to the knowledge of the Governor-General that a Persian army was besieging Hirat; that intrigues were actively prosecuted throughout Afghanistan, for the purpose of extending Persian influence and authority to the banks of, and even beyond, the Indus; and that the court of Persia had not only commenced a course of injury and insult to the officers of Her Majesty's mission in the Persian territory, but had afforded evidence of being engaged in designs wholly at variance with the principles and objects of its alliance with Great Britain.

"After much time spent by Sir A. Burnes in fruitless negotiation at Kabul, it appeared that Dost Mohammed Khan, chiefly in consequence of his reliance upon Persian encouragement and assistance, persisted, as respected his misunderstanding with the Sikhs, in urging the most unreasonable pretensions, such as the Governor-General could not, consistently with justice and his regard for the friendship of Maharajah Ranjit Singh, be the channel of submitting to the consideration of his Highness; that he avowed schemes of aggrandizement and ambition injurious to the security and peace of the frontiers of India; and that he openly threatened, in furtherance of those schemes, to call in every foreign aid which he could command. Ultimately, he gave his undisguised support to the Persian designs in Afghanistan, of the unfriendly and injurious character of which, as concerned the British character in India, he was well apprized, and by his utter disregard of the views and interests of the British government, compelled Sir A. Burnes to leave Kabul without having effected any of the objects of his mission.

"It was now evident that no further interference could be exercised by the British government to bring about a good understanding between the Sikh ruler and Dost Mohammed Khan, and the hostile policy of the latter chief showed too plainly that, so long as Kabul remained under his government, we could never hope that tranquillity of our neighbourhood would be secured, or that the interests of our Indian empire would be preserved inviolate.

"The Governor-General deems it in this place necessary to revert to the siege of Hirat and the conduct of the Persian nation. The siege of that city has now been carried on by the Persian army for many months. The attack upon it was an unjustifiable and cruel aggression, perpetrated and continued notwithstanding the solemn and repeated remonstrances of the English envoy at the court of Persia, and after every just and becoming offer had been made and rejected. The besieged have behaved with a gallantry and fortitude worthy of the justice of their cause; and the Governor-General would yet indulge the hope that their heroism may enable them to maintain a successful defence until succours shall reach them from British India. In the meantime the ulterior designs of Persia, affecting the interests of the British government, have been, by a succession of events, more and more openly manifested. The Governor-General has recently ascertained by an official despatch from Sir J. Macneil, Her Majesty's envoy, that His Excellency has been compelled, by a refusal of his just demands, by a systematic course of disrespect adopted towards him by the Persian government, to quit the court of the Shah, and to make a public declaration of the cessation of all intercourse between the two governments. The necessity under which Great Britain is placed of regarding the present advance of the Persian army into Afghanistan as an act of hostility towards herself, has also been officially communicated to the Shah, under the express of Her Majesty's Government.

"The chiefs of Qandhar (brothers of Dost Mohammed Khan of Kabul) have avowed their adherence to the Persian policy, with the same full knowledge of its opposition to the rights and interests of the British nation in India, and have been openly assisting in the operations against Hirat.

"In the crisis of affairs consequent upon the retirement of our envoy from Kabul, the Governor-General felt the importance of taking immediate measures for arresting the rapid progress of foreign intrigue and aggression towards our territories.

"His attention was naturally drawn at this conjuncture to the position and claims of Shah Shuja-ul-Mulk, a monarch who, when in power, had cordially acceded to the measures of united resistance to external enmity, which were at that time judged necessary by the British government, and who, on his empire being usurped by its present rulers, had found an honourable asylum in the British dominions.

"It had been clearly ascertained, from the information furnished by the various officers who have visited Afghanistan, that the Barakzai chiefs, from their disunion and unpopularity, are ill-fitted, under any circumstances, to be useful allies to the British government, and to aid us in our just and necessary measures of national defence. Yet so long as they refrained from proceedings injurious to our interests and security, the British Government acknowledged and respected their authority; but a different policy appeared to be now more than justified by the conduct of those chiefs, and to be indispensable to our own safety. The welfare of our possessions in the East requires that we should have on our western frontier an ally who is interested in resisting aggression and establishing tranquillity, in the place of chiefs ranging themselves in subservience to a hostile power, and seeking to promote schemes of conquest and aggrandizement.

"After serious and mature deliberation, the Governor-

General was satisfied that a pressing necessity, as well as every consideration of policy and justice, warranted us in espousing the cause of Shah Shuja-ul-Mulk, whose popularity throughout Afghanistan had been proved to his Lordship by the strong and unanimous testimony of the best authorities. Having arrived at this determination, the Governor-General was further of opinion that it was just and proper no less from the position of Maharajah Ranjit Singh, than from his undeviating friendship towards the British Government, that his Highness should have the offer of becoming a party to the contemplated operations.

"Sir William H. Macnaghten was accordingly deputed in June last to the court of his Highness, and the result of his mission has been the conclusion of a tripartite treaty by the British Government, the Maharajah, and Shah Shuja-ul-Mulk, whereby his Highness is guaranteed in his present possessions, and has bound himself to co-operate for the restoration of the Shah to the throne of his ancestors. The friends and enemies of any one of the contracting parties have been declared to be the friends and enemies of all.

"Various points had been adjusted which had been the subjects of discussion between the British Government and his Highness the Maharajah, the identity of whose interests with those of the Honourable Company has now been made apparent to all the surrounding states. A guaranteed independence will, upon favourable conditions, be tendered to the Mirs of Sindh, and the integrity of Hirat, in the possession of its present ruler, will be fully respected; while by the measures completed or in progress, it may reasonably be hoped that the general freedom and security of commerce will be promoted; that the name and just influence of the British government will gain their proper footing among the nations of Central Asia; that tranquillity will be established upon the most important frontier of India; and that a lasting barrier will be raised against hostile intrigue and encroachment.

"His Majesty Shah Shuja-ul-Mulk will enter Afghanistan, surrounded by his own troops, and will be supported against foreign interference and factious opposition by a British army. The Governor-General confidently hopes that the Shah will be speedily replaced on the throne by his own subjects and adherents; and when once he shall be secured in power, and the independence and integrity of Afghanistan established, the British army will be withdrawn. The Governor-General has been led to these measures by the duty which is imposed on him of providing for the security of the possessions of the British crown; but he rejoices that, in the discharge of his duty, he will be enabled to assist in restoring the union and prosperity of the Afghan people. Throughout the approaching operations, British influence will be sedulously employed to further every measure of general benefit, to reconcile differences, to secure oblivion of injuries, and to put an end to the distractions by which, for so many years, the welfare and happiness of the Afghans have been impaired. Even to the chiefs, whose hostile proceedings have given just cause of offence to the British Government, it will seek to secure liberal and honourable treatment, on their tendering early submission, and ceasing from opposition to that course of measures which may be judged the most suitable for the general advantage of their country.

"By order of the Right Honourable the Governor-General of India.

(Signed) "W. H. MACNAGHTEN,

"*Secretary to the Government of India,*

"*with the Governor-General.*"

Immediately after this a few men of war were ordered through the Bombay government to land troops in the Persian island named Kharak; and having taken possession of the place, waited there for further advice. It was also suggested that a large number of British forces should be collected at Firozpur, and proceeding thence in company with the Shah Shuja, should march upon Kabul, passing through Sindh, the Bolan Pass, Qandhar, and Ghazni; and that the Shah Zadah Taimur, with the Sikh contingent, should shape his course within the Panjab, so as to divert the attention of the Kabul chief from the Khaibar side. The rendezvous of the troops, now nominated the army of the Indus, was appointed to be at Firozpur, where the Governor-General had an interview with the Maharajah Ranjit Singh.

Let us turn back to the affairs in Persia. Sir John Macneil, who was compelled to leave the Persian camp, and who was on his way back to the Turkish frontier, was now apprised of the arrival of the man of war, and wrote immediately to Colonel Stoddart, still in the Persian camp, to inform the Shah of the proceedings undertaken by the British government, and if his Majesty were not to relinquish the siege of Hirat, the army now landed in the island of Kharak will be directed to march through Persia. The gallant colonel submitted the following proposal to the Shah, which perplexed and brought His Majesty to his senses, and the bugle of retreat was sounded, and the siege of Hirat raised.

"I AM directed by Her Britannic Majesty's Minister Plenipotentiary to state that he has been entrusted by Her Majesty's Ministers to inform your Majesty that the British Government look upon this enterprise in which your Majesty is engaged against the Afghans as being undertaken in a spirit of hostility towards British India, and as being totally incompatible with the spirit and intention of the alliance which has been established between Great Britain and Persia. That consequently, if this project is persevered in, the friendly relations which up to this time have so happily subsisted between Great Britain and Persia must necessarily cease, and that Great Britain must take such steps as she may think best calculated to provide for the security of the possessions of the British crown.

"I am further directed to inform your Majesty, that if Hirat should have surrendered to your Majesty, the British Government will consider your Majesty's continuing to occupy that, or any other portion of Afghanistan, as a hostile demonstration against England.

"Her Majesty's Minister Plenipotentiary anxiously hopes that, by speedily withdrawing the Persian army into your Majesty's own dominions, your Majesty will avert the inevitable consequences of persevering in a course of hostility to England.

"The British government also demands reparation for the violence offered to its messenger, which is a matter quite distinct from the question of Hirat. Her Britannic Majesty's Minister Plenipotentiary trusts your Majesty will grant that reparation in the manner which he pointed out, and thus relieve the British Government from the necessity of having recourse to other measures to exact it.

"Your Majesty is no doubt informed by the government of Fars that a body of British troops, and a naval armament consisting of five ships of war, have already arrived in the Persian Gulf, and that for the present the troops have landed on the island of Kharak. The measures your Majesty may adopt in consequence of this representation will decide the future movements and proceedings of that armament; but your Majesty must perceive, from the view which Her Majesty's Government has taken of the present state of affairs, and from the effect which must have been produced in the minds of Her Majesty's Ministers and the British authorities in India by the subsequent proceedings of the Persian Government, with which they were not then acquainted, that nothing but the immediate adoption of measures to comply with the demands of the British Government can induce the authorities acting under the order of that Government to suspend the measures which are in progress for the defence of British interests, and the vindication of British honour.

"In the meantime Her Britannic Majesty's Minister Plenipotentiary will pursue his journey to the Turkish frontier, and will remove all the English from the Persian territory; but he trusts that the bad counsel of the ill-disposed persons who have induced your Majesty to persevere in a course which has placed affairs in this position will no longer influence your Majesty; and that, guided by your own wisdom and by a regard to the true interests of Persia, your Majesty will adopt such measures as will enable Her Britannic Majesty's Minister Plenipotentiary to return to your Majesty's Court, and restore to its former footing of cordiality the alliance between the two governments. Your Majesty has seen that all Her Britannic Majesty's Minister Plenipotentiary has stated to your Majesty in regard to these matters, has been dictated by sincerity and truth, and by an anxious desire to avert the evils which it was obvious must result from a perseverance in the course which the Persian Government was pursuing; and he again assures your Majesty that nothing but immediate danger and injury to Persia can result from rejecting the demands of the British Government.

"That God may guide your Majesty to a wise decision, and that he may forgive those whose evil counsels have led to such a state of things, is the earnest prayer of an old and faithful servant, who has ever been a sincere well-wisher of the Shah and the Persian Government."

Many people, who pretended to be well informed in the affairs of Afghanistan, said, on the arrival of the dispatch of Colonel Stoddart, stating that the Persians had raised the siege of Hirat, that now there was no necessity any longer for the government of India to persevere in crossing the English army beyond the Indus into those distant regions. This circumstance, indeed, altered the disposition of the campaign in respect to the number of the troops, but it did not change the measures of the Governor-General; and in a political point of view his Lordship justly felt it incumbent upon himself to remember that there were many reasons in existence of great weight and importance which require the completion of his contemplated objects.

Firstly: Though the Persians had raised the siege of Hirat on the 9th of September, 1838, yet the forts and districts of Ghuryan, Kurukh, Sabzvar, and Farah, at two marches beyond the boundary of Qandhar, were still occupied by the Persian authorities; and from the following letters it will appear that the British officer at the court of Persia was urging upon the Persian government to give up the possession of those places to the Afghans, and that on the 29th of November, 1838, he had not succeeded in his negotiation; and I may safely state that the fort and district of Ghuryan were not restored by the Persians to the Hirat government till more than a year after the British had occupied Afghanistan, or long after the departure and failure of the mission of Major Todd from Hirat.

From Lieutenant-Colonel Sheil to His Excellency Mirza Masud, the Minister for Foreign Affairs.

Tehran, Nov. 22, 1838.

"In the communication which Colonel Stoddart conveyed to His Majesty the Shah, from his Excellency the British minister, subsequent to his departure from the Royal camp, his Excellency Sir John Macneil announced to His Majesty that if His Majesty should retain any portion of the Afghan territory, the British government will consider such a proceeding as a hostile proceeding against itself. Her Britannic Majesty's envoy extraordinary has now learnt that the troops which occupied Ghuryan, and also those which took possession of Farah, Sabzvar, and Khurrukh, in the name of the Shah of Persia, continue to hold those places in the name of His Persian Majesty.

"Agreeably to the instructions I have received from Sir John Macneil, I have the honour to request that your Excellency will furnish me with information on this subject, and I request you to state whether or not the troops which have occupied Ghuryan, Farrah, Sabzvar, and Khurrukh, hold these places for the Shah of Persia, or are subject to His Majesty's orders."

Tehran, Nov. 29, 1838.

"I HAVE the honour to acknowledge the receipt of your Excellency's letter of the 10th Ramadan (28th November), in reply to the communication which I addressed to you regarding the continued occupation by the Persian government of Ghuryan, Farah, Sabzvar, and Khurrukh.

"Your Excellency having given no reply sufficient to convey the information I sought, whether the above places were garrisoned by Persian troops, or were held by troops in the name of His Persian Majesty, I am obliged to conclude from your silence that the intelligence which had been received by His Excellency Sir John Macneil, on this subject, is correct, and that the above places are held by troops in the name of His Majesty the Shah, and are under His Majesty's orders.

"I am instructed by Her Britannic Majesty's minister plenipotentiary to intimate to His Persian Majesty's ministers, that he feels it to be his duty to protest against the continued occupation of Ghuryan by Persian troops being regarded as constituting any right on the part of Persia to retain permanent possession of that fortress or district.

"With regard to Farah, Sabzvar, and Khurrukh, I am directed by his Excellency Sir John Macneil to call on the Persian government to fulfil the engagement into which His Majesty the Shah entered at Hirat, of complying with the whole of the demands of the British government, and to issue the necessary orders for immediate evacuation of these places, furnishing me at the same time with an authentic copy of that order, for the information of the British government."

Secondly: If the army had not moved, the occupation of those places would not, in consequence of any negotiation, be abandoned by the Persians; and if they were allowed to keep it, the results were apparent, and are well described in a letter from Sir John Macneil to Lord Palmerston.

"If the Shah should effect the subjugation of any portion of Afghanistan, he will employ the influence of the chiefs who may have submitted to him to disturb the power and the quiet of those who have not; and when he has been elated with success, and has secured a footing in that country, from which it may be difficult to drive him, I fear that apprehension of a rupture with England would no longer deter him from prosecuting his conquests; and though he might hesitate to seek foreign aid for the purpose of getting possession of Hirat, he might not improbably be induced to have recourse to it for the purpose of enabling him to retain a conquest which he had already made."

Thirdly: M. Vikovich was even then distributing money to the chiefs of Qandhar, who, in adherence to the treaty concluded between them and Persia, and guaranteed by the Count Simonich, were acting inimically towards Hirat under the influence of the personal presence and guidance of Captain Vikovich.

Fourthly: If the Governor-General were to leave the chiefs of Qandhar and the Amir of Kabul to pursue their own plans, the result would be that Persian agents, superintended and directed by Russian officers, would be placed in the court of the above chieftains; and intrigues would have been conducted and extended by them even to the very heart of India; for branch missions of the united states of Persia and Russia had already been passing through Sindh, &c.

Fifthly: By the Tripartite treaty, which was already ratified, the British government and the Lahaur Court were bound to replace Shah Shuja, who at the time was earnestly sought by the Afghans, and in whose person the English found the means of holding a friendly relation with the kingdom of Afghanistan.

Under all the preceding grave and urgent considerations the Governor-General ordered the march of the army of the Indus; and it left Ferozpor on the 10th of December, 1838. The whole number of the force available for employment in the Afghanistan expedition, according to Major Hough's account, was as follows:—

	Men.
1st. The army of the Indus (from Bengal) under Major-General Sir Willoughby Cotton .	9,500
2nd. Major-General Duncan's reserve division, at Ferozpor, &c.	4,250
3rd. Shah Shuja's contingent	6,000
4th. The Bombay force under His Excellency Lieutenant-General Sir John (afterwards Lord) Keane	5,600

	Men.
5th. The Bombay reserve or Sindh force . . .	3,000
Total number to act in Sindh and Afghanistan	28,350

Previous to the opening of the campaign I was attached to the Mission, and the Governor-General, after a long conference with me on the various points connected with the progress of the army, and the advancement of the views of the government in Afghanistan, made me the bearer of his letters to the address of the bankers at Multan and to the Lohani merchants at Darahband, for the purpose of raising money, collecting supplies, and employing carriages for the use of the army. Sir Alexander Burnes was directed to go ahead of the army and negotiate an offensive and defensive treaty with the Mirs of Khairpur in the Upper Sindh; and Sir Henry Pottinger to form the same with the Mirs of Haidarabad in the Lower Sindh; while Major Mackison had to negotiate with the Navab of Bahavalpur, or the Daudpotra chief, to facilitate the progress of the army in his territory, and to supply Shah Shuja with certain equipage.

The bankers in Multan and the Lohanis in the

Derahbad were highly flattered with the contents of the letters from the Earl of Auckland. The former sent boats down the Chenab and the Indus, loaded with money and grain, to meet the wants of the army on its arrival at Shikarpur; and in addition to this they lent their personal assistance to Major Thompson and others, the commissariat officers who followed me into that city. The latter also collected a considerable number of camels, and brought provisions after the army to Qandhar.

The judicious proceedings and negotiations of Major Mackison with the Daudpotra chief gave ample comforts and easy means to get supplies to the army of the Indus; and I myself heard Sir Willoughby Cotton saying that every one in his camp seemed well satisfied while passing through the Bahavalpur territory.

As to the progress and results of the negotiations committed to Sir Alexander Burnes and to Sir Henry Pottinger in Sindh, I have only this remark to make in this place: that after a very short period of successful negotiations by those functionaries, and a short time of their absence from that country, the fate of that dominion has been finally doomed, and it is now connected to and joined with the British empire of India; wherefore I deem it desirable to reserve my saying on such grave subject, will put the whole matter briefly into one view in a separate chapter. It will prove amusing to the readers to find from what I have quoted, the highest and unquestionable authorities on this point, that how justly and how far back the Mirs of Sindh had discovered our ambitious designs for the conquest of their country; and how prudently they suspected our travellers and even myself, who went to examine their country; and how far they were right in their anticipations is now clearly understood, since we have become the masters of their country, and they are banished.

END OF VOL. I.

LIFE

OF THE

AMIR DOST MOHAMMED KHAN OF KABUL

LIFE

OF THE

AMIR DOST MOHAMMED KHAN OF KABUL

WITH HIS POLITICAL PROCEEDINGS TOWARDS THE ENGLISH, RUSSIAN, AND PERSIAN GOVERNMENTS

INCLUDING THE

VICTORY AND DISASTERS OF THE BRITISH ARMY

IN AFGHANISTAN

MOHAN LAL

IN TWO VOLUMES

VOL. II

WITH 8 ILLUSTRATIONS

Published by

Facsimile Publisher
12 Pragati Market
Ashok Vihar, Ph-2
Delhi-110052
facsimilepublisher.com

Distribution Network
gyanbooks.com
India, USA, Canada, UK, Australia, France

ISBN : 978-93-5324-437-8 (Set)
ISBN : 978-93-5324-439-2 Vol. 2 (HB)
First Published, London, 1846

2nd Impression 2020

Printed at: Gyan Press, Delhi.

LIfe of the Amir Dost Mohammed Khan of Kabul

Author: Mohan Lal

LIFE

OF THE

AMIR DOST MOHAMMED KHAN,

OF

KABUL:

WITH HIS POLITICAL PROCEEDINGS TOWARDS THE

ENGLISH, RUSSIAN, AND PERSIAN GOVERNMENTS,

INCLUDING THE

VICTORY AND DISASTERS OF THE BRITISH ARMY

IN

AFGHANISTAN.

By MOHAN LAL, Esq.,

KNIGHT OF THE PERSIAN ORDER OF THE LION AND SUN; LATELY ATTACHED TO THE MISSION IN KABUL.

IN TWO VOLUMES.

Vol. II.

LONDON:

LONGMAN, BROWN, GREEN, AND LONGMANS,

PATERNOSTER-ROW.

1846.

NOTICE.

The extracts which have unavoidably been briefly quoted in this Work, especially in the latter part of it, are meant neither in disrespect to the opinions of any authority whatever, nor to contradict or disprove the assertions of certain writers in Indian journals. That is the province of men of higher talents and abilities; nor are they meant as self-boasting by the Author. Far from it. They illustrate the pages merely as evidence to his statement, which otherwise might have been considered partial.

The Author.

CONTENTS OF VOL. II.

CHAPTER XIV.

CHAPTER XV.

CHAPTER XVI.

CHAPTER XVII.

CHAPTER XVIII.

ILLUSTRATIONS OF VOL. II.

LIFE

OF THE

AMIR DOST MOHAMMED KHAN

OF

KABUL.

CHAPTER XIV.

Affairs of Sindh—Geography—Political position—Mission to the Mirs—Difficulties attending its reception—It arrives at Tattah—Stay at that city—Negotiations—Departure—Captain Christie and Sir Henry Pottinger proceed in disguise through Sindh—Dr. James Burnes invited to Sindh—His testimony—Extracts from Sir John Malcolm—Mission of Sir Alexander Burnes—Various treaties—Further negotiations with the Mirs—Their harsh treatment by the British Government—Sir Charles Napier sent to Sindh—Continued oppression exercised towards the Mirs—the Bilochis revolt—Battle of Miani—The Mir of Mirpur is defeated—Capture of Omercote—Battle of Pir Assee—Victory gained by Col. Jacob—Conclusion of the history of Sindh.

THE country of Sindh is irrigated by the river Indus or Sindh, from which it takes its common appellation. On the north it is bounded by Kach Gandava, the Panjab, and the Daudpotra districts; and on the south side by the ocean. It has Rajvara on the east and Bilochistan on the west, making the area of the country about 100,000 square miles.* The revenue derived by the ex-Mirs of Sindh was from 3,500,000 rupees (35,000*l.*) to 4,000,000 rupees (40,000*l.*); and the expense in maintaining possession of that country is 8,000,000 rupees (80,000*l.*).†

When the successful career of Bonaparte had subverted the independence of many kingdoms in Europe, his thirst for the conquest of India, and the arrival of his mission on a large scale under General Gardanne at Tehran, excited great alarm in British India, and the Supreme Government deputed various missions in various directions to frustrate the designs of Napoleon. The Honourable Mountstuart Elphinstone, as already mentioned, went to the Durrani Court, Sir John Malcolm to the capital of Persia, and Nicholas Hankey Smith, Esq., of the Bombay Civil Service, was appointed as an envoy by the Governor-General of India to negotiate for and to secure the alliance of the Mirs of Sindh. Both the

* Visit to the Court of Sindh, by Dr. Burnes, K.H.

† Also in 1845 the expense has much exceeded the income. See Captain Postans's Observations on Sindh.

former kingdoms still retain their independence, but the latter dominion has fallen into our possession; and its rulers, who once possessed independence, and were soothed and courted by English ambassadors, and feared, flattered, and adored by European travellers, who explored their country in disguise, are now the prisoners of our Indian government!

In the number of the European gentlemen who composed the mission of Mr. Smith to the court of Sindh, I will only mention the name of Sir Henry Pottinger (then Lieut.), whose knowledge of that country became a guide to the ambition of others, and whose talents and judgment in all his diplomatic career, whether in Kach, in Sindh, or in China, have merited an extraordinary and yet just degree of estimation, and which are rewarded with the unanimous applause of all parties of the English nation at large. The departure of this officer brought the misfortune and sealed the fate of the Mirs of Sindh; and knowing as I do his just and noble principles, no one feels so bitterly distressed at the fall of the Mirs as he feels.

On the 27th of April, 1809, the mission, consisting of Mr. Smith and Sir Henry Pottinger, the former being the chief, embarked on board their ships to sail from Bombay, and on the 9th of May, at noon, they approached the harbour of Karachi, the Governor of which place was requested to supply pilots. Here I shall quote the Right Honourable Baronet himself,* and, in short, follow his steps until the valuable publication of "Napier's Conquest of Sindh."

"The Governor made some demur regarding the admission of the ships into the harbour, but his objections were overruled. About an hour after they had anchored, the Governor came on board to visit Mr. Smith, attended by several matchlockmen, and brought some sheep and vegetables as a present. The two succeeding days were lost in discussions respecting the disembarkation of the mission, which the Governor was anxious to delay until he should receive instructions from the Mirs. On the 12th he visited Mr. Smith a second time, when the latter took occasion to reprehend some improper assumptions in the correspondence that had taken place relative to the titles and rank of the Governor-General and the Mirs: at which he professed his regret, and said it arose from his ignorance of the

* Pottinger's Bilochistan. Mission to Sindh, p. 332.

Persian language; but that he was willing either to put the person who had written them to death, or to blind him, as the envoy chose. He was of course requested not to proceed to such violent measures, but to give orders for greater circumspection in future. The Governor seemed under great alarm throughout this visit, and, after his boat was alongside, hesitated whether he would come on board or not. On the 13th and 14th of May the tents and public stores of the mission were landed, and the former pitched on a spot pointed out by the Governor. Several of the gentlemen had gone on shore and learned that great consternation had been excited by our arrival; that orders had been issued not to let any of our people enter the fort of Karachi, and that a large body of troops, under one of their most distinguished Sardars, had encamped within eight miles of the place, with the evident intention of watching our motions; indeed, the whole of the Governor's conduct had evinced a medley of terror and dissimulation, and a jealousy of our acquiring the slightest information which could not have been exceeded had we come with declared hostile intentions. On the 16th of May the Envoy disembarked under salutes of fifteen guns from the two ships, and was received on the beach by the escort and gentlemen of the mission, amidst the acclamations of a vast concourse of natives, to whom money was distributed according to the Oriental custom. In the afternoon the Navab sent a man to intimate his intention of paying his respects to the Envoy; but as the order for debarring our servants from ingress to the fort was still in force, he was informed he would not be received. Mr. Ellis went to the Governor to explain the cause of this refusal, and had an interview with him at a house outside the walls. The Navab wished us to believe that a similar prohibition extended to all strangers: he said that he was very sorry it should give such offence; but whether Mr. Smith saw him or not, he would daily attend at his encampment; that he had his orders from the Mirs, his masters, and must obey them; and that when a Mihmandar* was sent from Haidarabad to conduct the mission to court, we should be convinced of the necessity of his non-compliance. A few days after a letter was received from the Mirs, acquainting the Envoy with their determination to depute two offi-

* Mihmandar, from Mihman, a guest and dar-a-keeper. He is a person appointed to conduct envoys, and see that they are supplied with the productions of the country. Usually his powers are very much abused, by making them a cloak for extortion.

cers of Government to treat with him at Karachi, and that he was to accept all they said as strictly official; but as the style of their language was in that strain of arrogance and superiority which it was so much the object of the mission* to check in its infancy, the letter was returned, accompanied by a light communication, acquainting the Mirs that, as it contained not merely an unwarrantable assumption of rank on their behalf, but a want of due acknowledgment of that of the exalted government of which the Envoy was the representative, it was impossible its contents could be attended to in any form. Reports of various natures now daily reached us. At one hour it was confidently affirmed that the mission was to advance to the capital, escorted by a large body of Sindhian horse, and to be treated with every mark of attention; at another, that the Envoy would be called upon to negotiate with officers that were to be dispatched to him for that purpose; and, at a

* An envoy on the part of the Government of Bombay had been deputed to Sindh the preceding year, and treated in a manner that was not deemed at all warranted by the relative rank of the two nations. The envoy from the Governor-General had therefore the most pointed instructions to repress every attempt at a similar impropriety, and to be scrupulously exact in resenting any omission of that respect due to the British power in India, as well as any superiority claimed by the rulers of Sindh.

third, that we were to be forced by a body of troops, then reported to be on its march to Karachi, to re-embark on board the ships and sail for India. All of them corresponded in one great feature, which was, that the Mirs entertained the utmost apprehensions of our designs on their territories; and, in fact, the hourly arrival of reinforcements for the garrison and defence of Karachi would have afforded sufficient evidence of this dread.

"Some days subsequent to the transmission of the letter to the Mirs, a friendly note reached the Envoy from Akhund Mohammed Baqa Khan, who had been at Bombay a few months before as an agent on behalf of the Sindhian government, announcing his being deputed to Mr. Smith, and his intention of making all possible haste to join him. The same messenger who brought this letter confirmed intelligence that we had obtained some time before of an army of three thousand men having been collected in the neighbourhood of the city of Tattah, and the probability of its moving towards us, in order, as we presumed, to enforce the Akhund's terms, which officer arrived at Karachi on the 23rd of May; and the following morning came to the British encampment, where he had a very long conference with the Envoy. He dwelt much on the fears that had been engendered in the minds of the Mirs by the presence of two armed ships in the harbour of Karachi; and concluded by avowing that their being dispatched to Bombay, or at least out of the Sindhian dominions, was a *sine quâ non* previous to the mission being allowed to move towards Haidarabad.

"Other subjects were also discussed of a political nature, and the consultation ended by a positive declaration of the envoy, that in preference to proceeding to the capital under the most trifling stipulation, he would go on board; and however great the risk might be of venturing to sea at that advanced season of the year,* sail for Calcutta, to lay the business before the Governor-General; that with regard to that part of the communication made by the Akhund, which relates to his powers to treat with the envoy, it was entirely out of the question, as the latter could only do so with the rulers of Sindh, to whom he was accredited. On the 26th May, the Governor sent a verbal message to the envoy, desiring he would issue orders for the ships

* The south-west monsoon had set in with great violence, and it was then blowing a tremendous gale.

to quit the harbour immediately; but he, as well as the Akhund, evaded, in the most artful manner, giving any written document to this effect. At length the former proposed to show any gentleman of the mission the official instructions he had received from the Mirs to enforce this demand; however, when Mr. Ellis and Captain Christie proceeded to the usual place of meeting, he declined to fulfil his proposal, on the grounds of not being authorised to do so by his masters. Under these perplexing circumstances, Mr. Smith came to the determination not to have any further official intercourse either with the Navab or the Akhund, but to write a letter to the Mirs, and to regulate his future measures in conformity with their answer. At the same time he announced his resolution to those officers, and requested that the latter of them would attend at the British encampment, in order that he might hear the proposed letter read, ere it was sent off to Haidarabad. He accordingly came, and, while it was preparing, a very long conversation took place, in which he laboured to convince the envoy that the mission had been received in the most friendly way; that the simple act of its being permitted to land, and to hoist the British flag, was decisive evidence of this assertion; 'for,' added he, 'if you had attempted to enter the port without leave, the guns of the fort would have sunk your vessels.' To this bravado it was replied, that had affairs come to that crisis it would have been seen whether English or Sindhian guns were best, and that the result was very obvious.

"The Akhund next adverted to the expressions which were complained of in the Mirs' correspondence, and endeavoured to prove that they were according to the idiom of the Persian language, as used in Sindh; he swore repeatedly that 'Mulazimat' (services) meant a friendly meeting; that 'Mavddat' (friendship) was highly disrespectful as used in the envoy's letters; and that 'Huzur' (the royal presence) had been the title of the Mirs for twenty years, and could not be altered without putting every man in Sindh to death. Mr. Smith reminded him that it was absurd to expect that he should be acquainted with the peculiar idiom of Sindh, or adopt it, even admitting he were so; that he used the two first words pointed out, and all other, agreeably to their general acceptation; that 'Huzur' was only applicable to an independent sovereign, and not to a tributary government like that of Sindh. The Akhund here interrupted the envoy by saying that the tribute was of late years only nominal, and that he might attribute his not receiving answers to his former letters to the diction used in them. The letter about to be dispatched to the Mirs was then read aloud by one of the Munshis or Persian writers, and the Akhund made the same ridiculous objections to the use of various words inserted in it, after which he took leave.

"All the Sindhians who had entered the public service were this forenoon expelled, with their families, from their houses in the fort of Karachi, and one of them, who was bringing some provisions for the use of the envoy's table, was seized and tied to a post in the centre of the Sindhian camp which now nearly encompassed our tents; but as we had Qanats* all round our encampment it did not inconvenience us. A remonstrance was instantly sent out by the Navab, who ordered the man to be released, and expressed his dissatisfaction at the act; but a few hours after his own people committed one of much

* Qanats are tent walls, made for the purpose of keeping tents private.

greater insolence, by beating the Lascars who were filling water for the consumption of the two ships' crews, and spilling all that was ready to be sent on board.

"In the evening the Akhund came to our encampment, accompanied by a person whom he introduced by the name of Musa Khan, informing the envoy that he was empowered to communicate the Mirs' desire that the ships should quit the harbour, and that the mission might afterwards advance to Haidarabad, with every honour and attention.

"We had been so narrowly watched since our arrival here, that it was quite unpleasant to venture beyond our camp limits; and matters began to assume so hostile an appearance from the increasing arrogance of the Navab, and the real or affected imbecility of Akhund Baqa Khan, that it was judged advisable to re-ship all the valuable part of the public property. Boats were consequently requested of the Governor, who avowed his positive determination not to permit a single article to be sent on board; and he effectually prevented any such precaution by denouncing the displeasure of the Mirs against whatever boatmen might dare to serve us. We were in reality now nothing better than prisoners at large, for the only communication we could have with the ships was by means of their boats, and every time that one of them came to the landing-place three or four armed men were placed near her to prevent things being put on board. We now also discovered that a guard was stationed at each corner of our encampment every night; which was so unequivocally meant to observe our proceedings, and consequently so undisguised an insult, that one of the Chobdars* was sent with a message to direct that they might not again come there under any circumstances: and this was attended with the proposed effect. The Hindus and other inhabitants of the town, who had been, at first, in the habit of occasionally visiting our encampment, had of late ceased to do so; and the Sindhians, who had been entertained in different capacities, were threatened with harsh treatment, unless they quitted our service.

"About a week after the transmission of the envoy's letter to the Mirs their reply was received, in which they entered into a prolix view of the

* Chobdar, a native mace-bearer; from *chob*, a mace, and *dar*, a bearer.

behaviour they had adopted towards the mission from the Bombay Government the antecedent year, contrasting it with the increased attention and respect which, as they wished to impress on Mr. Smith, had been observed with regard to the present one. The style of the letter was, however, highly domineering and imperious; and, among others, it contained an observation, that they knew not how to write to a person who had returned the Parvanah Huzur (royal mandate). They, however, revoked their orders respecting the dispatch of the ships,—a matter which they endeavoured to treat in the lightest manner, by inquiring of what importance it could be to them, though there were twenty British ships-of-war in the Karachi harbour?

"Political considerations induced the envoy to overlook, or at least to view in a secondary light, the exceptionable style of this communication, which was instantly returned; and as the question of any compromise of the dignity of the British Government was laid at rest by the rulers of Sindh having waved their stipulation on the subject of the vessels, he announced his determination to set out for Haidarabad in a few days."

On the 10th of June the mission quitted Karachi;

and after five marches arrived in the old and famous city of Tattah,* once the splendid capital of Sindh. A few days' stay in this place afforded a favourable opportunity for Sir Henry Pottinger to collect commercial and geographical information concerning this district; and the circumstances which took place during the space of his delay there will be better described in his own extracts.†

"Our stay at Tattah afforded us ample leisure to see every corner of it, and the surrounding district offered to the sportsmen of the party abundance of shooting at hares and partridges. We were not, however, exclusively indebted to these recreations for means to pass our time, as some acts of the officers of the Sindhian Government again called for all the firmness and address of the envoy to combat them, and had nearly led to the mission abruptly leaving the country. Shortly after we had taken up our residence at Tattah, a nobleman of high rank and station, of the name of Vali Mohammed Khan, came to that city on official business; and the very next morning sent a body of his troops, who made

* The Honourable East India Company had here a commercial Residency in Sindh for many years.

† Pottinger's Bilochistan, pp. 348-9.

prisoners of all the Sindhians that were employed by the mission.

"A second letter was received by the envoy from the Mirs while we were on the road, acquainting him that one of their jamptis, or state-boats, was about to be dispatched for the conveyance of himself and suite by water to Haidarabad; and that he might expect her in a few days. It had been previously decided that some plausible excuse should be fabricated to enable the gentlemen of the mission to separate here, in order to proceed to court by two routes, and thereby acquire the utmost geographical knowledge of the country possible under so jealous a government; and, therefore, so exactly the reverse was their proposal from being vexatious, that our plan was perfected by it, as the boat was found too small even to contain one half the mission; and Mr. Ellis, Captain Maxfield, and myself, were eventually accommodated on board of her, with some difficulty, while the envoy and the remainder of the officers proceeded by the land route.

"Mr. Ellis immediately waited on him by the envoy's directions, and reprobated in strong terms this unfriendly and unjustifiable measure. A very long conference ensued, in warm language, in the course of which the Khan asked who we (the English) were? and whether we fancied ourselves the lords of the land? He added that he would do as he chose with the subjects of Sindh; that he would flog them, cut their ears off, and put them to death; nay, that he would burn Tattah if he thought proper.

"The morning after the envoy reached Haidarabad the Mirs each sent a formal deputation out to our encampment, which was pitched on the bank of the Fuleli river, about one mile south-east of the fortress, to congratulate him on that event, and to inquire after his health; but as it was ascertained that none of the persons who brought these complimentary messages, and who were also charged with the delivery of many large trays of sweetmeats, were of higher rank than Khidmatgars,* it was not deemed

* Khidmatgars are personal servants, and we usually apply the term to every description of attendants at table. In Sindh the word appears to be more confined in its acceptation, and to signify inferior divans or stewards. They, however, wait on their masters, and perform several offices in the household. The Peish Khidmats of Persia are of the same class, and seemed to be employed on similar errands and duties.

consonant with the situation of affairs that Mr. Smith should receive them in person, and Mr. Ellis accordingly did so; at which arrangement they appeared considerably disappointed, though, when they found that they had a present notwithstanding, this feeling ceased, and they returned in perfect good humour. The Mirs did not, however, allow this alleged disrespect towards themselves to pass without a long expostulation, which was delivered by one of their divans, or managers, called Mushtaq Ram, who particularly enlarged on the policy of the envoy courting the favourable opinion of the Mirs by acts of pointed external respect, on which subject, he added, they were very tenacious. He likewise adverted, most opportunely, to its having been omitted by the envoy to make a return of complimentary inquiries for the Mirs, and was informed that that had not been neglected; but that the Munshi who was dispatched for that purpose had in vain endeavoured to gain entrance into the fort, and was actually obliged to wait outside until he sent a person back to Mr. Smith to ask what steps he should take towards delivering his messages; and that that gentleman had even waved ceremony so far as to direct he would do so to any of the officers of Government he should happen to meet with, in order that they might be conveyed to the Mirs through that channel.

"The divan was further reminded, that previous to the arrival of the envoy at the capital, Mr. Ellis found occasion, more than once, to have intercourse with the Mirs on official topics, and that the Munshi who was employed on those errands was invariably refused admission into the fort, and obliged to remain in the bazaar outside, until an answer was brought to him. It was therefore evident, if any unfriendly omission had occurred, that it originated on the side of the Sindhian Government; and it was equally obvious that the Mirs had no cause to feel any sort of chagrin at their Khidmatgars not being seen by any envoy, when they had declined to admit a Munshi, who was a person of much higher station and respectability, into their presence, even when charged with important verbal communications.

"A serious quarrel had nearly occurred between our people and the Sindhians, one of whom attempted to rush past a sentinel, and, on being prevented, struck him, and knocked off his cap. Exertions were made to seize the offender, but he effected his escape in the crowd; and the envoy's anxiety to obviate any similar occurrence, which might have led to the most fatal consequences, only for the forbearance displayed by the Sipahi, suggested the expedient of the sentries being posted inside the Qnats, which was accordingly resorted to.

"The second day after the envoy had got to Haidarabad, the ceremonials of his first audience at court were brought forward; when, as we had foreseen, the proposals made by the Mirs, through various people, induced a negotiation that delayed the final arrangements for nearly a week; and had once or twice led us to anticipate quitting Sindh without a personal interview of the rulers.

"It had been understood that the 'masnad,' or throne, was considerably elevated from the ground,* and the envoy therefore deemed it proper that he should have a chair to sit upon, and also that the three Mirs should rise on the entrance of the

* This mistake was immediately rectified, and the stipulation regarding the chair withdrawn, as it was ascertained that the Mirs sat upon a farsh, or quilted mattress, that did not raise them above two inches from the ground.

mission; while they, on the other hand, not only declined showing any outward mark of respect by standing up, but actually proposed that we should all be disarmed previous to coming into the hall of audience, grounding this unwarrantable proposition on a plea that proved it a still greater insult, of an attempt having once been made by two 'vakils' of the Jaipur Rajah to assassinate one of the Mirs at a public levee.

"The evening after the forms of our reception had been agreed upon we were introduced to the Mirs by Akhund Mohammed Baqa Khan, who came to the British encampment for the purpose of conducting us to court, and he severally announced the rank and station of the envoy and of the gentlemen of his suite.

"At last we got to the place where we were to dismount, and were there received by Vali Mohammed Khan and by several other officers of the highest rank, who preceded us to a large open platform, at the further end of which sat the three Mirs. The platform was spread with the richest Persian carpets, so that we here put off our shoes; and the moment the envoy made the first step to advance towards the princes, they all rose and stood upright until he reached his allotted place, which was distinguished from that of the remainder of the party by having an embroidered cloth laid over it.

"As soon as we had sat down a scene of confusion ensued, which it is difficult to describe, and could only be attributed to a distrust of our real designs; for the mass of attendants, matchlockmen, and swordsmen crowded into the place, and nearly overwhelmed us by their pressure. The foremost of them even placed their feet on the scabbards of our swords and on the skirts of our coats, which, from the manner in which we were sitting, lay along the carpet; but whether this was a preconcerted plan or the effect of chance it was impossible to guess. Subsequent interviews, however, incline me to lean to the former idea. The princes individually made polite inquiries for all our health. Indeed, nothing but compliments and expressions of politeness took place, as it was a mere audience of ceremony; and after we had been in the Darbar about half an hour, the eldest verbally signified their wish that we should retire, a hint that is given at all Indian levees by the introduction of 'pan supari'* and 'atr,' or oil of roses; but in Sindh they have no such custom, nor even the Persian one of Qalliyans and coffee.

"At this levee the Mirs were dressed still more superbly than when we first saw them; however, there was nothing so remarkable in the change of any part of their costume as to merit description. The eldest brother had some very long strings of beautiful pearls round his neck, and one in his hand, which he used as a rosary, the size of which I should have before regarded as perfectly incredible. One of the younger princes had a dagger in his sash, from the hilt of which was suspended a perfect emerald,—considerably larger than a pigeon's egg.

"Towards the close of this audience, the envoy retired with the Mirs, and had a private conference, when he explained to those princes the nature of the negotiations he was intrusted with by the Governor-General, and intimated his desire that they should nominate such officers of the government as they deemed qualified to conduct, on their behalf, the consideration of the various topics connected with his

* Pan is the leaf of the piper betel. The Supari is the fruit of the areca tree.

mission. To this proposal they gave their ready assent, and promised that their ministers should attend daily at the British encampment until all matters were finally arranged.

"The ministers fixed upon by the Mirs were Vali Mohammed Khan, Akhund Baqa Khan, and a Hindu called Mushtaq Ram,—all persons of acknowledged abilities, and high in the confidence of their masters; but it would be equally uninteresting and unprofitable here to enter into a prolix narrative of the progress of the negotiations which almost wholly engaged the attentions of the envoy during our further stay at Haidarabad. The very nature of them, although extremely delicate and perplexing, rendered the whole peculiarly devoid of interest; and as the rulers of Sindh had desisted from assuming the tone of imperious superiority that had guided their counsels on our first arrival in the country, the discussions thenceforward were purely of a political nature. It therefore is sufficient for me to add, that the result of them was in the highest degree satisfactory to the supreme British authority in India, and that the envoy received the merited approbation and thanks of his superiors for the firmness, dignity, and sound judgment he had evinced in fulfilling the orders with which he had been furnished. An envoy to the Governor-General was likewise appointed, to return with the mission, in order to receive the ratification of the treaty that was made then and there."

While the interviews and the negotiations between the Princes of Sindh and the English envoy were going on, Sir Henry Pottinger was engaged in collecting information as to what was necessary to be known. The objects of the mission were thus satisfactorily completed; and the British envoy, after appointing among them an Indian agent on the part of his government, quitted the court of Sindh on his way back to Bombay.

"Having had an audience of leave, we embarked on board three jamptis, or state barges, provided by the Mirs, on the morning of the 25th of August, the baggage being shipped into boats hired for the purpose, and dropped down the Fuleli, from Haidarabad, in a south-south-east direction, till we entered the mouth of the Guni."

At the time Sir John Malcolm was re-appointed on a mission to Persia, the government of India felt more anxiety than ever to make itself perfectly acquainted with the territory and resources bordering on Sindh, or the countries on the west of it. The information which was already gained, during the mission of Mr. Smith, appeared imperfect,—or in true words excited more curiosity than had existed before in the mind of the government. On this occasion Sir Henry Pottinger volunteered his services, together with Captain Charles Christie. This enterprising functionary, in order to facilitate the success of his mission, and the progress of his journey, did not only disguise himself, but also made himself known as the accredited agent of a rich Hindu,—a horse-dealer. On the 2nd of January, 1810, Sir Henry Pottinger and Captain Christie quitted Bombay; and on the 16th of that month they anchored at the harbour of Sonmiani. Here they thought proper to land in the darkness of night, so as to prevent the disclosure of their disguise; and on being introduced to the contractor of the Custom-house, Sir Henry Pottinger allowed them to say that he was in the service of Sundarji, the horse-dealer. Also at Bela, on the 26th of January, the Jam, or chief of the place, sent for one of the companions of Sir Henry

Pottinger, and pretended that he was anxious to show him civility and kindness, if the real character was known to him of that officer. It was, however, considered that the confession of his real character would be productive of serious trouble;—whereas the preservation of the disguise would facilitate the means of gaining information, and therefore the name of the horse-dealer was to be adopted as the safe passport for this bold traveller.

"Subsequent events, to dwell upon which would be entirely irrelevant to the subject of this narrative, induced the supreme government to recal Sir John Malcolm, and to postpone his mission until the latter end of the year 1809, when he arrived a second time at Bombay, on his way to the Persian capital. Captain Charles Christie, of the 5th regiment of Bombay Native Infantry, and I were then just returned from Sindh, whither we had accompanied the envoy on the part of the Governor-General, and on being made acquainted with the proposed plan, of exploring the regions between India and Persia, we volunteered to attempt the tour which is detailed in the following pages.*

* See Pottinger's Travels in Bilochistan.

"Our services having been accepted, and the authority of the government of Bombay obtained for their being thus appropriated, I was directed by General Malcolm to place myself under the orders of Captain Christie, who received his instructions from the General, and these instructions were of that indefinite tenor which the very nature of the service we were about to proceed upon demanded. They called our attention to such leading points as were most likely to merit the notice of government, and to meet the intentions of that enlightened policy that had sanctioned the original measure;—but at the same time they fully authorized us to select, with respect to our progress,—mode of travelling,—ultimate destination,—and, in fact, all minor points,—such a line of conduct as the circumstances we were placed in might render advisable, and were only peremptory in reminding us, that we were to regard our personal safety beyond every other consideration.

"It had been generally remarked that a very principal obstacle to the accomplishment of similar undertakings to that on which Captain Christie and myself were bent had originated at the very commencement of them, owing to the great difficulty attendant upon an advance from the sea-coast, where most Asiatics are known to be more suspicious of, and uncivil to European strangers, than at some distance inland; an arrangement, therefore, to effect our first outset from the port at which we might land, was considered of the last importance to us, and we were fortunate enough to succeed in making one, to which no possible objection could be discovered.

"A Hindu merchant of great respectability and wealth, called Sundarji Sevaji, who had been, for many years preceding, the contractor for supplying the government of Madras and of Bombay with horses, to mount the cavalry of those two Presidencies, offered (on being consulted as to the best mode for us to proceed) to furnish us with letters and bills,—accredited as his agents, and dispatched by him to Kelat, the capital of Bilochistan, to purchase horses, from which city he observed that we could follow such route as local knowledge might point out to us; and that even in the extreme case of being forced to fly, we could take a different road towards the sea-coast, from that which we travelled in going, and thereby secure, almost beyond a doubt, seeing a great portion of the country.

" The bills and letters for us were, therefore, prepared; and a Hindu Gumashtah, or agent of Sundarji named Pitambardas, was appointed to accompany us as far as Kelat for the purpose of giving a greater air of plausibility to our avowed characters. Captain Christie and myself also selected two Hindustani men, who were bound to secrecy by promises of large presents, and whose fidelity and honesty, in the result, proved most exemplary. We were also, each, furnished with a considerable sum of money in gold Venetians, intended to use as a dernier resort, in case of the utmost necessity. These we carried in belts, tied round our waists, underneath our clothes; and, in addition to this supply, Captain Christie was empowered to draw bills on the government of Bombay, in favour of Sundarji Sevaji, to any amount he might find necessary; so that nothing was omitted in our equipment which could enable us to surmount opposition, and extricate ourselves from difficulties or dangers. The month of December, 1810, elapsed in these preparations,— and I commenced my narrative from the day we quitted the Presidency of Bombay.

" Late in the evening of the 2nd of January, 1811,

Captain Christie and myself embarked on board a small native boat, in Bombay harbour, that had been hired for the purpose of conveying us to the port of Sonmiani, and we instantly got under way. At daylight, next morning, we found that our party, exclusive of the boatmen, consisted of two Hindustani servants, and a Gumashtah or agent of Sundarji, and his attendant,—besides several Afghan horse-dealers, on their return to their own country, to whom we had granted a passage, thinking such acquaintances might be useful on landing. We were introduced to them as Europeans in the service of Sundarji.

"In the forenoon of the 26th of January the Jam sent for our Hindu Tulsia, and after some desultory conversation, said to him, 'I am now going to speak to you on a subject which I have not hitherto hinted at, nor ever shall mention to any other person, not even to my own son. I do not think that the two Englishmen here are merchants:—it is neither my wish nor aim to inquire into their plans; but if they are officers, I ought, when they visited me, to have considered them as my equals, and to have treated them accordingly, I therefore request you will now inform me who they really are:—you may depend on the strictest secrecy, and if they belong to the British government it will give me additional pleasure to serve them.' The Hindu saw immediately into the drift of the Jam's curiosity, which he did not satisfy, but adhered to our original tale of being Sundarji's servants. The Jam next inquired what wages we had, and whether it would be possible to get, through our interest, two small guns or wall-pieces from Bombay. Tulsia replied he would mention the chief's wishes to us, and he then came away. We directed him to say that we could not venture to make any promises, but that on our return to India we would endeavour to have them sent."

On the 14th of July this brave and talented explorer of the regions quite unknown to the government of India in that period, came to Kashan, in Persia. The difficulties which he encountered, and the dangers he dared during his journey through Sindh and Bilochistan, bore a promising testimony to his worth, and gave hope of the career in which, at present, he has so successfully maintained his fame and honour. At Maraghah, south-west from

Tabriz, Sir Henry Pottinger joined Sir John Malcolm, after traversing a distance of two thousand four hundred and twelve miles, during the space of seven months ;—and on the 6th of January, 1811, he landed in Bombay after an absence of thirteen months.*

It would not much interest the readers to know the negotiations and correspondence which continued between our government and the Mirs of Sindh; let it therefore suffice to say, that on the 23rd of October, 1828, Dr. James Burnes, K.H., the surgeon to the Resident at Kach, was invited by the rulers of Sindh for medical advice. His reception was friendly, and his opinions on the political view of our government towards Sindh are remarkable. He was treated with the greatest kindness and respect on every stage, and in the places of note he was met by a nobleman deputed to him by the Mirs, till he was at length mounted on a horse and pompously conducted into the city. His reception by the rulers was gratifying, and expressive of the feelings of amity which they entertained towards the British government, and of their desire of cultivating its friendship, as well as of their sense of the dignified cha-

* See Pottinger's Travels in Bilochistan, pp. 245-6.

racter and high position which they enjoyed. He added that their names were worthy of their rank, and showed that good breeding which he seldom saw in an European character. The Mirs, after making inquiries after the health of the English King, and of the Governor of India, said that the present meeting will further strengthen the bonds of friendship between them and the British government. Here he also speaks of the value of the alliance which might be formed with that country.* "Ever since the final occupation of Kach by the British troops in 1819, our government has been brought into close connexion with Sindh, and attempts have been made on our part to cultivate an amicable intercourse with the Mirs. But these haughty and jealous chieftains, who, from the first, had perceived the extension of our empire in this direction with distrust and apprehension, uniformly maintained a cold and unfriendly attitude towards us. Treaties had been entered into, but without any feeling of cordiality on their part; no European officer was allowed to cross the frontier of Kach; and even an envoy, who had

* Visit to the Court of Sindh, by Dr. Burnes, K.H., pp. 1-3, 20-32, 33, 36-39.

proceeded from Bombay to Sindh, in 1820, on the invitation of their own minister, was coldly received at their court, and abused after he left it.

"It had been an object of policy to avoid a war with the Mirs; but the British government had, nevertheless, been forced on two occasions,—one so late as 1825,—to assemble large bodies of troops in Kach, to awe them into the maintenance of treaties, and to prevent them taking advantage of our being engaged in the Bhartpur and Barmis operations, in order to invade our territories, or those of our allies. It is scarcely to be doubted that the Court of Haidarabad gave protection and support to the Mianah plunderers who infested and devastated Kach in 1825; and, indeed, everything led to the impression, that it was the terror of our power alone which had prevented the Mirs from openly declaring war against us, and that they had no wish whatever to keep up friendly relations with us. Their distrust and jealousy were understood to extend equally to the government and to its European servants; and nothing appeared more improbable than that a British officer should be invited, on any pretence whatever, to visit Sindh.

"In this state of affairs considerable surprise was excited, when, on the 23rd October, 1828, a letter of the most friendly nature was received from the Mirs by the Resident in Kach, requesting that I should be permitted to proceed without delay to Haidarabad, on account of the alleged sickness of Mir Murad Ali Khan, one of the principal chiefs. As private reports did not represent the disease of His Highness as dangerous, it was now our turn to be suspicious; but many and various were the surmises formed as to the real object of the request. Some maintained that as peace had been restored in India by the fall of Bhartpur, and the termination of the Barmis war, and as the Russians had entered Persia, the Mirs had taken this mode of prudently making friendly advances to our government. Few gave them credit for sincerity in the reason assigned; and several of my friends were strongly of opinion that I ought not to venture into Sindh without some specific assurance of protection.

"For my own part I had ever felt a feverish anxiety to cross the forbidden frontier, and particularly to view the classic river Indus. Nothing could, therefore, be more satisfactory to me than the invitation; and, without considering whether the undertaking involved danger or not, I prepared to enter upon it with the best possible spirits, and without a moment's delay. My arrangements were soon completed; and, on the evening of the 25th, I commenced my march, accompanied by the Sindhian 'vakil' or agent at Bhuj, whom the Mirs had ordered to attend me, together with an escort composed of a small detachment of the 21st regiment of Native Infantry, a few troopers of the Punah auxiliary horse, and about a dozen horsemen in the service of His Highness the Rav of Kach.

"I waited with the greatest impatience till the morning of the 3rd of November, when the expected letter from the Mirs arrived. It was couched in the most friendly terms; begging me to come with all convenient speed to Haidarabad, and informing me that two noblemen, high in their favour, had been dispatched to meet me, and conduct me to their court.

"As I approached nearer Haidarabad (within thirty miles) I was met by Mohammed Khan Tora, a nobleman related to the family of the Mirs, who, together with another officer of rank, named Musa

Khan, had been sent to compliment me, and who brought with him a number of attendants.

"At the nearest stage to the capital I was received by the Navab Vali Mohammed Khan Laghari, the Prime Minister of Sindh, whom, as a mark of great respect, the Mirs had sent to congratulate me on my arrival.

"Within a mile of the city I was mounted on a large black horse, handsomely caparisoned, which had been brought out by Vali Mohammed Khan, and led slowly forwards.

"Viewing the family generally, I could not but admire their manners and deportment, and acknowledge that, in appearance at least, they seemed worthy of the elevation they had gained. The younger Princes, indeed, had an air of dignity and good breeding seldom to be met with, either in the European or native character.

"Several inquiries then followed regarding Mr. Elphinstone and Sir John Malcolm, Sir Evan Nepean, the Governor-General, and his Majesty King George the Fourth, for all of whom the Mirs professed the greatest respect and esteem. The resident in Kach, they observed, had acted the part of a friend in permitting me to visit Sindh; and by the grace of God, the friendship between themselves and the British government would now be greater than it had ever been at any former period."

Two years had not completely passed away from the time of the invitation to, and the return of Dr. Burnes from, the Court of Sindh; and the interest which his information created, both in England and in India, was clearly manifested in a general and strong desire to form a closer alliance with its rulers. This was evidently shown in sending another mission through that country in the course of such a short time.

In the year 1830, William the Fourth, King of Great Britain, sent a present of five horses to the Maharajah Ranjit Singh; and they arrived in Bombay while Sir John Malcolm was the Governor of that Presidency. There was also a letter from the Earl of Ellenborough, then President of the Board of Control, to the address of that chieftain, explaining the friendship which the British Government felt towards him. The Governor of Bombay selected and recommended Sir Alexander Burnes; upon which the Supreme Government of India nominated him to take charge of those presents, and to proceed to the capital of the Panjab. This produced a favourable opportunity to acquire a more familiar and accurate knowledge of the navigable state of the Indus, and of the country extending from its banks; and with this view it was resolved that the horses must be sent up by that river. It was at the same time considered advisable that a carriage should be purchased for the Maharajah, and sent with the horses. If the Mirs of Sindh, however, should happen to object to this measure, and should say that they will permit the horses to pass by land, Sir Alexander Burnes was to reply that the carriage, by a long journey on an uneven and irregular road, will be worn out and reduced to pieces; and that therefore he must go by water. I shall not fatigue the reader by adding observations on this subject, which fully shows that the suspicion and alarm of the chiefs of Sindh at the appearance of any British officer in their country, so evidently come to obtain information concerning it, were not groundless, since they have been deprived of it all at last. The intention which the English Government had towards that independent dominion, and the jealousy of the Mirs, which appears now to have been right and just, will be read with much interest from the following quotations from Sir Alexander Burnes.*

"Sir John Malcolm thus minuted in the records of the Government in August, 1830:—

"'The navigation of the Indus is important in every point of view; yet we have no information that can be depended upon on this subject, except of about seventy miles from Tattah to Haidarabad. Of the present state of the Delta we have native accounts, and the only facts which can be deduced are, that the different streams of the river below Tattah often change their channels, and that the sands of all are constantly shifting; but notwithstanding these difficulties, boats of a small draft of water can always go up the principal of them. With regard to the Indus above Haidarabad, there can be no doubt of its being, as it has been for more than two thousand years, navigable far up.'

"In addition therefore to the complimentary mission on which I was to be employed, I had my attention most specially directed to the acquisition of full and complete information regarding the Indus.

* Burnes's Travels into Bokhara, vol. iii. p. 2.

This was a matter of no easy accomplishment, as the Mirs or rulers of Sindh had ever evinced the utmost jealousy of Europeans; and none of the missions which visited the country had been permitted to proceed beyond their capital of Haidarabad. The river Indus, likewise, in its course to the ocean, traverses the territories of many lawless and barbarous tribes, from whom both opposition and insult might be dreaded. On these matters much valuable advice was derived from Lieutenant Colonel Sir Henry Pottinger, political resident in Kach, and well known to the world for his adventurous travels in Bilochistan. He suggested that it might allay the fears of the Sindh Government if a large carriage were sent with horses, since the size and bulk of it would render it obvious that the mission could then only proceed by water. This judicious proposal was immediately adopted by Government; nor was it in this case alone that the experience of Colonel Pottinger availed me, as it will be seen that he evinced the most unwearied zeal throughout the difficulties which presented themselves, and contributed in a great degree to the ultimate success of the undertaking.

"That a better colour might also be given to my deputation by a route so unfrequented, I was made the bearer of presents to the Mirs of Sindh; and at the same time charged with communications of a political nature to them. These referred to some excesses committed by their subjects on the British frontier; but I was informed that neither that nor any other negotiation was to detain me on my way to Lahaur. The authorities in England had desired that a suitable escort might accompany the party; but though the design was not free from some degree of danger, it was evident that no party of any moderate detail could afford the necessary protection. I preferred, therefore, the absence of any of our troops, and resolved to trust to the people of the country; believing that, through their means, I might form a link of communication with the inhabitants. Sir John Malcolm observed, in his letter to the Governor-General, that 'the guard will be the people of the country he visits, and those familiar with it, and Sir Alexander Burnes prefers such, on the justest grounds, to any others, finding they facilitate his progress, while they disarm that jealousy which the appearance of any of our troops excites.' Nor were my sentiments erroneous, since a guard of wild Bilochis protected us in Sindh, and allayed suspicion.

"When these preliminary arrangements had been completed, I received my final instructions in a secret letter from the chief secretary at Bombay. I was informed that the depth of water in the Indus, the directions and breadth of the stream, its facilities for steam navigation, the supply of fuel on its banks, and the condition of the princes and people who possess the country bordering on it, are all points of the highest interest to government, but your own knowledge and reflections will suggest to you various other particulars in which full information is highly desirable; and the slow progress of the boats up the Indus will, it is hoped, give you every opportunity to pursue your researches. I was supplied with all the requisites for surveying, as instruments, &c., and desired to draw bills on honour for my expenses."

With this view and with these directions the mission was formed, and Sir Alexander Burnes sailed from Mandvi in Kach on the 21st of January, 1831, and on the 24th he anchored near the mouth of Kori, which divides the country of Sindh from that of

Kach. He was turned out once by the Sindhians, but by communicating with the Mirs he sailed again for Sindh; and his letter to the agent at Daraji will not fail to point out how desirous we were to enter that country and to seek the friendship of the chiefs, notwithstanding their fearful hatred. Sir Alexander Burnes speaks thus of the circumstances and of himself.

"The jealousy of the Sindh government had been often experienced, and it was therefore suggested that we should sail for the Indus without giving any previous information. Immediately on anchoring, I dispatched a communication to the agent of the Mirs at Daraji signifying my plans.

"A day passed in anxious suspense, but on the following morning a body of armed men crowded round our boats, and the whole neighbourhood was in a state of the greatest excitement. The party stated themselves to be the soldiers of the Mir, sent to number our party and see the contents of all the boats, as well as every box that they contained. I gave a ready and immediate assent, and we were instantly boarded by about fifty armed men, who

* Burnes's Travels to Bokhara, vol. iii. p. 16.

wrenched open everything, and prosecuted the most rigorous search for cannon and gunpowder. Mr. Leckie and myself stood by in amazement till it was at length demanded that the box containing the large carriage should be opened, for they pretended to view it as the Greeks had looked on the wooden horse, and believed that it would carry destruction into Sindh. A sight of it disappointed their hopes, and we must be conjurors, it was asserted, to have come without arms and ammunition.

"When the search had been completed I entered into conversation with the head man of the party, and had hoped to establish, by his means, a friendly connexion with the authorities, but after a short pause this personage, who was a Rais of Lower Sindh, intimated that a report of the day's transactions would be forthwith transmitted to Haidarabad, and that in the meanwhile it was incumbent on us to await the decision of the Mir, at the mouth of the river. The request appeared reasonable, and the more so, since the party agreed to furnish us with every supply so situated. We therefore weighed anchor, and dropped down the river, but here our civilities ended. By the way we were met by several dingies full of armed men, and at night were hailed by one of them, to know how many troops we had on board. We replied, that we had not even a musket. 'The evil is done,' rejoined a rude Bilochi soldier; 'you have seen our country; but we have four thousand men ready for action.' To this vain-glorious observation succeeded torrents of abuse, and when we reached the mouth of the river the party fired their matchlocks over us; but I dropped anchor, and resolved, if possible, to repel these insults by personal remonstrance. It was useless; we were surrounded by ignorant barbarians, who shouted out in reply to all that I said, that they had been ordered to turn us out of the country. I protested against their conduct in the most forcible language, reminding them that I was the representative, however humble, of a great government, charged with presents from royalty, and added, that without a written document from their master, I should decline quitting Sindh. An hour's delay served to convince me that personal violence would ensue if I persisted in such a resolution, and as it was not my object to risk the success of the enterprise by such collision, I sailed for the most eastern mouth of the Indus, from which I addressed the authorities in Sindh, as well as Colonel Pottinger, the Resident in Kach.

"I was willing to believe that the soldiers had exceeded the authority which had been granted them, and was speedily put in possession of a letter from the Mir, couched in friendly terms, but narrating, at great length, the difficulty and impossibility of navigating the Indus.

"'The boats are so small,' said his Highness, 'that only four or five men can embark in one of them; their progress is likewise slow; they have neither masts nor sails, and the depth of water in the Indus is likewise so variable as not to reach, in some places, the knee or waist of a man.' But this formidable enumeration of physical obstacles was coupled with no refusal from the ruler himself, and it seemed expedient, therefore, to make a second attempt after replying to his Highness's letter.

"On the 10th of February we again set sail for Sindh. We now anchored in the Pikteani mouth of the Indus, and I forthwith dispatched the following document by a trustworthy messenger to the agent at Daraji.

"1st. Let it be known to the government agent at

Daraji that this is the memorandum of Mr. Burnes (sealed with his seal, and written in the Persian language in his own handwriting), the representative (vakil) of the English to the Mir of Sindh, and likewise the bearer of presents to Maharajah Ranjit Singh from the King of England.

"2nd. I came to the Indus a few days ago, and you searched my baggage, that you might report the contents thereof to your master. I have now returned, and await an answer.

"3rd. You may send any number of armed men that you please; my life is in your power; but remember that the Mir will hold every one responsible who molests me. Remember, too, that I am a British officer, and have come without a musket or a soldier (as you well know), placing implicit reliance on the protection of the ruler of Sindh, to whose care my government have committed me.

"4th. I send this memorandum by two of my own servants, and look to you for their being protected."

"This remonstrance drew no reply from the agent at Daraji; for the individual who had held the situation on our first visit to Sindh had been dismissed for permitting us to ascend the river; and our servants brought us notice that we should not be permitted to land, nor to receive either food or water. We observed, therefore, the greatest possible economy in the distribution of our provisions, and placed padlocks on the tanks, in the hope of reason yet guiding the councils of the Mir. When our supply of water failed I despatched a small boat up the river to procure some; but it was seized, and the party detained; which now rendered us hopeless of success, and only anxious to quit the inhospitable shores of Sindh.

"On the 22nd of February we weighed our anchor, at daylight, and sailed for Katch, and anchored in Mandivi Roads after a surprising run of thirty-three hours.

"It could not now be concealed that the conduct of the Mir of Sindh was most unfriendly, but he yet betrayed no such feeling in his letters. He magnified the difficulties of navigating the Indus, and arrayed its rocks, quicksands, whirlpools, and shallows, in every communication, asserting that the voyage to Lahaur had never been performed in the memory of man. It was evident that he viewed the expedition with the utmost distrust and alarm; and the native agent, who resides at Haidarabad on the part of the British Government, described, not without some degree of humour, the fear and dread of this jealous potentate. In his estimation we were the precursors of an army, and did he now desire to grant us a passage through Sindh, he was at a loss to escape from the falsehood and contradictions which he had already stated in his epistles. One letter went on to say, that 'the Mir of Sindh avoids giving any reply, lest he should be involved in perplexity; and he has stopped his ears with the cotton of absurdity, and taken some silly notions into his head, that if Captain Burnes should now come, he will see thousands of boats on the Indus, and report the same to his government, who will conclude that it is the custom of the Mir of Sindh to deceive on all subjects, and that he has no sort of friendship.' At length, after a remonstrance from Colonel Pottinger, both he and myself received letters from Haidarabad, offering a road through Sindh by land. As this might be fairly deemed the first opening which had presented itself during the whole negotiation, with the advice of Colonel Pottinger I set out a third time for the Indus. That officer, in the meanwhile, intimated my departure to the Mir, and pointed out the impossibility of my proceeding by land to Lahaur. He also intimated, in no measured language, that the vacillating and unfriendly conduct of the Mir of Sindh would not pass unnoticed, the more particularly since it concerned the passage of gifts which had been sent by His Most Gracious Majesty the King of Great Britain.

"On the 10th of March we once more set sail for the Indus; and reached the Hasamri, one of the central mouths of the river, after a prosperous voyage of seven days. We could hire no pilot to conduct us across the bar, and took the wrong and shallow mouth of the river, ploughing up the mud as we tacked in its narrow channel. We were now met by an officer of the Sindh government, one of the favourite descendants of the Prophet, whose enormous corpulence bespoke his condition. This personage came to the mouth of the river, for we were yet refused all admittance to the fresh water. He produced a letter from the Mir, and repeated the same refuted arguments of his master, which he seemed to think should receive credit from his high rank. It would be tiresome to follow the Sindhians through the course of chicanery which they adopted, even in this stage of proceedings. An embargo was laid on all the vessels in the Indus; and we ourselves were confined to our boats, on a dangerous shore, and even denied fresh water. The officers urged the propriety of our taking a route by land; and as a last resource, I offered to accompany him to the capital, and converse with the Mir in person. Having previously landed the horses, I made known this arrangement by a courier which I despatched to the Court; and on the following morning quitted the boats, along with Sayad Jindal Shah, who had been appointed our Mihmandar. No sooner had we reached Tatta, than the required sanction for the boats to ascend by the Indus was received, provided we ourselves took the land route; but I immediately declined to advance another step without my charge; and ultimately effected, by a week's negotiation at Tatta, the desired end. At the expense of being somewhat tedious, I will give an abstract of these proceedings, as a specimen of Sindhian policy and reasoning.

"A few hours after reaching Tatta, Sayad Zulfqar Shah, a man of rank, and engaging manners, waited on us on the part of the Mir. He was accompanied by our Mihmandar, and met us very politely. He said that he had been sent by his Highness to escort us to Haidarabad; to which I laconically replied, that nothing would now induce me to go, since the Mir had conceded the request which I had made of him. The Sayad here marshalled all his eloquence; asked me if I wished to ruin the Mihmandar, by making him out a liar, after I had promised to accompany him to the Court, and he had written so to the Mir? if I had no regard for a promise? that the capital was close at hand, and I could reach it in two marches; that, if I did not now go, it could only be inferred that I had been practising delusion, from a desire to see Tatta; for I had even been allowed to choose the route by that city, contrary to orders; and that I was not, perhaps, aware of the high character of the Sayad, who was a descendant of the holy Prophet, and honourable in this land; whose dignity the Christians, who preserved even the relic of Jesus Christ's nail, could well understand; and that it was not the part of a wise man to cavil like a mullah, since the Mir had sanctioned the advance of the mission by water if we embarked at Haidarabad, and would be answerable for the safety of the horses to that place; and finally, that if I persisted in taking the route by water, he was desired to say that it was a violation of the treaty between the States.

"I heard with attention the arguments of Zulfqar Shah; nor did I forget that the praises and respects which he claimed for his friend, as a descendant of the Prophet, likewise included himself; I replied, that there had existed a long-standing friendship between Sindh and the British Government; that I had been despatched by a well-frequented route, to deliver the presents of our gracious Sovereign to Ranjit Singh at Lahaur; that on reaching Sindh I had been insulted, abused, starved, and twice turned out of the country by low persons, whom I named; that my Government, which was ever considerate, had attributed this unheard-of insolence, not to their friends the Mirs of Sindh, but to the ignorance of mean individuals, and had despatched me a third time to Sindh; when I reached it, I found Sayad Jindal Shah ready to receive me, but although thoroughly satisfied that the presents of which I was in charge could never be forwarded by land, he offered me that route, and detained me on board ship for eleven days, till necessity had driven me to make a proposal of repairing in person to the presence of the Mir, in hopes of persuading that personage.

"The case was now altered; the water route had been granted, which rendered my visit to Haidarabad necessary; and I could only view the present procedure in the light of jealousy, which it was unbecoming in a government to entertain. I continued, that I had chosen the route by Tatta because my bills were payable at that city; and the sooner the Sayad got his master to meet my wishes the better, for the floods of the Indus were at hand, the hot season approached, and delay would increase the hazard; while no arguments but force would now induce me to visit the Court, or permit the horses to be moved without my presence. In fine, if it were not the intention of the Mir to act a friendly part, he had only to say so, and I would forthwith quit the country when I received a letter to that effect; and finally, that he had formed a very erroneous opinion of the British character, if he considered that I had been sent here in breach of a treaty, for I had come to strengthen the bonds of union; and, what was further, that the promise of an officer was sacred.

"An interview in the following morning brought a repetition of the whole arguments; and as we could not convince each other, we both agreed to address his Highness. After the style of Asiatic diplomacy, I informed the Mir that he had acted the part of a friend in first pointing out the difficulties of navigating the Indus, and now assisting me through them by giving his sanction to the water route; but since I was so thoroughly acquainted, through his Highness's kindness, with the dangers of the river, I dared not trust such royal rarities as the gifts of the King of Great Britain to the care of any servant. In three days I received a full and unqualified sanction to advance by water from the mouth of the Indus.

"On the morning of the 18th we moored opposite Haidarabad.

"Immediately on our arrival four different deputations waited on us to convey the congratulations of Mir Morad Ali Khan and his family at our having reached the capital of Sindh, and at the same time to tender the strongest professions of friendship and respect for the British government, to all of which I returned suitable answers.

"Tents were pitched, and provisions of every description sent to us; and it would, indeed, have been difficult to discover that we were the individuals who had so long lingered about the shores of Sindh, now the honoured guests of its jealous master. Great and small were in attendance on us: khans and Sayads, servants and chobdars, brought messages and inquiries.

"In the evening we were presented to the Mir of Sindh by his son Nasir Khan, who had previously received us in his own apartments to inform us of his attachment to the British government, and the state secret of his having been the means of procuring for us a passage through Sindh.

"We found the Mir seated in the middle of a room, begged that I would forget the difficulties and dangers encountered, and consider him as the ally of the British government and my own friend.

"Elephants and palanqueens were at our disposal if we would accept them; and he would vie in exertion with ourselves to forward in safety the presents of His Most Gracious Majesty the King of Great

Britain, and had nominated the son of his Vazir to accompany us to the limits of his territories.

"On the morning of the 23rd of April we embarked in the state barge of the Mir. On the day after quitting Sevan we were met by Mohammed Gauhar, a Bilochi chief, and a party, the confidential agents of Mir Rustam Khan, the Mir of Khairpur, who had been sent to the frontier, a distance of eighty miles, to congratulate us on our arrival and declare their master's devotion to the British government. We hardly expected such a mark of attention in Sindh, and were therefore gratified. The deputation brought an abundant supply of sheep, flour, fruit, spices, sugar, butter, ghee, tobacco, opium, &c. &c., on which our people feasted.

"In return for Mir Rustam Khan's kindness, I addressed to him a Persian letter in the following terms, which will serve as a specimen of the epistolary style used by the people of this country, which I imitated as closely as possible.

(After compliments.)

"I HASTEN to inform your Highness that I have reached the frontiers of your country in company with the respectable Sayad Taqi Shah, who has accompanied me on the part of Mir Morad Ali Khan from Haidarabad. As I have long since heard of your Highness from those who pass between Katch and Sindh, it forms a source of congratulation to me that I have arrived in your dominions, and brought along with me in safety the presents which have been graciously bestowed on Maharajah Ranjit Singh, by his Majesty the King of England,—mighty in rank; terrible as the planet Mars; a monarch great and magnificent; of the rank of Jamshaid; of the dignity of Alexander; unequalled by Darius; just as Naushervan; great as Faredun; admired as Cyrus; famed as the sun; the destroyer of tyranny and oppression; upright and generous; pious and devout; favoured from above, &c., &c. May his dominion endure for ever!

"It is well known that when a friend comes to the country of a friend it is a source of much happiness, and I have therefore written these few lines; but when I have the pleasure of seeing you, my joy will be increased.

"I had written thus far when the respectable Mohammed Gauhar, one of those enjoying your Highness's confidence, arrived at this place to acquaint me with your professions of respect and friendship for the British Government, bringing along with him many thanks of your hospitality. Need I say I am rejoiced? Such civilities mark the great."

"With the better orders of society we had frequent intercourse and conversation.

"Some of them felt interested about the objects of our mission to Lahaur. They did not give us much credit for sincerity in sending it by a route which they believed never to have been passed since the time of Noah.

"On the morning of the 14th we disembarked near the small village of Alipur, and were met by the Vazir of Mir Rustam Khan, who had come from Khairpur to receive us.

"Our reception was cordial and kind; the Vazir assured us of the high satisfaction with which his master had heard of our arrival, for he had long desired to draw closer to the British government, and had never yet had the good fortune to meet any of its agents. He said that Mir Rustam Khan did not presume to put himself on an equality with so potent and great a nation, but hoped that he might be classed among its well wishers, and as one ready to afford his services on all occasions.

"I thanked his Highness for the uniform attention and hospitality which we had received. He made a long address to me regarding his respect for the British government, and said that I had of course learned his sentiments from his Vazir.

"I must mention that the hospitality which he so modestly named consisted of eight or ten sheep, with all sorts of provisions for one hundred and fifty people daily; and that while at Khairpur he sent for our use, twice a day, a meal of seventy-two dishes."

The preceding contents which I have quoted will show how we were desirous to enter in Sindh to obtain political, geographical, and commercial information, and how the Mirs were flattered, civil, and hospitable, and what extraordinary forbearance was exhibited by our authorities to allay their suspicions, which appear now to be just. I shall preserve my saying on this subject of great moment, as I have said before, but will lead the readers to the trodden path of those high political characters whose remarks will themselves point out the object fully and clearly, which, if I were able to describe, would not be considered justifiable. So let the English public read the observations of their own countrymen and enterprising explorers.

On the 19th of May Sir Alexander Burnes took leave of Mir Rustam Khan of Khairpur, and his minister Fatah Mohammed Khan Ghori delivered to him the secret message with which he was entrusted by his master the good Mir.

"On the banks of the Indus we had a curious interview in the evening after our arrival with the Vazir from Khairpur, who had been sent by Mir Rustam Khan to escort us thus far, and see that we were furnished with boats.

"After requesting to be received privately, he renewed the subject of our first conversation, and said that he had been instructed by his master to propose a solemn treaty of friendship with the British Government on any terms that might be named. He then ran over the list of neighbouring states which owed their existence to an alliance,—the chief of the Daudpotras, the Raval of Jaisalmer, and the Rajah of Bikaner, &c. &c.,—and then concluded with a peroration full of gravity, that it was foretold by astronomers, and recorded in his books, that the English would in time possess all India, a prediction which both Mir Rustam and himself felt satisfied would come to pass, when the British would ask why the chiefs of Khairpur had not come forward with an offer of allegiance. I tried to remove, but without effect, the sad prognostication of the minister, and declared my incompetency to enter on such weighty matters as a treaty between the states, without authority, and before receiving a written statement under the Mir's seal. I said that I would make known the wishes that had been expressed to my government, which would be gratified to hear that they had such friends, which seemed to please the diplomatist. He begged that I would bear in mind what had passed, and exacted a promise that I would write to him when gone, and so water the tree of friendship that the object might be ultimately effected—'for the stars and heaven proclaimed the fortune of the English!'"

It has been already stated that though the Honourable East India Company had the commercial intercourse with the ruler of Sindh for a long standing period, there were no treaties of alliance contracted till 1809. Previous to the treaties of 1839, in which I was employed, it would make the matter more clearly to be understood that I should quote those which were successively framed during the space of those distant periods. Most of them, through the extraordinary tact and negotiations of Sir Henry Pottinger, produced a wonderful result, and success of the commercial measures at the time, and, above all, paved a peaceable path for our armies in their country, where, according to the first and second conditions of the third article of the treaty of the 20th April, 1832, it was engaged that no arms and military stores of any description shall be brought in their country.

Treaty with the Mirs of Sindh, of August 22, 1809.

"ART. 1. THERE shall be eternal friendship between the British Government and that of Sindh, namely, Mir 'Gholam Ali, Mir Karam Ali, and Mir Morad Ali.

"Art. 2. Enmity shall never appear between the two states.

"Art. 3. The mutual despatch of the vakils of both governments, namely, the British Government and Sindhian Government, shall ever continue.

"Art. 4. The Government of Sindh will not allow the establishment of the tribe of the French in Sindh.

"Written on the 10th of the month of Rajab-ul-Morajab, in the year of Hijri 1224, corresponding with the 21st August, 1809."

Treaty between the East India Company on the one hand, and the Mirs of Sindh on the other, of November 9, 1820.

"THE British Government and the Government of Sindh having in view to guard against the occurrence of frontier disputes, and to strengthen the friendship already subsisting between the two states, Mir Ismail Shah was invested with full power to treat with the Honourable the Governor of Bombay, and the following Articles were agreed on between the two parties :—

"Art. 1. There shall be perpetual friendship between the British Government on the one hand, and Mir Karam Ali and Mir Morad Ali on the other.

"Art. 2. Mutual intercourse by means of vakils shall always continue between the two governments.

"Art. 3. The Mirs of Sindh engage not to permit any European or American to settle in their dominions. If any of the subjects of either of the two states should establish their residence in the dominions of the other, and should conduct themselves in an orderly and peaceable manner in the territory to which they may emigrate, they will be allowed to remain in that situation; but if such fugitives shall be guilty of any disturbance or commotion, it will be incumbent on the local authority to take the offenders into custody, and punish or compel them to quit the country.

"Art. 4. The Mirs of Sindh engage to restrain the depredations of the Khosas and all other tribes and individuals within their limits, and to prevent the occurrence of any inroad into the British dominions.

Bombay, 9*th November*, 1820.

"*Note.*—The foregoing treaty was approved of by the Supreme Government on the 10th February, 1821."

Treaty of Peace between the East India Company and the State of Khairpur, April 4, 1832.

"ART. 1. THERE shall be eternal friendship between the two states.

"Art. 2. The two contracting powers mutually bind themselves from generation to generation never to look with the eye of covetousness on the possessions of each other.

"Art. 3. The British Government having requested the use of the river Indus and the roads of Sindh for the merchants of Hindustan, &c., the Government of Khairpur agrees to grant the same within its own boundaries on whatever terms may be settled with the Government of Haidarabad, namely, Mir Morad Ali Khan Talpur.

"Art. 4. The Government of Khairpur agrees to furnish a written statement of just and reasonable duties to be levied on all goods passing under this treaty, and further promises that traders shall suffer no loss or hindrance in transacting their business.

"Dated the 2nd of Ziqad, 1247 Hijri, corresponding with the 4th day of April, A.D. 1832."

Treaty concluded between the East India Company and Mir Morad Ali Khan, Ruler of Haidarabad, in Sindh, April 20, 1832.

"ART. 1. THAT the friendship provided for in former treaties between the British Government and that of Sindh remain unimpaired and binding; and that this stipulation has received additional efficacy through the medium of Lieut.-Colonel Pottinger, Envoy, &c.; so that the firm connexion and close alliance now formed between the said states shall descend to the children and successors of Mir Morad Ali Khan, principal after principal, from generation to generation.

"Art. 2. That the two contracting powers bind themselves never to look with an eye of covetousness on the possessions of each other.

"Art. 3. That the British Government has requested a passage for the merchants and traders of Hindustan by the river and roads of Sindh, by which they may transport their goods and merchandise from one country to another; and the said Government of Haidarabad hereby acquiesces in the same request, on the three following conditions:—

"I. That no person shall bring any description of military stores by the above river or roads.

"II. That no armed vessels or boats shall come by the said river.

"III. That no English merchants shall be allowed to settle in Sindh, but shall come as occasion requires, and, having stopped to transact their business, shall return to India.

"Art. 4. When merchants shall determine on visiting Sindh, they shall obtain a passport to do so from the British Government; and due information of the granting of such passports shall be made to the said Government of Haidarabad by the said Resident in Kach, or other officer of the said British Government.

"Art. 5. That the Government of Haidarabad, having fixed on certain proper and moderate duties to be levied on merchandise and goods proceeding by the aforesaid routes, shall adhere to that scale, and not arbitrarily and despotically either increase or lessen the same, so that the affairs of merchants and traders may be carried on without stop or interruption; and the custom-house officers and farmers of revenue of the Sindh Government are to be specially directed to see that they do not delay the said merchants on pretence of awaiting for fresh orders from the Government, or in the collection of the duties; and the said Government is to promulgate a tariff, or table of duties leviable on each kind of goods, as the case may be.

"Art. 6. That whatever portions of former treaties entered into between the two states have not been altered and modified by the present one remain firm and unaltered, as well as those stipulations now concluded; and, by the blessing of God, no deviation from them shall ever take place.

"Art. 7. That the friendly intercourse between the two states shall be kept up by the despatch of vakils, whenever the transactions of business or the increase of the relations of friendship may render it desirable.

"Written on the 18th Ziqad, 1247 Hijri, corresponding with the 20th of April, 1832."

Supplementary Treaty between the East India Company and the Government of Haidarabad in Sindh, which is to be considered as virtually annulled on the fulfilment of its Stipulations, April 22, 1832.

" Art. 1. It is inserted in the fifth article of the perpetual treaty, that the Government of Haidarabad will furnish the British Government with a statement of duties, &c.; and after that the officers of the British Government, who are versed in affairs of traffic, will examine the said statement. Should the statement seem to them to be fair and equitable, and agreeable to custom, it will be brought into operation, and will be confirmed; but should it appear too high, his Highness Mir Morad Ali Khan, on hearing from the British Government to this effect, through Colonel Pottinger, will reduce the said duties.

" Art. 2. It is as clear as noon day that the punishment and suppression of the plunderers of Parkar, the Thale, &c., is not to be effected by any one Government; and as this measure is incumbent on and becoming the states, as tending to secure the welfare and happiness of their respective subjects and countries, it is hereby stipulated, on the commencement of the ensuing rainy season, and of which Mir Morad Ali Khan shall give due notice, the British, Sindh, and Jodpur Governments shall direct their joint and simultaneous efforts on the above subjects.

" Art. 3. The Governments of the Right Honourable East India Company and of Khairpur, namely, Mir Rustam, have provided, in a treaty concluded between the states, that whatever may be settled regarding the opening of the Indus at Haidarabad shall be binding on the said contracting powers: it is therefore necessary that copies of the treaty should be sent by the British and Haidarabad Governments to Mir Rustam Khan, for his satisfaction and guidance.

"Written on the 20th of Ziqad, 1247 Hijri, corresponding with the 22d April, 1832."

Commercial Treaty between the East India Company and the Government of Haidarabad, in Sindh; published by Proclamation, on the 23*d of December*, 1834, *by order of the Governor-General in Council.*

"WHEREAS in the first article of the supplementary treaty concluded between the Honourable East India Company and the Government of Haidarabad, on the 22d day of April, 1832, corresponding with the 20th of Ziqad, 1247 Hijri, it was stipulated that the Government of Haidarabad was to furnish the British Government with a statement of duties, &c., and, 'After that, the officers of the British Government, who are versed in affairs of traffic, shall have examined the same statement, should the statement seem to them to be fair and equitable, and agreeable to custom, it will be brought into operation, and will be confirmed; but should it appear too high, his Highness Mir Morad Ali Khan, on hearing from the British Government to this effect, through Colonel Pottinger, will reduce the said duties.' Now, according to the terms of the above stipulation, the contracting States, having made due inquiry, hereby enter into the following agreement:—

"Article 1. In lieu of a duty on goods proceeding up and down the River Indus, in virtue of the fifth Article of the perpetual Treaty of Haidarabad, there shall be levied on the rivers, between the sea and Ropar, a toll on each boat of nineteen Tatta rupees, per Tatta kharah, of which amount eight rupees shall be receivable by the Government of Haidarabad and Khairpur, and eleven rupees by the other States possessing dominions on the banks of the rivers, namely:—His Highness Bahaval Khan, Maharajah Ranjit Singh, and the Honourable East India Company.

"Art. 2. To obviate any cause whatever of trouble or inconvenience to traders and merchants during their progress, and also to prevent disputes and doubts, and consequent altercations and delay, touching the size of boats, the toll is fixed at thirty Tatta kharahs. Be a boat large or small, she will pay toll according to this; and whether she measures five kharahs, or one hundred kharahs, she will be reckoned as one of thirty.

"Art. 3. The portion of the toll above described, appertaining to Sindh, and amounting to two hundred and forty Tatta rupees on each boat, shall be levied at the bandar or port at the mouth of the river, where the cargoes are transferred from the river to the sea-boats, and *vice versâ*, and divided as the Governments of Haidarabad and Khairpur may think best.

"Art. 4. For the purpose of assisting in the realization of the toll due to Sindh; also in the speedy and satisfactory adjustment of disputes, which may happen to occur amongst the merchants, boatmen, and others, on the question of hire, &c., as well as with a view to the preservation and augmentation of the amicable relations which happily subsist between the States—it is settled that a British agent (who shall not be an European gentleman), under the authority of Lieutenant-Colonel Pottinger, agent to the Governor-General of India, for the affairs of Sindh, shall reside at the bandar, or port, at the mouth of the river, where cargoes are transferred from one description of boats to another; and the British Government binds itself that the said agent shall neither engage in trade, nor interfere in any way with the fiscal or any other affairs of the Sindh Government. It is further settled, that when occasions connected with this Treaty may render it advisable, the Governor-General's agent for the affairs of Sindh shall have the power of deputing one of his assistants to the above described bandar, or port, to settle any discussion that may have arisen, after doing which he is to return to Bhuj.

"Art. 5. For the more perfect fulfilment of this treaty, it is hereby distinctly stipulated, that should any portion, however small or great, or of whatever description, of the merchandise or goods on board any boat passing up or down the river be landed for sale by a merchant or merchants, such portion of merchandise or goods, whatever may be its quantity or quality, shall instantly become subject to the existing local duties, as levied by the respective governments within their own territories; the purpose of the toll agreed to by this treaty being not to supersede or set aside the established dues of the different states, but to repay the expense to which the Government will necessarily be subjected in affording the customary protection to the trade in transit on the river. It will be perfectly understood, from this fifth Article, that the Governments have no claim to duties on merchandise merely passing up and down the river, and that the toll is all that is to be demanded; but should any portion, however small or large, of goods be landed and sold, then the usual duties will be levied."

Treaty between the East India Company and the Mirs of Sindh, concluded by Colonel Pottinger, Agent to the Governor-General for Sindh on one part, and their Highnesses Mir Nur Mohammed Khan, and Mir Nasir Khan on the other, April 20, 1838.

"ART. 1. IN consideration of the long friendship which has subsisted between the British Government and the Mirs of Sindh, the Governor-General in Council engages to use his good offices to adjust the present differences which are understood to subsist between the Mirs of Sindh and the Maharajah Ranjit Singh, so that peace and friendship may be established between the two states.

"Art. 2. In order to secure and improve the relations of amity and peace which have so long subsisted between the Sindh state and British Government, it is agreed that an accredited British minister shall reside at the Court of Haidarabad, and that the Mirs of Sindh shall also be at liberty to send a vakil to reside at the Court of the British Government; and that the British minister shall be empowered to change his ordinary place of residence as may from time to time seem expedient, and be attended by such an escort as may be deemed suitable by his Government.

"Ratified by the Governor-General at Simla, this 20th day of April, 1838."

Let us now relate the proceedings of Sir Henry Pottinger at the court of the Mirs at Haidarabad, and the negotiations of Sir Alexander Burnes in that of the Mirs at Khairpur, as well as the progress of the army of the Indus towards Sindh. The latter officer remained for a considerable time with the Mir Rustam Khan, and exerted himself very much to have the proposed treaty agreed to, and signed by him; but the Mir Mobarak evidently, and the arch intriguer the Mir Ali Morad secretly,

SIR HENRY POTTINGER G.C.B.

put many obstacles in the way of the Mir Rustam Khan, to prevent him from coming to an immediate conclusion with the English envoy. The former had naturally a disregard for, and a hatred against the English; and the latter, full of ambition and treachery, wished himself to prosper at the sacrifice of his brothers. Upon one hand his agents frequently visited Sir Alexander Burnes by night, and gave letters and messages from their master, presenting his profession of attachment to the British government, and saying that if he were to enjoy the confidence and friendship of that officer, he will at once beg his brother, the Mir Rustam, to sign the treaty, and will perform any other valuable services, which will cause the Mirs of Haidarabad to accede to the terms of Sir Henry Pottinger without further delay. On the other hand he prevented the Mir Rustam Khan from accepting our proposals, till there was first a treaty concluded in the lower Sindh; and said that if Sir Alexander were to insist upon the immediate settlement, he was to reply that the Mir Ali Morad, and Fatah Mohammed Khan Ghori, have full power to enter into any engagements for the alliance. Sir Alexander Burnes, from his knowledge and intercourse of ten or twelve years with the Sindh rulers, knew well the treacherous game which the Mir Ali Morad wished to play, and therefore he firmly refused to enter into any political conversation or convention with the junior members of the family, while the Mir Rustam Khan was alive. Ali Morad was now greatly disappointed; finding also that his brother seemed ready to consent to what the envoy had put on the paper, and sent to him for ratification: and he therefore contrived, through his Khas Khaili, to gain possession of the seal of the Mir Rustam, whom he frightened by saying that if he were to contradict him in what he says to Sir Alexander Burnes for the good of the family, he himself, the Mir Mobarak, and other members of the family, will make a separate division to receive the friendship and alliance of the British, who then, finding nearly the whole of the family on one side, and the Mir Rustam Khan alone on the other, will throw him off as nothing. While this crafty chief was thus causing the procrastination of the adjustment of affairs, he did not lose time to report the circumstances to Sir Alexander Burnes in a different garb. He stated that his brother, the Mir Rustam, had delivered to him the seal of his own free-will, and that he would at once agree to any terms he may propose; and in return he expects that, even while the Mir Rustam was alive, the British government would use its influence to aid him in taking an equal share in the revenues of the country with his brother; and that after his brother's death the English authorities would acknowledge him as the rightful successor. Sir Alexander Burnes gave a decided refusal to all these proposals of the Mir Ali Morad; finding that the Mir Rustam, the old and faithful friend of the government, was himself willing to seal the treaty, but that his brothers were preventing him, against his own wish, and will not come to any satisfactory terms before the flag of our approaching army floats on the boundary of Sindh. He therefore left Khairpur, without gaining the object of his mission, and came to Shikarpur, leaving at the Khairpur Court a sufficient intimation of his displeasure.

On his departure the friendly ties and cordial feelings he had shown among them made the Mir Rustam Khan feel uncomfortable, and the Ali Morad; so that when a few days had rolled on, the latter proceeded to his fort, Diji. Sensible as we were of the fidelity of that most excellent man the Mir Rustam Khan, I volunteered to go and undertake to settle the matter with him, if Sir Alexander Burnes would invite Fatah Mohammed Ghori to his camp, and permit me to confer and treat personally with the Mir Rustam Khan. Sir Alexander Burnes considered the plan proper, and while Fatah Mohammed Ghori was on his way to Shikarpur, I arrived at Khairpur by a different route, avoiding the chance of falling in with him.

I was very kindly received by the Mir Rustam Khan, who at once agreed to every article of the treaty, and stated that he will sign and seal it as soon as Sir Alexander Burnes comes to him. I did not approve of this plan, thinking that his coming will bring Fatah Mohammed Khan Ghori with him from Shikarpur, and will afford a fresh opportunity to the Mir, at the advice of the other persons, to alter certain words or conditions in the proposed treaty; while on being asked myself to do so, the answer was easy enough that I had not such power. With this view I wrote to Sir Alexander Burnes by express that he was to reply to the

Mir's request of visiting him, merely in one word, namely this: that when I return with the accepted treaty from the Mir's capital, he will visit him personally and congratulate him on the happy termination of such protracted negotiations, which have strengthened the bonds of amity between the two governments. Sir Alexander Burnes's letter came just at the time when the "Abdar" of Mir Ali Morad arrived from Diji, informing the Mir of his joining him to-morrow, and requesting him not to see me till he arrives. This I heard at a very late hour at night; and that night I passed in great anxiety, looking for the dawn of the morning.

It was still very early when I went to the private door of the residence of the Mir Rustam Khan, and sent in word to his Highness that I had received despatches, and was very desirous to see him on business of great moment. The good Mir came out in his night-dress, and placing me by his side, wished to know the object of my very anxious and early visit. I laid before him the treaty; and as I had taken with me the pen and ink, anticipating that the delay of asking for them might defer the accomplishment of my object, I begged the Mir to sign and read it at once. Some of his attendants said to him in the Bilochi language, that it would be better to wait the arrival of Ali Morad; but giving the pen into his hand, I desired him either to sign it without hesitation, or to say that he does not want the alliance of the British government. I of course said a few words in addition, which were delivered in a different tone of voice and meaning, while every respect and propriety of rank was strictly observed. On this the good-natured Mir was just at the point of putting his seal under his own hand-writing in word and name, when suddenly the Mir Ali Morad arrived and interrupted him in the act of sealing it. I again told the Mir that, though Ali Morad was his brother, yet certainly he was not his well wisher; and that when the British troops arrive at Sabzalkot, every one will feel, for his own safety, inclined to agree to all the terms we now do and might then propose; but that it will not reflect any light of credit or friendship on the Mir Rustam Khan to have delayed so long. He now, holding my hand, said in a most affectionate manner that he knew that I was not an Englishman, and that I had a real regard for the welfare of Sindh, and therefore I must tell him candidly whether the acceptance of the proposed treaty by him will really increase the friendship and satisfaction of the Governor-General and of the Sovereign in England, or that, after the present object was gained, he shall be put aside as useless. I assured the Mir, pledging my word and honour, as well as that of Sir Alexander Burnes on the part of the government (as he had told me), that every article of the treaty shall strictly be adhered to, and that the Mir and his descendants will from generation to generation enjoy the peaceable and independent authority of their possessions, without fearing any internal or external commotions: on which he affixed his seal, notwithstanding the open and repeated remonstrances of the Mir Ali Morad, whom the Mir Rustam Khan silenced by saying that he will get a separate agreement from Sir Alexander Burnes, stating that his (Ali Morad's) privileges will neither be interfered with nor coveted by the British Government; and at the Mir Rustam's repeated solicitation, that officer omitted the mention of the intrigues of Ali Morad in his despatch to the Governor-General.

Treaty between the Honourable the East India Company and the Khairpur State, or Mir Rustam Khan, on the 25th of December, 1838.

This Article requires no comment, being in the Treaty with Bhaval Khan, sent for my guidance.

" Article 1st.—There shall be perpetual friendship, alliance, and unity of interests between the Honourable the East India Company and the Mir Rustam Khan Talpoor, and his heirs and successors, from generation to generation, and the friends and enemies of one party shall be the friends and enemies of both.

As in Bhaval Khan's.

" Article 2nd.—The British Government engages to protect the principality and territory of Khairpur.

As in Bhaval Khan's.

" Article 3rd.—The Mir Rustam Khan, and his heirs and successors, will act in subordinate co-operation with the British Government, and acknowledge its supremacy, and not have any connexion with any other Chiefs and States.

As in Bhaval Khan's.

" Article 4th.—The Mir, and his heirs and successors, will not enter into negotiation with any Chief or State without the knowledge and sanction of the British Government; but the usual amicable correspondence with friends and relatives shall continue.

As in Bhaval Khan's.

" Article 5th.—The Mir, and his heirs and successors, will not commit aggressions on any one. If by accident any dispute arises with any one, the settlement of it shall be submitted to the arbitration and award of the British Government.

This Article differs materially from the others, and binds the Mir to all we wish, but in general terms.

The mention of not coveting a dam or drain is merely a repetition of what is already written in the Haidarabad Treaty, which the Governor General, *mutatis mutandis*, agreed to give to Khairpur.

The Persian words, left to explain this last clause, are their own, and not mine.

" Article 6th.—The Mir will furnish troops according to his means, at the requisition of the British Government, and render it all and every necessary aid and assistance throughout his territory during the continuance of war, and approve of all the defensive preparations which it may make, while the peace and security of the countries on the other side of the Indus may be threatened; but the British Government will not covet a dam or drain of the territories enjoyed by his Highness and his heirs, nor the fortresses on this bank or that bank of the river Indus.

This is the same as in Bhaval Khan's treaty, excepting the mention of our not listening to the complaints of the Mir's subjects, which is clearly implied in that treaty; for, without this mentioning of it, Rustam Khan declared he could not manage his country; and he is right, as appears to me.

" Article 7th.—The Mir and his heirs and successors shall be absolute rulers of their country, and the British jurisdiction shall not be introduced into that principality; nor will any of the Bilochis, servants, dependents, relatives, or subjects of the Mir be listened to, should they complain against the said Mir.

In this Article I have fulfilled his Lordship's instructions

" Article 8th.—In order to improve by every means possible the grow-to the letter, and I might have easily abolished the toll for ever; but this would be a hazardous step till we substitute our own influence in Sindh. The toll binds the Mir to protect property; the release from it would remove this duty from his shoulders.

ing intercourse by the River Indus, the Mir Rustam Khan promises all co-operation with the other Powers in any measures which may be hereafter thought necessary for extending and facilitating the commerce and navigation of the Indus.

A mere copy of the Article in the Haidarabad Treaty.

" Article 9th.—In order to still further secure the relations of amity and peace, which have so long subsisted between the Khairpur State and the British Government, it is agreed that an accredited British minister shall reside at the court of Khairpur, and that the Mir shall also be at liberty to depute an agent to reside at the court of the British Government; and the British minister shall be empowered to change his ordinary place of residence, as may from time to time seem expedient, and be attended by such an escort as may be deemed suitable by his Government.

As in Bhawul Khan's.

" Article 10th.—This Treaty of nine Articles having been concluded, and signed and sealed by Lieutenant-Colonel Sir A. Burnes, Knight, Envoy on the part of the Right Honourable George Lord Auckland, G.C.B., Governor-General of India, and the Mir Rustam Khan, on the part of himself, Chief of Khairpur, the ratification by the Right Honourable

N. B.—The separate Article on surrendering Bakkar is not added, as it required no comment.

the Governor-General shall be exchanged within forty-five days from the present date.

"Done at Khairpur, this 24th day of December, 1838, corresponding with the 6th day of Shaval, A. H. 1254."

After the Treaty was sealed by the Mir Rustam Khan, I put into his hand the separate article for the cession of the fort of Bakkar. It was intended that it should not be presented to the chief till the offensive and defensive Treaty was signed. On reading the article the Mir Rustam Khan referred to the fourth article of the Treaty, in which it is stated that the English Government will not covet a dam or drain of the territories enjoyed by his Highness and his heirs, nor any fortress on this bank or that bank of the river Indus. I replied to the Mir that the English Government will adhere to every word of the article in which it has engaged, and I shall be the last person to commit any unjust trespass or oversight of the conditions which might reflect any stigma or disgrace on the Government, and on his friend Sir Alexander Burnes, who has deputed me to perform such important transactions: adding that in the fourth article my Government has indeed bound itself not to covet any land or fortress on this or that bank of the Indus, but that the separate article strictly stands by that condition of the Treaty while it demands the possession of the fort Bakkar, which is situated in the island between the banks, and which is thus quite free of the argument now used by the Mir. Here, again, the Mir Ali Morad, shaking his head, and holding his own beard, said to the Mir Rustam, that the day is not far distant when his folly in attaching credit to us and in throwing himself entirely on the rumoured justice of the English, and on the sweet words and promises of Sir Alexander Burnes, and of myself on the part of the Governor-General, will bring a calamity over the whole family; and that we by some art, pointing out some day a new meaning of some other word in the Treaty, will desire him to deliver up his capital, as we have now done with regard to the fort of Bakkar. The good Mir's answer was, that his beard has been silvered by age, during which space no one has deceived him and betrayed his confidence. That he has now thoroughly attached himself to the British, and in the hope of good fortune he has "thrown himself into the ocean of the justice and generosity of that nation, and whether he comes out safe, and with his hands full of pearls or of shells only, remains to be seen hereafter, and that the result will be a lesson for other princes who may seek the alliance of the English." He added, moreover, that as he has entered into the Treaty of ten articles, he must accept the separate one too, on which he sealed it and returned it to me. I must here as well say that it was promised by Sir Alexander Burnes and by myself to the Mir Rustam Khan, that the article which he has now sealed shall be given to him after it is ratified by the Governor-General; and the fort, which is only required by necessity "in time of war as a depôt for treasure, and munition," shall be restored when such war is over.

"Separate Article. Since the British Government has taken upon itself the responsibility of protecting the state of Khairpur from all enemies now and hereafter, and has neither coveted any portion of its possessions nor fortresses on this side or that side of the Indus, it is hereby agreed upon by the Mir Rustam Khan, his heirs and successors, that if the Governor-General in time of war should seek to occupy the fortress of Bakkar as a depôt for treasure and munitions, the Mir shall not object to it.

"This separate Article having been concluded, signed, and sealed by Lieutenant-Colonel Sir Alexander Burnes,

Knight, Envoy on the part of the Right Honourable George Lord Auckland, G.C.B., Governor-General of India, and the Mir Rustam Khan, on the part of himself as chief of Khairpur, the ratification by the Right Honourable the Governor-General shall be exchanged within forty days of the present date.

"Done at Khairpur, this 24th day of December, 1838, corresponding with the 6th day of Shaval, A.H. 1254.

"A. BURNES,
"*Envoy at Khairpur.*"

After having thus obtained the object of the mission, I returned with the accepted and sealed Treaties from the Mir Rustam Khan to Sir Alexander Burnes, at Shikarpur, and he despatched them to the Earl of Auckland. He also officially wrote to me, acknowledging my zeal, and the share I had in these successful negotiations with the Khairpur state, but unfortunately that document was plundered, with my other property and papers, in the outbreak of Kabul. I shall, however, quote one extract from Sir Alexander Burnes' official Report, in which my name appears to be mentioned:—*

"I had the honour this morning to convey to you, for

* Sindh Blue Book.

the information of the Governor-General of India, the successful termination of my negotiations with the Khairpur state, ending in the cession of Bakkar, on his Lordship's own terms, and in Northern Sindh being henceforward dependant on the British nation.

"I now do myself the honour to enclose the Treaty for his Lordship's ratification, and to state in detail, though as briefly as possible, the discussions which terminated in the instrument now enclosed. To one copy I have appended notes, as a clearer method of showing the motives that have actuated this chief and myself.

"I therefore drafted the treaty as it now stands, making a separate article regarding the cession of Bakkar, but binding the chief to approve of all our defensive preparations. I did this in order to give to the Mir Rustam Khan an opportunity of concealing our requests, if he feared his relatives, till we could support him in his resolution to give us Bakkar, supposing he so intended it.

"I sent Mohan Lal with the treaty, signed and sealed, to Khairpur, on the 11th inst., first directing him to give the document to the minister, and then to wait on the chief, if invited. After a delay of four days it appeared that all would end well ; but the minister was then directed to wait upon me at Shikarpur, and he came full of grief and dismay at the demands made, and even stated that he had not shown the separate article to the Mir Rustam Khan from downright shame.

"Supposing such a statement to have been true, which I

do not believe, it was evident that the Mir must be made acquainted forthwith with our terms; and I demanded of Mohan Lal, at Khairpur, to deliver the treaty face to face; to tell his Highness that the treaty and the separate article were one, and that the separation entirely arose from an anxiety on my part to place it out of men's power to vex him, and that the cession of Bakkar was for his good as well as ours.

"The consternation caused by this public declaration was very great: the Mir first offered another fort in its stead; next to find security that our treasure and munitions were protected; but Mohan Lal, as instructed, replied to all, that nothing but the unqualified cession of the fortress of Bakkar, during the war, would satisfy me. He said it was the heart of his country; his honour was centred in keeping it; his family and children could have no confidence if it were given up; and that if I came to Khairpur he could speak in person to me many things. To this I had instructed Mohan Lal to say, that this was impossible till he signed the treaty, as I asked a plain question and wanted a plain answer.

"Yesterday morning the Mir sent for Mohan Lal, and told him that I had been the best and first friend of the Khairpur state; that I had made an unexpected demand upon him; that his name was irrecoverably gone if Lord Auckland did not seize upon Karachi or some other place from the Haidarabad family, who, as our enemies, now triumphed, while he, as our dearest friend, was thus depressed. If they were let off, his only resource was to commit suicide. With this, and saying, 'Bismillah' (in the name of God), he sealed the treaty and the separate article, before Ali Morad Khan, Mir Zungi, Sulaiman Abdar, and about twenty other people."

On the 24th of January, 1839, the Bengal column of the army of the Indus reached and joined Sir Henry Fane, the Commander-in-Chief, at Rori. It had been formerly agreed on by us that the army will cross it about six miles above Rori, but the able chief engineer, Major Thomson, after mature deliberation and experiments, found that it was impossible to throw a bridge anywhere on the Indus but under the very walls of the fort of Bakkar. On this another discussion arose between us and the Khairpur state, in which again the Mir Ali Morad took a prominent part. Major Leech was deputed, and I was ordered to follow him, to the court of the Mir Rustam Khan, with instructions to persuade that chief not to distrust us by following the evil counsels of his brothers. The Mir gave permission for the bridge, and that part of the army crossed the Indus.

Now we demanded the cession of the fortress of Bakkar, in accordance with the separate agreement, on which the Mir Rustam Khan, with his brothers Mirs Ali Morad, Mobarak, and Sangi, and his minister, Fatah Mohammed Ghori, justly remarked that we have not yet settled our differences, nor made any treaty of alliance with the Mir of Haidarabad in Lower Sindh; and having taken advantage of their sincere attachment to our government, we wish to make use of them as the first chiefs in Sindh who gave up their fort while the rest of the family held their independence. This, they said, will throw an everlasting stigma on the character of their descendants. We lent no ears to their reasonable and friendly remonstrance on this point; and I was ordered again to wait upon the chief, and to state to him, in the presence of all the members of the family, that if the fort was not instantly delivered, the troops shall be employed to possess it by force. Now a most overwhelming altercation commenced among them; in which the Mir Rustam Khan, in spite of all the frivolous, but mischievous excuses of his brothers, gave me the key of the fort, with one of his attendants to tell to the governor to quit it immediately. When I arrived at the gate of the fort, a swarm of Bilochis, about one hundred altogether came on the top of it, and said to the attendant sent with me by the Mir Rustam Khan, that they are servants of the whole family, and will therefore obey the united orders of the brothers. However, after a protracted discussion between him and the garrison, the gate was opened, where Lieut. Wood of the Indian navy followed me with the flag, and gave a sign for the movement of our forces. I gave up the key to Sir Willoughby Cotton, who, with the Commander-in-Chief and Sir Alexander Burnes, entered the fort, and the British flag was hoisted up and floated in the breeze, throwing a beautiful reflection in the waters of the Indus.

On the 26th of January, 1839, it was arranged that Mir of Khairpur, with his brothers, should wait upon Sir Henry Fane; and he was received by his Excellency with that respect and civility of which his friendship to the British government was deserving. With the view of giving stronger proofs of the British appreciation of the friendship of the Mir towards our government, the treaty ratified by the Governor-General was given to the Mir Rustam Khan by the Commander-in-Chief himself, with assurances of perpetual cordiality and amity. This was accompanied by a letter from the Earl of Auckland himself to the Mir, the copy of which, in the proper place, will much characterise the change of our policy in behalf of so well-deserving an ally as the Mir Rustam Khan.

The cession of the fort of Bakkar, and the march of the Bengal army towards Haidarabad, brought the judicious measures of Sir Henry Pottinger in that court to a favourable issue. Before the Commander-in-Chief moved with the forces, the Mirs of Khairpur objected to our march by the right bank of the Indus, and especially by the route leading to their capital. Colonel Gordon, the Quartermaster, did not receive any civility from the Bilochis, who had pitched in a considerable number between Rori and Khairpur, under the Mir Rustam Khan, and the Mir Ali Morad. Alarms of a night attack on our army at Rori were caused in the camp; and I was directed in that late hour to go to the Bilochi camp, escorted by ten of the cavalry. On my arrival in the Bilochi camp, I went straight to the tent of the Mir Rustam Khan; but the Mir Ali Morad, having received an intimation of my proceeding from Rori, had given orders that I was not to be announced to the Mir before the information was given to him. I did not dismount from my horse; and a reckless set of the Bilochis surrounded my party with drawn swords, and began to insult us by ill language and threats. I waited with patience the reply of the Mir Ali Morad; which having arrived, I immediately proceeded to his tent. I said to him that the object of my mission was to state to the Mir Rustam Khan that the British Government and the Khairpur Mirs had been united by an offensive and defensive treaty, and that it was not a friendly act of the Mirs to prevent the allied army from passing by their capital. The Mir Ali Morad said that the bridge was ready, and we could easily march our forces by the left bank. He added, in the strongest language possible, that if we will determine to proceed by the right bank great bloodshed will occur, and the Bilochis will not permit us to pass by Khairpur, where their wives and families reside; and that it will bring a stain on their national character to permit us to pass by their abode, and thus to expose them to a foreign army. I replied, that nothing could frighten the British-Indian army; and as to the threats of bloodshed of which the Mir speaks, our soldiers, who are led by brave officers, treat them as nothing. I stated that I had come to have a conference with the Mir Rustam Khan, who was the head chief; and that his suggestions on the points of my mission would provide my superiors with the opportunity of coming to a final decision. The Mir Ali Morad replied, that the Mir Rustam Khan had gone to bed, and had vested in him full powers to confer with us, and that he will therefore not allow me to go to his tent. I said no more, but left him. Finding, however, that his servant had not followed me, I stepped into the tent of the Mir Rustam Khan without permission; and he was sitting there, and was surprised to see me. I told him the Mir Ali Morad is causing ruin for him, in order to promote his own views; and that if the Mir were to follow his advice, which from the commencement had been injurious to him (Rustam), he will forfeit the kind feelings of our Government. He immediately broke up the camp, and gave orders that his tent and followers should follow him to the capital, and that no one belonging to him was to remain with the Mir Ali Morad. He stated "that he has planted the tree of friendship with the

British, and will never cease to water it, with the hope that he may enjoy the fruits hereafter." I returned to the camp of Sir Henry Fane, and reported the result of my mission to him. The army moved next morning; and I was directed, from the Political department, to proceed with Sir Willoughby Cotton as an agent, while Sir Alexander Burnes remained with the Commander-in-Chief one march in the rear. I was accompanied by the brother of the Khairpur minister; and during the march every thing necessary, as supplies or information, were gained to the satisfaction of Sir Willoughby Cotton: so that Major Havelock, C.B., writes in this manner:—

"The brother of Mir Rustam Khan's Vazir, with a considerable 'Savari' accompanied our advance; and we had the assistance, as an agent for the relief of our wants, and an interpreter, able in both capacities, of the celebrated Mirza Mohan Lal, who speaks English with a good accent and with much idiomatic propriety. This intelligent and amiable man accompanied Sir Alexander Burnes through his wanderings in Central Asia, displaying everywhere a rare union of zeal, tact, and fidelity. The educated people in Sindh all converse in Persian with fluency, with which 'lingua Franca,' as it may be justly esteemed, from the

Indus to the Caspian, the good Mirza was equally familiar."

The advance of the Bombay army under Lord Keane, and the co-operation of that sincere ally the Mir Rustam Khan of Khairpur, to facilitate the progress of our views, as well as the march of Sir Willoughby Cotton's force, induced the Mirs of Haidarabad to receive Captain Eastwick, and to accept the Treaty sent by Sir Henry Pottinger.

Draft of Treaty to be proposed to the Mirs of Haidarabad.

"WHEREAS treaties of friendship and amity have, from time to time, been entered into between the British and Haidarabad Governments; and whereas circumstances have lately occurred which render it expedient and necessary to revise those treaties; with a view to which this draft has been prepared, agreeably to instructions addressed by the Right Honourable George Lord Auckland, Governor-General of India, &c. &c. &c., to Colonel Henry Pottinger, Resident in Sindh.

"1st. That there shall be lasting friendship, alliance, and amity between the Honourable the East India Company and the Haidarabad Government; and the provisions of all former treaties, not modified or annulled by the present one, are hereby confirmed.

"2nd. The Governor-General of India has commanded

that a British force shall be kept in Sindh, and stationed at the city of Tattah, where a cantonment will be formed. The strength of this force is to depend on the pleasure of the Governor-General of India.

"3rd. Mir Nur Mohammed Khan, Mir Nasir Mohammed Khan, and Mir Mohammed Khan bind themselves to pay annually the sum of
in part of the expense of the force, from the presence of which their respective territories will derive such vast advantages.

"4th. The chiefs of Bilochi tribes, and all others holding grants (jaedads), pensions (vazifas), jagirs (tesols), &c., from the different Mirs, are to continue to enjoy them as they now do, the Mirs being answerable for their peaceful conduct towards the British Government and its subjects.

"5th. The British Government pledges itself neither to interfere, in any degree, great or small, in the internal management or affairs of the several possessions of the Mirs, nor to think of introducing, in any shape, its regulations or adalats.

"6th. The British Government pledges itself on no pretence to listen to the complaints of the Bilochi chiefs, or any other subjects, whether Musalmans or Hindus, or other castes, against their highnesses.

"7th. The British Government agrees to protect Sindh from all foreign possession.

"8th. The Company's rupee being exactly of the same value as that called the bakru or timure, it is to be considered current in the British cantonment and in this country at the same rate; but in every case, when the British Government may have to coin any of the rupees now in circulation in Sindh, the seignorage or dues of the Sindh Government shall be paid, agreeable to the custom of the country.

"9th. Should any Mir attack or injure the possessions of another Mir, or those of his dependants, the Resident of Sindh will, on receiving the sanction of the Governor-General of India, act as mediator between them; but it is to be distinctly understood that he (the Resident) is not to intermeddle with trifling points.

"10th. Should any Bilochi, or other chief, rebel against the authority of the Mir to whom he appertains, or attack the lands or other possessions of any other Mir or chief, and the Mir to whom he appertains shall declare his inability to coerce such chief, the Governor-General will take his case into consideration, on its being submitted to his Lordship by the Resident, and will, should his Lordship see sufficient reason, order such assistance to be given as may be requisite to punish the offender.

"11th. Their highnesses the Mirs agree to form no new treaties, or enter into any engagements with foreign states, without the knowledge and concurrence of the British Government; but their highnesses will, of course, carry on friendly correspondence, as usual, with all their neighbours.

"12th. The British Government agrees, on its part, not to form any treaty or enter into any engagement that can possibly affect the interest of Sindh, without the concurrence and knowledge of their highnesses the Mirs.

"13th. During the months of the year that vessels cannot enter the mouths of the Indus, the communication between Bombay and Sindh by sea is to be carried on by Karachi Bandar; and should it any time be requisite to send public stores to that place, every facility is to be afforded by the Sindh authorities to their being landed and forwarded under a guard, which will be sent from Tattah, to receive and watch them.

"14th. The Mirs agree to either build, or allow the British Government to build, an enclosure and storehouse at Karachi as a depôt for stores, their highnesses incurring no sort of expense on this account, and being repaid (should they build the enclosure, &c.) for any outlay they may incur.

"15th. Should any British merchants, or others, bring goods by way of Karachi Bandar, the duties of the Sindh Government (both import and transit) will be paid on them, agreeable to the custom of the country, and no exemption of such duties shall be claimed.

"16th. Amongst the great objects of the Governor-General in fixing a British force in Sindh, is that of perfecting the arrangements which have been in progress for several years for the opening of the Indus to traders; and as the thoroughfare (amad-o-raft) will now be increased an hundredfold, the contracting governments agree to abolish all tolls on the river from the sea to Firozpur.

"17th. To protect the interests of the different governments from any loss that might arise from the unrestrained intercourse provided for in the preceding article, it is hereby agreed, that all goods landed and sold (except those that are sold in the British camp or cantonment) shall be subject to duties agreeable to the usage of Sindh and the other states on that point, and no exception shall be made to this stipulation.

"18th. Goods of all kinds may be brought, by merchants and others, to the mouth of the Indus (Gorabi) at the proper season, and kept there, at the pleasure of the owners, till the best period of the year for sending them up the river; but should any merchant land and sell any part of his merchandise, either at Gorabari or any where else (except at the British cantonment or camp), such merchant shall pay the duties on them.

"19th. Should the British Government at any time require and apply for the aid of the army of Sindh, their Highnesses the Mirs agree to furnish it according to their means; and in any such case the Governor-General of India will take into consideration the expense the Mirs may incur, with a view to the diminution of the sum mentioned in the 3rd Article of this treaty.

"20th. The terms of this treaty are to be considered applicable to Mir Sobdar Khan, of Haidarabad.

"21st. A separate treaty has been made between the British Government and Mir Rustam Khan, of Khairpur.

"22d. Should Mir Shere Mohammed of Mirpur wish

it, a treaty, on the basis of this one, will be made with him.

"23rd. The British Government undertakes to guarantee to the different Mirs, their heirs and successors, on their acquiescing in the terms of this treaty, the perpetual enjoyment of their respective possessions; and the friends and enemies of one party shall be friends and enemies of the other.

"This treaty of Twenty-three Articles having been concluded, and signed and sealed, its ratification by the Right Honourable the Governor-General shall be exchanged within forty days from this date.

" Done at Haidarabad, on the day of , 1839, A.D., corresponding with the day of Hejri."

The objects of the Governor-General, both in Haidarabad and in Khairpur, were thus completed to the satisfaction of his Lordship, and in a manner becoming the dignity and honour of Britain, and which at the same time preserved the good feeling and the rights of the Mirs of Sindh. Before I proceed to my narrative of the progress of the army of the Indus on quitting the frontiers of Sindh *en route* to Afghanistan, it would be a matter of serious interest to read the fate of such faithful and independent allies as the Mir Rustam Khan, &c., who, both in the time of forming the expedition and during the disasters of Afghanistan, proved himself to be a sincere and cordial coadjutor in advancing our interests. But there are such grave subjects connected with the decline of the independence of Sindh, and the dethronement of our allies, that my observations on them will not be considered just and palatable. I shall therefore quote some impartial remarks on this subject from a most valuable work just published :—*

"The Resident had deferred making to the Mirs a definite communication of the views of the British Government as to their future position till this period; and as a diplomatist he acted rightly. The Mirs were intensely averse to even the passage of troops through their territories; the notion of a British force permanently occupying any part of those territories had never entered their minds.† The

* 'History of British India,' by Thornton, vol. vi. pp. 408–466.

† "This appears from the communications of Colonel Pottinger to his Government :—'I now beg to acknowledge the receipt of your letter of the 19th ultimo; and after most attentively studying the instructions conveyed by it, I am obliged

time at length arrived for suggesting it; and the draft of a Treaty was submitted to them, the second article of which declared that the Governor-General of India had commanded that a British force should be kept in Sindh, to be stationed at Tattah, where a cantonment was to be formed; and that the strength of this force was to depend on the pleasure of the said Governor-General. Thus in the outset it was assumed that the rulers of Sindh were dependent upon the Government of British India; for the stationing of a military force at Tattah, and the determining the amount of the force, were not made subjects of mutual contracts; the first point was rested on the Governor-General's command, and

candidly to confess that I feel myself placed in a situation in which I can indulge no hope of carrying the Governor-General's commands into effect on the principle prescribed. My despatches, subsequent to that of the 2nd of November, will have shown the abject state to which Nur Mohammed Khan has been reduced by my refusal to treat with him relative to the money payment to Shah Shujah-ul-Mulk; but even when labouring under his worst apprehensions, it will be observed that no such idea has apparently ever crossed his mind as that our ultimate plan was to station even a company of sepoys in Sindh; and the moment that intention is announced, I think it will be the signal for a cordial coalition to oppose our arrangements.'"—*Letter, December 15th*, 1838, *Sindh Papers*, p. 133.

the second was left to his pleasure. By the next succeeding article it was provided that the Mirs should pay a sum (left open in the draft) in part of the expense of the force, 'from the presence of which they will derive such vast advantages.' Such was the language employed; the chief advantage, as far as can be discerned, being the exchange of sovereignty for dependence.

"The draft treaty was laid before the Mirs, and Lieutenant Eastwick, with some other British officers, were admitted to an audience for the purpose of discussing and explaining this extraordinary document. On this occasion Nur Mohammed took from a box all the treaties that had formerly been entered into with the British Government, and significantly asked, 'What is to become of all these?' The question was not an inappropriate one, and it was followed by some observations not unfaithfully describing the progress of the intercourse between Sindh and the British Government. The Mir said, 'Here is another annoyance. Since the day that Sindh has been connected with the English there has always been something new; your Government is never satisfied; we are anxious for your friendship, but we cannot be continually persecuted. We have given a road to your troops through our territories, and now you wish to remain.'

"It would be useless to pursue the history of this period minutely. The Mirs of Haidarabad were well disposed to resist, and the Bilochi population not less ready to support their resistance. The British mission returned from the capital to the British camp, danger being apprehended from a continued stay at the former place. But difficulties, discouragements, and circumstances of embarrassment congregated thick and fast round the Mirs. The army of Sir John Keane was marching onward to Haidarabad; the reserve was in possession of Karachi; Sir Alexander Burnes had concluded a treaty with the Mirs of Khairpur, by which possession of Bakkar had been obtained; and Sir Willoughby Cotton, with the force under his command, was approaching from that quarter. In this situation the Mirs had no choice, but, in their own language, to become our humblest slaves: and the offensive treaty was accepted; the sum to be paid for the subsidiary force being fixed at three lakhs. But this treaty was not entirely approved by the government of British India. Three of the articles which related to the use of Karachi as a port during the months when other modes of communicating between Bombay and Sindh were not available, were struck out, inasmuch as the English were in possession of that place, and their Government meant to keep it. In the second article, as accepted by the Mirs, the exercise of the pleasure of the Governor-General, as to the force to be maintained in Sindh, had been restricted to the employment of five thousand men. This was qualified so as to declare no more than that it was not intended that the force should exceed five thousand fighting men, thus virtually restoring the article to its original state. By another modification the power of the British Government was almost indefinitely extended as to the choice of the locality in which this force should be stationed. Instead of being fixed absolutely at Tattah, it was to be either there or at such other place westward of the river Indus as the Governor-General might select. There were other alterations, the most important of which was the omission of an article restraining the British Government from forming any treaty or engagement which could possibly affect the interests of Sindh, without the knowledge and concurrence of the Mirs. The remainder it will not be requisite to notice. The result of the changes may readily be anticipated; the Mirs objected, implored, and finally gave way, by affixing their seals to the revised documents.

"Thus, in a very brief period, was Sindh reduced from a state of perfect independence to that of a feudatory of the British government. The modern history of India affords many instances of similar changes; but few, if indeed any, in which the incorporation has been effected so entirely without fair pretence. The Mirs of Sindh wished no alliance or connexion with us; they owed us nothing, and they had inflicted on us no injury; but it suited our policy to reduce them to vassalage, and they were thus reduced. If it be argued that we could not have prosecuted our views in Afghanistan without securing the dominion of Sindh, it must be answered, that if such were the case, they ought to have been abandoned. We had an object, and a legitimate one, to accomplish in Afghanistan; and as far as the rulers of that country, and those who claimed to rule it, were concerned, the prosecution of our policy did not violate the laws of justice; but if it could not be pursued without invading the rights of others, there ought to have been an end to all attempts for carrying it out. It might be, and without doubt it was, very convenient to pass through Sindh: but we might have confined the passage of our army to Upper Sindh, where the reluctance to grant the favour seems to have been less strong; or we might have entered Afghanistan without passing through Sindh at all. With Ranjit Singh we had a long-established alliance. Why should so old a friend distrust us? If he did, how could we expect to find greater favour from those who had always looked coldly upon us? And, finally, if both authorities refused us that which we wanted, upon what principle did we select Sindh for coercion? The principle was this:—we could not safely quarrel with Ranjit Singh, but we entertained little apprehension of danger from the Mirs of Sindh.

"When Lord Auckland retired from the government of British India, the subsidiary treaty was that which regulated the relations of that government with Sindh. Little of importance had occurred since its ratification, except the death of Nur Mohammed, the chief of the college of Mirs at Haidarabad, and some negotiations for transferring to the British the management of Shikarpur, which were never concluded. It was alleged that the Mirs had been engaged with various parties in correspondence of a dangerous tendency to British interests. The charge is not improbable, and may have been true; but it is remarkable that the terrible reverses which our army sustained in Afghanistan, and the consequent diminution of our military reputation, did not tempt the Mirs, writhing as they were under a deep sense of wrong, into any overt act of hostility. Indeed, the man likely to be best informed on the subject, Colonel Outram, political agent in Sindh, declared that nothing very definite had been resolved on, and expressed an opinion that such changeable, puerile, and divided chieftains were not ever likely to enter into deep, and consequently dangerous, conspiracy; nor did he consider that anything of the sort would be persevered in so long as no further disasters befel our arms in Afghanistan."

"This was written on the last day of May, 1842, when our prospects in Afghanistan were brightening.

"Early in the year 1842, Lord Ellenborough, as already mentioned, arrived in India as the successor of Lord Auckland. In May, from what especial cause does not appear, his Lordship transmitted to Colonel Outram letters addressed to the three divisions of the Mirs, threatening them with the confiscation of their dominions in the event of their proving faithless to the British government. The agent was allowed a discretion as to the delivery of these letters, and in the exercise of that discretion he withheld them.

"The Governor-General was prepared to dispossess the Mirs of their territories; but on the supposition that no sufficient, or ostensibly sufficient cause might be afforded for this step, he meditated an important change in their situation in regard to the British government. This was the commutation of the tribute payable by the Mirs to that government by the transfer of territory; and the localities where cessions of territory were to be derived were specified. Colonel Outram submitted to the Governor-General the sketch of a supplemental treaty embodying these views; but for some reason not explained, his Lordship deemed it not advisable to press negotiations on the Mirs precipitately, and determined to leave their minds for the present in tranquillity.*

"The tranquillity conceded was not of long duration. In the month following that in which expression has been given to the wish that the Mirs should enjoy this inestimable boon of tranquillity, Major-General Sir Charles Napier was ordered to proceed to Sindh to assume the chief military command there. This was not all; he was also to exercise the chief political and civil authority. Such an arrangement, under particular circumstances, may be sometimes beneficial. The present instance is pronounced by a writer, hostile to Lord Auckland, and generally favourable to Lord Ellenborough, to have been 'a step, at such a crisis, of very questionable policy.'†

"Sir Charles Napier, in accordance with the instructions of the Governor-General, proceeded to Sindh, and on the 5th of October reported that the

* "Letter to Political Agent in Sindh, 10th April, 1842.—*Sindh Papers*, p. 380."

† "'A Great Country's Little Wars,' by Henry Lushington, p. 221."

Mirs levied tolls on the river, contrary to the treaty. Without waiting for the result of the remonstrance which the British representative made on the subject, that functionary was, by instructions forwarded in answer to his communication, directed to intimate to the Mirs that he was authorised to treat for a revision of the treaty. The agent to whom these instructions were addressed was nothing loth to follow them; and, in a paper of extraordinary length, he recorded his conviction that the existing state of political relations between Sindh and the British Government could not last; that the more powerful government would at no very distant period swallow up the weaker; and that it would be better to come to the results at once, if it could be done with honesty. The difficulty of doing it with honesty was great; but Sir Charles Napier was not a man to despair. An array of charges against the Mirs, extending over a considerable period, was transmitted to the Governor-General; and was answered by the draft of a treaty to be presented for the acceptance of the alleged offenders. By this document, required to carry into effect the project of obtaining territory in place of tribute, certain places were pointed out as centres, to which a convenient arrondissement of country was to be assigned at the pleasure of the British general and political representative of his government. Another portion of territory was to be taken to reward the fidelity of the Khan of Bhavalpur as a British ally. The Mirs were to provide fuel for the steamers navigating the Indus; and if they failed, the servants of the British government were to be entitled to fell wood within a hundred yards of the banks of the river, within the territories of the Mirs. This was an offensive privilege, but not the most offensive that was claimed.

"By a series of articles in the treaty, which would seem to have been framed purposely with a view to insult, the Mirs were to cease to exercise the privilege of coining,—one of the chief characteristics of sovereignty. The British government were to coin for them; and, to aggravate the indignity offered to these wretched princes, the coin was to bear on one side the effigy of the sovereign of England. Thus, every transaction at every bazar throughout Sindh was to be made the means of publicly proclaiming that the Mirs had ceased to rule,—that they had become dependants of a foreign potentate, and held so much of authority as was allowed to remain with them only by the sufferance of a superior, or of the servants of that superior. Separate treaties were to be tendered to the government of Haidarabad and to those of Khairpur; but they were framed upon the same principles and directed to the same ends.

"The justice of imposing such severe terms was rested upon the authenticity of the letters said to have been written respectively by Mir Nasir Khan of Haidarabad and Mir Rustam Khan of Khairpur, and on the escape of an insurgent leader from the British authorities, through the agency of a servant of the latter prince. As to the letters, every one acquainted with Oriental affairs knows that correspondence is constantly fabricated to aid any purpose that may be in hand.

"It is not meant that any Englishman was connected with the fabrication in this case, supposing the process to have been resorted to, or had any acquaintance with the matter. The supposition is unnecessary; native adventurers have great tact in guessing what will be useful or acceptable to those above them, and a rare facility in counterfeiting both signatures and seals. The authenticity of the letters was denied by the alleged writers. The denial is certainly not to be received as conclusive against belief in their authenticity; but such belief is not warranted by any sufficient evidence. The seal attached to the latter, professed to be from Mir Nasir Khan, differed from the ordinary seal of that prince, but was said to correspond with another seal which he was represented to possess. The authenticity of the letter, however, was doubted by at least one very competent judge. The letter of Mir Rustam Khan, according to the admission of those who brought it forward in accusation against him, could not be traced to his cognizance; it was believed to have been written by his minister, but whether with or without his knowledge was not shown. And the escape of the prisoner from British custody was in like manner traceable no further than to the agent by whom it was effected. Certainly the rights of princes were never assailed on such slender ground as these charges afforded. But it was enough, for reasons not then disclosed; it was resolved to go forward with the process which had been commenced under a different administration, to tighten the grasp of the British government upon Sindh, and thus to accelerate the progress of the movement which was to convert that country into a British province in name as well as in fact.

"The treaties were presented for the acceptance of the Mirs both of Upper and Lower Sindh on the 6th of December; they were accompanied by letters from Sir Charles Napier, intimating his intention to take immediate possession of the districts which it was proposed to assign to the Khan of Bhavalpur. The letters were dated the 1st of the month, and on the 18th publicity was given to the intention by the issue of a proclamation signed by the British general; which, after reciting the orders under which he acted, and the purpose which he had in view, declared that if the Mirs should, after the commencement of the ensuing year, collect any revenue in advance, or impose any new tax within the districts which they were destined to lose, they should be punished by amercement. At this time the new treaties were matters for discussion—they had not been ratified—they were mere proposals from one party which the opposite parties might reject; subject, of course, to the penalty attached to rejection. But it cannot fail to be observed, that Sindh is dealt with by Sir Charles Napier as though the right of the Governor-General of British India to parcel it out at his pleasure were unquestioned and unquestionable; and moreover as if it were desired to exercise. The direct tendency of the proclamation was to render the Mirs contemptible in the eyes of those whom they were yet, perhaps for a time, to be permitted to regard as subjects. Such a course could not facilitate the acceptance of the proffered treaties; it was directly calculated to influence hostile feelings already believed to prevail in their minds; and had it been determined to hurry on an appeal to the sword, no more likely means could have been devised than the issue of this most injudicious and insulting proclamation.

"The extraordinary constitution of the Sindh government has already been adverted to. An incident arising from this cause has now to be noticed. Mir Rustam was the chief of the Mirs of Khairpur. He was above eighty years of age, and consequently no long tenure of life and power (such power as he was likely to retain) could be anticipated for him. According to the constitution of the Sindh state (if constitution it had), Ali Morad, brother of Mir Rustam, was the legitimate successor of the prince in the chieftainship. Mir Rustam, it was alleged, wished to divert the succession in favour of his own son; and Ali Morad applied to Sir Charles Napier for support against any such attempt, should it be made. It was promised on condition of the fidelity of Ali Morad to the British cause. But something further was wished. The unmanageableness of a government constituted like that of Sindh was obvious enough; and it occurred to Sir Charles Napier that the age of Mir Rustam, and a presumed indisposition on his part to be longer burthened with the toils and vexations of government, might afford means for effecting some modification favourable to British influence. The following statement rests upon the authority of Sir Charles Napier; but it is proper to observe in the outset that it is not in all points uncontroverted. Mir Rustam sent a secret communication to Sir Charles Napier, to the effect that he could do nothing, and would make his escape to the British General's camp. This step was not desired; it was regarded as inconvenient: and by a very adroit, if not a very straightforward, piece of diplomacy, the General was relieved alike from the embarrassment which would have resulted from entertaining Mir Rustam in his camp, and from that which would have followed his refusing him his refuge. As the transaction was in many points extraordinary, it will be best to relate it, as far as possible, in the words of the chief actor, Sir Charles Napier himself.

" It appeared then to him, that the only desirable system to follow in Sindh was that of making the chief powerful, and holding him under the power of the government—the British government being meant. 'This,' writes Sir Charles Napier, addressing the Governor-General, 'made me promise Ali Morad, your Lordship's support in having the turban,* which your Lordship has approved of. The next step was to secure him the exercise of its power now, even during his brother's life. This I was so fortunate to succeed in, by persuading Mir Rustam to place himself in Ali Morad's hands.'† Mir Rustam accordingly, instead of proceeding to the British camp, threw himself upon his brother, and surrendered to him the

* " The word turban, it will be perceived, is here used in the same sense as the word crown is frequently employed — to indicate the sovereignty."

† " Letter to Governor-General, 27th December, 1842.—*Sindh Papers*, p. 515."

chief authority. He seems, however, soon to have repented of the steps which he had taken, for in a very few days he escaped from the care of the person to whom he had been commended by the British General.*

"The flight of Mir Rustam — his first flight, namely, that which was followed by the surrender of his power to Ali Morad—excited great consternation among his family and followers. They forthwith fled; but not to the British camp, nor to Ali Morad. Their choice was the desert; and the greater portion were reported to have sought safety in a fort

* "That the intrigues of Oriental princes should be inexplicable is nothing new. Unfortunately, in this instance, the conduct of the British general is inexplicable also, and his statements irreconcileable until he shall furnish some further explanation. An account given by him has been closely followed in the narrative which will be found in the text, but it ought not to be concealed that the letters of the gallant general, written at different periods, contained discrepancies amounting to positive contradictions. The account followed above was written only eight days after the transactions recorded, and coincides with another more brief, which bears date on the day after Mir Rustam sought shelter with his brother. Any reader disposed to exercise his ingenuity in unravelling the perplexities and reconciling the discordance of this strange affair, all resting on the authority of Sir Charles Napier, will find abundant opportunity in the papers on the subject. Some notice of them will be found hereafter."

called Imam Ghar. Thither Sir Charles Napier resolved to follow them; and commenced his march without delay. No certain intelligence as to a supply of water being attainable, it was deemed prudent to take forward only a very small force. It consisted of three hundred and fifty men of the Queen's 22nd, mounted on camels (two on each animal), two hundred Sindhian horse, and two 24-pounder howitzers. The want of forage rendered it necessary to send back a hundred and fifty of the horse. The remainder of the force encountered the difficulties of the desert march, which were great, and reached Imam Ghar, which place was occupied without difficulty, and destroyed. The fort was stated to belong to Ali Morad, who consented to its destruction. The march of the British general, and the capture and destruction of a fortress belonging to some or other of the authorities of Sindh, took place at a time when we were professedly in a state of peace with all. It is greatly, therefore, to be desired, for the credit of the British name, that the statement above noticed should be correct. It has, however, been disputed, and with some appearance of truth. The fall of Imam Ghar took place early in the month of January, 1843.

"The event was not without effect, but the Mirs were yet naturally anxious to put off the evil day, which was to divest them of almost the very semblance of sovereignty. Major Outram, whose powers had been withdrawn, and who had consequently retired to Bombay, it was thought, might by his personal influence be able to effect something in the way of diminishing the reluctance of the princes to sign the sentence of their own virtual deposition. He returned, held various conferences with the Mirs, and finally prevailed on them personally to affix their seals to the treaties.* But there were other parties who claimed the privilege of judging beside the Mirs. The Bilochi tribes—bold, fierce, and intractable—were greatly excited againt the European intruders, who, by no slow advances, were establishing their own authority supreme in Sindh. As the British commissioner and his attendants departed from the final conference, they were assailed with execrations from an assembled crowd, who were restrained from more dangerous expression of their

* "With the exception of one of the Mirs of Khairpur, who alleged that his seal was in the possession of his brother, and promised to ratify the treaty at a future time."

feelings only by the presence of a strong escort of horse sent by the Mirs, under the command of some of their most influential chiefs.

"One great point on which the Mirs had dwelt in their conferences with Major Outram was the wrong which the British authorities had caused, and continued to uphold, in the transfer of authority from Mir Rustam to Ali Morad. It was stated that the surrender of power by the latter had been the effect of compulsion; and seeing that the aged chieftain was altogether in the hands of his brother, it is very probable such was the fact. The political move, which the British general thought a masterstroke of diplomacy, thus became a chief cause of embarrassing the negotiation; while it placed a chief, venerable for his years at least, in the position of an oppressed and injured man, and left on the shoulders of the highest British authority in Sindh the charge of being the principal author of the chieftain's degradation.*

* "The embarrassing situation in which Sir Charles Napier placed himself by his proceedings in regard to Mir Rustam and Ali Morad was obviously felt by him very deeply, as may be seen by a collation of his statement on the subject in the Sindh Papers and the supplementary collection. "The

"It was constantly represented by the Mirs that the continued advance of Sir Charles Napier would

"The first notice of the affair to be found in the printed papers occurs in a letter from Sir Charles Napier to the Governor-General, dated Sukkar, December 20th, 1842, which commences thus:—

"'I had a secret message from Mir Rustam. The bearer had an open letter in the usual unmeaning style of the Darbar; but the messenger privately informed Lieutenant Brown that Rustam could do nothing, and would escape to my camp. I did not like this, as it would have embarrassed me very much how to act; but the idea struck me at once that he might go to Ali Morad, who might induce him (as a family arrangement) to resign the turban to him (Ali Morad), especially as Rustam has long been desirous of getting rid of this charge of the Talpurs. I therefore secretly wrote to Rustam and Ali Morad; and about one o'clock this morning I had an express from Ali Morad to say that his brother is safe with him, and that he requested me not to move upon Khairpur before twelve o'clock to-day, to give time for his women to get away in safety. This I promised; and the more readily, as I could not (from other circumstances) move before to-morrow. Ali Morad is now virtually chief; for if Mir Rustam does not bestow the turban upon him, he will, at all events, be guided by Ali, into whose hands he has voluntarily thrown himself. Ali Morad was more powerful than any of the Talpurs, even when Mir Rustam's name and power were against him; now he is irresistible, and in alliance with us besides.' After a few further observations, Sir Charles Napier briefly sums up the results of the course which he had followed, and at the head of the summary stand the three points following:—First, that Ali Morad, the most powerful of the Talpur family, is secured to our interest by the promise of

exasperate the Bilochis, and cause them to resort to arms in defence of the independence of their country.

the turban. Second, that the chief of the Talpurs, frightened at the violence of his family, and at our steady operations to coerce them, has thrown himself into his brother's power by my advice; otherwise I should believe some trick was intended. Third, that we having complete power over the brother, have power over all without any chief making, or any apparent interference or any disturbance of the natural order of succession.

"In another letter to the Governor-General, dated 27th of December, Sir Charles Napier, after adverting to the duplicity of the Mirs, says, 'This conviction opened upon me a system which appears the only one to follow—making the chief powerful, and holding him under the power of the Government. This made me venture to promise Ali Morad your Lordship's support in having the turban, which your Lordship has approved of. The next step was to secure him the exercise of its power now even during his brother's life. This I was so fortunate to succeed in by persuading Mir Rustam to place himself in Ali Morad's hands. This burst upon his family and followers like a bomb-shell.' In a letter of a still later date (29th December), also addressed to the Governor-General, Sir Charles Napier, who had then become acquainted with Mir Rustam's flight from his brother, thus writes—'Mir Rustam had resigned the turban to his brother Ali in the most formal manner, writing his resignation in the Qoran before all the religious men collected to witness the resignation at Diji. Ali sent the Qoran to me to see it: I said that these family arrangements were their own, but that your Lordship would support the head of their family, whoever it might be, according to the spirit of the treaty. That I personally thought it better for Rustam to keep the turban, and let Ali Morad act for him; but that he was free to do as he

That officer, however, continued to advance, and on the 15th of February the long-threatened outbreak took

pleased ; it was a family arrangement with which your Lordship would not interfere.'

"This much is to be gathered from the first published collection of papers relating to Sindh, and the amount may be stated as follows :—That Mir Rustam proposed to escape to the British camp ; that Sir Charles Napier was desirous of averting such a movement, and suggested that the old chief should take refuge with his brother Ali Morad ; that in making this suggestion he was actuated by a wish to place Ali Morad, at all events, in possession of the actual power attached to what is called the turban itself. He abstained from suggesting the transfer, but thought it might be effected by a family arrangement. Mir Rustam acted on the British general's advice ; proceeded to join his brother, and by his own free consent, or as the result of compulsion, made the surrender of the turban as Sir Charles Napier had desired.

"The supplementary collection of papers contain the following letter from Sir Charles Napier to Mir Rustam, which it is to be presumed is the letter written in answer to the alleged communication from the chief to the British general—offering to come to his camp. 'My own belief is that, personally, you have ever been the friend of the English. But you are helpless among your ill-judging family. I send this by your brother his Highness Ali Morad. Listen to his advice, trust yourself to his care : you are too old for war ; and, if battle begin, how can I protect you? If you go with your brother, you may either remain with him or I will send an escort for you to bring you to my camp, where you will be safe.

"'Follow my advice, it is that of a friend. Why should I be your enemy? If I was, why should I take this trouble to save

place, the first object of attack being the residence of the British commissioner, Colonel Outram. A dense

you? I think you will believe me; but do as you please.' This letter, it will be observed, does indeed give the person to whom it is addressed the option of coming to the British camp after he had surrendered himself to his brother and successor Ali Morad, not at once and immediately; and Sir Charles Napier, in his correspondence with the Governor-General, declared that the presence of the Mir in his camp would embarrass him.

"In a paper drawn up by Sir Charles Napier, at a later period, and which will be found in the supplementary collection, pp. 112-115, as an enclosure in a letter to the Governor-General, dated 10th of August, 1843, numbered 155, the writer, after adverting to some conversations with Ali Morad, thus continues. 'Soon after, a message arriving from Mir Rustam, claiming my protection against the intrigues of his own family, offered an opportunity of having one man to deal with instead of a faction with whom it was impossible for a civilized government to deal, and into whose intrigues I considered it undignified for a powerful government to enter; and from the first I determined not to enter into them. I was determined that when there was a breach of treaty, whether great or small, I would hold all the Mirs responsible, and would not be played off like a shuttlecock, and told this was done by one Mir, and that by another, and have a week's inquiry to find out whom I was to hold responsible for aggression, for I at once saw, on arriving in Sindh, that this hide-and-seek shifting responsibility was the game which the Mirs had been playing. The proposal of Mir Rustam to come into my camp offered me an easy remedy for this evil, and having adopted the high opinion which Major Outram entertained of Ali Morad, I had no hesitation in recommending his brother to seek his protection, and be advised

body of cavalry and infantry took post in a manner to command three sides of the inclosure in which the

by him. But I beg the reader to bear in mind—for it is a matter of first-rate importance, and one upon which the whole gist of the matter depends—that while advising Mir Rustam to be guided by his brother, yet having suspicions in despite of the high character given to me by Major Outram of that brother, that some intrigue must be going on, I gave Mir Rustam the option and invitation of coming to my camp, and putting himself under my protection. I repeat the word must, because it is utterly impossible for me to believe that any Eastern divan can act without intrigue. By my advice to Mir Rustam, which, let the reader observe, was not given till it was asked, I secured to Mir Rustam the honourable and powerful protection of the British government. This he did not choose to accept; he went to his brother, and then he fled from that brother with his usual vacillating imbecility.'

"All this is reconcilable with what has been already quoted; but there is a colouring given to the transactions described, which in strict truth they will not bear. Mir Rustam denied that he had ever sent the message upon which Sir Charles Napier's interference with his movements was based; and the fact of his having sent it rests solely on the assertion of the Munshi by whom the message, real or pretended, was delivered. But presuming the message to be genuine (and upon this presumption Sir Charles Napier, throughout the papers, grounds his right to advise), it follows that Mir Rustam desired to place himself in the hands of the British general, but the latter did not wish to have him. He advised the aged chieftain to go to his brother; and with reference to his advice, and the manner in which it was given, it is not a fair statement to say that Mir Rustam did not choose to accept the protection of the British government.

residence was situated, the fourth being defended by a British steamer, which happily lay in the river at no

He did choose to accept it (supposing the message to have been sent), for he had applied for it; but he was recommended to take another course which suited Sir Charles Napier better. Let Sir Charles Napier speak for himself. In a letter to Mir Rustam, dated January 2nd, 1843 (in Supplementary Collection, p. 7, No. 17), he says:—'You know that you offered to come to my camp, and that I advised you to go to your brother's fortress instead of coming to my camp.'

"But a more extraordinary passage occurs in a later part of the paper, No. 155, in the Supplementary Collection: it follows. 'Another thing I have to observe—it is, that when I heard that he had resigned the turban to Ali Morad I disapproved of it, and Mr. Brown will recollect my sending Ali Morad's vakil back to him with this message. I even recommended him to return the turban, and merely act as his brother's lieutenant. His answer was, that the deed had been executed in due form before all the mullahs or priests, and that it was impossible to alter it. I, of course, had nothing to say; I had no business to interfere with the private arrangements of the Mirs.' And in a letter to the Governor-General in council, dated the 12th of August, 1843 (Supplementary Collection, No. 157), Sir Charles Napier says: 'I assuredly did not press the abdication of the turban by Mir Rustam, nor did I even advise it; on the contrary, my letters will show that I recommended that he should not.' In these two passages Sir Charles Napier asserts that he did not press the resignation of the turban; that he did not even advise it; that he recommended that it should not take place; and that on hearing that it had been effected he disapproved of the act, and suggested its avoidance. It may be granted that he did not openly advise the transfer of the turban, and consequently

great distance. A hot fire was commenced and kept up for four hours by the assailants; but their attempts to

that he did not press it; but from his own declaration it is clear that he wished it:—The idea struck me at once that he (Mir Rustam) might go to Ali Morad, who might induce him, as a family arrangement, to resign the turban to him (Ali Morad).' — Letter (above quoted), December 20th. In the hope of effecting this object, he advised Mir Rustam to place himself in his brother's hands, as appears from Sir Charles Napier's own declaration in his letter of December 27th, to the Governor-General above quoted, from the letter to Mir Rustam in answer to the message which has also been quoted above, where Sir Charles Napier says, 'You know that you offered to come to my camp, and that I advised you to go to your brother's fortress instead of coming to my camp.' Further, he recommended Mir Rustam not only to go to his brother, but to listen to his advice; and he knew full well what were Ali Morad's views. Sir Charles Napier laid the train, expecting and desiring that it should be fired by another—it was fired, and his language in explaining his own share in the transaction partakes more of the character of special pleading than might be looked for in a man bred, not in chambers, but in camps. In a note upon a statement made by Major Outram, p. 29, of the Supplementary Collection, Sir Charles Napier says, 'It (the transfer of the turban) was the positive act of Mir Rustam, without my connivance, or even knowledge, till it was done.' It was without the British general's knowledge; but, after reading his own account of his views in sending Mir Rustam to Ali Morad, can any one say that it was without his connivance?

"But, besides denying that he pressed or advised the abdication, Sir Charles Napier says that he recommended that it should not be made, and that his letters will show this. The only letter

effect an entrance were defeated by the judicious efforts of Captain Conway, the officer in command, ably and

found in the Collections which tends to bear out this assertion, is one addressed to Mir Ali Morad, under date of the 23rd of December, 1843 (Supplementary Collection, p. 6, No. 14), which commences thus:—'I think your Highness will do well not to assume the turban for the following reasons. People will say that the English put it on your head against the will of Mir Rustam. But do as you please; I only give you my advice as a friend, who wishes to see you great and powerful in Sindh. This is the wish of my government. The Governor-General has approved of all that I have said to you. If to be the chieftain gives you power, I would say, assume the turban. But it gives you none. You are strong without it. No one in Sindh can oppose you; no one out of Sindh can oppose you. The British government will secure you against all enemies.' Now, herein, Sir Charles Napier certainly does express an opinion unfavourable to the assumption of the turban by Ali Morad; but the force of that opinion is altogether neutralized by the words, 'Do as you please.' When a man has within his grasp the object of his highest ambition, and receives from a person of whose opinion he stands in awe, a mild dissuasive from possessing himself of it, qualified however by the gracious concession, 'Do as you please,' there can be no doubt as to the result—he will please to take that which he covets. Thus acted Ali Morad, and thus did Sir Charles Napier contend that he should act, notwithstanding the affectation of gently dissuading him from a step which the general had placed Mir Rustam in his hands for the very purpose of forwarding.

"The tortuous course of Sir Charles Napier in regard to the transfer of the turban is further illustrated by a proclamation which he issued from his camp at Khairpur on the 1st of Ja-

zealously supported by his subalterns, Lieut. Harding and Ensign Pennefather of her Majesty's 22nd; and

nuary, 1843, and which appears in the Supplementary Collection, No. 15, on p. 6. In this document he says: 'His Highness the Mir Rustam Khan sent a secret messenger to me to say that he was in the hands of his family, and could not act as his feelings of friendship for the English nation prompted him to do; and that if I could receive him he would escape and come to my camp. I answered his Highness that I would certainly receive him; but that my advice was, for him to consult with his brother the Mir Ali Morad Khan. He took my advice. He went to the fort of Diji to his brother. When I heard of this I was glad, for I thought that Sindh would be tranquil, that his Highness would spend his last days in honour and in peace. I moved with my troops towards Khairpur to force his violent family to disperse the wild bands that they had collected; I sent his Highness word that I should visit him; I wanted to ask his advice as to the arrangements for the new treaty; I thought that he had again become the friend of the government that I serve.

" 'That night I heard that he had solemnly conferred upon his brother, the Mir Ali Morad, the turban of command over the Talpur family, which brother is the heir to that honour. I thought this a very wise proceeding, and it added to my desire to meet his Highness, that I might hear from his own lips all about these things, and report the same to the Governor-General, being assured that these acts of his Highness would recover for him the good opinion and friendship of the Governor-General of India. My feelings towards his Highness were those of friendship, honour, and peace; I even advised his Highness's brother, Mir Ali Morad, not to accept the turban, and to assist his brother, the chief, in the care of government.'

" The above passage is not of great length; but, notwithstand-

by two volunteers, Captain Green of the 21st Native infantry, and Captain Wells of the 15th. Captain

ing, the writer seems to have found it impossible to preserve anything like consistency through it. He declares that he thought the surrender of the turban a very wise proceeding, and that he wished to report it as one among various acts (what were the others does not appear) which would recover for Mir Rustam the good opinion and friendship of the Governor-General; and yet he goes on to boast that he had advised Ali Morad not to accept the turban, not to concur in an act which was wise, and which, moreover, in the opinion of Sir Charles Napier, would be gratifying to the heads of the government which he served. It is proper to state that a version of Sir Charles Napier's proclamation, differing in some respects from that just quoted, appears in the Supplementary Collection; but the variations do not clear up the British general's character for consistency or plain dealing. In the second version the more important part of the passage extracted stands thus:—'That same evening I had intelligence that his Highness had conferred the turban of the Talpur family on his brother, Mir Ali Morad, because he was the rightful possessor of it. I considered that this was well, and desired more earnestly to meet his Highness, in order that I might hear from himself what he had done, and also, that I might be able to state the same to his Lordship the Governor-General; and I thought that, by his observing such a line of conduct, he would have re-established himself in the favour of the British government; my wish was, that friendship and honour should continue with Mir Rustam, and I gave his brother, Mir Ali Morad, advice that he should not take the turban, but that he should assist his Highness in the arrangements for his country.' The reader will see that this leaves the matter in question as it stood. The variations between the two

Brown, Bengal Engineers, was despatched to the steamer, and there rendered valuable assistance in

versions of the proclamation are greater than could have been expected; but they do not affect the views of Sir Charles Napier as to the transfer of the turban, nor the character of his proceedings in respect of that transfer.

"Sir Charles Napier alleges that he not only abstained from advising the transfer of the turban,—that he not only advised the direct contrary,—but that, after he heard of the transfer, he disapproved of it, sent a message recommending the rescission of the act, and acquiesced in giving it effect only on being assured that it was both regularly executed and irrevocable. Now, it is to be feared that the word 'disapproved' is here used in a manner which, if not altogether unwarrantable, is at least obscure and equivocal. How could Sir Charles Napier disapprove of that which he had taken pains to bring about, and which he invariably affirmed to be desirable for the British government? It is to be presumed, therefore, that in saying he disapproved, he means, not that he felt disapprobation, but that he expressed it. His communication to Mir Ali Morad must have been a deliberate piece of double dealing, or his avowal, several weeks before, of a desire that Mir Rustam should give the turban to Mir Ali Morad, must have been insincere. There is no reason for embracing the latter branch of the alternative, and, consequently, there is no choice but to accept the former.

"Mir Rustam, after going to his brother, Ali Morad, as advised by Sir Charles Napier, and surrendering to that brother the turban, as wished, though not advised, by Sir Charles Napier, subsequently fled from his brother, declared that the surrender of the turban was extorted from him (as most probably it was), and alleged that Sir Charles Napier had recommended him to go to his brother, and be governed by his advice, which

directing her fire. The number of men under Captain Conway was entirely inadequate to any pro-

recommendation he had followed. On this Sir Charles Napier remarked, in a letter to Major Outram, February 11th, 1843, Supplementary Collection, p. 32, No. 57:—'Rustam's plea of being sent to Ali Morad by me is a shallow affair, because, in the first place, he sent a secret message (by Moyadin, I believe Brown told me) to say he was, to all intents, a prisoner in Khairpur, and that he had tried to send away his family, and was obliged to bring them back after they were on their road, and that he would escape and come to my camp. Brown knows all this matter. The messenger said he (Rustam) would do whatever I advised. My answer was, Take your brother's advice; go to him, and either stay with him, or I will escort you to my camp. His flying from his brother's camp proves that he was not a prisoner; his not flying to mine proves either his duplicity or his imbecility, I believe the latter; but imbecility is not a legitimate excuse for rulers; I have only to deal with his acts. He played you the same trick; he even now stands out; he cannot say Ali Morad still influences him; I believe he did at first, but does not now, and I am half inclined now to doubt the fact, though I did not do so at first; but, as I said, the intrigues of these people are nothing to me, only I will not let his cunning attempt to cast his conduct upon my advice pass. He went contrary to my advice, and now wants to make out that he acted by it: I send you a copy of my letter.' A more extraordinary and painful specimen of floundering than is afforded by this passage is rarely to be found. Rustam's plea of being sent to Ali Morad by Sir Charles Napier was not a shallow affair; he was so sent, and no sophistry can explain the fact away. Indeed, a few lines after the above, Sir Charles Napier admits the fact. 'My answer was, Take your brother's advice; go to him, and

tracted defence, and the stock of ammunition was scanty. A reinforcement of men and a supply of

either stay with him, or I will escort you to my camp.' The reckless mode of arguing adopted by Sir Charles Napier in regard to Mir Rustam's flight from his brother is not less remarkable than the rest of the passage—'His flying from his brother's camp proves that he was not a prisoner.' Did Sir Charles Napier never know of a prisoner making his escape? 'His not flying to mine proves either his duplicity or his imbecility.' It proves neither one nor the other, though possibly the old chief might be under the influence of both; but, at all events, he had little cause for confidence in one who had recommended him to trust himself to the advice and keeping of a rival, by whose threats or cajolery his dignity had been subverted. The conclusion of the above extracts is worthy of all that precedes it. 'I will not let his cunning attempt to cast his conduct on my advice pass. He went contrary to my advice, and now wants to make out that he acted by it. I send you a copy of my letter.' On first reading this it is impossible not to suppose that the words 'he went contrary to my advice' must apply to the flight of Mir Rustam from his brother, not to his going to him; but the accuracy of this construction seems doubtful, because the letter, a copy of which is referred to, is that to Mir Rustam, in answer to his secret communication, and which is quoted above (p. 427). If it be meant that Mir Rustam went to his brother contrary to Sir Charles Napier's advice, the assertion is one of the boldest experiments upon the extent of human credulity ever hazarded. After the most careful consideration of this passage, no one can feel satisfied that he is in possession of its meaning, and the impression left on the mind is, that the writer felt that he was struggling with difficulties which could not be overcome, that he was conscious of the bad-plausible case in his favour. No ammunition were expected by another steamer; but she arrived without either; and it became obvious that there was nothing to be done but to effect a retreat with as little loss as possible. An attempt was made to remove the property within the residence; but the camp followers became alarmed, and after reaching the steamer with their first loads, could not be brought to return; while the fighting men had employment more important, as well as more stirring, than looking after baggage. The greater portion of the property was therefore abandoned, and the British party evacuated their quarters in a body, covered by a few skirmishers. The movement was effected with perfect order; and the British commander, with his

degree of ingenuity can give to the conduct pursued towards Mir Rustam the colour of straightforwardness and honesty.

"Throughout this inquiry the conduct of Sir Charles Napier has been tried solely upon his own testimony. Much might be added, if the statements made on the other side were admitted; but it is better that the case should be rested upon evidence to which even the friends and defenders of the British General cannot object. Upon such evidence it is clear that, though not in appearance, Sir Charles Napier was in substance the party chiefly instrumental in transferring the power and station of Mir Rustam to Mir Ali Morad, and that, subsequently finding that the act was regarded as odious, he vainly struggled to relieve himself from responsibility in respect to it."

brave escort, arrived in safety at the camp of Sir Charles Napier.

"There was now no mode of deciding the existing difference but by the sword. Sir Charles Napier accordingly advanced to a place called Miani, about six miles from Haidarabad, which he reached on the 17th of February, where he found the Mirs posted in great force. Their position was strong, their flank being protected by two woods, which were connected by the dry bed of the river Fulaili, having a high bank, behind which and in the woods were the enemy posted. In front of the extreme right, and on the edge of the wood protecting it, was a village. Having made his observations, the British general prepared for attack, posting his artillery on the right of the line, and sending forward skirmishers to drive out the enemy's force. The advance then took place from the right in echelon of battalions, the left being declined to escape the fire of the village. The artillery and her Majesty's 22nd formed the leading echelon, the 25th Native Infantry the second, the 12th Native Infantry the third, and the 1st Grenadier Native Infantry the fourth.

"About a hundred yards from the bank the

British opened the fire of their musketry in answer to that of the enemy. Thenceforward the official details of the battle are neither very full nor very clear. Thus much is certain,—that the conflict was obstinate and sanguinary, and that for a time the event was doubtful. The British, however, continued to press determinedly on their opponents, and a charge from the 9th Bengal light cavalry (which formed the reserve), aided by some Sindh horse, completed the discomfiture of the enemy, who slowly retired. The victory cost the British a loss of sixty-two killed and one hundred and ninety-five wounded. Among the number was a large proportion of officers;* the loss of the enemy was

* "The following is a list of the officers who suffered:—

"9th regiment light cavalry:—Lieut. Brevet Capt. Adjt. Cookson, killed; Capt. A. Tucker, Lieut. Brevet Capt. S. Smith, Lieut. H. G. C. Plowden, Ensign J. H. Firth, wounded.

"Her Majesty's 22nd regiment:—Capt. W. W. Tew, killed; Lieut.-Col. J. L. Pennefather, Ensign H. Bowden, wounded.

"12th regiment native infantry:—Capt. and Brevet Major Jackson, Lieut. and Brevet Capt. Meade, Lieut. Wood, killed; Ensign Holbrow, wounded.

"25th regiment native infantry:—Major Teesdale, killed; Lieut. Qr.-Mr. Phayre, Lieut. Bourdillon, wounded.

"Staff:—Major Wyllie, Assist. Adjt. Gen. S. and B., wounded.

estimated at five thousand, but this amount seems incredible.*

"Immediately after the battle six of the Mirs (three of Khairpur and three of Haidarabad) surrendered themselves prisoners; and on the 20th of February Sir Charles Napier entered the capital of Lower Sindh. But the contest was not yet at an end. Shere Mohammed, Mir of Mirpur, remained in arms; and on the 24th of March the British

* "One of the most pleasing duties of a general is to render just praise to those who have distinguished themselves under his command. It is scarcely a less gratifying duty to those whose humbler province it is to record the results of the soldier's efforts; but the list of officers favourably noticed by Sir Charles Napier is so long, that to introduce their names into the text would have the effect of converting a considerable portion of it into a mere catalogue. It is, however, not fitting that such names should be passed over, and they are consequently here presented. The officers named in the general's despatches are Major Teesdale (killed), Major Jackson (killed), Capts. Meade, Tew, and Cookson (all killed), Lieut. Wood (killed), Lieut.-Col. Pennefather (wounded), Major Wyllie (wounded), Capts. Tucker and Conway (both wounded), Lieuts. Harding and Phayre (both wounded), Lieut.-Col. Pattle, Major Story, Capt. Jacob, Major Lloyd, Capts. Whitlie and Hutt, Major Waddington, Major Reid, Major Poole, Capt. Jackson, Lieut. M'Murdo, Major M'Pherson, Lieut. Pelly, Lieut. Thompson, Lieut. Younghusband, Capt. Henderson, Lieut. Boileau, Lieut. Outlaw, Capt. Taite, Lieuts. Leeson and Brennan."

commander marched out of Haidarabad to attack him.

* * * * *

"Sir Charles Napier concluded his despatch to the Governor-General announcing the occupation of Umarkot with the words—'Thus, my lord, I think I may venture to say Sindh is now subdued; but the subjugation of a country inhabited, for the most part, by a wild and warlike population, is a thing easy to talk of, but not easy to accomplish.' The governor of Sindh (for to this office Sir Charles Napier had been appointed by his Lordship) for many months after uttering this declaration, found that he had something more to do than merely to make the requisite arrangements for carrying on the civil administration of the country which he represented as subdued. The Mir Shah Mohammed continued to break the tranquillity upon which Sir Charles Napier had calculated.

* * * * *

"Since this period Sindh has been more tranquil, but it will probably be long ere the irruptions of the wild Bilochi tribes shall cease to afford ground for alarm.

"The proceedings of the British government with regard to Sindh were never popular in England; and even the splendour of victory failed of securing public approbation to a course of policy believed to be based in injustice. The Governor-General, in a despatch to the Secret Committee, dated in June, entered into an elaborate defence of that policy, obviously under the impression that such a step was not unnecessary. As this document was the official vindication of a series of acts regarded by a great majority of observers as of very questionable character, some examination of its contents seems to be called for.*

* "With a view to fairness, the vindication itself, as given in the Parliamentary Collection, follows:—

"On the withdrawal of the British armies from Kabul to the Satlaj, I had to decide what course I should pursue with respect to the Lower Indus. I had to decide whether the Lower Indus should be altogether evacuated, and our armies everywhere resume the positions they occupied before the Afghan war, or whether, while the old positions were re-occupied upon the Satlaj, certain points should still be held upon the Lower Indus, which would insure the strict performance of commercial treaties, and give us the military command of that river.

"The withdrawal to the Satlaj, and the withdrawal from the Lower Indus, appeared to me to be very different questions. The withdrawal to the Satlaj was dictated by the clearest views

"The defence commences by a reference to the state of affairs at the time of the withdrawal of the

of military and political prudence. I shall not recapitulate the reasons for that measure, as they have been placed on record in what has been called my Proclamation of the 1st of October, 1842.

"I have adopted every measure which could have the effect of giving the appearance of triumph to the return of the armies from Kabul; but still it was a retirement from an advanced position, and it was the first retirement ever rendered necessary to a British army.

"I was deeply sensible of the impression which the reverses at Kabul had produced upon the minds of native princes, of the native population, and of our own troops. I knew that all that had taken place since, and all I had said and done, although it must have much diminished, could not have obliterated that impression, and restored to our government and to our army the place they had before held in the opinion of India.

"To have added to retirement to the Satlaj, retirement from the Lower Indus; to have abandoned every part of the advanced position we had taken up in 1839; to have withdrawn from Karachi and from Sakkar amidst the insults, and exposed, as we should have been, to the attacks of the Bilochis upon our rear-guard; to have practically abandoned, as we should thereby have done, all the benefits which we might expect ultimately to derive from the commercial treaties concluded in 1839 (for it was idle to imagine, after what had passed, that without the presence of force those treaties would be observed); to have abandoned also all the great prospective advantages which may be expected to be derived from substituting the Indus for the Ganges as the line of military communication between England and the north-west provinces, and to have left open to the am-

British army to the Satlaj; and it is urged that the question of withdrawing from the Lower Indus

bition of the Sikhs or of an European power that route of which we had demonstrated the practicability and the importance;—to have done all these things without positive instructions from you, or without some overpowering necessity, would have been, in my opinion, contrary to my duty, because inconsistent with our national interest and the national honour.

"Such a measure would have confirmed the most exaggerated accounts which had been circulated of our disaster,—it would have been humiliating to the army.

"There was no overpowering necessity for retirement. There is no difficulty in holding the positions of Karachi and Sakkar. The first is, during the largest portion of the year, accessible in a few days from Bombay; the latter is, during the whole year, accessible in less than three weeks from Firozpur. We can, besides, command the river by our steam-vessels, if we have a sufficient number of them well adapted to the navigation.

"The misinterpretations placed upon some provisions of the commercial treaty, and the various violations of its letters and its spirit, even while our armies were in force in Sindh, satisfied me that, unless some penalty were imposed upon the Mirs for such infractions of their engagements, there could be no security whatever for their future observance. I saw troops collected by the Mirs, contrary to their usage, and without legitimate cause; but such collections of troops in the presence of a British army is, in itself, an offence and an indication of hostility not to be misunderstood or overlooked.

"With respect to the authenticity of certain letters of hostile character, ascribed to the Mirs or to their agents, you will have observed how strongly I impressed upon Sir Charles Napier the necessity of caution in coming to a decision on that point. I

rested on very different grounds. The reasons assigned for the difference are that such a course

had, however, the fullest reliance upon his sense of justice; and with this reliance I felt that he, on the spot, with every opportunity of personal communication with those conversant with such matters, was infinitely more competent to form a correct conclusion than I could be, at Simla. To him, therefore, I confidently remitted the question.

"I am satisfied with the grounds upon which he decided that the letters were authentic.

"Major Outram's doubt as to the authenticity of the letter of Mir Rustam Khan to the Maharajah Sher Singh appears to have rested upon the circumstance of the party whose information led to the seizure of the letter being inimical to Mir Rustam Khan; but assuredly, information tending to criminate Mir Rustam could not be expected from one of his friends.

* * * * * *

"Much care appears to have been taken to investigate all the circumstances attending the escape of Mohammed Sharif. It seems impossible to doubt the participations of Mir Rustam's minister, in that escape of an enemy to the British government, proceeding to act hostilely against us.

"I cannot admit the convenient doctrine, that a chief is not to be responsible for the act of his minister. That minister, known to be so hostile to the British government, remained with Mir Rustam to the last.

"I have endeavoured to judge my own conduct as I could that of another; and I cannot think, on reviewing it, that in the circumstances in which I stood, I was unjustified in requiring from the Mirs the specific modification of their engagements, which I instructed Sir Charles Napier to propose to them.

"These modifications of the existing treaty involved on our

would have been humiliating; that there was no over-powering necessity for it; that our advanced position

part the abandonment of a considerable revenue, payable to us every year by the Mirs, under the name of tribute. They involved, undoubtedly, the sacrifice, on their part, of lands of more than equivalent value; but the penalty imposed did not seem disproportioned to the offence I had reason to believe they had committed.

"You have been long in possession of the reason which induced me to think that the abolition of tribute was in itself a good. You have also long been aware of the grounds on which I deemed it polite to make a gift to the Navab of Bhavalpur, of territory which formerly belonged to his state. Had you disapproved of the general principles upon which the new treaty proposed to the Mirs was founded; still more, had you disapproved of the intention I had announced, of holding military possession of certain points upon the Lower Indus, after the evacuation of Afghanistan; I presume that you would have acquainted me with that opinion. In the absence of any intimation to that effect, I had reason to suppose that a new treaty, based upon these principles, if legitimately obtainable, would not be unacceptable to you.

"Had the Mirs seen fit to reject the treaty proposed to them, and to support that rejection openly by arms, they would have pursued a legitimate course; and their defeat in fair fight would have admitted of subsequent arrangements on the basis of their retaining a portion of their territory, and the exercise of sovereign authority: but, from the first, while they of course denied the correctness of the charges made against them, they professed their willingness to submit to the penalty imposed, still they collected more troops. At last, having drawn the British general into the vicinity of Haidarabad, having then actually signed

was maintainable without difficulty; and that it was not desirable to abandon the Indus to the Sikhs, or

the draft of the treaty, they with a portion of their troops made a treacherous attack upon the residence of the British commissioner, and, with all their forces united, they opposed the further advance of our army at Miani.

* * * * * *

"The example of the Afghans at Kabul was to be followed by the Bilochis at Haidarabad; but the spirit in which they were met was different from that which at Kabul led to the destruction of a British army.

"It was my duty to mark such conduct by an extent of punishment which should be a warning to every chief and people in India, which should give future security to the persons of British ministers, and protect British troops from treacherous aggression.

"The battle of Miani entirely changed the position in which the British government stood with respect to the Mirs of Sindh.

"To have placed confidence in them thereafter would have been impossible.

"To have only exacted from them large cessions of territory would have been to give them what remained as the means of levying war for the purpose of regaining what was ceded.

"Foreigners in Sindh, they had only held their power by the sword, and by the sword they have lost it.

"Their position was widely different from that of a native prince succeeding a long line of ancestors, the object of the hereditary affection and obedience of his subjects.

"They had no claim to consideration on the ground of ancient possession or of national prejudice. Certainly they had none arising out of the goodness of their government. To take advantage of the crime they had committed to overthrow their

to a European power; that the Mirs had committed violations of the commercial treaty, and that the im-

power was a duty to the people they had so long misgoverned.

"It was essential to the settlement of the country that I should take at once a decided course with respect to the Mirs; and having no doubt that I was justified in dethroning them, I determined on at once adopting and announcing that decision.

"Their removal from the country with which they were no longer to be connected as sovereigns was a measure of obvious expediency. It has apparently had the beneficial effect I anticipated from it. The willing acquiescence of the people in our rule, and the adhesion of many of the chiefs to our government, are already the just rewards of an unhesitating and decisive policy which, in taking away every hope from the Mirs, has given confidence to their late oppressed subjects.

"Some resistance on the part of the Mirs I regarded as not an impossible event; and I considered that having once felt our strength, they might thereafter be more strict observers of their engagements. Treachery, such as that we experienced, had not come within my calculations. A victory, decisive as that at Miani, and gained under such circumstances, was to me a wholly unexpected event. As I have said, it entirely changed our position, and I was compelled at once to decide what policy should be adopted in the new state of things. I could not for the reasons I have given reinstate the Mirs. Any other arrangement than I have made would have imposed upon us all the burthen of protecting a government without affording us the means of benefiting the people or ourselves. Any half measure would have failed. Adopting the decisive measure of taking the province into our hands, I determined to adapt the means to the end, and

position of some penalty upon them was, therefore, expedient; that the Mirs were collecting troops; that they were charged with writing letters of hostile character which Sir Charles Napier determined to be genuine; that two of the Mirs entered into an agreement binding themselves to act together in every

not to omit any step by which security could be given to the new possession.

"The Mirs were removed beyond sea. All arrears of revenue due to them on the day of the battle of Miani were remitted, the transit duties were abolished, the neighbouring states of Jodpur and Jaisalmer were, as well as Bhavalpur, interested in the overthrow of the Bilochis, by the intimation that their ancient possessions would be restored. The inhabitants of Sindh were assured by proclamation that the property of all who laid down their arms would be respected.

* * * * * *

"The vast tracts which the Mirs have converted into Shikargahs will also be surveyed. Such of the woods as it may be necessary to retain will be carefully preserved, and extensive portions of land, having the richest soil, lately reserved for hunting-grounds by the Mirs, will be restored to cultivation.

"Some of these measures have originated with myself; in others, I have been anticipated by the Governor of Sindh. In all I know I shall have his most cordial co-operation.

* * * * * *

"You may be assured that no exertion of mine shall be wanting to make the conquest of Sindh by the British arms no less the source of happiness to the inhabitants of that country than of advantage to our own."

affair, whether for good or evil, peace or war; that the servants of some of the Mirs acted hostilely; and that their masters were accountable for their actions. These are the grounds from which the conclusion is deduced that it was just to demand the substitution in place of the existing treaty of one more favourable to the British government, which demand may be regarded as the first important step in the dealings of the Governor-General with Sindh.

"The withdrawing from the Lower Indus was in one view a very different measure from the withdrawal to the Satlaj. When it became a question whether or not the British should retain their positions on the Lower Indus, the impression produced by the disasters in Afghanistan had been in a great degree effaced by the triumphant march to Kabul. It will be recollected that before this march the British generals beyond the Satlaj had been urged to return with all speed. This would undoubtedly have been humiliating, and the effect might perhaps have been fatal. Happily, the officers commanding, both in Upper and Lower Afghanistan, were men not open to the influence of panic. They returned, but not till after they had vindicated their country's honour. Surely it could not be so humiliating, or so disastrous, to quit Sindh at a moment of triumph, as it would have been to quit Afghanistan under the disgrace of defeat. Yet the Governor-General, who was prepared for the latter step, shrank from the former. It was, at least, as safe to retire from Sindh victorious, as to retire from Afghanistan beaten, and the difference which exists between the two cases, as far as national military character is concerned, tells alike against the course urged upon the generals commanding in Afghanistan in the one case, and the opposite course voluntarily taken by the Governor-General in the other.

"To the argument that there was no overpowering necessity for retiring from Sindh, it is unnecessary to say anything further than that its adoption will justify a government in keeping any thing which it is strong enough to hold. And if a government may thus argue, why may not an individual? The British were in Sindh, and it was believed that they had the power to remain. The question of how they came there appears not to have been thought of. It is true, that the Governor-General was not accountable for the original wrong inflicted on the rulers of Sindh;

but he did not hesitate to add to that wrong, and thus to identify himself with an evil policy. Further—in the doctrine that nothing should be yielded except to an overwhelming necessity, we find a severe condemnation of the Governor-General's proposed policy in regard to Afghanistan—that of quitting the country without an effort to vindicate the national honour. There was no overwhelming necessity for this; yet he would have done it.

"But it was not to be expected that the Governor-General should sever the British connexion with Sindh before his arrival in India. The rights of the Mirs as independent rulers had been violated, by forcing upon them a treaty containing provisions which they regarded with great, and, as the event showed, with very just apprehensions. It would be too much to maintain that the Governor-General was bound to set aside this treaty, and to restore the state of affairs existing previously to its being made. Such things have occurred in India as for a Governor-General summarily to annul engagements solemnly concluded by his predecessor, even when one of the contracting parties was thereby exposed to ruin, and was most anxious to receive the protection of the great European power which now gives law to the Eastern world: but the Governor-General might justly hesitate at the adoption of such a course; and assuredly, had he adopted it in the case of Sindh, he would have been met in certain quarters by clamorous accusations of neglect of duty, in having abandoned the Indus, that great line of communication with Upper Asia, to which our merchants and manufacturers had been taught to look, as affording the means of deluging with British goods countries known only by name. The Governor-General could not reasonably be blamed, had he only endeavoured to maintain things as he found them; but with this he was not content. He was resolved to have a new treaty more humiliating and more hateful to the Mirs than that which preceded it; and in endeavouring to accomplish this object, he precipitated his government into a new and dangerous war,—ending indeed successfully, and thus saving the military reputation of the British from blot, but leaving on their character for honour and good faith a deep and enduring stain.

"The provisions of the commercial treaty, it was said, had not been strictly adhered to by the Mirs;

and the charge was probably true. But if every trifling breach of treaty committed by a native prince or by his servants were to furnish occasion for war, the British government of India would never be at peace for a single year with any of the states with whom it is in alliance. The alleged aggressions were all very slight; they afforded proper ground for remonstrance, but not for forcing on the Mirs at the point of the sword an entire change in their situation in regard to the British government. The Governor-General was for prompt and decisive measures: he deemed it necessary to inflict some penalty, because without it there would, in his judgment, be no security for the future observance by the Mirs of their engagements. What security was gained by the course which he took? He deposed the Mirs and took possession of their country, thus putting their future adherence to treaties quite out of the question. But this was but the clumsy expedient of an unskilful surgeon, who cuts off the limb which he is unable to restore to healthy action. Looking merely to the relations subsisting between the Mirs and the British, it is impossible to deny that the former were in the wrong; but if the means by which those relations were brought about be remembered, some degree of excuse will be suggested for men who had been coerced, by those whom they had never injured, into a position which they wished to avoid. The same remark will apply to the charge founded on the hostile letters (the authenticity of which is, to say the least, very doubtful) and to the other acts of an unfriendly character which the Mirs were charged with doing or tolerating. They had received gross provocations, and they might not unreasonably expect that remonstrance would be followed by some further period of probation before they were sentenced to descend still lower in the scale of dependency. But this was not granted. The charges were some of them trivial and some unproved, but they were sufficient to support a demand upon the Mirs for the execution of a new treaty, inflicting a penalty,—for that is the word employed by the Governor-General. It was not enough that the British government should be safe: it was deemed requisite that the Mirs should be punished. These princes had been subjected to much injustice: they were naturally dissatisfied; and it was therefore fitting that they should suffer more, especially as there was an opportunity for inflicting further injustice without much risk. If the Mirs gave cause for suspicion, it was right to watch their conduct narrowly; it was justifiable to require them to conform to the treaty which they had subscribed; it was lawful even to propose alterations in the treaty; but if they were declined, it was neither lawful nor honourable to treat an ally as a conquered enemy, and require submission to any terms which it might be the pleasure of the stronger power to dictate.

"The Mirs were blamed for not peremptorily rejecting the treaty and supporting the rejection by arms. This would certainly have been the more honourable course; but why should honour be expected to find a place in a native government when it had departed from that which had hitherto rested its claim to power in Asia upon its character for good faith? What measure of openness and fair dealing had the Mirs met with at the hands of the power which, within eleven years from the period when it obtained a reluctantly-granted permission to use the roads and rivers of Sindh for commercial purposes, and for these only, had by steps following each other in rapid succession advanced its claim even to the right of disposing of the territory of the Mirs at its pleasure? This is not an exaggerated representation. Sir Charles Napier assumed the right of transferring a portion of the territory of the Mirs of Sindh to the Navab of Bhavalpur, under orders from the Governor-General, and with reference to the provisions of a treaty which the Mirs had never executed. The General's proclamation announcing the transfer bears date the 18th of December. The Mirs did not subscribe the treaty till the 12th of February following. By threats or cajolery, by force or finesse, one sacrifice after another had been extorted from the Mirs.

"At length, at the end of the year 1842, the British Government being disembarrassed of all other difficulties, was able to deal very decidedly with the one which remained. It was thought no longer necessary to go through the forms of diplomacy, or to wear even a decent mask of friendship. It sufficed to declare that the British Government wanted certain portions of territory for their own objects, and forthwith to take them without reference to the treaty of 1839, though that was the only document which defined the relations of the Mirs and the British Government; and slight infractions of that treaty by the Mirs were represented by the other party as sufficient to stamp on those princes the character of the most faithless of men. If a few breaches of commercial regulations, some of which were doubtful, demanded the infliction of a penalty; what punishment was due to the seizure of a province in violation of treaty? The rulers of Sindh were guilty of the former offence, and lost a kingdom; the British Government committed the latter, and gained one. Affairs had indeed been for some time approaching a point where it was inevitable that disguise on both sides should be abandoned; it was maintained by one party as long as was practicable, by the other as long as was necessary. The British in the earlier of their proceedings had employed both cunning and force. They were now in a condition to rely solely on force, and accordingly they dispensed with the less dignified means by the use of which they had won their first steps. The situation of the Mirs was different. They could not afford to discard the use of temporizing, and accordingly they clung fast to it. There is this apology for them,—they were acting in self defence. This at no time could be said of their opponents; they were throughout acting aggressively. The contest on their part was an unrighteous one, and their triumph is felt by their countrymen to be almost as great a source of shame as would have been their defeat.

"The case properly rests on the grounds which have already been adverted to; but in the laboured defence of the Governor-General there are passages of wider and less special application, which claim some remark. They are those in which the situation of the Mirs in regard to their subjects, the character of their government, and the moral and social consequences of their dethronement, are referred to. 'Foreigners in Sindh,' writes his lordship, 'they had only held their power by the sword, and by the sword they have lost it. Their position was widely different from that of a native prince succeeding a long line of ancestors, the object of the hereditary affection and obedience of his subjects. They had no claim to consideration on the ground of ancient possession or of national prejudice.' The argument intended to be included in the word foreigner, obviously bears just as much against those who displaced the Mirs, as against the princes themselves, if not more strongly; and, though it be true that they held their power only by the sword, the British, according to the statement under examination, have no better tenure. They struck the sword out of the hand of the Mirs, and took it themselves. Another party, if strong enough, may wrest it from them; and thus the question is reduced to one of mere force.

"The position of the Mirs, it is said, 'was widely different from that of a prince succeeding a long line of ancestors, the object of the hereditary affection and obedience of his subjects. They had no claim to consideration on the grounds of ancient possession or national prejudice.' The length of the possession of their family was about sixty years. Our own standing in India is not so much more as to warrant us in despising a sixty years' possession. As to the case of a prince supposed not only to be derived from a long line of ancestors, but to be the object of the hereditary affection and obedience of his subjects, it may confidently be asked, Where within the wide expanse of India and the adjacent countries is such a prince to be found? For the most part the obedience rendered to native princes is very imperfect; but the Eastern potentate enjoying the affection of his subjects has still to be sought for. This imaginary case of a prince of ancient descent, and of such a character as shall command not only obedience but affection, is introduced merely for the purpose of a contrast with the Mirs, who, it is immediately added, had no claim to commendation arising out of the goodness of their government. This may readily be admitted. It may be at once allowed that the Mirs were not above the ordinary run of native princes—that they were very bad specimens of a very bad class; but why, it may yet be asked, were they selected for punishment by confiscation and imprisonment, while other royal profligates are permitted without restraint to cover with desolation some of the fairest portions of Asia? To take advantage of the crime they had committed to overthrow their power, it is said, was a duty to the people they had so long misgoverned; but how came it that the claims of the people of Sindh pressed so much more strongly upon the British government than those of other countries, with whom that government had been much longer connected? There was an opportunity, it seems—the Mirs had committed a crime. That crime consisted in a desire to keep to themselves the country from whose roads and river they had, down to the year 1832, excluded strangers at their pleasure; the country in which, down to the year 1839, they had exercised sovereign rule; the country in which they still retained the name and many of the functions of sovereignty, some of which, together with a large portion of territory, they were about to be deprived of. This was the crime of the Mirs; it was the crime of a man who resists an unlawful attempt to despoil him of his property. In all our disputes with these princes we had been the aggressors—we had dealt with their country as though it had been our own, and to suppose that they should regard us with friendly feelings was impossible. All that has been said of the bad government of the Mirs, and of the benefit likely to result from its transfer, is the result of after-thought. If a regard for the people of Sindh were the motive of our proceedings, why was it not avowed from the first? It was surely a more honourable one than some which could not fail to be imputed. Did we or did we not invade Sindh for the deliverance of its people from tyranny? If we did, why did we so long decline the honour attached to our chivalric movement? If we did not, how can we now pretend to any merit on such grounds? The government of the Mirs was bad; so is that of every other native state. The people will be more prosperous and more safe under British rule than under that of their native governors: so would the people of every other state of India. Are we, therefore, prepared to take possession of every state subject to native rule? The case, in truth, stands thus: the British were anxious for the possession of Sindh; they were strong enough to take it; and the people, it may be admitted, will be benefited by the change. But the motive which led to that change was ambition, not philanthropy—cupidity, not benevolence; and it is sheer hypocrisy to declaim on the vices of the Mirs and the wrongs of their people, while, if our own interest had not furnished a spur to interference, the rulers might, for us, have revelled in their vices, and the people bent under their wrongs, until the end of time.

"Thus, too, of the vapouring display which has been made of the advantages of opening the Indus. It need not be denied that some degree of benefit to commerce may follow; but how has it been secured? By a series of political crimes; and if the actors in them are to be justified by the results, then may we do evil that good may come. Men have ceased, in a great degree, from attempting to propagate religious truth by violence, and there are now few who will not admit the wickedness of such attempts. But it seems that it is quite lawful to open up new sources of trade by such means; and that when there may appear any chance of extending commercial operations, the sword may properly be employed to clear the way. Thus the errors and crimes of one age disappear in the next, but too often only to be replaced by others equally great and equally dangerous.

"And with such vindication of the policy of a British Governor-General, in dealing with an ally, as the letter of the Governor-General affords, closes, for the present, the history of Sindh, henceforth a British province."

Although I have swelled this chapter with the quotations and extracts of the best authorities and an impartial historian, I feel confident that the remarks of Captain William Eastwick, who, as a political agent in Sindh, was beloved by all, and possessed a most accurate knowledge of the politics of that country and the feelings of its inhabitants, will not be read without interest. He observes in his speech before the Court of Proprietors, that if such absurd rumours were listened to, no native prince would be then safe. He also states that if the Earl of Auckland had planned to subdue Sindh without any just reason, it was not necessary that the same error should be followed after his departure.

"Sir, before I conclude, I would advert to two points which catch the eye at the first glance; and with superficial observers, divert the attention from the glaring injustice of the previous proceedings. On the 5th March, 1843, the Governor-General issued a proclamation to the following effect:—'The Governor-General cannot forgive a treacherous attack upon a representative of the Government, nor can he forgive hostile aggression prepared by those who were in the act of signing a treaty.'

"Now, Sir, both these assertions distort the facts. The treaty was signed on the 12th, incorrectly stated by the Governor-General the 14th. The attack on Major Outram took place on the 15th. In the intermediate days Major Outram was distinctly warned, that the Mirs could not control the Bilochis. They had already saved his life once, and the lives of his escort, on their return from their conference.

"In 1839 I was placed in exactly the same position. Aware of the weakness of the internal government of Sindh, and the inability of the Mirs to protect me, I thought it my duty to withdraw in order to avoid collision. If I had been attacked after having been warned, could I have called the attack treacherous? Certainly not. Does Major Outram designate it as a treacherous act? He does not. Let him be summoned to the bar of the House of Commons, and answer for himself.

"Sir, the Mirs had not the power to prevent this attack. We have no right to judge them according to our European notions of a government. They were simply the heads of one of the principal tribes, the Talpurs, and the recognized channel of communication with foreign powers; but they had not even the jurisdiction of life and death amongst some of the other powerful tribes—the Lagharis for instance—they ruled through the Bilochi chiefs. They could influence and persuade, but they could not restrain nor enforce obedience when opposed to Bilochi prejudices. Captain Postans states, and I can confirm the statement, that the meanest Bilochi will, at times, unhesitatingly beard the Mirs in public Durbar.

"Sir, I feel convinced that the Mirs were not only not favourable to this attack, but exerted all their influence to prevent it, otherwise Major Outram must have been crushed. Will any man assert that the same troops who maintained such a desperate struggle at Miani against Sir Charles Napier's whole army, could not have destroyed a detachment of one hundred men?

"And now, Sir, let us turn to the charge of hostile aggressions prepared by those who were in the act of signing a treaty. Sir, the whole conduct of the Mirs show that their preparations were strictly defensive—that they had not the least notion of aggressive measures. The Governor-General himself writes on the 14th of November, 'The design of the Mirs would seem, by the intelligence transmitted, to be of a defensive character only.' We must recollect, Sir, that this is written after the assembly of a preponderating force at Sakkar, after the Mirs were aware of the provisions of the new treaty, and after it had been officially reported that the Mirs had been informed that the English meditated treachery.

"Sir, none but the most obstinately prejudiced or the wilfully blind could accuse these unhappy princes of a desire of hostile aggression. It is against all the evidence,—it is against all probability. Is it to be believed that the Mirs would have stood our staunch friends in the day of defeat and adversity to break with us at the moment when our armies were returning flushed with victory? Is it credible that, with the experience of our recent successes in Afghanistan, they would rush headlong into so unequal a contest? I would refer the Court to a most admirable letter of Sir Henry Pottinger, dated 20th June, 1839. It is too long to quote, but bears remarkably on this point.

"Sir, the Mirs knew their inability to cope with us in the field; they depended upon our sense of justice. What does Mir Nasir Khan write? 'I know that the Kings of England never sanction injustice.' In all their letters, in every conversation, they refer to the treaty of 1839. Mir Nasir calls it a wall, or bund. On signing the new treaty, they express their determination to petition the Governor-General.

"Let us read Mir Rustam's letter to Sir Charles Napier;

a more affecting document it never fell to my lot to peruse. He writes, 'God knows we have no intention of opposing the British, nor a thought of war or fighting; we have not the power. Ever since my possessions were guaranteed to me and my posterity by the British government under a formal treaty, I have considered myself a dependant of theirs, and have thought myself secure. I have always attended to the least wish of the British officers, and now that my territory is being taken from me, I am at a loss to find out the reason of so harsh a measure. I have committed no faults. If any is alleged against me, let me hear what it is, and I shall be prepared with an answer. I feel strong in the possession of that treaty, and I trust to the consideration of the British still. If, without any fault of mine, you choose to seize my territory by force, I shall not oppose you, but I shall consent to and observe the provisions of the new treaty. However, I am now, and shall continue to be, a suitor for justice and kindly consideration at your hands.' Sir, my very blood boils with indignation when I contemplate the wrongs of this old and venerable chieftain. When political agent in Upper Sindh, he treated me as a father does a son. I have sat with him in his inmost apartments, and heard him express his satisfaction that he had secured the friendship of the British government; there was nothing that he would not have done to show his devotion and good feeling; he proved it in a thousand instances; and what is his reward? He is hurled from his throne, torn from his wife and family, and sent to die in a prison in a foreign land. Sir, I am one of those who believe that retribution awaits the guilty even in this world, and it is my solemn conviction that some great calamity will overtake this country if such monstrous acts of injustice are sanctioned and upheld.

"But, Sir, I have shown what Mir Rustam writes. What does he do? He offers to throw himself into the hands of the British representative. Is it possible to show more plainly his submission and his reliance on the British government, his confidence in British faith, and strict observance of treaties; that confidence which has done more to raise up our wonderful empire in the East than all the exploits of British valour?

"Sir, notwithstanding Sir Charles Napier's repeated acts of hostility, notwithstanding his threatening and aggressive march on Haidarabad, all those who know Sindh must be aware that the Mirs could have no intention of proceeding to extremities. Sir, if they had meditated hostilities, they would have sent away their wives and families, they would have concealed their treasures, they would have called in all their levies, especially Mir Sher Mohammed, who was considered the bravest of their warriors, and who, on the prospect of hostilities with Lord Keane's army in 1839, brought his coffin and shroud to Haidarabad. And, Sir, if conscious of guilt, they never would have surrendered themselves immediately after the battle of Miani. Sir, I repeat, it is only those determined to convict against all evidence; it is only those prepared to trample upon all obligations, that will pronounce judgment against the unfortunate Mirs of Sindh.

"Sir, on the 4th of last April, I happened to be in the House of Commons, when a Noble Lord, an honour to his country, gave utterance to the following sentiments (I quote from memory, but the words made a deep impression upon me at the time, and found a responsive echo in my breast): 'England (he said), with one arm resting on the East, and the other on the West, is in too many instances trampling under foot all moral and religious obligations. If such is to be the course of our future policy; if our superiority in arts, in arms, in science, and in strength, is to be turned to the injury, and not to the advantage of mankind, I would much prefer that we should shrink within the proportions of our public virtue, and descend to the limits of a third-rate power.' While these words rang in my ears I cast a rapid glance at the events, which, within a brief space of time, have thrown such a fearful interest over our Eastern empire.

* * * * * *

"Sir, it is painful to reflect on the gallant lives thus uselessly sacrificed or the misery caused to hundreds of English families; and if we have suffered misery, we have inflicted a hundred times greater. That may be a consolation to some; but to me it only conveys deeper shame and sorrow. War at all times is a great evil, but an unnecessary and unjust war it is fearful to contemplate, and fearful the responsibility of those who throw their sanction over a crime of such magnitude.

" Sir, no wonder then that my mind turned with some sort of satisfaction to the reflection that these execrable wars were at an end ; that a new era was dawning on Hindostan ; and that, profiting by experience, we should direct all our energies to the maintenance of peace, and to the moral and physical advancement of the millions over whom we are permitted by a gracious Providence to preside. Little did I imagine that the very next mail would bring accounts of an act of aggression to which our Indian annals, unhappily so fertile in such acts, can afford no parallel. Little did I imagine that the very man who had denounced the Afghan expedition as a crime, who had gone out of his way to mark his total dissent from the policy of his predecessor, who had so recently put forth to the world that memorable declaration, that, 'content with the limits that nature appears to have assigned to its empire, the government of India will devote all its efforts to the establishment and maintenance of general peace ;' little did I think that the author of this declaration, without even the plea of an imaginary or real danger to the State, with all the aggravations of ingratitude for services rendered during a season of unwonted trial, would have grasped at frivolous and flimsy pretexts to goad a barbarous but brave people to desperation, and again to let loose all the horrors and calamities of war.

" Sir, it is my conscientious opinion that if the thinking part of this great Christian nation ; that if the independent portion of the public press could once be roused to the consideration of this question, such a storm of indignation would burst forth, that no ministry would be hardy enough to refuse a full and searching inquiry. Sir, the time is past, at all events in this free country, when the follies and passions of an individual can plunge the nation into all the calamities of war. Is it then to be permitted that the servants of the East India Company shall wantonly have recourse to such an extreme arbitrament? Is there to be no end of these wars of aggression? and no voice raised in their condemnation? If the Ministry of this country, oppressed with business, are unable or unwilling to grapple with Indian questions; if the great council of the kingdom have neither leisure nor inclination to enter upon an inquiry involving the rights of justice and humanity, involving the good name and good faith of the British nation, it is easy to predict that these acts of tyranny and aggression will continue, that one iniquity will only lead to another, and, to use the emphatic words of the unfortunate Mirs of Sindh, applied to their own case, 'There will be no justice for the natives of India until the Almighty sits on the judgment-seat.'

"Sir, I repeat this is no party movement; it is a step beyond the petty squabbles of political intrigue; it is an appeal to those loftier principles which alone ought to guide the councils of a great and enlightened Christian government. Every Englishman shares the responsibility of these acts, and we especially, as the intermediate body between the British public and the natives of India, bound as we are to that country by so many ties of friendship and gratitude.

Sir, are we also to remain silent, and to make no effort to awaken public attention to questions of such overwhelming national importance? Sir, I for one could not reconcile silence to my conscience. I believe it to be the duty of every member of this Court to record his opinion against a line of policy that reflects so much discredit on the British name, and entails so much misery upon our fellow-creatures. In this belief I second the motion, and call upon every independent man now present to support it."

I close this unavoidably lengthened chapter by adding one letter from the Earl of Auckland to the address of the Mir Rustam Khan* when he was in prosperity, and eagerly acknowledged and sought as a friend; and the petition of the latter to the Governor of Bombay† when dethroned by us.

The Governor-General to Mir Rustam Khan of Khairpur.

Camp, Bhagasar, Jan. 10, 1839.

"THE judicious mediation of your friend Sir A. Burnes, the highly esteemed and able agent of my Government now with you, has, by the blessing of God, brought about the establishing of our mutual good understanding by treaty on firm and lasting basis.

---

* As alluded to in page 96. See Sindh Blue Book, p. 117.

† Supplement to the Sindh Papers, page 76.

" The support afforded to you by the guarantee of the British Government will, I am well assured, prove a source of future strength, and, if it be God's will, of continued prosperity to your country; and I am glad to acknowledge the advantages which I hope to derive from your alliance and support in the warlike operations which I am about to undertake.

" Having entered into a treaty with your Highness in all honesty and good faith, I shall be very sorry to find any part of the written agreement between us so worded as to leave either your successors or mine under the supposition that we concluded our contract in a spirit, on the one side or the other, of anything like jealousy or distrust.

" The mention, however, of a previous written agreement in every instance, as to the temporary character of the occasional occupation of Sindh by the English, is calculated to convey this unpleasant idea.

" I have, therefore, struck it out; and, in place of inserting a sentence which casts a doubt on the sincerity of our intentions, I address you this friendly letter as a lasting assurance of the plain meaning and purpose of the words of the separate article, namely, that the British shall avail themselves of the fort of Bakkar, the citadel of their ally the Mir of Khairpur, only during actual and periods of preparing for war, like the present.*

* Not only kept the fort for ever, but the whole dominion afterwards conquered and the Mir banished ! !

"I trust that this mode of reassuring your Highness will have the double effect of setting your mind at ease and of putting you in possession of a written testimony to my intentions, such as may remain among your records in pledge of the sincerity of the British Government.

"I have, &c.

"(Signed) AUCKLAND."

Mir Rustam Khan, inhabitant of Khairpur, in Sakkar, Bakkar, in Sindh, town called Rori, to the Governor of Bombay in Council.

May 17*th*, 1843.

"Most respectfully sheweth,

"THAT your humble petitioner begs to lay this case before your Honour: that the General* and Mr. Outram told me from Rori town till Sabzal town to give to the Company. So I did, and made no row with him; and I gave to him, with my own wishes to the Company, and accepted of the town; and I gave him a writing for the same, that I have nothing to do with that town, and also he has given me one; and afterwards Mr. Outram told me to come with him to Haidarabad, and he will settle there, that I may receive ten annas from one rupee; and the rest six annas Company will take it. So I agree to that point, and when I reached Haidarabad I stopped in the house of Nasir Khan, and after a few days a row commenced with the Company, and the Nasir Khan was seized with the Mirs

* Sir Charles Napier.

of that country, and my son Mohammed Husain came with twelve thousand people to fight with the Company. I told him, you go back to your own country, that I have settled with the Company, so he went away; and afterwards a quarrel took place with the Haidarabad people, and in that row seized me, my young son, and my brother's son, with the Mirs, and brought to Bombay without any fault; and now I beg to lay this case before your Honour, that myself and my son, and my brother's son, and thirteen servants, are placed in a miserable condition to maintain upon, and heard that your Honourable Board wants to send me and my people to Poonah. I have no wrong to the Company, and beg that your Honourable Board will let me stop in Bombay, or else send me to my native country, that I may stop there, and receive whatever is in the agreement which has been made between me and Mr. Outram, and this charity will never be forgotten.*

"And your petitioner, as in duty bound, will ever pray.

"The ⋈ mark of Mir Rustam Khan, inhabitant of Khairpur, in Sakkar, Bakkar, in Sindh, town of Rori."

The contents of the former documents afford a fearful lesson to every human being, and inculcate

* Is not this petition of the most heart-rending nature when the writer was a faithful and veteran ally, whom at one time we flattered and begged to give us footing in his country for commerce, and now oppressed and reduced him to such begging state.

that if men in power are at one time flattered, respected, and assured of perpetual friendship, they ought neither rely upon those assurances, nor be forgetful of the adversity of their fortunes which is to follow them. The deplorable case of the Mir Rustam Khan, notwithstanding the open intrigues of his brother Mir Ali Morad, as reported by Colonel Outram* to Sir Charles Napier, punishing him

* *Colonel Outram to Sir C. Napier.*

January 22nd, 1843.

"My misgivings as to Mir Rustam have proved well founded. He has fallen into the snare Ali Morad laid for him, and, instead of marching to join me here, has gone off, I am informed, to consult with the other fugitive Mirs, who are somewhere near Kohera, between Dingi and Haidarabad, or thereabouts. Should this prove correct, there can be little expectation that he and they will meet me here; so I beg your orders in that case. I almost despair of saving these misguided chiefs from destruction now; but so far from feeling any irritation towards them for baulking all my earnest endeavours to avert their fate, I only experience deep regret that they should thus be sacrificed to the acts of their unprincipled relation.

"Should you, however, consider that enough has been done to prevent these people breaking their own heads, perhaps you will deem it but fair to make some attempt to save the Mirs of Haidarabad from a similar fate, if it can be done by fair means; and as I am confident I can prevent the latter committing themselves, by my personal appearance among them before they are too far pledged to the runaways, I deem it my duty to offer to go down to Haidarabad for that purpose; and, should I do so

(Rustam) merely on the assertion of his enemy, the arch intriguer Ali Morad,* is an extraordinary but sad proof on this point.

without much delay, and by the river, so as to enable me to shake off the creatures of Ali Morad, by whom I am beleaguered, I have no doubt that not only shall I prevent the Lower Sindh chiefs from giving aid or refuge to the fugitives of Upper Sindh, but, possibly, through the means of the Haidarabad Mirs (with the exception of the traitor Nasir Khan), may cause their submission or capture.—J. OUTRAM."—*Supplement to the Sindh Papers, No.* 13, *page* 16.

* "Woe attend those who conspire against the powerful arms of the Company. Behold the fate of Tipu Sultan, and the Peshva, and the Emperor of China. You know, for I had it from your own lips, that the Mirs of Upper and Lower Sindh were in league against us—all, except his Highness Mir Sabdar and yourself—therefore have they suffered."—*C. Napier to Mir Ali Morad. Supplement to the Sindh Papers,* 23*rd December,* 1843, *No.* 14, *p.* 6.

CHAPTER XV.

Affairs of Afghanistan—The British army crosses the Indus—Sir Alexander Burnes and Mohan Lal remain in the rear—They rejoin the army—Passage of the Bolan pass—Sir Alexander and his suite arrive at Kalat—Conduct of the Khan and his ministers—Treaty with him—His intrigues and bad faith—Progress of the Shah Shuja—Part of the Bombay army, under Major-Gen. Wilshire, sent against Mir Mehrab Khan—Storming of Kalat and death of the Khan—Shah Navaz Khan installed—Captain Loveday appointed resident—His conduct in that capacity—Unjust remarks of Mr. Masson.

I SHALL now resume again my narrative of the army of the Indus. On the 6th of February, 1839, the troops on the road to Haidarabad, under the Commander-in-Chief and Sir Willoughby Cotton, were ordered to return, and by the 18th the whole baggage and the ordnance had crossed the Indus. In Shikarpur we every day received numerous letters from the various chiefs of Bilochistan and of Afghanistan, all professing their joy at our approach, and all entertaining hopes of the reward that might be promised for co-operating with us in furtherance of the object of the expedition. Sir Alexander Burnes, feeling not inclined to enter Afghanistan subordinate to another political head, the envoy and minister, Sir William Macnaghten, suggested the propriety of his remaining at Shikarpur, in the rear of the army; and this was agreed to by his superior. It was evident, and a topic of conversation in the camp, that the two rival politicians do not wish to act jointly in one field of honour and fame. At the same time Sir Alexander Burnes requested the envoy to leave me with him for the purpose of settling the Commissariat and the Shikarpuri bankers' accounts, which, as I was desirous to proceed with the army to Kabul, gave me much disappointment. However, this arrangement was of a very short duration. Major Leech omitted no exertions in procuring supplies, digging wells for water, and inviting the petty chiefs to facilitate the advance of our army; but there were some of them who would communicate with none but Sir Alexander Burnes, and his accurate knowledge of the state of things in Afghanistan pressed upon the Commander-in-Chief the necessity of having that officer with the army. Sir William

Macnaghten in the mean time had appointed him Envoy to the Court of Mir Mehrab Khan of Kalat i Nasir: on which Sir Alexander Burnes stated that if he was to go as far as the Bilochi capital, he would proceed from thence to Kabul, and not return to Shikarpur; and to this the Envoy agreed.

Sir Alexander Burnes and myself quitted Shikarpur, and by a long march in the night, we reached the camp of Sir Willoughby Cotton. We were in great want of water and forage in the desert, which the troops traversed during the night. It was the month of February; yet the heat was intolerable, and the scarcity of water added to the inconvenience felt from the long marches of the army. Sayad Mohammed Sharif, Governor of Gandava, was sent by the Mir Mehrab Khan to wait upon Sir Alexander Burnes, who, leaving me with Sir Willoughby Cotton, went on before to Dadar to see that the supplies were got ready for the arrival of the forces.

On our arrival at Bhag, the brother of the Kalat chief was introduced by me to Sir Willoughby Cotton, who returned his visit on the following day. My servant, Mohammed Tahar, whom I had appointed as news-writer at Qandhar, was very active in inducing the various "Khavanins" (noblemen) to attach themselves to our interest, and to discourage the Barakzai chiefs of that city from offering us any opposition. He was also successful in conveying intelligence of the passing events in Afghanistan, and in securing the good offices of Mulla Nasu, the Prime Minister of the Sardar Kohandil Khan of Qandhar. This person, being a very rich merchant, had gained ascendency in the Court of that chieftain, and stood high in his favour as well as in his confidence. He undertook that he was to advise his master the Sardar either to surrender himself to us or to fly; and that he will continue to use such persuasions until he succeeds, even although the Sardar had really prepared to fight with us. In return for this service I sent him a letter from the Envoy and Minister, promising a pension for life and the preservation of his estate and property during the government of the Sadozais or Shah Shuja-ul-Mulk. In the mean time His Majesty the King was receiving assurances of submission from the Durrani nobles; and each march in advance was bringing several chiefs to the royal standard.

At Dadar Mohammed Hasan Khan, the minister

of the Mir Mehrab Khan, referred to the expectation which was afforded by our government to give two lakhs of rupees annually to the Mir for the purpose of binding him to keep the rear and route of our army clear from the predatory Bilochis, and added that he himself was in the hope of some substantial reward from the British. In this place Sir Willoughby Cotton halted, and Sir Alexander Burnes, with Colonel Curton and myself, penetrated the Bolan pass, and the engineers preceded us. We met no molestation from the robbers in the pass, who were reported afterwards to have caused great losses between Shikarpur and Dadar in regard to the followers of our army, our baggage, and camels.

In Shal or Koetta, Major Leech, by his usual indefatigable exertions, collected a great quantity of supplies, and remained with the British General; while Sir Alexander Burnes, with Captains Pattison of the 16th lancers, Simpson of the commissariat, and myself, bent his course towards Kalat; the former being directed to enter into alliance with the Mir Mehrab Khan, and the latter officer to purchase and send provisions to Shal for the army. After a march of two whole days we arrived at the capital of the Birohi chief, whose son, mounted on a noble charger, came out to receive the British envoy, Sir Alexander Burnes. The mission was accommodated outside of the town in a house which was considered to be one of the best buildings among the wild Bilochis. The civilities shown by the Mir or Khan to the mission, his frequent change in the colour of his face, and continued unsteadiness in his manners when conversing with us, caused suspicions of his perfidious and unfriendly intentions towards our government; but whether those feelings were disturbing the peace of his mind through the imaginary fear of our evil intentions towards himself, or through his own ill-will towards us, cannot easily be ascertained. Although Nayab Mulla Mohammed Hasan his minister, and Sayad Mohammed Sharif, were the medium of the negotiations between us and the Khan, yet neither of them possessed the entire confidence of his lord, nor stood so high in favour as the cunning Daroghah Gul Mohammed; and in justice to one observation of Mr. Masson, with regard to our proceedings in the Birohi Court, I should not pass this unnoticed. It is true that the Nayab, as well as the Sayad, threw many obstacles in our way, and delayed the termination of the friendly settlement between us and the Khan; but this they did neither with the intention to sacrifice the interest of their master, nor to impede the advance of our army towards Qandhar. Their object was to make a display of their talent in convincing us of their influence with the Khan, and thus to secure for themselves a handsome reward from us. They were, however, neither bought by Sir William Macnaghten, nor were any hopes of compensation held out to them for betraying their master. All they expected was that their services, like those of the other chiefs and people beyond the Indus, shall be duly appreciated. On the other hand, Daroghah Gul Mohammed, who was known as a celebrated man for intrigues and cruelties in the court of the Khan, was trying to become an important personage as the chief medium of our negotiations, to the end that he might thus profit himself as his rival courtiers had anticipated by our liberality. The drafts of the treaty were framed, and I conveyed them to the court for the approbation and seal of the Khan. Various topics of discussion at the ratification of it were raised and took place between myself and the Khan, who always, or I may say after every word he spoke, boasted of his superiority in command over the numberless warriors of the Bilochi tribes, and added that not only his animosity, but merely his neutrality during our advance upon Qandhar, would make it impossible for the British troops to pass unmolested through the Bolan Pass, and would encourage the Barakzai chiefs and the Ackzai Afghans to shut the Kojak or Khovajak pass upon our face, and annihilate every person of our army in the valley of Peshing or Faushinj. I of course having spoken freely but respectfully long before in the pompous, civilized, and haughty court of Persia, in intercourse with Abbas Mirza, could not bear the boasting and vain language of the Khan, which reflected a shadow of inferiority on the government which I served in the presence of the wild Bilochis. I therefore took away the treaty from the hands of the Khan with every respect, and begged to state a few words in reply to his most unwise speech. I said to him that the object of the British government was to treat the Khan as a friend and see him permanently established in his authority without any interference in the administration thereof; and that if he, undervaluing our good offices, cherished an idea that the English will not be powerful enough to advance unless the cordial aid of the Khan be obtained, I am sorry to find that he is so ill advised. This, I must be permitted to say, is an idea perfectly destitute of any sense, and those who have represented it to him are either men of the most childish intellect, or they are seeking for the destruction of the Khan. I added that if he was inclined to hope for any advantage in following the evil counsels of his disguised enemies and to be guided by such boasting sentiments, I would be the last person to ask him to accept the treaty which I held in my hand, and the first to recommend to him the undertaking of an immediate step to bring his own views into effect. This, I said, will at once decide the question whether or not the Khan's neutrality or animosity would check the progress of the army of the Indus, or whether the British soldiers will penetrate Afghanistan without sustaining any serious loss, and will soon plant the English flag on the tower of the Miri or palace of His Highness in the Kalat itself. On this the Bilochi chiefs around him appeared to be very extravagant in the words of their bravery while speaking to the

Khan, which I, of course, could not perfectly understand. But in justice to him I may say, that the Mir Mehrab Khan showed no apparent exasperation at my answer; but, taking the treaty again from my hand, he said that "I was a 'Sakhtgo,' or hard speaker—that the British have soldiers to frighten with their arms, and agents to cause alarm by their tongues, but that he will sign and seal the treaty free from those fears, and with the view only to secure our satisfaction." When Sir Alexander Burnes visited the Mir Mehrab Khan afterwards, he told that officer in my presence that I used hard words in treating with him, whereupon he inquired of the Khan whether they were bad words. On the contrary, replied Mehrab Khan, every one of them was good for the benefit of my government; and at the same time he said he had no reason to be dissatisfied with me. This is the real state of the thing, which any one present on the occasion of my conferring with the Khan might have alluded to afterwards in the presence of Mr. Masson, and he, altering the suggestion and remark from its real meaning, garbles it so as to suit his own purpose, with his undoubted and apt genius, so skilled in casting groundless accusations against nearly all who came into contact with this talented author.

The articles of the treaty, as far as I can remember, were that Mehrab Khan was to rule his own dominions as before, acknowledging the authority of Kabul; that Shah Navaz Khan his rival, the pretender from the elder branch of the family, was not to be recognised by the British and the Shah; that the Khan was to receive two hundred thousand rupees annually, and two thousand rupees cash at present; and that in return for this the Mir Mehrab Khan promised to keep the Bolan pass safe and open for our communications in the rear; that he was to wait upon the Shah and the British envoy at Koetta, and that he will exert himself as an ally in procuring, or rather facilitating the means of obtaining, provisions for our army.

The agreed sum in cash was paid to him by me in order to complete his equipage for the purpose of marching towards our camp; but yet several days passed away in fruitless preparations, and he did not start. Sir Alexander, finding that the Khan was neither sincere in his agreement nor in his deeds, quitted Kalat, leaving me with the Khan, and thus still continuing to entertain and cherish his hope of securing the co-operation of Mehrab Khan, and thus also, by preserving the articles of the treaty unviolated, to benefit the Brohi chief by the British alliance for ever. There were sufficient reasons to believe that a party of wild Bilochis had arrived in the town, whether by the direct advice of the Khan or through the agency of others, with the intention to massacre the mission by night; but the sudden and unexpected departure of Sir Alexander Burnes frustrated the foul design, whether that of the chief or of the Brohis. However this might be, the Khan sent for me, and said that the rumour of our bringing a line of camels loaded with treasure for the purchase of the grain had induced some of the distant robbers to commit the offence of stealing; but that it had pleased God that Sir Alexander Burnes had gone, and he will place a strong guard to protect me in the house where I live. It was all in vain to persuade the Khan to hasten his agreed departure to wait upon the Shah and the envoy. He gave orders one day to have the tents ready; next day to take them out of the fort; and the third day to pitch them. After this a discussion took place how to find and fix some lucky day that the Khan should leave his palace and go into the tent, which was pitched about a mile from the city. When he went there, some days were spent in patching the old "yakhdans," or leather baskets for the use of the kitchen of the Khan; and his object, I discovered, was to turn into ridicule the British authorities by showing off his marching preparations, while delaying it purposely with the frivolous excuse of getting ready, until the Shah and our army, being deficient in supplies, should be obliged to leave Shal for Qandhar; and in this view the Khan succeeded. Shah Shuja-ul-mulk, Sir William Macnaghten, and Lord Keane—the Commander-in-Chief, found at length that they could not stay and wait longer for Mehrab Khan; and Sir Alexander Burnes proceeded with the camp, directing me by express to quit Kalat immediately. This was all that Mehrab Khan wanted, by procrastinating his departure; and on my obtaining leave he told me to say to the envoy that the Khan was getting ready, and had pitched his tent to wait upon him; but that the intelligence of the Shah's quitting Shal prevented him from setting off. I replied that I shall be very happy to convey to the Envoy any message of which he wishes to make me the bearer; but as a well-wisher of the Khan, I must say that the excuse he makes for his not marching now was long previously fabricated along with the deliberate delay: and that if the Khan was sincerely desirous to show his attachment to the British he has an opportunity of proving it now in the most unqualified manner, by following and overtaking the camp in the valley of Peshing. He made no reply to this; but appointed Daroghah Gul Mohammed apparently to escort me to Shal, but secretly instructed him to stay in that place, and daily communicate to the Khan the news of our advance upon Qandhar.

The Mir Mehrab Khan did thus not only fail with deliberate intention in the agreement of his waiting upon the Shah and the Envoys, notwithstanding that a sum of money for the expenses of the march had been paid to him; but in reality he also failed to execute and fulfil the articles of the agreement by which he had bound himself to supply us with provisions, and to keep the roads open and safe in our rear. If he had no rule over the subjects of his dominions, why had he pledged himself to do what he was not able to do, and demanded annual payment to enable himself to maintain the tranquillity of the roads? Moreover, his not attending upon the Shah and the British envoy gave a sufficient proof to the Bilochis and to his neighbours the Kakars to persevere in their continued and augmented predatory habits, plundering our daks (or posts), stealing our camels, and cutting off our supplies. The treaty, signed and sealed by the Khan, and given by himself into the charge of the Sayad Mohammed Sharif,* for the purpose of giving to the envoy, was now taken by Darogh Gul Mohammed, who kept it, with the advice of his master, by himself, with the view of practising the deliberate treachery as to the end, that if the chiefs of Qandhar had defeated us, the production of that document would fairly show that he had not exchanged it, but had kept it, as he had no wish to form any connexion with us; and, on the other hand, if the British were victorious, it will be made to follow us to Qandhar, and the Khan thought that he will easily satisfy the Envoy by throwing the blame upon his agent for detaining it so long on the road. In April, 1839, when Haji Khan Kakar

* Not by Sir Alexander Burnes, as Mr. Masson says.

deserted the chiefs of Qandhar, and they fled towards their capital, now the agents of the Mir Mehrab Khan, agreeably to the previous arrangement, waited upon the envoy and Sir Alexander Burnes at Dandi Gulai, and delivered the treaty, saying, that the Khan will come and pay his respects in Qandhar. The conduct of the Khan * had been found to be from the beginning of an unfriendly nature, and therefore the treaty was given back to the agents, with this answer to the message of the Khan, which promised that he will wait upon the Shah at Qandhar, to the effect that the alliance shall be renewed then and there.

On the entering of the Shah into the city of Qandhar, and the flight of its chiefs towards Persia, it was expected that the chief of Kalat, according to

* "To judge rightly of the conduct of Mehrab Khan, who said to Sir Alexander Burnes—'You have brought an army into the country, but how do you propose to take it out again?' it is necessary to state that it was afterwards ascertained that the night before the departure of Sir Alexander Burnes a plan had been formed to murder the whole party, which was defeated by their unexpected departure. I was told so by Lieutenant Simpson, S. A. C. and G., one of the party. The Khan said, 'Your army will be starved, and the water of the country will kill your people.'"—*Major Hough's Campaign in Afghanistan*, pp. 73-74.

his recorded agreement at Dandi Gulai, will come personally, or at any rate will send congratulatory letters for our triumph; and it became known to us only by rumour that the Nayab Mohammed Hasan, in charge of the presents and dispatches from the Khan, was on his way to Qandhar, where he never made his appearance. Whether he missed his way by his own will, or by the directions of the Mir Mehrab Khan, who might have told him to stay in Shal, and wait to see how the affairs may go on in Ghazni and Kabul, thinking that the Amir of that place, with whom he was in correspondence, might gain the victory, and he might then be free to play the same game with him which he had hoped to play with the chief of Qandhar against our measures. Alas! in this, too, he was disappointed.

In the mean time our posts both east and west of the Bolan, as well as in the pass itself, were plundered, and the runners killed. The Governor of the Mir Mehrab Khan in Shal, instead of protecting our camels when grazing, employed men to carry them off to Sistan, where they were sold; for the Khan did not wish him to send them for sale in his capital of Kalat, as this would cast an open rebuke upon his character.

In process of time part of the Bombay army, after Shah Shuja-ul-Mulk was placed on the throne, quitted Kabul under Major-General Sir Thomas Wilshire. On the 25th of August the brave and just politician, Colonel Outram, was ordered to proceed with it, and received instructions from Sir William Macnaghten to the following effect, viz., to arrest the refractory Ghilzai chiefs, Mehtar Musa, Mama Khodai Nazar Khan, Abdulrahman Khan, and Gul Mohammed Khan, the plunderers of the Hindostan caravan at Maruf, to reduce the forts of Haji Khan, and to punish the perpetrators of the atrocious murder of Colonel Herring. He performed these duties to the satisfaction of his superiors, and introduced peace and homage in that part of the Ghilzai country.

On the 31st of October Sir Thomas Wilshire reached Koetta; and Captain Bean, the political agent, in answer to his communications for adjusting matters with the Mir Mehrab Khan, chief of Kalat, for the purpose of securing future tranquillity and the good offices of the Brohi chief, received threats of resistance, which obliged the British general to hasten his march towards his capital. On the 12th of November he encamped at Jiryani, a village within eight miles from Kalat. Next day the skirmishes commenced, and continued till the English force came in sight of Kalat. Now Sir Thomas Wilshire made the disposition of his forces, and planned to storm the town and citadel. The storming party was led in the most heroic and skilful manner by Brigadier Bomgardt, now commander of the 2nd Royal or Queen's regiment at Winchester.* The resistance made by the Mir Mehrab Khan in person was very brave, and he was killed fighting hard and with sword in hand. Such was the end of the Kalat chief, by whose instigation or imbecility hundreds of the followers of the British camp were slain in the Bolan Pass. The treachery and faults of the Khan in some cases in the time of the advance of the Army of the Indus were without any doubt; but I must say that the punishment, which ended his life, exceeded the crime. Shah Navaz Khan, the

* The services of this veteran officer were not rewarded as they ought to have been.

rival relation of the deceased chief, was installed, and Captain Loveday appointed as resident in his court. The charges made by Mr. Masson against this worthy and amiable officer, whom I had personally seen in Mastang, and of whom I heard the people talking in the most affectionate terms for his civil disposition, appear to me altogether incorrect. After he was most cruelly slaughtered, and the son of the late Mir Mehrab Khan was gained by the most skilful and wise measures of Brigadier Stacy, many influential men from Kalat came to Kabul. The British authorities of that day, as well as the chiefs of that place, made inquiries concerning the past but sad events of Kalat, and the proceedings of the much regretted Captain Loveday in that critical time. All of them unanimously, even those who had nothing to do with the good or bad manners and conduct of that officer, alleged that he was liked by every one for his civil and kind disposition, and he was disliked only by his political adversaries, namely, Darogh Gul Mohammed, with his party, to whose cruel passions he fell a victim at last. The truth stands thus: that the Earl of Auckland, with his secretaries Messrs. Maddock and Colvin, Sir William Macnaghten, Sir Alexander Burnes, Captain Bean, and Lieut. Loveday, were of course all men of eminent talents,—and they did not appoint Mr. Masson a political agent in Kalat, as he had requested; and moreover they suspected the usefulness of his travels in the Bilochistan country, which were followed by outbreaks. These were, I think, the reasons which excited Mr. Masson to throw abuse on the tombs of those lamented officers who sacrificed their lives in the service of their country, and to attack the reputation of those who are still alive. His own words will show that he was refused the situation he wanted, and was also suspected.* "As one of the principal points for which I was then contending was employment, from which my exertions might deserve and obtain credit, I could not forbear asking him if I might be allowed to go to Kalat and put everything to rights; but Sir Alexander hung down his head, and made no reply."

* Pp. 81-226.—Narrative of a Journey to Kabul by Charles Masson, Esq.

"The mystery of Mr. Masson's appearance at Kalat at the period of the present outbreak, combined with his clandestine residence at that place, has given rise to suspicions, in my mind, of that individual, which I have not failed to communicate to Government."

CHAPTER XVI.

Haji Khan joins the British—Other chiefs join the British force, and tender allegiance to Shah Shuja-ul-Mulk—The Qandhari chiefs consequently fly to Persia—Qandhar occupied by the British—Installation of Shah Shuja-ul-Mulk—The fugitive chiefs refuse the offers of the British—The Haji Dost Mohammed Khan—Violations of engagements—The army arrives at Kalat-i-Ghilzai—Joined by Abdulrashid Khan—Capture of Ghazni—Proposals of Dost Mohammed refused—Execution of Afghan prisoners—Flight of the Amir—Shah Shuja-ul-Mulk established in Kabul—Progress of the Shah Zadah Taimur—Movements of Akbar Khan—Gholam Khan Popalzai—The Amir at Bokhara.

THE judicious negotiations and secret correspondence of Major Leech were successful, and induced Haji Khan Kakar, whose name has been prominently mentioned in the first volume, to desert the chiefs of Qandhar at a very critical period, while the Sardar Kohandil Khan, the head chief, was at the head of three thousand or four thousand well-mounted cavalry, had quitted his capital to oppose our advance, as already noticed, and had pitched at Dandi Gulaï. The enemy diverted the stream of water from the side of our camp into another direction; and had carried off the two elephants, with their drivers, when they went in search of forage. The chiefs then planned for a night attack on our troops; but Lord Keane removed the Shah's camp and that of the Mission, and thus made an open field to meet the reported and expected attack of the Qandharis. The Sardar Kohandil Khan was told by Haji Khan Kakar, that it was not wise to attack our camp without first gaining proper information of our strength, and reconnoitring the position of our forces, and where the chance of any success might be anticipated. He added that, if permitted, he will go and bring back all this information in full to him. The Sardar, blind with regard to the intrigues of the Haji, permitted him to do this duty; but he came to our camp, whence he never went back to him.

It was the 20th of April, 1839, and about 10 A.M., when Haji Khan's messenger arrived in my tent with a letter to Sir Alexander Burnes, announcing that he had come over to us, but did not like to approach our picquets until some one was sent to meet him. The Envoy, on receiving this intelligence, desired me to go and conduct him to his tent, telling me at the same time not to go beyond the sight of the picquets, in case there might be a snare laid by the Afghan chief to get hold of one of us. However, I saw Haji Khan not far from our guards; and, after welcoming him, I conducted the famous Kakar to the Envoy. The desertion of Haji Khan, whose character and early life is well described in the valuable work of Mr. Masson, was a severe and fatal blow to the Barakzai chiefs of Qandhar, who fell back immediately on that city. They were now suspicious even of their own nearest dependents; and the safest course they were advised by Mulla Nasu now to pursue was to fly towards Persia, with the view to benefit themselves by the Russian security, which Count Simonich, the ambassador of the Emperor, and Mohammed Shah, the King of Persia, had given them, stipulating that if they (the Barakzai chiefs) are deprived of their country by the English, the ambassador and the Shah were to provide them (the chiefs) with maintenance equal to their loss, and sufficient to keep up their rank. When the news of Haji Khan's coming over to us was conveyed to the Amir Dost Mohammed Khan at Kabul, he was heard to say that the greatest mistake he committed in his life was that he did not put an end to the existence of the Haji when in Kabul.

The Haji Khan's coming to us was an example to others; and he was followed by other chiefs of considerable influence, as Abdulmajid Khan, the son of Shah Pasand Khan, governor of Lash, and Gholam Akhund Zadah, a priest, who was one of those that were most violent in exciting the religious hatred of the population against our march. While we were approaching Qandhar, all the men of consequence then in existence in that neighbourhood were joining our camp, tendering submission to His Majesty Shah Shuja-ul-Mulk, and expressing their joy at coming to closer acquaintance with the British. Whatever we might boast of our diplomatic successes during the campaign of Afghanistan, we were certainly very wrong in not keeping up our adherence, even for a short time, to those engagements and promises which we had so solemnly and faithfully made to the various chiefs, in return for their taking up our cause and abandoning their long-known and established masters. Our letters, pledging our honour and Government to reward and appreciate their services for our good, were in their hands; and as soon as we found that the chiefs of Qandhar were fled, and that there was no necessity for wearing longer the airy garb of political civilities and promises, we commenced to fail in fulfilling them. There are, in fact, such numerous instances of violating our engagements and deceiving the people in our political proceedings, within what I am acquainted with, that it would be hard to assemble them in one series. I shall, however, mention them in their proper places, and the time in which they were made, in order to show how soon they were forgotten through our vain pride of power and of our tact shown in the temporary and speedy gaining of the people.

The chiefs, on their return to Qandhar, after the Haji Khan came over to us, thought to secure themselves within the fortifications of the city; to sally out to have skirmishes with us, till our provisions are exhausted, our posts stripped in the rear, and the Mahomedans rise against us, either for the sake of religion, or through avarice of plunder and of theft. Mulla Nasu renewed his counsels, and succeeded at last in inducing the chiefs to quit the city, which was at the time of their departure suffering deeply through extortion and unjust outrages.

On the 25th of April the Shah Shuja-ul-Mulk and the British Envoy and Minister reached the city of Qandhar, the gates of which were already open to receive them. Lord Keane, with the English army, followed the Shah next day, and encamped in the neighbourhood. On a deliberate view of various points it was considered that His Majesty Shah Shuja-ul-Mulk should ascend the throne in a formal manner, and that the ceremony of installation should be publicly solemnized. Of course there was no proper throne that any one, after seeing even in a decayed state one of the poor descendants of the great Emperors of Dehli, might have supposed to be really a throne. However, a proper platform was erected in place of a throne, over which a canopy appeared to throw an ordinary light of pomp and show. It was placed out of the town in an open and extensive place, and the British army, amounting to 7500 men, was drawn up in a line. The Shah, mounted on a very superior horse, was accompanied by Lord Keane and Sir William Macnaghten: and his departure from the city was announced by the guns in the palace; and on his passing near the British lines a royal salute of

HIS LATE MAJESTY SHAH SHUJAH UL MULK.

twenty-one guns was fired. Afterwards there was a general salute; the colours were lowered; and on his ascending the throne a salvo was discharged from the whole of the artillery, 101 pieces, brought thither for the occasion.

Now the British Commander-in-Chief and the Envoy offered presents to the Shah on behalf of the English Government. Then the army of the Indus moved round in front of the Shah; and this grand ceremony was not only imposing for form's sake, but was caused with the view to awe the Afghans and the Ghilzais, through whose country we had yet to pass on our way to Kabul.

As to the fugitive chiefs of Qandhar. I introduced Mulla Nasu to the Envoy and Minister, and he once more tried, by negotiations, to induce the Sardars Kohandil, Rahamdil, and Mehardil Khan to accept our terms and proposals of returning to India. They had, however, already begun to know the value of our political promises, and had good reasons to believe that we shall never adhere to them. They therefore refused our offers; on which a detachment of troops was ordered to march and to overtake them at Girishk. In this enterprise we failed, just as we had begun knowingly and intentionally to fail in our dealings and promises.

From this time to the end of June the army halted at Qandhar to receive supplies and to restore confidence in the people. Proclamations and letters were circulated in the country, inviting the chiefs of the various tribes to tender homage, and promising rewards,—of course without an idea that they shall ever be fulfilled. Grain was very scarce in the mean time, and only through the most extraordinary exertions of Colonel Parsons and of Captain Watt it was brought by the Afghans from a distant part of the country.

It appeared very desirable that Haji Dost Mohammed Khan, a Durrani of high rank and of an influential family, should be invited, or rather induced, to wait upon the Shah and the British Envoy, with the view that his doing so might add much and favourable weight to our influence, and facilitate our progress through the Ghilzai, who would be thunderstruck, as well as the adherents of the Amir Dost Mohammed Khan, to think that the only remaining nobleman of consequence amongst the Durranis was also with us. Various communications passed between this chieftain, Sir William Macnaghten, and the Shah, but the result did not appear successful. In all the Oriental countries and courts correspondence in writing is not considered the proper channel for gaining any object; but on this point verbal conference and assurances in speech are more effectual.

My old friend of Hirat, Abdul Vahab Khan Mustaufi, was solicited by me, and assured of being replaced in his hereditary situation of Mustaufi, paymaster under the king, if he succeeded in bringing the Haji Dost Mohammed Khan. He received the paper sealed by the Shah; and the Envoy assured him of appreciation and reward. He was then employed as the bearer of similar kind letters to the Haji, whom, after a protracted space of time, he succeeded to bring with himself to Qandhar. He was received by us with consideration, but the great mistake committed in disturbing the ease of his mind was in requesting him to accompany the Shah to Kabul. This chief, like the other Durranis, brought up amidst intrigues and rapacity, suspected our good intentions towards him. Upon one hand he considered that the Shah and we would make him a prisoner and send him to Calcutta; and on the other hand he thought, like others, that after being thirty years on amicable terms with the Amir of Kabul, it would be painful to proceed with our camp and drawn sword upon a chief of so long standing. He therefore pretended to be unwell; but still we insisted upon his accompanying the Shah with our camp. Haji Khan Kakar was now elevated to the first situation under the King, and entitled Nasir ul-Doulah. He, as well as the Haji Dost Mohammed Khan, with other petty chiefs, hung back by slow marches to avoid their appearance in our camp, and to wait the result of our advance upon Ghazni. This we considered a treacherous design on their part, and we wished then to ensnare them, but did not warn them of their treachery at the time. Such were our political views and fair dealings.

After the Shah of Persia had raised the siege of Hirat, Colonel Stoddart was left with Prince Kam Ran and the Vazir Yar Mohammed Khan, to form a closer familiarity between the British Government and those personages. Sir William Macnaghten, who was desirous to act and be alone with the Shah, planned that Sir Alexander Burnes should be sent on a mission to the Prince of Hirat; while the latter officer, anxious to gain political fame and ascendancy, refused to undertake this mission, and persevered to remain with the Envoy, with the view of succeeding him. He even refused to be a Resident in Qandhar, which was long afterwards offered to him on a larger salary, by the Earl of Auckland. However, Major Todd was appointed, and sent on a mission to the Prince Kam Ran, with instructions to strengthen the fortifications of that city and form a treaty with him. His proceedings in the court of Hirat I shall notice at the time of the failure of our objects in that quarter.

The arrangements for the advance of the army of the Indus from Qandhar were completed on the 2d of June;* and one of the sons of Shah Shuja-ul-Mulk was appointed as Governor of this part of Afghanistan, and Major Leech was nominated as Political Agent. Since it became evident that we had nothing to contend with at Qandhar, Shah Shuja-ul-Mulk upon one hand, and the British on the other, commenced to throw off the mask of adhering to their engage-

* This day the Maharajah Ranjit Singh of the Panjab breathed his last.

ments with the people who had been recently detached from the enemy. The Shah, in conjunction with our chief men as advisers, made arrangements for the administration of the country; and various persons of much experience were entrusted with the different offices of the Government. The mint was farmed by Mulla Jalal, an Ackzai merchant of ordinary wealth, who offered the Shah to give double the sum which was paid by his predecessor to the ex-chiefs of Qandhar; and this was settled through our intervention. As soon as large sums of English money were circulated in the country, it became obvious that there would be a considerable increase in the revenues of the mint, for changing the Company's coin into that of the Shah Shuja-ul-Mulk. A different party, aware of the profit, offered more to the Shah than was agreed on by Mulla Jalal; and consequently avarice overpowered His Majesty, who expressed his wish to break off the agreement which had been contracted between him and the Mulla on our guarantee. Such was the state of things and of affairs in which the sovereign just now elevated to the throne began to disregard his own engagements, careless of all loss of reputation.

But now let us mention our own conduct. The co-operation of Mulla Nasu, the chief adviser of the ex-chiefs, was gained by us on giving a written agreement bestowing a pension upon him. In return, he was desired to dissuade the chiefs from opposing our army, which will cause a fruitless bloodshed on their part. He succeeded in his advice, and the chiefs fled to Persia. As we wished not to stand by our engagement, we pretended to find faults, and said that the chiefs had quitted Qandhar in order to fight with us, but that, seeing the strength of our forces, and the coming over of Haji Khan to us, this compelled them to fly, which was not brought about by the advice of Mulla Nasu, who therefore is not entitled to the agreed pension.

Abdul Vahab Khan was the second Durrani who suffered also by the violation of our engagements. This individual was deputed to Mir Mehrab Khan of Kalat from the chiefs of Qandhar, while Sir Alexander and myself were with him; and was accompanied by another Qazilbash of distinction, who had in his charge many valuable documents concerning the negotiations between the Sardars of Qandhar, the Russian agent, and the various chiefs of Bilochistan. He was a Durrani of the Popalzai clan, attached to the Sadozai, and thus hostile to the ascendancy of the Barakzai. Nevertheless, his father, as well as himself, were in the service of the usurpers. He offered his services to us in undertaking to deprive his companions of the alleged documents, for which we promised him a handsome reward from the British Government, and his nomination to the rank of the Mustaufi. In order to complete his promise, he set out from Kalat with his companion the Qazilbash, on his way back to Qandhar; but on the road, like a real Afghan, he broke off the bonds of long-standing amity with him, and respect to his employer the Sardar Kohandil Khan. He seized his comrade, and then let him off as a fugitive, and brought all the papers in his possession to us in Kalat. The next duty which was entrusted to him on our arrival at Qandhar was to induce Haji Dost Mohammed Khan of Garm Saial to come and wait upon the Shah and the British Envoy; and of his success in this affair I have made mention in the preceding pages. How we adhered to the engagements on our part is worthy of notice. We acknowledged his services by tongue as well as by pen; but, in order to avoid doing so by reward, we merely gave him a note to the Secretary of the Shah, saying that he was a well-wisher of His Majesty; who, as usual, said in reply to Abdul Vahab Khan, "Amar khavahad shud;" meaning, "the commands shall be issued." But this phrase of the Shah was still more an extraordinary piece of deception than our own political promises, for such commands were meant never to be issued. In this state of anxiety and hope, Abdul Vahab Khan spent all he had, and sold his horses to maintain himself; and at length we pretended to forget what we had first agreed to do, and the Shah's "Amar" never came to pass. Were such proceedings of the Shah Shuja-ul-Mulk, and our political conduct towards the people at Qandhar, prudent? Were Gul Mohammed (Guru) Abdurrahman and Sultan Mohammed Khans, the chiefs of the Hotak and Tokhi Ghilzais, amongst whom we had yet to pass on the road to Ghazni, to believe our sincerity in any engagement hereafter? However, we marched from Qandhar, and sent deputations and letters to the Ghilzai, promising the reward of rank and high pay, as we had done in the cases of Mulla Nasu, Abdul Vahab Khan, and the Haji Dost Mohammed

Khan. We were at once infringing the engagements behind our army, and making new ones a-head. But the Ghilzais were not such fools as we might have supposed from their being uncivilised; nor did they fear to vie with us in arms, though undisciplined. Having already heard of the insincerity of our promises towards Mulla Nasu, &c., the Ghilzais laughed at our proposals; and instead of joining us, and facilitating our march towards Ghazni, they moved their families with their valuables into the interior, and continued annoying and plundering us all the way on our flanks. We had undoubtedly planted in their hearts the dread of our arms, but certainly we failed in restoring confidence of our faith. They would neither believe our promises, nor even our written engagements. On our gaining the possession of Kabul, the Ghilzai chiefs considered their safety consisted in leaving Afghanistan; and they took refuge in the Sikh territory, whence we secured their persons through negotiations from our ally the ruler of the Panjab.

The head-quarters of the army and of the Shah arrived at Kalat-i-Ghilzai, on the 4th of July; and we halted for the 5th, to nominate rivals of Guru, &c.

to the chiefship of the Tokhis; and Mir Alam Khan, a man of weak mind, but of high family, was appointed. Some of the Shah's troops were to occupy the fort, for the purpose of keeping the communication in our rear uninterrupted. Sir William Macnaghten thought it advisable that I should be left as a political agent, to try to restore confidence amongst the Ghilzais; but, on mature deliberation, he considered that my services would be more useful in Ghazni and Kabul than they could be by keeping me in the rear of the army, and he therefore countermanded his orders on this point. Before our arrival at Mokar, we received intelligence at one time of opposition to be met at Ghazni, and at another time the Amir of Kabul had desired his son to leave that fort on our approach, and to join him with his force, in order to give us battle jointly in one place. However, we knew of the disaffected members of the family now within Ghazni; and I wrote a note to Abdulrashid Khan, the first nephew of Dost Mohammed, to quit the camp of Haidar Khan and join me instantly. I was on very intimate terms with this person from a long time before, and he fortunately attended to my advice. The bearer of my letter, a man from Istalif, was seized by Haidar Khan, just after he had delivered his charge to Abdulrashid. Here the sharpness of the Afghans in craft and planning of intrigues will not be deemed uninteresting. The seizure of my messenger, which was followed by putting him to death, deprived my friend of the opportunity to communicate with us, while he felt greatly anxious of necessity to do so. He taught one of his horsemen to counterfeit himself immediately as a fanatic and mad person, for the obtaining the martyrdom either by killing an infidel, or being himself killed by one of us. He shaved his beard, and clothed himself in green. He bore a drawn sword in hand, and, uttering the holy names of God and the Prophet, he proceeded in the direction of our camp, threatening to destroy any one who would dare to impede his progress. Besides the verbal messages and information from Abdulrashid Khan, he had contrived amazingly to conceal and bring a letter from him to us, which mode of hiding conveyance I had never dreamt of. Such was the successful contrivance of the nephew of the Amir, and thus the pretended thirst of martyrdom of the messenger was extinguished.

Abdulrashid Khan soon after stole his escape from Ghazni and joined our camp. I introduced him to the Envoy, who placed this same Abdulrashid Khan under the immediate disposal of Lord Keane. The information which he gave to Major Thomson, the chief Engineer, relative to the fortifications of Ghazni, was so valuable and necessary, that my friend Abdulrashid Khan was requested to attend upon him in all his reconnoitring expeditions. He told us that the Sardar Mohammed Afzal Khan, the eldest son of the Amir of Kabul, was, with a large troop of cavalry, outside the fort; and that the younger one, namely, Sardar Gholam Haidar Khan, was inside with a strong body of men, ready to defend himself to the last. On the 21st July, we came in front of Ghazni, and the fire of cannons from the ramparts bid us to form the disposition of the army. A council of war was held, and Lord Keane deemed it judicious that, instead of encamping opposite to the Qandhar gate of Ghazni, he had better move towards that of Kabul, and thus stop the reinforcement, if there was any sent, from the Amir Dost Mohammed Khan to the Governor of Ghazni. It became dark before we reached our ground; and the confusion and the irregularity in our movement was so great, that if the cavalry of Mohammed Afzal, under the cover of the guns of Ghazni, had fallen upon us in that hour, the consequences would have been fatal to us; but, fortunately for us, they misunderstood our movement. When the Sardar Haidar Khan surrendered himself to us, he told us that he and his brothers thought that we were advancing upon Kabul, and intended to leave Ghazni to submit on the occupation of the capital. He added that they both considered it right to allow us to move undisturbed till we were in the valley of Shekhabad, and then to annoy us in the rear, while their father the Amir would fall upon us in front, and therefore we escaped without molestation. We heard successive reports that the Amir had left Kabul, in order to reinforce Ghazni, and command there personally; and that the Sardar Mohammed Afzal Khan was joined by all the disaffected Ghilzai chiefs, and threatened an attack on our camp. These were considered to be about three thousand well-mounted fighting men; and the strength of the garrison was equally numerous and formidable.

The position of our camp had perfectly cut off the direct communication of the Amir Dost Mohammed

Khan with his sons at Ghazni; and skirmishing parties were every day sent out to divert the attention of the enemy. The Sardar Mohammed Afzal Khan discovered his weakness by remaining outside of the fort; and he sent a message to his step-brother the Sardar Haidar Khan, asking him to allow him and his followers to enter the fort, and promising that he will sally out to destroy our foraging parties. The younger brother, however, jealous and distrustful as he was of his brother Mohammed Afzal, like other Afghans, refused to admit him. He considered, moreover, the stronghold of Ghazni was never to be subdued by force of arms, and that when we were reduced in our supplies, and unable to maintain ourselves amidst the wrathful fanatics, the victory will result in favour of the garrison, and yet the credit of it will be shared, if not wholly claimed, by his brother. He also feared that the Sardar Mohammed Afzal Khan, by intriguing personally with his dependents in the garrison, might make him a prisoner and take possession of the fort. These were the suspicions of Gholam Haidar Khan in the garrison: and they wounded the brotherly feelings of Mohammed Afzal Khan, who was outside, by his being refused leave to enter the fort in such a critical time. He therefore moved far from Ghazni, abandoned the design of skirmishing with our forces, and left the garrison to its own fate.

Abdulrashid Khan gave such minute and correct information of the strength of the fortifications and of the chances of storming it, that all succeeded, and under the skilful and heroic superintendence of Major Thomson, the chief engineer, bags of leather filled with loose powder were attached to the Kabul gate. It was wonderful, indeed, how quietly and wisely the arrangements were made; but by 3 A.M. of the 23rd July, all the detachments ordered for the services were in their respective posts. Lord Keane, with his staff, as well as Sir Alexander Burnes and myself, stood upon the steep hill, which was frequently fired upon from the garrison, and Colonel Parsons was slightly wounded by a "Jozayar" ball, which fortunately had just missed me. The Commander-in-Chief had formed the disposition of the storming party so judiciously that it did not require his personal attendance at the time when the skilful and brave officers, Major Thomson and Captain Peat, blew up the gate. Immediately after the gallant Colonel Dennie led the storming party,—rushed in, and dislodged the enemy from the gateway. He was followed by the supporting or advance column, under Sir Robert Sale, and thus miraculously the capture of the strong fortress of Ghazni was accomplished in three quarters of an hour, while the Commander-in-Chief had anticipated the impossibility of gaining possession of it until long after breakfast, which he had therefore taken with himself to the hill, with the view of not returning to his tent till late in the evening. While a false alarm was given on the other side, the heroic rush-in of the storming party, just after the powder-bags exploded and burst the gates open, threw the Afghans into astonishment and consternation, and soon after this we heard the British soldiers under Sir Willoughby Cotton cheering on the Balahisar, or citadel of Ghazni. We then sighed often for the dawn, and when it came at length, discovered that all was in our possession, and the firing had ceased. The Shah Shuja-ul-Mulk, accompanied by Sir William Macnaghten, was conducted by Lord Keane into the fortress, and his Excellency gave immediate orders that no outrages and insults should be committed on the women of the garrison, and that every protection should be afforded to them. We entered the palace of the Sardar Gholam Haidar Khan, and there I saw his wife, the daughter of the late Sardar Mohammed Azim Kham, whom I had seen in 1832, when she was unmarried and about fourteen years of age, complaining of sore eyes, and asking the advice of the late Dr. Gerard. I gave her every assurance of protection on the part of my superiors, and of my endeavours to make her comfortable. She was accompanied by about thirty other females, relations and servants; and Captain John Conolly conducted them, with every mark of deference, to a house in the town, where it fell to my lot to provide them with every thing necessary which they wanted: and that responsible charge of them I had for a long time, and executed it to the satisfaction of the ladies, till they were sent to India. In the mean time the Governor of Ghazni, the Sardar, was not to be found, and the greatest doubts of his escape were entertained. After the Commander-in-Chief had returned to the camp, Major Macgregor found him concealed with an armed party, in the tower, waiting for the night, and intending then to effect their escape towards Kabul. His adherents would not surrender until the assurance of their personal safety was given, —and then the Sardar, mounted on a small horse, and accompanied by a few of his companions, was conducted by Major Macgregor to the tent of the Commander-in-Chief. Sir Alexander Burnes and myself were sent for, and as soon as the Sardar saw him he felt a little easy in his mind; and discovering me with him, the expression of his countenance was at once changed, and he asked me for a glass of water. Lord Keane allowed him to remain in my tent, under the charge of Sir A. Burnes. I clothed him with my own clothes every day, and he partook of my meals. All the time he continued with me, he repeated on every occasion his gratification and ease of mind, and his gratitude to the Commander-in-Chief and to the Envoy, for their placing him under my care, while the officer also of the Bombay Presidency,* at the head of the personal guard of our state prisoner, added to the satisfaction of the Sardar, by his strict adherence to the respect and civility which were due to him. He at first declined to wait upon the Shah Shuja-ul-Mulk; but the Commander-in-

* I unfortunately forget the name of that amiable officer.

Chief assuring him that there was no necessity for any kind of alarm, and that every respect should be shown to him, and that his Excellency would personally conduct him and bring him back from the presence of the king, he went; and the king received him of course, as was advised by us, with something like outward kindness.

A little before evening it was reported that a certain chief, a friend of our state-prisoner, at the head of about one hundred well-armed men, was still occupying his possessions, and resisting our forces in the town, and firing upon them from the top of his house, and would not listen to any proposals made to him by the officers of the garrison, unless Sir Alexander Burnes or myself were to speak to him. I was ordered to go and confer with the chief, taking with me the seals of the Envoy and of Sir Alexander Burnes, thus showing that I was empowered by them both to treat with him. The doors of his house were blockaded inside, and many of our soldiers and sepoys who had dared to attempt to break them open, were lying dead under the walls of the house, while the whole regiment and officers were standing round the building, under the cover of the different ruins.

They would have soon destroyed the house by cannonading, and would have killed and seized every one of the men who were killing our people after quarter had been granted;—but it contained many ladies of his family, and it was therefore considered proper to induce the chief to surrender by overtures, otherwise it would have involved the poor ladies also in the fatal consequences. In truth I must confess that I was not quite fearless on approaching the house; but the chief called me by my name, and swearing that there was no trap laid for my destruction, and that he only wished that I should take charge of his ladies, and place them with those of the Sardar Gholam Haidar Khan, pledging myself that no insult should be offered to them by our people, I agreed to all he had said, the doors were opened, and the ladies taken into my charge. The chief and his attendants now gave up their arms to the officers who were then around his residence; and from the most dark cellars he let loose a great number of his horses into the street, as they had been shut up for a long time, with the view that the fort would be besieged, and would hold out for a considerable time. Amongst these animals there was a most beautiful and valuable charger, of a grey colour, which he selected, and told me to accept from him, adding that he would be of great use to me if I were ever in danger, and wished to fly. The Commander-in-Chief kindly allowed me to keep that animal, and did not include him in the prize list of Ghazni.

The Sardar Mohammed Afzal Khan, who had encamped with his cavalry far from Ghazni, soon after the capture discovered that the British flag was waving on the citadel of that fortress. He thereupon broke up his camp and hastened on his way back to Kabul, whither he conveyed the melancholy news to his father of our brilliant victory at Ghazni. Lord Keane and Major Thomson recommended to the Envoy to confer a pension for the information which my friend Abdul Rashid had given them previous to the storming of the fortress. He was clothed by me in a dress of honour, and received a pension of five hundred rupees *per mensem* for his life, which unhappily did not last long.

On this the Navab Jabbar Khan, celebrated as a staunch friend of all Europeans, and especially of the English at that time, came on a deputation to us from the Amir Dost Mohammed Khan. Being from a considerable period endeavouring to establish the British influence against his brother in Kabul, and aware of the hospitalities, the kind, civil, and liberal protection with which he received the English officers frequently, and that at the same time conscious of his being in secret communication and correspondence with our government, in addition to the numerous claims which he had established by rendering valuable services to our state; he therefore, like other Afghans, or I may say naturally, felt confident that from the risk he ran in furthering the views of the English and the dethronement of his brother the Amir, he will, on the weight of the abovementioned claims, succeed in the object of his mission to us, and thus will show brotherly affection to the Amir in time of need. I went to receive him about five miles from our camp, and on arriving at the picquets he was met by Sir Alexander Burnes. He was accommodated in a tent next to the Envoy, but far from my place, with the view not to allow him to be near to our state-prisoner. He stated that his brother, the Amir Dost Mohammed Khan, was desirous to surrender on the condition that he be made the Minister (Vazir) of the Shah, which situation, by hereditary claim, he had a right to secure. Yet this was refused by us, and very properly. The mention of sending the Amir to India was not palatable to the Navab, who said that his brother the Amir will never agree to it. He then demanded the deliverance of his niece, the wife of Haidar Khan, which was also denied. This refusal I do not think was prudent. It was thus made evident how much the British were indebted to the Navab, and an Afghan cares very little for his wife or child in the hands of the enemy, when he has an opportunity to frustrate that enemy's designs. On the first ground it was incumbent upon us to oblige the Navab, and to give up his niece to him; for another reason, if the Afghans had means to resist our arms, and unforeseen circumstances should have thrown one of our officers into the hands of the Barakzai chiefs, the detention of the wife of Haidar Khan by us would have never induced them to save the life of our officer, when he became their prisoner, if they had thought it advisable to terminate his existence. With these views it was quite unnecessary to offend such a valuable friend as the Navab in this critical time, who justly and candidly said to us that "All Mahomedans know that I am the friend of the English, and that I am only the cause of my brother's ruin; and if I fail in gaining the appointment for him under the King, I shall still return proud amongst my equals if the wife of Gholam Haidar Khan was liberated and given back to him." As he was on the point of starting, he expressed his last wish to see his nephew Haidar Khan, who was in my tent, under the surveillance of Sir Alexander Burnes. It was promised that he should be permitted to see him, but on this point a little delay took place in obtaining the permission of the various political and military functionaries; and this delay gave the Navab reason to suppose that we were deceiving him. He was not only disappointed on this trifling matter, but he really lost confidence and hope in us. In the conversation which he had with us, the topic turned so as to speak of the Shah Shuja-ul-Mulk, whose name we of course mentioned with great deference; on which the Navab smiled, and said to the Envoy, "If Shah Shuja is really a king, and come to the kingdom of his ancestors, what is the use of your army and name? You have brought him by your money and arms into Afghanistan, and you have behaved toward him in a friendly and liberal manner in every way. Leave him now with us Afghans, and let him rule us if he can." Such plain language was not palatable to us; and he was requested to wait upon the Shah, who feigned to be civil to him, as His Majesty was advised by the Envoy to receive the Navab with kindness. The good Navab, sunk in disappointment and distress of mind by our unfriendly manner towards him, left our camp about noon of the 29th July. When the Shah and the Envoy offered him the situation of minister under His Majesty, he said he will share the fate of his brother the Amir, and not be flattered by such prospects and sweet promises. I was told to escort the Navab beyond our picquets; and on the road between the camp of the Envoy and the Commander-in-Chief we heard shrieks of some woman captured from the fortress of Ghazni. The Navab turned his face towards me, and nodding his head with an expression of inward abuse, said that we had boasted before him yesterday of our being fortunate in that no woman was ill treated by the captors. I assured the Navab that the person from whose tents the shrieks were heard must have brought her from some village in the vicinity; that every respect has been paid to the women in the fortress; but I immediately went in his own presence to the tent and got the poor female released, who was at that time captured by a waterman of the Sergeant of the Mission, who was afterwards discharged from the service. The tone of the language of the Navab, on his return to Kabul, was not friendly to the English. Disappointed as he was in regard to the success of his mission to our camp, and having expected little good from us, he unwisely, though justly, talked like others, saying that we political people show the prospect of a good harvest in distant promises, but that in the time of reaping we turn it into nothing but a "Darakht i hanzal," which looks green and beautiful, but bears no fruit. As he had been truly suspected for several years of intriguing with us to ruin his brother the Amir, therefore, to wipe away that stain from his name, he supported the Amir in encouraging the people to rise and oppose us, saying that otherwise we shall ill treat them and their females, and banish them from the country. I shall notice this latter part of the discourse of the Navab in its proper place hereafter, and go back to my narrative of the advance of the army.

The victory of Ghazni was undoubtedly brilliant and glorious; but the execution of numerous persons in the vicinity of the British camp threw a very unpleasant light on those triumphs. I do not mean that it took place either by our advice or without any offence; but surely no one in any country will admit and approve of the butchery of fifty men in the most cruel and barbarous way for the offence of one individual. It is true that such a massacre was perpetrated by an Afghan against the Afghans in Afghanistan: but every child in that country, as well as those well versed in the affairs of the Trans-Indus, will admit and say that the Shah would have never thought of beheading such a number of men in cold blood, who were fighting for their country, unless he was guarded by the British arms. If we had said in our proclamation that the Shah entertains the idea of murdering the persons who may fall his prisoners under the exertions of the English officers, we would have done the duty of just and humane beings in warning the population. The remarks of an English authority,* who was with

* Campaign of the Army of the Indus in Sindh and Kabul, by Dr. Kennedy, vol. ii. pp. 38-43 and 56-59.

the army at that time, will not fail to interest the reader :—

"The following day, the 22d July, was a day of no ordinary interest. Before us was the fort, firing its five-minute guns, apparently relying upon the noise to frighten us off, as crows are scared from a corn-field: they did not appear to fire at anything; the fire seemed for firing's sake; but the hill on our flank and rear presented a most formidable array of the enemy's rabble, covering the heights and clustering on the summits. It was not, I believe, considered desirable to employ the army generally against these people: had it been so, a fearful slaughter might have been made, for they put themselves most unaccountably forward, and showed the only spark of courage we had yet seen among them. Colonel Outram attacked them at the head of a part of the Shah's levies, and defeated them with a very trifling loss on our side, and not much on theirs; as they did not stand for any close-quarter work, and the force acting was too small for any flank movement to intercept their retreat.

"It was on this occasion that so many prisoners were beheaded by Shah Shuja's order. On being brought in, the King seems to have thought it would be agreeable to look at them, and have a little conversation with them; and they were consequently paraded in the royal presence! His Majesty upbraided them roundly as rebels, &c.; whereon one more heroic than the rest, or more probably intoxicated with opium, reviled the Lord's anointed, as an infidel at heart, and a friend and slave of infidels, and wounded one of the King's servants (a Pesh kidmat) with his dagger, on the menial, in the terror of horrified loyal sycophancy, attempting to stop his mouth, and the torrent of his abuse. The King, it is said, forthwith ordered the whole party, upwards of sixty in number, to be put to death.

"Captain Outram's narrative slurs over this affair in a manner that I hope silently shows his opinion of it; and his position may explain his motives for keeping such an opinion to himself. He describes the number of prisoners at about fifty; and says that one of them, 'on being brought into the King's presence, stabbed one of the principal officers of state in the open durbar,—an offence for which the whole are said to have atoned with their lives.'

"I heard that the person wounded was a Pesh

kidmat, and such a man may be a principal officer of state in an Asiatic darbar, where the scale of intellect and education betwixt the prince and his chief butler, and the baker and the prime minister, is not widely different; but why write that they were 'said to have atoned with their lives,' when every body knew that a great many prisoners, in reality upwards of sixty, had been put to death?

"A British officer of the Bombay column was said to have accidentally witnessed the destruction of these miserable creatures; and his statement, as it reached me, was, that they were huddled together pinioned, some sitting, some lying on the ground, some standing, and four or five executioners, armed with heavy Afghan knives—a something betwixt a sword and a dagger, the shape of a carving knife, two feet long in the blade, broad and heavy—were very coolly, and in no sort of hurry, hacking and hewing at their necks, one after the other, till all were beheaded.

"The Bengal papers have attempted to charge the responsibility of this on Lord Keane. I would hope that, when he heard of it, he may have given an English opinion in condemnation of it; but it is not likely that he could have had any intimation of it before it was all over. The Shah's camp was two miles from his tent; and it was a mere political question, which would not be referred to him by Sir W. Macnaghten.

"The first folly of having brought such people at such a moment into the King's presence, and so occasioning the outrage, should have palliated its atrocity, and mitigated its punishment, as the wounded man did not die. But allowing that one life was justly forfeited, and that the audacious criminal who struck the King's servant in the King's presence was beyond mercy, the remaining sixty-four were prisoners of war; and to call Dost Mohammed and his sons rebels, and to talk of sparing their lives on the one hand, or of executing them on the other, can be justified by no law, and upheld by no reasoning under heaven.

"It is little creditable to British honour to know that this could never have occurred but under the protection of the British artillery, and within the lines of the British camp. Even the Ghazni dispatch exhibits the British Commander-in-Chief soliciting the fulfilment of the Shah's promise to spare the life of his prisoner Haidar Khan, as if the bare possibility to the contrary could have been contemplated. But

Sir W. Macnaghten's letter to Colonel Outram, published by the latter as the twenty-fifth chapter of his Narrative, is enough, without further commentary, to show the courtier tone that was generally adopted. India was not won after this fashion: may God in his mercy grant that it be not lost thus!

" 'On the 25th July,' says Outram, 'the leader of the party which continued firing upon our soldiers on the 23d inst., after the town had surrendered, and who twice renewed hostilities after having actually sued for quarter, was this day shot by order of the Commander-in-Chief.'

" On the 16th of July, it is said, 'a native was shot by the sentence of a drum-head court-martial, for wounding and robbing some of the camp followers.' It might have been better had a drum-head court-martial preceded the business of the 25th. How any man, having the power to order a court to sit to try and condemn a person undoubtedly guilty, should prefer ordering the putting to death in the exercise of authority only, when the delay involves no risk of evil, seems inexplicable; nor should such a power be permitted to do this by the laws of any country, much less of a 'trial-by-jury' country.

"The power to put to death a prisoner in cold blood, without any public investigation or trial, supposes the power to destroy any other life whatsoever; and if we take into account the possibilities of insanity on the one hand, and blind obedience on the other, the hazards of the abuse of power are most fearful, and it is high time that such a law should be amended.

"The circumstances connected with the capture of the unhappy man who suffered, and whose name was Vali Mohammed, are most probably correctly stated by Colonel Outram. The manner of his death was very affecting. The Commander-in-Chief, having heard some such charge as Colonel Outram has related, probably the same verbatim, sent his Persian interpreter, Major Powell, on the evening of the 24th—that is to say, twenty-six hours after the capture—to single out the culprit from among the other prisoners. Major Powell called out, in a court-yard where the prisoners were, that he required Vali Mohammed; and he, little dreaming of what was intended for him, sprang up with alacrity, and at once presented himself to Major Powell, as one who probably fancied that he was 'a man whom the King might delight to honour.' He was led forth to the camp; and the next morning marched to the rear of the staff lines, and shot by a party of the Bengal 35th regiment of Native infantry.

"Much public discussion has been excited by this tragical occurrence. As to the guilt of the sufferer, I should hope it was so established, that, in a civilised country, and among educated men, the sentence of death would follow of strict necessity. But among such people as those with whom we were in collision, the turpitude and heinousness of guilt are to be weighed by other shades of criminality than those which operate in European warfare; and a high-toned generosity and clemency would have been the most honourable assumption of national and religious superiority."

One day after the capture of Ghazni, Haji Khan Kakar, along with Haji Dost Mohammed Khan and the other Durrani chiefs, who had designedly hung back from our camp on a former occasion, began now a new course of conduct. We knew of course the reason of this duplicity of their conduct, as I have noticed previously; but now they opened their tongue for flattery, showering the flowers of praise on our soldiers, which, indeed, they really deserved; and said that no one had ever thought in Afghanistan of our capturing the stronghold of Ghazni in such a short time, and that therefore they did not hurry themselves to join our camp, fearing to fatigue men and horses, and thus make them unfit for the active service which they expected we should want. On the 30th of July, the army of the Indus resumed its march in the direction of Kabul; and the Shah, with the Bombay brigade, preceded us to Shekhabad. About 3 A.M., on the 3d of August, a Persian friend of mine arrived in my tent, with the intelligence of the flight of the Amir Dost Mohammed Khan towards Bamian, leaving his artillery and ammunition at Maidan. I immediately conducted my friend to Sir Alexander Burnes; and though this news was satisfactory to the political functionaries, resulting as it did from their judicious negotiations in inducing the chiefs to abandon the cause of the Amir, yet it certainly disappointed the military authorities sadly, as I had seen many officers the previous evening sharpening their swords, rejoicing at the prospect of showing their true heroism. The brave Colonel Outram, with Captains Lawrence, Troup, Taylor,

Christie, Hogg, &c., volunteered immediately for special service, and started off at once to overtake the fugitive Amir of Kabul on his way to Bamian. Haji Khan Kakar or Nasir-ul-daulah accompanied the party, which amounted to about eight hundred foot and horse. I shall here leave the subject of the pursuit of the Amir at present, and resume it on the occasion of throwing Haji Khan into custody, and our administration in Kabul.

In Shekhabad my friend Khan Shirin Khan, the Persian chief, with a large retinue, and different other chiefs in it, joined ourcamp, after the Amir Dost Mohammed Khan had entered the valley of Sirchishmah. The Shah and the Envoy received him very kindly, and he was acknowledged as the first leader of the Persian tribe in Afghanistan. We moved on to Maidan, where the artillery and ammunition, with the other heavy baggage, had been left by the Amir, and which now became the property of the Shah Shuja-ul-Mulk. This day many Durrani chiefs came to meet the Shah, and were drawn up in lines on both sides of the road along which we passed, complimented and welcomed by them. The nearer we approached the city of Kabul, the more people of all ranks came in throngs to our camp. The fruits and the luxuries of ice, &c., as well as the picturesque view upon Kohdaman, Chardehi, &c., with the emerald-like gardens in the vicinity of the capital, intersected and washed as they are by the brooks of crystal-like water, though not foreign to me, yet induced me to partake of the astonishment and pleasure which suddenly but joyfully surrounded our army, particularly the natives of Bengal, of Madras, and of Bombay. It was the 7th of August, 1839, that the exiled king, Shah Shuja-ul-Mulk, after the lapse of thirty years, was reseated in the capital of his kingdom by the British army.

The Amir Dost Mohammed Khan would have certainly given us one or two battles before his flight to Bamian, had he had to oppose us only on one side. We, however, threatened him at once in three different directions, besides that we had to a considerable degree caused him to mistrust the chiefs and people around his own person. From the South, the army of the Indus, after obtaining possession of Qandhar, and taking the fortress of Ghazni, had reached within a few marches of his capital; and on the north, or in Kohdaman, at only about twenty

SIR CLAUDE WADE KT CB.

miles from the city, we had succeeded in inducing his own subjects, the Kohistanis, to stand up against him; and from the east side we had sent the Shah Zadah Taimur, the eldest son of the king, with about 10,000 foot and horse, through the Panjab, to divert the attention of the Amir towards Jelalabad and Khaibar; and we thus prevented his son the Sardar Mohammed Khan from joining his father in Kabul.

I have followed the "Army of the Indus" to its final destination, in its arrival at Kabul; and I shall now take a brief view of the proceedings of the Shah Zadah Taimur, and of the Khaibaris under the Sardar Mohammed Akbar Khan, before I touch upon the subject of raising a rebellion against the Amir in Kohistan.

In accordance with the Tripartite treaty, the Shah Zadah Taimur left Lodianah on his way to Peshavar through the Panjab, and Sir Claude Wade, having been invested with both the military and political powers, was appointed to accompany the Shah Zadah. They crossed the Satlaj on the 15th of February, 1839, and in the Panjab the whole of the troops under them, including the Sikh contingent, amounted to about 10,000 of all descriptions. A very interesting account of the daily progress of this part of the force advancing upon Kabul is well set forth in an amusing volume published by Lieut. W. Barr, one of the officers under Sir Claude Wade.*

Previous to the departure of the Shah Zadah Taimur from Lodianah, Mr. Lord was appointed as a political agent, and sent ahead to Peshavar to spread reports of the restoration of the Shah Shuja ul-Mulk to his kingdom of Afghanistan; to communicate with the various chiefs of the surrounding tribes, and to gain adherents for the purpose of advancing the views of the British Government; and he was authorised to spend the sum of one lakh of rupees, in order to effect this object. He had successfully negotiated with the Khataks, Bajauris, and Panjtaris, and had sent emissaries by a circuitous route to Qunduz and Khulam, inviting the co-operation of those chiefs against the Amir of Kabul. The instructions which were furnished to this officer from Sir Alexander Burnes, in addition to those given by

* Shahamat Ali, the Persian secretary to Sir Claude Wade, has written an able account of the advance of the Shah Zadah, which I hope he will amuse the public some day by publishing.

Sir Claude Wade, though abruptly and briefly stated, will not fail to show the outline of his guidance in those important transactions:—

"Be kind to the Divan of Sadat Khan Momand.

"Sadud Din has great influence with the tribes of the south of Peshavar; he is likely to be a useful man.

"Be careful how you deal with the Baujaur chiefs and the Shah of Kunar; do it secretly.

"Sadud Din will open the door to the Khataks.

"Do not carry on too much communication with Fatah Khan and Payandah Khan, or it may vex the Sikhs.

"Do not be open in your communications with Sadat Khan, or Mohammed Akbar Khan may injure him from Jalalabad.

"Mohammed Beg Qaflah Bashi is particularly to be well treated. Present him with one hundred rupees from me for bringing Gholam Khan's letter. Through him you can safely communicate with the Navab and with Gholam Khan; but beware of what you write, or these men will lose their lives.

"Employ the Qazis near, if you can, Qutab-alam. He is a shrewd, clever fellow; and his father being with the Shah gives to him an interest in doing good. He is, however, very thick with Avitabile. This has its advantages and its disadvantages."

The nearer to the Peshavar territory the Shah Zadah and Sir Claude Wade arrived, the more number of the Afghans joined their standard, and valuable advices reached them from Kabul. In Peshavar, on the 29th of March, 1839, that officer thought it advisable that the Shah Zadah should hold a public Darbar (levee), to receive the chiefs and bestow the dresses of honour on them. To excite the cupidity of the Afghans by such show, and to gain the services of the Khaibaris, it was necessary that the greatest splendour should be displayed on the occasion. A salute was fired. The French generals in the service of Ranjit Singh, Prince Hashim, the principal Arbabs, and the other Afghan chiefs, were introduced. The entrance of the Darbar tent was tastefully decorated by the Kashmir shawls. All the newly-raised officers exhibited the picture of the old system of the Sadozai state, and they stood all in an array before the Prince. Among them Akhund Mulla Shakur occupied a dignified post. To describe the series of the negotiations and the communication which took place between Sir Claude Wade and the chiefs of the Trans-Indus for the purpose of dethroning the Amir Dost Mohammed Khan, and the sound judgment, with able and unceased exertion which he showed in effecting this course, will be of great interest. I shall therefore quote his official reports to the Government of India.

To H Torrens, Esq., Officiating Secretary to the Government of India with the Right Honourable the Governor-General.

"Sir,

"I have the honour to transmit abstracts of letters received by me, by direct messengers from different parties across the Indus.

"2nd. Bad-rud-din is the son of a Sayad who was recommended to me by the late Mr. Moorcroft, and to whom some years ago I had an opportunity of showing such attentions as were in my power at Lodianah, which his son also visited for the purpose of interesting me in the settlement of some disputes or claim which he had in Peshavar; but as he possessed neither the influence nor ability of his father, and the request involved an improper interference, on my part, with the jurisdiction of the Sikhs, who had at that time established their authority in the place, I was able only to offer him my advice to conciliate that people.

"3rd. To the letter of Rahmut Khan Khaibari I have replied that I have been highly gratified by his assurances of attachment to the cause of Shah Shuja; that I had seen his agent, and heard what he had to state; that I felt fully assured of the good disposition of the writer, the praise of whose character was familiar to my ears; that I relied, with confidence, on the proofs of his devotion to the Prince, and that his agent, whom I had dismissed, would satisfy him of the nature of my friendly sentiments towards him.

"4th. By the agent himself I sent a verbal message to Rahmat Khan, to the effect that he might confidently rely on every attention being paid to his application for pecuniary assistance on the arrival of the Shah Zadah on the frontier; that it would not consist, in my opinion, with the interests of either side to make these open demonstrations now; but when the time came, the Shah Zadah would not be found wanting in the inclination to reward him and all those who might, like himself, profess their readiness to serve the cause of his father.

"In my letter to Shah Zadah Hashim I have deemed it right, from the intimacy which is supposed to exist between the Sikhs and himself, to inform him of the wish of my Government to see the Sadozai dynasty restored to the kingdom of Kabul; and while I have expressed my belief that as a member of that family Shah Zadah will contribute his means to the accomplishment of that object.

"To Amin Khan I have sent no reply, not being able to trace the channel by which his letter came.

"It is my intention to confine my replies at present to all communications of a tenor similar to those now reported to an intimation of the preparations in which I have been engaged, and that I have a firm reliance on the loyalty and devotion of the writers, when the time for the exhibition of these qualities may arrive. The Shah Zadah himself has replied to the letters received by him in the same manner, and he will continue to write in the same strain, as it is the best course which he can, I think, pursue until he is on the spot, and quite prepared to receive the allegiance, as well as to demand the services of his countrymen.

"I have, &c.,

(Signed) "C. M. WADE,

"*Political Agent.*"

To H. Torrens, Esq., Officiating Secretary to the Government of India with the Governor-General.

"SIR,

"MIR Baza Qasid, who was sent to Kabul about two months and a half ago, by Shah Shuja, with a letter for Dost Mohammed Khan of a conciliatory tenor, has just returned, and I collect the following information from him: that in consequence of the advice of Navab Jabbar Khan and Gholam Mohammed Khan Popalzai, who told him that he would lose his life if he attempted to deliver the Shah's letter openly, the Qasid had given it to a Faqir to deliver; that on opening and reading the letter, and finding from whom it came, he had thrown it into the fire, and said that he would never yield to the Shah; that he looked to Russia and Persia to rescue him from the threatened invasion.

"2nd. Strict orders were given to find out the bearer of the letter; but the Qasid managed to conceal himself, and only left Kabul fifteen days ago, the latest date to which my information, either direct or through Mr. Lord, extends. Mir Baz has been directed by the Shah Zadah to return to his father. He says that the Amir is apparently wrapt in utter carelessness as to his fate, making no visible preparations whatever of defences; that his son at Jelalabad has not above two thousand men with him; that the force sent to Qunduz is winter-bound in that country; that the people of Kabul are waiting with impatience for the appearance of the Shah and his son, and say that the present is the moment for their advance; that if we do not advance before the Nauroz the communication will then be open, and enable Dost Mohammed to receive succour both in men and money from Russia, who has promised aid in both.

"3rd. We may believe such portions of these reports as may seem probable. As I have said before, I shall be able to judge of the intentions of the Amir, the disposition of the people, and the best mode of meeting both.

"4th. Nearly the whole of Sultan Mohammed Khan's followers have now joined the Shah Zadah; and the report is that Ranjit Singh either has taken or intends to take the Jaghirs of the Peshavar chiefs from them, and give some land in the territory between the Bias and Satlaj. It is certain that Sultan Mohammed does not appear to retain any political influence now at Lahaur, a result which, proceeding as it does from the suggestions of the Maharajah's own mind, is better than if it had been effected by any pointed direction on our part, when such a course would have argued a groundless fear of the ex-chief's power to do us mischief, and a supercession of the just responsibility which attaches to Ranjit Singh for his conduct.

* * * * *

"With the command of Peshavar, the authority of the three brothers of Jammu would extend, almost without exception, to the whole country between the Jelum and Indus, south-west of Kashmir. Every day may be said to be adding weight to the power and importance of these great feudatories, and nothing but the personal character of Rajah Dhian Singh, whose moderation, when compared with his influence at the Court, redounds highly to his credit, restrains the ambitious projects of his brother, Gulab Singh.* Their object at present seems to be to consolidate their authority on the Afghan frontier; and I shall not be surprised to hear that ere long they succeed in forcing Peshavar and its dependencies from their master.

"When about to leave Lahaur, Faqir Azizuddin waited on me with the following questions, viz., that Qazi Mulla Hasan, in the service of Shah Shuja, had written to the Maharajah, requesting, on the part of the Shah, his Highness's assistance in procuring the immediate dispatch of

* His ambition has at last been successful; all that intermediate country has been added to his already overgrown possessions by the British government during the late war of the Panjab.

fifteen thousand rupees of shawls to His Majesty, and that the Maharajah wished to know what reply he should send.

"2nd. Whether I had any information to give regarding the receipt of the fifteen lakhs which the Maharajah is to receive from Sindh.

"3rd. That his Highness would be glad to learn when payment of the ten lakhs which he is to receive from the Government of Kabul is to commence.

"To the first question I replied that the Maharajah was the best judge of the reply to be sent to the Shah's request; to the second, that the contribution from the Mirs of Sindh had not yet been received, nor could it well be expected before the settlement of the existing affairs. With regard to the third question, I referred the Maharajah to the terms of the tripartite treaty, by which each party was bound to abide; the Faqir remarked that the words of the treaty were as 'ibtadar mamurr fany.'—I assent to this citation, adding, however, that the payment of the money could evidently not precede the establishment of the Shah on the throne for which the armies of the two states were preparing to invade the country. The Faqir did not again make any allusion to these subjects.

"I have, &c.,

(Signed) "C. M. WADE."

To the Officiating Secretary to the Government of India.

"SIR,

"I HAVE the honour to transmit a copy of a letter to my address from Mr. Lord, (the original sent to Mr. Torrens with private letter, and a copy with this letter,) dated the 31st ultimo.

"With regard to the attempt of Dost Mohammed Khan to exert the influence of religion in his favour with the people of Kabul, I may notice the arrival in my camp since the receipt of Mr. Lord's report, of a person from that city, who states that he has been deputed by Hafizji to assure the Shah Zadah and myself that though the force of circumstances has induced him and others to give a paper to the effect mentioned by Mr. Lord, their intentions towards the Shah are the same as before.

"As the man produced no letter authorising him, I rather distrusted the truth of his mission, but he said that his employer had desired him to inform me that he was afraid to write in consequence of the discovery of some letters that had been addressed by Shah Shuja to Hafizji, as well as others of his party in Kabul, from the effects of which on the mind of the Barakzai chief he had not been able to escape, by stating that he could not prevent the Shah addressing him, and by exclaiming against the injustice of suspecting him, until the Amir could prove that he had been writing to his Majesty.

"In the course of further conversation, I learned from the messenger, who is a respectable looking man, that after giving the Fatva, one of the Mullas expostulated with those who had put their seals to it, on the selfish violence of the deed which had been extracted from them, that Dost Mohammed Khan had not now the power of resisting the enterprise of Shah Shuja; that, therefore, by pronouncing an anathema against his Majesty, they were, in fact, sealing their own ruin, as it was not to be supposed that the Shah would forgive them for denouncing him whom they had hitherto regarded as their rightful sovereign, and on whose protection and favour their hopes of future peace and contentment rested.

"Though the story appeared to be a very plausible one, yet I saw an objection to my giving credence to it; and I accordingly told the person to go back to Kabul and inform Hafizji and the other friends of the Shah there of the danger that they would inevitably incur if they sided with the enemies of his Majesty; that I was disposed to place every confidence in their loyalty and devotion to his cause, but that the Shah would look for proofs of these sentiments; and as the time drew near when the Shah Zadah would arrive, I expected that they would prove their attachment, and avert the possible consequences of procrastination, by sending not a messenger known only to themselves, but one of their own body, which would give assurance of their fidelity, and establish their claim on the generosity of the Shah. The man is still, however, in the camp, and appears to be considered by the Shah Zadah's people as an authentic messenger; but I recommend that he should be allowed to return.

"I have written to Mr. Lord to encourage the overture which he has received from Sher Ali Khan Javansher, by offering a suitable provision for the present to himself and followers on their arrival in the Shah Zadah's camp, and that in the event of his compliance, a recommendation will be made to the Shah to receive him on the same terms as were conceded to his father. At the same time I have requested Mr. Lord to authorize Sher Ali Khan to draw to the extent of one thousand rupees on him, if he should be in want of money to extricate himself from his present situation. His father enjoyed much consideration with Shah Shuja during the monarchy among the leaders of the Gholam Khana, and is of the party of which Khan Shirin Khan is considered the head.

"Pir Mohammed Khan, as well as the other Barakzai chiefs subject to the Maharajah's authority, have, I understand, become alarmed at the suspicion with which they are at present viewed by the British and Sikhs. Impelled by his fears, it is said that Pir Mohammed Khan has, within the last few days, left Peshavar suddenly with his own family as well as that of his brothers, and retired to his estate with a view to secure a retreat if his liberty should be threatened.

"With respect to Sultan Mohammed Khan and Sayad Mohammed Khan, they are at present living in the city of Lahaur, where his Highness has allowed a spacious residence for them, and though they have repeatedly applied to return to Peshavar, they have as often been refused.

* * * * *

"While I was at Peshavar, Sultan Mohammed had made a representation both to the Maharajah and myself as to the conduct of the Afghans in leaving him, and that the arms, &c. which they had carried away with them were his property. He requested that I would order them to return; but I replied that they had come, neither on my invitation nor that of the Shah Zadah, and that it would be contrary to the usages of his own country as to that of any other, to force them back to his service; that I had heard that their complaint was that they had not been paid by him, but that into that subject I had no right to inquire; that they were free to remain wherever they pleased; that I did not desire to take any part in the affair; that if they had illegal possession of anything belonging to the Sardar he should apply to the Shah Zadah, who I doubted not would be ready to do impartial justice to both parties.

"Disappointed in my reply, I found that he interested Rajah Dhian Singh, who sent me a polite message to the effect of the complaint that Sultan Mohammed Khan had been making to me, while he told the Sardar himself, I learned, that people seek service where they were likely to be well paid. I replied to the Rajah by reporting the observations which I had used to Sultan Mohammed Khan, adding, however, that I thought, under the circumstances, that we should both consult our interests best by taking no part in the matter one way or the other; but a few days afterwards I heard that the Rajah had brought the complaints to the notice of Ranjit Singh, who took no notice of it. In consequence of his failure in these attempts, I presume the Sardar resolved, whether with or without the knowledge or instigation of any of the Sikh officers I cannot state, on pursuing a system of retaliation on the Afghans; having, therefore, waited some days for a confirmation of the report, and satisfied myself of its accuracy, I determined to address a notice on the subject to the Maharajah through the only direct channel of communication which I have of my own at present with the court, viz., the deputy news-writer at Lahaur; and I am happy to state that his Highness has noticed the conduct of his Barakzai dependant, and ordered the property and families to be released.

"The ground on which I have deemed it advisable to object to the part which Sultan Mohammed Khan has chosen to act is, that supposing the Afghans who have joined the Shah Zadah were possessed of any property belonging to the Sardar, he had no right to make his political duty to the Maharajah subservient to the gratification of a personal claim, or, in other words, to bring into jeopardy the obligation of the treaty which Ranjit Singh had contracted with our government.

"It will have been seen that his Highness has not returned any reply to the recommendation offered by me that some effectual means should be adopted to prevent the Barakzai chiefs owing allegiance to him from intriguing with impunity with the enemies of the Shah. These chiefs can evidently have no doubt of the jealousy and distance with which they are regarded, that in fact there is no way left to them of gaining the confidence of the British government;

and I am accordingly of opinion that I should hold the Maharajah responsible for their conduct in a more formal manner than he appears to consider himself at present required to do; I therefore intend to revert immediately to the necessity of his Highness taking such a pledge from them as I suggested.

"The Right Honourable the Governor-General is aware that, during the negotiations which led to the late treaty with the ruler of Lahaur, his Highness inquired what should be done with Sultan Mohammed during the contemplated operations. He was informed in reply that if agreeable to his Highness the Sardar might proceed with him. And on reference to the peculiar position of Sultan Mohammed Khan, it is I think greatly to be regretted that the mode in which it was arranged that he should be disposed of, during the actual progress of operations, was carried into effect. If it had been considered difficult to restrain him from engaging in intrigues to obstruct the success of our measures, the Shah's conformity with the disposal of him in the manner proposed would not have been more irksome to his Majesty than his acquiescence in other important objects of our contract with him. Though I am not prepared to say that he would have proved a faithful friend to the cause, whether placed with the Shah or with the troops of Ranjit Singh, yet his means of doing injury with the former would obviously have been neutralized by the presence of the overwhelming force with which his Majesty was moving, while by allowing him to remain where he is we have increased not alone his facilities, but those of the Sikhs, of intriguing against the Shah; and by declaring our suspicions of him, may be said to have converted a possibly useful partisan into an open enemy, and thus rendered the operations on the side of Peshavar more intricate and involved than they would otherwise have been.

"It is not improbable that the Maharajah may excuse himself for the acts of his Barakzai feudatory, by referring the rejection of the proposal which was made to remove him from a scene where his Highness no doubt saw that he could intrigue more readily than if he had been permitted to accompany the Shah, an event as matters now stand, and since his Lordship has not thought it a necessary precaution to insist on the course which was proposed, and Ranjit Singh does not seem inclined to adopt, or rather has not distinctly said that he would, the suggestion which I offered for guarding as effectually as I could against the intrigues of his vassal. I would beg to solicit the support of the Governor-General to the application which I am about to write to his Highness for the production of some real security for the future good conduct of Sultan Mohammed Khan. With a view to the same, I would also request that his Lordship would be pleased to send a duplicate of his letter to the Maharajah through the Agent at present with Mr. Clerk, while the original can be forwarded for transmission to me.

"Regarding the property claimed from the Afghans by Sultan Mohammed, although I have ascertained that they have brought nothing but their clothes and arms along with them, in lieu of long arrears of pay due to them when they left the Sardar's service, I intend to observe that he may bring a civil suit against them either through myself or through M. Avitabile, before the court at Peshavar, for the recovery of any property to which he may be found to have a just claim.

* * * * *

" The Shah Zadah has been joined by several other Afghans of note sent chiefly by Mr. Lord, who is ably and zealously engaged in securing the services of the tribes in favour of the Shah Zadah. I had informed the Prince on leaving Lahaur that I expected those who might join him on the road would be entertained out of the fixed sum for his monthly expenses; but as the seceders from Sultan Mohammed Khan had now regularly attached themselves to the service of the Shah Zadah, and the time appeared to me to have arrived when both his Highness and myself should adopt some plan by which, while treating his countrymen, who were the first to flock to his standard, with his princely liberality, he should possess something more substantial than their mere verbal assurances of devotion to him, and that I should satisfy myself that the public money of which I had the disposal was not heedlessly squandered away, I deemed it advisable to suggest to Shah Zadah Taimur that he should explain to the Afghans with him, that before they could be finally enrolled in his service they should give him their written pledge of fidelity, and moreover that they should not hold any correspondence or communication whatever with the enemies of his house without his previous knowledge and consent.

"The Prince approved entirely of my proposition, and I am happy to say that the parties who have been required to conform to it have at once admitted the reasonableness and justice of the measure, and cheerfully signed, sealed, and delivered to the Shah Zadah a paper to the effect desired.

"I have pointed out the necessity of pursuing the same plan with others who may arrive, being decidedly of opinion that it is better to incur all the risk of foregoing the services of men who may refuse to sign such a declaration, than expend the money of Government in entertaining them without any security between them and the Shah Zadah.

"I have, &c.,

(Signed) "C. M. Wade."

On the 20th of July, the Shah Zadah came to Jam Road; and by the 22d his force marched to enter the Khaibar Pass. Sir Claude Wade, Major Mackison, Captains Cunningham, Ferris, &c., ascended the heights of the pass by the different routes. There were many Afghans who had espoused the cause of the Prince, some by love of loyalty, others by cupidity; but there were still many of them in the Khaibar who did not tender their homage to the Shah Zadah, and intended to resist. The Sardar Mohammed Akbar Khan had encamped at the western extremity of the pass, near Dakka. He did not like to enter the pass to impede the progress of the Shah Zadah; for he thought that if he was routed by the united force of the Sikhs and the Prince, he will be plundered by the very Khaibaris, who will stand by him for a time, and most probably caught and delivered to Sir Claude Wade. However, he did not fail in spreading false reports of the arrival of the Persian army in Ghuryan for the aid of the Barakzais, and thus encouraged the Khaibaris to oppose us.

Substance of a Letter addressed by Mohammed Akbar Khan to the Khaibaris, received on the 22nd of May.

"Accompanied by all my troops and the peasantry of the country around, I have to-day left Jalalabad with a view to commence a religious war against the detested infidels, and to sacrifice my life in the way of God, and have halted at Ali Boghan. The next stage will be Chahardehi, and from thence to Basaul and Dakka, where I shall arrive soon.

"About five thousand Jazayarchis and an equal number of people from Kohistan have been dispatched from Kabul by my father, to assist me. Please God they will join me at Basaul, after which I will proceed forthwith to Khaibar. By the favour of the Almighty and his prophet, the bravery of his faithful servants, the devotion of experienced warriors, and the assistance of my troops and artillery, you will witness the proofs of courage that will be displayed on the field of battle in defending the honour of my nation.

"Correct intelligence has been received from Ahmad Shahi to the effect that the Persians and Russians had arrived with a large army at Ghuryan, that they would soon be able to assist the chiefs of Qandhar, and contend with the British army and Shah Shuja-ul-Mulk, who by the blessing of God will be disgraced, and that on the receipt of this news had recalled his 'Pesh Khana' (tent), which he had sent in advance to the fort of Azam Khan on the way to Kabul, and that he was preparing for a siege at Qandhar."

Before the Shah Zadah's forces reached Ali Masjid, Major Mackison came into contact with the Khaibaris; and because the Sikh Najibs showed cowardice on the occasion, he was compelled to erect a breastwork; and with extraordinary bravery and presence of mind he continued the unequal contest with the enemy, till assistance, with ammunition, was dispatched to him from Sir Claude Wade. The Khaibaris were, however, successful in carrying off some of the camels laden with the baggage; and after a succession of petty attacks, they escaped, leaving the impregnable fort of Ali Masjid quite empty; and it was soon discovered and occupied by one of the Afghan officers under Captain Ferris; and on the 27th of July the British flag and that of the Shah Zadah were displayed on the top of that fort. After leaving a garrison there, the Prince and Sir Claude Wade arrived on the 6th of August, 1839, at Dakka, which had been abandoned by the Sardar Mohammed Akbar Khan, when he was recalled by his father on the fall of Ghazni.

The chief of Dakka, Sadat Khan Momand, who resided in the opposite fort of Lalpurah, was always considered to be in favour with the Shah Shuja-ul-Mulk; but when the Shah Zadah Taimur and Sir Claude Wade arrived in Peshavar, the Momand lord behaved in a manner which gave cause of suspicion in the mind of that British officer. However, he invited him again to wait upon the Shah Zadah, but received no satisfactory reply. Next day it was reported that he with his Momand followers had decamped, either with a deliberate intention of rebelling, or in consequence of the alarm which was created by the precautionary measures of Sir

Claude Wade, as it is described by Lieut. Barr.* The British officers crossed the river and took possession of the fort of the fugitive chief; and Turrah Baz Khan was made head of the Momand tribe under the government of the Shah Shuja-ul-Mulk. The policy of Sir Claude Wade, in dispossessing Sadat Khan Momand, and substituting Turrah Baz Khan in his place, was palatable neither to the Shah nor to the political head of Afghanistan. However, the conduct of Sadat Khan was really suspicious; and if Sir William Macnaghten and the Shah were

* "Our camp was pitched on the banks of the Kabul river, which flowed silently and swiftly by, and opposite to the village of Lalpurah, the principal residence of Sadat Khan, who has erected a small fort close to it. Intimation has been received from that chief, avowing his willingness to come to terms; but the unceasing enmity that he had evinced towards the Shah Zadah, since our arrival in Peshavar, rendered it necessary to be prepared to act on the offensive, in case he should change his mind. Accordingly some troops were ordered on this service, and cannon were planted opposite to his stronghold; but no further acts of hostility ensued, and on the following morning the colonel was informed that the Momand lord, with his followers, had decamped during the night, and gone off in the direction of Bajaur. Sir C. Wade, on this, crossed the river and took possession of Lalpurah and the fort, the government of which he conferred on Furrah Bâz Khan, a chief who had proved a most faithful ally to us."—'Kabul and the Panjab,' by Lieut. W. Barr, pp. 353-4.

on the spot, they would have done the same, I believe, that Sir Claude Wade was obliged to do. This change undoubtedly kept our troops employed against many tribes, who were sometimes conducted personally by Sadat Khan, and sometimes only instigated by him, to resist us for a long period. But the measure and the choice of Sir Claude Wade, in dethroning one chief of suspicious character and elevating another, appeared most judicious in the time of the disasters of 1841-2; for it was Turrah Baz Khan who stood by the British when all the Afghan chiefs had deserted them. It was the new chief of Lalpurah who became the medium of our communication between our heroic garrison of Jelalabad and the Peshavar authorities; and above all it was he who escorted the supplies of ammunition, grain, and money to them, when they were in great need. The Shah Zadah Taimur and Sir Claude Wade, after adjusting matters in Lalpurah and Dakka, reached Kabul without any further annoyance. On the 3d of September, the entry of the Shah Zadah into the capital of his father was solemnised with the display of much military splendour. Lord Keane ordered some of the regiments to be arranged for the occasion, making a street to the city; and the Prince passed along this through the concourse of the population and of our camp. The Shah Shuja-ul-Mulk did not like this mode of our showing respect to the Prince, as his jealousy and pride neither permitted him to witness nor hear of the honour or consideration paid to others.

Now I will briefly take a view of the circumstances which had alarmed the Amir Dost Mohammed near his capital in Kohistan, and principally caused him to abandon his design of proceeding to the assistance of any of his sons, either to the south or to the east, and at last compelled him to precipitate his flight towards Bamian. The readers of this book should bring back into their mind the name of Gholam Khan Popalzai, a liberal friend of the Amir in the days of his poverty. When the Dost became Amir, and had the supreme power in Kabul, he made no good return to his early friend for his kindness in supporting him in distress, and in taking his part against his rival and wealthy brothers. Being disgusted with this ingratitude in the Amir, Gholam Khan turned his mind to pursue the usual line of conduct of his family, who always were the well-wishers of the Sadozai, or royal family. Gholam Khan was now evidently sighing, praying, and exerting himself for the restoration of the monarchy instead of anarchy. He knew that the Shah Shuja-ul-Mulk had taken asylum in the British territories, which Gholam visited in search of a medical adviser. The late William Fraser, Resident at Dehli, and Sir Claude Wade, treated him with great consideration in consequence of his high birth, and as the son of Nasaqchibashi, who was of some service to the Hon. Mountstuart Elphinstone. The civilities shown to him in India made a deep impression upon the mind of this noble man; and when I returned from Mashad to Peshavar, on my way to Calcutta,* he made his acquaintance with me, and invited me to dinner, and at last became my correspondent in Afghanistan. On the arrival of the mission of Sir Alexander Burnes, I introduced my Durrani friend to him, who felt gratified by making the acquaintance of one whose name he had so often heard previously. The first words poured out from the lips of this visitor were that we were quite mistaken in the idea of the success of our mission to the

* Page 357 of Mohan Lal's Travels in the Panjab and Afghanistan.

Amir of Kabul; whose treacherous and faithless disposition cannot sufficiently be fathomed by any human being. He afterwards was my constant visitor; and the information and opinions he gave appeared to be authentic and sound. The mission failed, as he had foretold; and on our departure towards India, he said that we must rest assured that the Shah Shuja, if he is ever brought by the English, will enter Afghanistan without meeting any opposition from the ruling chieftains, who will be most fortunate persons to be deserted, if not killed or plundered, by their own adherents. It is a most extraordinary coincidence that all his forebodings on the politics of that day, as well as on the course and extent of our disasters, came to pass without the slightest difference. In the meantime the Mission left Kabul, and the army of the Indus, with the Shah Shuja-ul-Mulk, obtained possession of Qandhar; and during this space of time Gholam Khan was exerting himself, in the face of every personal risk, to gain friends for the British, to create disturbance against the Barakzai, and, above all, to transmit the most valuable intelligence to Sir Claude Wade in Peshavar, and to us in Sindh and Qandhar. From the latter place, under the direction of my superiors, I sent him a note of credit for forty thousand rupees, which was wonderfully procured at such a crisis by Pokhar, a Shikarpuri broker in Kabul. Gholam Khan, whom we instructed to raise disturbances against the Amir, gained the great priest of Kabul, "Hafiz Ji," the son of the late Mir Vaiz, the most turbulent heretic and hypocrite in the kingdom. He also gained in the same manner the Khavajah Khanji of Ashqan-i-Arifan, with many other petty chiefs or ringleaders, both Durranis, and the Qizalbashes. He then disguised himself as a woman, and covering himself with the veil or Burqah from head to foot, he mounted a donkey at sunrise and went out to a distance from Kabul. Thus he cunningly succeeded in avoiding the seizure of his person by the people of the Amir, who had lately appointed some men to get hold of him.

Gholam Khan afterwards rode on horseback and hastened his departure to Tagav, the ruler of which place, Milak Shahdad Khan, commonly called "Bachai Mazu," gave him refuge, raised his own tribe to espouse our cause, and went with him to Kohistan, where all the chiefs, as Mir Misjadi, Mir Darvesh,

Mir Khoja, Khalifah Ibrahim, Mir Sikandar Shah, Saif-ul-Din, Milak Esa Khan, and other chiefs of Nijrav, Panjsher, Ghorbard, Kohistan, and Koh-deman, rose in arms to further the views of Gholam Khan. He thus distributed the money we had sent him from Qandhar amongst his followers, and threatened an attack upon the Amir in Kabul. Hafiz Ji, in the mean time, made a pretence of suppressing the Kohistanis (who worshipped him as their religious guide), and joining the Amir against the English; yet he received secretly a present of 8,000 rupees from our friend, and instead of bringing his followers the Kohistanis to the assistance of the Amir against us, he co-operated with Gholam Khan in our favour. At this time one of the descendants of the "Sadozai," or Royal Family, had joined the insurgents in Kohistan, and was proclaimed as Prince, under the Shah Shuja-ul-Mulk. The Amir seized upon Pokhur, and confined and tortured him for lending the money to Gholam Khan, whose property also he confiscated, and razed his house to the ground. Hafiz Ji's junction with Gholam Khan was a plain cause and evidence that none of the Sunnis of Kabul would exert themselves in his favour; while the Qizalbashes fortunately embraced a favourable opportunity by this change of the Sunnis, and stated to the Amir that if they were to go with him either to oppose the English towards Ghazni, or to oppose Sir Claude Wade in the direction of Khaibar, the Kohistanis, who were ready to pour down upon Kabul with Gholam Khan, and Hafiz Ji, will join the Sunnis of the city, will massacre their families, and reduce the Chandoul, or the Persian quarters, to ashes, not under the prompt encouragement of their leaders, but under the influence of their religious prejudices. The citizens said to the Amir, that his silence, and his holding consultations every day, and not taking any step to quell the progress of the Kohistanis, is causing them very much loss in their bargains, and keeping up danger amongst their neighbours. They added, that he ought not to leave the town unprotected; and, in short, they insisted upon him to take clearly, decidedly, and at once, any of the measures, whether to decide for war with us, or to flee into Turkistan. The Amir called an assembly in the garden which surrounds the tomb of Taimur Shah, and made a speech, petitioning his subjects to support him in maintaining his power, and in driving off the infidels (us) from the Mahomedan country. Many people who were present, stated to me that the words of the Amir were most touching and moving, but they gained no friends. The Amir also frightened the ignorant people by fabricating and telling them monstrous falsehoods, such as that we have continued, during our march from Sindh to Ghazni, in the practice of seizing and abusing the women, and perpetrating the most barbarous deed of boiling the little infants for our meals. The Navab Jabbar Khan confirmed the assertion of the Amir, with the view that the people will thus be induced to rise in his cause, but all this was in vain. In the mean time Gholam Khan with the Kohistanis began to descend from their native valley with the intention to annoy and fright the Kabulis if they will allow the Amir to remain any longer in their city. To the end that I may show the importance of the services of this individual, which he rendered to the British government at the risk of his life and to the loss of his estate, I shall not let the readers pass away from this subject, without quoting parts of his voluminous communications to our government, which will give a clear view of his proceedings.

Translation of the Extracts of a Letter from Gholam Khan Papalzai.

"THE chief of Kabul is exceedingly distracted in mind. He lately sent for some of his courtiers one night in secresy, and observed that as information was constantly arriving of the advance of Shah Shuja-ul-Mulk against him, with the British troops on one hand and the Sikhs on the other, he requested they would give him their opinions as to the course which his interest required him to adopt. They replied that he was wise and should follow the dictates of his own judgment, while their duty was to serve him. Dost Mohammed Khan repeated his request, and desired every one of those in attendance to express his sentiments; but they all maintained a perfect silence. The Sardar became dejected and retired to his harem. On the retreat of Dost Mohammed Khan, some of the members of the meeting, such as Navab Jabbar Khan, Amir Akhundzadah, and Abdullah Khan, that the time for consultation was when Sir A. Burnes had visited Kabul; that he should then have formed some connexion with the British government,—but that at that period being led away by the representations of the Russian agents, the Persians, and the Amir of Bokhara, he did not listen to their advice. These courtiers also retired afterwards to their homes, saying that they would now see how the Russians, the Persians, and the Amir of Bokhara would assist the Amir, of which they talked so much of doing; that at present there was no remedy but fighting.

"God knows what may come to pass; but it is certain Dost Mohammed Khan is alarmed and distressed.

"The reason of Dost Mohammed Khan's sending Akram Khan along with Mirza Abdul Sami towards Bamean was that the Persians should not raise the siege of Hirat, and with the same view he continued to supply Mohammed Shah and the Russian Ambassador with fabricated news regarding the English and the Sikhs. The substance of the letter written by the Amir to the Ambassador of Russia after the retreat of the Persians from Hirat, is as follows:

"'In persuasion of your letter, sent by the hand of Captain Vikovich, and the delusive overtures made by him, I sacrificed my alliance with the British Government, and consequently dismissed Sir A. Burnes. The Persians and the Russians, notwithstanding their united efforts, have not been able to capture Hirat, defended by four thousand men, who were like the dead in their tombs, and had retired to Persia. How is it reconcileable with your ideas of conquering India to Calcutta? Hirat was neither assisted by Bokhara, nor by Afghánistan; nor had you sustained any defeat which should have occasioned your retreat. If you had shame you would not have caused the enmity which has taken place between me and the British Government; for your sake the foundation of my house has been destroyed, though my nation never attempted to save Hirat, yet it has been liberated by the hostile exertions of two important powers.'

"On the arrival of the news of the Persian retreat at

Kabul, the Qizalbashes seemed much dejected and vexed, while the Sunnis expressed exceeding joy on the occasion. For instance, a party of poor merchants who trade between Qandhar and Kabul having collected about one hundred rupees by subscription, held a party in a temple outside the city, and illuminated the place. Dost Mohammed, on being informed of the fact, sent for the ringleaders, severely rebuked and disgraced them for their merriment. They answered that God had aided in defeating the arms of the infidels, and had thus defended the faith and reputation of the whole Afghan nation; that in consequence they had held a party of pleasure, and that they not alone, but the whole nation, were delighted at the event. The very Akhundzada, who is the minister, and is called Naib, was heard in the Darbar to offer thanksgiving to God for the retreat of the Persians. It offended the Amir very much; and he observed that the retribution of the Qajars was his own, when the Naib, who was one of the favourites of the Amir, was so actuated, what would be the sentiments of the Kabulis, Durranis, and Ghilzais; the fact is, the Sunnis are all discontented with Dost Mohammed, and so are the Qizalbash, since the Persian retreat, and every one now looks towards the English. The chiefs and people will rebel, and the country will fall into your hands without fighting.

" A letter had been received from the Qandhar chiefs confirming the news of the Persian retreat, and announcing the return of Captain Vikovich to them; that he had already reached Farah, had brought ten thousand ducats for them, with a message that they were to make every necessary preparation of defence, and that after the Nauroz the Persians would return. It is rumoured that the Russian ambassador has also remitted about twenty thousand ducats for the Amir, who on account of delay in the operations on your part and the arrival of the ducats, is pleased and re-assured. He is now employed in repairing the Bala Hisar, and Mohammed Akbar Khan has been sent to Jalalabad, where he is engaged in building a fort.

"The Dastkhats sent by his Majesty for different people have been distributed to them; assurances had been held out by the writer to the Arabs of Balahisar, &c. He states that he had done his best to awaken them from their lethargy; but it should be recollected that he could manage the affair merely by empty words. When the Shah reaches Shikarpur, if he would remit him money, the writer would raise the people. Those who are sincerely affected towards his Majesty, from their forefathers, are now in great distress for want of subsistence. The writer observes that he had tried to induce Hafizji to proceed to the Kohistan to collect the people; and his reply was that without means his journey there would be useless, and would be like erecting a wall without a foundation. Those who appear in the least disaffected towards the Amir, I send them Dastkhat of his Majesty.

"Lately I forwarded a Dastkhat to Mir Morad Beg, and one to Abdulakhan Achakzai, who is displeased with the Qandharis. The people of Mavarulnahar are discontented with the Amir of Bokhara because he did not receive the son of Shah Zadah Kamran with proper distinction, and refused to give him assistance against the infidels. They call the Amir also an infidel. Morad Beg and others are all waiting for his Majesty's advance to throw off the mask. If his Majesty is determined to proceed to this quarter, he should remit a sufficient sum of money by the hand of a confidential person, so that the people be secured by him, and they may have some assurance of the Shah's intentions.

"On the 31st of October, Captain Vikovich reached Qandhar with ten thousand ducats, and has held out to them assurances that Mohammed Shah would return after Nauroz; that if in the mean time the English should attack them and reduce them to extremity, they were to apply for assistance to the troops that were left at Ghuryan, and that Afghanistan had now become the country of the Russians. The said officer has also written to Dost Mohammed Khan that in a day or two the Amir would receive six lakhs rupees, with which he was desired to defend himself until the return of the Persians, when the whole country, including Hirat, should belong to him. The Amir is highly delighted by the receipt of this intelligence. He is now preparing to dismiss Abdul Vahab, who brought him a Khilat on the part of the Russian Emperor. Favour me with an immediate reply."

I have now shown the method of our operations against the Amir of Kabul by the three different directions, which distracted his mind so painfully that he at once resolved to fly, but yet implored the Qizalbashes to prevent the people from plunder, and to escort him safely to Sar Chishmah. Thus he was compelled to relinquish all thoughts of opposition, and, leaving his elephants and warlike stores in "Arghandi," where his son the Sardar Mohammed Akbar Khan joined as an invalid, he made the best of his escape towards Bamian, as previously noticed.

Gholam Khan Popalzai entered the city of Kabul with his Kohistan auxiliaries, one day before the arrival of the Shah and the British, and proclaimed the authority of his Majesty. He was of great assistance to our authorities as well as to those of the Shah, in the administration of the country, and more particularly at the appearance of the Amir in Kohistan against us, and during the unfortunate disasters of 1841-2. Throughout the account of those events his name will frequently be read with interest; but here I shall add only the final termination of his history, with the end of his life. In return for his services we had engaged ourselves, both in writing and in words, to replace him in his hereditary rank, and to honour him with permanent rewards, both from our government and from the Shah; but yet none of those promises were ever fulfilled in any degree. We on our part continued to make one promise after another, without doing more than merely to promise; and Gholam Khan, still relying upon the virtue of our words, did not cease to devote himself to our interest on his part, until we were compelled to leave Afghanistan. He then followed us with his family to Lodianah, as his stay in Afghanistan would endanger the safety of his life in our absence. He thus lost his estate, his house, and his relations in attaching himself to us in spite of his countrymen, and he became an exile in our territory. How we fulfilled our promises and appreciated his services is not unworthy to be mentioned here. We gave him a dress of honour in Kabul; and yet we allowed the Shah and his ministers, Mulla Shikur and Nizam-ul-Daulah, to treat him slightingly even there and then, and to levy taxes on his very small private property, which was free in the time of the Amir. This threw him into such poverty, that at Lodianah he dismissed his adherents, sold all his horses and every article he had, and afterwards he was starved, having fallen sick: he expired, leaving a family in the most distressed and impoverished state!!

Having recorded in detail the circumstances which occurred from the commencement of the expedition, I shall now pursue the course of the Amir Dost Mohammed Khan to Bokhara.

When Colonel Outram, in company with several English officers, and the Afghans under Haji Khan Kakar, as mentioned before, started from Shekhabad in pursuit of the Amir Dost Mohammed Khan, the fugitive, with Nayab Zulfqar and the Navab Jabbar Khan, as well as his immediate adherents, was three marches beyond Maidan. On the 21st of August the brave Colonel was informed that the object of his pursuit was at Urt, only one march a-head; but it appears from the official report of Colonel Outram, that the escape of the Amir Dost Mohammed Khan was in consequence of the treachery of Haji Khan, or the new Nasir-ul-Daulah. I do neither doubt the authenticity of the assertion of that impartial officer, nor do I seek to excuse or to deny the treacherous intention of the Khan; but there was no communication of the kind between the traitor and the fugitive. When the ministers and a good many followers of the Amir returned from Turkistan, they told us that he, the Amir, instead of having the slightest hope or thought of the good offices of Haji Khan in delaying the march of the English, did not only throw loads of abuse on his head, whenever his name was mentioned, but concluded that he will do all to facilitate the means of his being overtaken. He therefore became more alarmed, and precipitated his advance from Hunai to Gardan Divar, bearing the diseased Mohammed Akbar Khan in a litter, and leaving his family with the Navab to follow him. At night the Hazarahs stole about twenty horses of the Amir, which reduced the number of his confidential attendants considerably. The party of Colonel Outram arrived at last in Bamian, while the Amir Dost Mohammed Khan had succeeded to get into Aqrabad long before the arrival of his pursuers. He then went to Saighan, and next morning to Qilai Sar-i-Sang, which was still in the possession of the people of the ex-Amir; and now at length he found himself out of the reach of the British officers and Haji Khan, whom I shall leave here for the present.

In Qilai Sar-i-Sang, Mohammed Ali Beg, the Uzbeg chief, waited upon the Amir Dost Mohammed Khan, and presenting him with a beautiful horse, he gave his son as hostage to the Amir. In return, he requested the Amir to give him the charge of the abovementioned fort, and promised to deliver it to the Vali of Khulam if he and the Amir did ever ask for it. The Amir accepted his terms; and while the son of Mohammed Beg, who was left as hostage, was marching with him towards Khulam, Farhad Beg, the rival of his father, shot him dead on horseback. The Amir was met on the road by all the Uzbeg chiefs, Sufi Beg, Qalich Ali Beg, and Mir Baba Beg, who paid him every consideration; and meanwhile he arrived in Khulam. Here the Mir Vali allotted the best apartments for the residence of the Afghan guests; and soon after they all assembled in the tent of the Sardar Mohammed Akbar Khan, to consult about what course should be most advantageously adopted for the future good of the Amir and of his family. The Sardar stated that the best thing for them would be to go to Persia; on which the Vali promised to escort them all safely to Shibarghan and Hazarahjat.

In the meantime the Amir Dost Mohammed Khan dispatched his own peshkhidmat, named Mohammed

Azim, towards Maimanah, to bring him the intelligence of that road to Persia; and deputed Mirza Sami Khan to the Amir or King of Bokhara, to request the favour of his Majesty to allow him to remain in Balkh; and himself, with the Mir Vali, set out for Qunduz, to co-operate with the Mir Mohammed Morad Beg in suppressing the tumultuous Uzbegs, as requested by that chieftain. The Amir settled the affairs of the Qunduz chief, who of course paid him a sum of money to defray the expenses of his journey, and consequently the Amir returned to Khulam. Mirza Sami Khan, with the agent of the King, returned from Bokhara, and communicated to the Amir that his Majesty thinks it impossible that the chiefs of Qunduz, Khulam, or the revenues of Balkh, should be able to maintain the followers of the Amir; and that if he comes personally to Bokhara, he will not only be treated with distinction, but will receive military assistance to enable him to recover his country. However pleasing this intelligence was to the Amir, yet nothing was resolved; for one day he thought it better to accept the offer of the King, but various fears gave him reason to put it off; while on another day, when the thoughts of better fortune entered his mind, he fancied going over to Persia. During these speculations grain began to be scarce in Khulam; and the Amir again called Mohammed Akbar Khan, the Navab, Mirza Sami Khan, and the Vali, and asked their opinion for his guidance. The former persevered in his advice of going to Persia, while the latter suggested the propriety of waiting upon the King of Bokhara. Mirza Sami Khan stated that although he did not hear any thing unsatisfactory from the lips of the Uzbeg monarch, yet his minister Nur Mohammed Bi mentioned to him that the sovereignty of Kabul has been restored to its hereditary royal master, and that the Amir Dost Mohammed Khan ruled only as an usurper. He would advise, therefore, that he should wait in patience till affairs appear to take a favourable turn. Nayab Abdul Samad, added the Mirza, mentioned that the King of Bokhara will not have reliance on the fidelity of the Afghans, unless the Amir comes into Bokhara with his family. The Navab Jabbar Khan, in junction with the Vali, and the Peshkhidmat Mohammed Azim, suggested the almost insurmountable difficulties of the road to Persia, which was already impassable on account of the snow; and allowing the chance of the fears which were afforded by the reports of the Mirza, he advised the Amir to go to the Uzbeg king. At last, however, the Amir Dost Mohammed Khan determined upon going to Bokhara. And now the question of the expenses of the road demanded and occupied the Amir's attention; on which the Sardar Mohammed Akbar Khan gave him about fourteen thousand rupees, and the Vali six thousand on mortgage of the jewels. He thereupon left his family in Khulam, and set out with all his sons and the Navab towards the Oxus. In Balkh, the Governor received the ex-chief of Kabul with honour, and gave him five hundred out of one thousand tilas.* The Navab had remained behind in Mazar, and did not join the Amir for three days, when he plainly refused to accompany him. The Amir left Balkh; and all the way to and in Qarshi, Nur Mohammed Bi provided him with all the necessaries of life. At Qaraval, the principal officers of the Bokhara court came to receive the Amir, and requested him, on the part of the King, to proceed at once with his mounted retinue into the presence of his Majesty.

* Gold coin of Bokhara, fifteen shillings each.

The Afghan guest agreed to this; and after paying his respects to the King, returned with his sons and followers to the quarters assigned for his residence. During five days' dinner all the luxuries of the court were sent to the Afghans from the royal kitchen; and on the sixth his Majesty sent a person named Mirza Khan to the Amir, and inquired by him what were his wishes, saying that, if possible, they shall be gained for him. Dost Mohammed Khan sent reply that he does not expect anything from the King, but the royal aid to regain his authority, which has been snatched away from him by the enemies of their mutual religion (namely, by the English). In return to this, the Amir was told that he should recover first from his fatigue; and as the winter was fast approaching, he would do well to keep about two hundred men only with himself, and the rest of his followers should be divided into small numbers, so as to reside in the villages, where, in this manner, they will be all lodged; and that in the summer his case shall be taken into the royal consideration. The Amir was also requested to send for his family from Khulam. On this all the members of the Afghan party assembled, and the Amir stated to them the message of the King, with his own opinion that its adoption would be a hazardous step. All of them replied, that as they were now in a foreign country, and in the hands of the foreigners, it would be better to act on their guidance. While the Amir was about to inform the King of the result of his decision, Qazi Badruddin stepped into his presence, and on hearing the circumstances of the assembly, he dissuaded the Amir from taking any advice of the kind from the King, adding, that if once his family was in the power of the Uzbegs, and his followers divided into separate and small parties, the Afghans will be reduced into worse slavery than the Qizalbashes. The Amir, finding trust in the soundness of the Qazi's sentiment, sent word to his Majesty that he had come to Bokhara in the hope of better fortune; that if the King was desirous to show his liberality to the Afghans, he begs to have some land on the other side of the river towards Balkh, to maintain himself with his family; and that otherwise he wants permission to proceed on his pilgrimage.

The King of Bokhara replied to the Amir Dost Mohammed Khan, that since he had come into his court, he would do better to act as he is advised;

and that if he insists on being dismissed, he is at liberty to go wherever he likes. The Afghans prepared to start for Mecca; and the Court appointed some of the Uzbegs to see them soon out of the city. The night was passed in tents outside of the gates; and in the morning another party of the Uzbegs was sent with the message that they are to break up from the ground immediately, and take the route of Khiva, and not of Charju. This perplexed the Afghans, who sent a petition through Mohammed Afzal Khan and Abdul Ghani, stating that none of them will pass alive through the waterless deserts of Khiva; and therefore they hope that the King will pardon them for the offence which they give him by refusing to act on his advice. His Majesty allowed them again to return to Bokhara, but ceased from showing them the former hospitality. The meal of food from the royal kitchen was now stopped; and a very trifling sum in cash was paid to the Amir for maintaining himself.

In the meantime the Amir Dost Mohammed Khan selected two of his best horses, with about ten fine swords and a few daggers, and sent them through his son Mohammed Amin Khan for the acceptance of the

Amir-ul-momnin, as the king was called. In return five dresses of honour were sent by his Majesty, with the message, that Mohammed Afzal Khan was forthwith to fetch the Amir's family from Khulam. Mohammed Akbar Khan did not approve of the going of his elder brother, on which the "Badshah" of Bokhara desired them to send any of the confidential Afghans. This concerned very much the whole party; and the Sardar Mohammed Akbar Khan, after consulting with his brothers, resolved to steal their way towards Shahar-i-Sabz. The Amir being informed of the flight of his sons, immediately informed the King of the circumstance, and requested him to effect their return. Orders were accordingly issued in all parts of the kingdom; and the sons of the Amir, unfortunately losing the road, came near Qarshi, where they found two shepherds, one of whom undertook to lead them in the right way, and the other went and reported the affair to Nur Mohammed Bi, the governor of Qarshi. He started immediately with the ruler of Chiraghchi, and about 3000 horsemen, and overtook the Afghans very near to the boundary of Shahar-i-Sabz. He sent them a message that their leaving Bokhara without the permission of the Badshah was an insult to his authority, and degrading to the character of their father, who was still in the city; and he would therefore advise them to return. The Sardar Mohammed Akbar Khan and his brothers promised to go with him if he will allow them to rest and to halt for the night. This was agreed to by Nur Mohammed Bi, who provided them with all the necessaries of life. At night the Afghans held a council of war; and in the morning, after arming and mounting themselves, they rushed into the lines of their pursuers the Uzbegs, and there ensued then a hard fight, in which many of the Uzbegs were killed. At the close of the contest the Afghans became exhausted, and destitute of ammunition, on which the Uzbegs attacked and killed about fifteen of them, with Samandar Khan, and made the rest, with Akbar, prisoners. All their property and horses were plundered; and the Governor of Qarshi, agreeably to his commands from the throne, sent all of them to Bokhara, where his Majesty ordered them to live with their father the Amir. Not long time had passed after this, when the Badshah again requested the Amir either to leave his kingdom, or to send for his family. The answer returned was this,—"The Navab Jabbar Khan has the charge of the whole family, and I do not think that the Navab will pay attention to even my request, with regard to sending them to Bokhara." The Badshah said, if the Amir consents to write a letter and to send a confidential servant with it, he will not blame him if the Navab Jabbar Khan does not act upon his command. Husain Khan Shah Samand was entrusted with the letters to Khulam, to whom the Amir secretly said, that he was to tell the Navab that he should not lose time in taking off his family anywhere out of the reach of the Uzbegs. The King of Bokhara, by the same opportunity, wrote letters to the Vali of Khulam, and to the Mir of Qanduz, to facilitate the departure of the family of the Amir Dost Mohammed Khan from their territory. Ghanichah, the agent of the King of Bokhara, accompanied Husain Khan Shah Samand to Khulam, where he was rebuked by the Navab and the rulers for the ill behaviour of his employer towards the Amir. He returned therefore without obtaining the object of his mission, and the Badshah, incensed at this, ordered the Amir

Dost Mohammed Khan to quit Bokhara with his retinue, and issued commands to provide him with every thing necessary on the road to Charju. Here the "Mahram"* of the king desired the Amir and his sons and relatives to occupy one boat to cross the Oxus, while his servants were said to be about to follow him afterwards. To this plan, however, he did not agree, and while the matter was in discussion, one of the boatmen desired the Mahram, in the Turkish language, to quit the boat,—which the Amir Dost Mohammed Khan understood, and instantly jumped out of the vessel, and rode his horse back to Bokhara. He was thus saved from being drowned in the river, which the king had faithlessly contrived and had wished to be his fate. On his arrival in the city, he informed the king of the reason of his return, and he, after some delay, ordered him to occupy his former apartments, stating that he plainly saw that an Afghan chief was afraid to travel in Turkistan. No food nor servants, as usual, were sent for three days to the Amir Dost Mohammed Khan, who at last applied to his Majesty for his daily expenses. The Badshah sent a message to say that there was

* Confidential, or literally, familiar attendant.

no necessity for maintaining two hundred followers, and that the Amir had better keep only thirty of them. In the meantime Nayab Abdul Samad secretly informed the Amir that he had spoiled all his prospects by his own conduct, which made him the more perplexed in his mind. He then proposed his desire to marry his daughter with the king, who accepted it, and Abdul Ghani and Mohammed Azim Khan were ordered to go to Khulam and bring the daughter of the Amir for marriage. Mohammed Amin, Sharif, Azim, and Sherjan Khan, the four younger sons of the Amir, also got permission to join their mother at Khulam; and Mirza Imam Vardi made himself appear to be insane, and thus secured his release, and Mustaufi Abdul Razzaq also obtained leave and followed him.

Now the Amir Dost Mohammed Khan was removed to another house, and during a few days he was well treated. In the meantime the manners of the Uzbegs now waiting upon him excited some suspicion of the evil intention of the king, in the mind of the Amir. When the Mirza Sami Khan was brought from a separate residence to live with the Amir, and the Mustaufi ordered back from the way to Khulam, it increased the apprehension of the Afghan chiefs, who thought that they were collected for the purpose of being massacred. They were only permitted to make their prayers in the mosque; and one day some of the people who were engaged in the prayers made their heads bare and prayed for the good fortune of the Amir, which was reported to the king. His Majesty was incensed as well as alarmed by the partiality of the people towards the Amir, and therefore gave orders that they are to discharge their religious functions inside of the house, and never should go out of the doors. Now the Amir Dost Mohammed Khan, with his sons Mohammed Akbar, Afzal Khan, and his minister, was a regular prisoner.

CHAPTER XVII.

Occurrences at Kabul—Disaffection—Expedition against Pusht —Extracts from various correspondence—Dost Mohammed Khan escapes from Bokhara—Takes up arms—Is defeated by Col. Dennie—Movements of Sir R. Sale—The ex-Amir is again defeated—He surrenders himself to Sir W. Macnaghten —Increasing discontent.

HAVING pursued the course of the ex-chief till his confinement by the barbarous King of Bokhara, it would not be improper to mention the occurrences which took place in Kabul during the period of his imprisonment, till he surrendered himself to Sir William Macnaghten.

On the return of Colonel Outram from Bamian, Haji Khan was accused of his deliberate treachery in causing the escape of the Amir Dost Mohammed Khan. I have said that I do not doubt the grounds which Colonel Outram had for suspecting his fidelity, but I say it was not then the proper time for punishing the treacherous. In the first place, it was utterly far from policy to expect good service from Haji Khan on such a critical point as the pursuit of the Amir Dost Mohammed Khan, after every one of us had expressed our conviction of his duplicity in remaining behind till the fortress of Ghazni was stormed and taken. In the second place, I cannot see how wisdom could dictate to place confidence in one whom we had induced to betray his former master of twenty years.

Whatever the faults of Haji Khan Kakar were, it was very impolitic to punish him. He was three months ago nominated Nasir-ul-daulah, with a considerable salary; and now we made him a prisoner, and banished him to India. We gained no good by all this, but rather we shook the confidence of many other chiefs. Immediately when his fate was known in the capital of Afghanistan, Aziz Khan, the principal chief of the eastern Ghilzais, fled from Kabul, fearing that he might be forced to share the fate of Haji Khan; and Yar Mohammed Khan, the Vazir of Hirat (as it will be observed by the official extracts), called us the "faithless dogs" in the presence of Major Todd, the British Envoy, alluding to the case of Haji Khan. Sir Claude Wade was in the meantime directed to conciliate the Aziz Khan Ghilzai chief, and endeavour to restore confidence enough to induce him to wait upon the Shah and the Envoy. He had great difficulty to efface from his mind the suspicion and fear which had been already implanted in his heart by the example of our treatment of Haji Khan, yet at length he succeeded in persuading him to meet the expectations of the Kabul Government. He gave him letters of recommendation, pledging his word for honourable treatment, in addition to the reward he was promised; but very little attention was paid by us to his stipulation.

I have particularly stated the just and sound reasons which led the Earl of Auckland to place an allied sovereign on the throne of Kabul, and the judicious measures which dictated his policy in that crisis, and which ended in the successful termination of his enterprise. If mistakes or wrongs, whether arising from the pride of power, or from the misunderstandings or the jealousies of the parties invested with chief authority, were committed on the acquisition of the objects of the Governor-General, this cannot with impartiality be attached to the originator of that enterprise. The object of the Governor-General was to annihilate the Russian and Persian influence and intrigues in Afghanistan, both at that time and for all time to come, unless they adopt open measures; and this object he fortunately and completely attained in a manner worthy of the British name, and laudable to himself as a statesman. If he had not taken these open measures, disasters and outbreaks would have soon appeared in the very heart of India. The only mistakes which his lordship committed during the whole Afghanistan affair were on these two points of the gravest importance,—one, in appointing two such talented men as Sir William Macnaghten and Sir Alexander Burnes to act at the same time in one field of honour; and the second was that, on hearing of the outbreak at Kabul, he delayed in insisting upon the Commander-in-Chief to order an immediate dispatch of the troops towards Peshavar, as was judiciously advised by Mr. Clerk. Though this outbreak had nothing to do with the line of policy which the Governor-General had adopted in the origin, and was caused by the most extraordinary circumstances of quite a contrary nature, which I shall hereafter describe; yet, he being the superior head of the Government, he ought not to allow hesitation to approach and to embarrass his sound judgment at the crisis when immediate and energetic attention was required. But the motive for not doing so was that his lordship had already made every arrangement to retire from the Indian government, and therefore did not wish to prolong the time for his departure by embarking in other and new operations. I shall therefore leave this matter here, and proceed to tell the causes of our triumph, without opposition from the people or chiefs of Afghanistan, men who in customs and in religion were perfectly different from us.

Firstly. The inhabitants of Afghanistan, whether the Durranis, Tajaks, or partly the Persians, are by nature habituated to and fond of the vicissitudes of times; and thus, in consequence of the tranquillity established by the iron rod, not the popularity of their ruler, and the destruction of the ringleaders of every description caused by the Amir Dost Mohammed Khan, they became tired of his government.

Secondly. The Amir had confiscated the estates of all the Durranis; and the authority of the districts and towns was entrusted to his personal adherents; and those who suffered thereby were always desirous to see his government overthrown.

Thirdly. His force, which in a great proportion consisted of cavalry, was discontented in consequence of their small pay, and the long journeys which they were sometimes obliged to make under great personal fatigue and expense.

Fourthly. The Amir had deprived the Navab Mohammed Zaman Khan, his uncle, of the Jalalabad country, and had given it in charge to the Sardar Mohammed Akbar Khan, his own son. He had behaved in the same manner with his nephew, the Sardar Shamshuddin Khan, the ruler of Ghazni, and appointed his second son, the Sardar Gholam Haidar Khan, as ruler in this stronghold of Afghanistan.

Fifthly. The Navab Jabbar Khan, the elder brother (but step-brother) of the Amir, was deprived by him of the government of the Ghilzai country, which had compelled the Navab to pursue a hostile course towards him, and to become a willing friend of the English.

Sixthly. The Amir had killed and had caused the murder of many rebellious chiefs of Kohistan; and therefore their survivors were always anxious to co-operate with those who may seek for his ruin.

Seventhly. The poor as well as the men of business were harassed by being employed without pay, or with very little wages from the Amir Dost Mohammed Khan.

Eighthly. The merchants of all descriptions on various occasions, and especially in the time of any internal or external demand for military aid, were forced to lend large sums of money, which were scarcely repaid by the Amir.

Ninthly. The Amir was also disliked for fixing several unjust demands for revenues upon the land, in addition to what his servants, when abroad on duty, gained as food from the cultivators by the use of force, and paid no value for it.

Tenthly. The allowances of the Mullas, the Sayads, and the priests of all denominations, which were granted by the late sovereigns of Afghanistan, were in some instances forfeited, and in others reduced.

Eleventhly. The friendly correspondence and amicable intercourse which continued between the Amir Dost Mohammed Khan and Mohammed Shah of Persia, as well as the siege of Hirat by that monarch, stimulated the religious enthusiasm and hatred of the majority of the Afghans against his conduct and policy, because his countrymen, being Sunnis by sect, were fatal and deadly enemies to the Shias of Persia.

Previous to my taking a view of the various points of policy and the line of conduct which we pursued after taking Kabul, a glance on the reasons of our popularity and esteem in Afghanistan would not be destitute of interest, because those manifold reasons, added to the discontented feelings of the Afghans against the Amir, formed a favourable instrument and occasion for our triumph.

Firstly. The golden days of the liberality of the mission of the Honourable Mountstuart Elphinstone were always in fresh remembrance with the inhabitants of Afghanistan; and as they are by nature the most avaricious of mankind, they entertained very high hopes of deriving emoluments from his countrymen, and thus they wished our influence established for some time in that country, for their own advantage.

Secondly. The city of Kabul in particular has always been involved in the mutual contest of the two parties, the Sunnis and Shias, and these two sects maintain religious animosity between themselves at all times, and the bloodshed of the one party is considered a virtue by the other. The English, on the contrary, were none of them; and being free from their religious prejudices, were inclined to act only as impartial mediators, endeavouring to annihilate this evil. The Shias, being themselves foreigners in Afghanistan, liked the foreigners (the English) more than the Sunnis, and they always stood high as men of the sword amongst the latter.

Thirdly. The chiefs of the country entertained an opinion that if they were to render service to the British, their descendants from generation to generation will derive benefit from this service; and thus we had gained their good opinion very effectually.

Fourthly. The merchants and the people of the lower class, such as the cultivators of the land, &c., were desirous to see our authority established in Afghanistan; because the former suffered much under the Amir Dost Mohammed Khan, through the heavy duties which he imposed; and the latter suffered also in extortions of every kind.

Fifthly. There were also a few men of rank in the country, who, being moved by vanity, and proud of the well-known superiority of their blood, were jealous of the usurpers (the Amir, &c.), and zealous to serve us under the name of their long-exiled but legal monarch; and therefore thus they caused disunion against the Barakzai chiefs on our approach to Afghanistan.

Under the above-mentioned circumstances, which had made the populace of Afghanistan the desperate foes of the Barakzais upon one hand, and had made the English more popular on the other hand, there appeared no evident sign of discontent, nor of such resistance or commotions as would require an immediate recourse to arms. Undoubtedly we alone held possession of Kabul, but in the meantime its ruler was not in our hands, and there was therefore sufficient reason for apprehension that as long as he, or any of his sons, was at liberty, and a fugitive on our northern frontiers, there would be no difficulty for the people of Kabul to invite him whenever we give them any annoyance by our conduct. Notwithstanding all these points of grave concern, we sent a large portion of the army back with Lord Keane to India, and yet we interfered in the administration of the country, and introduced such reforms amongst the obstinate Afghans just on our arrival, as even in India, the quietest part of the world, Lords Clive and Wellesley had hesitated to do but slowly, and to extend them over many years.

Captains Taylor and Trevor, with some other officers, were appointed nominally to act under the Shah, and to enlist Afghan forces; and all the chiefs were desired to give "San," that is, to pass with their mounted followers for inspection, under the eyes of the above-mentioned officers, who discarded the unfit, and enlisted the fit ones as servants of the Durrani states. All those who were gained by Sir Claude Wade on his advance upon Kabul with the Shah Zadah, and all those chiefs whom we had secured to our interest during our progress to, and residence in, Kabul, had of course the strong testimonials from us, and were therefore entered into the service. Here we committed another fatal error, knowingly, I may say, in that we did not till then at once reduce the number of their followers, but allowed them to be enrolled on that occasion, and after a few months began to show them signs of our further intentions in dismissing them, which they reasonably attributed to our deliberate treachery.

All the principal towns on the frontiers of Afghanistan were now placed under the administration of the officers of the Shah, while our political assistants to the Envoy were everywhere watching their conduct, and interfering in the jurisdiction of the country; and yet as this interference was not open, it did no good to the people, while it caused a disregard for the local authorities of the kingdom.

The more we found the people quiet, the more steps we took in shaking off their confidence. We neither took the reins of government in our own hands, nor did we give them in full powers into the hands of the Shah Shuja-ul-Mulk. Inwardly or secretly we interfered in all transactions, contrary to the terms of our own engagement with the Shah; and outwardly we wore the mask of neutrality. In this manner we gave annoyance to the king upon the one hand, and disappointment to the people upon the other.

The Shah Shuja-ul-Mulk began to become jealous of our power, and of the influence which he thought we were daily gaining for our own benefit, contrary to treaty, and to suspect that all the people looked upon us as the sovereigns of the land. We did indeed give a kind reception to some of the heads of the tribes, but this was merely temporary, to ensure the stability of the Shah's kingdom, and to provide for ourselves some means of cure or of safety against any internal commotions in future. It is sad to state, however, that all our liberalities were showered upon intriguing men of low birth, and not upon the chiefs of high estimation, who would have stood by us in time of need.

Akhund Mulla Shakur, an old sharer of the misfortunes of the Shah, was the head manager of the affairs of government, commonly called Vazir, but neither we nor the Shah ever allowed him to assume that title. Having passed all the former part of his life in exile with the king at Lodianah, where he had only to distribute about 4000 rupees *per mensem* amongst the dependents of his Majesty, little good might have been expected from such a manager in the administration of the kingdom. He had no relation to claim his aid and attention; and whatever money he gained by public or private means he added to the coffers of the Shah, and he was therefore in great favour and confidence with the king. Mulla Shakur was however very old, and totally unfit to occupy this high post. He had lost his memory to such an extent that he could not recognise a person whom he had well known before, if he had not seen him even for a day; but he had perfectly understood the real meaning of our treaty with the king, and by it he knew that we had no right in the administration of the country, and therefore our position was not favourably looked on by him nor by the Shah. Mulla Shakur appointed Sher Mohammed and Daya Ram as his deputies,—men too well known for tyranny and unjust principles. Sir Alexander Burnes introduced a system for the reduction of duties on all articles of commerce, which undoubtedly grew thence more prosperous; but the men of Mulla Shakur treated those alterations slightingly, and took from the merchants more than was fixed by us. Every day complaints were made to us, and we permitted ourselves to interfere by giving notes to the complainants, requesting the Mulla to settle their cases; but this did no good, for instead of having redress to their grievances they were beaten, and sometimes confined, for coming and complaining to us against the Shah's authority. All the chiefs or heads of tribes received their allowances from certain villages, by obtaining an order from Mulla Shakur. If there was any man among them known to us, and whom we would wish to favour, the Mulla took care to annoy and vex him by giving him an order to a distant village for such sums, which he would likely spend during his journey, or else to poor villages, where there was very little chance of gaining anything. Gholam Khan Popalzai, whose services and melancholy death I have already mentioned, was appointed, by our advice, to settle some disputes in Charkar. Mulla Shakur, whether by himself or with the consent of the Shah, sent criers to notify in the streets that Gholam Khan, being a protégé of the infidel English, was (himself) an infidel, and acting for the ruin of the Shah, and of the faithful of the country. In a very short time, it became manifest that the Mulla was not acting to our satisfaction ;—whether he acted to the satisfaction of his own master or not is another question. He was now trying to form a party in favour of the king separately from us, with the view to make his Majesty entirely independent of our support. Instead of acting wisely on such a critical subject, he made use of such foolish sentiments as afforded a good opportunity for the chiefs and intriguers to play their own cards. Instead of telling the people that the Shah was an independent sovereign, and, being an ally of the British, was protected by the British troops, which will retire on the settlement of the country, he said to the people that the Shah looks upon us as the violators of the treaty by keeping the force in the country; interfering with the business thereof, and inducing the people to go to us for favour. He added that, as soon as the family of the Shah had arrived in Kabul from Lodianah, His Majesty will be quite fearless of our injury, and then, by the assistance of his faithful subjects, the followers of "Islam," he will take the reins of government into his own hands, will reward his friends and punish his enemies. Such expressions of Mulla Shakur gave an excuse to the bigoted malcontents to look upon us and the Shah as disunited, and, in fact, they considered him to be our slave by necessity. The priests, therefore, omitted the performance of the usual ceremony of reciting the "Khutbah" with the name of king, after the prayers in the mosque. We had indeed heard this privately, and now Mulla Shakur waited upon us and informed us of the circumstance, in the show and manner as if he had no concern with the affair, nor any knowledge of the reason of it. He added that the priests, according to the Mahomedan faith, cannot recite the Khutbah for any one but an independent sovereign, while the Shah under our arms cannot be recognised in that position. Mulla Shakur, by such ruinous absurdity, did not really exert himself to put a stop to such insolence of the priests, because he had two objects in view.

In the first place, he wished to excite the religious hatred of the Musalmans against us, and by allowing such thoughts to pass quietly, he meant to show the natives of the country that though the omission of the oration or Khutbah was an insult to the king, yet being faithful himself, he would not urge the Mullas to read it, since it was contrary to their law to do so during our occupation of the country.

In the second place, he thought that our interference in such matters would involve us in great difficulties and even in religious warfare; and that if we were to bear such disrespect of the people with toleration, we shall of course be looked at as more weak than it is politic for us to appear.

Soon after this, another occasion of disorder and

confusion was caused in the city by our disagreeing with Mulla Shakur on the subject of grain. In this affair, I may say, he was right, and we were wrong; and the wrong we then did hastened our ruin in that country. The purchase made by our Commissariat officers of grain from the various parts of the country raised the price too high and placed it utterly beyond the means of the population in general. The landlords, knowing the advantage of the sale at such a price, keeping only as much as would meet their own immediate demand, used to send all their produce to our camp, without selling the smallest quantity to the poor in the country or in the towns. Grass for cattle, meat and vegetables, and in short all the necessaries of life, rose to a considerable price, and the cry of starvation was universal, and there were very many hardly able to procure a piece of bread even by begging in the streets, while every thing would have been in abundance but for our purchase. Mulla Shakur in the first instance gave orders, by beating the drum, that if any one shall either sell articles necessary for subsistence higher than the fixed price, or store up the grain more than is necessary for the consumption of his family, shall suffer a severe penalty. To this notification of the Government of the Shah, there was no attention paid at all. The necessaries of life continued to rise higher in value, and the poor to suffer more than before, and Sir Alexander Burnes was obliged to order the distribution of about one thousand loaves of bread amongst the poor, who assembled in throngs around his house. Mulla Shakur was now compelled to adopt such measures as are usual in Afghanistan, by seizing the shop-keepers and forcing them to sell the grain at a moderate price. All of them were well aware that we will interfere in this determination of the Mulla, and will prevent him from forcing the sellers to conform to orders; and thus, therefore, shut up their shops and ceasing to dispose of anything for sale, they came in throngs to complain to us. I was ordered to wait upon Mulla Shakur, and to request him to release the traders, who, in fact, had taken the advantage of our interference, with the deliberate intention of starving the people in general, and of filling up their own pockets, while they sold the grain very dear. The result of our stopping the Mulla from executing his plans in cheapening the grain was that there appeared a universal cry throughout the whole kingdom that we are killing the people by starvation. As a natural consequence of this, all of them became tired of our presence in the country; and at length they joined and swelled the number of the rebellious. After the outbreak of Kabul, when I was concealed in the Persian quarters, I heard both the men and the women saying that the English enriched the grain and the grass sellers, &c., while they reduced the chiefs to poverty, and killed the poor by starvation.

Whenever any article rose high in price in the time of the Amir Dost Mohammed Khan, he used to make it cheap by forcing the traders to sell cheaper, as Mulla Shakur attempted to do on this occasion, but we unwisely objected to his proceedings. The full force of power in a despotic country and among a reckless people is a law suited to the taste and habits of its inhabitants, and simple justice produces there most bitter fruits. We adhered to this mode of lenity in Afghanistan, and allowed the traders to sell provisions at their own price; but we thereby raised the indignation of the population while supporting the wicked principles of a few, and in return we were turned out of the country. What Navab Jabbar Khan did on such occasions is not unworthy of mentioning here. During the disasters of 1842, when Mohammed Akbar Khan had gained the supreme power, and the rumour was spread that the British army was advancing upon Kabul, the grain began then to rise high in price. The traders ceased to sell anything to the people at low prices, having the prospect of much gain from us. The Navab sent for one man belonging to each of the different trades, as one butcher, one grass and grain seller, &c., and persuaded them to sell cheap, so as not to produce famine. They made an excuse, that their supply or store of grain is not in the vicinity, and that to bring it into the market requires a longer notice. The Navab gave no heed to such excuses, but ordered his men to pierce an iron nail through the corner of the trader's ear; and then in the case of the butcher, to fasten the point of it in the block of wood over which he used to hang the killed sheep in his shop. Thus he was forced to stand there for a whole day, passing a stream of blood from his ear; and the meat was next morning so cheap as to be within the reach of all classes. Such was the example put upon all traders, and the effect was satisfactory. I confess, such punishment in a civilized country must be considered to exceed the crime, and barbarous; but in Afghanistan it annoyed only a few persons, and it did good to very many, for it gained both provisions for all, and the good-will of the people at large.

Another discussion ensued between us and Mulla Shakur, with respect to the wages of certain people in the employ of the Shah. Our engineer officers in building the cantonments employed the workmen at a much higher price than was usual, so that hundreds of the people of the country, leaving the plough in the field, ran to seek work in our cantonment. Mulla Shakur had orders to repair the gardens of the king, and could not get one man but on wages higher than we had promised to pay. The treasury of the Kabul government could not afford such payments; and the Mulla was therefore obliged to force the people to work in the garden of the Shah, and accept the regular wages of the country. This produced a clamour, and they came complaining to us. The Mulla was informed that if he does not satisfy the people by payment, we shall open our treasury and pay them for the Shah.

However, our differences on all subjects with Mulla Shakur grew every day more and more. We submitted all his proceedings to the Shah Shuja-ul-Mulk, and requested him to dismiss the Mulla; but as he was adding to the private treasury of the Shah, and foolishly intriguing against us, His Majesty paid little attention to our warnings, and thought that we are desirous to lower his dignity by causing the dismissal of his minister, the old Mulla Shakur, while he himself was aware that if we put anything in order one day, the Mulla spoiled it again next day, even from spite.

The jealousy of the Shah Shuja-ul-Mulk grew stronger. He complained to Sir William Macnaghten against Colonel Dennie, who had taken up his quarters at the palace-yard in the absence of the Shah. He said that it was showing disrespect to his royal dignity by that officer's occupying that part of the palace. Such was the Afghan gratitude which the Shah felt for one of the bravest officers who had taken a prominent part in storming and subduing the fortress of Ghazni for him. A king, moreover, who had lived for thirty years on the bounty of his countrymen, who freely shed their blood and spent their money in placing him on the throne; that he should consider his dignity lowered by the occupation of a room where formerly the sweepers lived!!* When the communication on this subject was made to Colonel Dennie, he most resolutely but justly replied, "that he declares before God that it shall be the Governor-General alone who shall turn him out." His Majesty also suggested the impropriety of our keeping ammunition and provisions in the Bala hisar, while the country was not perfectly tranquillized, and the Russian army was moving towards Khiva. He stated that it will reduce him to be the neighbour of the commissariat and ordnance officers. In this department no one showed a determined disposition like Colonel Dennie, and so the cellars were evacuated.

How unwisely we paid attention to such absurd ideas of the king! Had our commissariat stores

* What Sir Willoughby Cotton said on this occasion was this:—"In Persia, in Egypt, in Masqat, the greatest sovereigns allow the officers to occupy palaces; and Shah Shuja declares he will resign his throne if he be so insulted by the contamination of those men who bled for him, and placed him where he is!"

remained in the Bala hisar, where Captain Watt had judiciously placed them on the arrival of the army, how different would have been the circumstances during the insurrection, when our troops were starving in the cantonment! The Shah did not stop here, but pursued a jealous and unprincely course on all occasions. I shall notice one case here, though perfectly foreign to the subject of the book. During the mission of Sir Alexander Burnes to the Amir Dost Mohammed Khan, Qadirju, a Kashmirian musician, with his band, entered my service; and when our army advanced upon Kabul he reoccupied his situation under me. His musical instruments were always in my house; and, according to the custom of the country, no one asked his attendance without my permission. The Shah Shuja-ul-Mulk, having heard of their excellence in music, ordered them to wait upon His Majesty; but Qadirju remonstrated that he was in my service, and that his instruments were in my house. The king stated to the Envoy that I had kept the musical instrument by force in my house, although they belonged to His Majesty. The Envoy, on investigating the case, found that the musician was never in the service of the king, and that the musical instruments were purposely made by my orders. He informed the Shah of the result of his investigation, saying that he could not force me to give them up to the king, even if I were his own private servant. However, after some time, when his minister called upon me, I made over the charge of the musician to him, for the satisfaction of the Shah; but this fairly shows how destitute his suggestion was of truth, and how easily accessible he was to jealousy. Another complaint he made of me to the Envoy was in consequence of my building a house, of which he became jealous, and thought that no one should have a good thing but himself. He made an excuse, and said that I had built such a high and large house, which overlooked all the neighbours; and that they have privately complained to him on account of their inconvenience. On this my neighbours made a petition, sealed and signed by all, stating that I had built the house with their permission, and that they look upon me as one of themselves, and had never thought of any inconvenience from my erecting the house. Here, again he was disappointed, or rather ashamed, through telling such stories which he could never prove.

There was now one general impression amongst us that the country was all quiet; but this idea soon began to be effaced. Colonel Herring, escorting the treasury from Qandhar, was murdered near Ghazni. Sayad Hashim rebelled, and disturbed the authority of the Shah Shuja-ul-Mulk, in the direction of Kunar. Major MacGregor, C. B., whose diplomatic talents and military skill will demand a prominent place in the account of the victorious garrison of Jelalabad, was appointed political agent in that place, and accompanied the expedition. All the troops of the Shah marched against the fort of Pushut, the residence of the refractory chief Sayad Hashim, excepting the brigadier; which exception was amusing enough, since a report stated that the said brigadier withdrew from mess because an officer spoke slightly of the Envoy in his presence, and refused to apologise to him when asked to do so. Colonel Orchard was appointed to lead the expedition, and the fort of the enemy did not fall in our hands so easily as was anticipated. These are the words of Sir William Macnaghten:—

"I have just heard from Major MacGregor. The forts are stronger than we were led to expect. The account is not

MAJOR Mc GREGOR C B.

so favourable as I could wish. The gate of Pushut resisted our powder-bags, and all our ammunition being expended, we were obliged to retire with a loss of forty or fifty killed and wounded. Collinson severely, and Hicks of the European regiment slightly wounded. Hashim has, I grieve to say, escaped, and taken with him eighty thousand rupees. The rain was sadly against us. The garrison evacuated during the night, and are gone God knows where."

While such disorder was prevailing at home, we were not altogether free from receiving the stirring news of the movements of Russia towards Khiva, and we aimed at political fame by recommending the military occupation of Balkh, and of the eastern banks of the Oxus, and thus establishing our influence in the kingdoms of Bokhara and Khavarazm to counteract the advance of Russia. Mr. Lord was appointed political agent on the north-west frontier of Afghanistan, and resided in Bamian, where he was negotiating with the Navab Jabbar Khan to deliver the family of the Amir Dost Mohammed Khan to us, and from whence he was the direct channel of communication with the chiefs of Turkistan. Sir Alexander Burnes coincided in these opinions; but the Earl of Auckland placed not much importance on the movements of Russia, and considered it a most hazardous work to employ any force on the other side of Bamian. After a great deal of correspondence had passed between the Kabul authorities some time in favour and some time against the movement of our troops towards Turkistan, and the repeated intelligence of the Russian army, despatched by our news-writers in Bokhara and in Khiva, as well as the reports of Mohammed Husain Kashi (who was deputed to the King of Bokhara); Lord Auckland thought it advisable that a messenger should be sent to Khiva to examine the real state of affairs, and to find out the real object of the Russian expedition. We knew that the Amir Dost Mohammed Khan was nearer to Persia and Russia, though a prisoner, and we were aware that the Shah of Persia, under the advice of the Russian ambassador, had written to the King of Bokhara to release the Amir of Kabul; and that Major Todd, the envoy at Hirat, had discovered at last the duplicity of Yar Mohammed Khan Vazir. The latter had abused our government for faithlessness, called our officers "dogs," and had offered to tender Hirat to the Persian government, after we had employed our engineers, spent thirty-six lakhs from our treasury, and exerted our skill in repairing and strengthening the fortifications, and in encouraging agriculture and commerce of the country. In short, Major Todd's mission to Hirat failed, and he also advised the military operations against Kam Ran, in which we all coincided, as well as the home authorities; but the Governor-General did not think it prudent to enter into an undertaking of such great magnitude; and at the same time he strictly observed the engagements of the tripartite treaty. Colonel Arthur Conolly, whose sad fate will be noticed together with the melancholy end of Colonel Stoddart, was the officer selected by Sir William Macnaghten to go to Khiva instead of a messenger. No better officer could be found to conduct political duties of such a nature than Colonel Arthur Conolly, who succeeded in forming a treaty with the Khan of Khiva.* Before his arrival in that country,

* The relation of the King of Bokhara had also come to the Envoy at Hirat, demanding the British aid against His Majesty; and if we had made a declaration on the part of Shah Shuja-ul-Mulk, without compromising the English government, there was a prospect of success in the release of Colonel Stoddart from the dungeon of that savage king. However, the policy of the time was not favourable to effect this step, which I must confess was a very dangerous one.

Lieutenant Shakespear (afterwards Sir Richmond Shakespear) was deputed by the Envoy at Hirat to the Khan of Khiva, and had wonderfully succeeded in obtaining the release of the Russian slaves. Yet the expedition of Russia, under General Petrowik, had created so much political discussion in our quarters, that Sir Alexander Burnes, who had once expressed that "no move of any kind, political or military, may take place beyond the passes," had now volunteered to proceed to the general's camp if he were invested with full powers. But again the Governor-General hesitated in sanctioning such measures, which he wisely considered would lend our political influence far from our support, and at the same time make us a close neighbour with Russia. It would be highly interesting if I were to quote the extracts of some correspondence which took place between the authorities of that day.

From Mr. Lord.

"I have received Sir William Macnaghten's official, and your private reply to my propositions of sending in the troops to Khulam.

"Meanwhile, that I am not to have the advantage which would arise from the immediate execution of it, both in getting me into the country and Dost Mohammed out of it."

From Sir Alexander Burnes.

"I have just received your very interesting letter of the 13th, with its enclosure, an extract from the Governor-General's letter regarding the designs of Russia. I now feel somewhat at ease since his Lordship has become cognizant of the real state of affairs on our frontier, as we shall no longer be acting on a blind reliance that the expedition to Khiva was small, and would be unsuccessful, when it is an army composed of the *élite* of their empire, and has made good its lodgment in the Delta of the Oxus. After the Punic faith which Russia has exhibited, I confess I was astonished to see Lord Clanricarde put trust in what Count Nesselrode told him on the strength of the Russian force, and you may rely on it that we are better judges of what Russia is doing in Turkistan, than our ambassador at Saint Petersburg; and I hope the correctness of all our information from first to last will now lead to implicit reliance being hereafter placed upon it. One correspondent may exaggerate and distort; but it is not in the nature of falsehood to be consistent: and of inconsistency we have none, the cry being that Russia has entered Turkistan with the design of setting up her influence there, and that (whether her ruler or ministers admit it or not) her object is to disturb us in Afghanistan. European intelligence confirms all this; and with a policy peculiarly her own, Russia has for the present left the Turkish question to be settled by England and France, and even in her generosity agreed to open the Black Sea.

"Firmly impressed with these views they torture all my thoughts and opinions; and, in consequence, lead me to hope that our every nerve will be strained to consolidate Afghanistan, and that no move of any kind, political or military, may take place beyond the passes. Had we force sufficient the occupation of Balkh might not be a bad military move, and one which would, in truth, show an imposing attitude. * * * The attitude of the Sikhs towards us is that of undisguised hostility, and on both our front and rear we have cause for deep reflection—I will not say alarm, for I do not admit it; we have only to play the good game we have begun, and exhibit Shah Shuja as the real King, to triumph over our difficulties. * * *

"I regarded * * * deputation to Khiva as the most unhappy step taken during the campaign: * * * it places us in a position far more equivocal than Russia was placed in by Vikovich being here. We had no ground of complaint against Dost Mohammed (till he joined our enemies), and two great European powers merely wished for his friendship; * * * * * * but release her slaves and have done with her. Does he remember that Russia has extensive trade passing through Khiva, and that the proclamation of war declares that the object of the expedition is to protect the merchants? Is England to become security for barbarous hordes, some thousands of miles from her frontier? If not, * * * * such promises or speeches must compromise us.

"I observe you proceed on the supposition that Russia

wants only her slaves released; but this is one of her demands only; and instead of our language, therefore, being permanent on that head that we insist on her relief, it means nothing, for Captain Abbott tells us that the Khan had offered to release them all; and I know that the King of Bokhara has made a treaty to that effect, and acts, too, upon it, for Captain Abbott likewise confirms the information frequently reported. * * * We have, in consequence, I think, no business in Khiva, and, however much we may wish it, none in Bokhara. The remaining state is Kokan; and we shall now state the probable good of a connexion with it.

"In my letter to Colonel A. Conolly, I enclosed some 'observations on sending the mission to Khiva:' but I did not then discuss the policy of the thing; I merely, in reply to Colonel Conolly's request for hints, pointed out the difficulties of the road and communication when there.

* * * * *

For the chances are that Russia will at once march on Balkh to assert her just position, as she calls it, in Central Asia; and then, indeed, the Governor-General's surmises will be proved; it will give measures to all surrounding states, and add difficulty to the game which we have to play. But one very serious obstacle to all interference with Turkistan has apparently been overlooked. Russia is not engaged alone in the enterprise; she has her ally of Persia in too, and ambassadors who seek the release of the Persian slaves. Are we prepared to insist on this, and reconstruct the whole fabric of society by marching back some two or three hundred thousand slaves? If not, our proceedings are neither consonant with humility nor the rights of nations. * * *

"I have been thus earnest on these very momentous questions, from the anxiety which I have to see our cause flourish, and our good name preserved. It is not the question of Mr. Lord or Colonel Conolly going; that is a mere trifle, which does not call for a moment's consideration.

* * * * *

Let us crown the passes; let an engineer forthwith be sent to map them; and let grain (as you have just proposed) be stored behind them at Bamian. Let alarm be allayed by our not appearing to stir over, for Kabul is the place for the coup de main, and not Bamian, which should be its outwork, and as such, strengthened. * * * We have our agent detained in Bokhara; for Colonel Stoddart's captivity reflects seriously upon our character and damages it here: while in Kokan I see possibly good likely to flourish, even from the most splendid success attending the agent, and on the contrary, much chance of evil.

"I sent off your letter to Mr. Lord, and yours to Major Todd is now being despatched. I shall keep Nicolson fully informed of the proceedings of the Ghilzais.

"I am in constant correspondence with Sir James Carnac himself, and your views are almost on all points my own. The Governor-General and his private secretary are, it seems, resolved on giving no credence to the Russian attack on Khiva, in spite of all your and my letters. This short-sightedness is distressing.

"I have just got your long official, and the private letter accompanying. The latter, stripped of the two last sheets, has gone on with the official. You ask me what I think of the latter. I can say in truth that it is a very clear and convincing document; but you will not move the Envoy or his Lordship at all. Lord Auckland must see that it is his duty to counteract Russia either from this or Europe; and he leaves the ministers at home to work. I must confess that I should like to see Balkh and the country south of the Oxus restored to Shah Shuja; but when Russia is in the field, if we are not able to render them to his dominions by force, the less we do in that quarter the better; and to this conclusion you seem to have come, from the papers which I have now received. Lord Auckland took a step in sending an army into this country contrary to his own judgment. * * * All the dispatches plainly prove this. * * * The Envoy sees that Russia is coming on; that Hirat is not what it ought to have been—ours; and his dawning experience tells him, that, if not for us, it is against us. What says Lord Auckland?—'I do not agree with you; Yar Mohammed is to be conciliated. Russia is friendly to England, and I do not credit her advance on us, though she may have an expedition against Khiva. I wonder,' adds his Lordship to the Envoy, 'that you should countenance attack on Hirat, contrary to treaty; that you should seek for more troops in Afghanistan; it is your duty to rid Afghanistan of troops;' all very fine. * * *

"I find my yesterday's letter did not go on account of snow. I have just had long letters from Sir W. Macnaghten, with three sheets from the Governor-General.

"His Lordship mentions yourself, and I quote the passage through, 'not authorised to prevent you saying more. Mr. Lord's letters are a little mild, and he appears to me to be too restless. It was clearly out of the question that any of the regular troops at Kabul should be sent to him. You will restrain him from pushing too rashly forward. Upon this point however I much rely upon your judgment, for I am far from able to decide where occupation should end and the exercise of peaceful influence begin.' This latter sentiment will please you much, and show you what might be done to meet your wishes, if the Envoy wish. But at present I am even a conservative as to movements beyond Bamian, *i. e.* we will not set our house right at Hirat, and with Russia in the field and Dost Mohammed not dissolved. What we should do requires great caution. I am, however, of your opinion that Russia should have one side of the Oxus and we the other; but I would not be in too great a hurry, but to Balkh I would ultimately go."

While these signs of discontent were attracting our attention in Afghanistan, we were suddenly informed of the escape of the Amir Dost Mohammed Khan from Bokhara. This was effected in the most extraordinary mode, and for such tact the early life of the Amir has always been signalized. The king of Persia rebuked the Bokhara ambassador for the harsh conduct of his master to the Amir of Kabul, on which the king took him out from the prison and lodged him in the house of the daughter of Shah Zaman, and fixed five hundred tankas * for him as monthly expenses. He was allowed to take exercise in riding, and to make his prayers in the mosque, without any personal guard, but was entrusted to the care of one of the priests or Sahabzadahs from Sarhind. In the mean time, his eldest son, the Sardar Mohammed Afzal, became an invalid; and after the king had given him permission to join his family, he was stopped on his way for some days, and then allowed again to start at the earnest request of his father. After this, the Amir lost no time in contriving his own escape. After discharging the evening prayers in the mosque, he assembled Mohammed Akbar Khan, Sultan Jan, and Alahvardi, and consulted with them on schemes of escape. He said, to flee in one body and together would be an unwise thing, while it would be better that

* Twenty-two tankas make fourteen or fifteen shillings.

Mohammed Akbar, with Sultan Jan and a guide, should take the Andkho road, and he himself with Alah Vardi and one guide should flee towards Shahar Sabz; and in this manner, if one party is overtaken by the pursuers, the other one is sure of success in the enterprise. The Amir set out accordingly, but unfortunately, by traversing a long, circuitous, and wrong road, he tired and killed his horse. Yet then he luckily met a caravan on the road, and was provided with a camel, bearing baskets on both sides; and in these baskets the Amir and his companion placed themselves, under the pretence of indisposition. In Chiraghchi, the servants of the Bokhara government, being previously informed of the escape of the Amir from the city, suspected his being in the caravan. They examined every camel basket, but could not discover him, since he had cunningly coloured his silver beard with ink, which he found by himself on the occasion, and the informer was punished by the officers for bringing them into ridicule with his false report. Mohammed Akbar Khan and Sultan Jan were still in Bokhara, and the Amir, by a providential escape, arrived at Takyah, in the suburbs of the Shahar Sabz. Here he sent for Kabir Khan, a merchant, who provided him with clothes, on which the Amir sent information of his arrival to the Mir of that place. The latter, accompanied with about a thousand horsemen, came to receive the Amir Dost Mohammed Khan, and conducted him with all possible honour to his princely apartments; and now he was free from the fear of the Bokhara tyrant. The ruler of Shahar Sabz however soon received a letter from the king of Bokhara, desiring him not to allow the Amir to go towards Khulam, at least if he will not send him back to the Badshah; but he replied that his custom was to pay every attention and respect to a guest, while those of his Majesty are contrary, and that he shall therefore do what will be suitable to the Amir Dost Mohammed Khan.

After resting there a few days, the Amir Dost Mohammed Khan quitted the Shahar Sabz, escorted by a large body of horse, and the ruler presented him with a beautiful charger, with a sword, and with money for the expenses of the road. Passing by the town of Hisar, he safely crossed the Oxus, where Yahabeg the boatman brought dinner for the Amir. The Vali of Khulam came to receive him, and was delighted to see him again in his country. In Khulam, both of these chiefs, in conjunction with many other adherents, held councils as to the future proceedings of the Amir. He proposed to disturb our tranquillity, and try to recover his lost government in Kabul; and the Vali was promised to be his vazir. The latter chief had not succeeded in having his affairs settled with us to his satisfaction before, and he now thought that his co-operation with the Amir at this time will induce our policy to meet his wishes; and he therefore collected money, horses, and auxiliary forces from the chiefs of Mazar and Qunduz and marched towards Bamian; and the Mir Baba beg, the chief of Haibak, being our friend against his brother the Vali of Khulam, was dispossessed of his place by the united force of the Amir and the Vali. It is well to state here, that the family of the Amir Dost Mohammed Khan, with the Navab Jabbar Khan, was in our hands, and the son of Mir Vali was in attendance upon the Shah and the Envoy. Yet these ties had no power either on the Uzbeg or Afghan mind; for they knew that the British rules will neither permit us nor the Shah to ill-treat their relations for their advancing against us. At this time affairs were indeed of a more seriously alarming nature than ever was known before in Afghanistan. The chiefs and the people of the country, being disappointed by our fruitless promises, were desirous to see us involved in difficulties;—disturbances were brisk in Kohistan, and no favourable tidings sent from Hirat, Kalat, and Bajaur. Yet the well known activity and prudence of Major MacGregor, the Political Agent, had in the meantime settled everything favourably in the latter direction.

The affairs in Kohistan demanded the immediate attention of our authorities; and we began now to suspect almost every one for intriguing with the Amir Dost Mohammed Khan, and for being ready to join the Kohistanis in their attack on the city. There were, indeed, many people innocent of any such intention; yet our own fault making our conscience uneasy gave us a strong reason to fear and doubt every one. Haji Dost Mohammed Khan of Garm Sail, Agha Husain, Mulla Rashid, Nayab Amir, Mahmoud Khan Bayat, with many other chiefs, were now placed in custody, and Hafizji was sent as a prisoner to India, and thence to Mecca. These our measures in some respects put a check upon intrigues in certain quarters; but on the other hand many individuals of consequence lost their confidence in us. The people in Kohistan were the warmest and stoutest friends of the Shah and of the English in July, 1839; and they were now reckoned our enemies, in consequence of the judicious measures of Gholam Khan Popalzai, who had purchased them with money and with promises of reward; for in both of these they were disappointed by us on gaining the possession of Kabul. In this district, as I said before, the poor people were discontented, because of oppression; while those of rank were intriguing in consequence of our neglecting their privileges.

On the 30th of August the Sardar Mohammed Afzal Khan, eldest son of the Amir Dost Mohammed Khan, came with five hundred horsemen to attack our post at Bajgah, and was driven off. Information reached us the same evening that the Amir was in great force on this side of Haibak; on which Captain Rattray, with the Janbazes, fell back upon Saighan. All our outposts were now left to the Amir; and even Saighan was evacuated, leaving a good deal of private property for the use of the enemy. All our troops were now in Bamian, from whence one company* of the Afghan regiment, raised by Captain Hopkins, went over to the Amir, and the rest were disarmed and ordered to go back to Kabul.† On the 7th of September the brave Colonel Dennie left Kabul to reinforce Bamian; and on the 18th the Amir attacked a fort dependent upon Kabul. It was now ascertained that the allied forces of the Amir and of the Vali were more in number than had been stated previously; and Colonel Dennie did not think it prudent to wait for aid from Kabul nor yet to retire: and so he at once charged and drove the enemy from their position. The cavalry, consisting of Captain Anderson's horse Janbazes, and of Mr. Lord's and Captain Conolly's escort, spread in every direction, and cut off great numbers of the fugitive Uzbegs; and no mercy was shown to the deserters of Captain Hopkins's regiment. The Amir Dost Mohammed Khan, with his son and the Vali, had a very narrow escape, after losing about six hundred men in the field of battle, and leaving all

* Headed by Salah Mohammed, who in 1842 changed sides and gave up the British prisoners.

† Amir Khan, brother of our pensioner Abdulrashid, also followed their example.

their tents and stores behind for our possession. Colonel Dennie moved on to Saighan, but the fugitives were so precipitate in their flight that it was considered not prudent to pursue them any further.

On the 28th the Vali of Khulam sent an agent to our political agent, Mr. Lord, and accepted the proposed offers. The Amir was refused any further assistance by the Uzbeg chiefs, and Mohammed Afzal Khan, having fortunately met the men of a caravan of Bokhara, levied the customary duties, and thus obtained about a thousand rupees to provide his routed father with a few necessary things. In the meantime the spirit of rebellion and of insurrection in Kohistan grew daily more and more restless. Shah Zadah Taimur, with a few hundreds of the Afghans, was sent towards that district; and Captain Edward Conolly was attached to his Highness. The royal person, without the British troops, was not considered to throw any weight on the people of Kohistan, nor to ensure their respect; and therefore Her Majesty's 13th Light Infantry, together with two native regiments under Sir Robert Sale, was ordered to follow the Shah Zadah, and Sir Alexander Burnes and myself accompanied it as political agent to negotiate with the rebels.

Sultan Mohammed Khan, a steadfast adherent of the Amir Dost Mohammed Khan, was at this crisis in Nijrav, and was exhorting the Kohistanis to espouse his cause; and did not lose a moment to dispatch a paper, signed and sealed by a good many chiefs of that district, inviting the Amir into that quarter. The Amir, after being routed by Colonel Dennie, had no hopes whatever from the Uzbegs, and therefore was glad to take advantage of this invitation, as well as of our unfavourable state of things; and he was also informed of our forces moving to Kohistan, and meeting opposition in every direction. After a few long and most tiresome marches he arrived in the valley of Ghorband, through Qilai Surkh, but was deserted by Sultan Hazarah, at the head of about seven hundred foot, although the Amir had only one day before presented him with a handsome horse, ornamented with silver trappings.

On the 29th of September Sir Robert Sale surrounded the forts of Ali Khan, who was in special or close communication with the Amir Dost Mohammed

Khan, and was an active person in exciting the rebellion. He had taken a very strong position in the fort, and on the heights which commanded it, as well as the suburbs, and resisted our troops with vigour for a short time. At length, however, the fort was deserted by Ali Khan, and destroyed by our troops. In this warfare of Tutamdrah we suffered a severe loss by the death of Captain Edward Conolly. Notwithstanding his political duty, and merely to see the fun, as he called it, he wished to be in the battle, and thus had volunteered himself to be the aide-de-camp of the general; and while he was galloping his horse on the advance of the troops towards the fort was shot through the heart, and he was then brought in a litter, and placed by me under the tree. This was indeed a heart-rending sight to me, since I was on terms of most intimate familiarity with him, and with his brothers, all men of noble character and benevolent disposition.

The Shah Shuja-ul-Mulk had sent Munsur Khan Chaus Bashi, an officer of the court, to co-operate with us in gaining the notice and favour of the people, as well as all necessary information. The Shah had also asked the Envoy to supply him with cash* wherewith to corrupt the adherents of the rebels: but it was stated at that time, that his Majesty added much out of that sum to the stores in his own treasury; and it is certain that the Chaus Bashi did us harm rather than good. He advised the rebels to resist us a little, in order to show Afghan bravery, and then to go straight seeking the pardon and reward from the Shah. Sir Alexander Burnes objected to such measures, and pointed out to the Envoy the injury that must arise from employing various channels of intercourse in gaining over the enemies.

Gholam Khan Popalzai, zealous as usual, had considerately rendered us the most valuable services during this crisis. He brought over and persuaded many influential chiefs, as Khojah Khanje and Khojah Abdul Khaliq, to tender their submission to us; and settled that Mir Misjadi Khan was to go the next day to Kabul, and to take refuge in the mausoleum of Taimur Shah, and thence to proceed to wait upon the Shah and the Envoy, as he was afraid to come to our camp. Sir Alexander Burnes agreed to this plan; yet at night, contrary to the previous arrangements, and without the knowledge of Gholam

Khan, the Afghan chiefs, with the Shah Zadah, were excited by us to go and invest the stronghold of Julgah, the residence of Mir Misjadi Khan; and on the 3rd of October, early in the morning, we marched, regardless of the entreaties of Gholam Khan, and besieged Julgah. He suggested and urged the impropriety of the measure, which will never restore confidence in the Mir Misjadi Khan; but we lent no ear to his solicitations, and thus we made the Mir our enemy for ever. The walls of the Julgah were exceedingly strong, and our guns made no practicable breach.

The storming party, consisting of five companies of Her Majesty's 13th Light Infantry, as well as detachments of Indian infantry, under their respective officers, was commanded by Lieut.-Colonel Tronson, who led it up to the walls with the most determined bravery. The conduct of the troops, under the heavy and close fire of the enemy, was conspicuous; but the breach being not practicable to ascend, the troops were compelled to retire. At night Mir Misjadi Khan, who was severely wounded, opened the gate of the fort, and stole his escape, to our bitter disappointment, towards the valley of

Nijrav. If we had taken due caution to prevent the chance of his flight, and had placed proper guards around the fort, he never would have succeeded in getting away so quietly. The fort of Julgah was then destroyed, and we remained there for a few days to receive the submission of the other chiefs; and we gave the charge of Julgah to Khojah Padshah, the rival of Mir Misjadi Khan.

On the 8th of October the troops marched to Chakar, anticipating to meet the Amir Dost Mohammed Khan in his coming out from the valley of Ghorband near Tutamdrah. In the meantime information was received of the departure of the Amir to Nijrav, and the rumours were in circulation that he still keeps himself with his followers (who had now surrounded his standard to a considerable number) along the skirt of the mountains, and purposes to join the rebels of Kahdrah and of Baba Qushqar, and then to fall upon the city of Kabul. Desertion now commenced to show itself among the native troops, and on the 14th a whole company of Lieutenant Moul's Kohistanis went over to the Amir Dost Mohammed Khan; yet under all these circumstances, we moved and pitched our camp near Qarabagh on the 15th of

October. In the neighbourhood the fort of Boaba Qushqar, which was considered a very strong one, was in possession of another rebel chief, the Mir Darvesh Khan, who, in consequence of the earnest supplications of the mother of Madad Khan, one of the sisters of the Amir Dost Mohammed Khan, had espoused the cause of the latter. This lady was equally conspicuous in intrigues as her brother the Amir was. I was informed by her own adherents, that since the attack of her brother upon Bamian, and his defeat there, she has been day and night paying visits to the chiefs in Kohistan, producing the Holy Qoran before them, tying knot at their garment,* and thus securing their co-operations in behalf of her brother. Knowing this, I addressed a letter to the Mir Darvesh, on the ground of my former acquaintance with him, advising him to put away all rebellious thoughts from his mind, and to acknowledge the authority of the Shah. His reply was, that he was not a rebel, but that he feared to wait upon us or the Shah, as his enemies had im-

* This is a great token of humiliation in imploring mercy and support amongst the Afghans, which by the national rule cannot be refused.

planted evil suspicions of his conduct in our mind. He added, that if we will use our force against him, he will shut himself up in the fort, which is much stronger than that of Julga, which we could not take after a whole day's battering; and therefore that he will there fight to the last, and not be so mean as to stoop before the enemies of his religion. On this the forces moved with the intention to fight; but it was soon discovered by the reconnoitring party under Colonel Sanders, that the Mir Darvesh Khan had fled, and thus the fort of Baba Qushqar fell into our possession, and we blew it up immediately.

There was another rebel in Kahdrah who had been exceedingly insolent in his language towards us and the Shah, writing in letters that he was stimulated by the sweet thirst for martyrdom, to do all he can to kill us the infidels, or to fall in battle by our foul hands. All negotiations failed on this occasion, and recourse to arms was considered necessary. It was a very dark night when the Kahdrah chief Milak Saifuddin Khan attacked the front and rear of our camp with about five hundred men, but caused no injury of consequence; and on the 21st, our troops advanced in three divisions, and got possession of that place reckoned by him impregnable. Saifuddin Khan, with his family and adherents, escaped to the mountains, and we destroyed the town of Kahdrah with flames of fire.

On the 22nd, the troops under Sir Robert Sale encamped at aq-Sara-i, commanding the road to Kabul, and thus impeded the progress of the Amir Dost Mohammed Khan, if he was attempting a surprise in that quarter.

Leaving Nijrav, the Amir arrived at Durnamah on the 28th, and on the next day the Shah Zadah Taimur, with our camp, moved in the direction to meet him, and halted at Bagh-i-alam. He was now at the head of about five thousand, but as he was gradually and cautiously descending the hills and approaching the capital, he was securing the assistance of other chiefs, by whose forts he passed, taking hostages and provisions during his march, till he reached the valley of Parvan. Sir Alexander Burnes and myself were actively engaged in detaching from him as much as we could the number of adherents. We sent our servants, natives of Kabul, with money into the different forts and villages; and by paying the people in small sums of money, we deprived the Amir of gaining any additional number to his standard, which he had exhibited, under the pretence of maintaining a religious war. The rumour of our distributing money amongst the people in order to prevent their junction with the Amir, had circulated amongst his followers, and he appeared distrustful of their fidelity, and feared that they might seize or destroy his power in the hope of receiving a reward from us. However, on the morning of the 2nd of November,* we came in sight of the Amir Dost Mohammed Khan. The information was received of his endeavouring to retreat, on which Colonel Salter detached two squadrons of the 2nd cavalry, and resolved to intercept the fugitives; but it was said that these troops followed slowly, and paid no attention to the orders of that officer, who repeatedly, but in vain, cried out "Charge! charge!" The Amir took advantage of this disorderly state on our side, and drawing the sword, he with his followers fell upon our force and routed our cavalry.

* The very same day in the following year, *i. e.* 2nd of November, 1841, the insurrection took place in Kabul; Sir Alexander Burnes was murdered, and Mohammed Akbar headed the rebels at last.

Majors Ponsonby and Fraser were severely wounded, and Mr. Lord, the political agent, and Lieutenant Broadfoot and Adjutant Crispin, were killed. The two former of the killed officers had also volunteered to accompany the advance; and if they had not gone out, but had adhered to the rules of their own duty, they would not have been killed. The Amir Dost Mohammed Khan was seen on a charger, with a white turban, and a blue flag by his side, haranguing and cheering his men to attack us. Notwithstanding this confusion on our side, the Amir felt himself still overwhelmed by numerous difficulties, and in personal danger. The people employed by us were diminishing the number of his followers by the distribution of money among them, and the Amir knew that the Kohistanis around his person will not hesitate to shoot him if they were sure of the Shah's approbation and reward for that deed. He therefore was obliged to leave the field of battle without the knowledge of any of his followers, or even of his son, Mohammed Afzal Khan. About half an hour after his escape, the intelligence was brought to me by a person who had seen him passing through a village only four miles distant; but no credence was placed on this report. In this case, we pitched our camp on the battle-field, and the insurgents crowned the tops of the hills. All night there was heard here and there the sound of firing; and the fall of our officers and the flight of the cavalry had produced a bad impression in the minds of the Afghans of the Shah Zadah. His Highness was so afraid that he sent for me at about ten o'clock at night, and represented the dangerous position he was in, and said that if he sees any signs of mutiny amongst the soldiers of his camp, or any of the chiefs going over to the Amir, he will come quietly to my tent. We also now felt the delicacy of our position, for all the forts in the rear were rebellious, and the mountains in front covered with the enemies. Sir Alexander Burnes prepared an official letter at three o'clock in the morning for Sir Robert Sale, advising him to march back upon Charkàr, stating that we had withstood the Amir with bravery, notwithstanding our own disorders, and had pitched our camp on the ground lately occupied by the enemy; suggesting, however, that by remaining long here, we shall induce the countless swarms of people to pour down upon us from all the different valleys opposite to us, while by taking the central position at Charkar, we will closely watch the movement of the Amir along the hills, on both sides, leading to Kabul. The general moved his force agreeably to the advice of Sir Alexander Burnes, and came to Charkar.

Repeated information of the movements of the Amir reached us, but they all differed from each other; and on the 4th of November, early in the morning, a letter from Sir William Macnaghten arrived, conveying the happy tidings of the surrender of the Amir Dost Mohammed Khan; and then all the authorities agreed that my information of the escape of the Amir just after the battle of Parvan was correct and authentic. The Amir, as I said previously, thought it safer not to trust himself any more to the Kohistanis; and therefore passing through Nijrav he came straight to Kabul with his friend the Sultan Mohammed Khan. It was in the evening of the 3rd of November, when Sir William Macnaghten was riding with two officers and deliberating on the sad contents of the report of the battle of Parvan, and on the uncertainty of the movements of the Amir, that one horseman galloped up and said to him, "Are you Lord Sahab?"* "Yes," replied the Envoy. "Then," rejoined the Afghan, "I come to tell you that the Amir is arrived." "What Amir? Where is he?" "Dost Mohammed Khan," was the answer. After a minute the Amir appeared, and dismounted from his horse, and claimed the protection of the British Envoy. The Envoy took his arm, and conducted him with all respect to his own residence, where the Amir one year before held his court, swayed his country, and now surrendered his sword as a state-prisoner! Such are the decrees of fate!! However the Envoy, by the nobleness of his mind, begged the Amir to keep it; and Lady Macnaghten kindly sent for one of his wives, the daughter of Nazir Khair-ullah, who was still in Kabul, and, supplying her with everything necessary, conducted her to the presence of her long separated Lord—the Amir. The reception and the generosity of the Envoy delighted the Amir Dost Mohammed Khan beyond all limits, and he wrote letters to his sons, as Mohammed Afzal Khan, &c., to come to us, as he had surrendered and met every

* The Envoy by the natives of the country was addressed as Lat Sahab or Lord for respect.

kind consideration. After a few days, the necessary arrangements having been made, the Amir started for India, and all his family were escorted from Ghazni to join him at Peshavar.

Our position in the month of October, 1840, before the surrender of the Amir Dost Mohammed Khan, was a hundred times more dangerous than it was in October, or even on the 2nd of November, 1841. The whole of Kohistan was in rebellion, the people and chiefs being equally discontented by our not adhering to the engagements and promises we had made with them. Above all, the Amir Dost Mohammed Khan was personally encouraging and regulating the insurrection. What was then the reason that we encountered the surrounding difficulties with success on all sides? What was it that kept in order Abdullah Khan Achakzai, and the Amin Ullah Khan, and the tumultuous people, or Sunnis, of Kabul, even though we had imprisoned their priest Hafiz Ji? What was it then that procured success and maintained an honourable name for the British when our negotiations had failed at such a crisis? It was only the determined heroism and perfect skill of Sir Willoughby Cotton which annihilated all the impending dangers that were ready to fall on our heads. His eyes, his ears, and his mind were directed on all sides, and attentive to what was going on in all places; and wherever the presence of his troops was considered to produce good, he was ready and active to effect such good most successfully. But alas! neither he nor any officer like Sir H. Smith or General Littler was in Kabul to preserve the British name from the stigma which the disasters of November, 1841, have stamped on the English character in Central Asia, and I may safely add, in India too.

As soon as we became free from anxiety and elated at the time on seizing and banishing the Amir Dost Mohammed Khan, we thought that we had nobody to disturb the peace of our mind any more for ever; but such peace was imaginary only, and perfectly at variance with the results which our own proceedings were sure to create. On the surrender of Dost Mohammed Khan a bag full of letters was found in the field of the Parvan battle, and among them were the letters generally from Sultan Mohammed Khan of Nijrav, and Saifuddim of Kahdrah, signed also and sealed by a hundred persons more, inviting the Amir to protract the contest; promising to join his standard, and stating merely the names of some men of rank in the city who would also espouse his cause: and I received orders to translate these letters, the contents of which were undoubtedly offensive. On my part, however, I would have treated them as nothing, and even would never have confessed to having them in our possession after the Amir was in our hands; while the disclosure of them made the writers and the other parties concerned with them always fearful of our suspicions of them, and thus caused the loss of mutual confidence. To mention them at all served also to open a field for the vagabonds of Kabul; for it was universally known that we were in search of such letters as might show the intrigues of certain people. There were many such characters as would be ready to fabricate and to write such letters, in order to become our familiar associates for having produced them.

I forgot to mention in its proper place, that just at the time of the attack of the Amir Dost Mohammed Khan on Bamian, all of us had discovered a most singular proof of the existence of certain people who had made it their profession to forge letters, in order to gain our bread and intimacy.

There was a very respectable person of Kohat, by the name of Sayad Ahmad Khan, in the service of Captain Edward Conolly; and this person reported to that officer an account of his seizing a messenger bearing a communication from the Sardar Sultan Mohammed Khan, or from the Sikhs to the address of the Navah Jabbar Khan, then residing in Kabul. He thought this a discovery of some great treasury, or of a plot against the English; and so the messenger was placed clandestinely in a house, and his letters submitted to the Envoy. They were translated: and they acknowledged the receipt of the letter from the Navab, and, coinciding with his opinion, requested him to raise disturbances in Kabul, while the Sardar Sultan Mohammed Khan, with the pecuniary aid from the Sikhs, would disturb the peace of Jellalabad, from the Bajaur side, and the Amir Dost Mohammed Khan was to threaten us at Bamian. Such letters were truly in plain meaning and understanding sufficient grounds to accuse and banish the Navab from the kingdom of Afghanistan, and such appeared the intention of the authorities. Sir Alexander Burnes was consulted, and he desired the original letters to be produced. If I am not mistaken, there was Captain Johnson, paymaster of the Shah's force, with him; and I suggested to Sir Alexander Burnes that it would be desirable to send for the man who had charge of the letters. He came, and on my asking him the date of his arrival in Kabul, he mentioned a day which I pretended to say was not right; and to find out the truth, I added that I had a man in my room who had seen him two days before in Kabul, riding on horseback, in a fine dress; and that he was neither a messenger, nor could make a trip in such a short time to Peshavar and back here on the day he describes. This puzzled the man, and we offered him a reward of fifty rupees if he were to make the whole truth known to us. He at once said that if we promised a pardon to him, he would disclose the whole secret. We accordingly complied with his request; on which he stated that he was not a messenger, but the horseman of Sayad Mohammed, who wrote the letters, and gave them into his hands, and told him to appear as a messenger before Captain Conolly!!

This was reported to the Envoy, who, of course, ordered the forger to leave the Mission Compound; but no punishment was inflicted upon such a culprit, which might have served to stop all such ruinous intrigues hereafter. We all indeed allowed such things to go on smoothly, and this encouraged the writers continually.

Here were three more persons of the same character as Sayad Mohammed Khan, all of them known as an abandoned set of men. One, with the name of Shah Ji, became an agent of the Envoy; and another, named Mir Hasan, gained the favour of Sir Alexander Burnes for having acted in the same capacity; while a third, named Ahmad Khan, obtained our patronage by forging letters on the part of Nazir Khan Ullah and other men at Bokhara, and filling them with fabricated accounts concerning the movements of Russia and Colonel Stoddart, who was a prisoner at Bokhara.

Meanwhile Mulla Shakur was dismissed by the Shah at our repeated solicitations; and our recommendation for nominating Mohammed Usman Khan or Nizam-ul-daulah as a minister was forced upon the Shah in a great measure. This showed the people in the country that the King had no power, and the new minister truly looked upon us as his patrons rather than upon His Majesty. Every evening he came to report to us what he had done during the day, and he executed our orders with more celerity and attention than those of the Shah Shuja-ul-mulk, whose minister he was appointed to be. Our choice fell upon him merely because he was a Sadozai; but certainly he possessed no abilities for administering a kingdom, having passed all his previous life as a subordinate servant of the Barakzais. Our selection of Mohammed Usman increased the jealousy of the Shah upon one hand, and the hatred of the chiefs of the country upon the other. His late father, Vafadar Khan, had been equally obnoxious to dislike in the employment of his capacities as his son was now; and the son was inclined to seek revenge against those noblemen who had taken part in the murder of his father, in the reign of Shah Zaman, and always to insult those who stood higher than himself, rather than to restore confidence for the public good. Mirza Imam Vardi, a great hypocrite, became his deputy, or under secretary, and his career in the service of the Barakzai chiefs has always been stained with deeds proceeding from principles highly injurious to the welfare of the Government. He, along with Abdul Razzaq Khan, Mustaufi, and Sayad Husain Daftri, took advantage of the ignorance and inexperience of the new minister in the affairs of the realm, and thus enriched themselves by the unjust exercise of their influence. At the same time they were old servants of the Barakzai chiefs; and being the relations and friends of Mirza Sami Khan, the minister of the Amir Dost Mohammed Khan, they were endeavouring to excite confusion in the country in order to act against the new Sovereign. While Mohammed Usman Khan was proud of our protection, he did not care for the good or bad opinion of the people, nor for the satisfaction of the Shah, and the following is a remarkable instance of this fact. A Sayad, the spiritual guide of the Shah, was deprived of his land, which was attached by the minister to that of his own servant. He complained to the Shah, whose repeated injunctions could not induce the minister to restore to the Sayad what was his by right. He waited again upon the Shah, and on representing the result of his interview with the minister, the Shah told him the truth in reply—that he had no power over his Vazir, and therefore that the Sayad should curse him, and not trouble the Shah any more, because he is no more a King, but a slave.

While the dissatisfaction of the Shah and the discontent of the chiefs and people became stronger, Nizam-ul-daulah, the minister, took care to bribe Shah Ji and Mir Hasan, the news-writers of the Envoy and of Sir Alexander Burnes; and they received a monthly sum for engaging to praise his administration and popularity.* In this manner the envoy was kept unacquainted with the proceedings of the Nizam-ul-daulah. Sir Alexander Burnes was also informed by me, by Nayab Sharif, and by many other persons of rank and trust, that such was the state of things; but he felt himself in an awkward position, and considered it impossible to cause the dismissal of one whose nomination he had with great pains so recently recommended, together with

* The circumstance which led us to know of the bribe received by our news-writers was curious. While the Shah, the Envoy, and the Minister were passing the winter in Jellalabad, Sir Alexander Burnes, being the resident in Kabul, received orders from the Governor General to examine the custom duties; and while reading over the items of expenditure, a sum appeared to be paid monthly to the Shah Ji.

causing the discharge of Mulla Shakur, the favourite of the King.

I cannot omit to express here my agreement in opinion with Sir James Hogg, M.P., now the Chairman of the East India Company, when he spoke in the House of Commons, alluding to the deplorable case of the Rajah of Satarah, "that paid agents are a curse to their employers and to the country." So Ahmed Khan Mandival or Biranjfrosh, Mir Hasan, and Shah Ji, have proved to be amid our ruin. Their names will appear on several occasions hereafter; but a glance at their history will not be entirely uninteresting here. I must say that they never gave me any reason whatever for private offence, and so I do not entertain the private resentment against them which persons unacquainted with the state of things might fancy.

Shah Ji was formerly in the service of the Barakzai chiefs in Peshavar, and having committed an offence, was obliged to take refuge and service under the government of the Amir of Kabul. Here he did some other mischief, and to avoid punishment he escaped to Peshavar, where the sons of the Qazi Mulla Hasan took him under their protection, and put him in the employ of the Sardar Sayad Mohammed Khan. He continued in the mean time to furnish intelligence secretly to our news-writers in Kabul till the British army arrived in that country, and he then got an appointment under us, and became a corrupted supporter of the minister.

Mir Hassan, a Sayad by birth and Mufti by rank, was a person of a most bitter and degraded character. Every boy in Kabul knew that he was matchless in forging letters, seals, and lies. He was several times put in prison, and was once saved of his ears and beard through the applications of the good Navab Mohammed Zaman Khan, when the vigilant Dost Mohammed Khan found him guilty, and wished to deprive him of them.

Ahmad Khan Mandival, or Biranjfrosh (one of the rice-merchants, or sellers in the market), assumed a respectable surname, and wished to be called Mulla Ahmad Khan. He pretended to set himself up for a rich merchant, and as connected with the mercantile people of Bokhara. He was notorious in Kabul for lies and intrigues; yet he gained the favour of Sir Alexander Burnes by fabricating news, and enriched himself by the charges he made for obtaining information from Bokhara, and by the wages of the messengers.

Such were the characters of the individuals who stood high in our estimation, while the chiefs and persons of respectability were refused access into our presence.

Sir Alexander Burnes proposed a valuable paper regarding the administration of the government of Kabul, in which he recommended the introduction of reform in the military department. All the chiefs who were enlisted about a year ago with a certain reduced number of their followers, were now informed that they were to re-pass under the eyes of Captain Trevour, who will keep and discharge such of them as he shall think proper, and that they are hereafter to bear the name of "Hazarbashes," to live in tents and to be ready to start at a moment's notice. To this all the Durrani and the Persian chiefs objected; stating that they were not brought up to bear such reform, and that if we were determined to diminish the number of their retinue, they would bring with them only such a number for the inspection of Captain Trevour as we were inclined to allow each of them to maintain, as this would prevent disgrace to their character; for that otherwise our interference was sure to lower them in the eyes of their dependants. We, however, refused to them even this means of pacifying their feelings. All the chiefs, with much unwillingness, went with their followers for inspection to Captain Trevour, who regulated their number, and retained, and dismissed them as he liked. Each of the nobles, gnawing his beard and hanging his head with fury, left the residence of that officer, who, irritating the chiefs, employed any one without distinction, whether he was a vegetable seller or a soldier. Some of them, who still bore patiently this violent insult to their pride and feelings, were on several occasions reduced to suffer the harsh treatment and ill words which we sometimes use in our intercourse with the low class of people in India. Under all these just causes of offence and of indignation there were no bounds to the fury of the chiefs, and of the descendants of the old soldiers of the country. Abdullah Khan Achakzai, Mulla Momin took a prominent part in showing discontent against our reforms and against that officer, by whom they appeared to be introduced. Khan Shirin Khan repeatedly said to us that our reforms in the military class of Afghanistan would involve us in fatal difficulties—that every one of the "Hazarbashes" would think himself independent of the chiefs, and in time of need would act according to his own plans, disobeying them without fear—and that thus the English officers, not acquainted with the custom of the country, would not know how to manage them; at least these officers would either be trifled with or be killed by them. This was too truly and really the case at the insurrection of Kabul and of Qandhar.

While we were making the nobles of the country our enemies by introducing these reforms, Mir Hasan, our news-writer, forged another letter on the part of the Sikh government to the address of the Amir Dost Mohammed Khan, and produced it to Sir Alexander Burnes, who received it of course as a matter of caution, and according to the existing custom of the time considered it to be a genuine document. Translations and copies were sent to the Government, and thus we were anxiously seeking for a rupture with the Lahaur government, but as we had not secured safety for ourselves in Kabul, we did not think it prudent to kindle a fire immediately in our rear. However the reward which Mir Hasan received for this discovery of his own fabrication gave him ample encouragement to establish fresh claims upon our thirst for news of every kind.

After a few days he went to a Khatri merchant at Moradkhani, in the city, and demanded of him a sum of money, threatening to have him seized by us if he refused. When disappointed in regard to the money, he came with great pride, under the pretence of discovering a plot, and desired us to seize the merchant immediately, while in his shop. His plan was, that then he would go to the merchant's wife, pretending to be his friend, and would request her to deliver to him a bag of papers for her husband, and thus he would have all the papers before us. We had placed so much confidence in him, notwithstanding the unanimous reprobation of the public, that we desired the apprehension of the poor trader; on which Mir Hasan, with a bag full of forged letters in his pocket, entered the room of his house, where his wife saw him taking out the bag from his own pocket. Now Mir Hasan, himself a forger, discoverer, and our protegé, astonished the trader's wife by saying that her husband was an intriguer, and was therefore imprisoned by us. All the merchants came forward as witnesses for the innocence of the victim of Mir Hasan, but we lent a deaf ear to them. In the bag were found numerous letters of the various chiefs conspiring against us, and some bearing the seal of Shah Shuja-ul-Mulk. Under the pretence of protecting the chiefs who were thus exposed, he managed, by his artifice, to snatch money from several of them, and thus also he kept them always fearful of our suspicion. The letters of the Shah were addressed to the various chiefs in the Kohistan, desiring them to rise up against us; but neither the style nor the handwriting gave reason to believe that they were authentic. On examination it appeared that the words which had formerly been in the paper were washed out and fresh ones had been replaced; but as we knew that neither the Shah was satisfied with our interference nor the chiefs with the failure of our promises, it became a matter of grave discussion whether they were really sent by His Majesty or were the production of the intrigues of Mir Hasan. However, they were shown to the king, who, either justly or unjustly, denied being ever concerned in them in any way. We gained no good by this exposure; we did not punish the doer of the evil, but on the contrary we implanted distrust in the mind of the Shah; and the Khatri merchant was punished by being placed on the back of a donkey and proclaimed as an offender of the state.

In the mean time the Shah Shuja-ul-Mulk despatched Mansur Khan Chaus Bashi to Qandhar, stating to us that the Governor of that city, Mohammed Taqi Khan, had been negligent in his duties, and the Chaus Bashi was ordered to regulate his conduct. On his arrival at Qandhar he desired the governor to assemble the Durrani chiefs privately, because he had a Royal message to deliver to them. They appeared all in the assembly, on which the Chaus Bashi requested them to join in his plan, and to show signs of disturbance in the country, which would compel us to act agreeably to the wishes of the Shah, and suitably to the dignity of the chiefs. The governor, Mohammed Taqi Khan, considered himself our protegé, and having informed Major Rawlinson, the political agent, of the object of the mission of the Chaus Bashi, requested him to allow one of his confidential men to be concealed behind the screen in the house of the said governor, where he would call another assembly of the nobles to have the repetition of the Shah's message from Mansur Khan. This was all managed wonderfully, and the whole proceedings were reported and laid before the king, who, like other Afghans, at once threw the whole blame, justly or unjustly, upon the Chaus Bashi, and denied having anything to do in the matter.

The Chaus Bashi, Mansur Khan, was ordered back to Kabul, where, at our urgent request, as well as to show his neutrality, the Shah Shuja-ul-Mulk blackened the face of his officer, mounted him on an ass, and ordered him to be conducted through all the streets. The cries of the criminal were—"He who will serve the Shah Shuja-ul-Mulk in confidence will suffer such penalty," meaning that whatever service he had performed was in pursuance of His Majesty's secret orders.

To give the substance of the discovered or forged letters of Mir Hasan would fill up the pages of these volumes; but the translation of the document supposed to be sent by the Lahaur government to the Amir Dost Mohammed Khan, when attacking Bamian, will at once show the fabrication of the whole proceedings by our protegés, Mir Hassan, Shah Ji, and Ahmed Khan.

Letter from the Lahaur Government to the Amir Dost Mohammed, intercepted or forged by Mir Hasan.

To Dost Mohammed, Mohammed Afzal, and Akbar Khan, Nau Nehal Singh, Sultan Mohammed Khan, and Sayad Mohammed Khan, from Lahaur, send their salam.

"YOUR letter mentioning your release from Bokhara and arrival at Khulam reached. They are much pleased thereat. The Sarkar has ordered me to write and say that he is your friend; rest satisfied. The Sarkar desires that you should send by Qasids all the intelligence you may wish; that he is on your side. The Sarkar has sent these things to you: 10,000 rs. hundi, 60 abrahs, 60 shawls, which Jewahire Singh will cause to be delivered to you secretly. The Sirkar says that you will be seized if you go to Kabul; you had better come to him. If you can get troops where you are, the Sarkar will send you (ferèman) lots of money by the Kohistan route. Any papers you may wish to send have them written by Raghu Shikarpuri, and send by Sultan Khan and Salem Khan. Have no fears for your family, we will send for them. Nau Nehal Singh says if you come towards Peshavar he will send Ayob's son to meet you. Bajaur and Runar have tendered their allegiance; everybody is with you. The Biloches of Kalat, the Talpurs and Kakars have all sent papers. The Sarkar is very kind to us. The Farangis have not more than five to seven thousand men altogether, and have disgusted all the country, which is with us.

Write constantly, for we day and night look for your letters. Now is the time for exertion. Be bold. Write us all the Turkistan news. Do not be alarmed about the Qajars; they too have sent letters. I will send you money through Kunar. Ata Mohammed does you great service here—be satisfied.

"13th Savan, 1897, Sammat, corresponding with 7th August, 1840.

"The Sarkar did not do anything for you when you went to Bokhara, though your letters reached; such shall not now be the case.*

(True translation. ALEX. BURNES.)"

To Lallu Mal, Javahare Singh's salam.

"I HAVE sent you 10,000 rs. and 60 shawls for Dost Mohammed Khan by a Qafila; get a receipt and send it to me. Be careful that no one discovers this. Send me intelligence of what force collects that I may send you money. Do not send by the Bamian but the Hindu Kush road and Charkar. Whatever the expense is, that is the road to be used.

"Savan Badi, 8th (22nd) August, 1897.

(True translation. ALEX. BURNES.)"

While in every direction we had unquestionable

* Every word and style of this is a plain fabrication of Mir Hasan, and never used in Panjab.

proofs of discord and malcontent, we now commenced to hasten the calamities by causing the adoption of economy in the kingdom of Afghanistan. Upon one hand we were sending the British troops back to India, and, on the other, raising low and petty persons into the corps of "Hazarbashes," namely, Kohistanis and Khaibaris; and neither would the British Government pay these new levies, nor could the revenues of the country, unless the allowances of the chiefs should be reduced: wherefore our policy and the advice of our appointed minister, Nizam-ul-daulah, dictated the adoption of the latter plan. The sum of two lakhs of rupees was considered necessary to be deducted from the allowances of the Ghilzais, the Mullas, the Durranis, and the other chiefs; and all the Afghans who were employed by Prince Taimur at Peshavar, on the guarantee of Sir Claude Wade, were turned out of the service; and this proposition caused a general disorder in the circle of the nobles. On this Nizam-ul-daulah advised us to force the discontented chiefs to subscribe a document to the King, binding themselves to perpetual fidelity, and never to enter into any intrigues, but to agree to the terms of the new system in the

Government, otherwise to leave the dominions of the Shah. To this the chiefs replied that they were servants of the state; and that it was not the custom of kings to mistrust their servants, and to demand a paper bond of this nature from them. On this we requested the Shah not to allow them to attend the court, and to send them orders to quit the country. They knew that the Shah was not willing to give them such disgraceful annoyance, and that it was Nizam-ul-daulah who, with the use of our influence, was at the bottom of such administration.

Under these circumstances the chiefs saw no remedy for their evils, and therefore they prepared and signed a paper as we had desired. After this the minister advised us to tell the noblemen that it was necessary to seek his satisfaction and approbation on every occasion, and this was another bitter stroke to their pride. The minister thus, instead of gaining their good will for the interest of the Government, was really actuated by old family differences to treat them with contempt. Amin Ullah Khan Logri was requested either to give up the chiefship of that district, or to increase the sum of the revenue paid by him. He then appointed his own son the governor of Jelalabad; and intending to nominate Mirza Imam Vardi under him, and to extend his influence by attaching the Ghilzai districts to Jelalabad, he presented a series of complaints, some just, and some partial and unjust, against Hamzah Khan, and at length succeeded in persuading us to cause the dismissal of that governor; and this also was perfectly against the wish of the Shah. Now, therefore, Hamzah Khan had also good reason to join those who had already been plotting against us.

These rumours of the disaffection of the chiefs under the Durrani regime were not slow in reaching the ears of Yar Mohammed Khan, the cunning vazir of Hirat. He wisely thought that the result of our proceedings in Kabul will be a general tumult, and he took the first step to show want of respect to our envoy, Major Todd, who was thus compelled to quit Hirat and come to Kabul; and this gave fresh encouragement to the designs of the malcontented personages of the capital.

Besides all these alarming occurrences in our administration, the state of the government in the city wore a fearful aspect. Whenever the chiefs or the poor had any complaint to make to the Shah, even if access were obtained, the Shah, having no power to decide, referred the case to the minister; while the latter, by his natural vanity and selfish motives, was adding to their distresses. It was then represented to Sir Alexander Burnes, who was to tell them to wait upon his superior the Envoy, who having formed a good opinion of the Nizam-ul-daulah from the perusal of the news written by the corrupted Shah Ji, only disappointed their expectations by ordering them to seek justice from that minister. He, on the other hand, would not give them any relief, unless his avidity, jealousy, and old animosity against them were satisfied; and thus by disappointing them under the influence of these reasons, he was sure to tell them that he acts as advised by the Shah and by the British authorities, and thus people were lost in uncertainty about where to go and seek redress for their grievances.

One day, however, the noblemen waited upon the King in the Bala Hisar, and submitted their deplorable state to his Majesty, adding, that they are quite at a loss as to what would be the best course for them to adopt in order to secure their own good. The Shah, in the hope that some unpleasant disturbance will induce us to seek his consultation and dependance upon the one hand, and show the chiefs that his Majesty was inclined to promote their interest on the other, replied that he was a King only by title and not by power, and that they cannot do any thing; meaning that they are cowardly, and cannot persevere so as to mount to the national honours of the Durrani kingdom ("Az roe shuma hech nameshavad, kenam qaum koned"). These were indeed sad and severe words of the Shah; and, in my opinion, though guilty of such unwise utterance of them, he had never anticipated that they will stimulate the chiefs to open rebellion, and that they will go so high as to be beyond his power to suppress. His object in speaking these imprudent words was to convince us of the unpopular character of the Nizam-ul-daulah, and of the bad policy of our reforms, and of our other measures; and that thus we shall be forced to give up all the affairs of state into the entire management of the Shah himself.

After the interview with the King the chiefs assembled at the end of September, 1841, and sealed an engagement written on the holy leaves of the Qoran, binding each other to rebel against the existing government, and thus to annihilate our influence in the country. One of the parties concerned in the plot called "Bacha-i Pahalvan," a neighbour of Nayab Mohammed Sharif Khan, came and informed me of the circumstances, adding, that if we wish he will go and seize the Qoran from the bearer who has it now to take it to certain chiefs in the country. I reported the whole circumstance to Sir Alexander Burnes, and Nayab Sharif persisted in giving him leave to gain this object; but he did not place any value on this discovery, which could at once show who were the chiefs inimical or friendly to us.

The eastern Ghilzais stopped our communications and disturbed the peace of the road between the city of Kabul and Jelalabad. They plundered the merchants near Tezin, and refused to acknowledge our orders to restore their property to them. On this a brigade, under Sir Robert Sale, was sent to punish them, and bravely succeeded in clearing off the pass of the Khurd Kabul. In consequence of Major Macgregor's absence with the Zurmat expedition I was ordered to go with Sir Robert Sale from the political department, and I executed the duties entrusted to me till the return of that officer. On my return to Kabul the state of things and the spirit of the inhabitants seemed to threaten our stability, and gave ample reasons for alarm. It has been stated in many papers, and by many authorities, that neither Sir William Macnaghten nor Sir Alexander Burnes had information of the existing discontent and conspiracy of the chiefs; yet, on the contrary, the following quotations will fairly show that they were both well informed several months before; but that the pride of power, and the disunion of opinion caused by two able men acting in one field of notoriety, always prevented them from taking the necessary measures to meet the reverse. Sir Alexander Burnes's opinion about stirring, and being alert was, that this will show our alarm, and make things much worse; while on the other hand, being silent and treating these reports as nothing will show our unshaken intrepidity, and will be likely to produce favourable results. But this was not the time to speculate.

"My dear Burnes,

"I heard a report yesterday which I cannot believe, to the effect that Khan Shirin Khan is intriguing with certain parties; yet it is certain that he is disaffected, as are many of the great men of these parts; and with Akbar Khan on the frontier, and determined, as I hear, not to come in, it might be just as well to watch the proceedings of these gentry; not that they could do much harm, but a row would be unpleasant. So pray keep the Sayad (Mir Hasan) on the alert.

"Yours sincerely,

17th July. "W. H. MACNAGHTEN."

From Sir Alexander Burnes.

"I WAS again called by the King in the afternoon. I see a deep-rooted jealousy against the Vazir (minister). Though he must and ought to be supported, I still think the King should be made more conversant with the passing affairs than he is.

"The King gave me at greater length his feeling and his sufferings. He said he had not a trustworthy man in his country;—that all were engaged in setting him against us, and us against him—that his enemies were allowed to continue in power—that the portion of his revenue set aside for him was not collected and paid—that his adherents were discontented—that he was kept under by us in all things, yet that they had not gone right;—that a pilgrimage to Mecca was his only alternative, and that at Lodianah he had had much power as compared with this part of his reign.

"More fighting still! when will this country be pacified?"

Another symptom of discord among the Shah's people was known during the night attack of the Ghilzais on Colonel Monteith's camp in the Khurd Kabul Pass. Mohammed Ali Khan, who had gone to co-operate with that officer on the part of the Shah, neither fired on the enemy before nor after the assailants were defeated, and forced back through his camp. The Khan was in consequence of this seized under our advice to the King.

After the victory of Khurd Kabul Sir Robert Sale was opposed by a larger body of the Ghilzais at Tezin, but the very brave bearing and wise negotiations of Major Macgregor made a peace for a short time, though there was still some annoyance experienced by our troops near Jagdalak. These little temporary patches of peace with the Ghilzais made us to hope for the cessation of further disturbances, especially as they were assured upon our granting them again the rank and allowances which they had formerly enjoyed, besides some reward from the British Government.

In the meantime a circular letter was secretly sent round to all the Durrani and Persian chiefs in the city and suburbs, falsely intimating to them an idea of our designs to seize and send them all to India with Sir William Macnaghten, who was about to proceed as governor to Bombay in the course of three days. The authors of this atrocious letter were afterwards proved to be Mirza Iman Vardi, Mulla Ahmad Khan, and Mir Hasan. The object of every one of these was to signalise himself as our friend during the outbreak, if we were able to maintain our part. The Mulla was also reported to have stated verbally the contents of this letter to Mirza Sayad Husain, Mohammed Husain (the son of the Dost's minister), Mirza Abdul Razaq Mustaufi, Mirza Ali Akbar, Mohammed Mirza Khan, Javan Sher, and Hasham Kah Frosh. These persons, in the habit of deriving advantage from the revolutions in the previous reigns, wrote the contents of the report of the Mulla; and these they distributed amid all the petty chiefs through their own confidential men, who without showing themselves to the chiefs, gave them into the hands of their servants at the door when the night was quite dark, without waiting for a minute for the fear of being recognised and seized by any of the chiefs who might feel still favourably disposed towards us.

As the chiefs of all denominations were extremely distressed by the decrease of their allowances, and also vexed by the injurious conduct of the Nizam-ul-daulah, they were thunderstruck by the perusal of such vouchers, and with the idea of being banished from their native land. Under these painful thoughts, Abdullah Khan Achakzai, with his relatives, went to Amin Ullah Khan Logri, and, holding the Qoran in his hands, implored him to be their comrade in exciting a sedition in the city. When he had agreed to this, some other discontented chiefs, as Sikandar Khan, Abdul Salam Khan, Mir Afzal, Mir Ahmad Khan, Samad Khan, and Mohammed Husain Khan Arzbegi of Chandaul, Haji Ali and Hazar Khan Kotval, Mir Junaid, Mahmud Khan Bayat, Mohammed Azim Peshkhidmat, Nazir Ali Mohammed, Mir Aftab, Mirza Mir, Abdulrahim Mohtsib, Mir Mahbub, Mir Haji, Mir Said Khan, Mir Gholam Qadir, Agha Husain, Tabchibashi, relations of the Dost, sons of Mir Dad Khan Hotak, and Vali Mir Akhor, Akbar Khan Khabgahi, Abdulraihman

Usmanlu, were sent for into the house of the Ackzai chief. The whole of the party now solemnly entered into an engagement with each other, and determined to stand up against us. Some of them suggested that it would be a better plan to murder the Envoy on the road to visit the Shah; and others proposed that they should secretly set fire to our magazine in the cantonment; but Amin Ullah, in conjunction with Abdullah Khan Achakzâi, considered this whole talk childish, and proposed that first of all they should attack the houses of Sir Alexander Burnes, of other officers, and myself, residents of the city; and this plan was admired and chosen by the rest of the party.

Before I commence the narrative of the insurrection, I feel compelled to touch on a subject which has so often been talked of, and believed in the circles of the high authorities both in Europe and in India. This is a most unjust and misrepresented accusation against Sir Alexander Burnes, for intriguing with the ladies of Abdullah Khan, the Achakzai chief. I know well that the exposure of the truth on this subject will cause the animosity of many persons towards me; but I feel assured that the vindication of the character of that deceased officer in a just cause and that the performance of this duty will not cause that feeling in the impartial and pure mind. However, I shall not mention the names of the persons, and shall not hesitate to say how far Sir Alexander Burnes was to be blamed in this matter, which sadly terminated in the loss of his life on the fatal morning of the 2nd of November.

Abdullah Khan Ackzai could not bear the treatment we gave to the chiefs when they visited Sir Alexander Burnes. They were kept waiting for hours near the door-keeper, and then referred to me, as he did not like to see them, for fear of being supposed desirous of interfering with the business of the Envoy, as he notes himself in these words:—"I am hardly to be blamed, for I have no responsibility, and why should I work?" In the meantime our old friend Phokar Shikarpuri, a broker in Kabul, had some claim for debt against Abdullah Khan; and to show his own influence, he asked Sir Alexander Burnes to give him two of his attending servants (peons) to go with the message to the chief that he must pay immediately his debt. The Achakzai chief justly replied that his allowances and followers are diminished, and that he cannot pay his creditor in one sum. Again the peons went with the broker with fresh orders that he must sell his horses to pay his debt, and not think to show himself a great man. They spoke to him with some sharp words and in an insolent tone, and of course no Afghan chief would bear insults, even though his head was placed in danger. Neither did Abdullah Khan forget the disgraceful conduct of the bearers and the tone of their message; nor did Sir Alexander Burnes drop from his memory that the Achakzai chief never waited upon him, nor acted as ordered; and hence it came that their misunderstanding grew daily stronger.

After a few days one of the favourite concubines of Abdullah Khan left his house, and took shelter in the house of a "Sahab Log"* residing between his house and the Chandaul. He could not get her back through polite applications to that officer, and he therefore sent his nephew to complain to Sir Alexander Burnes. He did not wish to write, but ordered one of his peons to go with the complainant, and restore the lady to him if she is there.

* All the English were addressed after this name.

On his approaching the house, she was concealed, and the gentleman of the house turned furious, and accused the Ackzai of a false complaint, notwithstanding they saw her running into the back room. They returned to Sir Alexander Burnes, who, instead of giving soft words to the sufferer, said angrily that he was making false accusations against "Sahab Log," and then turned him out of the presence.

Another case was similarly brought to the notice of our authorities. A gentleman who had taken up his quarters at the house of the Navab Jabbar Khan, won the heart of the favourite lady of his neighbour Nazir Ali Mohammed, and she, crossing the wall by the roof, came to him. The Nazir waited upon me, and I reported the circumstance to Sir Alexander Burnes while the defendant was breakfasting with him. He of course denied having ever seen the lady, on which the Nazir was dismissed, and I myself was always disliked from that day by that gentleman for reporting that fact. The Nazir then complained to the minister of the King, and he sent us a note demanding the restoration of the fair one. The constable saw her in the house, and gave his testimony to this as a witness; but Sir

Alexander Burnes took the part of his countryman, and gave no justice. One night the very same gentleman was coming from the Bala Hisar, and abused the constable for challenging him, and next day stated to Sir Alexander Burnes that he was very ill used, on which Sir Alexander Burnes got the man dismissed by the King. The lady was openly sheltered at the house of the same gentleman after some time, and came to India under the protection of his relatives. Nazir Ali Mohammed and the constable (Hazar Khan Kotval) never forgot these acts of injustice of Sir Alexander Burnes, and thus they were stimulated to join with Abdullah Khan Ackakzai, and to strike the first blow in revenging themselves on that officer.

A rich merchant of Nanchi, near the city, had two years previously fallen in love with a lady at Hirat, and after great pains and exorbitant expense he married her, and placed her under the protection of his relations while he went on to Bokhara to transact his commercial business. In the absence of the husband a European subordinate to the staff officer contrived her escape to his residence in the cantonment. The wretched man on hearing this catastrophe left all his merchandise unsold, and hastened back to Kabul; and there were no bounds to his tears and melancholy. He complained to all the authorities, and offered a very large sum to the King to have his fair wife restored to him; but she was not given up. He at last sat at the door of Sir William Macnaghten, and declared that he had resolved to put an end to his own life by starvation. When that authority appeared partly determined to order the lady to be given to her lawful husband, she was secretly removed to a house in the city. Hereupon the Envoy appointed two of his orderly men to enter the house, and to give her into the charge of the plaintiff; but now the very officer who had offended Nazir Ali Mohammed and Hazar Khan Kotval came to Sir Alexander and begged him to pacify the Envoy, which he agreed to do. On this a sum of four hundred or five hundred rupees was offered to the husband if he will give up his claim to his wife; and Sir Alexander Burnes employed Nayab Sharif and Hayat Qaflahbashi to persuade the poor husband of the lady to accept these terms, stating that otherwise he will incur the displeasure of that authority. The poor man had no remedy but to fly to Turkishtan, without taking the above mentioned sum. When her paramour was killed during the retreat of our forces from Kabul, she was also murdered by the Ghazis, with the remnant of our soldiers who had succeeded in making their way forcibly as far as Gandumakh.

Two other gentlemen lived opposite to the house of the Navab Mohammed Zaman Khan, and Quddos Khan, and wrought a change upon the affections of their respective favourites. When all endeavours failed to get them back, the good Navab wrote a civil note to the possessor of his fair one, saying that he himself had no need for her, and that he (the Englishman) had better keep her for ever. That gentleman having now been joined by his own wife has at length left her, I think, in an unprovided and destitute condition. But the other one, belonging to Quddos Khan, is well and respectably treated by her paramour, who has made a will to say that she was to claim his property in case of his death, in preference to any of his own relatives.

Mir Ahmad Khan, brother of Abdullah Khan Achakzai, was returning from Qandhar to marry a lady with whom he was engaged a long time before in Kabul. On his arrival near Ghazni he heard from his friends that she had left the roof of her parents, and taken shelter in the house of a "Sahab Log." He was incensed beyond all description, but could not show his face in Kabul; wherefore he turned back from the road and afterwards joined his brother in the insurrection in order to gain his revenge upon us; and the woman is now, I think, left unprovided at Lodianah.

These instances of gallantry in the gentlemen, with numerous cases of the same nature, were disgraceful and abhorrent to the habits and to the pride of the people whom we ruled; and it was the partiality of Sir Alexander Burnes to his friends in these circumstances which made him obnoxious to dislike, and wounded the feelings of the chiefs, who formerly looked upon him as their old friend and guardian. It was not he who committed himself in any sort of intrigue; but yet it was his duty to restore the ladies to their relations, and not to sacrifice his public name and duty through any private regard to his friends,—who, in return, never contradicted the accusations which were attached to him personally instead of to them. All of those friends knew well that Major Leach, Sir Alexander Burnes, his brother, and those who were subordinate to him, had Kashmerian females in their service, ever since he proceeded on a mission to Kabul, and no just man will deny this, and allow that they were persons to intrigue with the ladies in Kabul. Sir Alexander Burnes, indeed, bitterly suffered, or I may say lost his life, for the faults of others, as far as he appears concerned at all in such intrigues.

Exasperated and disgraced as the chiefs felt by the whole line of our conduct, they resolved first to attack the house of Sir Alexander Burnes; and they determined not to delay in perpetrating their deed to the fullest extent, lest, in the meantime, the plot might be discovered. Nayab Mohammed Sharif, and Taj Mohammed Khan, informed Sir Alexander Burnes of the conspiracy, and Mohammed Mirza Khan Javan Sher, one of the conspirators, called upon me the same evening in the house of that officer; and on my telling him that the Ghilzais were pacified by Major Macgregor, and that the force under Sir Robert Sale was victoriously proceeding towards Jelalabad, he seemed to laugh at my expression about pacifying the Ghilzais, and said seriously that to-morrow morning the very door I was sitting at will be in flames of fire, and yet still we pride ourselves in saying that we are safe. I told all this to Sir Alexander Burnes, whose reply was, that we must not let the people suppose that we are frightened, and that he will see what he can do in the cantonment; whither he started immediately. While I was talking with Sir Alexander Burnes an anonymous note reached him in Persian, confirming what he had already heard from me and from other sources, on which he said, "The time is arrived that we must leave this country."

CHAPTER XVIII.

The 2nd of November, 1841—Sir Alexander Burnes's house fired—His hard fate—How he might have been saved—The Shah's regiment defeated—Insurgents increase—Stores plundered—Hard fighting, on the 13th—Promised reward to Akbar Khan—Sir William Macnaghten shot by Akbar Khan—Unaccountable conduct of the troops—On the 6th of January the troops commenced their march—Lieutenant Eyre's account — Jelalabad maintained — Akbar Khan defeated—Government notification—The Shah fired upon and killed—Amin Ullah Khan defeated—Akbar gains Bala Hisar—Mohan Lal communicates with Sir George Pollock—Mohan Lal's services denied—Authorities quoted—The Amir restored.

THE sad dawn of the 2nd of November, 1841,—a Tuesday,—appeared awful to our wearied eyes, and an outbreak in the city immediately followed. It was about seven o'clock in the morning when the maid-servant knocked loudly at the door of my bed-room, and cried, "Agha * shuma khab hasted va shahar chappa shudah," meaning, you are asleep and the city is upset. I came out into my garden, and saw the people moving their goods to some secure place from my neighbourhood. The merchants were

* Masters are always addressed by servants in that name.

taking off their commodities from their shops, and the whole city appeared in commotion. Mirza Khodadad, secretary to the Sultan Jan, came to my house, and being my old acquaintance, warned me of the danger in which I was then standing, by remaining in my house, and not sending away my property. Nayab Mohammed Sharif also sent his father-in-law Mohammed Kamal, to fetch me to the Persian quarters, with all my valuable things. But I refused to attend to all their kind advice, fearing that my stirring from the house might increase the apprehension of the impending danger, and I sent my servant Abdullah Kashmiri, with a note to Sir Alexander Burnes* conveying to him the messages I had received, and desiring his advice for my guidance. His reply was, that I must remain in my house, and that he has sent for the troops, and that they will soon be in town. Half an hour after this, my servant informed me that the Nizam-ul-Daulah was advising that officer to quit his house and to proceed with him to the Bala Hisar, as there was very great

* His residence was separated by a few buildings from my house, on the right, and that of Captain Trevor was by my garden, on the left.

risk and danger to his personal safety. He then ordered his horse to be saddled, but his "Jamadar Nathu" from Bhuj reminded him of his sending a note to Sir William Macnaghten, and of the propriety of waiting for his answer. This changed the mind of Sir Alexander Burnes, who, from that time, repeatedly said to the Nizam-ul-Daulah, that he will not leave his place. On this the Minister proceeded towards the Bala Hisar, and was fired on from the top of the houses in the street, but unfortunately he did not part some of his guard, which was composed of sixty of the best Jazayarchis, but said that he will bring the Shah's own regiment for his protection. The principal rebels, as Abdullah Khan Achakzai, Amin Ullah, Sikandar, and Abdul Salam Khan, mounted their horses and came to the garden, very near to the residence of Sir Alexander Burnes. He sent a Sayad in his employ, with another horseman named Hamid, with a message to them, inquiring the reason of their thus suddenly appearing in open rebellion, and assuring them of his wish to restore their privileges to them. Before an answer was made to the Sayad, Sikandar Khan, one of the party, stood up and cut off his head with one stroke of his sword, without regarding the respect which was due to the blood of the poor Sayad, the descendant of his Holy Prophet. This caused the other servant of Sir Alexander Burnes to make his way back as fast as possible, and gave an ample proof to the lower class of the citizens of the determined resolution of the above-mentioned chiefs to overthrow our influence. On this, they ordered their handful of men to ascend the tops of the houses of the Tabchi bashi, and of the Agha husain, and to penetrate the garden attached to the Presidency, by the direction of Mirdad Khan's lodgings, and to open a fire on Sir Alexander Burnes. The door was ordered to be shut, and the guards of Sepoys were still prevented from using their muskets. Now about two hundred people assembled on all sides, and Sir Alexander Burnes, from the window of his upper room, demanded the insurgents to pacify themselves, and promised a handsome reward to all. While he was thus haranguing the mob, Captain Broadfoot received a ball just below his breast, and was brought down by Sir A. Burnes, and Charles Burnes, and placed in the room down stairs, and the guard being now under a sharp fire from the rebels, was compelled to oppose the advance. Some of the servants of Sir Alexander Burnes desired him to permit himself to be concealed and wrapped up in a tent, which they will carry off on their shoulders, like as others are carrying off plunder, but he said that he can neither leave his own brother nor his wounded friend Captain Broadfoot. Now Hazar Khan Kotval, whose bosom was full of revenge against Sir Alexander, came with Haji Ali, Hashim Kah Farosh, Kaka Husain, Abdul Rahim, Mohammed Husain Khan Arezbegi, and they set fire to the very door which Mohammed Mirza Khan Javan sher had mentioned to me the previous evening. The flames extended to the room where Sir Alexander and his brother were standing, looking at the multitude and begging for quarter, and Captain Broadfoot was consumed in it. Lieutenant Charles Burnes then came out into the garden and killed about six persons before he was cut to pieces. The people now became a large mob, and the balls passing the house of Sir Alexander Burnes were breaking the glass windows of my house, from the top of which I was witnessing this unhappy progress of the enemy. Some of them now came towards my house, and I ordered the door to be shut, and I went out through a hole in the neighbouring wall belonging to the Nazir Zafar, with the intention to bring Khan Shirin Khan, the Persian chief, to the assistance of Sir Alexander, and some of his men, to save my house from plunder. In the street I was seized by Nazir Ali Mohammed, and by several other "Khabgahis," who proposed to murder me on the very spot, and Shuja-ul-Daulah * gave hints to perpetrate the deed, while he was arming himself to join Abdullah Khan in attacking Sir Alexander Burnes. Providentially his father, the famous, kind-hearted Navab Mohammed Zaman Khan, came out of his house and upbraided those who had seized me, and snatching me from their hands, took me away and placed me among his ladies, who having received some assistance from me some time before, brought a sumptuous dish of "Pulav" for my breakfast. To enjoy this hospitality from the hands of the Afghan fair on other occasions would have been an unexpected and highly valued nourishment, but at the present disastrous moment every grain of the rice seemed to choak me in my throat, and I refused to touch the dish. I was now locked up in a dark room, and the

* He afterwards murdered the Shah Shuja-ul-mulk.

good Navab desired me to take off the rings from my fingers, and to conceal them somewhere, so that the avarice of his son might not tempt him to cut off my fingers with them! All my house was in the meantime plundered, and Khan Shirin Khan having heard on the road that Sir Alexander Burnes, to whose aid he was proceeding, was murdered by the rebels, went to protect Captain Trevor and his family.

The Shah's own regiment, under Mr. Campbell, came to support Sir Alexander Burnes, and had a hard conflict with the rebels, and as they received no succour, they were at last obliged to give way, nearly all of them being cut to pieces, and their guns captured.

Shah Zadah Fatah Jang was ordered by the king to pass into the city and to restore tranquillity, but this prince, whether with or without the permission of the Shah, or in consequence of the danger of his position amidst the rebellious mob, instead of adjusting matters, encouraged them to persevere in their tumult, adding "Prove yourselves to be the champions of the faith, and destroy the infidels (English)." My guardian the Navab became very apprehensive on hearing the name of the king connected with the rebels, who under such authority might attack his house, in order to get hold of my person. He therefore filled his house with armed men to protect me, and desired me to write to Sir William Macnaghten, on his part, that the Navab will remain in person in the cantonment, and will render service under his guidance to pacify all the insurgents, who, if the Shah is not their instigator, will not dare to stand up against him or his advice; and Navab sent this letter by his own men to the envoy, but no answer was returned.

I was now very anxious to be let out of the room, and to look from the top of the Navab Mohammed Zaman Khan's house (which commanded the residence of Sir Alexander Burnes), to find if possible what has befallen to that officer. The Navab took me up, and we saw that it was all in flames, and that the people were plundering his property, and even the wood of the house. The servants or guards of the Navab, who were on the top of the house watching the proceedings of the rebels, stated that after Charles Burnes was killed, and the fire had consumed the whole of the room, Sir Alexander Burnes was obliged to come to the door opening to his garden. Here he implored the multitude to save his life, but receiving a torrent of abuse from Nazar Ali Mohammed, Hazar Khan Kotval and the nephew of the Achkzai chief, and many others, whom he had unjustly offended by taking the part of his countrymen, he abandoned all hopes of safety. On this he opened up his black neckcloth and tied it on his eyes, that he should not see from what direction the blow of death strikes him. Having done this, he stepped out of the door, and in one minute he was cut to pieces by the furious mob. The treasury and house of Captain Johnson was also plundered and levelled with the ground, and a poor female was burnt in it.

While affairs were wearing such a sad and unfavourable aspect, and even Lieutenant Sturt was attacked and wounded in the presence of the Shah Shuja-ul-Mulk at the Bala Hisar, and Captain Lawrance at great personal risk made his way towards the cantonment, no defensive measures were taken on our part. Brigadier Shelton came and kept himself with his troops within the walls of the Bala Hisar, whereas, had he entered the city by any side, the life of Sir Alexander Burnes would have been saved, and that movement would have not only preserved the lives of thousands, but even would have suppressed the insurrection at the moment, for the rebels had secured the means of escape for themselves, and would have fled on the appearance of our troops; moreover, if Brigadier Shelton had arrived in the Bala Hisar while Sir Alexander Burnes was still alive in his own house in the city, order would have been restored.

In the evening, the Navab Mohammed Zaman Khan kindly offered to escort me either to the cantonment or into the Persian quarters, and he even accompanied me himself to the latter. The whole town was now in great alarm, and every minute they were expecting the arrival of our troops to blow up the town in order to revenge the murder of Sir Alexander Burnes, but none of the troops were ordered to move. On my arrival in the house of our kind host of Kabul, Nayab Mohammed Sharif Khan, the Persian chief, Khan Shirar Khan, an old and intimate friend of mine, thought it advisable that I should remain in his house, which will be a safer place than the house of the Nayab. I was now in great and painful anxiety and in a very disturbed state

CAPT^{N} COLIN MACKENZIE.

of mind at one time, thinking of my own safety, and at another time thinking of the melancholy loss I had suffered in the untimely end and most cruel murder of Sir Alexander Burnes, who had gained my attachment and respect by his continued desire to treat me as a friend. Khan Shirin Khan told me that, as soon as the outbreak took place in the city, he sent his officer Shah Ghasi to the envoy, requesting him to command his services, and that the answer was not so favourable as the chief had anticipated. The envoy sent him a message, that he will look upon him as an enemy if he will not seize Abdullah Khan. Nevertheless being unable to do this, Khan Shirin Khan remained, and saved Captain Trevor with his family for two days, and at last conducted them safely to the cantonment.

In the meantime Captain Colin Mackenzie still held possession of the fort "Qilai Nishan Khan," although no reinforcement was sent to him: but at length he and his party felt themselves in a state of great danger, and boldly made their way through the enemy to the cantonment, yet he was wounded on the road. In fact, all the brave commanders of our troops were paralyzed at this outbreak; and without using any of those energies which have always been displayed in the power and skill of the British arms, they let such awful deeds grow and prevail. While Captain Mackenzie held out the fort in the city against the rebels, he hoped that reinforcements will arrive and enable him to keep its possession. But when he had spent all his ammunition, and had lost every hope of receiving aid, he was compelled at length to leave it. The number of the insurgents from the country now increased, and the Navab Jabbar Khan, who had always until then proved himself hospitable and friendly to the British, entered the town accompanied by a large number of the villagers, beating a drum and haranguing the faithful to stand up against us: and the people from Kahdrah, Logar, and Vardak came in swarms to swell the number of our enemies in the city. In the former place also, Lieutenants Maul and Wheeler were barbarously murdered by the people of their own Kohistani regiment. On the 4th of November the rebels, having stationed themselves in the King's garden and the fort of Mohammed Sharif, destroyed the communication between our cantonment and the commissariat fort which stood outside of it. They then attacked the fort, and plundered all our commissariat stores, while no exertions were made to preserve such necessaries on which the life of the warriors depended: and thus the enemy was daily gaining spirit while it was sadly sinking amongst our troops. General Elphinstone was said to be in a weak state of bodily health, and Brigadier Shelton was desired to come to the cantonment from the Bala Hisar. He appeared from the commencement of the outbreak to despair of success, which produced a baneful effect in every fighting man. In short, he recommended to evacuate Kabul and to retreat to Jelalabad. Sir William Macnaghten, however, was averse to this plan, and taking the whole responsibility upon himself, he urgently desired the General to storm the fort of Rikabashi. While such uncertainty prevailed, I was negotiating with the Ghilzai chiefs through Nayab Mohammed Sharif, and my protector Khan Shirin Khan was promising every aid, and preparing to take our side, yet was still fearful to declare for us. In the mean time Sir William Macnaghten wrote to me as follows: "I am very glad to find that you are doing excellent service. Enclosed are two letters for Khan Shirar Khan and

Mohammed Hamzah.* You may assure them both, that, if they perform the service they have undertaken, the former shall receive one lakh and the latter fifty thousand rupees, and everything else they require. I hope you will encourage Mohammed Yar Khan, the rival of the Amin Ullah, and assure him that he shall have the chiefship. You may give promises in my name to the extent of five lakhs, and I fully approve your having raised thirty thousand rupees for distribution amongst those disposed to assist our cause, but I would not advance more than fifty thousand rupees before some service is actually rendered." We had not only sheltered our enemies under our own wings in the city, but had neglected the overtures made to us by the stern and hostile person on the frontier. In the city, the Navabs Jabbar Khan, Mohammed Zaman Khan, and Usman Khan, all Barakzais, were allowed to remain, after the Amir Dost Mohammed Khan was sent to India, and our conduct was daily adding to their

* He was deprived of the governorship of the Ghilzais, and confined by Nazam-ul-daulah ; and on the appearance of the insurrection he obtained his liberation, and took a leading part with the rebels against us.

discontent. On the frontier Mohammed Akbar appeared, and requested us to fix a separate allowance for him from that of his father, promising that then he will surrender himself to us. But the Envoy most likely was right to refuse such a proposal, and he wrote in this manner in reply, "That Mohammed Akbar's arrival at Bamian is likely enough. There can be little use, I fear, in offering him a separate remittance if the rebels have made overtures to him already."

On the 13th a hard day of fighting continued between our troops and the rebels till the evening, but our success of this day was destined to be the last one ;. and from this time misfortunes and blunders of every description surrounded the British arms and honour. Major Pottinger, with Lieutenant Haughton, were the only surviving officers of the unfortunate Gorkha regiment of Charkar, and they made their way, under great risk and fatigue, to the cantonment, while suffering from wounds. In Charkar, on the 3rd of November, when Major Pottinger was conferring with the Kohistan chiefs in the garden, and his assistant, Lieutenant Rattery, at a little distance, was negotiating with the other petty chiefs, the latter was suddenly shot, and the former obliged to secure himself within the fort; and all the negotiations failed. The cantonment, which was most unwisely situated far from water, could not be preserved under thirst, hunger, and the attack of the enemy, and it was therefore abandoned. The regiment, having fallen into confusion, was cut off by the rebels in all directions, and their females, with many other surviving Gorkhas, were distributed and sold as slaves. Sir William Macnaghten, on the arrival of Major Pottinger, wrote to me as follows:—"The Charkar regiment behaved ill, and has been for the most part destroyed; but Major Pottinger is safe in the cantonment."

Quandhar, Kelat-i-Ghilzai, Ghazni, and Jelalabad, were soon after surrounded by the swarms of rebels. The whole of Afghanistan was in a state of rebellion, and the Hazarbash cavalry had mutinied, and murdered their English officers. The Navab Mohammed Zaman Khan was elevated as a king, and the other rebel chiefs, though acting on their own judgment, did in some measure acknowledge his superiority. Mohammed Akbar Khan, taking the advantage of such a disastrous state of things, hastened to reach Kabul from Bamian. He wisely agreed to act under the Navab, but yet he was carrying on negotiations with the Envoy upon one hand, and making a separate party for himself on the other. The Ghilzais took his part, and did all to promote his interest, while they were not forgetful to desire money from us by promising their services to us, to the Shah, the Navab, and his coadjutors. Nayab Mohammed Sharif, under great personal risk, did all he could to buy over the Ghilzais in our favour. Sir William Macnaghten at first hesitated to advance the stipulated sum without having any security for the fulfilment of their agreement; but to this they objected on many groundless excuses, and the circumstances were so unfavourable, that we were compelled to accede to their demands. They wrote an agreement on the leaf of the Qoran, pledging themselves to wait upon the Shah, to open communication between us and Jelalabad, to supply us with provisions, and to espouse our cause openly. Upon this some of the Ghilzais came to the Envoy in the cantonment, and he advanced them money. They continued promising everything, and yet putting off the fulfilment from day to day. In the mean time the Envoy had lost every hope of aid from the troops, and was distressed to find that, if he fails in his negotiations, he cannot use force to make the Ghilzais or other chiefs adhere to their agreements. Thrown into such a dilemma, the Envoy and all his subordinates, like myself, had no other means but still to persevere in treating with the rebels, hoping perhaps we might yet succeed, though we had failed before. As our troops were daily losing their soldier-like spirits under the discouraging talk of retreat by their commander, Brigadier Shelton, this sad intelligence, being circulated in the cantonment, was thence unfortunately conveyed to the rebels by their countrymen who were in the service of our several officers. This made them perfectly careless about the claim of our power, and aware that we will neither sally out, nor keep our ground much longer without provisions. It was through the most active and extraordinary exertions of Captain Boyd, and especially of Captain Johnson,* that now and then a

* No one is better acquainted than myself of the influence he had on certain grain-sellers. His efforts in getting the supplies were miraculous, and successful in that crisis.

quantity of grain was brought for sale secretly into the cantonment.

However, this mode of obtaining supplies was not of long duration: and the military authorities, as they were always anxious about this affair, insisted upon the Envoy's negotiating with the chiefs for a retreat, whilst he entreated them either to keep their ground, or to go into the Bala Hisar, and thus to keep up the name and honour of the English government. In reply, a great many obstacles and dangers were thrown on the idea of the safety of the troops and camp-followers in passing between our cantonment and the Bala Hisar, a distance of nearly two miles and a half; while to travel for eight or ten days to go to Jelalabad through the frozen passes of the Khurd Kabul, Tezin, and Jagdallak, which were occupied by the ferocious and plundering Ghilzais, was considered by our military superiors far from dangerous!! Thus Sir William Macnaghten was forced to open the negotiation with the Barakzais; and the principal article of his agreement with Mohammed Akbar Khan and the other Barakzai chiefs was to evacuate Afghanistan, if all classes were desirous of our doing so. This article, however, retained for us the privilege of still remaining in Afghanistan, if a portion of the people or chiefs wished us to remain. Sir William Macnaghten had secured a good deal of grain through the Ghilzais; but as the military people were so obstinately desirous of a retreat, he feared to offend the Barakzais by having the grain thrown in, and therefore with much reluctance he wrote to me on the evening of the 22nd December, "Pray forbid the Ghilzais to bring up grain to-night. The sending grain to us just now would do more harm than good to our cause." The same night Mohammed Saddiq, accompanied by Captain Skinner and the treacherous Sarvar Khan Lohani, waited upon the Envoy, and offered, on the part of the Sardar Mohammed Akbar Khan, that if the Envoy was to promise a certain sum of money, the Sardar will seize Amin Ullah Khan, on receiving such a promise in the form of a written document. The offer was not received by the Envoy altogether without suspicion; but as he had no hope of military aid, and considered the idea of retreat disgraceful to the British name, he was just like a drowning man catching at straws, and sensibly running the risk of all sorts of evils, with the view of reserving any chance of success. On this he wrote the paper required, saying that if Mohammed Akbar Khan performs the service he has undertaken, he will be rewarded. Mohammed Saddiq and Sarvar Khan Lohani assured the Envoy of the sincerity of Mohammed Akbar Khan, who, in consequence of his parents and family being in the power of the British general, will faithfully promote the objects of the Envoy; and they requested the Envoy to keep this secret from every one, lest it might reach the ears of Amin Ullah Khan.

Mirza Khodadad, the Secretary to the Sultan Jan, and Mohammed Saddiq Khan, who was present in the room with them when Mohammed Akbar Khan consulted with Mohammed Shah Khan, for perpetrating this deed of blood, informed me secretly of the plot. He stated that Akbar has laid a deep scheme to entrap the Envoy, and that if he succeeds in bringing him alive into the city, he will force him to give up to him all the ammunition, the treasury, &c., and will then cause his death by poison, and that otherwise he will shoot him with the very pistols the Envoy presented to him the other night. This was said to me by the Mirza about 10 A.M., on the 23rd of December, 1841, and I sent Qurban Ali* to the Envoy with a note and the message which Mirza Khodadad had related. The Envoy was just then conversing with the Mustaufi, on the deputation of Akbar, and just preparing to start for the fatal conference with him, when my messenger delivered to him the note, and told him in the ear what a conspiracy had been formed against him. Sir William Macnaghten changed the colour of his countenance as if he were either annoyed with the information or alarmed at the intelligence. He had now no other remedy, however, but to run personal risks in order to preserve the honour of his country and of the government, for even the troops left him alone at the time when his life was in danger. He entreated the military authorities to have two regiments ready outside the cantonment, with the view that, if Mohammed Akbar Khan was sincere, he might employ them for offensive acts against Amin Ullah Khan,

* This person stood in great confidence and esteem with Sir Alexander Burnes for taking despatches to Hirat and the Persian camp; and the Envoy wrote to me once in his behalf as follows: "I should be glad if you would send with the Ghilzais this evening the messenger you were formerly in the habit of sending, as he is well acquainted with this place."

THE LATE SIR WILLIAM HAY MACNAGHTEN BART.

and if he was not sincere, they would take a defensive part and protect his person. Alas! all his extraordinary exertions to keep the honour of Great Britain from disgrace at such a crisis, which would have melted an iron framed body by care and alarm, were useless, and produced not the slightest shadow of energy in the bosom of the officers and soldiers of his country. Captains Lawrance, Mackenzie, and perhaps Trevor, warned him of the danger; to which he replied, "Dangerous it is, but, if it succeeds, it is worth all risks; the rebels have not fulfilled one article of the treaty, and I have no confidence in them, and if by it we can only save our honour, all will be well; at any rate, I would rather suffer a hundred deaths than live the last six weeks over again."

"A plot! let me alone for that,—trust me for that!"

In short Sir William Macnaghten went out of the cantonment to meet Mohammed Akbar, and looked back and saw that no troops were ordered according to his suggestion, and knew even that the military authorities made an excuse to employ them on such an occasion. While conferring with the treacherous

Akbar, the Envoy was suddenly caught by him and Sultan Jan, and when he refused to mount on horseback, he was dragged down from the cliff, shot by Mohammed Akbar Khan with the very same pistols, and wonderful to add, loaded and then presented by the Envoy himself.* Mohammed Shah Khan Ghilzie, and his brother Dost Mohammed Khan, saved Captains Lawrance and Mackenzie,† and brought them on their own horses into the fort of Mahmud Khan Bayat, and Captain Trevor fell a victim to the revenge of Mulla Momin, whom, with many other chiefs, he had most imprudently offended by discharging a great number of his followers, when introducing the fatal reform in the military class, which deprived them of their livelihood, and which was also wrong in principle.

* In him I lost the best and noblest friend in the world. I knew him from 1834, and he was the best judge of his placing confidence in me, being a constant medium of my communications with the Supreme Government. Some misinformed person, if not malicious, put in the Indian papers that I had cast some slanders on the character of that dignified and lamented authority. It is utterly false. No one regrets his loss so bitterly as I do, and no one more gratefully feels pride in speaking of his high talents and character than I do.

† Read their letters on the murder of their political chief, Sir William Macnaghten.—*Eyre's Diary.*

On the fall of Sir William Macnaghten, Mohammed Akbar Khan put the first stroke of his sword on his throat, and then his head was severed from his body, and brought into the house of the Navab Mohammed Zaman Khan. His body was dragged away and was hung up in the Bazar for the public view, while the assassin, Mohammed Akbar Khan, triumphed by, bearing the drawn and bloody sword in his hand when returning to the city, and receiving with pride the congratulations of the Ghazis. There has been a good deal of difference of opinion whether Mohammed Akbar Khan shot the Envoy, or if the deed was perpetrated by the Ghazis. He formerly repeatedly expressed with pride, that he was the assassin of the Envoy, in the presence of many noblemen and of myself.* The difference of opinion and the doubt on the subject have not unjustly been raised by those who, while dining and conversing with the assassin during their imprisonment, flattered him most imprudently by giving him the views of all the parliamentary speeches, and by assuring him that England will not keep possession of Afghanistan, but

* He confessed in a letter to his murdering the Envoy, which was intercepted by the illustrious garrison of Jelalabad.

that it disapproved of the policy of the Indian Government, and has ordered the evacuation of that country. Why such information and speeches were translated by some of us to please Akbar Khan is a matter for others to determine, and is not one of my suggesting. The body of the Envoy, after hanging for three days in the public street, was thrown into a ditch, behind the treasury of Captain Johnson, and his head was sent to the Vali of Khulam, and this statement was confirmed by several servants of Colonels Stoddart and Conolly, who had seen it in returning from Bokhara. They affirm that they saw it with their own eyes conveyed in the nose-bag of the horse.* Such was the deplorable end of Sir William Macnaghten, who, unassisted by troops, preferred the loss of his life to that of the honour of his country and government, by evacuating Kabul while himself was alive; and very extraordinary indeed was the heroism of the British officers and troops, to see their chief murdered within the distance of musket-shot, in the face of the English camp, and

* Never was his real head found. It was merely to deceive and take money from Major Leech when a man came from Kabul, and presented an account of his finding it, and bringing it at great risk to India.

yet not to fire a gun on the perpetrators of the murder, nor on the draggers of his body which lay for some time in the plain! I repeat it here again, that if the pride of power had not wrought upon the minds of political chiefs, they were sufficiently aware of the impending danger, and fully able to destroy it before it broke open on our heads; and the insurrection would not have grown so fatally strong, and continued from the 2nd of November to the 22nd of December, if four companies of soldiers from the cantonment had been sent to save Sir Alexander Burnes in the commencement of the outbreak. And if the two regiments, as ordered by Sir William Macnaghten, had been sent out when he proceeded to treat with Mohammed Akbar Khan, the Envoy in all probability would not have been murdered. With his sad loss came the loss of spirits to every one in the cantonments; the loss of the British honour in Central Asia, and an open field was left for certain military men, who were insisting upon him to negotiate for retreat.

Major Pottinger took the political charge after the death of Sir William Macnaghten,* and he found all

* If the Envoy had not been murdered, he would have re-

the demands of the rebels increased, and that in spite of all his own judgment, as well as that of others of his department, he also was urged to quit the capital; a negotiation which commenced with the chiefs, and ended at the evacuation of the cantonment. No regard was shown to the articles of the tripartite treaty, and the Shah Shuja-ul-Mulk was left at the mercy of his enemies, to whom we had given shelter during his government of the last two years. Had it not been for us, he, acting as an independent sovereign, and on the usual customs of the country, would have destroyed all the Barakzais, and have thus freed us and himself from these fatal consequences; herein, however, we interfered, and allowed Jabbar Khan, Zaman Khan, Usmán Khan, and other Barakzais, to remain and now intrigue

mained in Kabul, or at least in the Bala Hisar, till the spring would have brought reinforcements from India, and there was plenty of provisions and wood. All his letters in my possession show his disgust at the word of retreat; and up to the 22nd of December he was trying to gain his object, and was expressing his opinions thus to me: "If the people quarrel amongst themselves, and we are allowed to remain, it would be very agreeable to stop here for a few months, instead of having to travel through the snow. I will spend any sum to effect that purpose; but no time is to be lost."

with the malcontents against us. By the new agreements the chiefs became possessed of the magazine fort, the guns, and bills of money to be drawn on India, and in return they were to escort our troops safely to Jelalabad. This was not indeed their intention, for their object was to see us once out of the cantonment, and then to plunder and imprison us. Khan Shirin Khan, the Persian chief, informed me of this fact, and desired me to dissuade our authorities from marching towards Butkhak, and said that we had better enter the Bala Hisar. I accordingly wrote what the Khan stated to my political chief in the cantonment, and the secretary replied thus:—"Thanks for your kind letter, and the hints it contains. The chiefs you name have signed the treaty, and the most of them accompany us. As for others attacking us on the road, we are in the hands of God, and in him we trust. We hope to be off tomorrow."

On the 6th of January, the British army, consisting of 4500 fighting men and nine guns, commenced the march from the cantonment. The Persian chief Khan Shirin Khan forced me to go back with him to Kabul; and our forces, as soon as they were out of the cantonment, were in confusion and disorder. The enemy were soon busy plundering and burning the cantonment, and soon after commenced firing upon us. The guns were then left, and the sepoys as well as their European brothers in arms were exhausted by hunger and fatigue, and equally paralysed with the havoc caused by the Ghazis. When Mohammed Akbar Khan joined with the avowed intention to annihilate our army, and to make the English ladies and gentlemen his prisoners, the Afghans were more ferocious in their attacks. He spoke to them in Persian, seemingly to prevent them from committing offence, and then in Turkish, engaging them to plunder and seize us, as some of the officers could not understand that language. Many officers, soldiers, and sepoys, with numerous followers, were shot, wounded, and left on the ground to perish by cold; and thousands being unable to move, sank down in despair. Soon afterwards they were seen perished and frozen to death, exhibiting a fearful group of snow-burnt bodies, which covered the face of the road, and particularly of the pass. The treacherous Mohammed Akbar was also gradually getting possession of several officers as hostages, so that by these means the strength of the force was totally weakened, and by the 13th of January all the officers became prisoners to the assassin of the Envoy, and the whole army was thus annihilated. No better account is given of these disasters than that of Lieutenant Eyre, who, as a Christian and an upright person, has spoken the truth freely; and I can promise all persons interested in those sad affairs that they will not be disappointed if they throw a glance over his most interesting 'Diary.'

On the 18th of January, the Sardar Mohammed Akbar Khan, with Sultan Jan, Mohammed Shah Khan, and the other Ghilzai chiefs, proceeded on an expedition to reduce Jelalabad, and left all the British prisoners, or rather the survivors of the retreating force of General Elphinstone, in Badiabad. When Sir R. Sale and Major Macgregor refused to evacuate Jelalabad, as ordered by General Elphinstone and by Major Pottinger, Mohammed Akbar Khan could not be convinced of the reasonableness of the rule that a *prisoner*, however exalted in rank, is not obeyed by any subordinate, however inferior he may be. He assembled a considerably large force of

Ghazis in the mean time, and gradually approached to and besieged Jelalabad. He was every day attacking our foraging parties, planning the storm of the place, and endeavouring to mine it, and he was at the same time laying a trap by negotiations for Major Macgregor, who was however too wise to be deceived by him. Mohammed Akbar Khan used his influence more powerfully in Kabul, and made the Shah Shuja-ul-Mulk to write to Major Macgregor to leave Jelalabad, and to say that His Majesty will escort the garrison safely to Peshavar. The fortress of Ghazni was also surrendered to the enemy, and the Kelat-i-Ghilzai abandoned. Sir William Nott was surrounded by the rebels, headed by Prince Safdar Jang, and, though always victorious, he could not move towards Kabul before the harvest was ripe. Sir George Pollock's army was detained in Peshavar longer than was anticipated, and Colonel Moseley's retreat from Ali Makjid gave further signs that no reinforcement can immediately be expected. The supply of provisions, of ammunition, and of money fell short, and the communication was entirely cut off from Peshavar with the brave garrison of Jelalabad. It was only through the able and extraordinary exertions of Major Mackison that now and then small sums of money, &c. were conveyed by Turrah Baz Khan to Major Macgregor. In the mean time, Mohammed Akbar Khan was accidentally wounded in the arm by the musket of his servant being fired off by chance when helping him to mount his horse. This created a strong impression in the mind of Akbar, who burnt alive the innocent man, and being incensed by the false idea that he had been induced to shoot him either by the Shah or by Major Macgregor, he furiously determined to gain possession of Jelalabad, and of the persons of its gallant officers, whether by force of arms or by the means of negotiation. Mohammed Akbar Khan wrote to the rebel chiefs in Kabul, and I read the letter myself (whether what it told was true or false), stating that the "Kafir" (infidel) Macgregor will not negotiate in any way with him, and that he has been informed from an authentic source that he (Macgregor), Colonel Dennie, Major Broadfoot, and Captain Abbot have taken a prominent part in persevering to maintain the possession of Jelalabad, which they declare they will not quit while they bear heads on their shoulders. The ramparts of the town were made defensible by the extraordinary abilities of Major Broadfoot, and Major Macgregor never placed any reliance on the negotiations of Mohammed Akbar Khan, and always insisted on preserving the British honour by a firm stand at Jelalabad.

In writing to Major Mackison, the Political Agent at Peshavar, he appears still persevering in the same sound opinion, even up to the 23rd of March, two weeks before the signal defeat of Mohammed Akbar. "Pray, tell the General (Sir George Pollock) that no good can possibly arrive from entering into a negotiation with this young Hotspur Akbar."

On the 5th and 6th of April, 1842, the heroic garrison of Jelalabad heard rumours of the reverses of Sir George Pollock's army in the Khaibar Pass, and resolved at once to strike a blow on the enemy's camp, and thus to relieve itself from further vexation in being starved and invested by the merciless Afghans. It was the ever-memorable morning of the 7th, which gloriously dawned on this brave garrison, who, having been formed into three columns, attacked and surprised the camp of Mohammed Akbar. The centre was led by the heroic and deeply-lamented officer Colonel Dennie, who was shot just after securing the honour of the British name and arms in the face of an inveterate enemy. Mohammed Akbar Khan fled with precipitate haste towards Lamghan; and Mohammed Husain Khan Arzbegi, with numerous other chiefs, followers of Akbar, were so much alarmed by an idea of being pursued and overtaken by Sir Robert Sale, that they hurried their flight and arrived the next morning in Kabul, some without shoes, some without clothes on their person, and others riding the unsaddled horses. This glorious victory, gained by such a small garrison, has for ever established the martial name of the English army, with fear and praise. The Government of India acknowledged the services of Major Macgregor, on the 19th May, in the most flattering manner:—"I am directed by the Governor-General [Lord Ellenborough] to offer you his Lordship's acknowledgments for the indefatigable zeal and assiduity, and the unbending spirit with which you executed your duty in Jelalabad, from the entrance of Major-General Sir Robert Sale into that place, to the period of its ultimate relief by the advance of the army under Major-General Sir George Pollock; and his Lordship will be happy should any suitable opportunity offer itself of evincing his sense of your merit."

Let me return to the state of things in Kabul. After the departure of General Elphinstone's force from the cantonment, and its annihilation on the road to Jelalabad, Amin Ullah Khan Logri, the Durrani chiefs, and Khan Shirin Khan, declared themselves openly, and waited upon the Shah Shuja-ul-Mulk. It was indeed necessary that the Navab, Mohammed Zaman, who was a few weeks ago acknowledged as a sovereign, and called Shah Zaman, should give up that title—should tender his homage to the Shah Shuja—should assume the station of Vazir (minister) under him—and that the Amin Ullah himself, the agent of the latter, should submit in like manner. Confidence could neither be procured by the Navab Mohammed Zaman Khan, by the Barakzais, nor by the Shah Shuja-ul-Mulk, the Sadozais. The former hesitated to wait upon the Shah for fear of being apprehended; and the latter was afraid that, by opening the gates of the Bala Hisar, and allowing the Barakzais to be inside of it, he might lose the place altogether. Oaths after oaths were exchanged; and the Amin Ullah, with the

Persian chief, assured the Shah of the fidelity of all classes of the people. His Majesty, finding his situation very delicate and not safe, pretended to harangue the "faithful" to destroy and discard us from Jelalabad; and he distributed dresses of honour and sums of money to divert their attention. The King had his trust entirely in the Logri chief; and Mohammed Zaman Khan, with his Barakzai clansmen, was watching for a favourable opportunity to upset the influence of the Amin Ullah, and to extricate the Sadozais from Kabul. All the Barakzais could not bear the overgrown power of a commoner of Logar, who was always in their employ. Letter after letter was received from Akbar Khan, urging the necessity for a reinforcement from Kabul; but the family jealousy between the Barakzais, and their joint hatred of Amin Ullah Khan, upon one hand, and the old rivalry of the Durranis of all classes with the Barakzais; the daily growing dependence of the Shah on the Logar chief, and a desperate thirst of all in general for snatching money from the King, upon the other, became a chief topic of the concerns of the day, and thus no attention was paid to the affairs of Jelalabad.

Meanwhile the intelligence of the movement of the British army towards Peshavar, and a copy of the notification issued by the Earl of Auckland, was brought by a merchant from Peshavar, and given to the Navab Mohammed Zaman Khan. He came to the Persian chief, Khan Shirin Khan, and asked him where was his (Navab's) "Rafiq," friend, meaning myself. I was sent for, and the Navab was very courteous, and told me before the whole assembly that I must rest assured that the British army will soon come to Kabul; and then, taking out of his pocket the copy* of the said noti-

* *Notification by the Government of India.*

"INTELLIGENCE having been received which leaves no room to doubt that, after the British force at Kabul had maintained its position against overpowering numbers of insurgents for more than six weeks, the officer commanding had judged it necessary, in consequence of a failure in provisions, to agree to a convention with the enemy, and to retire, in reliance on the faith of that convention, towards Jelalabad, when the troops, exposed to the worst rigours of cold and privation on the mountain defiles, and harassed by treacherous attacks, suffered extreme disasters,—the Governor-General (Earl of Auckland) in Council deems it proper to notify that the most active measures have been adopted, and will be stedfastly prosecuted, for expediting powerful reinforcements to the Afghan frontier, and for assisting such operations as may be required in that quarter for the maintenance of the honour and interest of the British Government.

"The ample military means at the disposal of the British

fication, he requested me to read. It was indeed a masterly resolution; but, as I said before, it was not put into execution immediately. This notification created so much alarm and consternation, that the wealthy persons removed their property to a distance, and did not return to town till long after the retreat of Sir George Pollock's army from Kabul.

However, the rebel chiefs insisted upon the Shah Shuja-ul-Mulk marching in person towards Jelalabad, and checking the progress of the British troops in the Khaibar. The Shah, having already suffered by his unwise speech with the Durranis previous to the

Government will be strenuously applied to these objects, so as at once to support external operations and to ensure efficient protection to its subjects and allies.

"A faithless enemy, stained by the foul crime of assassination, has, through a failure of supplies, followed by consummate treachery, been able to overcome a body of British troops, in a country removed, by distance and by the difficulties of the season, from the possibility of succour. But the Governor-General in Council, while he most deeply laments the loss of the brave officers and men, regards this partial reverse only as a new occasion for displaying the stability and vigour of the British power, and the admirable spirit and valour of the British Indian army.

"By order of the Right Honourable the Governor-General of India in Council.

"T. H. Maddock."

outbreak, was soon sensible of his error and the dilemma in which he was placed. He was consequently very unwilling to proceed; and therefore he put it off from day to day, hoping that the reinforcements from India might soon arrive, and that he might then co-operate with them to destroy the enemy. The rebels began to suspect him for being friendly disposed to the British; and Mir Haji, the fanatic priest of Kabul, pitched out his tent, and proclaimed his avowed intention of proceeding to Jelalabad, and inviting all the Musulmans to join him. The Navab Mohammed Zaman Khan was secretly intriguing with the Haji against the Amin Ullah, and at the same time desirous to become a powerful man in Kabul. All the nobles insisted upon the Shah marching with the Haji; and the Navab sent his wife at night to the King in the palace, with a written agreement in the Qoran that he was devotedly attached to his Majesty, and will faithfully promote the interest of his government. On this assurance of the Navab Mohammed Zaman Khan, the head of the Barakzais, being conveyed and communicated to his Majesty by a female of such distinction as his (the Navib's) wife, he fixed the day of his march for the

5th of April. Shuja-ul-Daulah, whether with the knowledge of his father the Navab or not, but certainly instigated by the Sardar Mohammed Usman Khan, and by the Navab Jabbar Khan, on the one hand, and incensed at the appointment of the son of the Amin Ullah Khan as governor of the city during the absence of the Shah and the chiefs, on the other, determined to revenge himself upon the Shah, and thus to gain a higher name than Mohammed Akbar Khan did in murdering Sir William Macnaghten. He consulted with some adventurers, as Shahghasi Dilavar and Nur Mohammed Khan-i-Reka, &c., in all about sixty well-armed persons; and he went early in the morning and placed himself on the road between the Bala Hisar and the royal camp. The Shah, attended by a few Hindostanis, came out of his palace in a litter (jampan), and was first fired upon by Shuja-ul-Daulah. In the hope of still being saved, he threw himself out of it, and ran towards the small ditch of an adjoining field, but was overtaken and again fired upon. His Majesty implored the mercy of the assassin, and cried out, "Az barai khoda Sardar Sarkar che gunah kardak?" ("For God's sake, save me!—what offence have I done?")

Shuja-ul-Daulah paid no attention to this; and then a volley of musketry was poured upon the Shah, who instantly fell lifeless. The assassin fled to his house, and the corpse of the Shah was left lying for several hours on the ground.* The report of the murder of the Shah was soon spread, to the surprise and in-

* It was the custom of the Shah Shuja-ul-Mulk to have all his precious diamonds and valuable stones in a bag always in his pocket, in the fear that he might meet some reverse unexpectedly, and that he should not lose them by keeping them in a box at his palace. When he was fired at, he took the bag out of his pocket and threw it in the field, in the hope of having it again if his life were saved. His assailants did not perceive it; but an Afghan, who was merely a spectator at a distance, saw the Shah throwing something aside, and came there afterwards at night, and picked up the bag full of diamonds. He was a real Afghan, a savage of the mountains, and thought the prize nothing but common stones of different colours. He showed it to a Khatri in Charsu, who, taking advantage of the ignorance of the Afghan, told him they were common stones, but he would give him ten pounds if he would part with them. They were valued at nearly a million, yet he gave up the stones for this trifling sum. A third person saw this, and after taking five pounds from the purchaser to keep the matter secret, he went to Shuja-ul-Daulah, and reported the circumstance. The purchaser was immediately summoned, tied to the mouth of a gun, and threatened to be blown up if he did not give up the whole of the diamonds. The poor man was thus compelled to deliver up his prize, and was not paid his expenses. Thus fell the property of the Shah into the hands of his assassin.

dignation of all the chiefs; and the Amin Ullah Khan, taking their side, became a powerful opponent of the Barakzais. Prince Fatah Jang was placed on the throne, and called on the chiefs to punish the murderers of his father.

Hence a deep-rooted misunderstanding took place between the Navab Mohammed Zaman Khan, who also proclaimed himself to be the king, in opposition to the Amin Ullah Khan and the Durrani chiefs. Now, there were thus two kings in one town. However, the Amin Ullah Khan, at the instigation of Ahmad Khan Biranj Farosh, desired Navab Mohammed Zamar Khan to deliver up the person of Captain John Conolly, and of other hostages, to remain in the charge of Mir Haji the priest. He succeeded in this; and that officer, with other of his companions, was now under a strict watch; and no one was allowed to see him, except Ahmad Khan, whose object was to procure bills in large sums for paying small amounts, and thus to keep the whole management of affairs in his own hands, without the slightest interference of any other person. He, of course, paid something now and then to the Amin Ullah Khan, whom he convinced that he was his friend and an enemy to us; and at the same time he stated to Captain Conolly that he was doing service to him under great personal risk. Captain Conolly told me himself that this scoundrel, in conjunction with his own writer, Haji Mir, kept all his separate bills of different amounts, after taking one in total amount for them all.

In the mean time the Amin Ullah Khan, influenced by the money of Fatah Jang, and the association of the Durrani chiefs, proposed to fight with the Navab Mohammed Zaman Khan, and by persuading the Priest Mir Haji to speak in favour of the latter, he was attacked by every citizen on every side, defeated, and obliged to take refuge with the Prince Fatah Jang in the Bala Hisar. This was indeed a proper time and a favourable field open for the display of the tact and intrigues of the Sardar Mohammed Akbar Khan. He lost no time in making his appearance during these internal commotions, and gained universal applause by declaring with cunning hypocrisy that it was the time that all home quarrels and interests should be buried under ground, and that all should join together to put off the external enemy (English) of the religion and honour of the "faithful." He accordingly opened negotiations with the Amin Ullah Khan, and addressed letters to him, calling him his father, and stating his attachment to the distinguished person of the Amin Ullah Khan, who had taken so prominent a part in protecting the "Islam" or Mohammedan faith. Meanwhile he was siding with the Navab Mohammed Zaman Khan against the Prince Fatah Jang and the Amin Ullah Khan, till after many skirmishes and much warfare the latter was obliged to confer with the Sardar Mohammed Akbar Khan, with whom he entered into treaty and begged His Royal Highness to go and meet him outside of the Bala Hisar. It is stated that he and Akbar had basely conspired to lay hold of the Prince, and therefore the Arabs of the citadel objected to the going out of Fatah Jang, and Mohammed Akbar could not trust himself to come in, and so the Amin Ullah left the royal family to join his new ally. Several days rolled on, and the Bala Hisar was closely invested and attacked by the united forces of the Navab Mohammed Zaman and of the Sardar Mohammed Akbar Khan. The Durranis stood by in a cowardly state of neutrality and there was only the Prince Fatah Jang with the other royal descendants, the Hindostanis, and his secretary Merza Haidar Ali, repelling bravely the repeated assaults of the overpowering number of the Barakzais. Money was not spared, and every exertion was used to uphold the citadel, to preserve the honour of the royal family, and to act on the advice of Sir George Pollock. The Prince Fatah Jang, in time of need, himself headed the party to repel the enemy from the ramparts; but the ammunition was exhausted, and there was no other means to procure it for any sum but by a little now and a little then through my agency. The Sardar Mohammed Akbar Khan at last conducted a mine under the large tower of the Bala Hisar called Burj-i-Majanju, and the mine was blown, and the battering guns which had been left by us in the cantonment, and which were now in possession of the Barakzais, were opened on the same tower. On the 7th of June Mohammed Akbar Khan became master of the fortress, and of the guns, &c., through the treachery of Darvesh Mohammed Khan, the Arab chief, who allowed Amin Ullah with his party to enter it, and thus forced the Prince to surrender. The Sardar Mohammed

Akbar Khan was not forgetful of the designs of the Navab Mohammed Zaman Khan by taking a share in storming the Bala Hisar, knowing that it was done in order to establish his own influence as an equal if not a superior to Akbar; and he therefore took precaution whereby to avoid this, and he succeeded.

The Sardar Mohammed Akbar Khan did neither allow the Shuja-ul-Daulah, the son of the Navab Mohammed Zaman Khan, to go inside of the Bala Hisar, nor to station any of his men at the gate. This caused a fatal disappointment to the Navab, and Mohammed Akbar soon bought over to his own side the Sardar Mohammed Usman Khan, Mir Haji the priest, and other staunch adherents of his rival uncle. After this he waited upon the Prince Fatah Jang, and in order to deceive him, he did not sit down in his presence, but continued to show him the highest nominal respect till he got plenty of money from him; and after a hard fight of a whole day he deprived Mohammed Zaman Khan of his guns and of all the weapons of war. His followers were all dispersed or gained over, and himself made a secondary chief. Mohammed Akbar Khan was now without the fear of an internal rival, and there was no hinderance for him to accomplish his objects with the Prince. He placed him on the throne and became himself his minister, and continued to show him some outward respect until he extorted all the money and a great part of the jewels and of the silver and gold utensils from that helpless king Prince Fatah Jang, and then confined him at last in a room out of the palace, whence he made his escape to the Persian quarters, and then was escorted by the brother of Amin Ullah Khan to the camp of Sir George Pollock. The Sardar Mohammed Akbar Khan had now gained possession of all things belonging to the royal household, and found himself in the zenith of glory.

I shall now invite the attention of the readers to the hardships and the anxiety under which the British prisoners laboured who were in the hands of Mohammed Akbar Khan, and were dragged about from one place to another. I shall also briefly touch upon the circumstances which occurred during our imprisonment, and which were connected with us and Akbar, as well as the duties which fell to my lot to perform. It must be recollected, that on the departure of the forces of General Elphinstone, I was brought back from Siah Sang to the Persian quarters in Kabul, and remained under the protection of the Persian chief, Khan Shirin Khan, nearly to the end of June. I was treated by him with much consideration, and enjoyed within my allotted room all the blessings of freedom; but I was not allowed to go out of the room to see any one secretly from him. His son-in-law, my old friend Sultan Mohammed Khan, also slept in the room where I was living, and he amused me always with his conversation and anecdotes, as did also the Nayab Mohammed Sherif. He knew that I was corresponding with Sir George Pollock, but he had plainly told me, that if any of my letters was intercepted by our enemy, he should not then be able to protect me, and would be compelled to give me up; and I therefore took all the responsibility on my own shoulders. Various chiefs, while in power, demanded Khan Shirin Khan to deliver me to them, but he was ever ready to abuse them for the idea of disgracing his name by taking me off from his protection; and the divisions amongst the chiefs were so numerous, that no one could exactly use force against him without offending others. Though

I was not free from external danger, yet I did not fail to negotiate with the chiefs, to detach them from the enemy, to communicate with the Prince, to send ammunition into the Bala Hisar, for the use of his Royal Highness; and, above all, to send regularly the intelligence of the state of things and of parties in Kabul to the Government and to Sir George Pollock.

On the 22nd of June, Mohammed Akbar Khan, having gained superiority over all the chiefs, sent a party into the house of Khan Shirin Khan, which seized and conducted me into the house where Major Pottinger and Captain Mackenzie lived. From thence I was taken and placed in the house of Mohammed Mirza Khan, in charge of Sultan Jan, and thence delivered to Mulla Jalal Achkakzai, who tortured me and ill-treated me in other ways. It was only the tone of dissatisfaction which the letter from the Governor General showed, and the conversation of Sir George Pollock with Haji Bakht Yar Khan, that after some time produced a change in the steps of Mohammed Akbar, who stopped in his ill-treatment, and moved me from the house of that cruel Mulla Jalal on the 29th of July, and lodged

CAPT^N JOHN CONOLLY.

me where Major Pottinger, and the Captains John Conolly, Drummond, Troup, Lawrence, and other hostages had been living ever since Mohammed Akbar Khan had possession of the Bala Hisar; and even here, while under the same guard as other officers were, I contrived to keep up my communication with Sir George Pollock, under great personal risk. A few extracts which I quote here will explain the nature of my duties, and the difficulties and dangers which I encountered in executing them. The regular messengers to carry out my letters could not be employed for fear of being intercepted on the road, which was on every inch watched by the people of Mohammed Akbar Khan. I therefore ran the risk of securing the aid of the very men of Akbar himself and of the other rebel chiefs, by money, and I fortunately succeeded. They accordingly took my letter, which was very closely written on the small thin paper, and concealed it under the lock of their musket, which they bore on their shoulder, and proceeded in this manner as if they were really going to harass the camp of Sir George Pollock.

While living with the hostages near the house of Mohammed Akbar Khan, I had frequent conversations with Captain John Conolly, an officer of the most amiable and noble character. I was intimately acquainted with him, as well as with his two brothers, the one killed in Tutam Drah, as I mentioned already, and the other murdered by the savage king of Bokhara. Captain John Conolly spoke very firmly on my behalf to Mohammed Akbar Khan, when I was suffering in person from his cruel treatment, and also by the extortion of money; and on my joining the hostages, he was so good as to give up his bed and room to me. With him I was perfectly easy and happy; but unfortunately this enjoyment was not of long duration. He was suffering ever since the disasters mentioned above by a sad pain at the heart, caused through the public misfortunes; and he could not bear to think a moment of the disgrace and misfortunes which had stained the arms and honour of his country; and thus his mind was agitated so much that at length it produced disease. No one was so much liked by the people of the country as Captain John Conolly was. He was a universal favourite; and it was his amiable disposition and polite manners which induced the people to lend him large sums of money, wherewith to feed, to heal, and to clothe, hundreds of the sick and wounded of our soldiers and camp-followers.

In addition to all the calamities of Kabul, he had the melancholy news to hear, that his brother, Captain Arthur Conolly, had been murdered by the King of Bokhara, which sad tidings hastened to increase his illness; and this advanced so fast, that in a very short time he breathed his last, on the 7th of August. His loss was sincerely lamented by us all, and, I may say, by every one in Kabul.

Captain Arthur Conolly was in England when the army of the Indus marched into Afghanistan, to place Shah Shuja on the throne of Kabul. He arrived there after six or nine months, and, as I stated before, he went on a mission to Khiva, where he completed the object of his embassy. He went thence to Kokan, and when there, a very worthy feeling of ambition induced him to think that his presence might aid to throw a light on the dark mind of the Uzbeg king, which he considered Colonel Stoddart was unable to do alone. While we were in power at Kabul, the King of Bokhara set the latter officer at liberty, and treated him with consideration; and there was an open communication kept up by that officer with us, through Agha Hamza at Kabul, an intimate friend of Nayab Abdul Samad, with whom Colonel Stoddart was then living in Bokhara. The king gave him permission to return to Kabul, and, besides that, there were favourable opportunities on several occasions, which might have easily permitted the escape of that lamented officer. We also employed men to bring him to Kabul, but, after promising frequently to start, he put it off from day to day: and he wrote, and asked for rarities from us to present to the king, such as buffaloes, clocks, &c., which we sent him. The changed manner, and the attention of the king, gave reason to Colonel Stoddart to hope that he will at last succeed in bringing His Majesty to a favourable opinion towards the English Government, and that he himself will no doubt be made an ambassador to his court. He would have certainly gained his object, had the disasters of Kabul not occurred; and he, as well as his fellow-prisoner, Colonel Arthur Conolly, would not have been murdered by that cruel monarch had our army started immediately for Afghanistan, and re-occupied Kabul as soon as the winter was over. Herein the unfortunate delay occurred, and the King of Bokhara put them both to death, merely to show forth and to satisfy his vanity, in being able to say he also had shed the blood of two "infidels," as the faithful of Kabul shed that of thousands. The report of their being thus murdered was repeatedly confirmed; wherefore altogether in vain were Captain Grove's friendly pains and anxiety to ascertain this, as also the incurring such expense by sending that enterprising missionary, Dr. Wolff, to ascertain the fate of those brave officers. What was done for this purpose was certainly extraordinary, and few friends would have done so much as Captain Grove did; and he would have received thanks from their relations, and from other authorities, if he had not published the "Victims of Bokhara," which could not be acceptable, however right he was in his opinions.

Sardar Mohammed Akbar Khan was on several occasions inviting me to dine and converse with him; and on the march of the army of Sir George Pollock towards Kabul, he often asked my advice (of course not sincerely), what course he should pursue. He said he knows well that he cannot stand our troops in the field, and that our money will, in its influence, pursue and oppose him wherever our arms cannot reach; he asked if I thought there was any chance of his being safe if he were to throw himself upon the honour of the British Government, as his father did in time of need. I replied to him, that though my advice to him would appear a partial one, yet still I would not hesitate in saying that his life will be safe, and that he will likely be forgiven for the outrages he has committed against the English, if he wait upon Sir George Pollock. To this he answered that we may give him every assurance, but yet we will not act upon it. He had become so conversant with all the affairs of England by newspapers, and the old histories read to him, or related by some of us, the prisoners, that he perfectly made me silent by saying that Napoleon, who was not considered a murderer, as he fears himself to be of the English Envoy, relied upon the British justice, and in time of difficulty went on board an English ship; and that the English Government, instead of showing him the privilege of the liberty of their land, made him a prisoner, and sent him to a distant island, where he died. He added, also, that since the disasters took place in Afghanistan, and Lord Auckland departed for Europe, there has been a universal outcry against his political measures, and that in almost every newspaper which we—the prisoners—receive, men do not accuse him so much for the offences he has committed as they accuse and find fault with their own countrymen and authorities; and he added, that seeing this, he cannot rely on any assurances he might receive for his waiting upon the General;—and in justice to him I must say that he was right. We had given numerous wretched grounds and causes for our words and assurances both to be suspected; and instead of endeavouring to wipe away the stain, and to preserve the English honour, by forgetting all party feelings, and by striking a severe blow at once on our offenders, we were accusing and abusing those who had planned and acted in the expedition. How different was the time, and how unjustly partial were the people of these days in comparison to those who had to deal with men who met similar reverses when wars were waging with Hulkars and other chiefs in India. The retreat of Colonel Monson was disastrous in that period, but how nobly did Lord Wellesley * sympathise with his

* "Grievous and disastrous as the events are, the extent of the calamity does not exceed my expectation. I fear my poor friend Monson is gone. Whatever may be his fate, or whatever

misfortunes when writing to Lord Lake. The disasters at Kabul were exaggerated by want of confidence and perseverance among us; and the brave and noble general, Sir William Nott, writing to the Governor General, stated that all the disasters which befell us in Kabul were extremely exaggerated. The delay in the movement of Sir George Pollock towards Kabul, and the general complaint now of the past and once-praised expedition, gave us, the prisoners of Mohammed Akbar Khan, a sad idea that the British Government will not like to incur another heavy expense and hazard by sending an army again into Kabul. While we were thus speculating and lamenting our fates, the overland mail brought us the intelligence of the views of the Government of England with regard to Afghanistan, and in a most welcome and long speech of Sir Robert Peel, we read an extract * which convinced us that we are

the result of his misfortune to my own fame, I will endeavour to shield his character from obloquy; nor will I attempt the mean purpose of sacrificing his reputation to save mine."—*Sir John Hobhouse's Speech.*

* "I trust that in any course that Her Majesty's Government may pursue, they will not forget to ensure that the honour of the British army shall be fully maintained; and that no instances of gross treachery and perjury shall pass altogether unpunished."

not forgotten, and that the Government was determined to frighten (if not chastise) the enemy; and in the meantime I received a communication from Sir George Pollock * which dispelled all doubts of his coming to Kabul.

I shall now briefly describe how the government of India and Sir George Pollock received intelligence of the events passing at Kabul, and what measures were taken for the rescue of our prisoners. Whatever humble share I fortunately took in these transactions when myself a prisoner, and ill-treated by Mohammed Akbar Khan, was long before, without my wish, published in the "Englishman" of Calcuttta,† and then in the Delhi Gazette, but no one then had appeared to contradict any part of my assertions. On my submitting a memorial to the Court of Di-

* "You ought not to despair of British troops advancing on Kabul; and you must not, on any account, sell the grain which has been collected for the use of the army."

† That letter, with the following remark of the editor, has received an honourable place in the Appendix of Lieut. Eyre's Diary: "Mohan Lal's brief and unassuming account of his own exertions, intrepidity, risks, and sufferings, is very little calculated to do him full justice; but his great merits are well known to, and will be amply appreciated and rewarded by, the Government of India."

rectors, some persons accused me most cruelly and unjustly. In writing out their accusations, some of them took the credit of knowing every thing of the political and secret department, because, indeed, he could prove this merely by signing himself a prisoner, or by being in Afghanistan! Undoubtedly I should have been guilty of a gross crime had I not established my claims by the original documents of the authorities under whom I served, and also I should have felt ashamed of doing so if any of the political authorities whose name I have mentioned, and who are now living,* could contradict any of my statements. I sincerely say that I am not one of those who would boast of great doings and snatch at the merits of others, or who would have ever felt inclined to disrespect and be ungrateful to the officers, both military and civil, who were in Afghanistan. I do not presume to say that none but myself took a share in transmitting intelligence and negotiating the release of the prisoners,—far from it. There might be many more persons besides Captain John Conolly

* Sir George Pollock, Sir Richmond Shakespear, Major Mackison, in India; Major Macgregor, Captains Lawrence and Mackenzie, in London.

and Majors Pottinger and Lawrance, but I fully trust that the same persons who were so good as to cast a stigma on my reputation, will, on the perusal of the quotations, feel to what extent I had the good fortune to be serviceable at that time, and how far this credit was allowed to me by very many, from the Governor General, Lord Ellenborough, down to the principal authorities in Afghanistan. I call upon any one who may doubt the authenticity of the letters I quote, to throw off the mask of anonymous writing, and like an honourable man, openly to demand the perusal of the original documents.*

Captain John Conolly sent always information while he was a hostage in the house of the Navab Mohammed Zaman Khan, but when he was placed

* Nothing gave me so much satisfaction as the calling of Mr. or Professor Houghton, the father of the gallant Lieutenant Houghton, of Charkar, upon me in London, and telling me in a straightforward and honourable manner that his son, being one of the prisoners, had never mentioned my name in taking any share in the release of the prisoners. He desired me to show him the original letters of Major Pottinger and Sir Richmond Shakespear, whom the people had considered to be the sole negotiators. On reading their documents, quoted hereafter, he most affectionately shook hands with me, adding that he was thankful to me on account of his son, and that those who denied my services were malicious and partial accusers.

in the charge of the head priest, Mir Haji, he had less opportunity, and when brought thence by Mohammed Akbar, he had it not at all. Major Pottinger also wrote, but only when Mohammed Akbar wished him to communicate his negotiations with Sir George Pollock. But while in the house of Khan Shirin Khan I had ample and uninterrupted opportunities of writing, but the danger of transmitting the letters to Jalalabad was just the same as I had when suffering under the cruelties of Mulla Jalal, and when afterwards placed under the guard of Mohammed Akbar Khan, and living with Major Pottinger, Captains Conolly, Drummond, Airy, and Welch, &c. I shall henceforth quote only the authorities, and shall not make any more remarks on my behalf.

Lord Ellenborough.

"THE subsequent information has confirmed the report of the Shah's murder, and the elevation to the throne of Prince Fatah-Jung, who has opened a communication with Sir George Pollock, and professes a strong inclination to co-operate with our Government. For particulars of the state of parties and affairs at Kabul, I beg to refer your Honourable Committee to the letters from Mohan Lal, enclosed in General Pollock's despatch of the 30th ultimo."

"In a letter from Mohan Lal, dated Kabul, 9th May, your Honourable Committee will observe that, notwithstanding the vigilance observed in strictly guarding Dost Mohammed Khan within our provinces, it is alleged that he had found means to communicate with his son, Mohammed Akbar."

"The intelligence which has been lately received by Sir George Pollock from Kabul, with great despatch and regularity, contains a clear and connected account, mostly* from the pen of Mohan Lal, of the progress of events at that capital."

"The letters from Prince Fatah-Jang and Mohan Lal, previous to the capture of the Bala Hisar, had repeatedly urged the expediency of the advance of the British army, even as far as Gundamuk, as a measure which would lead

* Can any higher testimony than this be shown of my being the regular and constant correspondent while a prisoner, and living in the same house, and under the same guard, where Major Pottinger, Captain Troup, &c. &c., prisoners, were living? I wish "Quorum Pars," the correspondent of the Delhi Gazette (December 13, 1845), to read this. If he does not know the difference between Baboo and other Orientals, how can he know what Major Pottinger and other political people were doing in behalf of the prisoners, which was all secret? He might be one of the Bamian captives, but he was not a political officer, who could only know what we were doing. If he has means to throw a glance on the pages of the Blue Book, he will there see whose name is most frequently mentioned by Lord Ellenborough. This I do not say by way of boasting, but to show how unjustly I have been accused by some worthy writers of the Indian papers, as himself.

almost certainly to the dispersion of the Barakzai party, and the probable flight of Mohammed Akbar Khan, and the liberation of the British prisoners."

"Mohammed Akbar has told Mohan Lal that, in the event of the British army advancing, he shall not meet it in the field, but defend the town of Kabul, upon which I immediately sent 400 more rockets to Sir George Pollock."

"I have continued to receive constant reports,* furnished by Mohan Lal, of the progress of events at Kabul. Your Honourable Committee will learn that Mohammed Akbar was installing himself in the office of Vizier to Prince Fatah-Jung, whom he has formally proclaimed King."

Sir George Pollock.

"MOHAN LAL has proved himself to be a very intelligent and useful public servant. He was of essential service in sending me information from Kabul, until I reached that capital with the army under my command."

"I have already had occasion to bring to the notice of the Right Honourable the Governor-General the valuable services performed by Mohan Lal, in keeping me informed, at considerable personal risk,† of the state of affairs at Kabul."

* This will further show from whom Lord Ellenborough received much and regular information.

† It will separately show Mr. "Quorum Pars" and others what risks I encountered in sending the communications to the army.

Sir R. Shakespear.

"It is, indeed, very cruel to keep Mohan Lal in any doubt. His services to the state were of great value; and if any of his letters had fallen into the hands of the enemy, his life would have been forfeited." *

"Mohan Lal has performed very valuable service to the British Government during the campaign of 1842.

"While at Jalalabad we were entirely† dependent on him for intelligence of the state of affairs and of parties at Kabul. His letters in general reached us twice a-week; and I do not remember a single instance of the information which he gave being incorrect; and his arrangements were so good, that not a single letter sent by any of his messengers fell into the hands of the enemy."

Major Macgregor, Political Agent.

"I HAVE known and have served with Mohan Lal in Afghanistan for several years. At the risk * of his life he did serve his Government faithfully, and his services are too well known to render it necessary that I should here detail them. A more intelligent person I have never met with, and I trust that his meritorious services will be duly rewarded by a lucrative appointment. His qualifications and judgment render him equal to a difficult enterprise."

* See preceding Note.

† Does not this say that the entire dependence was on my information?

Sir Richmond Shakespear, Secretary, to Mohan Lal.

"YOUR very interesting letters, of date the 6th June, reached me this morning at 9 A.M. They have been shown to the General, and copies forwarded to Government."

"We are very anxious to hear from you again.

"I trust you continue to give intelligence of the state of affairs at Kabul, as all your letters are forwarded to Government."

"SIR,

"THE General is very sorry that you have been seized by Mohammed Akbar Khan, but hopes that you will still be able to write us intelligence occasionally of the state of affairs.* The General has to-day written to the Governor-General, pointing out the zeal and perseverance which you have displayed in sending such regular and correct information."

Sir George Pollock to the Governor-General (Lord Ellenborough).

Political Department.

"I REGRET to have to report the seizure of Mohan Lal by Mohammed Akbar Khan. I venture to take this oppor-

* These letters will further show the brave "Quorum Pars" and others in what personal danger I performed my duty, and what was expected and spoken of me by the first authorities of India, if not by the good "Quorum Pars" and his worthy companions.

tunity of bringing to the notice of the Right Honourable the Governor-General the zeal and perseverance of Mohan Lal, who, under very difficult circumstances, and at very great personal risk,* has contrived to send me regular and correct information of the state of the different parties at Kabul.

"The Cossid brought the scrap of paper, a copy of which I have now the honour to enclose."

Governor-General (Lord Ellenborough).

"I HAVE the honour to acknowledge the receipt of your letter, No. 132, dated 26th June, reporting the seizure of Mohan Lal by Mohammed Akbar Khan.

"In reply I am directed to inform you that the Governor-General duly appreciated the zeal and intelligence displayed by Mohan Lal * during late events at Kabul, and regrets that the state is likely to be deprived for a time of that officer's services."†

Sir Richmond Shakespear, Secretary, to Mohan Lal.

"SIR,

"I AM very sorry to hear that you have been so ill-

* See preceding Note.

† Lord Ellenborough and the quoted authorities will show how ill I was treated when a prisoner, and that the Government expects and appreciates the services of Asiatics as well as those of Englishmen, which Mr. "Quorum Pars" takes all to himself.

treated, and trust that such disgraceful conduct will not be repeated.*

"I have received your letters of the 17th and 19th, and am much distressed to hear of your sufferings. The General will have it explained (to Akbar) that there can be no possible faith in negotiations while any of our prisoners are ill treated.

"Mohammed Akbar has been told that we have heard of his ill-treatment of you, and reminded that *our* prisoners are well treated.*

"I trust that you will not be ill-treated again, as it has been explained to Mohammed Akbar that the treatment of the Afghans in our possession will depend on his treatment of our prisoners."*

Governor-General to Sir George Pollock.

"I am directed by the Governor-General (Lord Ellenborough) to acknowledge the receipt of your letter of the 3rd instant, and to communicate to you his Lordship's entire approval of the measures adopted of extending to Mohan Lal the protection of the British Government.

"It is his Lordship's intention to remove Mohammed Akbar Khan's family from Lodianah; and it is under his Lordship's consideration whether Mohammed Akbar Khan's wife and children should not be immediately sent to Calcutta, and eventually to England.

"Mohammed Akbar Khan must be aware that the Go-

* See preceding Note.

vernment in England cannot afford to any one education in the Mohammedan faith, and there are no means of obtaining it there."*

Sir George Pollock to Mohan Lal.

"We are glad of your being released from your sufferings, and allowed to join Major Pottinger."

In reading the preceding extract of a letter from the Earl of Ellenborough, and also the forthcoming ones, it will be observed how deeply concerned and anxious his Lordship was, as were also Sir George Pollock and Sir Richmond Shakespear, about obtaining the liberty of the prisoners. In order to effect this object, the exchange of the Afghan prisoners, and also large sums of money, were offered to Mohammed Akbar. There were also in the mean time numerous negotiations in existence through highly esteemed and able officers, such as Major Pottinger, and Captains Lawrance, Troup, Drummond, Johnson, and I may also say every prisoner! but the treachery of Mohammed Akbar Khan was always an obstacle to our success. Proclamations

* This letter from Lord Ellenborough, and a closer confinement of the Amir and his family by Mr. Clerk, made a favourable change in the condition of the prisoners then in the hands of Mohammed Akbar Khan.

desiring the citizens to interfere in rescuing us, with promises of rewards and threats of punishment, were issued and caused by us to be thrown unknown into the houses of the various rebels. Several promised to render us service, and openly to declare for our release; but the dread of the cruel disposition of Mohammed Akbar was always a hinderance in the way to our objects. Sir George Pollock, with Sir Richmond Shakespear and Major Macgregor, had from the beginning entertained a good wish towards me, and therefore in order to bring me kindly forward they always encouraged me to exert myself in every way and degree to have us released, and the same was the aim and endeavour of every officer who had an opportunity of being acquainted with the influential men. The time however came when I was the first to say to Major Pottinger, in the presence of Captain Drummond, that we were ordered to go to Turkistan. Mohammed Akbar had often expressed his intention to fulfil his threats of distributing us, and of selling us as slaves in Turkistan; and nothing could have prevented this gratification of his cruelty and vanity if we were once on the other side of Bamian. Colonel Palmer, who was disgracefully ill-treated and tortured by Shamshuddin Khan, at Ghazni, was now, with other officers, brought and placed with the rest of the prisoners by Mohammed Akbar. This was managed through our friend Khan Shirin Khan, who excited the suspicion of Mohammed Akbar by saying that Shamshuddin Khan was negotiating with us separately from him, and thus would get the upper hand of him through our influence. All of us were ordered to be ready to start in the dusk of the evening of the 25th of August, as Mohammed Akbar was a little afraid of the rising of the people to force our liberation. I waited upon him, and reminded him of his swearing on the Qoran, and promising to release me after I had given him the sum of eighteen thousand rupees. I added that he had failed in this, and still kept me a prisoner, and that he was now going to send me off to Turkistan. His sister, the wife of Sultan Jan, to whom I had shown every attention in my power while she was the only member of the Amir Dost Mohammed Khan's immediate family that was allowed to remain at my request in Kabul, interposed on my behalf, and begged her brother to keep me under the same guard and in the same house where I was living with the other prisoners, and then take me with himself to the camp when he went to fight with Sir George Pollock, instead of sending me to Bamian. He agreed to this, but next day he got into a great passion with me on hearing that I was intriguing with the chiefs, and he ordered the door of my room to be locked, and gave orders that I must not be permitted to step out under any circumstances.

On this I again begged him to relax his hard treatment, and I gave a handsome present to Yaqub Khan, the commandant of our guard, and begged him to allow to come to me Sayad Murtza Shah, a Kashmirian draper, pretending that I wished to buy some clothes for myself. He came, and was good enough to undertake the hazardous mission to Salah Mohammed Khan, then in charge of the prisoners in Bamian. As Sir George Pollock had approved of my proposal, I wrote letters, and made Sayad Musiza Shah the bearer of them, and he succeeded in inducing Salah Mohammed to accept my proposals of a pension for life, and that of twenty thousand rupees in cash, as well as of a pardon for his past offences. On the successful termination of these negotiations by Sayad Murtza Shah, Major Pottinger wrote to me immediately a letter (1),* which I forwarded immediately to Sir George Pollock, and he submitted the information to the Governor-General (2, 3). Before Akbar Khan started to oppose Sir George Pollock, I made my escape from his custody, and went with Nayab Mohammed Sherif Khan to the Afshar fort, where my friend Khan Shirin Khan, the Persian chief, joined me with all his followers. Captain Troup, with Captain Anderson and his family, were left by Mohammed Akbar Khan in the fort of Shevki, and it became now important to secure their safety; and Khan Shirin Khan, on my paying a small sum,† despatched a strong body of horse, which was accompanied by Sayad Mohammed Khan (Janfishan) Ali Jan, the son-in-law of our stedfast friend Nayab Mohammed Sherif Khan, and I was soon delighted to hear from Captain Troup (4) that all of them were safe. He came next day to see me in the fort, and

* Every mark from Number 1 will regularly guide to the quotations inserted pp. 473—483.

† It was distributed amongst the horsemen by Nayab Sharif, and I also gave two gold makeers to Janfishan, as his expenses.

as I had resolved to send a Persian party to meet our prisoners (5), he readily offered to accompany them if there was any necessity for the appearancce of an European officer with them. In the mean time another letter from Major Pottinger came to my address (6), on which Sir Richmond Shakespear boldly accompanied the Persian party, and his person gave great weight to the measures. By the quotations (7) it will be observed that I was in communication with Salah Mohammed before I had received the orders of any of my superiors, and had also secured the highly valuable services of Agha Hamza, which we should have used if Salah Mohammed had declined to meet my wishes. It will be seen in an extract from Major Pottinger's report (8), the authenticity of which a recent misunderstanding between several officers obliged Captain Lawrence (9) to confirm, that before the arrival of my friend Sayad Murtza Shah, Salah Mohammed had distinctly refused the offers of other officers, and it will at the same time show how far their share is allowed in the report of Major Pottinger. On the successful and happy release of the prisoners, and the signal victory gained by Sir

George Pollock over Mohammed Akbar Khan, that just and impartial General writes to the Governor-General (10); and Sir Richmond Shakespear afterwards, on receiving the thanks of the prisoners for his gallant exertions in order to meet them while with the Persian party, writes (11) in my behalf, and so does Colonel Outram, the late Resident in Sindh, in a letter to the Viscount Jocelyn (12). Major Macgregor, the political agent, who had also negotiated (13) with Mohammed Shah Khan Ghilzai, offering him two lakhs of rupees to have the prisoners released, finding that the sum I promised to pay to Salah Mohammed (twenty thousand rupees) and to Sayad Murtza Shah (five thousand rupees), as well as their pension, was much less than what Mohammed Shah Khan was offered, kindly and justly stated (14) these particulars of my economy on behalf of the Government.

It is my pleasing duty now to mention that Lord Hardinge has shown much liberality to my friend Sayad Murtza Shah, and has fixed a pension of five hundred rupees *per mensem* for him instead of one hundred only, which Lord Ellenborough had granted to him in accordance to my promise.

(1)

Major Pottinger, C.B., Political Agent, with the Prisoners, to Mohan Lal.

"SIR,

"YOUR agent Sayad Murtza Shah has arrived and concluded the arrangements; Salah Mohammed Khan agrees to it. The agent wants money, and says that it and aid of troops should be sent; if the troops follow quickly, the country will aid them, and the Minister may be taken. Let General Pollock or General Nott know.

"Yours obediently,

"ELDRED POTTINGER."

(2)

Sir George Pollock to the Governor-General of India.

"SIR,

"I HAVE the honour to forward, to be laid before the Governor-General, the accompanying report forwarded to me by Major Pottinger. The return in safety of the prisoners may be attributed, in a great measure, to the negotiations of Mohan Lal, and the active co-operations of the Kizulbash chiefs.

"GEORGE POLLOCK."

(3)

The Governor-General of India to the Secret Committee.

"HONOURABLE SIRS,

"I RECEIVED last night a letter from Major-General Pollock, dated the 21st ult., of which I enclose an extract, by which you will perceive that all the European prisoners, except Captain Bygrave, are in our hands, and that Sir Robert Sale, at the head of a light force, was bringing them into Kabul, where they were expected to arrive on the 22nd.

"I have, &c.,

"ELLENBOROUGH."

(4)

Letter of the Shevki Prisoners to the Address of Mohan Lal.

"MOHAN LAL,

"SIR,

"JAN Fishan Khan, Mehar Ali Khan, Sher Ali Khan, Ali Mirza Khan, Abbas Khan Shahghasi, have just reached us, with a note from you for Sir R. Shakespear. I beg you will offer our best thanks to Khan Shirin Khan, Gholam Mohammed Khan, Nezamul Daula, Gholam Hasan Khan, Naib Sharif, Mehar Ali Khan, and all the other chiefs, for their great kindness to us. I mention the names of the gentlemen here in order that you may make the chiefs acquainted with them—Captain Anderson, with his wife and children; Mrs. Trevor and her children; Captain Troup, Dr. Campbell.

"Your obedient servants,

"EDWARD CAMPBELL,

"W. ANDERSON,

"C. TROUP."

(5)

Sir George Pollock, C.B., to the Commander-in-Chief.

"SIR, *21st Sept.* 1842.

"I HAVE the honour to report, for the information of His Excellency the Commander-in-Chief, that having received intimation from Bamian, * * * * * * * * I, at the suggestion of Mohan Lal, with the concurrence of Khan Shirin Khan, chief of the Qizalbashes, sanctioned the speedy departure of seven hundred of his horse on the 15th inst., the day of our arrival here, to meet the party. Some difficulty occurring on the score of money, I advanced ten thousand rupees (1000*l.*), which were delivered by Sir R. Shakespear, who accompanied the Qizalbashes.

"I cannot conclude without recording my opinion, that to Khan Sheereen Khan and Mohan Lal may be attributed the safety of the prisoners, and I have reason to believe the chief of the Qizalbashes to be a stedfast adherent to the British Government.*

"I have, &c.,

"GEORGE POLLOCK, *Major-General,*

" *Commanding in Afghanistan.*"

* This letter is quoted in Stocqueler's (formerly Editor of the 'Englishman,' Calcutta, and now of the 'English Gentleman' in London,) 'Memorials in Afghanistan,' and also printed in the Parliamentary Blue Book.

(6)

Major Pottinger, C.B., Political Agent, with the Prisoners, to Mohan Lal.

"SIR, *Bamian, 16th September*, 1842.

"Your good agent Sayad Murtza Shah Kashmiri arrived a few days ago, and has succeeded in getting Salah Mohammed Khan to change sides, and in consequence of the letters from the Qizalbash, most of the Hazarah chiefs have come in. Give my best thanks to the Qizalbash chiefs engaged in the business, and tell them that neither my fellow prisoners nor myself shall ever forget their kindness. I trust we may be strong enough to move into the Afghan country in a few days; but lest we should not, I have written to General Nott to send some troops if he possibly can.

"Your obedient servant,

"ELDRED POTTINGER,

"*Political Agent, T. F.*

"I enclose a letter for General Pollock, C.B."

(7)

Sir R. Shakespear, Secretary, to Sir George Pollock, to the Address of Mohan Lal.

"I need hardly tell you that if you can obtain the release of the prisoners, and particularly of the ladies, you will perform a most valuable service to Government.

"You may consider this as security for the payment of

any sum of money thus expended, when the service has been performed.

"It is impossible to come to terms with Mohammed Akbar; and Mohammed Shah Khan has been written to, but has not replied.

"There is now an opportunity of doing good service by detaining our prisoners and getting grain and supplies for our troops, and we trust to you to make every exertion to effect them both. * * *

"If Salah Mohammed secures the prisoners, as his expenses to the amount as mentioned shall be paid, he may be quite sure that he will be forgiven, and well rewarded if we get the prisoners.

"Agha Hamza's conduct is very gratifying, as we are most anxious to get all the prisoners. Agha Hamza has offered to raise a corps to cut off the retreat, and states that it would cost 10,000 rupees (1000*l.*). The General would willingly pay that, or even two or three thousand more."

(8)

Extracts from Major Pottinger, C.B., Political Agent, to the Address of Sir George Pollock, G.C.B.

"I HAVE omitted to state that on the 29th and 30th of August the prisoners having agreed among themselves that they would raise a subscription for their release, and the party having selected Captain Lawrance, Captain Johnson, and myself as their agents, we opened a negotiation with Salah Mohammed Khan, by Captain Johnson and Captain

Lawrence severally offering to engage themselves for the payment of a lakh of rupees to Salah Mohammed Khan, if he would agree to aid in our release; and Captain Johnson explained to him that, if he (Salah Mohammed) would delay our march, when Major-General Nott's army reached Maidan, we might, by a forced march, join his camp. To both these proposals Salah Mohammed Khan returned distinct refusals, and afterwards treated us with considerable harshness, giving orders that no one should go beyond the line of sentinels round our tents, threatening to kill us if any escaped, and in other ways showing himself displeased with our propositions."

Editorial remark of the Delhi Gazette.

"The following letter, relating to a correspondence which appeared in our columns some time since, bearing on the part which Colonels Shelton and Palmer were said *not* to have taken in the liberation of the prisoners at Bamian, ought to have reached us by the April mail, but in consequence of being sent to a distant station, was not placed in our hands till Monday last. Any of our readers anxious to connect the present with the former correspondence will find the same by referring to the 'Gazettes' of the 30th December, 1843, of the 6th January, 1844, and of the 17th of the same month.—Ed."

(9)

To the Editor of the Delhi Gazette.

"Sir,

"Your overland summary of January 21st reached me

by the last mail, and with reference to the correspondence in it between Captain H. Johnson, 26th N. I. and a 'Quondam Captive,' in justice to the late Major Pottinger I deem it incumbent on me thus publicly to state that the Major's account of our negotiations with Salah Mohammed in the matter of our release, as contained in his official letter to Major-General Sir George Pollock, K.C.B., of the 21st September, 1842, No. 512 of the Afghanistan Blue Book, is perfectly correct, and further that Captain Johnson not only saw but read the said letter previously to its despatch! I myself having taken it to him!! the only remark he made on it was that Pottinger had taken to himself all the credit!!! hardly naming us, which remark led me to get Pottinger to add the concluding paragraph, commencing 'I have omitted to state,' &c.!!!! In a letter to a near relative, of 27th September, 1842, which is now lying before me, is the following paragraph—'On the 11th Salah Mohammed asked to speak to Pottinger, Johnson, and myself; immediately Pottinger told me, I said it must be about our release, and so it proved. We three, with Mackenzie (Shelton and Palmer refusing, *being afraid of compromising themselves with Mohammed Akbar*), signed a paper giving Salah Mohammed," &c. &c.*

"Captain Johnson should have known that this was the

* It is very strong evidence of the authenticity of my statement. Had I done otherwise, it would have been contradicted by Captains Lawrance, Mackenzie, and Major Macgregor, who were in London on submitting my Memorial.

paper alluded to by Pottinger; when he reported to Government that Shelton and Palmer declined affixing their signatures to it. Shelton in particular said he would have nothing to do with it; that we were premature, and would compromise ourselves; that it was a trap, &c. &c. The paper which the Captain parades as bearing the Brigadier's signature at the top, was one subsequently prepared, and was merely, as it sets forth, to bind the subscribing parties to abide by what the Committee should apportion to each in the event of Government not sanctioning our engagements with Salah Mohammed.

"Captain Johnson says 'that Pottinger, Lawrance, and self never thought of asking Shelton or any other officer to attach his signature to the bond drawn up by Suyud Mustza Shah,' he seems altogether to forget what passed at the meeting when Colonels Shelton and Palmer positively refused to have anything to do with it. Does he forget what Salah Mohammed said to Shelton at the time? if he does, I do not. Had not we broken up the meeting, leaving Shelton and Palmer in the room, and taken Salah Mohammed into Lady Sale's, and then signed the bond, my firm opinion is that not one of us would now be alive to tell the tale.*

"I am, Sir, yours, obediently,

(Signed) "G. St. P. Lawrence,

"Captain 11th Cavalry."

"*Bath*, *5th April*, 1844."

* If such difference of opinion or disunion is in existence amongst such distinguished officers, how can an Asiatic, as my-

(10)

Sir George Pollock, G.C.B., to the Governor-General.

"I HAVE already had occasion to bring to the notice of the Right Hon. the Governor-General the valuable service performed by Mohan Lal in taking a prominent part in the arrangements which so happily terminated in the release of the prisoners from Bamian * * * * *; and he was also greatly instrumental in effecting the escape of the prisoners from Bamian.

"GEORGE POLLOCK."

(11)

"Above all, Mohan Lal deserves the credit of having been the first to open the negotiation with Saleh Mohammed, which so happily terminated the release of our prisoners. * * * * *

"R. SHAKESPEAR."

(12)

"Mohan Lal, of Indian celebrity, of whom you have read and heard as the travelling companion of Burnes, and the

* * * * *

man who, amongst all the British prisoners at Kabul, did

* * * * *

most to uphold our honour and rescue our countrymen: I am sure I need say no more to interest your Lordship; but I may add, that you will find him most intelligent on all

self, dare to claim any share, unless the quoted authorities—Sir George Pollock, Sir R. Shakespear, &c.—should speak for me?

Indian subjects, and particularly conversant with all relating to the Sikhs and our north-western frontier.

"J. OUTRAM."

(13)

Mohammed Shah Khan to Major Macgregor.

"YOUR letter has been received and has afforded me much pleasure; I have been much pleased with what you say regarding the release of the English gentlemen who are under my protection, and the friendship which you express for my relations, and the message which you sent by the bearer of the letter desiring me to send, or cause to be sent, the gentlemen to Major-General Pollock, as the English Government would reward such service. My friend, ingratitude is not permitted in your religion, nor in mine."

(14)

"I FEEL assured that, so long as he (Mohan Lal) is employed by the Government, he will not only serve it with the utmost fidelity, but also with advantage to the State.

"G. H. MACGREGOR,

"*Political Agent.*"

On the successful arrival of Sir George Pollock's army in Butkhak, I had received instructions to bring all the chiefs to meet Prince Fatah Jang, who was to enter the city along with him, and other high officers of the British army. In the morning of the 16th of

September I proceeded with the chiefs, and met Sir George Pollock with the Prince, and came back with them to the Bala Hisar. The Prince, accompanied by all who attend of use and wont on such an occasion, entered the court and sat on the throne of his father, while Sir George Pollock and Sir Robert Sale sate by his side, each on a chair, and Majors Macgregor, Lawrence, and myself, with some other staff officers, stood by his Highness, I may say by his Majesty. All the Afghan and Persian chiefs stood in a row to offer their submission and their congratulations upon his restoration to the throne of his father; and a salute was also fired, but whether for his installation, or for honouring the British flag, which was then on the top of the citadel, is a matter beyond my discovery.

A brigade under Sir — MacCaskill was now sent to punish the rebellious chiefs in Kohistan, and after destroying all their fortifications and the places where they had committed their atrocities, we returned to Kabul; but yet Fatah Jang, whom the British generals had accompanied, and caused to ascend the throne, refused to stay there after the return of our army. All the Musalmans of the city had gone off with all their moveable property, and there were only the Khatris and Shikarpuris now left living in the town. They remained on assurances of protec-tection, and they deserved it; for after the force of General Elphinstone was destroyed in the retreat, that class of the inhabitants of Kabul had behaved most liberally towards our half-dead, lame, and handless sepoys and camp-followers. They indeed clothed, fed, and warmed them during the winter, and continued their generosity till the arrival of Sir George Pollock. They therefore deserved, and were sure of protection; but unhappily, when a small part of the Kabul Bazar was blown up (where the bodies of Sir William Macnaghten and Captain Trevor had been hung up by Akbar Khan), these poor people in that time of confusion suffered by being plundered; and all their families, which had once given our people shelter, were pillaged of all their property, and driven from their houses.

Mohammed Akbar Khan had in the meantime fled towards Ghorband, and thence to the frontier of Bamian; and had not Sir George Pollock been re-peatedly ordered to march back from Kabul, many of the rebel chiefs, as well as Mohammed Akbar

Khan, the assassin of the British Envoy, would have been easily seized. To have punished our enemies by the stay of our army for six months at least in Jalalabad, if not in Kabul, would have shown the people of Central and of all Asia, that we possessed an abundance of means, both defensive and offensive, not only to disperse our enemies, but also to occupy their fields and their cities.

In the mean time we might have buried the bodies of thousands of our brave soldiers and of our poor camp-followers, which were lying scattered about in every direction, calling us to avenge them on their destroyers. Moreover, if we had found during our stay there that the Sadozais, whom we are bound by treaties to support, were unfit to rule the country, and that to maintain a military post there would cost us much money and blood, we might have then honoured our name by releasing and placing the Amir Dost Mohammed on the throne, and afterwards withdrawn wholly our armies. If we had thus completed these chivalrous objects, then we would be both right and proud to say that "our victorious armies, after retrieving the loss of our honour, have been withdrawn." We have now, on the contrary, left an impression for ever in Central Asia that we are so rare of high honour that we could not punish those who had offended us, and that we were afraid to stop among them, and too weak to sway the haughty and bold Afghans.* This is the opinion now of all the chiefs and natives of India and of Central Asia, and this was the notion which emboldened the Sikhs to oppose our arms, though at last this proved ruinous to themselves.

I said before that the Prince Fatah Jang would not endanger his personal safety by attempting to keep the sovereignty at Kabul without our arms; and so he, with all the royal family, followed our camp to India. In the moment of departure, I cannot understand whether political considerations or the supplications of certain chiefs induced our authorities to think that the Prince Shahpur should

* "They were taught that England is powerful to punish as well as to protect; but not one benefit, either political or military, has England acquired by the war. Indeed, our evacuation of the country resembled almost as much the retreat of an army defeated as the march of a body of conquerors, seeing that to the last our flanks and rears were attacked, and that such baggage as we saved was by dint of hard fighting."—P. 128, *Sale's Brigade in Afghanistan*, by the Rev. G. R. GLEIG, M.A.; published by JOHN MURRAY, 1846.

be seated on the throne in the presence of some of us, but so it was done, and the poor boy was left at the mercy of his powerful enemies, and had to incur much personal danger, with the loss of property, when obliged to run away from Kabul on the approach of Mohammed Akbar Khan from Bamian. By such a precipitate withdrawal from Afghanistan we did not show an honourable sentiment of courage, but we disgracefully placed many friendly chiefs in a serious dilemma. There were certain chiefs whom we detached from Akbar Khan, pledging our honour and word to reward and protect them; and I could hardly show my face to them at the time of our departure, when they all came full of tears, saying that "we deceived and punished our friends, causing them to stand against their own countrymen, and then leaving them in the mouths of lions." As soon as Mohammed Akbar occupied Kabul, he tortured, imprisoned, extorted money from, and disgraced all those who had taken our side. I shall consider it indeed a great miracle and a divine favour if hereafter any trust ever be placed in the word and promise of the authorities of the British governments throughout Afghanistan and Turkistan.

We thus left the country where the bravest officers and soldiers of our army had been treacherously destroyed, supplying our enemies at the same time with money and the weapons of war! Yet such was called the retrieving of the lost reputation of the British arms!!!

Mohammed Akbar Khan, on hearing that Salah Mohammed had given up all the prisoners, and that there was only one of them, Captain Bygrave, remaining with him, felt that he had no remedy, but was forced to show pretended feelings of generosity by sending that officer also to our camp. His release indeed was without any negotiation on our part, and he therefore owes it to himself and to Akbar.

The victorious force at Qandhar, under Sir William Nott, whose name will never die, had, by the orders of the Governor-General, gained possession of the celebrated Sandal-wood gates which had been long before carried away by the bigoted Sultan Mahamud of Ghazni from the temple of Somnath * in India, about eight hundred years ago, if

* Baron, or Captain Von Orlich, the celebrated Prussian traveller, has lately published an account of his travels in India

tradition speaks the truth. This was indeed a masterly stroke, and never to be forgotten by the religious class of Afghanistan; but Mohammed Akbar Khan and the others who had offended us, did not care for them, whether we bore them away as our trophy to India, or might have burnt them to warm ourselves in the chilling breeze of the Khurd Kabul pass. On their entering Peshavar, their fortune, after eight hundred years, became brighter, for, passing through the Panjab and Sarhand, they were glorified by the attendance of the British officers, such as my friend Major Leech, &c., and were carried with much pomp. The notification of the Governor-General,* and the respect we paid to the old gates, undoubtedly gained the attachment of those to whom it was addressed; but some even of the followers of Somnath said that we ought to have glorified, and shown the superiority of our arms and power by bringing Mohammed Akbar Khan, the murderer of the British Envoy, instead of the holy

and Lahaur, replete with valuable information and amusing anecdotes. That work is illustrated with a drawing of those gates.

* The reader will find this notification in the Blue Book of Parliament, and also in Stocqueler's Memorials of Afghanistan, p. 302, published in Calcutta.

gates. The learned Musalmans contented themselves by saying, that as those gates were foul in reality, and taken from the foul temple of Somnath, they could no longer continue to be gates of the pure and holy tomb of Mahmud, since Mohammed, the prophet, has foretold that "Kulle shayan yarjo ala aslahi;" meaning all things go back to their origin.

No honour can be more sufficiently shown than was paid by Lord Ellenborough to the well-deserving garrison of Jalalabad. At Qasur, on the other side of the Satlaj, medals were received that had been transmitted thither for the brave officers and soldiers of Sir Robert Sale. On the ferry of Firozpur also a beautifully decorated bridge of boats was thrown across the river, to carry over that illustrious garrison; and triumphal arches were erected, where the Governor-General was himself seen courteously showing his feelings of pride and of gratification in the heroic conduct of the lions of Jalalabad, and where the whole of the army of reserve formed a street, and presented arms to their victorious brother officers and soldiers. Here was the termination of all the campaigns of Afghanistan!!

Let me return now to the hero of my tale, the Amir Dost Mohammed Khan. After his surrender and departure to India, he expressed his wish to wait upon the Earl of Auckland, the Governor-General of India. His family was accommodated in the house where his unfortunate successor, the Shah Shuja-ul-Mulk, had lived, at Lodianah, and the Amir himself was sent to Calcutta. His son, Haidar Khan of Ghazni, was despatched from Bombay to join his father. Every attention and respect were shown to him by the Governor-General; and this not only delighted the Amir, but astonished him with an idea of wonder to see and to feel with what deference and generosity state-prisoners are treated by the British. His Lordship fixed a sum of three lakhs per annum for the expenses of his household; and the Amir, in seeing all the curiosities of Calcutta, and the improvements introduced by the British in all the imaginable and useful departments, together with the command and management of the military and naval stores, was astonished beyond all measure. He was heard to say, that if he had known of all these warlike means, and of the extraordinary power of the English before, he would never have thought to oppose our views. The dinners and balls in the Government-house gave him also a grand idea of British splendour and hospitality. During his sojourn in Calcutta he became indisposed in health, and was so much alarmed about the probable consequences to his health from his staying any longer in that metropolis, that he repeatedly begged the Governor-General to send him to Lodianah to join his family, often and earnestly saying to Mr. Colvin, the private secretary to his Lordship, "Sahab mara zud nazdik ayal i ma bifresed vagarnah inja bimari mara me kusbad va nam argrez dar tamam alam badnam kavahad shud;" meaning, "Send me, Sir, quick to join my family, else the illness will kill me here, and the English will get a bad name—it will be said he was poisoned." The Amir was accordingly sent into the upper provinces, and afterwards to the hills, where he enjoyed the climate and the cold in some degree of his own country. During the insurrection of Kabul he had managed wonderfully to communicate with his son Mohammed Akbar Khan, advising him to do all in his power to destroy us; yet when I met and dined with him at Lodianah, on his being released, and on his way to Lahaur, in order to proceed to Afghanistan, he said, to please me, that the conduct of Ákbar was obnoxious to much blame, and that he believes there is some fault in his birth, and that he does not think him his own son.

On crossing the river Satlaj he was accompanied by Captain Nicolson to the court of the Maharajah Sher Singh,* with whom he entered into a secret treaty of alliance. With regard to the proclamation, which was published by the Earl of Ellenborough, no man of impartial feeling can deny the nobleness and generosity of his Lordship in treating the Amir honourably, and in releasing a prisoner in so dignified a manner. The release of the Amir, said some chiefs of the Panjab, was in variance with the tripartite treaty, while Shahpur and Safdar Jang, the sons of the Shah Shujah-ul-Mulk, were in Afghanistan, and contrary to our then existing alliance with the Lahaur court. However, it was a noble act, and universally admired.

From Lahaur the Amir Dost Mohammed Khan was escorted to the Khaibar Pass by the Sikh authorities, where he was received by his son the Sardar

* He was shot dead by Ajit Singh; and since that the Panjab has been suffering by anarchy, murders, and bloodshed.

THE LATE MAHARAJAH SHER SINGH

Mohammed Akbar Khan and the other chiefs of Afghanistan. There was no limit to the rejoicings of this chieftain at the circumstances which induced our Government to release and restore him to his kingdom. In Kabul, after a few months, he adopted all his old tyrannical system of extortion; and he grew unpopular so suddenly that he was once fired upon, but escaped. He wished to add another to the number of his wives, and fixed his eyes on the daughter of a Morad Khani chief. The intended bride being young, refused to marry the old Amir, but he instantly coloured dark his silvered beard and told her that he was now young, and he must have her. She was forced by her parents to consent to his proposal.

The Amir is now enjoying the authority in Kabul, and the superiority of his family. He is now fearless of an invasion from the West as well as from the East, and he has given himself up again to drinking and to dancing parties, which habits he had forsaken on assuming the title of "Amir-ul-momni." It is said he believes that while he was an enemy to wine he was always involved in difficulties, and that since he drinks he is prosperous, and has gained his liberty after being in "Qaid i Frang," meaning in an English prison!

THE END.